OXFORD PAPERBACK REFERENCE

A Dictionary of
Finance and
Banking

Oxford Paperback Reference

The most authoritative and up-to-date reference books for both students and the general reader.

ABC of Music
Accounting
Allusions
Animal Behaviour*
Archaeology
Architecture
Art and Artists
Art Terms
Astronomy
Better Wordpower
Bible
Biology
British History
British Place-Names
Buddhism
Business
Card Games
Catchphrases
Celtic Mythology
Chemistry
Christian Art
Christian Church
Chronology of English
    Literature
Classical Literature
Classical Myth and Religion
Computing
Contemporary World History
Countries of the World
Dance
Dates
Dynasties of the World
Earth Sciences
Ecology
Economics
Encyclopedia
Engineering*
English Etymology
English Folklore
English Grammar
English Language
English Literature
Euphemisms
Everyday Grammar
Finance and Banking
First Names
Food and Drink
Food and Nutrition
Foreign Words and Phrases
Geography
Humorous Quotations
Idioms
Internet
Islam

Kings and Queens of Britain
Language Toolkit
Law
Linguistics
Literary Quotations
Literary Terms
Local and Family History
London Place-Names
Mathematics
Medical
Medicinal Drugs
Modern Design*
Modern Slang
Music
Musical Terms
Musical Works
Nicknames*
Nursing
Ologies and Isms
Philosophy
Phrase and Fable
Physics
Plant Sciences
Plays*
Pocket Fowler's Modern
    English Usage
Political Quotations
Politics
Popes
Proverbs
Psychology
Quotations
Quotations by Subject
Reverse Dictionary
Rhyming Slang
Saints
Science
Shakespeare
Slang
Sociology
Space Exploration*
Statistics
Synonyms and Antonyms
Weather
Weights, Measures, and Units
Word Games*
Word Histories
world History
World Mythology
World Place-Names*
World Religions
Zoology

*forthcoming

A Dictionary of
Finance and
Banking

THIRD EDITION

OXFORD
UNIVERSITY PRESS

OXFORD

UNIVERSITY PRESS

Great Clarendon Street, Oxford OX2 6DP

Oxford University Press is a department of the University of Oxford.
It furthers the University's objective of excellence in research, scholarship,
and education by publishing worldwide in

Oxford New York

Auckland Bangkok Buenos Aires Cape Town Chennai
Dar es Salaam Delhi Hong Kong Istanbul Karachi Kolkata
Kuala Lumpur Madrid Melbourne Mexico City Mumbai Nairobi
São Paulo Shanghai Singapore Taipei Tokyo Toronto

Oxford is a registered trade mark of Oxford University Press
in the UK and in certain other countries

First published 1993 as *A Dictionary of Finance*
Second edition 1997
Third edition 2005

British Library Cataloguing in Publication Data

Data available

Library of Congress Cataloging in Publication Data

Data available

ISBN 0-19-860749-0
ISBN 978-0-19-860749-6

1

Typeset in Swift by Market House Books Ltd.

Printed in Great Britain by Clays Ltd, St Ives plc

Preface

A Dictionary of Finance and Banking, which is a companion volume to *A Dictionary of Business* and *A Dictionary of Accounting*, is intended for students and professionals in the fields of finance and banking as well as for private investors and the readers of the financial pages of newspapers.

The 5000 entries in the dictionary provide up-to-date coverage of the vocabulary used in banking, money markets, foreign exchanges, financial futures and options, commodity markets, and takeovers and mergers, as well as business loans and debt-collecting. Public finance is also included, with a substantial coverage of the terms used in government finance, the money supply, public-sector borrowing, local finance, central banking, and European finance. The private investor and borrower will find entries for terms relating to savings, stock-exchange dealing, mortgages, pensions, life assurance, and taxation.

The coverage is wide and international, with entries for all the world's standard currency units and many of the financial institutions in London, New York, Tokyo, Hong Kong, Frankfurt, and Paris.

For this edition over 1000 new entries have been added and the text has been fully revised and expanded to take account of such developments as European Monetary Union and the increasing importance of derivatives markets. International coverage has also been increased to reflect the ongoing globalization of financial markets.

The editors of this book have been at great pains to make the entries as clear and as easy to understand as possible. Although jargon is avoided wherever possible in definitions, many jargon words and phrases are included and defined.

JS
JL
2005

Note: An asterisk (*) placed before a term in a definition indicates that this term can be found as an entry in the dictionary and will provide further information. Synonyms and abbreviations are usually found within brackets immediately following a headword.

Credits

Editors
John Smullen BSc(Econ), MA, MSc(Econ), MBA (Senior Academic Associate,
  University of Greenwich)
Nicholas Hand MSc, BComm (Senior Lecturer, University of Greenwich)

Market House Books Ltd Editorial Staff
Jonathan Law
Peter Lewis

Contributors
Barry Brindley
Brian Butler
David Butler
Brian Clutterbuck
Nicholas Hand
Alan Isaacs
Brian Johnson
Graham Sidwell
John Smullen
R. M. Walters
Andrew Wood
Matthew Wright

A1 A description of property or a person that is in the best condition. In marine insurance, before a vessel can be insured, it has to be inspected to check its condition. If it is "maintained in good and efficient condition" it will be shown in *Lloyd's Register of Shipping as 'A' and if the anchor moorings are in the same condition the number '1' is added. This description is also used in life assurance, in which premiums are largely based on the person's health. After a medical examination a person in perfect health is described as "an A1 life".

AADFI Abbreviation for *Association of African Development Finance Institutions.

abandonment 1. The surrender of title, rights, or claim to financial assets or any other type of property. **2.** Not exercising an *option at expiry.

ABC method *See* ACTIVITY-BASED COSTING.

ABI Abbreviation for *Association of British Insurers.

abnormal return A rate of return for taking a particular risk that is greater than that required by the market. The excess return is usually measured as being relative to that which the *capital asset pricing model or the *arbitrage pricing theory requires. *See also* ACTIVE MANAGEMENT; ANOMALY; EFFICIENT MARKETS HYPOTHESIS.

above par *See* PAR VALUE.

above-the-line 1. Denoting the upper part of a company's *profit and loss account, ending with the profit (or loss) for the financial year and excluding the entries explaining the distribution of profit. **2.** Denoting advertising expenditure on mass media advertising, including press, television, radio, and posters. It is traditionally regarded as all advertising expenditure on which a commission is payable to an advertising agency. **3.** Denoting transactions concerned with revenue, as opposed to capital, in national accounts. *Compare* BELOW-THE-LINE.

absolute rate An interest rate expressed as a percentage rather than in relation to a *reference rate.

absolute-rate swap An *interest-rate swap in which the fixed interest rate is expressed in terms of an *absolute rate.

absorption costing (**total absorption costing**) The process of costing products or activities by taking into account the total costs incurred in producing the product or service, however remote. This method of costing ensures that full costs are recovered provided that both the implied full-cost price and forecast sales volumes are achieved. *Activity-based costing is an attempt to allocate costs on a more sophisticated basis. *Compare* MARGINAL COSTING.

ACA Abbreviation for Associate of the *Institute of Chartered Accountants.

ACCA Abbreviation for Associate of the Chartered Association of Certified Accountants. *See* CERTIFIED ACCOUNTANT; CHARTERED ACCOUNTANT.

acceptance   1. The signature on a *bill of exchange indicating that the person on whom it is drawn accepts the conditions of the bill. **2.** A bill of exchange that has been so accepted. Acceptances are divided into two categories: *banker's acceptances and trade acceptances. **3.** Agreement to accept the terms of an offer; for example, the agreement of an insurance company to provide a specified insurance cover or of a trader to accept a specified parcel of goods at the offer price.

acceptance credit A means of financing the sale of goods, particularly in international trade. It involves a commercial bank or merchant bank extending credit to a foreign importer, whom it deems creditworthy. An acceptance credit is opened against which the exporter can draw a *bill of exchange. Once accepted by the bank, the bill can be discounted on the *money market or allowed to run to maturity. In return for this service the exporter pays the bank a fee known as an **acceptance commission**.

acceptance supra protest (acceptance for honour) The acceptance or payment of a *bill of exchange, after it has been dishonoured, by a person wishing to save the honour of the drawer or an endorser of the bill.

accepting house An institution specializing in accepting or guaranteeing *bills of exchange. A service fee is charged for guaranteeing payment, enabling the bill to be discounted at preferential rates on the *money market. The decline in the use of bills of exchange has forced the accepting houses to widen their financial activities, many of whom have returned to their original role as *merchant banks.

Accepting Houses Committee A committee representing the 17 *accepting houses in the City of London. Members of the committee are eligible for finer discounts on bills bought by the Bank of England, although this privilege has been extended to other banks.

acceptor The drawee of a *bill of exchange after acceptance of the bill, i.e. the acceptor has accepted liability by signing the face of the bill.

accommodation bill A *bill of exchange signed by a person (the accommodation party) who acts as a guarantor. The accommodation party is liable for the bill should the *acceptor fail to pay at maturity. Accommodation bills are sometimes known as **windbills** or **windmills**. *See also* KITE.

accommodation endorser A person or a bank that endorses a loan to another party; for example, a parent company may endorse a bank loan to a subsidiary. The endorser becomes a guarantor and is secondarily liable in case of default. Banks may endorse other banks' acceptance notes, which can then be traded on the secondary market.

account   1. A statement of indebtedness from one person to another; an invoice. A provider of professional services or of goods may render an account to a client or customer. A solicitor selling a house on a person's behalf will render an account of the sale, which may show that the solicitor owes the seller the proceeds of the sale, less expenses. **2.** A named segment of a ledger recording transactions relevant to the person or the matter named. Accounts consist of two sides; increases are recorded on one side and decreases on the other. These entries are often referred to as **debit** and **credit** entries. Accounts may be kept in a written form in a ledger, they may be on loose cards, or they may held in a computer. **3.** An account maintained by a *bank or a *building society in which a depositor's money is kept. *See* CHEQUE ACCOUNT; CURRENT ACCOUNT; DEPOSIT ACCOUNT. **4.** A period during which dealings on the London Stock Exchange were formerly made without immediate cash settlement. Up to the end of each account, transactions were recorded but no money changed hands. Settlement of all transactions made within an account was made ten days after the account ended. This practice changed in 1996 when the account system was abandoned. **5.** In an advertising, marketing, or public-relations agency, a client of the agency from whom a commission or fee is derived, in return for the services. **6.** *See* ANNUAL ACCOUNTS.

accountability An obligation to give an account. For limited companies, it is assumed that the directors of the company are accountable to the shareholders and that this responsibility is discharged, in part, by the directors providing an annual report and accounts (*see* ANNUAL ACCOUNTS). In an accountability relationship there will be at least one principal and at least one agent. This forms the basis of an *agency relationship.

accountant A person who has passed the accountancy examinations of one of the recognized accountancy bodies and completed the required work experience. Each of the bodies varies in the way they train their students and the type of work expected to be undertaken. For example, accountants who are members of the Chartered Institute of Public Finance and Accountancy generally work in local authorities, the National Health Service, or other similar public bodies, while members of the Chartered Institute of Management Accountants work in industry (*see* CHARTERED ACCOUNTANT; MANAGEMENT ACCOUNTING). Wherever accountants work, their responsibilities centre on the collating, recording, and communicating of financial information and the preparation of analyses for decision-making purposes.

account day (settlement day) The day on which all transactions made during the previous *account on the London Stock Exchange were formerly settled. Since the account system was abandoned in 1996, transactions have to be settled within a few days.

accounting concepts (accounting principles) The basic theoretical ideas devised to support the activity of accounting. As accounting developed largely from a practical base, it has been argued that it lacks a theoretical framework. Accountants have therefore tried to develop such a framework; although various concepts have been suggested, few have found universal agreement. However, four are deemed to be fundamental: the first, the *going-concern concept, assumes that the business is a going concern until there is evidence to the contrary, so that assets are not stated at their break-up value; the second, the *accruals concept, involves recording income and expenses as they accrue, as distinct from when they are received or paid; the third, the *consistency concept, demands that accounts be prepared on a basis that clearly allows comparability from one period to another; and the fourth, the *prudence concept, calls for accounts to be prepared on a conservative basis, not taking credit for profits or income before they are realized but making provision for losses when they are foreseen. These four principles are recognized in the European Union *Fourth Directive and the Companies Acts together with a fifth, the *separate-entity concept. Other accounting concepts might include *depreciation and *deferred taxation, which are concepts relating to accounting, but which are not usually considered when reference is made to fundamental accounting concepts.

accounting package *See* BUSINESS SOFTWARE PACKAGE.

accounting period **1.** The period for which a business prepares its accounts. Internally, management accounts are usually produced either monthly or quarterly. Externally, *financial statements are produced for a period of 12 months (interim accounts are often produced for the first six months), although this may vary when a business is set up or ceases or if it changes its accounting year end. *See* FINANCIAL ACCOUNTING; MANAGEMENT ACCOUNTING. **2. (chargeable account period)** A period in respect of which a *corporation tax assessment is raised. It cannot be more than 12 months in length. An accounting period starts when a company begins to trade or immediately after a previous accounting period ends. An accounting period ends at the earliest of:
• 12 months after the start date,
• at the end of the company's period of account,
• the start of a winding-up,
• on ceasing to be UK resident.

accounting principles *See* ACCOUNTING CONCEPTS.

accounting rate of return (ARR) An accounting ratio that expresses the profit of an organization before interest and taxation, usually for a year, as a percentage of the capital employed at the end of the period. Variants of the measure include using profit after interest and taxation, equity capital employed, and the average of opening and closing capital employed for the period. A variation of this measure can be used to forecast return on an investment project although *discounted cash flow measures are acknowledged to be superior for this purpose.

Accounting Standards Board (ASB) The recognized body for setting accounting standards in the UK. It was established in 1990 to replace the Accounting Standards Committee (ASC) following the recommendations contained in the *Dearing Report. Under the Companies Act 1985, companies (except *small companies and *medium-sized companies) must state whether their accounts have been prepared in accordance with the relevant accounting standards and give details and reasons for any material departures from those standards. The ASB issues Financial Reporting Exposure Drafts (FREDs), *Financial Reporting Standards (FRS), and through its offshoot, the Urgent Issues Task Force, reports known as Abstracts. The ASB is a subsidiary of the *Financial Reporting Council.

account payee only Words printed between two vertical lines in the centre of a UK cheque that, in accordance with the Cheque Act 1992, make the cheque non-transferable. This is to avoid cheques being endorsed and paid into an account other than that of the payee, although it should be noted that banks may argue in some circumstances that they acted in good faith and without negligence if an endorsed cheque is honoured by the bank. In spite of this most cheques are now overprinted 'account payee only', and the words 'not negotiable' are sometimes added.

accounts **1.** The *profit and loss account, *balance sheet, and *cash-flow statements of a company. *See* FINANCIAL STATEMENTS. **2.** *See* ACCOUNT.

accounts payable (trade creditors) The amounts owed by a business to suppliers (e.g. for raw materials). Accounts payable are classed as *current liabilities on the balance sheet, but distinguished from *accruals and other non-trade creditors (such as the Inland Revenue).

accounts receivable (trade debtors) The amounts owing to a business from customers for invoiced amounts. Accounts receivable are classed as *current assets on the balance sheet, but distinguished from prepayments and other non-trade debtors. A provision for bad debts is often shown against the accounts receivable balance in line with the *prudence concept. This provision is based on the company's past history of bad debts and its current expectations. A general provision is often based on a percentage of the total credit sales, for example 2% of credit sales made during the period.

accreting cap An interest-rate *cap on an increasing principal.

accreting swap A *swap in which the principal increases over time.

accrual (accrued charge) An amount incurred as a charge in a given accounting period but not paid by the end of that period, e.g. the last quarter's electricity charge. *See* ACCRUALS CONCEPT.

accruals concept One of the four fundamental concepts contained in Statement of Standard Accounting Practice 2, 'Disclosure of Accounting Policies', and one of the principles in the Companies Act 1985. It requires that revenue and costs are recognized as they are earned or incurred, not as money is received or paid. Income and expenses should be matched with one another, as far as their relationship can be established or justifiably assumed, and dealt with in the *profit and loss account of the period to which they relate. However, if there is a conflict between the accruals concept and the *prudence concept, the latter prevails. *Accruals and prepayments are examples of the application of the accruals concept in practice. For example, if a rates bill for both a current and future period is paid, that part relating to the future period is carried forward as a current asset (a prepayment) until it can be matched to the future periods.

accrued benefits Benefits due under a pension scheme in respect of service up to a given time, irrespective of whether the rights to the benefits are vested or not. Accrued benefits may be calculated in relation to current earnings of protected final earnings. *Statement of Standard Accounting Practice 24, 'Accounting for Pension Costs', contains mandatory regulations on accounting for pension costs in financial accounts.

accrued income scheme An arrangement that applies in the UK to the disposal of interest-bearing securities. The purpose of the scheme is to prevent the avoidance of an income tax liability on *accrued interest. The interest accrued between the date of the last interest payment and the date of disposal is regarded, for tax purposes, as the income of the transferor. The transferee is able to deduct this sum from taxable income. The scheme does not apply to non-residents or if the transfer is part of a trade. Exemption also applies to individuals (husband and wife being regarded as one) if the total nominal value of the securities held does not exceed a certain amount.

accrued interest The amount of interest earned by a bond or other security since the last interest payment, but not yet received. *See* ACCRUED INCOME SCHEME.

accumulated depreciation (aggregate depreciation) The total amount of the *depreciation written off the cost price or valuation of a *capital asset since it was brought into the balance sheet of an organization.

accumulated dividend A dividend that has not been paid to a holder of *cumulative preference shares and is carried forward (i.e. accumulated) to the next accounting period. It represents a liability to the company. The Companies Act requires that where any fixed cumulative payments on a company's shares are in arrears, both the amount of the arrears and the period(s) in arrears must be disclosed for each class of shares.

accumulated profits The amount showing in the *appropriation of profits account that can be carried forward to the next year's accounts, i.e. after paying dividends, taxes, and putting some to reserve.

accumulating shares Ordinary shares issued to holders of ordinary shares in a company, instead of a dividend. Accumulating shares are a way of replacing annual income with capital growth; they avoid income tax but not capital gains tax. Usually tax is deducted by the company from the declared dividend, in the usual way, and the net dividend is then used to buy additional ordinary shares for the shareholder.

accumulation The gradual purchase of a large number of shares or other securities, so as to increase an investor's holding without driving up the share price.

accumulation area In *chartist analysis, a range in the price of a security that tends to attract buyers.

accumulation trust *See* DISCRETIONARY TRUST.

accumulation unit A unit in a *unit trust or an *investment trust in which dividends are ploughed back into the trust, after deducting income tax, enabling the value of the unit to increase. It is usually linked to a life-assurance policy.

acid-test ratio *See* LIQUID RATIO.

ACII Abbreviation for Associate of the *Chartered Insurance Institute.

acquisition **1.** The purchase of an asset. **2.** The process of taking a controlling interest in a business (*see* MERGER).

acquisition accounting The accounting procedures followed when one company is taken over by another. The fair value of the purchase consideration should, for the purpose of consolidated financial statements, be allocated between the underlying net tangible and intangible assets, other than goodwill, on the basis of the fair value to the acquiring company. Any difference between the fair value of the consideration and the aggregate of the fair values of the separable net assets (including identifiable intangibles, such as patents, licences, and trademarks) will represent goodwill. The results of the acquired company should be brought into the consolidated *profit and loss account from the date of acquisition only.

In certain circumstances *merger accounting may be used when accounting for a business combination. Acquisition accounting differs from merger accounting in that shares issued as purchase consideration are valued at their market price, not par value (*see* SHARE PREMIUM ACCOUNT), a goodwill figure may arise on consolidation, and pre-acquisition profits are not distributable. Merger accounting treats both parties as if they had always been combined, and values the purchase consideration at par.

Acquisition accounting and merger accounting are covered by Financial Reporting Standard 6, 'Acquisitions and Mergers', and Financial Reporting Standard 7, 'Fair Values in Acquisition Accounting'.

across-the-board movement A movement in all sectors of a market, as when the shares of all companies listed on the stock market rise or fall in price.

ACT **1.** Abbreviation for *advance corporation tax. **2.** Abbreviation for *Association of Corporate Treasurers.

active management A method of portfolio management in which individual investments are selected with an eye to earning *abnormal returns. The general academic view is that this approach runs counter to the *efficient markets hypothesis and is therefore unlikely to be successful. The strategies of *diversification and following a market index are thought more likely to provide greater returns. *Compare* PASSIVE MANAGEMENT.

active partner A partner who has contributed to the business capital of a partnership and who participates in its management. All partners are deemed to be active partners unless otherwise agreed. *Compare* SLEEPING PARTNER.

active stocks The stocks and shares that have been actively traded.

active underwriter A managing agent in *Lloyd's who underwrites on behalf of a syndicate. *See* UNDERWRITER.

activity-based costing (ABC method) A system of costing proposed by Professors Johnson and Kaplan in their book *Relevance Lost: The Rise and Fall of Management Accounting* (1987), in which they questioned accounting techniques based on *absorption costing. Their method recognizes that costs are incurred by each activity that takes place within an organization and that products (or customers) should bear costs according to the activities they use.

actuals (physicals) 1. Commodities that can be purchased and used, rather than goods traded on a *futures contract. **2.** In futures contracts or forward dealing, the commodity underlying a contract. **3.** Expenses or receipts that have actually occurred, as opposed to targets, budgets, or other projections.

actuarial surplus The surplus that arises as a result of *overfunding.

actuary A professional trained in the application of mathematics and statistics to issues relating to general insurance and *life assurance. Some are employed by insurance companies to calculate probable lengths of life and advise insurers on the amounts that should be put aside to pay claims and the amount of premium to be charged for each type of risk. They advise on the pricing of insurance contracts and also on the administration of pension funds. *See also* INSTITUTE OF ACTUARIES.

adaptive expectations In economic theory, a hypothesis explaining how economic agents form forecasts or expectations of the future values of certain economic variables by adjusting past values of the variable.

adaptive exponential smoothing A quantitative forecasting method in which averages derived from historical data are smoothed by a coefficient, which is allowed to fluctuate with time in relation to changes in demand pattern. The larger the coefficient, the greater the smoothing effect.

additional paid-in capital In the USA, the excess received from stockholders over the *par value of the stock issued.

additional voluntary contributions (AVCs) Extra contributions made by employees either into an employers' pension scheme or into a scheme of their own choice (free-standing AVCs) in order to increase benefits available from their pension fund on retirement. In the UK, AVCs are subject to tax concessions and are limited – together with standard pension contributions – to 15% of current salary.

adjudication 1. The judgment or decision of a court, especially in bankruptcy proceedings. **2.** An assessment by the Commissioners of Inland Revenue of the amount of stamp duty due on a document. A document sent for adjudication will either be stamped as having no duty to pay or the taxpayer will be advised how much is due. An appeal may be made to the High Court if the taxpayer disagrees with the adjudication.

a

adjustable peg *See* CRAWLING PEG.

adjustable-rate mortgage (ARM) A *mortgage in which the interest rate is adjusted at periodic intervals, usually to reflect the prevailing rate of interest in the *money markets. Borrowers are sometimes protected by a *cap, or ceiling, above which the interest rate is not allowed to rise.

adjustable-rate preferred stock (ARP) Stock or cumulative preference shares in the USA whose dividends are linked to Treasury Bill interest rates. Minimum and maximum rates are specified by the application of a *collar. **Convertible adjusted-rate preferred stock** can be converted to common stock at a fixed price at specified dates.

adjusted present value A calculation of the *all-equity net present value of an investment or project that is then adjusted to allow for any other impacts, for example any tax concessions on financing. *See also* NET PRESENT VALUE; PRESENT VALUE.

adjusted strike price A new *exercise price (strike price) for an option that arises from an unexpected event, such as a stock dividend or split.

adjustment bond A *bond issued in exchange for existing bonds when a business in financial difficulties is being restructured.

adjustment credit An advance made by a US Federal Bank to smaller banks to satisfy short-term lending needs. The loans may be made for as short a term as 15 days. Adjustment credits are most often used when interest rates are high and money supply is short.

administration order **1.** An order made in a county court for the administration of the estate of a judgment debtor (*see* JUDGMENT CREDITOR). The order normally requires the debtor to pay the debts by instalments; so long as this is done, the creditors referred to in the order cannot enforce their individual claims by other methods without the leave of the court. Administration orders are issued when the debtor has multiple debts but it is thought that *bankruptcy can be avoided. **2.** An order of the court under the Insolvency Act 1986 made in relation to a company in financial difficulties with a view to securing its survival as a going concern or, failing that, to achieving a more favourable realization of its assets than would be possible on a *liquidation. While the order is in force, the affairs of the company are managed by an *administrator and the firm is protected from legal action by the creditors to wind up the business.

administrative receiver A *receiver appointed by the holder of a *floating charge covering the whole, or substantially all, of a company's assets in order to recover money due to a secured creditor. The administrative receiver has the power to sell the assets that are secured by the charge or to carry on the company's business.

administrator **1.** Any person appointed by the courts, or by private arrangement, to manage the property of another. **2.** Any person appointed by the courts to take charge of the affairs of a deceased person, who died without making a will. This includes collection of assets, payment of debts, and distribution of the surplus to those persons entitled to inherit, according to the laws of *intestacy. The administrator must be in possession of *letters of administration as proof of the authority vested by the courts. **3.** Any person appointed by the courts to implement an *administration order or undertake the duty of an *administrative receiver.

ADR Abbreviation for *American depositary receipt.

ad valorem (Latin: according to value) Denoting a tax or commission calculated as a percentage of the total invoice value of goods or services rather than the number of items. For example, *value added tax is an ad valorem tax, calculated by adding a fixed percentage to an invoice value.

advance corporation tax (ACT) Formerly, an advance payment of *corporation tax payable when a company made a *qualifying distribution. The requirement for such payments was abolished in 1999, although rules exist to permit the recovery of payments prior to this date. Larger companies must now pay corporation tax in instalments.

advance–decline ratio The ratio of the number of companies whose share prices have risen to the number whose prices have fallen on a stock exchange over a given period, often a single day. A fall in the ratio can be interpreted as an impending overall fall in prices. Its value is a measure of *market sentiment, positive being bullish, and negative being bearish.

adventure A commercial undertaking of a speculative nature, often associated with overseas trading.

adverse balance A deficit on an account, especially a *balance of payments account.

adverse opinion An opinion expressed by an *auditor in an *auditors' report to the effect that the financial statements do not give a true and fair view of the organization's activities. This situation usually arises if there is a disagreement between the auditor and the directors, and the auditor considers the effect of the disagreement is so material or pervasive that the financial statements are seriously misleading. Audit reports are covered by the Auditing Practices Board's Statement of Auditing Standard 600, 'Auditors' Reports on Financial Statements'.

adverse selection In the market for insurance products and loans, the tendency for the most risky customers to be the most likely to demand products that exempt them from disclosing their status. To reduce their exposure to large claims on this basis, sellers often raise premiums generally or exclude high-risk customers from such products. *See also* ASYMMETRIC INFORMATION; MORAL HAZARD.

advice of acceptance An acknowledgment from a *collecting bank to the bank from which the collection was received, detailing the funds transferred, confirming that the collection has been made, and giving details of charges, deductions, etc.

advised line of credit Confirmation by a bank or other lender of the specific *credit line available to a particular customer.

advise fate A request by a collecting bank wishing to know, as soon as possible, whether a cheque will be paid on its receipt by the paying bank. The cheque is sent direct and not through the Bankers' Clearing House, asking that its *fate should be advised immediately.

advising bank A bank in an exporter's own country that informs the exporter that a *letter of credit has been opened with a foreign bank.

advisory broker A *broker who provides advice concerning share investments.

advisory funds Funds placed with an intermediary who has full discretion in the matter of their investment.

a

AFBD Abbreviation for *Association of Futures Brokers and Dealers Ltd.

Affärsvarlden General Index An index of security prices on the *Stockholm Stock Exchange.

affiliate *See* ASSOCIATE COMPANY.

affinity card A *credit card issued to members of a particular group (such as a club, college, etc.) or to supporters of a particular charity; the credit-card company pledges to make a donation to the charity or organization for each card issued and may also donate a small proportion of the money spent by card users. In the UK, affinity cards are sometimes called **charity cards**.

afghani (AF) The standard monetary unit of Afghanistan, divided into 100 puli.

afloat Denoting goods, especially commodities, that are on a ship from their port of *origin to a specified port of destination; for example, "afloat Rotterdam" means the goods are on their way to Rotterdam. The price of such goods will usually be between the price of spot goods and goods for immediate shipment from origin.

African Development Bank A regional bank, based on the model of the *International Bank for Reconstruction and Development (World Bank), created by independent African nations in 1964 to provide long-term development loans. Membership was originally restricted to African countries but was widened in 1989.

after date The words used in a *bill of exchange to indicate that the period of the bill should commence from the date inserted on the bill, e.g. '... 30 days after date, we promise to pay ...'. *Compare* AFTER SIGHT; AT SIGHT.

after-hours trading Transactions made on a market after its official close at the end of its mandatory quote period. These deals are recorded as part of the next day's trading and referred to as early bargains.

after market *See* SECONDARY MARKET.

after sight The words used in a *bill of exchange to indicate that the period of the bill should commence from the date on which the drawee is presented with it for acceptance, i.e. has sight of it. *Compare* AFTER DATE; AT SIGHT.

after-tax basis The calculation of returns after tax has been deducted.

AG Abbreviation for *Aktiengesellschaft*. It appears after the name of a German, Austrian, or Swiss company, being equivalent to the British abbreviation plc (i.e. denoting a public limited company). *Compare* GMBH.

against actuals In a *commodity market, describing transactions in *futures contracts that are offset against transactions in the cash market. *See* ACTUALS.

against the box Denoting a situation in which a dealer who holds a *long position in a security makes a short sale in the same stock (*see* SHORT SELLING).

ageing schedule A breakdown of *accounts receivable by time period.

agency **1.** A relationship between two parties; one, the principal, on whose behalf some action is being taken by the other, the **agent**. An agency agreement might exist, for example, when one person gives a power of attorney to another to negotiate a contract on his or her behalf, or when a bank purchases securities for a customer. **2.** (*or* **agent**) An organization or individual that provides such an agency service. **3.** Securities issued in the USA by non-Treasury Department sources, such as the National Mortgage Association. **4.** One bank that acts as the organizer for a group of banks lending money to a corporation.

agency agreement An agreement between a customer and a bank allowing the customer to bank cheques at a branch of that bank, usually for logistical reasons. The cheques thus enter the clearing system, although the customer does not have an account with that bank. A charge is made by the bank for this service.

agency bill *See* INLAND BILL.

agency fee (facility fee) An annual fee paid to an agent for the work and responsibility involved in managing a loan after it has been signed.

agency loan A loan available for local-government authorities, public organizations, etc., from the *European Investment Bank.

agency problem The problem, first systematically identified by Jensen and Meckling (1976), that arises when the shareholders of a firm and its managers have different interests. There is consequently a need for appropriate supervision of the actions of managers. The agency problem was brought into sharp focus by the collapse of the US companies Enron and WorldCom in 2002. *See* ASYMMETRIC INFORMATION; SIGNALLING HYPOTHESIS.

agent *See* AGENCY.

agent de change A stockbroker or securities house on the Paris Bourse (*see* BOURSE).

age relief An additional *personal allowance set against income for income-tax purposes in the UK for both single people and married couples over 65. At the age of 75 both the personal allowance and the married couple's allowance are increased. These allowances are subject to restriction based on level of income. *See also* INCOME-TAX ALLOWANCES.

aggregation The netting of assets and liabilities in relation to a particular counterparty.

aggregator A firm that collates and presents information about an individual's bank accounts, investments, insurance policies, etc. so that the person concerned can manage all his or her financial affairs via a single website.

agio **1.** The fee charged by a bank or other financial institution for changing one form of money into another, e.g. coins to notes, or one currency to another. **2.** The difference between a bank's interest rate for borrowing money and the rate at which it is prepared to lend it, also known as the **turn** or **spread**.

agora (*plural* **agorot**) A monetary unit of Israel worth one hundredth of a *sheqel.

agreed bid A *takeover bid that is supported by a majority of the shareholders of the target company, whereas a **hostile bid** is not welcomed by the majority of the shareholders of the target company.

agreed-value policy An insurance policy in which the sum to be paid out under any claim is set out in the policy agreement.

agreement value The value of a *swap in the event of early termination.

Agricultural Bank (Land Bank) A credit bank specifically established to assist agricultural development, particularly by granting loans for longer periods than is usual with commercial banks.

AIBD Abbreviation for Association of the International Bond Dealers. *See* INTERNATIONAL SECURITIES MARKET ASSOCIATION.

AIM **1.** Abbreviation for *Alternative Investment Market. **2.** Abbreviation for *Amsterdam Interprofessional Market.

Aktb Abbreviation for *Aktiebolaget*. It appears after the name of a Swedish joint-stock company.

Aktiengesellschaft A German, Austrian, or Swiss public limited company. *See* AG.

ALCO Abbreviation for *asset and liability management committee.

all-equity net present value A calculation of *net present value made as if the firm, project, or investment were funded entirely by equity. In such cases, the *discount rate is the discount rate for equity. *See also* ADJUSTED PRESENT VALUE; PRESENT VALUE.

Allfinanz *See* BANCASSURANCE.

alligator spread An options *spread in which any potential gain is annulled by the high cost of commissions.

All-Ordinaries share index The most widely quoted index of Australian shares; it is a capitalization-weighted arithmetic average of 245 ordinary shares quoted on the *Australian Stock Exchange. The index encompasses two others, which are sometimes quoted independently: the All-Mining index (accounting for 17.6% of the All-Ordinaries) and the All-Resources (34.1%).

all-or-nothing option *See* BINARY OPTION.

allotment A method of distributing previously unissued shares in a limited company in exchange for a contribution of capital. An application for such shares will often be made after the issue of a *prospectus on the *flotation of a public company or on the privatization of a state-owned industry. The company accepts the application by dispatching a **letter of allotment** to the applicant stating how many shares have been allotted; the applicant then has an unconditional right to be entered in the *register of members in respect of those shares. If the number of shares applied for exceeds the number available (oversubscription), allotment is made by a random draw or by a proportional allocation. An applicant allotted fewer shares than applied for is sent a cheque for the unallotted balance (an application must be accompanied by a cheque for the full value of the shares applied for). *See also* MULTIPLE APPLICATION.

allotted shares Shares distributed by *allotment to new shareholders (allottees). The shares form part of the **allotted share capital**. *See also* SHARE CAPITAL.

all-risks insurance An insurance policy that provides full coverage, excepting specific exclusions. It is the standard form of marine insurance contract.

ALM Abbreviation for *Association of Lloyd's Members.

alpha coefficient A measure of the return on a share compared to the expected return on shares with a similar *beta coefficient. It identifies the *specific risk associated with a particular share as opposed to the *systematic risk associated with securities of the same class. Sometimes referred to as **Treynor's alpha**, it is formally calculated as:

$$R_i - R_f - \beta_i[E(R_m) - R_f],$$

where R_i = the returns on the asset under consideration, R_f is the risk free return, $E(R_m)$ is the average or expected returns on a market portfolio, and β_i is the beta of the asset or portfolio i.

alpha stocks The most actively traded securities in the *Stock Exchange Automated Quotations System (SEAQ); it was a measure of market liquidity used by the *London Stock Exchange from October 1986 until January 1991, when the system was replaced by the *Normal Market Size (NMS) measure of dealings in a company's shares. The system divided the approximately 4000 securities quoted into four categories, alpha, beta, gamma, and delta, according to the frequency with which they were traded. The classification defined the degree of commitment to trading that had to be provided by market makers.

alteration of share capital An increase, reduction, or any other change in the authorized capital of a company (*see* SHARE CAPITAL). If permitted by the *articles of association, a limited company can increase its authorized capital as appropriate. It can also rearrange its existing authorized capital (e.g. by consolidating 100 shares of £1 into 25 shares of £4 or by subdividing 100 shares of £1 into 200 of 50p) and cancel unissued shares. These are reserved powers, passed – unless the articles of association provide otherwise – by an ordinary resolution.

alternate director A person who can act temporarily in place of a named director of a company in his or her absence. An alternate director can only be present at a meeting of the board of directors if the *articles of association provide for this eventuality and if the other directors agree that the person chosen is acceptable to undertake this role.

alternative currency option An *option in which the *underlying is priced in one currency and the payoff is in another.

alternative delivery procedure Non-standard delivery terms in an *options or *futures contract.

alternative investment **1.** Anything purchased for the pleasure of owning it as well as the likelihood that it will increase in value. **2.** *See* ALTERNATIVE INVESTMENT MARKET.

Alternative Investment Market (AIM) A market of the *London Stock Exchange that opened in June 1995 to replace the Unlisted Securities Market, with the object of allowing small growing companies to raise capital and have their shares traded in a market, without the expense of a full market listing. Since its formation over 600 smaller companies have traded their shares on this market and the number of institutions investing in the market is increasing.

amalgamation The combination of two or more companies. The combination may be effected by one company acquiring others, by the merging of two or more companies, or by existing companies being dissolved and a new company formed to take over the combined business. Financial Reporting Standard 6, 'Acquisitions and Mergers', regulates the accounting of business combinations. *See also* ACQUISITION ACCOUNTING; MERGER ACCOUNTING.

American depositary receipt (ADR) A receipt issued by a US bank to a member of the US public who has bought shares in a foreign country. The certificates are denominated in US dollars and can be traded as a security in US markets. The advantages of ADRs are the reduction in administration costs and the avoidance of stamp duty on each transaction.

American option *See* OPTION.

American Stock Exchange (AMEX) A stock exchange in New York, on which second-tier securities are traded. Listing requirements on AMEX are less stringent than on the *New York Stock Exchange. AMEX pioneered touch-screen technology and, in linking with the Toronto Stock Exchange in 1985, established the first international link between primary equity markets. AMEX has developed a market in options and futures. AMEX is now a member of the NASDAQ group.

American terms A quotation of an exchange rate in terms of how many US dollars can be exchanged for one unit of another currency. *Compare* EUROPEAN TERMS.

AMEX Abbreviation for *American Stock Exchange.

amortization **1.** The process of treating as an expense the annual amount deemed to waste away from a fixed asset. The concept is particularly applied to leases, which are acquired for a given sum for a specified term at the end of which the lease will have no value. It is customary to divide the cost of the lease by the number of years of its term and treat the result as an annual charge against profit. While this method does not necessarily reflect the value of the lease at any given time, it is an equitable way of allocating the original cost between periods. *Compare* DEPRECIATION.

  Goodwill may also be amortized. Financial Reporting Standard 10, 'Goodwill and Intangible Assets', requires the writing-off of goodwill to the *profit and loss account in regular instalments over the period of its economic life. However, non-amortization is an option in exceptional circumstances. **2.** The repayment of debt by a borrower in a series of instalments over a period. Each payment includes interest and part repayment of the capital. **3.** The spreading of the *front-end fee charged on taking out a loan over the life of a loan for accounting purposes. **4.** A contribution to a *sinking fund to repay a debt. **5.** In the USA, another word for *depreciation.

amortization schedule A schedule that summarizes the dates on which specified amounts must be paid in the repayment of a loan.

amortizing cap An interest-rate *cap on a reducing principal.

amortizing collar An interest-rate *collar on a reducing principal.

amortizing mortgage A *mortgage in which all the principal and all the interest has been repaid by the end of the mortgage agreement period. Although equal payments may be made during the term of the mortgage, the sums are divided, on a sliding scale, between interest payments and repayments of the principal. In the early years most of the payments go towards the interest charges, while in later years more repays the sum borrowed, until this sum is reduced to zero with the last payment. *Compare* BALLOON MORTGAGE.

amortizing option An *option in which the notional principal reduces over the life of the option.

amortizing swaption A *swaption in which the notional principal reduces over the life of the swaption.

amount at risk **1.** The difference between the current forced-sale value of a
lender's security and the *principal owed to the lender, excluding both
uncapitalized interest and any security over which the lender does not have power
of sale. **2.** The portion of an insurer's risk under an insurance policy that is not
covered by the insurer's reserves against that risk.

amounts differ The words stamped or written on a cheque or bill of exchange by
a banker who returns it unpaid because the amount in words differs from that in
figures. Banks usually make a charge for returning unpaid cheques.

Amsterdam Interprofessional Market (AIM) A market set up by the banks,
commission houses, and institutions in 1986 on the *Amsterdam Stock Exchange to
transact large business at negotiated commissions without the use of brokers.

Amsterdam Stock Exchange Amsterdam first established a stock exchange in
1602 to trade in shares of the Dutch East India Company; it thus claims to be the
world's oldest stock exchange. On the Amsterdam Stock Exchange only members
(*hoekmen*) can deal. *See also* AMSTERDAM INTERPROFESSIONAL MARKET; EUROPEAN
OPTIONS EXCHANGE.

analyst A person trained to examine statistics and other information regarding
past, present, and future trends or performance of an operation. *See also* INVESTMENT
ANALYST.

ancillary credit business A business involved in credit brokerage, debt
adjusting, debt counselling, debt collecting, or the operation of a credit-reference
agency (*see* CREDIT RATING). **Credit brokerage** includes the effecting of introductions
of individuals wishing to obtain credit to persons carrying on a consumer-credit
business. **Debt adjusting** is the process by which a third party negotiates terms for
the discharge of a debt due under consumer-credit agreements or consumer-hire
agreements with the creditor or owner on behalf of the debtor or hirer. The latter
may also pay a third party to take over an obligation to discharge a debt or to
undertake any similar acitivity concerned with its liquidation. **Debt counselling** is
the giving of advice (other than by the original creditor and certain others) to
debtors or hirers about the liquidation of debts due under consumer-credit
agreements or consumer-hire agreements. A **credit-reference agency** collects
information concerning the financial standing of individuals and supplies this
information to those seeking it. The Consumer Credit Act 1974 provides for the
licensing of ancillary credit businesses and regulates their activities.

Andean Pact An association set up by Columbia, Ecuador, Peru, and Venezuela in
1978 to enhance economic cooperation.

anergy The condition arising when, far from adding value, a business merger
produces an outcome that is less than the sum of the parts. It is the opposite of
*synergy.

angel An investor in a high-risk enterprise. Traditionally, the term was applied to
the financial backers of stage productions but it is now used increasingly for
investors in e-business.

annual accounts (annual report; report and accounts) The *financial statements
of an organization, generally published annually. In the UK, incorporated bodies
have a legal obligation to publish annual accounts and file them at Companies
House. Annual accounts consist of a *profit and loss account, *balance sheet, *cash-
flow statement (if required), and *statement of total recognized gains and losses,

a

together with supporting notes and the directors' report and *auditors' report. Companies falling into the legally defined *small companies and *medium-sized companies categories may file abbreviated accounts that may not have been audited. Some bodies are regulated by other statutes; for example, many financial institutions and their accounts will have to comply with their own regulations. Non-incorporated bodies, such as partnerships, are not legally obliged to produce accounts but may do so for their own information, for their banks if funding is being sought, and for the Inland Revenue for taxation purposes.

annual depreciation allowance The reduction in the book value of an asset at a specified percentage rate per annum.

annually compounding yield (annual percentage yield) The annual *rate of return on an investment calculated on the assumption that interest payments are reinvested at the yield rate.

annual percentage rate (APR) The annual equivalent *rate of return on a loan or investment in which the rate of interest and charges are specified in terms of an annual rate of interest. Most investment institutions are now required by law to specify the APR when the interest intervals are more frequent than annual. The use of an APR is required by the *Consumer Credit Act 1974 in the UK and the Truth in Lending Act in the USA. Similarly those charge cards that advertise monthly rates of interest (say, 2%) must state the equivalent APR. In this case it would be $[(1.02)^{12} - 1]$ = 26.8%.

annual report *See* ANNUAL ACCOUNTS.

annual return A document that must be filed with the Registrar of Companies within seven months of the end of the relevant accounting period (ten months for private companies). Information required on the annual return includes the address of the registered office of the company and the names, addresses, nationality, and occupations of its directors. The *financial statements, *directors' report, and *auditors' report must be annexed to the return. Legally defined *small companies and *medium-sized companies may file abbreviated accounts. Unlimited companies are exempt from filing the financial statements and dormant companies may not have to be audited. There are penalties for late filing of accounts.

annuitant A person who receives an *annuity.

annuity 1. A contract in which a person pays a premium to an insurance company, usually in one lump sum, and in return receives periodic payments for an agreed period or for the rest of his or her life (*see* LIFE ANNUITY). An annuity has been described as the opposite of a life assurance as the policyholder pays the lump sum and the insurer makes the regular payments. Annuities form the basis for private pensions in many developed countries. *See also* ANNUITY CERTAIN; DEFERRED ANNUITY. **2.** A payment made on such a contract.

annuity certain An *annuity in which payments continue for a specified period irrespective of the life or death of the person covered. In general, annuities cease on the death of the policyholder (*see* LIFE ANNUITY) unless they are annuities certain.

annuity finance A loan that is repaid by a set of payments involving principal and interest.

anomaly An opportunity for *abnormal returns in financial markets. If markets are efficient there should be no anomalies (*see* EFFICIENT MARKETS HYPOTHESIS), and the assumption that this will indeed be the case dictates the pricing of many financial obligations, notably derivatives (*see* ARBITRAGE-FREE CONDITION).

ANRPC Abbreviation for *Association of Natural Rubber Producing Countries.

ante-date To date a document before the date on which it is drawn up. This is not necessarily illegal or improper. For instance, an ante-dated cheque is not in law invalid. *Compare* POST-DATE.

anticipatory hedge A *hedge for a transaction that is expected to take place on a future date.

antidilution clause A term in a *warrant designed to protect the share price (and dividends per share) against such actions as *scrip issues.

antitrust legislation Laws that restrict monopolistic practices and are designed to encourage competitive behaviour among businesses.

APACS Abbreviation for *Association for Payment Clearing Services.

APCIMS Abbreviation for *Association of Private Client Investment Managers and Stockbrokers.

application form A form, issued by a newly floated company with its *prospectus, on which members of the public apply for shares in the company. *See also* ALLOTMENT; MULTIPLE APPLICATION; PINK FORM.

application for quotation An application by a *public limited company for a quotation on a *stock exchange.

appreciation **1.** An increase in the value of an asset, through inflation, a rise in market price, or interest earned. The directors of a company have an obligation to adjust the nominal value of land and buildings and other assets in balance sheets to take account of appreciation. *See* ASSET STRIPPING. **2.** An increase in the value of a currency with a *floating exchange rate relative to another currency. *Compare* DEPRECIATION; DEVALUATION.

appropriation **1.** An allocation of the net profit of an organization in its accounts. Some payments may be treated as expenses and deducted before arriving at net profit; other payments are deemed to be appropriations of profit, once that profit has been ascertained. Examples of the former are such normal trade expenses as wages and salaries of employees, motor running expenses, light and heat, and most interest payments on external finance. Appropriations of the net profit include payments of income tax or corporation tax, dividends to shareholders, transfers to reserves, and, in the case of partnerships, salaries and interest on capital paid to the partners. *See also* ACCUMULATED PROFITS. **2.** The allocation of payments to a particular debt out of several owed by a debtor to one creditor. The right to make the appropriation belongs first to the debtor but if the debtor fails to make the appropriation the creditor has the right to do so.

approved deferred share trust (ADST) A trust fund set up by a British company, and approved by the Inland Revenue, that purchases shares in that company for the benefit of its employees. Tax on dividends is deferred until the shares are sold and is then paid at a reduced rate.

approved list A list of suitable investments drawn up by a financial institution.

APR Abbreviation for *annual percentage rate.

APT Abbreviation for *arbitrage pricing theory.

arbitrage The entering into a set of financial obligations to obtain profits with no risk, usually by taking advantage of differences in interest rates, exchange rates, or commodity prices between one market and another. Arbitrage is non-speculative because an arbitrageur will only switch from one market to another knowing exactly what the rates or prices are in both markets and will only make the switch if the profit to be gained outweighs the costs of the operation. Thus, a large stock of a commodity in a user country may force its price below that in a producing country; if the difference is greater than the cost of shipping the goods back to the producing country, this could provide a profitable opportunity for arbitrage. Similar opportunities arise with *bills of exchange and foreign currencies.

arbitrage-free condition (no-arbitrage condition) The assumption, important in financial modelling, that there are no opportunities for risk-free excess returns in financial markets and no market *anomalies. These premises inform many aspects of finance, notably option pricing.

arbitrage pricing theory (APT) A model proposed by Stephen Ross in 1976 for calculating security returns in terms of the *arbitrage-free condition. It is an alternative to the *capital asset pricing model (CAPM). APT assumes a number of different *systematic risk factors without, however, definitively identifying the various types of risk. In setting *discount rates for decisions or valuations, companies therefore generally prefer to base their calculations on the CAPM.

arbitration A means of settling disputes without recourse to law. The arbitrator will hear the case of the parties and make either a binding or an indicative judgment.

ARBs Abbreviation for arbitrageurs, i.e. dealers specializing in *arbitrage.

arithmetic mean (arithmetic average) An average obtained by adding together the individual numbers concerned and dividing the total by their number. For example, the arithmetic mean of 7, 20, 107, and 350 is 484/4 = 121. This value, however, gives no idea of the spread of numbers. *Compare* GEOMETRIC MEAN; MEDIAN; WEIGHTED AVERAGE.

ARM Abbreviation for *adjustable-rate mortgage.

arm's length **1.** Denoting a transaction in which the parties to the transaction are or behave as if they are financially unconnected. For example, a transaction between two subsidiaries of the same parent organization could only be said to be at arm's length if it could be shown that the deal had been carried out at current market prices with no preference of any kind being shown in the trading terms. **2.** Denoting a portfolio in which the owner is not aware of the transactions entered into or its asset composition. *See* BLIND TRUST.

ARP Abbreviation for *adjustable-rate preferred stock.

ARR Abbreviation for *accounting rate of return.

arrangement **1.** A method of enabling a debtor to enter into an agreement with any creditors (either privately or through the courts) to discharge his or her debts by partial payment, as an alternative to bankruptcy. This is generally achieved by a **scheme of arrangement**, which involves applying the assets and income of the debtor in proportionate payment to the creditors. For instance, a scheme of arrangement may stipulate that the creditors will receive 20 pence for every pound that is owed to them. This is sometimes also known as **composition**. Once a scheme of arrangement has been agreed a **deed of arrangement** is drawn up, which must be registered with the Department of Trade and Industry within seven days. **2.** *See* VOLUNTARY ARRANGEMENT. **3.** A transaction or sale arranged by an intermediary, as in the case of an estate agent selling a mortgage as an agent for a bank.

articles of association The document that governs the running of a company. It sets out voting rights of shareholders, conduct of shareholders' and directors' meetings, powers of the management, etc. Either the articles are submitted with the *memorandum of association when application is made for incorporation or the relevant model articles contained in the Companies Regulations (Tables A to F) are adopted. Table A contains the model articles for companies limited by shares. The articles constitute a contract between the company and its members but this applies only to the rights of shareholders in their capacity as members. Therefore directors or company solicitors (for example) cannot use the articles to enforce their rights. The articles may be altered by a special resolution of the members in a general meeting.

ASB Abbreviation for *Accounting Standards Board.

ascending tops A series of market peaks, each of which represents a higher level of prices than its predecessor. In *chartist analysis such a series is seen as a sign of a *bull market. *Compare* RISING BOTTOMS. *See also* DOUBLE TOP.

A shares In the USA, the most important class of *ordinary shares. A shares usually have greater voting power than *B shares and may carry various other privileges.

Asian option (average rate option) An *option in which the *exercise price is arrived at with reference to the average price of the underlying.

asked price The price at which a security or commodity is offered for sale.

as per advice Words written on a *bill of exchange to indicate that the drawee has been informed that the bill is being drawn on him or her.

assented stock A security, usually an ordinary share, the owner of which has agreed to the terms of a *takeover bid. During the takeover negotiations, different prices may be quoted for assented and **non-assented stock**.

assessment The method by which a tax authority raises a bill for a particular tax and sends it to the taxpayer or the taxpayer's agent. The assessment may be based on figures already agreed between the authority and the taxpayer or it may be an estimate by the tax authorities. The taxpayer normally has a right of appeal against an assessment within a specified time limit. A **Notice of Assessment** is, under UK income tax legislation, essential before a legal liability to income tax can arise. The assessment must also be served on (or delivered to) the person being assessed. *See also* SELF-ASSESSMENT.

asset Any object, tangible or intangible, that is of value to its possessor. In most cases it either is cash or can be turned into cash; exceptions include prepayments, which may represent payments made for rent, rates, or motor licences, in cases in which the time paid for has not yet expired. Tangible assets include land and buildings, plant and machinery, fixtures and fittings, trading stock, investments, debtors, and cash; intangible assets include goodwill, patents, copyrights, and trademarks. *See also* DEFERRED DEBIT.

For *capital gains tax purposes, an asset consists of all forms of property, whether situated in the UK or abroad, including options, debts, incorporeal property, currency (other than sterling), and any form of property either created by the person disposing of it or owned without being acquired. It must, however, consist of some form of property for which a value can be ascertained. Some assets are exempt from capital gains tax.

asset and liability management committee (ALCO) A senior management committee of a bank or financial institution that has overall responsibility for setting and overseeing risk-control policies in relation to the balance sheet (*see* ASSET–LIABILITY MANAGEMENT; GAP ANALYSIS). In some cases it will also be responsible for general management policy.

asset-backed fund A fund in which the money is invested in tangible or corporate assets, such as property or shares, rather than being treated as savings loaned to a bank or other institution. Asset-backed funds can be expected to grow with inflation in a way that bank savings cannot. *See also* EQUITY-LINKED POLICY; UNIT-LINKED POLICY.

asset-backed security A bond or note whose *collateral is the cash flows from a pool of financial obligations such as mortgages, car loans, or credit-card receivables. *See* SECURITIZATION.

Asset card *See* DEBIT CARD.

asset constraint A restriction on the *assets that can be contained in a portfolio.

asset cover A ratio that provides a measure of the solvency of a company; it consists of its *net assets divided by its *debt. Those companies with high asset cover are considered the more solvent.

asset financing Funding arranged by using assets as collateral. Examples of asset financing are *factoring and *hire purchase agreements.

asset–liability gap *See* GAP.

asset–liability management The management of assets and liabilities in order to influence the *credit risk, *interest-rate risk, and *liquidity risk of a bank. *See* ASSET AND LIABILITY MANAGEMENT COMMITTEE; GAP ANALYSIS.

asset management **1.** The management of the financial assets of a company in order to maximize the return on the investments. **2.** An investment service offered by banks and some other financial institutions. In the UK some private banks offer an asset management service for wealthy customers. *See also* PORTFOLIO.

asset securitization The process of turning assets into securities. In *mortgage-backed securities, for example, the cash flows of a mortgage portfolio are packaged and sold to an investor in the form of a security.

asset-sensitive Describing a situation in which a bank's assets are of shorter *duration or have a shorter time until repricing than its liabilities. This situation may make a bank vulnerable to falls in interest rates, since interest income falls will predate falls in interest cost on liabilities. *See* GAP.

asset stripping The acquisition or takeover of a company whose shares are valued below their *asset value, and the subsequent sale of the company's assets. Having identified a suitable company, an entrepreneur would acquire a controlling interest in it by buying its shares on the stock exchange; after revaluation, properties or other assets held could be sold for cash, which would be distributed to shareholders (now including the entrepreneur). Subsequently, the entrepreneur could either revitalize the management of the company and later sell off the acquired shareholding at a profit or, in some cases, close the business down. Because the asset stripper is totally heedless of the welfare of the other shareholders, the employees, the suppliers, or creditors of the stripped company, the practice is highly deprecated.

asset swap A *swap designed to alter the cash flows of the holder of a particular asset. For example, if the asset provides a variable cash flow it can be swapped with one providing a fixed cash flow.

asset valuation **1.** The assessment of the value of assets, most usually by a *present value calculation. **2.** An assessment of the value at which the *assets of an organization, usually the *capital assets, should be entered into its balance sheet. The valuation may be arrived at in a number of ways; for example, a revaluation of land and buildings would often involve taking professional advice.

asset value (per share) The total value of the assets of a company less its liabilities, divided by the number of ordinary shares in issue. This represents in theory, although not in practice, the amount attributable to each share if the company was wound up. The asset value may not necessarily be the total of the values shown by a company's balance sheet, since it is not the function of balance sheets to value assets. It may, therefore, be necessary to substitute the best estimate that can be made of the market values of the assets (including goodwill) for the values shown in the balance sheet. If there is more than one class of share, it may be necessary to deduct amounts due to shareholders with a priority on winding up before arriving at the amounts attributable to shareholders with a lower priority. If a company goes into liquidation or receivership, the break-up value of the assets may well be below their book value, especially if the assets include specialized or obsolete machinery saleable only for its scrap value.

assignment The act of transferring, or a document (a **deed of assignment**) transferring, property to some other person. Examples of assignment include the transfer of rights under a contract or benefits under a trust to another person.

assignment of insurable interest Assigning to another party the rights and obligations of the *insurable interest in an item of property, life, or a legal liability to be insured. This enables the person to whom the interest is assigned to arrange insurance cover, which would not otherwise be legally permitted.

assignment of life policies Transfer of the legal right under a life-assurance policy to collect the proceeds. Assignment is only valid if the life insurer is advised and agrees; life assurance is the only form of insurance in which the assignee need not possess an *insurable interest. In recent years policy auctions have become a popular alternative to surrendering *endowment assurances. In these auctions, a policy is sold to the highest bidder and then assigned to him or her by the original policyholder.

associate company (affiliate) A company that is partly owned by another and over which the investing company exercises a significant influence.

Association for Payment Clearing Services (APACS) An association set up by the UK banks in 1985 to manage payment clearing and overseas money transmission in the UK. The three operating companies under its aegis are: BACS Ltd, which provides an automated service for interbank clearing in the UK; Cheque and Credit Clearing Co. Ltd, which operates a bulk clearing system for interbank cheques and paper credits; and CHAPS, which provides same-day clearing for high-value cheques and electronic funds transfer. In addition EftPos UK Ltd is a company set up to develop electronic funds transfer at the point of sale. APACS also oversees London Dollar Clearing, the London Currency Settlement Scheme, and the cheque card and *eurocheque schemes in the UK.

Association of African Development Finance Institutions (AADFI) An organization set up in 1975 in Abidjan, Côte d'Ivoire, to encourage and support funding for economic and social development projects in African countries.

Association of British Insurers (ABI) A trade association representing over 440 insurance companies offering any class of insurance business, whose members transact over 90% of the business of the British insurance market. It was formed in 1985 by a merger the British Insurance Association, the Accident Offices Association, the Fire Offices Committee, the Life Offices Association, and the Industrial Life Offices Association.

Association of Corporate Treasurers (ACT) An organization set up to encourage and promote the study and practice of treasury management in companies. A small organization in relation to the professional accounting bodies, it has become influential in the field of corporate treasurership. Fellows of the Association are designated FCT and members as MCT.

Association of Futures Brokers and Dealers Ltd (AFBD) A former Self-Regulating Organization (SRO) set up under the *Financial Services Act 1986 to regulate the activities of brokers and dealers on the London International Financial Futures and Options Exchange. It merged with The *Securities Association Ltd in 1991 to form the *Securities and Futures Authority Ltd (SFA). In November 2001, with the implementation of the Financial Services and Markets Act 2000, the SFA was absorbed into the *Financial Services Authority.

Association of International Bond Dealers (AIBD) *See* INTERNATIONAL SECURITIES MARKET ASSOCIATION.

Association of Lloyd's Members (ALM) A voluntary advisory organization of the *external members of *Lloyd's aimed at exploring and promoting their views on the Lloyd's insurance market.

Association of Natural Rubber Producing Countries (ANRPC) An organization of countries that produce natural rubber. Its aims are to foster mutual pricing, marketing, and the technical development of natural rubber.

Association of Private Client Investment Managers and Stockbrokers (APCIMS) A representative body for private-client investment managers and stockbrokers, formed in June 1990. It aims to improve the environment and expand the market in which private-investors' business is transacted. The association represents 95% of eligible firms with a network of over 250 offices throughout the UK. It publishes a directory of private-client stockbrokers, with details of members and the services they provide. It is run by an elected committee with a small permanent secretariat based in London, assisted by specialist practitioner committees.

Association of Tin Producing Countries (ATPC) An organization of countries that produce tin. Its aim is to control the market price of mined tin by means of export quotas.

assurance *Insurance against an eventuality (especially death) that must occur. *See* LIFE ASSURANCE.

assured The person named in a life-assurance policy to receive the proceeds in the event of maturity or the death of the *life assured. As a result of the policy, the person's financial future is 'assured'.

AST Abbreviation for *automated screen trading.

asymmetric information **1.** An aspect of the *agency problem in which managers have superior information to shareholders regarding the state of the shareholders' investment. *See* SIGNALLING HYPOTHESIS. **2.** The situation in which the purchaser of an insurance contract knows more about the nature of the risks than the seller of the contract (*see* ADVERSE SELECTION).

asymmetric margining A situation in which different parties in a transaction are subject to different margin conditions, which may reflect their creditworthiness.

asymmetric payoff The situation in which the *payoff profile of a financial instrument is different according to whether the market rises or falls. For example, this is the case with option values in relation to changes in the price of the *underlying and with bond values in relation to changes in interest rates.

at A monetary unit of Laos, worth one hundredth of a *kip.

at best An instruction to a broker to buy or sell shares, stocks, commodities, currencies, etc., as specified, at the best possible price at the time of transaction. It must be executed immediately irrespective of market movements. *Compare* AT LIMIT.

at call Denoting secured money that has been lent on a short-term basis and must be repaid immediately on demand. Discount houses in the City of London are the main borrowers of money at call.

Athens Stock Exchange The only stock exchange in Greece. It was established in 1876 and privatized in 1988, with a new supervisory board and central depository.

at limit An instruction to a broker to buy or sell shares, stocks, commodities, currencies, etc., as specified, at a stated limiting price (i.e. not above a stated price if buying or not below a stated price if selling). When issuing such an instruction the principal should also state for how long the instruction stands, e.g. for a day, a week, etc. *Compare* AT BEST.

ATM Abbreviation for *automated teller machine.

at par *See* PAR VALUE.

ATPC Abbreviation for *Association of Tin Producing Countries.

at sight The words used on a *bill of exchange to indicate that payment is due on presentation. *Compare* AFTER DATE; AFTER SIGHT.

attachment The procedure enabling a creditor, who has obtained judgment in the courts (the judgment creditor), to secure payment of the amount due from the debtor. The judgment creditor obtains a further court order (the garnishee order) to the effect that money or property due from a third party (the garnishee) to the debtor must be frozen and paid instead to the judgment creditor to satisfy the amount due. For instance, a judgment creditor may, through a garnishee order, attach the salary due to the debtor from the debtor's employer (the garnishee).

at-the-money option A call or put *option in which the exercise price is approximately the same as the current market price of the underlying security.

ATX Abbreviation for Austrian Traded Index. *See* OTOB.

auction A method of selling in which goods, securities, rights, etc., are sold in public to the highest bidder. In an **English auction** the potential buyers make bids and the highest bid is accepted. In a **Dutch auction** the price begins high and is gradually lowered until a buyer agrees to pay it. Auctions are also used to sell government, debt and many diverse financial obligations. *See* DOUBLE AUCTION.

auction market preferred stock (AMPS) A US floating rate preferred stock whose dividend is set by Dutch auction.

audit An independent examination of, and the subsequent expression of opinion on, the financial statements of an organization. This involves the auditor in collecting evidence by means of compliance tests (tests of control) and substantive tests (tests of detail). External audits (i.e. audits performed by an auditor external to the organization) are required under statute for limited companies by the Companies Act and for various other undertakings, such as housing associations and building societies, by other acts of parliament. Internal audits are performed by auditors within an organization, usually an independent department, such as an internal-audit department. Internal auditors examine various areas, including financial and non-financial concerns, with emphasis on ensuring that internal controls are working effectively. Internal auditors may assist the external auditor of an organization. Non-statutory audits can be performed at the request of the owners, members, or trustees of an undertaking, for example. Forms of *financial statements, other than the annual accounts, may also be audited; for example, summaries of sales made or stocks held by an organization in a specified period. *See also* STATUTORY AUDIT; AUDITORS' REPORT; INTERNAL AUDIT.

audit fee (auditors' remuneration) The amount payable to an *auditor for an *audit; this has to be approved at the annual general meeting of a company. In the *financial statements, audit fees must be distinguished from fees payable to the auditor for non-audit work.

auditor A person or firm appointed to carry out an *audit of an organization. In the UK, since the Companies Act 1989 an external auditor must be a registered auditor or a member of a recognized supervisory body and be eligible for appointment under the rules of that body (*see* CERTIFIED ACCOUNTANT; CHARTERED ACCOUNTANT). The four recognized bodies, given approval in 1991, were the Association of Chartered Certified Accountants (ACCA), the Institute of Chartered Accountants in England and Wales (ICAEW), the Institute of Chartered Accountants of Scotland (ICAS), and the Institute of Chartered Accountants in Ireland (ICAI). Since 1991, the Association of Authorized Public Accountants (AAPA) has also been recognized in principle. The recognized supervisory bodies are required to have rules designed to ensure that persons eligible for appointment as company auditors are either individuals who hold the appropriate qualification or firms controlled by properly qualified persons. These bodies must also ensure that eligible persons continue to maintain the appropriate level of competence and must monitor and enforce compliance with their rules. These rules do not apply to internal auditors.

auditors' report (audit report) A report by the auditors appointed to *audit the accounts of a company or other organization. Auditors' reports may take many forms depending on who has appointed the auditors and for what purposes. Some auditors are engaged in an internal audit while others are appointed for various

statutory purposes. The auditors of a limited company are required to form an
opinion as to whether the annual accounts of the company give a true and fair view
of its profit or loss for the period under review and of its state of affairs at the end of
the period; they are also required to certify that the accounts are prepared in
accordance with the requirements of the Companies Act 1985. The auditors' report
is technically a report to the members of the company and it must be filed together
with the accounts with the Registrar of Companies under the Companies Act 1985.
Under this Act, the auditors' report must also include an audit of the directors'
report with respect to consistency. *See also* QUALIFIED AUDIT REPORT.

audit trail The ability to trace the details of past transactions through accounts. It
is usually applied to computer files and is important in securities dealing to enable
supervisory bodies to follow transactions and ensure that fair prices have been paid.
It is sometimes called a **paper trail**.

aurar The plural of *eyrir.

Australian Stock Exchange (ASX) The stock exchange based in Sydney, which
in 1987 superseded the exchanges in Brisbane, Adelaide, Hobart, Melbourne, and
Perth. It abolished fixed-rate commissions in 1984 and adopted fully automated
trading in October 1990. ASX issues the *All-Ordinaries share index as well as the
subsidiary indices, the All-Industrials share index and All-Resources share index.

authorized auditor An individual granted authorization by the Board of Trade or
the Secretary of State to be the auditor of a company under the Companies Act
1967. Authorizations were granted to individuals not otherwise eligible to act as
auditors on the basis of their experience. The power to grant authorizations ended
in April 1978. Under the Companies Act 1989 an authorized auditor is eligible for
appointment as an auditor of an unquoted company but is not qualified to be the
auditor of any other company. *See also* AUDITOR.

authorized financial adviser An investment and finance adviser authorized
under the UK *Financial Services Act 1986.

authorized investments Legally authorized investments suitable for trust funds.
See also GENERAL POWER OF INVESTMENT.

**authorized share capital (nominal share capital; nominal capital; registered
capital)** The maximum amount of *share capital that may be issued by a company,
as detailed in the company's memorandum of association. The authorized share
capital must be disclosed on the face of the *balance sheet or alternatively in the
notes to the accounts.

autocorrelation In statistics, the correlation of error terms produced by a
regression (*see* REGRESSION ANALYSIS). It may make the regression and its estimated
coefficients less reliable. *See* CORRELATION COEFFICIENT.

automated screen trading (AST) Electronic dealing in securities using visual-
display units to display prices and the associated computer equipment to enter,
match, and execute deals. The system does away with the need for face-to-face
trading on a formal stock-exchange floor, and even dispenses with telephone
dealing. It potentially reduces or eliminates paperwork.

automated teller machine (ATM) A computerized machine often attached to
the outside wall of a High-Street bank or building society that enables customers to
withdraw cash from their accounts, especially outside normal banking hours. The
machines may also be used to pay in cash or cheques, effect transfers, and obtain

statements. They are operated by *cash cards or *multifunctional cards in conjunction with a *PIN. ATMs are often known colloquially as **cash dispensers**.

automatic debit transfer *See* GIRO.

available earnings *See* EARNINGS PER SHARE.

aval **1.** A third-party guarantee of payment on a *bill of exchange or promissory note; it is often given by a bank. **2.** A signature on a bill of exchange that endorses or guarantees the bill.

AVCs Abbreviation for *additional voluntary contributions.

average **1.** A single number used to represent a set of numbers; mean. *See* ARITHMETIC MEAN; GEOMETRIC MEAN; MEDIAN. **2.** A method of sharing losses in property insurance to combat underinsurance. This is usually applied in an **average clause** in a fire insurance policy, in which it is stated that the sum payable in the event of a claim shall not be more than the proportion that the insured value of an item bears to its actual value. **3.** A partial loss in marine insurance.

average rate option *See* ASIAN OPTION.

average stock A method of accounting for stock movements that assumes goods are taken out of stock at the average cost of the goods in stock. *See* BASE STOCK; FIRST IN, FIRST OUT; LAST IN, FIRST OUT.

averaging Adding to a holding of particular securities or commodities when the price falls, in order to reduce the average cost of the whole holding. **Averaging in** consists of buying at various price levels in order to build up a substantial holding of securities or commodities over a period. **Averaging out** is the opposite process, of selling a large holding at various price levels over a long period.

avo A monetary unit of Macao worth one hundredth of a *pataca.

baby bonds **1.** In the USA, bonds having a denomination lower than $1000. **2.** Bonds offered by tax-exempt friendly societies, which produce maturing funds for an infant over a period (minimum 10 years). Under current UK rules, up to £25 a month (or £270 a year) may be invested tax free in a baby bond. **3.** An informal name for *child trust funds.

back contract The *futures contract on an exchange with the latest (i.e. most distant in time) expiry date.

backdate **1.** To put an earlier date on a document than that on which it was compiled, in order to make it effective from that earlier date. **2.** To agree that salary increases, especially those settled in a pay award, should apply from a specified date in the recent past.

back door One of the methods by which the *Bank of England injects cash into the *money market. The bank purchases Treasury bills at the market rate rather than by lending money directly to the discount houses (the **front-door method**) when it acts as *lender of last resort.

back-end load The final charge made by a *mutual fund or *investment trust when an investor sells shares in the fund.

backing away The failure of a *market maker in a particular security to fulfil a *bid for the minimum quantity. This is considered unethical conduct. *See* MAKING A PRICE. *See also* GOING AHEAD.

back month The latest (i.e. most distant in time) expiry month for a *futures contract.

back office A section of a financial firm not directly involved in trading, but rather dealing with administration, documentation, and *compliance with regulatory restrictions. *Compare* FRONT OFFICE; MIDDLE OFFICE.

back-office crunch A situation in which the *back office of a financial firm is overwhelmed by the administrative implications of a high level of business.

back spread The strategy of selling an *option near to or at the money (*see* AT-THE-MONEY OPTION) and using the premium to buy a number of the same types of option out of the money (*see* INTRINSIC VALUE). If this is a call option, a profit will be made if the price of the *underlying rises markedly. If the option is a put, then money will be made if the value of the underlying falls dramatically.

back-to-back credit (countervailing credit) A method used to conceal the identity of the seller from the buyer in a credit arrangement. When the credit is arranged by a British finance house, the foreign seller provides the relevant documentation. The finance house, acting as an intermediary, issues its own documents to the buyer, omitting the seller's name and so concealing the seller's identity. The reason for not revealing the seller's identity is to prevent buyer and seller dealing direct in future transactions and thus cutting out the middle man.

b

back-to-back loan One loan of a matching pair of loans in different currencies: A lends to B and B lends to A where the loans are of the same value. The back-to-back loan was a precurser of the *currency swap and can be used to avoid currency restrictions.

back-to-back swaps Two *swaps that have been combined, sometimes as a method of winding up a swap position. However, the obligations mean that such a combination still has residual risk, so swaps are usually wound up by a final payment reflecting the current market value of the swap.

back-up credit An alternative source of funds arranged if an issue of *commercial paper is not fully taken up by the market. Back-up credit is provided by a bank for a fee or by the deposit of credit balances at the bank of the issuer. The back-up is often a stand-by facility provided by the bank, which may be drawn upon if the paper is not placed.

backwardation **1.** The difference between the spot price of a commodity, plus any carrying costs, and the forward price, when the spot price is the higher. **2.** A situation that occasionally occurs in which a market maker quotes a buying price for a share that is lower than the selling price quoted by another market maker. **3.** On a stock exchange, a percentage paid by the seller to delay delivery by one account period.

backwardation swap A commodity *swap in which the payments are based on the spot and futures prices. *See* BACKWARDATION.

BACS Abbreviation for *Bankers Automated Clearing System. *See also* ASSOCIATION FOR PAYMENT CLEARING SERVICES.

bad debt An amount owed by a debtor that is unlikely to be paid; for example, due to a company going into liquidation. The full amount should be written off to the *profit and loss account of the period or to a provision for bad and doubtful debts as soon as it is foreseen, on the grounds of prudence. Bad debts subsequently recovered either in part or in full should be written back to the profit and loss account of the period (or to a provision for bad and doubtful debts).

badges of trade The criteria that distinguish trading from investment for taxation purposes. They were set out by the Royal Commission on the Taxation of Profits and Income in 1954. Dealing on the *commodity markets is normally regarded as trading and profits are subject to income tax or corporation tax; dealing on security markets is often (but not always) treated as investment and profits are subject to lower taxation by the capital gains tax.

baht (B) The standard monetary unit of Thailand, divided into 100 satang.

baiza A monetary unit of Oman worth one thousandth of a *rial.

balance concentration In banking, the practice of consolidating the bank accounts of a group of companies in order to minimize overdraft costs.

balanced-budget multiplier (BBM) The effect on the gross national product caused by a change in government expenditure that has been offset by an equal change in taxation. For example, an increase in government spending will inject more demand into the economy than the equal increase in taxation takes out, since some of the income absorbed by the tax would have been used for savings and therefore did not contribute to the aggregate demand. In effect, individuals have reduced savings, they feel worse off, and therefore work harder to build up their savings again. The balanced-budget multiplier is not usually pursued explicitly as an instrument of fiscal policy as taxation is generally unpopular.

In traditional Keynesian goods-sector models the BBM will equal one. In other words, the change in gross national product is equal to the change in government expenditure or the change in taxation, i.e.:

$$BBM = \frac{\Delta Y}{\Delta G} = 1,$$

where ΔG is the change in government expenditure and ΔY is the change in gross national product.

balanced mutual fund A low-risk *unit trust in which the investment strategy is to balance growth and income. This is achieved by purchasing a mix of *ordinary shares, *preference shares, and bonds.

balance of payments The accounts setting out a country's transactions with the outside world. They are divided into various sub-accounts, notably the **current account** and the **capital account**. The former includes the trade account, which records the balance of imports and exports (*see* BALANCE OF TRADE). Overall, the accounts must always be in balance. A deficit or surplus on the balance of payments refers to the level of purchases or sales of the currency by the national government, usually through its central bank. The conventions used for presenting balance-of-payments statistics are those recommended by the *International Monetary Fund.

balance of trade The accounts setting out the results of a country's trading position. It is a component of the *balance of payments, forming part of the *current account. It includes the *visibles (i.e. imports and exports in physical merchandise) but not the *invisible balance (receipts and expenditure on such services as insurance, finance, freight, and tourism).

balance sheet A statement of the total assets and liabilities of an organization at a particular date, usually the last day of the *accounting period. The first part of the statement lists the fixed and current assets and the liabilities, the second part shows how they have been financed; the totals for each part must be equal. Under the Companies Act the balance sheet is one of the primary statements to be included in the financial accounts of a company. The Companies Act requires that the balance sheet of a company must give a true and fair view of its state of affairs at the end of its financial year, and must comply with statute as to its form and content. There are two possible balance-sheet formats. In both formats, corresponding amounts for the preceding financial year should be shown. A balance sheet does not necessarily value a company, as some assets may be omitted, or given an unrealistic value.

balance-sheet hedge A *hedge against *translation exposure.

balancing charge The charge that may be assessable to *corporation tax on the disposal of an asset when the proceeds realized on the sale of the asset exceed the *written-down value, for tax purposes. The balancing charge amounts to the difference between the proceeds and the written-down value. For example, if the written-down value is £23,000 and the proceeds on disposal were £30,000, there would be a balancing charge of the difference of £7000. The balancing charge is deducted from the other allowances for the period. If the charge exceeds the allowances available, the net amount is added to the profit for the period and assessed to tax.

balboa (B) The standard monetary unit of Panama, divided into 100 centésimos.

balloon A large sum repaid as an irregular instalment of a loan repayment. **Balloon loans** are those in which repayments are not made in a regular manner, but are made, as funds become available, in balloons.

balloon mortgage A *mortgage in which one or more large payments may be made as part of the repayment profile; it is also called a **non-amortizing mortgage**. With a balloon mortgage a lump sum often has to be repaid at the end of the term to cover the remaining debt.

ballot A random selection of applications for an oversubscribed *new issue of securities (see also FLOTATION). The successful applicants may be granted the full number of securities for which they have applied or a specified proportion of their applications. Applicants not selected in the ballot have their applications and cheques returned.

Baltic Exchange A former commodity and freight-chartering exchange in the City of London. It took its name from the trade in grain with Baltic ports, which was the mainstay of the business in the 18th century. Its activity is now undertaken by the London *Futures and Options Exchange.

Baltic International Freight Futures Exchange (BIFFEX) See FUTURES AND OPTIONS EXCHANGE.

ban (*plural* **bani**) A monetary unit of Romania and Moldova worth one hundredth of a *leu.

bancassurance (Allfinanz) The combination of traditional loan and savings bank products with such assurance products as *life assurance and *pensions. It is now common for major UK banks to provide this combined service and the practice is spreading worldwide.

band **1.** A trading range, set by upper and lower limits, of a commodity or currency. The *European Monetary System and Bretton Woods system (see BRETTON WOODS CONFERENCE) both established such ranges within which currencies were permitted to move. **2.** Four ranges of maturities set by the Bank of England to influence short-term interest rates in the money market. They are set on *Treasury bills, *local authority bills, and eligible bank bills (see ELIGIBLE PAPER); band 1 is from 1 to 14 days, band 2 from 15 to 33 days, band 3 from 34 to 63 days, and band 4 from 64 to 91 days.

bank A commercial institution that takes deposits and extends loans. Banks are concerned mainly with making and receiving payments on behalf of their customers, accepting deposits, and making short-term loans to private individuals, companies, and other organizations. However, they also provide money transmission services and in recent years have diversified into many areas of financial services. In the UK, the banking system comprises the *Bank of England (the central bank), the *commercial banks, *merchant banks, branches of foreign and Commonwealth banks, the *National Savings Bank, and the National Girobank (see GIRO). The first (1990) *building society to become a bank in the UK was the Abbey National, after its public *flotation; many other building societies have now followed this precedent. In other countries banks are also usually supervised by a government-controlled central bank.

bank account See ACCOUNT; CHEQUE ACCOUNT; CURRENT ACCOUNT; DEPOSIT ACCOUNT; LOAN ACCOUNT; SAVINGS ACCOUNT.

bank advisory committee A group of leading banks in a foreign debtor country that draws up plans for rescheduling that country's debts. These plans are submitted to the debtor country's government. *See* LONDON CLUB; MULTI-YEAR RESCHEDULING AGREEMENT.

bank bill A bill of exchange issued or guaranteed (accepted) by a bank. It is more acceptable than a trade bill as there is less risk of non-payment and hence it can be discounted at a more favourable rate, although to some extent this depends on the bank's credit rating.

bank certificate A certificate, signed by a bank manager, stating the balance held to a company's credit on a specified date. It may be asked for during the course of an audit.

bank charge The amount charged to a customer by a bank, usually for a specific transaction, such as paying in a sum of money by means of a cheque or withdrawing a sum by means of an automated teller machine. However, modern practice is to provide periods of commission-free banking by waiving most charges on personal current accounts. Business customers invariably pay tariffs in one form or another.

bank deposit A sum of money placed by a customer with a bank. The deposit may or may not attract interest and may be instantly accessible or accessible at a time agreed by the two parties. Banks may use a percentage of their customers' deposits to lend on to other customers; thus most deposits may only exist on paper in the bank's books. Money on deposit at a bank is usually held in either a *deposit account or a *current account, although some banks now offer special high-interest accounts.

bank draft (banker's cheque; banker's draft) A cheque drawn by a bank on itself or its agent. A person who owes money to another buys the draft from a bank for cash and hands it to the creditor who need have no fear that it might be dishonoured. A bank draft is used if the creditor is unwilling to accept an ordinary cheque.

banker's acceptance 1. A *time draft that promises to pay a certain sum and has been accepted by a bank. It is a form of promissory note, widely used in international trade; once signed and dated it can be traded before its maturity. *See also* THIRD-COUNTRY ACCEPTANCE. **2.** The *acceptance by a bank of a *bill of exchange, thereby increasing its negotiability.

Bankers Automated Clearing System (BACS) A company owned by the UK banks that operates a computerized payments clearing service. It is commonly used by companies for paying employees. *See also* ASSOCIATION FOR PAYMENT CLEARING SERVICES.

banker's bank 1. A bank created by a group of independent banks in order to set up a *clearing cycle. **2.** A *central bank that holds accounts for banks within its jurisdiction.

banker's cheque *See* BANK DRAFT.

banker's reference (status enquiry) A report on the creditworthiness of an individual supplied by a bank to a third party, such as another financial institution or a bank customer. References and status enquiries are often supplied by specialist credit-reference agencies, who keep lists of defaulters, bad payers, and people who have infringed credit agreements. References must be very general and recent legislation has given new rights to the subjects of such reports, which restrict their value even further.

Bank for International Settlements (BIS) An international bank originally established in 1930 as a financial institution to coordinate the payment of war reparations between European central banks. It was hoped that the BIS, with headquarters in Basle, would develop into a European central bank but many of its functions were taken over by the *International Monetary Fund (IMF) after World War II. Since then the BIS has fulfilled several roles, including acting as a trustee and agent for various international groups, such as the OECD, European Monetary System, and IMF. The frequent meetings of the BIS directors have been a useful means of cooperation between central banks, especially in combating short-term speculative monetary movements. The BIS also sets *capital adequacy ratios for banks. The original members were France, Belgium, West Germany, Italy, and the UK but now most European central banks are represented as well as the USA, Canada, and Japan. The London agent is the Bank of England, whose governor is a member of the board of directors of the BIS.

Bank Giro *See* GIRO.

bank guarantee An undertaking given by a bank to settle a debt should the debtor fail to do so. A bank guarantee can be used as a security for a loan but the banks themselves will require good cover in cash or counter-indemnity before they issue a guarantee. A guarantee has to be in writing to be legally binding. Such guarantees often contain indemnity clauses, which place a direct onus on the guarantor. This onus leaves the guarantor liable in law in all eventualities.

bank holding company A corporation that has a bank as one of its major subsidiaries.

Bank Holidays In the UK, public holidays on which the banks are closed. In England and Wales they are New Year's Day, Easter Monday, May Day (the first Monday in May), Spring Bank Holiday (the last Monday in May), August Bank Holiday (last Monday in August), and Boxing Day. In Scotland, Easter Monday is replaced by 2 January and the August Bank Holiday is on the first Monday in August. In Northern Ireland St Patrick's Day (17 March) and the Battle of the Boyne (12 July) are added. In the Channel Islands Liberation Day (9 May) is included. Bank Holidays have a similar status to Sundays in that *bills of exchange falling due on a Bank Holiday are postponed until the following day and also they do not count in working out *days of grace. Good Friday and Christmas Day are also public holidays, but payments falling due (including bills of exchange) on these days are payable on the preceding day. When Bank Holidays fall on a Sunday, the following day becomes the Bank Holiday.

banking The activities undertaken by banks; this includes personal banking (non-business customers), commercial banking (small and medium-sized business customers), and corporate banking (large international and multinational corporations). In the UK most banking for both business and personal customers is undertaken through the High-Street banks, known as **branch banking** (*see also* COMMERCIAL BANK).

Banking Acts 1979 and 1987 UK Acts of Parliament defining a bank as a taker of deposits and investing supervision of banks in the *Bank of England. The Acts created safeguards to ensure that only proper persons should be managers, directors, or controllers of banks. The Acts also stipulate that the paid-up capital reserves of such an institution should be not less than £1 million. The only exceptions to this limit are authorized *building societies, municipal and school

banks, and some central or international development banks. The UK legislation
was made necessary by the European Community's First Banking Directive.

banking book A record of the banking activities of a bank as distinct from its
trading activities. This division is often used for the purposes of organizational and
risk management. For example, the banking book will register the impacts of the
competitive advantage that may be obtained from raising and lending retail funds
on particular terms and of the *credit risk and *operational risk associated with
those activities. However, rates of interest and exchange are likely to be swapped
out of the banking book, because they are regarded as being managed by the
trading activity of the bank. *Compare* TRADING BOOK.

banking directives Directives on various aspects of banking practice issued by
the EU parliament and Council of Ministers for implementation in member states;
they include directives on solvency ratios, large exposures, and money laundering.
The most important is the *Second Directive, which concerns the licensing of banks
in EU countries other than their domicile; it also makes stipulations about *capital
adequacy. The *Investment Services Directive seeks to apply the principles outlined
in the Second Directive to investment products.

Banking Ombudsman *See* FINANCIAL OMBUDSMAN SERVICE.

bank loan (bank advance) A specified sum of money lent by a bank to a customer,
usually for a specified time, at a specified rate of interest. In most cases banks
require some form of security for loans, especially if the loan is to a commercial
enterprise, although if a bank regards a company as a good credit risk, loans may
not be secured. *See also* LOAN ACCOUNT; OVERDRAFT; PERSONAL LOAN.

bank mandate A document given by a customer of a bank to the bank,
requesting that the bank should open an account in the customer's name and
honour cheques and other orders for payment drawn on the account. The mandate
specifies the signatures that the bank should accept for transactions on the account
and also contains specimens of the signatures.

banknote An item of paper currency issued by a central bank. Banknotes
developed in England from the receipts issued by London goldsmiths in the 17th
century for gold deposited with them for safekeeping. These receipts came to be
used as money and their popularity as a *medium of exchange encouraged the
goldsmiths to issue their own banknotes, largely to increase their involvement in
banking and, particularly, moneylending. Now only the Bank of England and the
Scottish and Irish banks in the UK have the right to issue notes. Originally all
banknotes were fully backed by gold and could be exchanged on demand for gold;
however, since 1931 the promise on a note to "pay the bearer on demand" simply
indicates that the note is legal tender. *See also* PROMISSORY NOTE.

Bank of England The central bank of the UK. It was established in 1694 as a
private bank by London merchants in order to lend money to the state and to deal
with the national debt. It came under public ownership in 1946 with the passing of
the Bank of England Act. The Bank of England acts as the government's bank,
providing loans through ways and means advances and arranging borrowing
through the issue of gilt-edged securities. The bank helps to implement the
government's financial and monetary policy as directed by the Treasury. Since May
1997 its Monetary Policy Committee has had sole authority for setting the *base
rate, which was formerly a joint decision of the Chancellor of the Exchequer and
the Governor of the Bank of England (although the Chancellor retains the right to
overrule the Governor in exceptional circumstances). It had wide statutory powers

to supervise the banking system, including the commercial banks. However, it was announced in May 1997 that these supervisory powers would pass to the restructured *Securities and Investment Board, subsequently the *Financial Services Authority. The bank, however, retains its responsibility for systemic stability and that of *lender of last resort.

The Bank Charter Act 1844 divided the bank into an issue department and a banking department. The issue department is responsible for the issue of banknotes and coins as supplied by the *Royal Mint. The banking department provides banking services (including accounts) to commercial banks, foreign banks, other central banks, and government departments. The bank manages the national debt, acting as registrar of government stocks. It also administers *exchange control, when in force, and manages the *exchange equalization account. The bank is controlled by a governor, deputy-governor, and a court (board) of 16 directors, appointed by the Crown for periods of 4–5 years. *See also* BANKING ACTS 1979 AND 1987.

Bank of Japan (BOJ) The Japanese central bank, which controls monetary policy but does not regulate Japanese banks.

bank rate The rate at which the central bank, in the UK the *Bank of England, is prepared to lend to the other banks in the banking system. It is now more commonly known as the *base rate.

bank reconciliation statement A statement that reconciles the bank balance in the books of an organization with the *bank statement. Differences may be due to cheques drawn by the organization but not yet presented to the bank, bank charges deducted from the account not yet notified to the organization, and payments made to the bank but not yet recorded by the organization. Bank reconciliations are usually performed weekly or monthly and are a form of internal control check.

bank release A document that allows an importer to take physical possession of goods purchased by means of a bank credit to the importer.

bankruptcy The state of an individual who is unable to pay his or her debts and against whom a **bankruptcy order** has been made by a court. Such orders deprive bankrupts of their property, which is then used to pay their debts. Bankruptcy proceedings are started by a petition, which may be presented to the court by (1) a creditor or creditors; (2) a person affected by a voluntary arrangement to pay debts set up by the debtor under the Insolvency Act 1986; (3) the Director of Public Prosecutions; or (4) the debtor. The grounds for a creditors' petition are that the debtor appears to be unable to pay his or her debts or to have reasonable prospects of doing so, i.e. that the debtor has failed to make arrangements to pay a debt for which a statutory demand has been made or that a judgment debt has not been satisifed. The debts must amount to at least £750. The grounds for a petition by a person bound by a voluntary arrangement are that the debtor has not complied with the terms of the arrangement or has withheld material information. The Director of Public Prosecutions may present a petition in the public interest under the Powers of Criminal Courts Act 1973. The debtor may also present a petition on the grounds of being unable to pay his or her debts. Once a petition has been presented, the debtor may not dispose of any property. The court may halt any other legal proceedings against the debtor. An interim receiver may be appointed. This will usually be the *official receiver, who will take any necessary action to protect the debtor's estate. A *special manager may be appointed if the nature of the debtor's business requires it.

The court may make a bankruptcy order at its discretion. Once this has happened, the debtor is an undischarged bankrupt, who is deprived of the ownership of all property and must assist the official receiver in listing it, recovering it, protecting it, etc. The official receiver becomes manager and receiver of the estate until the appointment of a **trustee in bankruptcy**. The bankrupt must prepare a statement of affairs for the official receiver within 21 days of the bankruptcy order. A **public examination** of the bankrupt may be ordered on the application of the official receiver or the creditors, in which the bankrupt will be required to answer questions about his or her affairs in court. Within 12 weeks the official receiver must decide whether to call a **meeting of creditors** to appoint a trustee in bankruptcy. The trustee's duties are to collect, realize, and distribute the bankrupt's estate. The trustee may be appointed by the creditors, the court, or the Secretary of State and must be a qualified insolvency practitioner or the official receiver. All the property of the bankrupt is available to pay the creditors, except for the following: equipment necessary for him or her to continue in employment or business, necessary domestic equipment; and income required for the reasonable domestic needs of the bankrupt and his or her family. The court has discretion whether to order sale of a house in which a spouse or children are living. All creditors must prove their claims to the trustees. Only unsecured claims can be proved in bankruptcy. When all expenses have been paid, the trustee will divide the estate. The Insolvency Act 1986 sets out the order in which creditors will be paid (*see* PREFERENTIAL CREDITOR). The bankruptcy may end automatically after two or three years, but in some cases a court order is required. The bankrupt is discharged and receives a certificate of discharge from the court.

Bankruptcy Reform Act 1978 A US law that brought about major changes to bankruptcy law. The reforms made it easier to file petitions, amended the previous absolute rule giving priority to secured creditors in all cases, and gave federal bankruptcy judges more powers to hear cases. The reforms also added a clause covering tests for ability to pay under chapter 13 of the Bankruptcy Act. Under *chapter 11 a firm can apply to the court for protection from its creditors while it undergoes a reorganization in an attempt to pay its debts.

bank statement A regular record, issued by a bank or building society, showing the credit and debit entries in a customer's account, together with the current balance. The frequency of issue will vary with the customer's needs and the volume of transactions going through the account. Cash dispensers enable customers to ask for a statement whenever they are needed.

bank transfer (bank giro credit; BGC) A method of making payments in which the payer may make a payment at any branch of any bank for the account of a payee with an account at any branch of the same or another bank.

banque d'affaires The French term for a *merchant bank or an *issuing house as well as an *investment bank.

Banque de France The central bank of France, which has approximately the same status as the Bank of England. Established in 1800 and nationalized in January 1946, it has some 214 branches.

barbell A *portfolio made up predominantly of short- and long-term obligations, notably in bonds. Its name derives from the idea of such a portfolio being "weighted" at both ends like a barbell or dumb-bell.

bargain **1.** A transaction on the London Stock Exchange. The bargains made during the day are included in the *Daily Official List*. **2.** A sale made at a specially low price, either as a means of sale promotion or to clear old stock.

barometer stock A security whose price is regarded as an indicator of the state of the market. It will be a widely held *blue chip with a stable price record.

barratry Any act committed wilfully by the master or crew of a ship to the detriment of its owner or charterer. Examples include scuttling the ship and embezzling the cargo. Illegal activities (e.g. carrying prohibited persons) leading to the forfeiture of the ship also constitute barratry. Barratry is one of the risks covered by marine insurance policies.

barrier option (trigger option; up and in or **up and out option)** An *exotic option that is activated or deactivated if the price of the *underlying reaches or fails to reach a certain level during its life. *See* IN-BARRIER OPTION; KNOCK-IN OPTION; OUT-BARRIER OPTION.

base currency The currency used as the basis for an exchange rate, i.e. a foreign currency rate of exchange is quoted per single unit of the base currency, usually US dollars.

base rate 1. The rate of interest used as a basis by banks for the rates they charge their customers. In practice most customers will pay a premium over base rate on loans and will receive below the base rate on deposits with banks. **2.** An informal name for the rate at which a country's *central bank lends to the banking system, which effectively controls the lending rate throughout the banking system. The abolition of the *minimum lending rate in 1981 heralded a loosening of government control over the banking system, but the need to increase interest rates in the late 1980s (to control inflation and the *balance of payments deficit) led to the use of this term in this sense. In 1997 sole responsibility for setting the base rate was given to the Bank of England. The base rate is more formally known as the *bank rate.

base stock A certain volume of business stock, assumed to be constant in that stock levels are not allowed to fall below this level. When the stock is valued, this proportion of the stock is valued at its original cost. This method is not normally acceptable under Statement of Standard Accounting Practice 9 for financial accounting purposes.

base-weighted index Any index in which the values are compared with those of a *base year or base point.

base year (base date) The first of a series of years in an index. The value of the index in that year is often denoted by the number 100, enabling percentage rises (or falls) to be seen at a glance. For example, if a price index indicates that the current value is 120, this will only be meaningful if it is compared to an earlier figure. This may be written: 120 (base year 1985 = 100), making it clear that there has been a 20% increase in prices since 1985.

basic rate of income tax A rate of income tax between the starting rate and the higher rate. In the UK it is 22%, which is applied to that part of *taxable income in the band £2,020 to £31,400 (2004–05). *See also* HIGHER RATE OF INCOME TAX; STARTING RATE OF INCOME TAX.

basis point One hundredth of one per cent; this unit is often used in finance when prices involve fine margins.

basis price The price, based on the return on investment, used by a dealer when selling a security.

basis risk **1.** The *risk associated with changes in the *gross redemption yields of a bond. **2.** The risk arising from possible changes in the difference between the spot and futures price of a particular commodity, security, etc. It is associated with the use of *futures contracts as hedging instruments (*see* HEDGE).

basis swap A *swap in which the payments are based on two variable interest rates. The swap may be either in a single currency or across currencies. *See* CROSS-CURRENCY INTEREST-RATE SWAP; INTEREST-RATE SWAP.

basket of currencies A group of selected currencies used to establish a value for some other unit of currency.

basket pegger A country that fixes its exchange rate by averaging a *basket of currencies.

Basle Concordat The basis for cooperation between central banks. The Concordat was agreed in 1975 and revised in 1983. It provides a moral rather than practical obligation for banks to be supervised and to help one another. The Concordat also considered the supervision of foreign branches of domestic banks.

Basle Convergence Accord An agreement reached in 1988 by the *Group of Ten (G10), and enacted through the *Bank for International Settlements, concerning *capital adequacy regulations for banking in G10 countries. It suggested that banks should have specific liabilities to cover a minimum of 8% of their *capital at risk. Capital at risk was defined in terms of a set of multipliers to be attached to a number of different asset classes and multiplied by their balance-sheet worth. For example, lending commitments to public sector counterparties had a multiplier of zero, OECD banks and municipalities 20%, and other private sector institutions 100%. The 8% of the total value of their capital at risk has to be covered by shareholder funds, which are defined as *Tier 1 capital, and the rest covered by *Tier 2 capital, in the form of specifically designated funding instruments. *See also* BASLE TWO.

Basle Market Risk Amendment A 1996 amendment to the *Basle Convergence Accord that allows the use of internal risk models based on *value-at-risk to be used in the calculation of a bank's risk capital.

Basle Two An accord, implemented in 2004, that supplants the *Basle Convergence Accord of 1988. It establishes a new framework for defining *risk capital and weightings, based to a greater extent than previously on credit ratings and internal models. It also puts in place a supervisory process to ensure that banks have adequate internal systems to understand and establish their *capital at risk and assess its adequacy. There are also additional requirements for disclosure of risk-related information.

Bay Street **1.** The street in Toronto in which the Toronto Stock Exchange is situated. **2.** The Toronto Stock Exchange itself. **3.** The financial institutions of Toronto collectively.

bazaar A derogatory name for a market that is unregulated.

B2B Abbreviation for business-to-business; denoting direct Internet trading between commercial organizations.

BBA Abbreviation for *British Bankers Association.

BBM *See* BALANCED-BUDGET MULTIPLIER.

BCG matrix *See* BOSTON MATRIX.

beamer A US name for a mortgage-backed annuity.

bear A dealer on a stock exchange, currency market, or commodity market who expects prices to fall. A **bear market** is one in which prices are falling or expected to fall, i.e. a market in which a dealer is more likely to sell securities, currency, or goods than to buy them. A bear may even sell securities, currency, or goods without having them. This is known as selling short or establishing a **bear position**. The bear hopes to close (or cover) a short position by buying in at a lower price the securities, currency, or goods previously sold. The difference between the purchase price and the original sale price represents the successful bear's profit. A concerted attempt to force prices down by one or more bears by sustained selling is called a **bear raid**. A successful bear raid will produce a sharply falling market, known as a **bear slide**. In a **bear squeeze**, sellers force prices up against someone known to have a bear position to cover. *Compare* BULL.

bear closing The purchase of securities, currency, or commodities to close an open *bear position. Bear closing can have the effect of firming up a weak market.

bearer A person who presents for payment a cheque or *bill of exchange marked "pay bearer". As a bearer cheque or bill does not require endorsement it is considered a high-risk form of transfer.

bearer security (bearer bond) A security for which proof of ownership is possession of the security certificate; this enables such bonds to be transferred from one person to another without registration. No register of ownership is kept by the company in whose name it is issued. This is unusual as most securities are registered, so that proof of ownership is the presence of the owner's name on the security register. *Eurobonds are bearer securities, enabling their owners to preserve their anonymity, which can have taxation advantages. Bearer bonds are usually kept under lock and key, often deposited in a bank. Dividends are usually claimed by submitting coupons attached to the certificate.

bear hug An approach to the board of a company by another company indicating that an offer is about to be made for their shares. If the target company indicates that it is not against the merger, but wants a higher price, this is known as a **teddy bear hug**.

bear market *See* BEAR.

bear note *See* BULL NOTE.

bear position *See* BEAR.

bear raid *See* BEAR.

bear slide *See* BEAR.

bear spread A position in the bond market that is long in short-dated securities and short in longer dated securities; it is intended to take advantage of a fall in commodity or security prices. If the *yield curve becomes steeper, then it can be closed out at a profit. *Compare* BULL SPREAD.

bear squeeze *See* BEAR.

bed and breakfast An operation on the London Stock Exchange in which a shareholder sold a holding one evening and made an agreement with the broker to buy the same holding back again when the market opened the next morning. The object was to establish a loss, which could be set against other profits for calculating capital gains tax or to take advantage of the rule that allowed the first part of any gain in one year to be free of capital gains tax. In the event of an unexpected change in the market, the deal was scrapped. Tax changes have made this set of transactions less attractive as the time elapsed between sale and repurchase must now be above 30 days.

Beige Book The report on the current economic climate prepared by the US *Federal Reserve Board ahead of one of the meetings (held eight times a year) of the *Federal Open Market Committee.

Belfox Abbreviation for the Belgian Futures and Options Exchange. Based in Brussels, it opened April 1991 and trades in Belgian government bond futures and stock index options.

bells and whistles Additions (such as *options or *warrants) made to a financial product to increase its appeal to the market.

bellweather security In the USA, a security considered to be a good guide to the direction in which the market is moving.

below par *See* PAR VALUE.

below-the-line **1.** Denoting the lower part of a company's *profit and loss account, which contains the entries explaining the distribution of profit. **2.** Denoting advertising expenditure in which no commission is payable to an advertising agency. For example, direct mail, exhibitions, point-of-sale material, and free samples are regarded as below-the-line advertising. **3.** Denoting transactions concerned with capital, as opposed to revenue, in national accounts. *Compare* ABOVE-THE-LINE.

benchmark **1.** A standard used to measure the performance of an investment or portfolio. **2.** A standard specification of a contract, for example a futures contract. **3.** A base price or interest rate (*see* BASE RATE).

benchmark bond A *bond that is regarded as a key indicator of market prospects.

beneficial interest The right to the use and enjoyment of property, rather than to its bare legal ownership. For example, if property is held in trust, the trustee has the legal title but the beneficiaries have the beneficial interest in equity. The beneficiaries, not the trustee, are entitled to any income from the property.

beneficial owner The true owner of an asset; the owner of the *beneficial interest of property. It is usually the person whose funds were used for its purchase. The beneficial owner is not necessarily the *legal owner.

beneficiary **1.** A person for whose benefit a *trust exists. **2.** A person who benefits under a will. **3.** A person who receives money from the proceeds of a *letter of credit. **4.** A person who receives payment at the conclusion of a transaction, e.g. a retailer who has been paid by a customer by means of a *credit card.

benefits in kind Benefits other than cash arising from employment. The UK tax legislation seeks to assess all earnings to tax, whether they be in the form of cash or in kind. The treatment of benefits depends on the level of total earnings, including the value of any benefits, and whether the employee is a director of a company. The general rule is to value benefits at their cash equivalent although some specific benefits (e.g. company cars) are subject to specific valuation rules. For employees earning less than £8500, the benefits are only assessable if they are living accommodation or if they are capable of being turned into cash, such as credit tokens or vouchers. For all directors and higher-paid employees, with total earnings (including benefits) in excess of £8500, the benefits must be reported on form P11D by the employer at the end of the *fiscal year. This form will include details of company cars and associated fuel provided by the employer, beneficial loans, mobile telephones, medical insurance provided by the employer, subscriptions paid, and any costs paid on the employee's behalf. These benefits will be assessed to tax. This often takes the form of a restriction to the *income tax code.

Benelux An association of countries in western Europe, consisting of Belgium, the Netherlands, and Luxembourg. apart from geographical proximity these countries have particularly close economic interests, recognized in their 1947 *customs union. In 1958 the Benelux countries joined the *European Economic Community.

Berne Union The informal name for the International Union of Credit and Investment Insurers, an association of credit insurers from the main industrial countries, except Japan. Its main function is to facilitate an exchange of information, especially over credit terms. The *Export Credits Guarantee Department of the UK government is a member.

BES Abbreviation for business expansion scheme. *See* ENTERPRISE INVESTMENT SCHEME.

best advice *See* INDEPENDENT FINANCIAL ADVISER.

best efforts A term used in US agreements for underwriting a stock issue in which the securities house undertakes to use its best efforts to sell an issue for the issuer, but makes no guarantee that it will sell all of the issue at the offer price.

best price An order placed with a dealer to buy or sell a security, commodity, etc., at the best price available when the order is given.

beta coefficient A measure of the volatility of a share. A share with a high beta coefficient is likely to respond to stock market movements by rising or falling in value by more than the market average. It is thus a measure of the *systematic risk associated with a particular security. *See also* ALPHA COEFFICIENT; CAPITAL ASSET PRICING MODEL.

beta stocks The second rank of liquidity of shares quoted on the London Stock Exchange, under the former classification system now replaced by *Normal Market Size. *See also* ALPHA STOCKS.

better-of-two-assets option An *exotic option in which payoff is on the better of two *underlyings.

BGC Abbreviation for bank giro credit. *See* BANK TRANSFER.

bid 1. The price or yield at which a buyer indicates that he or she is willing to buy a financial obligation. *See* BID PRICE; BID RATE. **2.** An offer by one company to buy the share capital of another; an attempted takeover.

bid–offer spread The difference between an *offer price and the *bid price.

bid price The price at which a *market maker will buy shares: the lower of the two figures quoted on the *TOPIC screens of the *Stock Exchange Automated

Quotations System, the higher being the *offer price. Some dealers prefer to rely on the figure quoted, others prefer to haggle over the price.

bid rate **1.** Short for *London Inter Bank Bid Rate (LIBID). **2.** The price or yield at which a financial obligation is purchased.

biennial bond A *bond in which the first coupon payment takes place after two years.

BIFFEX Abbreviation for Baltic International Freight Futures Exchange. *See* FUTURES AND OPTIONS EXCHANGE.

bifurcation The divestment of part of a business to improve the strategic focus of the remaining part.

Big Bang The upheaval on the *London Stock Exchange (LSE) when major changes in operation were introduced on 27 October 1986. The major changes enacted on that date were: (a) the abolition of LSE rules enforcing a rigid distinction between jobbers and brokers; (b) the abolition of fixed commission rates charged by *stockbrokers to their clients. The measures were introduced by the LSE in return for an undertaking by the government (given in 1983) that they would not prosecute the LSE under the Restrictive Practices Act. Since 1986 the Big Bang has also been associated with the *globalization and modernization of the London securities market.

Big Blue Colloquial name for the US information-systems group, IBM (International Business Machines Inc.).

Big Board Colloquial name for the *New York Stock Exchange, on which the stocks of the largest corporations in the USA are traded. *Compare* LITTLE BOARD.

Big Four **1.** The major High-Street or *commercial banks in the UK: Barclays, Lloyds TSB, HSBC (formerly Midland), and NatWest (now owned by the Royal Bank of Scotland). In terms of market capitalization the four were joined in the 1990s by Abbey National (now Abbey), the Woolwich, and the Halifax (now HBOS following its merger with the Bank of Scotland), which changed their status from *building societies to banks. **2.** The four largest firms of accountants in the world, i.e. Deloitte and Touche, Ernst and Young, KPMG, and Price WaterhouseCooper. **3.** In Japan, the four largest securities houses: Daiwa, Nikko, Nomura, and Yamaichi.

bilateral bank facility A *facility provided by a bank to a corporate customer. The agreement is restricted to the two parties, which enables a relationship to develop between the bank and the customer (*see* RELATIONSHIP BANKING). *Compare* SYNDICATED BANK FACILITY.

bilateral netting **1.** An agreement between two counterparties that mutual obligations will be settled by a single payment. **2.** A method of reducing bank charges in which two related companies offset their receipts and payments with each other, usually monthly. In this way a single payment and receipt is made for the period instead of a number, which saves on both transaction costs and paperwork. *See also* MULTILATERAL NETTING.

bill **1.** A short-term financial instrument used by agencies, firms, or government. **2.** Short for *bill of exchange. **3.** Colloquial name for an invoice.

bill broker (**discount broker**) A broker who trades in *bills of exchange.

billion One thousand million (10^9).

b

bill leak A device used by UK banks to circumvent the restrictions by the Bank of England on lending and on interest-bearing eligible liabilities (*see* CORSET) by lending outside the banking sector to non-banking organizations by means of the acceptance of bills. It was a means of avoiding monetary control regulations in the UK in the period 1973–80.

bill mountain Bills that have been discounted and are held at the Bank of England.

bill of exchange An unconditional order in writing, addressed by one person (the drawer) to another (the drawee) and signed by the person giving it, requiring the drawee to pay on demand or at a fixed or determinable future time a specified sum of money to or to the order of a specified person (the payee) or to the bearer. If the bill is payable at a future time the drawee signifies *acceptance, which makes the drawee the party primarily liable upon the bill; the drawer and endorsers may also be liable upon a bill. The use of bills of exchange enables one person to transfer to another an enforceable right to a sum of money. A bill of exchange is not only transferable but also negotiable, since, if a person without an enforceable right to the money transfers a bill to a *holder in due course, the latter obtains a good title to it. If the drawee or acceptor of the bill is a bank, the bill is known as a *bank bill or in the USA as a *banker's acceptance. If it is a trader, it is called a **trade acceptance**. These bills have a standard 90 days to maturity and their attractiveness will depend on whether they are eligible for rediscounting at the central bank. *See* ACCOMMODATION BILL; BILLS IN A SET; DISHONOUR.

bill of lading A document acknowledging the shipment of a consignor's goods for carriage by sea. It is used primarily when the ship is carrying goods belonging to a number of consignors (a general ship). In this case, each consignor receives a bill issued (normally by the master of the ship) on behalf of either the shipowner or a charterer under a charterparty. The bill serves three functions: it is a receipt for the goods; it summarizes the terms of the contract of carriage; and it acts as a document of title to the goods. A bill of lading is also issued by a shipowner to a charterer who is using the ship for the carriage of his or her own goods. In this case, the terms of the contract of carriage are in the charterparty and the bill serves only as a receipt and a document of title. During transit, ownership of the goods may be transferred by delivering the bill to another if it is drawn to bearer or by endorsing it if it is drawn to order. It is not, however, a negotiable instrument. The bill gives details of the goods; if the packages are in good order a **clean bill** is issued; if they are not, the bill will say so (a **dirty bill of lading**).

bill of sight A document that an importer, who is unable fully to describe an imported cargo, gives to the Customs and Excise authorities to authorize them to inspect the goods on landing. After the goods have been landed and the importer supplies the missing information the entry is completed and the importer is said to have **perfected the sight**.

bill rate (discount rate) The rate on the *discount market at which *bills of exchange are discounted (i.e. purchased for less than they are worth when they mature). The rate will depend on the quality of the bill and the risk the purchaser takes. First-class bills, i.e. those backed by banks or well-respected finance houses, will be discounted at a lower rate than bills involving greater risk.

bills in a set One of two, or more usually three, copies of a foreign bill of exchange. Payment is made on any one of the three, the others becoming invalid on the payment of any one of them. All are made out in the same way, except that each refers to the others. The first copy is called the **first of exchange**, the next is the **second of exchange**, and so on. The duplication or triplication is to reduce the risk of loss in transit.

bills payable An item that may appear in a firm's accounts under current liabilities, summarizing the *bills of exchange being held, which will have to be paid when they mature.

bills receivable An item that may appear in a firm's accounts under current assets, summarizing the *bills of exchange being held until the funds become available when they mature.

BIMBO Abbreviation for buy-in management buy-out: a form of *management buy-out in which management invests in the venture together with outsider venture capitalists, who have more managerial control than is usual with a management buy-out.

binary option (all-or-nothing option; cash-or-nothing option; digital option) An *exotic option in which the payoff is either a given value or nothing.

binomial process A process consisting of several stages, at each one of which there are two possible outcomes with separate probabilities. In finance, models based on binomial processes are used to consider the value of financial obligations, most notably certain option-pricing models. *Compare* TRINOMIAL TREE.

birr (Br) The standard monetary unit of Ethiopia, divided into 100 cents.

BIS Abbreviation for *Bank for International Settlements.

black box syndrome A general term for the problems that may arise in using complex mathematical and statistical models in finance. For example, it may be difficult to model transparently the impacts of trading on the overall exposure of a complicated set of positions.

black knight A person or firm that makes an unwelcome *takeover bid for a company. *Compare* GREY KNIGHT; WHITE KNIGHT.

Black Monday Either of the two Mondays on which the two largest stock market crashes occurred in the 20th century. The original Wall Street crash occurred on Monday, 28 October 1929, when the *Dow Jones Industrial Average fell by 13%. On Monday, 19 October 1987, the Dow Jones Average lost 23%. In both cases Black Monday in the USA triggered heavy stock market falls around the world.

black money (dirty money; grey money) Money earned illegally, especially through the international drugs market.

Black–Scholes option-pricing model The first successful option-pricing model, published in 1973 and based on stochastic calculus. It focuses on the pricing of European options, in which the underlying does not pay a dividend in the option period. The option is priced according to the value of the underlying, the volatility of the value of the underlying, the *exercise price, the time to maturity, and the risk-free rate of interest. The model provided a general approach to option pricing and has given rise to a number of other option-pricing models.

Black Wednesday Wednesday 16 September 1992, when sterling left the Exchange Rate Mechanism (*see* EUROPEAN MONETARY SYSTEM), which led to a 15% fall in its value against the Deutschmark. Owing to the improved economic performance of the UK following this event, it is also sometimes known as **White Wednesday**.

blank bill A *bill of exchange in which the name of the payee is left blank.

blank cheque A cheque in which the amount payable is not stated. The person writing the cheque (the drawer) may impose a maximum amount to be drawn by the cheque by writing on it, for example, 'Not more than £100'.

blank endorsed See ENDORSEMENT.

blanket policy An insurance policy that covers a number of items but has only one total sum insured and no insured sums for individual items. The policy can be of any type, e.g. covering a fleet of vehicles or a group of buildings.

blank transfer A share transfer form in which the name of the transferee and the transfer date are left blank. The form is signed by the registered holder of the shares so that the holder of the blank transfer has only to fill in the missing details to become the registered owner of the shares. Blank transfers can be deposited with a bank, when shares are being used as a security for a loan. A blank transfer can also be used when shares are held by *nominees, the beneficial owner holding the blank transfer.

blind trust A trust that administers the private financial affairs of a person in public office without informing him or her of the transactions entered into, so that there can be no conflict of interest. See also ARM'S LENGTH.

block A large quantity of securities.

blocked account 1. A bank account from which money cannot be withdrawn, for any of a number of reasons, of which the most likely is that the affairs of the holder of the account are in the hands of a receiver owing to *bankruptcy (or *liquidation in the case of a company). **2.** A bank account held by an exporter of goods in another country into which the proceeds of the sale of the goods have been paid but from which they cannot be transferred to the exporter's own country. This is usuly a result of a government order, when that government is so short of foreign currency that it has to block all accounts that require the use of a foreign currency.

blocked currency A currency that cannot be removed from a country as a result of *exchange controls. Trading usually takes place in such currencies at a discount through brokers specializing in blocked-currency trading, who convert it to other funds for importers and exporters with blocked currency accounts.

block order exposure system (BLOX) A UK stock-market system for making quotes on large blocks of securities.

block positioner A *broker/dealer who acts as a counterparty to a large sale.

block trade 1. The sale or purchase of large quantities of a security, normally in excess of 10 000 securities. **2.** The situation in which the sponsoring managers of a certificate of deposit or floating rate certificate of deposit buy an entire issue for later distribution. **3.** The situation in which the *lead manager of a securities issue underwrites the whole issue.

block volume A total volume of block trades in stocks in a given time period.

Bloomberg A US-based financial information service.

BLOX Acronym for *block order exposure system.

Blue Book **1.** *See* UK NATIONAL ACCOUNTS. **2.** In the USA, the review document of monetary control options produced by members of the *Federal Open Market Committee.

blue chip Colloquial name for any of the ordinary shares in the most highly regarded companies traded on a stock market. Originating in the USA, the name comes from the colour of the highest value chip used in poker. Blue-chip companies have a well-known name, a good growth record, and large assets. The main part of an institution's equity portfolio will consist of blue chips.

blue month The month in which the trading activity in a *derivative is greatest.

blue-sky law In the USA, a law providing for state regulation and supervision for issuing investment securities in that state. It includes broker licensing and the registration of new issues.

Board of Customs and Excise The government department responsible for collecting and administering customs and excise duties and *value added tax. The Commissioners of Customs were first appointed in 1671 by Charles II; the Excise department, formerly part of the Inland Revenue Department, was merged with the Customs in 1909. The Customs and Excise have an investigation division responsible for preventing and detecting evasions of revenue laws and for enforcing restrictions on the importation of certain goods (e.g. arms, drugs, etc.). Their statistical office compiles overseas trade statistics from customs import and export documents. In 2004 plans were announced to merge the Board with the Inland Revenue, thereby bringing it under the direct control of the Treasury.

Board of Inland Revenue A small number of higher civil servants, known individually as Commissioners of Inland Revenue, responsible to the Treasury for the administration and collection of the principal direct taxes in the UK, but not the indirect VAT and excise duties. They are responsible for income tax, capital gains tax, corporation tax, inheritance tax, petroleum revenue tax, and stamp duties. Under the Taxes Management Act 1970, they are under a duty to appoint inspectors and collectors of taxes who, in turn, act under the direction of the board. They also advise on new legislation and prepare statistical information.

boilerplate A copy intended for use in making other copies. The term is sometimes used to mean a group of instructions that is incorporated in several different places in a computer program or the detailed standard form of words used in a contract, guarantee, etc.

boiler room A colloquial name for a *bucket shop that specializes in the selling of high-pressure securities over the telephone.

bolívar (B) The standard monetary unit of Venezuela, divided into 100 céntimos.

boliviano ($b) The standard monetary unit of Bolivia, divided into 100 centavos.

bolsa A Spanish or Portuguese or South American *stock exchange. These include the Bolsa Brasileira de Futuros, the Bolsa de Bogota SA, the Bolsa de Comercio de Buenos Aires, the Bolsa de Comercio de Santiago, the Bolsa de Madrid, the Bolsa de Valores de Lisboa, the Bolsa de Valores de São Paulo, the Bolsa de Valores do Rio de Janeiro, and the Bolsa Mexicana de Valores.

Bombay Stock Exchange India's leading stock exchange, listing more than 2000 companies. British influence brought share trading to India, where trading began in the 1830s on an informal basis in Bombay, the commercial gateway from the West;

exchanges now exist in seven other cities. The Indian government has created a Securities and Exchange Board of India (SEBI) to regulate the market. SEBI operates in much the same way as the *Securities and Exchange Commission in the USA and the *Securities and Investment Board in the UK.

bond An IOU issued by a borrower to a lender. Bonds usually take the form of *fixed-interest securities issued by governments, local authorities, or companies. However, bonds come in many forms: with fixed or variable rates of interest, redeemable or irredeemable, short- or long-term, secured or unsecured, and marketable or unmarketable. Fixed-interest payments are usually made twice a year but may alternatively be credited at the end of the agreement (typically 5 to 10 years). The borrower repays a specific sum of money plus the face value (PAR) of the bond. Most bonds are unsecured and do not grant shares in an organization (*see* DEBENTURE). Bonds are usually sold against loans, mortgages, credit-card income, etc., as marketable securities. A discount bond is one sold below its face value; a premium bond is one sold above par. *See also* EUROBOND; INCOME BOND; PREMIUM BONDS. *Compare* NOTE.

bond basis A method of calculating the *accrued interest on bonds.

bond broker A *broker who carries out bond transactions.

bond conversion The right to convert from one bond to another, which may have different terms.

bond covenant A term in a bond contract that restricts the behaviour of the issuer.

bond futures A *futures contract to buy or sell a specific bond on a future date for an agreed price.

bond risk The *risk associated with holding bonds, which falls into two categories. In *interest-rate risk, the value of a bond falls if the rate of interest rises; in *credit risk, the rating of the bond may deteriorate, payments may be delayed, or the bond may default.

bond swap The simultaneous sale of one bond and purchase of another. *See* SWAP.

bond washing *See* DIVIDEND STRIPPING.

bond yield The *internal rate of return on the cash flows of a bond.

bonus 1. An extra payment made to employees by management, usually as a reward for good work, to compensate for something (e.g. dangerous work), or to share out the profits of a good year's trading. **2.** An extra amount of money additional to the proceeds, which is distributed to a policyholder by an insurer who has made a profit on the investment of a life-assurance fund. Only holders of *with-profits policies are entitled to a share in these profits and the payment of this bonus is conditional on the life assurer having surplus funds after claims, costs, and expenses have been paid in a particular year. **3.** Any extra or unexpected payment. *See also* NO-CLAIM BONUS; REVERSIONARY BONUS; TERMINAL BONUS.

bonus dividend A *dividend issued to a shareholder in addition to those expected. Typically, two dividends are issued each year. If an additional dividend is paid to shareholders, perhaps because of a takeover, this is known as a bonus dividend.

bonus shares (bonus issue) Shares issued to the existing shareholders of a company following a *scrip issue. The number of shares received depends on the level of the shareholding prior to the bonus issue. The number of bonus shares is usually one share for a specified number of shares held before the issue. For example, if the specified number is four this would be denoted as a 1:4 bonus issue. It is also possible to have a 2:1 bonus, when two shares are issued for every one held.

book **1.** The totality of the purchases and sales that make up a trader's *position. The terms **long book**, **short book**, and **open book** are used synonymously with *long position, *short position, and *open position. *See* MAKING A BOOK. **2.** To find purchasers for a new issue. **3.** To record an item in the accounts, usually a sale. **4.** Short for *book value.

book value The value of an asset as recorded in the books of account and stated in the *balance sheet of an organization. This is normally the historical cost of the asset reduced by amounts written off for *depreciation. If the asset has ever been revalued, the book value will be the amount of the revaluation less amounts subsequently written off for depreciation. Except at the time of purchase of the asset, the book value will rarely be the same as the market value of the asset.

bootstrap **1.** A cash offer for a controlling interest in a company. This is followed by an offer to acquire the rest of the company's shares at a lower price. The purpose is twofold: to establish control of the company and to reduce the cost of the purchase. Multiple price offers are not permitted in the UK, but they are in other countries, notably Germany and the USA. **2.** A technique enabling a computer to load a program of instructions. Before computer hardware can function, a program must be loaded into it. However, as a program is needed in the computer to enable it to load a program, preliminary instructions are stored permanently in the computer making it possible for longer programs to be accepted. **3.** A technique by which parameter estimates and their confidence intervals are calculated by creating new samples by draws with replacement from existing samples.

borrowed reserves Loans made to US banks from the Federal Reserve, which allow reserves in individual banks to remain at acceptable levels. This is usually only necessary when excessive lending is being undertaken, because otherwise reserves are kept to a workable minimum as they do not attract interest for the banks.

BOT Stockbrokers' shorthand for "bought".

Börse A German stock exchange.

Boston matrix (BCG matrix) A means of analysing and categorizing the performance of business units in large diversified firms by reference to market share and growth rates. It was developed by the Boston Consultancy Group (BCG), a leading firm of strategic consultants. Four main categories are displayed in a two-dimensional matrix, which seeks to identify those business units that generate cash and those that use it, and then to relate the position of the business units to the formulation of an overall business strategy. The Boston matrix has also been applied to a company's product range so that an overall product development strategy can be implemented.
Cash cows: mature businesses or products with a high market share but low growth rate. Typically, most fixed investment has already been made and a substantial cash flow is generated, the surplus being used to develop and support other businesses or products requiring higher levels of investment and marketing support.
Stars: businesses or products with a high rate of growth, which are often able to generate sufficient cash to fund the high investment necessary to meet increasing

demand. As the market matures, such businesses or products should be managed in order to become future cash cows.

Question marks (or **problem children**): although operating in a growth market, the low market share is likely to mean that these business units are unable to sustain the required level of investment needed in order to try and turn them into stars. Competitor pressures may result in such a business or product becoming a dog.

Dogs: the combination of low growth rate and market share is typical of these businesses and products, which operate in mature markets. Firms frequently face strategic decisions regarding whether to continue to support dogs or to implement a divestment strategy. Barriers to exit would also need to be considered.

Boston option *See* BREAK-FORWARD.

bottom fishing The practice of seeking out very low-priced shares to invest in, or of waiting until the market as a whole is low before investing, in the hope of making a profit when prices rise.

bottom line Colloquial expression for *net profit.

bought deal 1. A method of raising capital for acquisitions or other purposes, used by quoted companies as an alternative to a *rights issue or *placing. The company invites *market makers or banks to bid for new shares, selling them to the highest bidder, who then sells them to the rest of the market in the expectation of making a profit. Bought deals originated in the USA and are becoming increasingly popular in the UK, although they remain controversial as they violate the principle of *pre-emption rights. *See also* VENDOR PLACING. **2.** A *management buy-out or one in which the finance is obtained from a single institution.

bought ledger 1. Historically, the book of account in which a business records its purchases. Now it often refers to the credit-control department of a retailer or manufacturer. **2.** The computer program that deals with all the purchase accounts of a large company. *See* BUSINESS SOFTWARE PACKAGE.

boundary condition A restriction in a mathematical problem. Boundary conditions are used in some option-pricing models.

bourse The French name for a *stock exchange (from the French *bourse*, purse). 'The Bourse' usually refers to the stock exchange in Paris (*see* PARIS BOURSE), but some other stock markets are also known by this name, e.g. the Bourse de Genève, the Bourse de Luxembourg, and the Bourse de Montréal. In Belgium, the term denotes foreign-exchange dealing.

boutique 1. An office, usually with a shop front and located in a shopping parade, that offers financial advice to investors, often on a walk-in basis. **2.** Specialist investment bankers, who cover a particular sector of the market, e.g. management buy-outs, acquisitions, etc. They are sometimes known as **niche players**.

box A storage location for securities.

Box–Jenkins model A method for *time-series forecasting in econometrics.

box spread A combination of call and put *options held at the same exercise price.

bracket 1. Any of several categories of *underwriter in the *primary market. Financial institutions are classed as **major bracket** or **minor bracket** according to the extent of their commitment to buy new issues of a security. *See also* BULGE BRACKET. **2.** *See* TAXATION BRACKETS.

bracket indexation A change in the upper and lower limits of any particular *taxation bracket in line with an index of inflation. This is needed in times of inflation to avoid fiscal drag (the tax system collecting unduly large amounts of tax).

Brady bond A bond issued in conjunction with the *International Bank for Reconstruction and Development (World Bank) to help refinance less developed countries. US Treasury zero-coupon bonds are used as collateral.

Brady Commission A US presidential commission set up under Nicholas Brady, the Secretary of the Treasury, to investigate the 1987 stock market crash (*see* BLACK MONDAY).

Brady Plan A plan in which the International Monetary Fund and the *International Bank for Reconstruction and Development (World Bank) attempted to improve the debt funding for less developed countries and solve their immediate debt crises.

Brazilian Stock Exchange *See* SÃO PAULO STOCK EXCHANGE.

break A major fall in prices on a financial market.

break-even analysis A technique, used in evaluating a decision, that considers revenues and costs in relation to sales and determines the level of sales at which the activity will begin to make a profit. If this level is much lower than the expected level of sales, the decision is thought to be less risky than would be the case otherwise.

break-forward (Boston option) A contract on the money market that combines the features of a *forward-exchange contract and a currency option. The forward contract can be undone at a previously agreed rate of exchange, enabling the consumer to be free if the market moves favourably. There is no premium on the option; the cost is built into the fixed rate of exchange.

breaking a leg (lifting a leg) Closing out one part of an arbitrage or spread transaction, while leaving the other part open. *See also* LEG; STRADDLE.

breakout In *chartist analysis, a movement in the market price of a security above or below the limits within which it has recently fluctuated. When a security's price moves to a level above the usual price ceiling or below the usual price floor, this is thought to herald a continuing move in the same direction. *See also* RESISTANCE LEVEL.

break-up value **1.** The value of the assets of an organization on the assumption that it will not continue in business. On this assumption the assets are likely to be sold piecemeal and probably in haste. **2.** The *asset value per share of a company.

Bretton Woods Conference A conference (formally, the United Nations Monetary and Financial Conference) held in July 1944 at Bretton Woods, New Hampshire, in the USA, at which the representatives of 44 countries, most importantly the UK and USA, established a system of international finance, resulting in the setting up of the *International Monetary Fund and the *International Bank for Reconstruction and Development.

bricks-and-clicks Denoting a business that trades from physical premises ("bricks") as well as on the Internet ("clicks").

bridging loan A loan taken on a short-term basis to bridge the gap between the purchase of one asset and the sale of another. It is particularly common in the property and housing market.

Britannia coins A range of four British *gold coins (£100, £50, £25, and £10 denominations). They were introduced in October 1987 for investment purposes, in competition with the *Krugerrand. Although all sales of gold coins attract VAT, Britannia coins are dealt in as bullion coins.

British Bankers Association (BBA) A London-based organization that represents the views of all the banks recognized in the UK. Founded in 1919, it is regarded as the banks' trade association. It established model contracts for financial instruments and publishes daily market interest rates in major eurocurrencies. It collects and publishes London Inter Bank Offer Rate Quotes, which are the basis for many financial contracts expressed on BBA terms.

British Insurance and Investment Brokers Association A trade association for insurance brokers registered with the *Insurance Brokers Registration Council and investment brokers registered under the Financial Services Act 1986. Formed in 1977 as the British Insurance Brokers Association by the amalgamation of a number of insurance broking associations, it changed to its current name in 1988 to widen its membership to include investment advisors. It provides public relations, free advice, representation in parliament, and a conciliation service for consumers.

British Technology Group (BTG) A government-appointed organization formed in 1981 by the merger of the **National Enterprise Board** (NEB) and the **National Research and Development Corporation** (NRDC). Its purpose is to encourage technological development by providing finance for new scientific and engineering products and processes discovered through research at UK universities, research councils, and government research establishments. It was privatized in 2000.

broad money An informal name for M3 or any wide definition of the *money supply). *Compare* NARROW MONEY.

broker An agent who brings two parties together, enabling them to enter into a contract to which the broker is not a principal. A broker's remuneration consists of a **brokerage**, which is usually calculated as a percentage of the sum involved in the contract but may be fixed according to a tariff. Brokers are used because they have specialized knowledge of certain markets or to conceal the identity of a principal, in addition to introducing buyers to sellers. *See* BILL BROKER; COMMODITY BROKER; INSURANCE BROKER; STOCKBROKER.

brokerage The commission earned by a *broker.

broker/dealer 1. An agent for buyers and sellers who also trades on his or her own account. **2.** A member of the *London Stock Exchange who, since the *Big Bang, has functioned both as a stockbroker and a jobber, but only in a single capacity in one particular transaction.

B shares 1. In the USA, a category of less important *ordinary shares. B shares are usually distinguished from *A shares by their limited voting power. **2.** A class of shares traded on Chinese stock markets.

BTG Abbreviation for *British Technology Group.

bubble (speculative bubble) A situation in which asset prices are seriously inflated. The unstable boom thus created may lead to a market crash. The most infamous example of this was the *South Sea Bubble of 1720 in Great Britain. A more recent example was the so-called 'dot.com bubble' of 1999–2000.

bucket shop A derogatory term for a firm of brokers, dealers, agents, etc., of questionable standing and frail resources, that is unlikely to be a member of an established trade organization.

budget 1. A financial or quantitative statement, prepared prior to a specified accounting period, containing the plans and policies to be pursued during that period. It is used as the basis for *budgetary control. Generally a functional budget is drawn up for each functional area within an organization, but in addition it is also usual to produce a *capital budget, a *cash-flow budget, stock budgets, and a master budget, which includes a budgeted profit and loss account and balance sheet.
2. (the Budget) In the UK, the government's annual budget, which is presented to parliament by the Chancellor of the Exchequer (traditionally, but not always, on a Tuesday in March). It contains estimates for the government's income and expenditure, together with the tax rates and the fiscal policies designed to meet the government's financial goals for the succeeding fiscal year.

budget account (continuous credit account) A loan account conducted by a bank, in which the borrower decides the monthly repayment instalments and can continue to borrow up to a ceiling, which is expressed as a multiplier of the instalment. The multiplier is often 24 times (e.g. if the repayment instalment is £100 per month, the borrowing limit is £2400).

budgetary control The process by which *financial control is exercised within an organization. *Budgets for income and expenditure for each function of the organization are prepared in advance of an accounting period and are then compared with actual amounts. Differences arising are usually investigated using *variance analysis.

budget deficit The excess of government expenditure over government income, which must be financed either by borrowing or by printing money. Keynesians have advocated that governments should run budget deficits during *recessions in order to stimulate aggregate demand. Monetarists and new classical macroeconomists, however, argue that budget deficits simply stimulate *inflation and crowd out private investment. Most economists now agree that, at least on average, governments should seek a balanced budget and that persistent deficits should be eliminated, either by reducing expenditure or increasing taxation. In some cases a **budget surplus** can be used during a boom to collect more revenue than is being spent.

Buenos Aires Stock Exchange (Mercado de Valores de Buenos Aires) The oldest of the four stock exchanges in Argentina. Opened in 1872, it is also the oldest stock exchange in Latin America.

buffer stock A stock of a commodity owned by a government or trade organization and used to stabilize the price of the commodity. Usually the manager of the buffer stock is authorized to buy the commodity in question if its price falls below a certain level, which is itself reviewed periodically, to enable producers to find a ready market for their goods at a profitable level. If the price rises above another fixed level, the buffer stock manager is authorized to sell the commodity on the open market. Thus, producers are encouraged to keep up a steady supply of the commodity and users are reassured that its price has a ceiling. It may lead to over-production of the commodity if the intervention prices are set too high. *See also* UNITED NATIONS CONFERENCE ON TRADE AND DEVELOPMENT.

Building Societies Act 1986 A UK Act of Parliament regulating the activities of *building societies. It widened their powers to include making unsecured loans and offering a range of financial services, such as providing cheque accounts, credit cards, foreign exchange, buying and selling shares, managing unit-trust schemes and personal equity plans, arranging and giving advice on insurance, etc. It also allowed building societies to own estate agencies and indulge in property development. The Act subjected building societies to a new regulatory agency, the Building Societies Commission, and additionally allowed societies to issue shares and become public limited companies (demutualize), subject to the agreement of their members.

Building Societies Ombudsman *See* FINANCIAL OMBUDSMAN SERVICE.

building society Traditionally, a financial institution that accepts deposits, upon which it pays interest, and makes loans for house purchase or house improvement secured by *mortgages. They developed from the *Friendly Society movement in the late 17th century and were non-profitmaking, with *mutual status. These institutions can be found in the UK, Australia, South Africa, Ireland, and New Zealand. In the USA *savings and loan associations are broadly similar organizations. In the UK, since the *Building Societies Act 1986 they have been able to widen the range of services they offer; this has enabled them to compete with the High-Street banks in many areas. They offer cheque accounts, which pay interest on all credit balances, cash cards, credit cards, loans, money transmission, foreign exchange, personal financial planning services (shares, insurance, pensions, etc.), estate agency, and valuation and conveyancing services. The distinction between banks and building societies is fast disappearing: indeed, many building societies have obtained the sanction of their members to become *public limited companies. They then become profit-making banks, owned by their shareholders, instead of non-profitmaking societies owned by their subscribing members. These changes have led to the merger of many building societies to provide a national network that can compete with the *Big Four banks. Competition is well illustrated in the close relationship of interest rates between banks and building societies as they both compete for the market's funds. Moreover, the competition provided by the building societies has forced the banks into offering free banking services, paying interest on current accounts, and Saturday opening. Similar change has taken place in all the other countries that have building societies. The UK building societies are now regulated by the *Financial Services Authority.

bulge bracket The leading investment banks in the capital markets.

bull A dealer on a financial market who expects prices to rise. A **bull market** is one in which prices are rising or expected to rise, i.e. one in which a dealer is more likely to be a buyer than a seller, even to the extent of buying without having made a corresponding sale, thus establishing a **bull position** or a **long position**. A bull with a long position hopes to sell these purchases at a higher price after the market has risen. *Compare* BEAR.

bulldog bond A fixed-interest sterling *bond issued in the UK by a foreign borrower.

bullet **1.** A security offering a fixed interest and maturing on a fixed date. **2.** The final repayment of a loan, which consists of the whole of sum borrowed. In a **bullet loan**, interim repayments are interest-only repayments, the principal sum being repaid in the final bullet.

bullion Gold, silver, or some other precious metal used in bulk, i.e. in the form of bars or ingots rather than in coin. Central banks use gold bullion in the settlement of international debts. In the **London bullion market**, bullion brokers act as agents for both buyers and sellers and also trade as principals.

bull market *See* BULL.

bull note A bond whose redemption value is linked to a price index (e.g. FT-SE 100 Index; *see* FINANCIAL TIMES SHARE INDEXES) or a commodity price (e.g. the price of gold). Thus, a holder of a bull note will receive on redemption an amount greater than the principal of the bond if the relevant index or price has risen (but less if it has fallen). With a **bear note** the reverse happens. Bull and bear notes are therefore akin to an ordinary bond plus an *option, providing opportunities for hedging and speculating.

bull position *See* BULL.

bull spread The simultaneous buying and selling of options on the same commodity or security to take advantage of an anticipated rise in the price of the *underlying. *Compare* BEAR SPREAD.

Bundesbank The German central bank (literally, federal bank). It controlled the 11 regional banks in the former West Germany and now oversees all German banks. It implemented Germany's monetary policy until the introduction of the euro in January 1999, when responsibility for rate setting was centralized for the Eurozone and executed by the *European Central Bank.

Bundesbond A German government bond issue.

bunny bond A bond that gives the holder the option of receiving interest or additional bonds.

burn-out turnaround The process of restructuring a company that is in trouble by producing new finance to save it from liquidation, at the cost of diluting the shareholding of existing investors.

burn rate The rate at which a new company or project uses up its funding before cash begins to come in from its trading activities. It is frequently used to evaluate high-tech or venture capital investments.

business combination The combining of two or more companies by means of acquisition or merger. *See* ACQUISITION ACCOUNTING; MERGER ACCOUNTING.

business cycle (trade cycle) The process by which investment, output, and employment in an economy tend to move through a recurrent cycle of upturn, prosperity, downturn, and *recession. The cycle does not describe a regular pattern in either length or amplitude. Cycles in the immediate postwar period were of historically low amplitude, while those of the late 1970s and 1980s had greater amplitude and involved much deeper recessions. The reasons for the business cycle remain little understood.

business expansion scheme (BES) *See* ENTERPRISE INVESTMENT SCHEME.

business-interruption policy (consequential-loss policy; loss-of-profits policy) An insurance policy that pays claims for financial losses occurring if a business has to stop or reduce its activities as a result of a fire or any other insurable risk. Claims can be made for lost profit, rent, rates, and other unavoidable overhead costs that continue even when trading has temporarily ceased.

business judgment rule The rule that the courts will not generally interfere in the conduct of a business. For example, the courts will not substitute their judgment for that of the directors of a company unless the directors are acting improperly. The rule is often invoked when directors are accused of acting out of self-interest in *takeover bids.

business plan 1. A detailed plan setting out the objectives of a business over a stated period, often three, five, or ten years. A business plan is drawn up by many businesses, especially if the business has passed through a bad period or if it has had a major change of policy. For new businesses it is an essential document for raising capital or loans. The plan should quantify as many of the objectives as possible, providing monthly *cash flows and production figures for at least the first two years, with diminishing detail in subsequent years; it must also outline its strategy and the tactics it intends to use in achieving its objectives. Anticipated *profit and loss accounts should form part of the business plan on a quarterly basis for at least two years, and an annual basis thereafter. For a group of companies the business plan is often called a **corporate plan**. **2.** A forecast of the activity volumes and cash flows relating to a specific project within an organization.

business property relief An *inheritance tax relief available on certain types of business property. For a business or interest in an unquoted business, including a partnership share, the relief is 100%. Land or buildings owned and used in a company under the control of the donor, or in a partnership in which the donor was a partner, attract 50% relief. A majority controlling interest in a quoted company also attracts 50% relief.

business rates The local tax paid in the UK by businesses. It is calculated annually by the local authority in which the business is situated and is based on the rateable value of the property occupied by the organization and the *Uniform Business Rate set by central government.

business risk The *risk that a business may be unable to meet its financial obligations.

business software package One of a wide range of software programs sold in packages to enable computers to be used for a variety of business uses. They range in complexity and expense from those needed to operate a PC to the suite of programs required by a mainframe or a network. A typical package would include one or more of: book-keeping programs, which provide facilities for keeping sales, purchase, and nominal ledgers; accounting packages, enabling balance sheets, budgetary control, and sale and purchase analysis to be undertaken automatically; payroll packages, dealing with wages, salaries, PAYE, National Insurance, pensions, etc.; database management systems to maintain company records; communications software to allow two or more computers to work together; and wordprocessors. The programs comprising the package are designed to work together and use each other's data; sometimes a single program provides one or more of these functions.

business strategy An overall practical policy for a firm that coordinates the separate functional areas of a business. It defines the business objectives, analyses the internal and external environments, and determines the direction of the firm. Each firm operates in a competitive environment and seeks to formulate a strategy that will provide it with an advantage over its rivals: design, quality, innovation, and branding are examples of ways in which competitive advantages may be established. Some firms may seek to diversify into new markets, either through *internal growth (i.e. by expanding their existing products or introducing new ones) or by *external growth through mergers, takeovers, joint ventures, or strategic partnerships (*see* DIVERSIFICATION). Each of these methods carries different levels of risk.

busted bond (old bond) A bond issued by a government or corporation that has already defaulted on the loan on which the bonds are based. Busted bonds are now collectors' items, especially those from prerevolutionary Russia and those issued by US railroad companies. Occasionally promises are made to honour Russian or Chinese bonds.

butterfly A strategy used by dealers in traded *options. It involves simultaneously purchasing and selling call or put options at different *exercise prices. A butterfly is most profitable when the price of the underlying security fluctuates within narrow limits but the losses from the strategy are limited. *Compare* STRADDLE.

butut A monetary unit of the Gambia worth one hundredth of a *dalasi.

buy and hold An investment strategy that involves the purchase and holding of securities to provide long-term returns.

buy and write An investment strategy that involves writing (selling) an option on a security that one has bought. This enables the investor to benefit from the *call premium and to hedge any risk relating to the option payoff. *See* COVERED CALL WRITING.

buy-back 1. The buying back by a company of its shares from an investor, who put venture capital up for the formation of the company. The shares are bought back at a price that satisfies the investor, which has to be the price the company is willing to pay for its independence. The buy-back may occur if the company is publicly floated or is taken over. **2.** The buying back by a corporation, especially in the USA, of its shares to reduce the number on the market, either to increase the return on those shares still available or to remove threatening shareholders. **3.** Action by a developing country's government to reduce some or all of its debt to overseas banks by buying back that debt at the market price or at a substantial discount. The attraction for the banks is the removal of a damaging and negative debt, which may already have been provided for in its balance sheet. The advantage to the country in debt is a return to creditworthiness and the possibility of acquiring new loans.

buy earnings To invest in a company that has a low *yield but whose earnings are increasing, so that a substantial capital gain can be expected.

buyer credit A loan granted to the buyer of exported goods.

buyers' market A market in which prices are falling as a result of supply exceeding demand. *Compare* SELLERS' MARKET.

buyers over A market in securities, commodities, etc., in which the sellers have sold all they wish to sell but there are still buyers. This is clearly a strong market, with an inclination for prices to rise. *Compare* SELLERS OVER.

buy-in 1. The purchase of a holding of more than 50% in a company by (or on behalf of) a group of executives from outside the company, who wish to run the company. **2.** The buying of a security to complete the delivery of a failed transaction. **3.** The closing out of a short position in an options market by 'buying-in' the same option that has been sold.

buying forward Buying commodities, securities, foreign exchange, etc., for delivery at a date in the future in order to establish a *bull position or to cover a forward *bear sale. In the case of foreign exchange, a forward purchase may be made to cover a payment that has to be made at a later date in a foreign currency. *See also* FUTURES CONTRACT.

buying in The buying of securities, commodities, etc., by a broker because the original seller has failed to deliver. This invariably happens after a rise in a market price (the seller would be able to buy in himself if the market had fallen). The broker buys at the best price available and the original seller is responsible for any difference between the buying-in price and the original buying price, plus the cost of buying in. *Compare* SELLING OUT.

buy-out 1. An option, open to a member of an *occupational pension scheme on leaving, of transferring the benefits already purchased to an insurance company of his or her own choice. **2.** The acquisition of its own shares by a company with a listing on a stock exchange, either by purchasing them on the open market or by means of an offer to purchase. The aim is to revert to private-company status. **3.** *See* LEVERAGED BUY-OUT. **4.** *See* MANAGEMENT BUY-OUT; EMPLOYEE BUY-OUT.

BV Abbreviation for *Besloten Vennootschap*. It appears after the name of a Dutch company, being equivalent to the British abbreviation Ltd (denoting a private limited company). *Compare* NV.

CA **1.** Abbreviation for *chartered accountant. **2.** Abbreviation for *Consumers' Association.

CAC Abbreviation for Cotation Assistée en Continue. *See* PARIS BOURSE.

CAC General Index *See* PARIS BOURSE.

CAD Abbreviation for *cash against documents.

Cadbury Code A UK code of best practice concerning appropriate senior management remuneration, produced by the 1992 Cadbury Committee on the Financial Aspects of Corporate Governance.

cafeteria plan An agreement that permits employees to choose from a range of *benefits in kind. These include retirement plan assets and health insurance.

calendar convention A convention in *euromarkets that the maturity date of short-term bonds, etc., is the same as the date of issue.

calendar spread An *options strategy that involves the sale of an earlier expiry option and purchase of a later expiry option on the same *underlying.

call **1.** A demand for a payment due on nil or partly paid stocks; this procedure has been common with the privatization programme of the UK government since 1979. It consists of a demand to pay a specified amount of money by a specified day; if payment is not made by the due date the shares can be forfeit. **2.** A notification that redeemable shares or bonds should be presented for repayment. **3.** A demand made on a client by a securities house, stockbroker, etc., for a partial payment of the client's debt because the value of the collateral so far provided has fallen.

callable bonds Fixed-rate bonds, usually *convertibles, in which the issuer has the right, but not the obligation, to redeem (call) the bond during the life of the bond. The call exercise price may be at par, although it is usually set at a premium. A **grace period** (i.e. a period during which the borrower is unable to call the bond) will usually be included in the terms of the agreement; conversion after the grace period will only be possible if certain conditions are met, usually related to the price of the underlying share. *See also* CALL PROVISION; FREELY CALLABLE. *Compare* PUTTABLE BONDS.

called-up capital *See* SHARE CAPITAL.

call money **1.** Money put into the money market that can be called at short notice (*see also* MONEY AT CALL AND SHORT NOTICE). **2.** *See* OPTION MONEY.

call-of-more option *See* OPTION TO DOUBLE.

call option *See* OPTION.

callover A meeting of commodity brokers and dealers at fixed times during the day in order to form a market in that commodity. The callover is usually used for trading in futures, in fixed quantities on a standard contract, payments usually being settled by differences through a *clearing house. Because traders usually form a ring around the person calling out the prices, this form of market is often called **ring trading**. This method of trading is also called **open outcry**, as bids and offers are shouted out during the course of the callover. The price agreed for a transaction at a callover is called the *callover price.

callover price The price agreed for a transaction at a *callover; it may be used subsequently by the general market dealers. Callover prices, though verbal at the outset, may later be formally printed.

call premium 1. The premium paid to purchase a call *option. **2. (redemption premium)** The amount over par value that the bond issuer must pay an investor if the security is redeemed early. *See* CALLABLE BONDS; CALL PROVISION.

call price (redemption price) The *exercise price of a bond's *call provision.

call provision A clause in the agreement between the issuer and the holder of a bond that entitles the issuer to redeem the bond before maturity. The bond may be redeemed either at or slightly over par value (*see* CALL PREMIUM). *See also* CALLABLE BONDS; FREELY CALLABLE.

call risk The *risk to a bond holder that a *call provision will be exercised, i.e. that the bond will be redeemed before its maturity date.

call spread The strategy of buying a call *option at one *exercise price and selling the same call at a higher exercise price.

Calvo clause A clause in a contract relating to a foreign investment stating that the parties to the contract agree to rely exclusively on the legal remedies available in that foreign country in the event of a dispute. The principle was established by the Argentinian jurist Carlos Calvo (1824–1906).

CAMEL A mnemonic for the five principal areas to be examined in evaluating a banking organization:
C – capital adequacy,
A – asset quality,
M – management quality,
E – earnings,
L – liquidity.

cancellation price The price at which a unit trust will redeem units.

candlestick chart A type of graph used by *chartists in which each trading period is represented by a separate histogram. The blocks of the diagram represent the opening and closing prices, while the high and low periods are represented by vertical lines from the opening and closing prices, which in the case of the highs resemble candlewicks.

cap 1. A ceiling on a price; for example, an interest-rate cap would set a maximum interest rate to be charged on a loan, regardless of prevailing general interest-rate levels. A lender would charge a fee for including a cap at the outset to offset this risk. Caps may also limit annual increases to a certain level. *Compare* FLOOR. *See also* COLLAR. **2.** A feature of an option that sets a maximum cost, payout, or return.

CAP Abbreviation for *Common Agricultural Policy.

cap and collar mortgage A *mortgage in which the variable interest rate paid by the borrower cannot rise above or fall below specified levels; such a mortgage may be granted for the first few years of a loan. *See also* CAPPED MORTGAGE.

capital 1. The total value of the assets of a person less liabilities. **2.** The amount of the proprietors' interests in the assets of an organization, less its liabilities. **3.** The money contributed by the proprietors to an organization to enable it to function; thus **share capital** is the amount provided by way of shares and the **loan capital** is the amount provided by way of loans. However, the capital of the proprietors of companies not only consists of the share and loan capital, it also includes retained profit, which accrues to the holders of the ordinary shares. *See also* RESERVE CAPITAL. **4.** The market value of a firm's equity and long-term debt. **5.** In economic theory, the man-made factor of production, usually either machinery and plant (**physical capital**) or money (**financial capital**). However, the concept can be applied to a variety of other assets (e.g. *human capital).

capital account 1. An *account recording capital expenditure on such items as land and buildings, plant and machinery, etc. **2.** A budgeted amount that can only be spent on major items, especially in public-sector budgeting. *Compare* REVENUE ACCOUNT. **3.** An account showing the interest of a sole trader in the net assets of a business. **4.** A series of accounts recording the interests of the partners in the net assets of a partnership. Capital accounts can embrace both the amounts originally contributed and the *current accounts; it may also refer, more narrowly, to the amounts originally contributed, adjusted where necessary by agreement between the partners. **5.** Part of a set of *balance-of-payments accounts recording flows of money between currencies for investment purposes.

capital adequacy The ability of a bank to meet the needs of its depositors and other creditors. It is the proportion of risk capital to risk-adjusted assets in a bank. Many US, European, and Japanese banks are signatories to the *Basle Convergence Accord, an agreement with the *Bank for International Settlements that requires them to maintain 8% of their risk-adjusted assets as capital, and the Accord's successor, *Basle Two.

capital allocation The allocation of *risk capital to particular units within an organization on the basis of possible losses, which are calculated by *value-at-risk or *expected tail loss techniques. This is particularly common in financial insititutions. Capital allocation may also be related to the funding structure of units and is often used as a basis for the calculation of *shareholder value or *economic value added. *See also* RETURN ON RISK-ADJUSTED ASSETS.

capital allowances Allowances against UK income tax or corporation tax available to a business, sole trader, partnership, or limited company that has spent capital on plant and machinery used in the business. Capital allowances are also given on commercial buildings in enterprise zones, agricultural buildings, industrial buildings, and hotels. The level of allowances varies according to the different categories of asset. Plant and machinery qualifies for a 25% *writing-down allowance and small to medium-sized businesses may claim a 40% *first-year allowance on certain assets. An allowance of 4% calculated by the straight-line method (*see* DEPRECIATION) is available on industrial buildings, with no initial allowance. An allowance of 6% is also available for certain long-life assets expected to last for 25 years or more. The allowances are treated as an expense in the computation of taxable profit and the capital allowance period reflects the period during which the accounts are prepared.

capital asset (fixed asset) An asset that is expected to be used for a considerable time in a trade or business (*compare* CURRENT ASSETS). Examples of capital assets in most businesses are land and buildings, plant and machinery, investments in subsidiary companies, goodwill, and motor vehicles, although in the hands of dealers these assets would become current assets. The costs of these assets are normally written off against profits over their expected useful life spans by deducting an item for *depreciation from their book value each year.

capital asset pricing model (CAPM) A statistical model to explain the expected or average return on an investment. It assumes that this return will be composed of the *risk-free rate of return and a *risk premium. The risk premium is related to risks that cannot be avoided when holding the market portfolio (*see* MARKOWITZ MODEL). Formally, the CAPM is based on the equation:

$$E(R_i) = R_f + \beta_i[E(R_m) - R_f],$$

where $E(R_i)$ is the expected/average return on the assets in portfolio i, R_f is the risk-free rate of return, $E(R_m)$ is the expected/average return on all assets, and B_i is the *beta coefficient of the asset or the portfolio i. The beta is the percentage that the return in i will change with a 1% change in R_m. The CAPM is a measure of the risk in the asset or the portfolio. It is the basis for calculating the required return on an investment and is frequently used to calculate the discount rate for a *net present value calculation. *See also* SECURITY MARKET LINE.

capital at risk 1. An element in the calculation of the capital requirements of a bank, under the system that was put in place by the *Basle Convergence Accord (*see* COOKE RATIO). **2.** A measure of worst-case losses in excess of the average that is used in banking to calculate both capital requirements and certain performance measures, such as *risk-adjusted return on capital (RAROC). It is usually based on the *value-at-risk methodology.

capital bond National Savings Capital Bond; a type of UK bond, introduced by the Department of *National Savings in 1989, that offers a guaranteed rate of return over a five-year period. Tax is not deducted at source from the interest. The bonds may be bought in units of £100; the maximum holding of all series of capital bonds, excluding any holding of Series A, is £250,000.

capital budget The sums allocated by an organization for future *capital expenditure. The capital budget may well encompass a longer period than the next accounting period.

capital commitments (commitments for capital expenditure) Firm plans, usually approved by the board of directors in the case of companies, to spend sums of money on *capital assets. Capital commitments must by law be shown by way of a note in the company accounts.

capital consumption The total depreciation in the value of the capital goods in an economy during a specified period. It is difficult to calculate this figure, but it is needed as it has to be deducted from the *gross national product (GNP) and the *gross domestic product (GDP) to obtain the net figures.

capital-conversion plan An *annuity that converts capital into income. Capital-conversion policies are often used to provide an income later in life for a person who might be liable to capital gains tax if his or her capital is not reinvested in some way.

capital employed Either the sum of the shareholders' equity in a company and its long-term debts or the *capital assets of a company plus its *net current assets. However, this term is neither legally defined nor required to be disclosed in a *balance sheet, although it is an important element of *ratio analysis, particularly in the calculation of *return on capital employed.

capital expenditure (**capital costs; capital investment; investment costs; investment expenditure**) The expenditure by an organization of a significant amount for the purchase or improvement of a *capital asset; the amount expended would warrant the item being depreciated over an estimated useful life of a reasonably extended period. Capital expenditure is not charged against the profits of the organization when it takes place, but is regarded as an investment to be capitalized in the *balance sheet as a fixed asset and subsequently charged against profits by depreciating the asset over its estimated useful life. Relief against taxation is available through *capital allowances.

capital flight The rapid withdrawal of capital (flight capital) from a country as a result of loss of confidence in its government.

capital formation *See* FIXED CAPITAL FORMATION.

capital gain (**capital profit**) The gain on the disposal of an asset calculated by deducting the cost of the asset from the proceeds received on its disposal. Under *capital gains tax legislation the *chargeable gain for individuals may be reduced by *taper relief (and also by *indexation if the asset was purchased prior to April 1998). Capital gains by companies are adjusted by indexation and are chargeable to *corporation tax.

capital gains tax (**CGT**) A tax on *capital gains. Most countries have a form of income tax under which they tax the profits from trading and a different tax to tax substantial disposals of assets either by traders for whom the assets are not trading stock (e.g. a trader's factory) or by individuals who do not trade (e.g. sales of shares by an investor). The latter type of tax is a capital gains tax. Short-term gains taxes are taxes sometimes applied to an asset that has only been held for a limited time. In these cases the rates tend to be higher than for the normal capital gains tax. In the UK, capital gains tax applies to the net gains (after deducting losses) accruing to an individual in any tax year, with an exemption to liability if the individual's gains do not exceed a specified figure (£8200 for 2004–05); this exemption applies separately to husbands and wives. Other exemptions include gains on assets sold for less than £6000, private cars, government securities and savings certificates, loan stocks, options, gambling, life-assurance and deferred-annuity contracts, main dwelling house, and works of art. Certain reductions also apply to gains from employee shares held for more than four years. The rate of tax is 10%, 20%, or 40% depending on the taxpayer's marginal rate of income tax. *Taper relief may be available to reduce a chargeable gain and *indexation is available to companies and to individuals who purchased the asset prior to April 1998.

capital gearing *See* GEARING.

capital goods Long-term man-made factors of production, such as factories and machinery.

capital growth An increase in the value of invested capital. Investment in *fixed-interest securities or bonds provides income but limited capital growth (which may be improved in index-linked *gilt-edged securities). To have a chance of making substantial capital growth it is necessary to invest in equities (*see* ORDINARY SHARE), the value of which should increase more rapidly than *inflation. Investing in equities is thus said to be a hedge against inflation. *See* GROWTH STOCKS.

capital impairment A situation in which a bank has insufficient *capital at risk to cover the risks it is undertaking, either from a risk-management or a regulatory perspective.

capital inflow An increase in a country's foreign assets within its own country or a decrease in its assets held abroad. *Compare* CAPITAL OUTFLOW.

capital-intensive Denoting a technique of production that requires a high ratio of capital to labour costs. *Compare* LABOUR-INTENSIVE.

capital investment *See* INVESTMENT.

capitalism An economic system in which the factors of production are privately owned. In this system the market and the profit mechanism will play a major role in deciding what is to be produced, how it is to be produced, and who owns what is produced.

capitalization 1. The act of providing *capital for a company or other organization. **2.** The structure of the capital of a company or other organization, i.e. the extent to which its capital is divided into share or loan capital and the extent to which share capital is divided into ordinary and preference shares. *See also* THIN CAPITALIZATION. **3.** The conversion of the reserves of a company into capital by means of a *scrip issue.

capitalization issue *See* SCRIP ISSUE.

capitalized value 1. The value at which an asset has been recorded in the balance sheet of a company or other organization, usually before the deduction of *depreciation. **2.** The capital equivalent of an asset that yields a regular income, calculated at the prevailing rate of interest. For example, a piece of land bringing in an annual income of £1000, when the prevailing interest rate is 10%, would have a notional capitalized value of £10,000 (i.e. £1000/0.1). This may not reflect its true value.

capital lease In the USA, a lease that does not legally constitute a purchase although the leased asset should be recorded as an asset on the lessee's books if any one of the following four criteria is met:
- the lease transfers ownership of the property to the lessee at the end of the lease term;
- a **bargain purchase option** exists; i.e. an option exists enabling the lessee to buy the leased property at the end of the lease for a minimal amount or to renew the lease for a nominal rental (a **bargain renewal option**);
- the lease term is 75% or more of the life of the property;
- the *present value of minimum lease payments equals or exceeds 90% of the fair value of the property.

See also FINANCE LEASE.

capital loss (allowable capital loss) The excess of the cost of an asset over the proceeds received on its disposal. *Indexation is not permitted to create or increase a capital loss. Both individuals and companies may set capital losses against *capital gains to establish tax liability.

capital maintenance concept 1. The **financial capital maintenance concept** is that the capital of a company is only maintained if the financial or monetary amount of its *net assets at the end of a financial period is equal to or exceeds the financial or monetary amount of its net assets at the beginning of the period, excluding any distributions to, or contributions from, the owners. **2.** The **physical capital maintenance concept** is that the physical capital is only maintained if the physical productive or operating capacity, or the funds or resources required to achieve this capacity, is equal to or exceeds the physical productive capacity at the beginning of the period, after excluding any distributions to, or contributions from, owners during the financial period.

capital market A market in which long-term *capital is raised by industry and commerce, the government, and local authorities. The money comes from private investors, insurance companies, pension funds, and banks and is usually arranged by *issuing houses and *merchant banks. *Stock exchanges are also part of the capital market in that they provide a market for the shares and loan stocks that represent the capital once it has been raised. It is the presence and sophistication of their capital markets that distinguishes the industrial countries from the developing countries, in that this facility for raising industrial and commercial capital is either absent or rudimentary in the latter.

capital market line *See* MARKOWITZ MODEL.

capital movement The transfer of capital between countries, either by companies or individuals. Restrictions on *exchange controls and capital transfers between countries have been greatly reduced in recent years. Capital movements seeking long-term gains are usually those made by companies investing abroad, for example to set up a factory. Capital movements seeking short-term gains are often more speculative, such as those taking advantage of temporarily high interest rates in another country or an expected change in the exchange rate.

capital outflow A decrease in a country's foreign assets held in its own country or an increase in its assets held abroad. *Compare* CAPITAL INFLOW.

capital profit *See* CAPITAL GAIN.

capital rationing A shortfall in a company's *capital budget, impairing its ability to invest in projects that would otherwise be financially viable. The *profitability index is used to determine which projects should receive the limited funds available.

capital reserves *See* UNDISTRIBUTABLE RESERVES.

capital shares *See* INVESTMENT TRUST.

capital stock In the USA, the equity shares in a corporation. The two basic types of capital stock are *common stock and *preferred stock.

capital structure (financial structure) The balance between the assets and liabilities of a company, the nature of its assets, and the composition of its borrowings. The assets may be fixed (tangible or intangible) or current (stock, debtors, or creditors); the borrowings may be long- or short-term, fixed or floating, secured or unsecured. Ideally the assets and liabilities should be matched. *See also* GEARING.

capital surplus In the USA, the difference between the *par value of a share and its *issue price. It is the equivalent of a *share premium in the UK.

capital transfer tax A tax levied when capital is transferred from one person's estate usually into that of another, as by lifetime gifts or inheritances. There was such a tax in the UK from 1974 to 1986, when it was replaced by *inheritance tax.

capital turnover (asset turnover) The ratio of sales of a company or other organization to its *capital employed (i.e. its assets less liabilities). It is presumed that the higher this ratio, the better the use that is being made of the assets in generating sales.

CAPM Abbreviation for *capital asset pricing model.

capped floating rate note A floating rate note (*see* EUROBOND) with an upper limit on the coupon rate.

capped mortgage A *mortgage in which the variable interest rate paid by the borrower cannot rise above a specified level, usually for the first few years of the loan. The interest rate can, however, be reduced if interest rates fall generally. *See also* CAP AND COLLAR MORTGAGE.

capped option An *option in which the payout on exercise has a maximum limit.

capped prime loan A loan in which the interest rate cannot exceed a maximum level.

caption An *option on an interest-rate *cap.

captive finance company A finance company controlled by an industrial or commercial company.

captive insurance company An insurance company that is totally owned by another organization and insures only, or mostly, the parent company's risks. In this way the parent organization is able to obtain insurance cover (particularly those classes that are compulsory by law) without having to pay premiums to an organization outside its trading group.

CAR Abbreviation for *compound annual return.

care and maintenance (c & m) Denoting the status of a building, machinery, ship, etc., that is not currently in active use, usually as a result of a fall in demand, but which is being kept in a good state of repair so that it can be brought back into use quickly, if needed.

carry back (carry forward) The ability of a taxpayer to move a tax advantage from one taxation year to another.

carrying amount The balance-sheet value of an asset or liability. For example, a *capital asset, such as a building, will be shown at the historical cost less the accumulated *depreciation to date, using the rules of *historical cost accounting. Under alternative accounting rules it can be shown at the revalued amount less the accumulated depreciation to date.

carrying market A *commodity market in which goods for delivery, storage, and resale can be carried over from month to month because the particular commodity does not perish.

carry-over 1. The quantity of a *commodity that is carried over from one crop to the following one. The price of some commodities, such as grain, coffee, cocoa, and jute, which grow in annual or biannual crops, is determined by the supply and the demand. The supply consists of the quantity produced by the current crop added to the quantity in the hands of producers and traders that is carried over from the previous crop. Thus, in some circumstances the carry-over can strongly influence the market price. **2.** To delay delivery or payment from one payment date to the next, usually with the consent of the counterparty.

cartel An association of independent companies formed to regulate the price and sales conditions of the products or services they offer. A cartel may operate nationally or internationally, although some countries, including the UK and the

USA, have legislation forbidding cartels to be formed on the grounds that they are *monopolies that function against the public interest.

cascade shareholdings A form of *pyramiding in which a holding company has a controlling interest in a company that in turn has a controlling interest in further companies, and so on.

case of need An endorsement written on a *bill of exchange giving the name of someone to whom the holder may apply if the bill is not honoured at maturity.

cash *Legal tender in the form of banknotes and coins that are readily acceptable for the settlement of debts.

cash accounting **1.** An accounting scheme for *value added tax enabling a *taxable person to account for VAT on the basis of amounts paid and received during the period of the VAT return. Relief for bad debts is automatically available under this scheme. In order to qualify for the scheme, expected turnover should not exceed £660,000 in the next 12 months. A business already in the scheme is allowed a 25% tolerance limit above this threshold. **2. (cash-flow accounting)** A system of accounting that records only the cash payments and receipts relating to transactions made by a business, rather than when the money is earned or when expenses are incurred, as in *accrual accounting. UK legislation does not permit this system of accounting to be used for *published accounts.

cash against documents (CAD) **1.** The simultaneous exchange of assets and payment. **2.** Payment terms for exported goods in which the shipping documents are sent to a bank, agent, etc., in the country to which the goods are being shipped, and the buyer then obtains the documents by paying the invoice amount in cash to the bank, agent, etc. Having the shipping documents enables the buyer to take possession of the goods when they arrive at their port of destination; this is known as **documents against presentation**. *Compare* DOCUMENTS AGAINST ACCEPTANCE.

cash and carry **1.** A wholesaler, especially of groceries, who sells to retailers and others with businesses at discounted prices on condition that they pay in cash, collect the goods themselves, and buy in bulk. **2.** An operation that is sometimes possible on the futures market (*see* FUTURES CONTRACT), especially the *London Metal Exchange. In some circumstances the spot price of a metal, including the cost of insurance, warehousing, and interest for three months, is less than the futures-market price for delivery in three months. Under these conditions it is possible to buy the spot metal, simultaneously sell the forward goods, and make a profit in excess of the yield the capital would have earned on the money market.

cash budget *See* CASH FLOW.

cash card A plastic card enabling customers of retail banks to obtain cash from *automated teller machines, in conjunction with a *personal identification number. Many cash cards also function as *cheque cards and *debit cards.

cash cow *See* BOSTON MATRIX.

cash cycle In manufacturing industry, the interval between an outlay of cash to buy raw materials and the receipt of payment for the manufactured goods produced from them.

cash discount A *discount receivable or allowable for settling an invoice for cash, or within a specified period. In the *profit and loss account, discounts receivable are classed as revenue; discounts allowable as expenditure.

cash dispenser *See* AUTOMATED TELLER MACHINE.

cash dividend A *dividend paid in cash rather than shares. Cash dividends are paid net of income tax, credit being given to the shareholder for the tax deducted. *See also* ADVANCE CORPORATION TAX.

cash flow 1. The amount of cash being received and expended by a business, which is often analysed into its various components. A **cash-flow projection** (or **cash budget**) sets out all the expected payments and receipts in a given period. This is different from the projected profit and loss account and, in times of cash shortage, may be more important. It is on the basis of the cash-flow projection that managers may arrange appropriate financing facilities and may also arrange for employees and creditors to be paid at appropriate times. *See also* DISCOUNTED CASH FLOW; FREE CASH FLOW. **2.** In finance, the net income from a particular transaction after all cash expenses have been met (noncash expenses such as depreciation being specifically excluded from the calculation).

cash flow at risk A measure of the risks to a firm's cash flows, calculated by applying the concept of *value-at-risk.

cash instruments Financial instruments and obligations that are sold for immediate delivery.

cash management The planning, monitoring, and execution of a firm's policy regarding *liquidity.

cash management account A bank account in which deposits are invested by the bank, usually on the money market; it is, however, a cheque account and the client is able to obtain loans if required.

cash market A market in which delivery and settlement is within a few days.

cash-or-nothing option *See* BINARY OPTION.

cash price The price at which a seller is prepared to sell goods provided that payment is received immediately in cash, i.e. no credit or commission to a credit-card company has to be given. This is invariably below the price that includes a *hire-purchase agreement.

cash ratio (liquidity ratio) The ratio of the cash reserve that a bank keeps in coin, banknotes, etc., to its total liabilities to its customers, i.e. the amount deposited with it in current accounts and deposit accounts. Because cash reserves earn no interest, bankers try to keep them to a minimum, consistent with being able to meet customers' demands.

cash settlement (cash deal) 1. A settlement made on a cash market. **2.** An alternative to physical delivery in derivatives markets.

cash unit trust *See* MONEY-MARKET UNIT TRUST.

casting vote A second or deciding vote. It is common practice to give the chairman of a meeting a second vote to be used to resolve a deadlock. In the case of a company meeting, the chairman is generally given this right by the articles of association, but has no common-law right to a casting vote.

CAT Abbreviation for *computer-assisted trading.

catching bargain (unconscionable bargain) An unfair contract, often one in which one party has been taken advantage of by the other. Such a contract may be set aside or modified by a court.

CATS Abbreviation for *Certificate of Accrual on Treasury Securities.

CBOE Abbreviation for *Chicago Board Options Exchange.

CBS Index The share index of the Amsterdam Stock Exchange.

CCA Abbreviation for *current cost accounting.

c.c.c. Abbreviation for *cwmni cyfyngedig cyhoeddus: the Welsh equivalent of plc.

CD Abbreviation for *certificate of deposit.

CEC Abbreviation for Commodities Exchange Center Inc.

CEDEL Abbreviation for *Centrale de Livraison de Valeurs Mobilières.

cedi The standard monetary unit of Ghana, divided into 100 pesewas.

cent 1. A monetary unit of American Samoa, Antigua and Barbuda, Australia, the Bahamas, Barbados, Belau, Belize, Bermuda, the British Virgin Islands, Brunei, Canada, the Cayman Islands, Dominica, East Timor, Ecuador, El Salvador, Fiji, Grenada, Guam, Guatemala, Guyana, Hong Kong, Jamaica, Kiribati, Liberia, Malaysia, the Marshall Islands, Micronesia, Namibia, Nauru, New Zealand, Puerto Rico, Saint Kitts and Nevis, Saint Lucia, Saint Vincent and the Grenadines, Singapore, the Solomon Islands, Taiwan, Trinidad and Tobago, Tuvalu, the USA, the Virgin Islands, and Zimbabwe, worth one hundredth of a *dollar. **2.** A monetary unit of Andorra, Austria, Belgium, Bosnia and Hercegovina, Finland, France, French Guiana, Germany, Greece, Guadeloupe, Ireland, Italy, Kosovo, Luxembourg, Madeira, Martinique, Mayotte, Monaco, Montenegro, The Netherlands, Portugal, Réunion, San Marino, and Spain, worth one hundredth of a *euro. **3.** A monetary unit of Ethiopia, worth one hundredth of a *birr. **4.** A monetary unit of Kenya, Somalia, Tanzania, and Uganda, worth one hundredth of a *shilling. **5.** A monetary unit of South Africa, worth one hundredth of a *rand. **6.** A monetary unit of Mauritius, the Seychelles, and Sri Lanka, worth one hundredth of a *rupee. **7.** A monetary unit of Swaziland, worth one hundredth of a *lilangeni. **8.** A monetary unit of Surinam and the Netherlands Antilles, worth one hundredth of a *guilder. **9.** A monetary unit of Sierra Leone, worth one hundredth of a *leone. **10.** A monetary unit of Malta, worth one hundredth of a *lira. **11.** A former monetary unit of The Netherlands, worth one hundredth of a guilder (until 2002).

centas (*plural* **centai** or **centas**) A monetary unit of Lithuania worth one hundredth of a *litas.

centavo 1. A monetary unit of Bolivia, worth one hundredth of a *boliviano. **2.** A monetary unit of Brazil, worth one hundredth of a *real. **3.** A monetary unit of Argentina, Chile, Colombia, Cuba, the Dominican Republic, Mexico, and the Philippines, worth one hundredth of a *peso. **4.** A monetary unit of El Salvador, worth one hundredth of a *colón. **5.** A monetary unit of Guatemala, worth one hundredth of a *quetzal. **6.** A monetary unit of Honduras, worth one hundredth of a *lempira. **7.** A monetary unit of Nicaragua, worth one hundredth of a *córdoba. **8.** A monetary unit of Peru, worth one hundredth of a *new sol. **9.** A monetary unit of Cape Verde, worth one hundredth of an *escudo. **10.** A monetary unit of Mozambique, worth one hundredth of a *metical. **11.** A monetary unit of São Tomé e Príncipe, worth one hundredth of a *dobra. **12.** A former monetary unit of Portugal and Madeira, worth one hundredth of an escudo (until 2002).

centesimo (*plural* **centesimi**) A former monetary unit of Italy and San Marino, worth one hundredth of a lira (until 2002).

centésimo **1.** A monetary unit of Panama worth one hundredth of a *balboa. **2.** A monetary unit of Uruguay worth one hundredth of a *peso.

centime **1.** A monetary unit of Benin, Burkina-Faso, Burundi, Cameroon, the Central African Republic, Chad, Comoros, Congo, Congo-Brazzaville, Côte d'Ivoire, Djibouti, Equatorial Guinea, Gabon, Guinea, Liechtenstein, Madagascar, Mali, Niger, Rwanda, Senegal, Switzerland, Tahiti, and Togo, worth one hundredth of a *franc. **2.** A monetary unit of Algeria, worth one hundredth of a *dinar. **3.** A monetary unit of Haiti, worth one hundredth of a *gourde. **4.** A monetary unit of Morocco, worth one hundredth of a *dirham. **5.** A former monetary unit of Andorra, Belgium, France, Luxembourg, and Monaco, worth one hundredth of a franc (until 2002).

céntimo **1.** A monetary unit of Costa Rica, worth one hundredth of a *colón. **2.** A monetary unit of Paraguay, worth one hundredth of a *guaraní. **3.** A monetary unit of Venezuela, worth one hundredth of a *bolívar. **4.** A monetary unit of Peru, worth one hundredth of a *new sol. **5.** A former monetary unit of Spain and Andorra, worth one hundredth of a peseta (until 2002).

central bank A bank that provides financial and banking services for the government of a country and its commercial banking system as well as implementing the government's monetary policy. The main functions of a central bank are: to manage the government's accounts; to accept deposits and grant loans to the commercial banks; to control the issue of banknotes; to manage the public debt; to help manage the exchange rate when necessary; to influence the interest rate structure and control the money supply; to hold the country's reserves of gold and foreign currency; to manage dealings with other central banks; and to act as lender of last resort to the banking system. Examples of major central banks include the *Bank of England in the UK, the Federal Reserve Bank of the USA (*see* FEDERAL RESERVE SYSTEM), and the *European Central Bank.

Central Bank Advisory Board *See* WORLD GOLD COUNCIL.

central bank discount rate The rate of interest charged by a *central bank for discounting *eligible paper.

Centrale de Livraison de Valeurs Mobilières (CEDEL) A settlement service for *eurobonds based in Luxembourg. It is owned by a consortium of international banks. *See also* EUROCLEAR.

Central Fund A fund maintained at *Lloyd's to pay claims by policyholders in the event of the financial failure of a Lloyd's underwriter.

Central Government Borrowing Requirement (CGBR) In the UK, the *Public Sector Borrowing Requirement (PSBR) less any borrowings by local authorities and public corporations from the private sector. Since local authorities and public corporations both have a measure of freedom in deciding how much they borrow, the government does not have the complete control over the PSBR as it does over the CGBR.

central limit theorem A set of mathematical propositions stating that the distributions of certain statistics will converge to a *normal distribution over a large number of samples.

Central Registration Depository (CRD) The computerized directory set up in the USA by the *National Association of Securities Dealers Inc. (NASD), listing the employment, qualifications, and curricula vitae of more than 40 000 professional members of the investment industry, who deal with the public.

Central Statistical Office *See* OFFICE FOR NATIONAL STATISTICS.

central treasury A single organizational unit that provides services in dealing on financial markets, trading, and liquidity.

certain annuity (terminable annuity) A form of investment contract that pays fixed sums at scheduled intervals to an individual after he or she attains a specified age; it runs for a specified number of years.

certainty equivalent method In a *capital budget, a method of expressing a particularly risky return in terms of the *risk-free rate of return that would be its equivalent.

Certificate of Accrual on Treasury Securities (CATS) A *zero-coupon bond issued by the US Treasury.

certificate of deposit (CD) A negotiable certificate issued by a bank in return for a term deposit of up to five years. CDs originated in the USA in the 1960s. From 1968, a sterling CD was issued by UK banks. They were intended to enable the *merchant banks to attract funds away from the *clearing banks with the offer of competitive interest rates. However, in 1971 the clearing banks also began to issue CDs as their negotiability and higher average yield had made them increasingly popular with the larger investors.
   A secondary market in CDs has developed, made up of the *discount houses and the banks in the interbank market. They are issued in various amounts between £10,000 and £50,000, although they may be subdivided into units of the lower figure to facilitate negotiation of part holdings. *See also* ROLL-OVER CD.

certificate of incorporation The certificate that brings a company into existence; it is issued to the shareholders of a company by the Registrar of Companies. It is issued when the *memorandum and *articles of association have been submitted to the Registrar of Companies, together with other documents that disclose the proposed registered address of the company, details of the proposed directors and company secretary, the nominal and issued share capital, and the capital duty. The statutory registration fee must also be submitted. Until the certificate is issued, the company has no legal existence.

certificate of quality A certificate to provide proof that goods to be traded in a *commodity market comply with an agreed standard.

certificate of value A statement made in a document certifying that the transaction concerned is not part of a transaction (or series of transactions) for which the amount involved exceeds a certain value. The statement is made in relation to stamp duty, denoting that either it is not payable or it is payable at a reduced rate.

certificate to commence business A document issued by the *Registrar of Companies to a public company on incorporation; it certifies that the nominal value of the company's allotted share capital is at least equal to the authorized minimum of £50,000. Until the certificate has been issued, the company cannot do business or exercise its borrowing powers.

certified accountant A member of the Chartered Association of Certified

Accountants. Its members are trained in industry, in the public service, and in the offices of practising accountants. Membership is granted on the basis of completion of the Association's examinations and of sufficient relevant work experience. Members are recognized by the UK Department of Trade and Industry as qualified to audit the accounts of companies. They may be associates (ACCA) or fellows (FCCA) of the Association and although they are not *chartered accountants, they fulfil much the same role. In the USA the equivalent is a certified public accountant (CPA), who is a member of the Institute of Certified Public Accountants.

CET Abbreviation for *Common External Tariff.

CFC Abbreviation for Common Fund for Commodities. *See* UNITED NATIONS CONFERENCE ON TRADE AND DEVELOPMENT.

CFTC Abbreviation for *Commodity Futures Trading Commission.

CGBR Abbreviation for *Central Government Borrowing Requirement.

CGT Abbreviation for *capital gains tax.

chaebol A large, often family-owned, conglomerate in South Korea. The Hanbo Business Group, which collapsed in 1997 with debts of $US6 billion, is an example of a *chaebol*.

chamber of commerce In the UK, a voluntary organization, existing in most towns, of commercial, industrial, and trading businessmen who represent their joint interests to local and central government. The London Chamber of Commerce is the largest such organization in the UK; it also fulfils an educational role, running several commercial courses, for which it also sets examinations. Most UK chambers of commerce are affiliated to the Association of British Chambers of Commerce. *Compare* CHAMBER OF TRADE.

chamber of trade An organization of local retailers set up to protect their interests in local matters. They are a much narrower organization than a *chamber of commerce and most in the UK are affiliated to the National Chamber of Trade (NTC).

Chambre Agent General Index An arithmetically weighted index of 430 shares on the Paris Bourse.

chaos theory A set of mathematical models according to which simple equations and initial conditions give rise to complicated paths for variables. Some of these models have been applied to financial markets.

CHAPS Abbreviation for Clearing House Automatic Payments System. *See* ASSOCIATION FOR PAYMENT CLEARING SERVICES.

chapter 7 In the USA, the statute of the Bankruptcy Reform Act 1978 that refers to liquidation proceedings. It provides for a trustee appointed by the court to make a management charge, secure additional financing, and operate the business in order to prevent further loss. The intention of the statute, which is based on fairness and public policy, is to accept that honest debtors may not always be able to discharge their debts fully and to give them an opportunity to make a fresh start both in their business and personal lives. *Compare* CHAPTER 11.

chapter 11 In the USA, the statute of the Bankruptcy Reform Act 1978 that refers to the reorganization of partnerships, corporations, and municipalities, as well as sole traders, who are in financial difficulties. Unless the court rules otherwise, the debtor remains in control of the business and its operations. By allowing activities to continue, debtors and creditors can enter into arrangements, such as the restructuring of debt, rescheduling of payments, and the granting of loans. *Compare* CHAPTER 7.

chapter 13 In the USA, a statute of the Bankruptcy Reform Act (1978) that refers to debt restructuring and provides for individuals to repay creditors over time.

charge 1. A legal or equitable interest in land, securing the payment of money. It gives the creditor in whose favour the charge is created (the **chargee**) the right to payment from the income or proceeds of sale of the land charged, in priority to claims against the debtor by unsecured creditors. **2.** An interest in company property created in favour of a creditor (e.g. as a *debenture holder) to secure the amount owing. Most charges must be registered by the *Registrar of Companies (*see also* REGISTER OF CHARGES). A *fixed charge (or specific charge) is attached to a specific item of property (e.g. land); a *floating charge is created in respect of circulating assets (e.g. cash, stock in trade), to which it will not attach until **crystallization**, i.e. until some event (e.g. winding-up) causes it to become fixed. Before crystallization, unsecured debts can be paid out of the assets charged. After, the charge is treated as a fixed charge and therefore unsecured debts (except those given preference under the Companies Acts) rank after those secured by the charge (*see also* FRAUDULENT PREFERENCE). A charge can also be created upon shares. For example, the articles of association usually give the company a *lien in respect of unpaid *calls, and company members may, in order to secure a debt owed to a third party, charge their shares, either by a full transfer of shares coupled with an agreement to retransfer upon repayment of the debt or by a deposit of the share certificate.

chargeable assets Forms of property, wherever situated, that are subject to *capital gains tax. Exempt assets include motor cars, National Savings Certificates, foreign currency for private use, betting winnings, life-insurance policies for those who are the original beneficial owners, works of art of national importance given for national purposes, principal private residences, *gilt-edged securities, certain low-value items, and investments under *personal equity plans and *individual savings accounts.

chargeable event Any transaction or event that gives rise to a liability to income tax or to capital gains tax.

chargeable gain In the UK, that part of a *capital gain arising as a result of the disposal of an asset that is subject to taxation. The exceptions are:
• gains resulting from proceeds that are taxable under *income tax or *corporation tax;
• gains covered by various exemptions and reliefs (e.g. an annual personal exemption from capital gains tax of £8200 for 2004–05;
• gains not charged in full, as part of the gain occurred before 6 April 1965.
See also INDEXATION; TAPER RELIEF.

chargeable transfer Certain lifetime gifts that are transfers of value not covered by any of the exemptions and are therefore liable to *inheritance tax. If such a lifetime gift is not a *potentially exempt transfer, it is a chargeable transfer. If the gift is a potentially exempt transfer, but death of the donor occurs within seven years, then that potentially exempt transfer becomes a chargeable transfer.

charge account A credit facility offered by a retailer to enable customers to settle (usually) monthly accounts, instead of paying for items as they are purchased. *See* CHARGE CARD.

charge card A plastic card entitling the holder to purchase goods or services, usually up to a prescribed limit, and requiring payment in full, or of an agreed proportion, at regular intervals (usually monthly). Charge cards usually only cover purchases from the issuers' retail outlets. However, some banks issue charge cards (e.g. American Express, Diners' Club), which have a wide acceptability similar to *credit cards but they do not have the facility to roll over credit. *See also* CHARGE ACCOUNT.

charitable trust A trust set up in the UK for a charitable purpose that is registered with the **Charity Commissioners**, a body responsible to parliament. Charitable trusts do not have to pay income tax and may have other indirect taxes reduced or exempted if they comply with the regulations of the Charity Commissioners.

charity card *See* AFFINITY CARD.

chartered accountant (CA) A qualified member of the *Institute of Chartered Accountants in England and Wales, the Institute of Chartered Accountants of Scotland, or the Institute of Chartered Accountants in Ireland. These were the original bodies to be granted royal charters. Other bodies of accountants now have charters (the Chartered Association of Certified Accountants, the Chartered Institute of Management Accountants, and the Chartered Institute of Public Finance and Accountancy) but their members are not known as chartered accountants. Most firms of chartered accountants are engaged in public practice concerned with auditing, taxation, and other financial advice; however, many trained chartered accountants fulfil management roles in industry.

Chartered Association of Certified Accountants *See* CERTIFIED ACCOUNTANT; CHARTERED ACCOUNTANT.

chartered bank A bank in the USA that is authorized to operate as a bank by a charter granted either by its home state (**state-chartered bank**) or by the federal government (**nationally chartered bank**). In Canada, a similar charter is granted to banks by the Comptroller of Currency. The use of charters dates back to the use of Royal Charters, which predated Acts of Parliament.

Chartered Institute of Management Accountants *See* CHARTERED ACCOUNTANT.

Chartered Institute of Public Finance and Accountancy *See* CHARTERED ACCOUNTANT.

Chartered Insurance Institute (CII) An association of insurers and brokers in the insurance industry. Its origins date back to 1873; its first Royal Charter was granted in 1912. It provides training by post and at its own college, examinations leading to its associateship diploma (ACII) and fellowship diploma (FCII), and sets high standards of ethical behaviour in the industry.

chartist An *investment analyst who uses charts of prices and volumes in an attempt to predict what will happen in financial markets. Most chartist analysis is based on the assumption that history repeats itself and that the movements of share prices conform to a small number of repetitive patterns.

cheapest to deliver In *futures contracts, the most cost-effective form of security (usually a Treasury security) for the seller to buy and deliver on the fixed date.

cheap money (easy money) A monetary policy of keeping *interest rates at a low level. This is normally done to encourage an expansion in the level of economic activity by reducing the costs of borrowing and investment. It was used in the 1930s to help recovery after the depression and during World War II to reduce the cost of government borrowing. *Compare* DEAR MONEY.

check The US spelling of *cheque.

checkable Denoting a bank account in the USA upon which a check can be drawn. *See also* CHECKING ACCOUNT.

checking account US name for a *current account, i.e. a bank account upon which checks can be drawn.

cheque A preprinted form on which instructions are given to an account provider (a bank or building society) to pay a stated sum to a named recipient. It is a common form of payment of debts of all kinds (*see also* CHEQUE ACCOUNT; CURRENT ACCOUNT). In a **crossed cheque** two parallel lines across the face of the cheque indicate that it must be paid into a bank account and not cashed over the counter (a **general crossing**). A **special crossing** may be used in order to further restrict the negotiability of the cheque, for example by adding the name of the payee's bank. An **open cheque** is an uncrossed cheque that can be cashed at the bank of origin. An **order cheque** is one made payable to a named recipient 'or order', enabling the payee to either deposit it in an account or endorse it to a third party, i.e. transfer the rights to the cheque by signing it on the reverse. In a **blank cheque** the amount is not stated; it is often used if the exact debt is not known and the payee is left to complete it. However, the drawer may impose a maximum by writing 'under £…' on the cheque. A **rubber cheque** is one that is 'bounced' back to the drawer because of insufficient funds in the writer's account. In the USA the word is spelled **check**. *See also* BANK DRAFT; CHEQUES ACT 1992; RETURNED CHEQUE; STALE CHEQUE; TRAVELLER'S CHEQUE.

cheque account An account with a *bank or *building society on which cheques can be drawn. In general, building societies pay interest on the daily credit balances in a cheque account but banks traditionally did not; they are now often doing so to meet competition from building societies. *See also* CURRENT ACCOUNT.

cheque card A plastic card issued by a retail bank to its customers to guarantee cheques drawn on the customer's current account up to a specified limit. The card carries the account number, the name of the customer, and has to be signed by the customer. The card number must be written on the reverse of the cheque that it is guaranteeing. Many cheque cards have now been replaced by *multifunctional cards, which also function as *cash cards and *debit cards.

cheque clearing *See* CLEARING CYCLE.

Cheques Act 1992 A UK Act of Parliament that gives legal force to the words *account payee on cheques, making them non-transferable and thus stopping fraudulent conversion of cheques intercepted by a third party. Banks require the express permission of a customer to cash an endorsed cheque. Within weeks of the legislation most High-Street banks introduced new cheque books with the words 'account payee' printed on each cheque.

cherrypicking The act of choosing the best or most profitable items for oneself out of a range of items, as in *asset stripping a company.

chetrum A monetary unit of Bhutan, worth one hundredth of a *ngultrum.

Chicago Board of Trade (CBOT) The main US exchange for trading *financial futures. It started in 1848, trading in grain, and in the 1970s extended its business to financial futures.

Chicago Board Options Exchange (CBOE) A major US financial institution trading in *options. It was set up in 1973.

Chicago Mercantile Exchange (CME) The prime US futures and options market. It trades in financial and commodity contracts. It was started in 1919 as a commodity futures market, currencies trading being introduced in 1972.

child trust funds (baby bonds) A government-backed savings scheme for children introduced from 6 April 2005. On that date, the UK government will provide every child born on or after 1 September 2002 with £250 (£500 for the poorest families) to invest in an approved scheme; children born subsequently will receive this sum at birth. A further government payment will be made on the child's seventh birthday and parents and others will be allowed to top up the funds to a maximum of £1200 a year. The funds will mature when the child is 18.

China International Trust and Investment Corporation (CITIC) A Chinese government organization that provides finance for capital ventures in China in conjunction with foreign entrepreneurs, through the issuing of bonds.

Chinese wall A notional information barrier between the parts of a business, notably between the market-making part of a stockbroking firm and the broking part. It would clearly not be in investors' interests for brokers to persuade their clients to buy investments from them for no other reason than that the market makers in the firm, expecting a fall in price, were anxious to sell them.

chip card A type of *debit card that incorporates a microchip in order to store information regarding the transactions for which it is used. *See also* SMART CARD.

CHIPS Abbreviation for *Clearing House Inter-Bank Payments System.

chon A monetary unit of North Korea and South Korea, worth one hundredth of a *won.

chooser option An *option in which the holder has the freedom to decide, up to a specified point before expiry, whether it is a put or a call option.

churning 1. The practice by a broker of encouraging an investor to change investments frequently in order to enable the broker to earn excessive commissions. **2.** The practice by a bank, building society, insurance broker, etc., of encouraging a householder with an endowment *mortgage to surrender the policy and to take out a new one when seeking to increase a mortgage or to raise extra funds, instead of topping up the existing mortgage. The purpose is to increase charges and commissions at the expense of the policyholder. **3.** A government policy of paying a benefit to a wide category of persons and taxing it so that those paying little or no taxes receive it while the well off return it through the tax system. There have been suggestions that a higher child benefit is suitable for churning.

CII Abbreviation for *Chartered Insurance Institute.

circuit breakers Measures put in place by the major stock and derivatives exchanges to prevent very large market movements; for example, suspending trading on a particular market when certain extreme price fluctuations take place.

These provisions were first instituted after the major stock market crash on *Black Monday 1987.

circuity of action The return of a *bill of exchange, prior to maturity, to the person who first signed it. Under these circumstances it may be renegotiated, but the person forfeits any right of action against those who put their names to it in the intervening period.

circular letter of credit *See* LETTER OF CREDIT.

circular transaction An artificial transaction between companies in a group, or under a single control, the purpose of which is to inflate the *turnover of one or more of the companies.

CISCO Abbreviation for *City Group for Smaller Companies.

Citibank A major US *commercial bank with a worldwide network of branches.

CITIC Abbreviation for *China International Trust and Investment Corporation.

City The district of London in which the head offices of many financial institutions are situated. Occupying the so-called *square mile on the north side of the River Thames between Waterloo Bridge and Tower Bridge, the City has been an international merchanting centre since medieval times. Although many institutions remain in the Square Mile, others have migrated east along the river, to new offices in the Docklands area.

city bank **1.** Any one of the major 13 Japanese banks, which operate a national network. **2. (reserve city bank)** In the USA, a bank situated in a city with a Federal Reserve Bank.

City Call A financial information service provided by British Telecom over the telephone in the UK. It gives nine bulletins of updated information each day.

City Code on Takeovers and Mergers A code first laid down in 1968, and subsequently modified, giving the practices to be observed in company takeovers (*see* TAKEOVER BID) and *mergers. Encouraged by the Bank of England, the code was compiled by a panel including representatives from the London Stock Exchange Association, the Issuing Houses Association, the London Clearing Bankers, and others. The code does not have the force of law but the panel can admonish offenders and refer them to their own professional bodies for disciplinary action.

The code attempts to ensure that all shareholders, including minority shareholders, are treated equally, are kept advised of the terms of all bids and counterbids, and are advised fairly by the directors of the company receiving the bid on the likely outcome if the bid succeeds. Its many other recommendations are aimed at preventing directors from acting in their own interests rather than those of their shareholders, ensuring that the negotiations are conducted openly and honestly, and preventing a spurious market arising in the shares of either side. One of its rules is that if the number of shares controlled exceeds 30% of the total, a general offer should be made for all the shares in the business. *See also* MANDATORY BID.

City Group for Smaller Companies (CISCO) A pressure group formed in December 1992 by 17 firms, ranging from venture capitalists to brokers, to represent the interests of smaller companies on the London Stock Exchange in anticipation of the closure of the Unlisted Securities Market. Its aims are to advocate the need for a market for smaller company shares; to examine alternatives to the

London Stock Exchange market; to chart investment trends of smaller companies; and to influence regulatory bodies in decisions which might affect smaller companies.

claim **1.** A right to assets held by another individual or organization. *See* LIEN. **2.** A right to all or part of the estate of a deceased person. **3.** An application by a policyholder for reimbursement for loss or damage, within the terms of an *insurance policy.

class A type or category of *security. The two principal classes are *stocks and *bonds.

class action A legal action in which a person sues as a representative of a class of persons, e.g. the shareholders of a company or the members of a society, who share a common claim.

classical system of corporation tax A system of taxing companies in which the company is treated as a taxable entity separate from its own shareholders. The profits of companies under this system are therefore taxed twice, first when made by the company and again when distributed to the shareholders as dividends. *Compare* IMPUTATION SYSTEM.

clawback **1.** Money that a government takes back from members of the public by taxation, especially through the *higher-rate of income tax, having given the money away in benefits, such as increased retirement pensions. Thus the money is clawed back from those who have no need of the extra benefit (because they are paying higher-rate taxes). **2.** An agreement requiring the sponsors of a project to repay past profits in the event of a shortfall in later periods. This may be a condition in project-finance agreements.

Clayton Act US *antitrust legislation passed in 1914; it placed restrictions on mergers and acquisitions that limited competition and debarred individuals from holding directorships on the boards of competing companies.

clean floating A government policy allowing a country's currency to fluctuate without direct intervention in the foreign-exchange markets. In practice, clean floating is rare as governments are frequently tempted to manage exchange rates by direct intervention by means of the official reserves, a policy sometimes called **managed floating** (*see also* MANAGED CURRENCY). However, clean floating does not necessarily mean that there is no control of exchange rates, as they can still be influenced by the government's monetary policy. *See also* DIRTY FLOAT.

clean price The price of a *gilt-edged security excluding the *accrued interest since the previous coupon payment. Interest on gilt-edged stocks accrues continuously although coupons are paid at fixed intervals (usually six months). Prices quoted in newspapers are usually clean prices, although a buyer will normally pay for and receive the accrued income as well as the stock itself.

clear days The full days referred to in a contract, i.e. not including the days on which the contract period starts or finishes.

cleared balance A balance on a bank account, excluding any receipts that do not yet represent *cleared value.

cleared for fate Denoting the date on which the payer's bank has confirmed that funds are available to provide value for a transfer in accordance with the instructions given in a cheque, etc. *See* CLEARING CYCLE.

cleared value Denoting the time at which a credit to a customer's bank account becomes available to him. The *cleared balance is used for calculating interest and for establishing the undrawn balance of an agreed overdraft facility. *See also* CLEARING CYCLE.

clearing bank 1. In the UK, a bank that is a member of the bankers' *clearing house, to enable passage and clearance of cheques. It is often used as an alternative description for the major High-Street or joint-stock banks. **2.** In the USA, a bank that settles federal, agency, and corporate securities for its customers.

clearing cycle The process by which a payment made by cheque, etc., through the banking system is transferred from the payer's to the payee's account. Historically, in the UK the average time for the clearing cycle to be completed was three days, although by 1994 this had been reduced to two days in many cases. However, with this reduction in the cycle, the payee's bank may not have received confirmation from the payer's bank that funds are available to provide value, *cleared for fate.

clearing fee The sum charged by the agency affiliated to a commodity exchange for settling the exchange's transactions.

clearing house A centralized and computerized system for settling indebtedness between members. The best known in the UK is the *Association for Payment Clearing Services (APACS), which enables the member banks to offset claims against one another for cheques and orders paid into banks other than those upon which they were drawn. Similar arrangements exist in some commodity exchanges, in which sales and purchases are registered with the clearing house for settlement at the end of the accounting period. *See* LONDON CLEARING HOUSE.

Clearing House Inter-Bank Payments System (CHIPS) A US bankers' *clearing house for paying and accepting funds. It is an electronic system operated through terminals in bank branches. Participating banks must be members of the New York Clearing House Association or affiliates of it, for example foreign banks operating in the USA can only take part through selected correspondents among the 12 New York Clearing Houses. Outside New York, similar transactions are undertaken through Fedwire, a clearing system for members of the *Federal Reserve System.

Clearing Houses Automated Payment System (CHAPS) *See* ASSOCIATION FOR PAYMENT CLEARING SERVICES.

client account A bank or building society account operated by a professional person (e.g. a solicitor, stockbroker, agent, etc.) on behalf of a client. A client account is legally required for any company handling investments on a client's behalf; it protects the client's money in case the company becomes insolvent and makes dishonest appropriation of the client's funds more difficult. For this reason money in client accounts should be quite separate from the business transactions of the company or the professional person.

clientele effect The impact on a financial firm's policy of its desire to attract and retain particular types of investors. For example, the dividend policy of a firm may be determined by its investors' particular tax requirements.

close company A company resident in the UK that is under the control of five or fewer participators or any number of participators who are also directors. There is also an alternative asset-based test, which applies if five or fewer participators, or any number who are directors, would be entitled to more than 50% of the company's assets on a winding-up. The principal consequences of being a close company are that the provision of certain *benefits in kind to shareholders can be treated by the Inland Revenue as a *distribution, as can loans or quasi-loans. Close investment companies do not qualify for the reduced rate of *corporation tax. There are a number of other consequences. In the USA close companies are known as **closed companies**.

closed economy An economic system that does not trade outside its national borders.

closed-end fund A fund set up by an *investment trust that issues a fixed number of shares to its investors. *Compare* OPEN-END TRUST.

close investment holding company A *close company that does not exist wholly or mainly as a trading company, a property company letting to third parties, or a holding company of a trading company.

closely held corporation In the USA, a public corporation that has only a limited number of stockholders and consequently few of its shares are traded.

close out To close an *open position by buying or selling a financial obligation to create a net zero position with an initial position.

closing balance The debit or credit balance on a ledger at the end of an *accounting period, which will appear on the *balance sheet at that date and will be carried forward to the next accounting period. A debit closing balance (such as an *accrual) will be carried forward to the credit side of a ledger and a credit closing balance (such as a prepayment) will be carried forward to the debit side of a ledger.

closing deal A transaction on a commodity market or stock exchange that closes a long or short position or terminates the liability of an *option holder.

closing prices The buying and selling prices recorded on a financial market at the end of a day's trading. *See* AFTER-HOURS TRADING.

club deal *See* SYNDICATED BANK FACILITY.

CME Abbreviation for *Chicago Mercantile Exchange.

CMO Abbreviation for *collateralized mortgage obligation.

CNMV Abbreviation for Comisión del Mercado de Valores. *See* MADRID STOCK EXCHANGE.

coemption The act of buying up the whole stock of a commodity. *See* CORNER.

COFACE Abbreviation for *Compagnie Française pour l'Assurance du Commerce Exterieur.

Coffee, Sugar and Cocoa Exchange Inc. of New York (CSCE) A major world market dealing in coffee, sugar, and cocoa *futures contracts and *options.

Coffee Terminal Market Association of London Ltd A former trading market in London dealing in *futures contracts for Robusta coffee. It is now incorporated into the *London Commodity Exchange.

cofinancing Loans of a very high value that are obtained from commercial lenders, especially banks, acting in partnership with a government or a government-sponsored organization, such as the *International Bank for Reconstruction and Development.

COIN Abbreviation for *continuously offered intermediate note.

coinsurance The sharing of an insurance risk between several insurers. An insurer may find a particular risk too large to accept because the potential losses may be out of proportion to their claims funds. Rather than turning the insurance away, the insurer can offer to split the risk with a number of other insurers, each of whom would be asked to cover a percentage of the risk in return for the same percentage of the premium. The policyholder deals only with the first or leading insurer, who issues all the documents, collects all the premiums, and distributes shares to the others involved. A coinsurance policy includes a schedule of all the insurers involved and shows the percentage of the risk each one is accepting.

A policyholder can also become involved in coinsurance. In this case, a reduction of the premium by an agreed percentage is given, in return for an acceptance by the policyholder that all payments of claims are reduced by the same proportion.

collar 1. Two interest-rate *options combined to protect an investor against wide fluctuations in interest rates. One, the **cap**, covers the investor if the interest rate rises against him or her; the other, the **floor**, covers the investor if the rate of interest falls too far. **2.** A ceiling and floor put on the coupon rate for a *floating-rate note.

collateral A form of *security, especially an impersonal form of security, such as life-assurance policies or shares, used to secure a bank loan. In some senses such impersonal securities are referred to as a secondary security, rather than a primary security, such as a guarantee.

collateralized mortgage obligation (CMO) A US bond secured by a portfolio of mortgages and offering a restricted redemption profile or, for example, rapid prepayment.

collecting bank (remitting bank) The bank to which a person who requires payment of a cheque (or similar financial document) has presented it for payment.

collection The act of sending a *cheque, *bill of exchange, or other financial instrument to the prospective payment source (usually a bank) for payment. *See also* ACCEPTANCE; COLLECTING BANK.

collection order A written order that advises a bank under what conditions it may release documents relating to funding for importing and exporting.

colón (*plural* **colónes**) **1.** The standard monetary unit of Costa Rica, divided into 100 céntimos. **2.** The standard monetary unit of El Salvador, divided into 100 centavos.

COLTS Abbreviation for *continuously offered longer-term securities.

COMEX Abbreviation for *Commodity Exchange Inc. of New York.

Comit Index The share index of the *Milan Stock Exchange.

commercial bank A privately owned bank that provides a wide range of financial services both to the general public and to firms. The principal activities are operating cheque current accounts, receiving deposits, taking in and paying out notes and coin, and making loans. Additional services include trustee and executor facilities, the supply of foreign currency, the purchase and sale of securities, insurance, a credit-card system, and personal pensions. They also compete with the *finance houses and *merchant banks by providing venture capital and with *building societies by providing mortgages.

The main banks with national networks of branches in the UK are Abbey,

Barclays, HBOS (Halifax Bank of Scotland), HSBC, Lloyds TSB, The Royal Bank of Scotland Group (including NatWest), and the Woolwich. They are also known as *joint-stock banks, retail banks, or High-Street banks. *See also* CLEARING BANK.

commercial banking Banking services offered to business customers rather than private individuals.

commercial bill Any *bill of exchange other than a *Treasury bill. *See* BANK BILL; TRADE BILL.

commercial collection agency *See* DEBT COLLECTION AGENCY.

commercial credit company A US finance house that gives credit to businesses rather than individuals.

commercial loan selling A transaction involving two banks and one business customer. Bank A grants a loan to the customer and then sells that loan agreement to Bank B. Bank A makes a profit on the sale; Bank B has a loan book it would not otherwise achieve; and the customer borrows at a favourable rate. Commercial loan selling is common in the USA.

commercial paper A relatively low-risk short-term (maturing at 60 days or less in the US but longer in the UK) unsecured form of borrowing. Commercial paper is often regarded as a reasonable substitute for Treasury bills, certificates of deposit, etc. The main issuers are large creditworthy institutions, such as insurance companies, bank trust departments, and pension funds. In the UK, sterling commercial paper was first issued in 1986. Commercial paper is now available in Australia, France, Hong Kong, The Netherlands, Singapore, Spain, and Sweden.

Commerzbank Index An arithmetically weighted index of 60 German shares.

Commissão de Valores Mobiliaros (CVM) The securities commission that regulates Brazilian securities markets.

commission A payment made to an intermediary, such as an agent, salesman, broker (*see also* BROKERAGE), etc., usually calculated as a percentage of the value of the goods sold. Sometimes the whole of the commission is paid by the seller (e.g. an estate agent's commission in the UK) but in other cases (e.g. some commodity markets) it is shared equally between buyer and seller. In advertising, the commission is the discount (usually between 10% and 15%) allowed to an advertising agency by owners of the advertising medium for the space or time purchased on behalf of their clients. A **commission agent** is an agent specializing in buying or selling goods for a principal in another country for a commission.

commission broker In the USA, a stock-exchange dealer who executes orders to buy or sell securities on payment of a fee or a commission based on the value of the deal.

Commissione Nazionale per le Società e la Borsa (CONSOB) The supervisory body of the Italian Stock Exchange.

commitment fee An amount charged by a bank to keep open a line of credit or to continue to make unused loan facilities available to a potential borrower. *See* FIRM COMMITMENT; FRONT-END FEE.

commitments for capital expenditure *See* CAPITAL COMMITMENTS.

committed facility An agreement between a bank and a customer to provide funds up to a specified maximum at a specified *interest rate (in the UK this is usually based upon an agreed margin over the *London Inter Bank Offered Rate) for a certain period. The total cost will be the interest rate plus the *mandatory liquid asset cost. The agreement will include the conditions that must be adhered to by the borrower for the facility to remain in place. *Compare* UNCOMMITTED FACILITY. *See also* REVOLVING BANK FACILITY.

Committee on Uniform Securities Identification Procedures (CUSIP) A UK regulatory oganization responsible for allocating to all securities issued in the UK a unique nine-digit identification number, which must be shown on all documents relating to that security.

commodity 1. A *good regarded in economics as the basis of production and exchange. **2.** Any raw material or primary product. **3.** A raw material traded on a *commodity market, such as grain, coffee, cocoa, wool, cotton, jute, rubber, pork bellies, or orange juice (sometimes known as *soft commodities) or metals and other solid raw materials (known as *hard commodities). In some contexts soft commodities are referred to as **produce**.

commodity-based Denoting any financial obligation related to the behaviour of commodity markets.

commodity broker A *broker who deals in *commodities, especially one who trades on behalf of principals in a *commodity market (*see also* FUTURES CONTRACT). The rules governing the procedure adopted in each market vary from commodity to commodity and the function of brokers may also vary. In some markets brokers pass on the names of their principals, in others they do not, and in yet others they are permitted to act as principals. Commodity brokers dealing in soft commodies are often called **produce brokers**.

commodity exchange *See* COMMODITY MARKET.

Commodity Exchange Inc. of New York (COMEX) A commodity exchange in New York that specializes in trading in metal *futures contracts and *options.

Commodity Futures Trading Commission (CFTC) A US government body set up in 1975 in Washington to control trading in commodity futures (*see* FUTURES CONTRACT) and *options.

commodity market A market in which *commodities are traded. The main *terminal markets in commodities are in London and New York, but in some commodities there are markets in the country of origin. Some commodities are dealt with at auctions (e.g. tea), each lot being sold having been examined by dealers, but most dealers deal with goods that have been classified according to established quality standards. In these commodities both *actuals and futures (*see* FUTURES CONTRACT) are traded on **commodity exchanges**, often with daily *callovers, in which dealers are represented by *commodity brokers. Many commodity exchanges offer *option dealing in futures, and settlement of differences on futures through a *clearing house. As commodity prices fluctuate widely, commodity exchanges provide users and producers with *hedging facilities with outside speculators and investors helping to make an active market, although amateurs are advised not to gamble on commodity exchanges.

The fluctuations in commodity prices have caused considerable problems in developing countries, from which many commodities originate, as they are often important sources of foreign currency, upon which the economic welfare of the country depends. Various measures have been used to restrict price fluctuations but none have been completely successful. *See also* INTERNATIONAL PETROLEUM EXCHANGE;

LONDON CLEARING HOUSE; LONDON COMMODITY EXCHANGE; LONDON INTERNATIONAL FINANCIAL FUTURES AND OPTIONS EXCHANGE; LONDON METAL EXCHANGE.

Common Agricultural Policy (CAP) A policy set up by the *European Economic Community to support free trade within the Common Market and to protect farmers in the member states. The *European Commission fixes a **threshold price**, below which cereals may not be imported into the European Union (EU), and also buys surplus cereals at an agreed **intervention price** in order to help farmers achieve a reasonable average price, called the **target price**. Prices are also agreed for meats, poultry, eggs, fruit, and vegetables, with arrangements similar to those for cereals. The European Commission is also empowered by the CAP to subsidize the modernization of farms within the community. The common policy for exporting agricultural products to non-member countries is laid down by the CAP. In the UK, the Intervention Board for Agricultural Produce is responsible for the implementation of EU regulations regarding the CAP.

Common Budget The fund, administered by the *European Commission, into which all levies and customs duties on goods entering the European Union are paid and from which all subsidies due under the *Common Agricultural Policy are taken.

Common External Tariff (CET) The tariff of import duties payable on certain goods entering any country in the European Union from non-member countries. Income from these duties is paid into the *Common Budget.

Common Fisheries Policy A fishing policy agreed between members of the European Community (EC) in 1983. An earlier agreement of 1971 introduced the principle of free access to European Community waters and a single fishing market. The key elements resulting from the 1983 agreement were: the setting of a Total Annual Catch (TAC) for the Community, which aimed to ensure conservation of stocks; a national TAC allocation; schemes for fleet restructuring; and negotiation with 'third party' nations. A radical reform of the policy imposing severe cuts in fishing quotas was agreed in 2002.

Common Market *See* EUROPEAN ECONOMIC COMMUNITY; EUROPEAN UNION.

common stock The US name for *ordinary shares.

commutation The right to receive an immediate cash sum in return for accepting smaller annual payments at some time in the future. This is usually associated with a pension in which certain life-assurance policyholders can, on retirement, elect to take a cash sum from the pension fund immediately and a reduced annual pension.

Compagnie Française pour l'Assurance du Commerce Exterieur (COFACE) The French equivalent of the UK *Export Credits Guarantee Department.

Companies Acts Legislation governing the activities of companies. In the UK, the first Companies Act was passed in 1844; the current comprehensive legislation is contained in the 1985 Companies Act.

Companies House (Companies Registration Office) The office of the *Registrar of Companies, formerly in London but now in Cardiff. It contains a register of all UK private and public companies, their directors, shareholders, and balance sheets. All this information has to be provided by companies by law and is available to any member of the public for a small charge.

company A corporate enterprise that has a legal identity separate from that of its members; it operates as one single unit, in the success of which all the members participate. An **incorporated company** is a legal person in its own right, able to own property and to sue and be sued in its own name. A company may have limited liability (a *limited company), so that the liability of the members for the company's debts is limited. An **unlimited company** is one in which the liability of the members is not limited in any way. There are various different types of company: a **chartered company** is one formed under Royal Charter. This was the earliest type of company to exist and they were influential in the development of both foreign trade and colonization; an example is the Hudson's Bay Company. Chartered companies, however, are now rare, unless a charter is required for prestige purposes, as it might be for a new university. A **joint-stock company** is a company in which the members pool their stock, trading on the basis of their joint stock. This differs from the earlier **merchant corporations** or **regulated companies** of the 14th century, in which each member traded with his own stock but agreed to obey the rules of the company.

A **registered company**, one registered under the Companies Acts, is the most common type of company. A company may be registered either as a public limited company or a private company. A **public limited company** must have a name ending with the initials 'plc' and have an authorized share capital of at least £50,000, of which at least £12,500 must be paid up. The company's memorandum must comply with the format in Table F of the Companies Regulations (1985). It may offer shares and securities to the public. The regulation of such companies is stricter than that of private companies. Most public companies are converted from private companies, under the re-registration procedure laid down in the Companies Act. A **private company** is any registered company that is not a public company. The shares of a private company may not be offered to the public for sale. The legal requirements for such a company are less strict; for example, there is no minimum issued or paid-up share capital requirement and small and medium-sized private companies need not file full accounts. A **statutory company** is a company formed by special Act of parliament. These are generally public utilities that were either not nationalized (for example, certain water authorities) or that have been privatized (such as British Gas and British Telecom). Their powers and privileges depend upon the Act under which they were formed.

company auditor A person or firm appointed as an *auditor of a company under the Companies Act, which requires that a company's annual *financial statements must be audited. Since 1989 only registered auditors are eligible for appointment.

company doctor An executive or accountant with wide commercial experience, who specializes in analysing and rectifying the problems of ailing companies. He or she may either act as a consultant or may be given executive powers to implement the policies recommended.

company formation The procedure to be adopted for forming a company in the UK. The *subscribers to the company must send to the *Registrar of Companies a statement giving details of the registered address of the new company together with the names and addresses of the first directors and secretary, with their written consent to act in these capacities. They must also give a declaration (**declaration of compliance**) that the provisions of the Companies Acts have been complied with and provide the *memorandum of association and the *articles of association. Provided all these documents are in order the Registrar will issue a *certificate of incorporation and a certificate enabling it to start business. In the case of a *public limited company additional information is required.

company limited by guarantee An incorporated organization in which the liability of members is limited by the *memorandum of association to the amount they agree to pay in the event of a *liquidation. Such a company does not issue shares to its members.

company limited by shares An incorporated organization in which the liability of members is limited by the *memorandum of association to the amounts paid, or due to be paid, for shares. In the UK this is the most popular form of company.

compensation for loss of office A payment, often tax-free, made by a company to a director, senior executive, or consultant who is forced to retire before the expiry of a service contract, as a result of a merger, takeover, or any other reason. This form of **severance pay** (*see also* REDUNDANCY) may be additional to a retirement pension or in place of it; it must also be shown separately in the company's accounts. Because these payments can be very large, they are known as **golden handshakes**. *See also* GOLDEN PARACHUTE.

compensation fund A fund set up by the *London Stock Exchange, to which member firms contribute. It provides compensation to investors who suffer loss as a result of a member firm failing to meet its financial obligations.

competition and credit control The subject of an important paper issued in 1971 by the *Bank of England. It outlined a number of changes affecting the banking system and the means of controlling credit. From October 1971 a new system of reserve requirements was implemented, the banks agreed to abandon collusion on setting interest rates, and the Bank of England changed its operations in the gilt-edged securities market. The main aim of these changes was to stimulate more active competition between the banks and to move towards greater reliance upon interest rates as a means of credit control. It was a prelude to the most rapid expansion in the availability of credit in the 20th century.

Competition Commission A commission established in 1948 as the Monopolies and Restrictive Practices Commission, renamed the **Monopolies and Mergers Commission** in 1973, and given its present title in 1999 under the Competition Act 1998. It investigates questions referred to it on monopolies and mergers and its Appeals Tribunal hears appeals against decisions by the *Office of Fair Trading and utility regulators relating to anticompetitive trade practices.

competitive devaluation The devaluation of a country's currency to make its economy more competitive in international trade, rather than to correct an ongoing disequilibrium in the exchange rate.

completion The conveyance of land in fulfilment of a contract of sale. The purchaser will have obtained an equitable interest in the land at the date of the *exchange of contracts but will not become the full legal owner until completion. If the seller refuses to complete, the court may grant a decree of specific performance. The date on which completion must take place is stated in the contract of sale.

completion risk The inherent risk in *limited recourse financing of a project that it will not be completed. *Compare* TECHNOLOGICAL RISK; SUPPLY RISK.

compliance Mechanisms in a financial institution whose purpose is to ensure that the institution meets its legal and regulatory obligations.

composite insurance company A company that offers a full range of insurance services, including accident, fire, health, investment, life, and pensions.

compound annual return (CAR) The total return available from an investment or deposit in which the interest is used to augment the investment. The more frequently the interest is credited, the higher the CAR.

CAR = 1 + (nominal rate/number of times interest paid per annum)

The CAR is usually quoted on a gross basis. The return, taking into account the deduction of tax at the basic rate on the interest, is known as the **compound net annual rate (CNAR)**.

compound interest *See* INTEREST.

compound net annual rate (CNAR) *See* COMPOUND ANNUAL RETURN.

comprehensive income tax An income tax for which the tax base consists not only of income but also of *capital gains as well as other accretions of wealth, such as legacies. Although this is not a tax currently levied in the UK, tax theorists find it attractive since sometimes clear distinctions between income, capital gains, etc., are difficult to sustain.

comptroller The title of the financial director in some companies or chief financial officer of a group of companies. The title is more widely used in the USA than in the UK.

Comptroller of the Currency A US Treasury Department official, appointed by the president, who is responsible for the regulation of the national banking system.

compulsory liquidation (compulsory winding-up) The winding-up of a company by a court. A petition must be presented both at the court and the registered office of the company. Those by whom it may be presented include: the company, the directors, a creditor, an official receiver, and the Secretary of State for Trade and Industry. The grounds on which a company may be wound up by the court include: a special resolution of the company that it be wound up by the court; that the company is unable to pay its debts; that the number of members is reduced below two; or that the court is of the opinion that it would be just and equitable for the company to be wound up. The court may appoint a *provisional liquidator after the winding-up petition has been presented; it may also appoint a *special manager to manage the company's property. On the grant of the order for winding-up, the official receiver becomes the *liquidator and continues in office until some other person is appointed, either by the creditors or the members. *Compare* MEMBERS' VOLUNTARY LIQUIDATION.

compulsory purchase annuity An annuity that must be purchased with the fund built up from certain types of pension arrangements. When retirement age is reached, a person who has been paying premiums into this type of pension fund is obliged to use the fund to purchase an annuity to provide an income for the rest of his or her life. The fund may not be used in any other way (except for a small portion, which may be taken in cash).

computer-assisted trading (CAT) The use of computers by brokers and traders on a market, such as a stock exchange or foreign-exchange market, to facilitate trading by displaying prices, recording deals, etc.

computer-to-computer interface (CTCI) The link between a securities house in the USA and the *National Association of Securities Dealers Automated Quotation System (NASDAQ) computer, which allows the simultaneous reporting of a trade to NASDAQ and the recording of the same trade on the securities house's own data store.

concentration The degree to which an industry is dominated by a small group of firms and thus closed to competitive pressure.

concentric merger The combining of two or more businesses in order to pool expertise.

concert-party agreements Secret agreements between apparently unconnected shareholders to act together to manipulate the share price of a company or to influence its management. The Companies Act 1981 laid down that the shares of the parties to such an agreement should be treated as if they were owned by one person, from the point of view of disclosing interests in a company's shareholding.

conditional bid *See* TAKEOVER BID.

conditionality The terms under which the *International Monetary Fund (IMF) provides balance-of-payments support to member states. The principle is that support will only be given on the condition that it is accompanied by steps to solve the underlying problem. Programmes of economic reform are agreed with the member; these emphasize the attainment of a sustainable balance-of-payments position and boosting the supply side of the economy. Lending by commercial banks is frequently linked to IMF conditionality.

conditional order An instruction to a broker contingent on some event.

conditional sale agreement **1.** A contract of sale under which the price is payable by instalments and ownership does not pass to the buyer (who is in possession of the goods) until specified conditions relating to the payment have been fulfilled. The seller retains ownership of the goods as security until being paid in full. **2.** A sale subject to conditions, as for example, with a merget being subject to a *due diligence condition.

Confederation of British Industry (CBI) An independent non-party organization formed in 1965, by a merger of the National Association of British Manufacturers, the British Employers Confederation, and the Federation of British Industry, to promote prosperity in British industry and to represent industry in dealings with the government. The CBI represents some 250 000 UK companies; its governing body is the Confederation of British Industry Council, which meets monthly; there are 13 Regional Councils.

confidentiality clause A clause in a contract of employment that details certain types of information the employee will acquire on joining the firm that may not be passed on to anyone outside the firm.

confiscation risk The risk that assets in a foreign country may be confiscated, expropriated, or nationalized; a non-resident owner's control over the assets may also be interfered with.

conflict of interests A situation that can arise if a person (or firm) acts in two or more separate capacities and the objectives in these capacities are not identical. The conflict may be between self-interest and the interest of a company for which a person works or it could arise when a person is a director of two companies, which find themselves competing. The proper course of action in the case of a conflict of interests is for the persons concerned to declare their interests, to make known the way in which they conflict, and to abstain from voting or sharing in the decision-making procedure involving these interests.

conglomerate A business made up of entities from different *value chains. In general, investors dislike conglomerates since they often lack strategic focus and are an inefficient way of spreading risks for the investor.

conglomerate merger A merger between firms that have no industrial relation to each other. *See* CONGLOMERATE.

connected person In the context of the Companies Act (disclosure requirements of *directors' interests), a director's spouse, child or stepchild (under 18 years of age), a body corporate with which a director is associated, a trustee for a trust that benefits a director or connected person, or a partner of a director.

consequential-loss policy *See* BUSINESS-INTERRUPTION POLICY.

consideration **1.** A tangible benefit that is exchanged as part of a contract. It is essential if the contract is to be valid. **2.** The money value of a contract for the purchase or sale of securities on the London Stock Exchange, before commissions, charges, stamp duty, and any other expenses have been deducted.

consistency concept The accounting concept that ensures consistency of treatment of like items within each accounting period and from one period to the next. It also ensures that accounting policies are consistently applied. It is a principle contained in the Companies Act and in the Statement of Standard Accounting Practice 2, Disclosure of Accounting Policies.

CONSOB Abbreviation for *Commissione Nazionale per le Società e la Borsa.

consolidated accounts *See* CONSOLIDATED FINANCIAL STATEMENTS.

consolidated annuities *See* CONSOLS.

consolidated balance sheet The balance sheet of a group providing the financial information contained in the individual financial statements of the parent company of the group and its subsidiary undertakings, combined subject to any necessary *consolidation adjustments. *See also* CONSOLIDATED FINANCIAL STATEMENTS.

consolidated financial statements (consolidated accounts; group accounts; group financial statements) The financial statements of a group of companies obtained by *consolidation. These are required by the Companies Act and Financial Reporting Standard 2, 'Accounting for Subsidiary Undertakings'. The information contained in the individual financial statements of a group of undertakings is combined into consolidated financial statements, subject to any *consolidation adjustments. The consolidated accounts must give a true and fair view of the profit or loss for the period and the state of affairs as at the last day of the period of the undertakings included in the consolidation. Subsidiary undertakings within the group may be excluded from consolidation, and the parent company itself may be exempt from preparing consolidated accounts.

Consolidated Fund The Exchequer account, held at the Bank of England and controlled by the Treasury, into which taxes are paid and from which government expenditure is made. It was formed in 1787 by the consolidation of several government funds.

consolidated profit and loss account A combination of the individual *profit and loss accounts of the members of a *group of organizations, subject to any consolidation adjustments. A parent company may be exempted, under section 230 of the Companies Act, from publishing its own profit and loss account if it prepares group accounts. The individual profit and loss account must be approved by the directors, but may be omitted from the company's annual accounts. In such a case, the company must disclose its profit or loss for the financial year and also state in its notes that it has taken advantage of this exemption. *See also* CONSOLIDATED FINANCIAL STATEMENTS.

Consolidated Quotation Service (CQS; consolidated tape) A service provided by the National Association of Securities Dealers Automated Quotation Service (NASDAQ) in the USA, offering all available quotations on stocks listed on the *New York Stock Exchange and *American Stock Exchange and selected securities on regional stock exchanges.

consolidation 1. An increase in the *nominal price of a company's shares, by combining a specified number of lower-price shares into one higher-priced share. For example five 20p shares may be consolidated into one £1 share. In most cases this can be done by an ordinary resolution at a general meeting of the company. **2.** The inclusion of one or more subsidiary companies in a parent company's financial statements. *See also* CONSOLIDATED FINANCIAL STATEMENTS.

Consols Government securities that pay interest but have no redemption date. The present bonds, called **consolidated annuities** or **consolidated stock**, are the result of merging several loans at various different times going back to the 18th century. Their original interest rate was 3% on the nominal price of £100; some now pay 2½% and therefore stand at a price that makes their annual *yield comparable to long-dated *gilt-edged securities, e.g. at £31 they yield about 8%.

consortium A combination of two or more businesses formed on a temporary basis. Consortia often involve the setting up of a *special-purpose vehicle or a *joint venture. They are often set up to quote for a large project, such as a new power station or dam. The companies would then work together, on agreed terms, if they were successful in obtaining the work. The purpose of forming a consortium may be to eliminate competition between the members or to pool skills, not all of which may be available to the individual companies. *See also* CONSORTIUM RELIEF.

consortium relief A modified form of *group relief applying to consortia. A consortium exists if 20 or fewer companies each own at least 5% of the ordinary share capital of the consortium company and together the consortium members hold at least 75% of the ordinary shares of the consortium company. Losses can be surrendered between the consortium members and the consortium company provided they are all resident in the UK. The loss that can be surrendered is restricted to the proportion of the claimant's profits that corresponds with the surrendering company's interest in the consortium.

constant-dollar plan The US name for *pound cost averaging, i.e. the investment of a specified sum of money at regular intervals in the acquisition of assets. It is sometimes called **dollar-cost averaging**.

consumer credit Short-term loans to the public for the purchase of goods. The most common forms of consumer credit are credit accounts at retail outlets, personal loans from banks and finance houses, *hire purchase, and *credit cards. Since the *Consumer Credit Act 1974, the borrower has been given greater protection, particularly with regard to regulations establishing the true rate of interest being charged when loans are made (*see* ANNUAL PERCENTAGE RATE). The Act also made it necessary for anyone giving credit in a business (with minor exceptions) to obtain a licence. *See* CONSUMER-CREDIT REGISTER.

Consumer Credit Act 1974 A UK Act of Parliament aimed at protecting the borrower in credit agreements, loans, and mortgages. The Act requires full written

details of the true interest rate (i.e. *annual percentage rate) to be quoted, a
*cooling-off period to be given, during which borrowers may change their minds
and cancel agreements, and all agreements to be in writing. The Act does not cover
overdrafts.

Consumer Credit Protection Act 1969 The US equivalent of the UK
*Consumer Credit Act 1974.

consumer-credit register The register kept by the Director General of Fair
Trading, as required by the Consumer Credit Act 1974, relating to the licensing or
carrying on of consumer-credit businesses or consumer-hire businesses. The register
contains particulars of undetermined applications, licences that are in force or have
at any time been suspended or revoked, and decisions given by the Director under
the Act as well as any appeal from them. The public is entitled to inspect the
register on payment of a fee.

consumer instalment loan The US name for *hire purchase.

consumer price index *See* RETAIL PRICE INDEX.

Consumers' Association (CA) A UK charitable organization formed in 1957 to
provide independent and technically based guidance on the goods and services
available to the public. The Consumers' Association tests and investigates products
and services and publishes comparative reports on performance, quality, and value
in its monthly magazine *Which?* It also publishes *Holiday Which?* and *Gardening From
Which?* as well as various books, including *The Legal Side of Buying a House*, *Starting Your
Own Business*, and *The Which? Book of Saving and Investing*. The US equivalent is the
Consumer Advisory Council.

contango 1. The value by which the price for future delivery is greater than the
spot price. Also called **forwardation**. **2.** The former practice of carrying the purchase
of stocks and shares over from one account day on the London Stock Exchange to
the next.

contingency insurance An insurance policy covering financial losses occurring
as a result of a specified event happening. The risks covered by policies of this kind
are various and often unusual, such as a missing documents indemnity, the birth of
twins, or pluvial insurance.

contingent agreement *See* EARN-OUT AGREEMENT.

contingent annuity (reversionary annuity) An annuity in which the payment is
conditional on a specified event happening. The most common form is an annuity
purchased jointly by a husband and wife that begins payment after the death of one
of the parties (*see* JOINT-LIFE AND LAST-SURVIVOR ANNUITIES).

contingent interest *See* VESTED INTEREST.

contingent liability A liability that, at a balance sheet date, can either not be
measured or can only be anticipated to arise if a particular event occurs. Typical
examples include a court case pending against the company, the outcome of which
is uncertain, or loss of earnings as a result of a customer invoking a penalty clause
in a contract that may not be completed on time. Under the Companies Act 1985,
such liabilities must be explained by a note on the company balance sheet.

continuous compounding The assumption made in many financial analysis
models that *interest is paid continuously, and hence that interest is also
continuously paid on interest.

continuous credit account *See* BUDGET ACCOUNT.

continuously offered intermediate note (COIN) A type of medium-term *euronote.

continuously offered longer-term securities (COLTS) Bonds of various types offered by the *International Bank for Reconstruction and Development (World Bank).

continuous net settlement The daily settlement of transactions on a net basis by a *clearing house. It reduces the need for the delivery of certificates and cash payments to settle individual transactions, by producing daily net accounts in each security for each security firm as well as accounts recording the transaction of each firm with the clearing house.

contract A legally binding agreement. Agreement arises as a result of an *offer and *acceptance, but a number of other requirements must be satisfied for an agreement to be legally binding. There must be *consideration (unless the contract is by *deed); the parties must have an intention to create legal relations; the parties must have capacity to contract (i.e. they must be competent to enter a legal obligation, by not being a minor, mentally disordered, or drunk); the agreement must comply with any formal legal requirements; the agreement must be legal (*see* ILLEGAL CONTRACT); and the agreement must not be rendered void either by some common-law or statutory rule or by some inherent defect.
    In general, no particular formality is required for the creation of a valid contract. It may be oral, written, partly oral and partly written, or even implied from conduct. However, certain contracts are valid only if made by deed (e.g. transfers of shares in statutory companies, transfers of shares in British ships, legal *mortgages, certain types of lease) or in writing (e.g. *hire-purchase agreements, *bills of exchange, promissory notes, contracts for the sale of land made after 21 September 1989), and certain others, though valid, can only be enforced if evidenced in writing (e.g. guarantees, contracts for the sale of land made before 21 September 1989).

contract for service A contract undertaken by a self-employed individual. The distinction between a contract for service (self-employed) and a *service contract (employee) is fundamental in establishing the tax position. With a contract for service the person may hire and pay others to carry out the work, will be responsible for correcting unsatisfactory work at their own expense, and may make losses as well as profits.

contract grade A specification of the exact grade and quality of the commodity to be delivered in a *futures contract.

contract guarantee insurance An insurance policy designed to guarantee the financial solvency of a contractor during the performance of a contract. If the contractor becomes financially insolvent and cannot complete the work the insurer makes a payment equivalent to the contract price, which enables another contractor to be paid to complete the work. *See also* CREDIT INSURANCE.

contracting out *See* STATE EARNINGS-RELATED PENSION SCHEME.

contract note **1.** A document containing details of a contract sent from one counterparty to the contract to the other. **2.** A document sent by a stockbroker or commodity broker to a client as evidence that the broker has bought (in which case it may be called a **bought note**) or sold (a **sold note**) securities or commodities in accordance with the client's instructions. It will state the quantity of securities or goods, the price, the date (and sometimes the time of day at which the bargain was struck), the rate of commission, the cost of the transfer stamp and VAT (if any), and the amount due and the settlement date.

contract of employment See SERVICE CONTRACT.

contract of service See SERVICE CONTRACT.

contributory Any person who is liable to contribute towards the assets of a company on liquidation. The list of contributories will be settled by the liquidator or by the court. This list will include all shareholders, although those who hold fully paid-up shares will not be liable to pay any more.

contributory pension A *pension in which the employee as well as the employer contribute to the pension fund. *Compare* NON-CONTRIBUTORY PENSION.

controller In the USA, the chief accounting executive of an organization. The controller will normally be concerned with financial reporting, taxation, and auditing but will leave the planning and control of finances to the *treasurer. *See also* COMPTROLLER.

controlling interest An interest in a company that gives a person control of it. A shareholder having a controlling interest in a company would normally need to own or control more than half the voting shares. However, in practice, a shareholder might control the company with considerably less than half the shares, if the others shares are held by a large number of people. For legal purposes, a director is said to have a controlling interest in a company if he or she alone, or together with a spouse, minor children, and the trustees of any settlement in which he or she has an interest, owns more than 20% of the voting shares in a company or in a company that controls that company.

convenience yield The price that users of a commodity are willing to pay rather than suffer from future shortages.

convergence The movement of the futures price towards the spot price (*see* SPOT GOODS) as a *futures contract approaches expiry.

conversion exposure The risk attached to converting one currency into another.

conversion premium The cost of converting a share at the current market price into a *convertible security or warrant. It is normally expressed as a percentage of the market price of the convertible security, by means of the formula:

$$\left(\frac{P_s - P_c}{P_c^m}\right) \times 100 \geq 0$$

where P_s is the market price of shares, P_c is the price at which the convertible may be exchanged for shares, and P_c^m is the market price for the convertible.

conversion ratio An expression of the number of units of another security that a *convertible security can be exchanged for. It is set at the time of issue of the convertible bond.

convertibility The extent to which one currency can be freely exchanged for another. Since 1979 sterling has been freely convertible. The *International Monetary Fund encourages free convertibility, although many governments try to maintain some direct control over foreign-exchange transactions involving their own currency, especially if there is a shortage of hard-currency foreign-exchange reserves.

convertible 1. A *bond or preferred stock that can be changed into other securities, usually equity, on predetermined conditions. **2.** A government security in which the holder has the right to convert a holding into new stock instead of obtaining repayment. *See also* CONVERTIBLE UNSECURED LOAN STOCK.

convertible adjusted-rate preferred stock *See* ADJUSTABLE-RATE PREFERRED STOCK.

convertible revolving credit A *revolving credit that can be converted by mutual agreement into a fixed-term loan.

convertible term assurance A *term assurance that gives the policyholder the option to widen the policy to become a *whole life policy or an *endowment assurance policy, without having to provide any further evidence of good health. All that is required is the payment of the extra premium. The risks of AIDS has meant that policies of this kind are no longer available, as insurers are not now prepared to offer any widening of life cover without evidence of good health.

convertible unsecured loan stock (CULS) Unsecured *debenture that entitles the holder to exchange the debenture for another security, usually ordinary shares in the company, at some future date.

convexity A mathematical expression of how the *duration of a bond will change when its yield changes. It measures the stability of the relationship between the price of a bond and its yield, when the yield changes.

Cooke ratio The minimum ratio of *capital at risk to *risk-adjusted assets established under the 1988 *Basle Convergence Accord.

cooling-off period 1. In the USA, the time between registration and when an issue is offered to the public. **2.** The time that must elapse after a failed bid before a new takeover bid can be made. **3.** The 14 days that begins when a life-assurance policy, credit agreement, etc., is effected, during which new policyholders, borrowers, etc., can change their minds. During this period any policies or agreements entered into can be cancelled with a full refund of any premiums, arrangement fees, etc.

córdoba (C$) The standard monetary unit of Nicaragua, divided into 100 centavos.

CORES Abbreviation for Computerized Order Routing and Execution System. *See* TOKYO STOCK EXCHANGE.

corner An individual or organization that acquires a controlling influence over the supply of a particular good or service (often referred to as 'cornering the market'). It can then force the price up until further supplies or substitutes can be found. This objective has often been attempted, but rarely achieved, in international *commodity markets. Because it is undesirable and has antisocial effects, a corner can now rarely be attempted as government restrictions on monopolies and antitrust laws prevent it. An example of an attempt to corner a market was Nelson Bunker Hunt's attack on the silver market in the USA in the early 1980s.

corporate anorexia A malaise that affects businesses after a severe cost-cutting phase. The firm's ability to expand production to maintain its competitive position in the market may, for example, be compromised by a misguided pressure to reduce costs by *downsizing, resulting in the elimination of personnel who made a long-term contribution to the company's viability.

corporate bond A bond issued by a private corporation.

corporate finance **1.** A branch of financial economics devoted to business funding, decision making, and mergers and acquisitions. **2.** An activity in investment and merchant banks in which advice and funding for mergers and acquisitions, etc., is provided to large corporations. **3.** Loans made to large companies by banks.

corporate governance The way in which companies are managed and organized, ensuring in particular that the interests of shareholders are given sufficient weight.

corporate raider A person or company that buys a substantial proportion of the equity of another company (the target company) with the object of taking it over, inducing takeover bids, or forcing the management of the target company to take certain steps to improve the image of the company sufficiently for the share price to rise enough for the raider to sell the holding at a profit.

corporate venturing The provision of venture capital by one company, either directly or by means of a venture-capital fund, for another company. This may be undertaken as a means of obtaining information about the company requiring venture capital or its market, of taking a first step towards acquiring the company, or of moving into a new market cheaply and without needing to acquire the relevant expertise and personnel.

corporate venturing scheme (CVS) A scheme designed to encourage established companies to invest in the full-risk ordinary shares of companies of the same kind as those qualifying under the *enterprise investment scheme; the scheme encourages the investing and qualifying companies to form mutually beneficial corporate venturing relationships. Companies investing through the CVS may obtain *corporation tax relief (at 20%) on the amount invested provided that the shares are held for at least three years after issue or, if later, three years after the trade for which the money was raised begins. Investing companies also obtain relief for most allowable losses on the shares and deferral of corporation tax when a chargeable gain from the disposal of CVS shares is reinvested in a new CVS investment.

corporation A succession of persons or body of persons authorized by law to act as one person and having rights and liabilities distinct from the individuals forming the corporation. The artificial personality may be created by royal charter, statute, or common law. The most important type is the registered *company formed under the Companies Act. **Corporations sole** are those having only one individual forming them; for example, a bishop, the sovereign, the Treasury Solicitor. **Corporations aggregate** are composed of more than one individual, e.g. a limited company. They may be formed for special purposes by statute; the BBC is an example. Corporations can hold property, carry on business, bring legal actions, etc., in their own name. Their actions may, however, be limited by the doctrine of *ultra vires. See also* PUBLIC CORPORATION.

corporation tax (CT) Tax charged on the total profits of a company *resident in the UK arising in each *accounting period. The rate of corporation tax depends on the level of profits of the company. The **small companies rate** of 20% applies to companies with total annual profits of £300,000 or less: since 2002 very small companies with total annual profits of £10,000 or less pay no CT. Full-rate corporation tax of 30% applies to companies with total annual profits of over £1.5 million. There is a *marginal relief for those companies with total profits plus franked investment income between £300,000 and £1.5 million or between £10,000 and £50,000.

correlation A statistical measure of the relationship between two variables. It is the *covariance of the variables divided by the product of their *standard deviations.

correlation coefficient In statistical analysis, a measure of the *correlation between one variable and another. The correlation coefficient ranges from minus one, when the two variables are perfectly inversely linearly related, to plus one, when the two variables have a perfect direct linear relationship. If the correlation coefficient is zero, then the variables have no linear relationship. *See* REGRESSION ANALYSIS.

correspondent bank A bank in a foreign country that offers banking facilities to the customers of a bank in another country. These arrangements are usually the result of agreements, often reciprocal, between the two banks. The most frequent correspondent banking facilities used are those of money transmission.

corset 1. A restriction of the movements of currency exchange values imposed by certain formal market mechanisms. **2.** A restriction on the activity of the UK commercial banks, known as the Supplementary Special Deposits scheme, which was in force between 1973 and 1980. The scheme was designed to limit the growth of bank deposits, i.e. interest-bearing eligible liabilities, and thus indirectly control bank lending and the money supply, which depended on them.

cost accountant Formerly, an *accountant whose principal function was to gather and manipulate data on the costs and efficiency of industrial processes. This function is now generally subsumed within the activity of *management accounting.

cost-benefit analysis A technique used in decision making that takes into account the estimated costs to be incurred by a proposed decision and the estimated benefits likely to arise from it. In a *financial appraisal the benefits may arise from an increase in the revenue from a product or service, from saved costs, or from other cash inflows, but in an *economic appraisal the economic benefits, such as the value of time saved or of fewer accidents resulting from a road improvement, often require to be valued.

cost effectiveness 1. Achieving a goal with the minimum of expenditure. **2.** Achieving a goal with an expenditure that makes the achievement viable in commercial terms.

cost of capital The return, expressed in terms of an interest rate, that an organization is required to pay for the capital used in financing its activities. The capital of an organization can be a mix of *equity share capital and *debt. The cost of capital is the *weighted average cost of capital, based on its particular mix of capital sources. The cost of capital is often used as a *hurdle rate in *discounted cash flow calculations.

The weighted average cost of capital (WACC) is expressed in the formula:

$$\text{WACC} = r_e\left(\frac{V_e}{V_e + V_d}\right) + r_d(1 - T_c)\left(\frac{V_d}{V_e + V_d}\right),$$

where r_e is the required returns on equity, r_d is the required returns on debt, T_c is a firm's average corporation tax rate, V_d = the value of a firm's long-term debt, and V_e is the value of a firm's equity.

cost of carry **1.** The degree to which funding costs exceed the returns of a position. **2.** The costs of holding the underlying in a futures contract.

cost of funds **1.** The cost to banks of borrowing in the principal *money markets, which determines their rates of interest when lending to their customers. **2.** The cost of raising additional finance for a firm.

cost-plus contract A contract in which the price paid for a product or service is based on the costs incurred in making or providing it, plus an agreed mark-up to cover any unforeseen additional costs arising and a profit margin.

cost-push inflation An increase of the price level in the economy caused by a reduction in the aggregate supply. This may be caused by growing pressure from trades unions for higher wage settlements or to the increasing cost of importing raw materials.

cote officielle **1.** The official price for a security as quoted on a French stock exchange. **2.** The *Paris Bourse itself, to distinguish it from the *coulisse*.

coulisse The unofficial market in securities attached to the Paris Bourse.

council tax A UK local-government tax raised according to property valuation. Replacing the community charge from 1993–94, the tax is charged on the value of a property as defined by a series of bands. Different bands apply to different regions of the UK. Council tax assumes that two people live at the address, with rebates for single occupancy, and provides for a scale of earnings exemptions. *See also* UNIFORM BUSINESS RATE.

counterparty A person who is a party to a contract.

counterparty risk The *risk that either of the parties to a contract (counterparties) will fail to honour their obligations under the contract. In such organized markets as the *London Commodity Exchange and *London International Financial Futures and Options Exchange, this risk is reduced by the *London Clearing House (LCH) becoming counterparty to the contract, i.e. the buyer contracts to buy from LCH and the seller contracts to sell to LCH (*see* NOVATION). The risk of default by either the buyer or the seller is thus assumed by LCH, the buyer and seller being left with the greatly reduced counterparty risk that LCH will fail. The risk is, however, greater in over-the-counter (OTC) transactions.

countertrading The practice in international trading of paying for goods in a form other than by hard currency. For example, a South American country wishing to buy aircraft may countertrade (usually through a third party) by paying in coffee beans.

countervailing credit *See* BACK-TO-BACK CREDIT.

country risk The *risk of conducting transactions with, or holding assets of entities within, a particular country.

coupon **1.** One of several dated slips attached to a bond, which must be presented to the agents of the issuer or the company to obtain an interest payment or dividend. *See also* COUPON SECURITY. They are usually used with *bearer bonds; the **coupon yield** is the *yield provided by a bearer bond. **2.** The rate of interest paid by a fixed-interest bond. The annual payment is a percentage of the bond's nominal value. **3.** A general name for bonds and notes on US Treasury Markets. **4.** A fixed-rate payment on an interest or currency swap.

coupon security A US government stock (Treasury bond or Treasury note) that pays interest on a *coupon.

coupon stripping A financial process in which the *coupons are stripped off a *bearer bond and then sold separately as a source of cash, with no capital repayment; the bond, bereft of its coupons, becomes a *zero-coupon bond and is also sold separately.

covariance A statistical measure of the relationship between two variables. Negative covariance occurs when the variables have an inverse relationship; positive covariance occurs when they have a direct relationship. Covariance has similar though not identical attributes to *correlation.

covenant A promise made in a deed, which may or may not be under seal. Such a promise can be enforced by the parties to it as a contract, even if the promise is gratuitous: for example, if A covenants to pay B £100 per month, B can enforce this promise even without having done anything in return. Covenants were formerly used to minimize income tax by transferring income from taxpayers to non-taxpayers, such as children or charities; however, only gifts made to charities now offer much scope for tax planning (*see* DEED OF COVENANT; GIFT AID).

   Covenants may be entered into concerning the use of land, frequently to restrict the activities of a new owner or tenant (e.g. a covenant not to sell alcohol or run a fish-and-chip shop). Such covenants may be enforceable by persons deriving title from the original parties. This is an exception to the general rule that a contract cannot bind persons who are not parties to it. If the land is leasehold, a covenant "touching and concerning land" may be enforced by persons other than the original parties if there is "privity of estate" between them, i.e. if they are in the position of landlord and tenant. If the land is freehold, the benefit of any covenant (i.e. the rights under it) may be assigned together with the land. The burden of the covenant (i.e. the duties under it) will pass with the land only if it is a restrictive covenant. This means that it must be negative in nature, such as a covenant not to build on land.

cover **1.** The security provided by *insurance or *assurance against a specified risk. **2.** *See* DIVIDEND COVER. **3.** Collateral given against a loan or credit, as in option dealing. **4.** A *hedge purchased to safeguard an open position. **5.** Money set aside from income to meet potential bad debts or losses. **6. (covering bid)** The second bid in competitive bidding for bonds.

covered bear (protected bear) A person who has sold securities, commodities, or currency that they do not have, although they do have a hedge that they could sell at a profit if the market moves upwards.

covered call writing Selling (writing) a call *option on assets one owns. Thus, if the manager of a portfolio expects the price of a certain holding in the portfolio to remain unchanged or to fall, he or she can increase the portfolio income by the amount of the premium received for the call option sold. If the asset price rises the manager has to deliver it at the exercise price. *Compare* NAKED CALL WRITING. *See also* BUY AND WRITE.

covered interest arbitrage Borrowing in one currency to deposit funds in another currency, in order to take advantage of a margin in interest rates between the two countries, at the same time purchasing a forward contract (*see* FORWARD DEALING) to cover the exchange risk.

covered interest-rate parity A relationship between spot and forward exchange rates and interest rates that should apply provided that the *arbitrage-free condition holds. If, for example, a person invests in a UK short-term security, such as a Treasury Bill, then this is equivalent to exchanging the same principal from pounds into dollars at the spot rate, entering into a forward contract to change the dollars obtained at the expiry of the investment into pounds, and buying US short-term securities, such as US Treasury bills. The return on both investments is known, and both have the same *credit risk. They are therefore equivalent, and so should provide the same sterling return. If that is the case, the relationship between spot rates, forward rates, and short-term interest rates in the two countries is the covered interest-rate parity. *See also* INTEREST-RATE PARITY THEORY.

covered position A *position in which all risks are hedged (*see* HEDGE). *Compare* OPEN POSITION.

CP Abbreviation for *commercial paper.

CPA Abbreviation for certified public accountant. *See* CERTIFIED ACCOUNTANT.

CPP accounting Abbreviation for *current purchasing power accounting.

C2 Principles A code of best practice, established by Thomas Dunfee and David Hess of the University of Pennsylvania, describing how a company and its employees should deal with any attempt to make or solicit improper payments.

CQS Abbreviation for *Consolidated Quotation Service.

crash **1.** A rapid and serious fall in the level of prices in a market. **2.** A breakdown of a computer system. A program is said to crash if it terminates abnormally. A computer is said to crash either if it suffers a mechanical failure, or if one of the programs running on it misbehaves in a way that causes the computer to stop.

crawling peg (adjustable peg; sliding peg) A method of exchange-rate control that accepts the need for stability given by fixed (or pegged) exchange rates, while recognizing that fixed rates can be prone to serious misalignments, which in turn can cause periods of financial and economic upheaval. Under crawling-peg arrangements, countries alter their pegs by small amounts at frequent intervals, rather than making large infrequent changes. This procedure provides flexibility and, in conjunction with the manipulation of interest rates, reduces the possibility of destabilizing speculative flows of capital. However, it is exposed to the criticism made against all fixed-rate regimes, that they are an inefficient alternative to the free play of market forces. At the same time, the crawling peg loses a major advantage of fixed rates, which is to inject certainty into the international trading system and more stable inflationary expectations. The rates may move as frequently as daily under a crawling-peg policy.

CRD Abbreviation for *Central Registration Depository.

creation price The cost to the managers of a *unit trust of creating the units, i.e. the underlying cost of the securities plus the accrued income.

creative accounting Misleadingly optimistic, though not illegal, forms of accounting. This can occur because there are a number of accounting transactions that are not subject to regulations or the regulations are ambiguous. Companies sometimes make use of these ambiguities in order to present their financial results in the best light possible. In particular, companies often wish to demonstrate increasing accounting profits and a strong balance sheet. Examples of transactions in which creative accounting has taken place concern consignment stocks and sale and repurchase agreements. In these contexts, creative accounting will involve the separation of legal title from the risks and rewards of the activities, the linking of several transactions to make it difficult to determine the commercial effect of each transaction, or the inclusion in an agreement of options, which are likely to be exercised. These policies are often referred to as *off-balance-sheet finance and *window dressing. Creative accounting is now less prevalent than it was in the 1980s. This is due both to a number of scandals that have raised the profile of issues such as *corporate governance and *auditors' responsibilities, and to the activities of the *Accounting Standards Board, which has addressed some of the worst abuses.

credit 1. The reputation and financial standing of a person or organization. **2.** The sum of money that a trader or company allows a customer before requiring payment. **3.** The funding of members of the public to purchase goods and services with money borrowed from finance companies, banks, and other money lenders. **4.** An entry on the right-hand side of an *account in double-entry book-keeping, usually showing a sale or a liability. **5.** A payment into an account.

credit balance A balancing amount of an account in which the total of credit entries exceeds the total of debit entries. Credit balances represent revenue, liabilities, or capital.

credit brokerage *See* ANCILLARY CREDIT BUSINESS.

credit card A plastic card issued by a bank or finance organization to enable holders to obtain credit in shops, hotels, restaurants, petrol stations, etc. The retailer or trader receives monthly payments from the credit-card company equal to its total sales in the month by means of that credit card, less a service charge. Customers also receive monthly statements from the credit-card company, which may be paid in full within a certain number of days with no interest charged, or they may make a specified minimum payment and pay interest on the outstanding balance. Credit cards may be used to obtain cash either at a bank or its ATMs. *See also* CHARGE CARD; DEBIT CARD; GOLD CARD.

credit control 1. Any system used by an organization to ensure that its outstanding debts are paid within a reasonable period. It involves establishing a **credit policy**, *credit rating of clients, and chasing accounts that become overdue. *See also* FACTORING. **2.** Control of bank lending as part of central bank monetary policy.

credit crunch A period during which lenders are unwilling to extend credit to borrowers. *See also* CREDIT SQUEEZE.

credit default option An *option in which the payoff is related to the credit rating or payment performance of the *underlying.

credit derivative A *derivative in which the payoff is related to the credit rating or payment performance of the *underlying.

credit enhancement Techniques for raising the credit rating of *asset-backed securities.

credit guarantee 1. A type of insurance provided by credit guarantee associations, government institutions, or lenders to enable small firms to obtain credit from banks. **2.** Companies providing undertakings for their subsidiaries. **3.** Individuals providing undertakings for borrowers.

credit insurance 1. An insurance policy that continues the repayments of a particular debt in the event of the policyholder being financially unable to do so because of illness, death, redundancy, or any other specified cause. **2.** A form of insurance or **credit guarantee** against losses arising from bad debts. This is not usually undertaken by normal insurance policies but by specialists known as factors (*see* FACTORING). *See also* EXPORT CREDITS GUARANTEE DEPARTMENT.

credit line 1. The extent of the credit available to a borrower or the user of a *credit card as set down in the initial credit agreement. **2.** The facility for borrowing money over a given period to a specified extent.

CreditMetrics A *value-at-risk approach to credit risk established by J. P. Morgan Chase and a number of other banks. *See also* RISKMETRICS.

creditor One to whom an organization or person owes money. The *balance sheet of a company shows the total owed to creditors and a distinction has to be made between creditors who will be paid during the coming accounting period and those who will be paid later than this.

creditors' committee A committee of creditors of an insolvent company or a bankrupt individual, which represents all the creditors. They supervise the conduct of the administration of a company or the bankruptcy of an individual or receive reports from an administrative *receiver. If large debts are involved, the creditors' committees are often run by creditor banks.

creditors' voluntary liquidation (creditors' voluntary winding-up) The winding-up of a company by special resolution of the members when it is insolvent. A **meeting of creditors** must be held within 14 days of such a resolution and the creditors must be given seven days' notice of the meeting. Notices must also be posed in the *Gazette* and two local newspapers. The creditors also have certain rights to information before the meeting. A *liquidator may be appointed by the members before the meeting of creditors or at the meeting by the creditors. If two different liquidators are appointed, an application may be made to the court to resolve the matter.

credit rating An assessment of the creditworthiness of an individual or a firm, i.e. the extent to which they can safely be granted credit. Traditionally, banks have provided confidential trade references (*see* BANKER'S REFERENCE), but recently **credit-reference agencies** (also known as **rating agencies**) have grown up, which gather information from a wide range of sources, including the county courts, bankruptcy proceedings, hire-purchase companies, and professional debt collectors. Credit referencing may be divided into individual referencing, rating for small businesses, and rating for large corporations. The credit ratings for large corporations are provided for the debt instruments by such institutions as Moody's Investor Service and Standard and Poor. *See also* ANCILLARY CREDIT BUSINESS.

credit reference An indication of a borrower's previous borrowing record, usually given by a bank or other lender to enable a borrower to extend an existing credit line or open new credit facilities. Such information is also provided by **credit-reference agencies**. *See* ANCILLARY CREDIT BUSINESS; BANKER'S REFERENCE; CREDIT RATING.

credit risk The *risk that a counterparty will default or delay payment on an obligation or that the value of a flow of payments will decline due to an adverse movement in the counterparty's *credit rating.

credit-risk insurance Insurance against the *credit risk to which an institution may be exposed.

credit-risk premium The excess in yield above the *risk-free rate that is owing to *credit risk. *See* RISK PREMIUM.

credit sale agreement *See* HIRE PURCHASE.

credit spread The differences in yield resulting from different levels of *credit risk.

credit squeeze A government measure, or set of measures, to reduce economic activity by restricting the money supply. Measures used include increasing the interest rate (to restrain borrowing), controlling moneylending by banks and others, and increasing down payments or making other changes to hire-purchase regulations.

credit transfer An electronic system of settling a debt by transferring money through a bank or post office. The payer completes written instructions naming the receiver and giving the receiver's address and acount number. Several receivers may be listed and settled by a single transaction. The popularity of this system in the UK led the banks to introduce a credit-clearing system in 1961 and the Post Office to do so in 1968. *See also* GIRO.

credit union A non-profitmaking cooperative that functions as a *savings bank, taking deposits from savers and lending. A *share account with a credit union pays a dividend rather than interest. These institutions can be found in the USA, Japan, and Europe.

creditworthiness An assessment of a person's or a business's ability to pay for goods purchased or services received. Creditworthiness may be presented in the form of a *credit rating.

creeping takeover The accumulation of a company's shares, by purchasing them openly over a period on a stock exchange, as a preliminary to a takeover (*see* TAKEOVER BID). There are regulations governing this process and stipulating the maximum number of shares that can be acquired before formal notification must be made and a bid undertaken.

CREST An electronic share settlement system created by the Bank of England for the securities industry that began operation in 1996. Using CREST, shares are registered electronically, purchases and sales are settled instantaneously on the due date, and the dividends can be paid electronically direct to the shareholder's bank. Paper certificates and associated paperwork have been abolished for those who join CREST. As with paper shares, the company register of shareholders provides proof of ownership. Those wishing to retain paper certificates are able to do so.

cross-border listing The practice of listing shares in a company on the stock exchanges of different countries in order to create a larger market for the shares.

cross-currency interest-rate swap A *swap of two different interest rates in two different currencies. This usually involves swapping a fixed rate for a floating rate (or vice versa); if both rates are floating it is known as a *basis swap. *See* CURRENCY SWAP; INTEREST-RATE SWAP.

crossed cheque *See* CHEQUE.

cross-hedge A *hedge created by selling a forward contract or futures contract in a different security or commodity than the one being hedged, or by taking a *short position in this second *underlying. For a cross-hedge to be effective, the two underlyings should usually have similar price movements.

cross-holding A situation in which two or more companies hold shares in each other in order to cement business ties and forestall takeovers.

crossing A practice that occurs on the London Stock Exchange when the same broker or securities house buys and sells a block of securities, instead of allowing the sale to cross the market in accordance with Stock Exchange rules. In the USA, such a transaction is known as a **wash sale**.

cross-over A term used by *chartists and technical analysts for two series that cross at a particular point on a graph. If, for example, a short-term *moving average crosses a longer term moving average for an equity price from below, this may indicate an auspicious time to buy.

cross rate *See* FOREIGN CURRENCY CROSS-RATE.

crowding out **1.** The effect of increased government borrowing in raising interest rates, causing some investment projects to become less viable. **2.** Adverse impacts on the demand for a security caused by activity in substitute asset markets.

crown jewel option A form of *poison pill in which a company, defending itself against an unwanted *takeover bid, writes an *option that would allow a partner or other friendly company to acquire one or more of its best businesses or assets at an advantageous price if control of the defending company is lost to the unwelcome predator. The granting of such an option may not always be in the best interests of the shareholders of the defending company.

CSCE Abbreviation for *Coffee, Sugar and Cocoa Exchange Inc. of New York.

CTCI Abbreviation for *computer-to-computer interface.

cum- *See* EX-.

cum-dividend *See* EX-.

cum-new Denoting a share that is offered for sale with the right to take up any *scrip issue or *rights issue. *Compare* EX-NEW.

cumulative preference share A type of *preference share that entitles the owner to receive any dividends not paid in previous years. Companies are not obliged to pay dividends on preference shares if there are insufficient earnings in any particular year. Cumulative preference shares guarantee the eventual payment of these dividends in arrears before the payment of dividends on ordinary shares, provided that the company returns to profit in subsequent years. If the dividends are in arrears, then shareholders may have some rights as ordinary shareholders.

cumulative preferred stock In the USA, stock in which the dividends accumulate if not paid out in a particular financial period.

currency **1.** Any kind of money that is in circulation in an economy. **2.** Anything that functions as a *medium of exchange, including coins, banknotes, cheques, *bills of exchange, promissory notes. etc. **3.** The money in use in a particular country. *See* FOREIGN EXCHANGE. **4.** The time that has to elapse before a bill of exchange matures.

currency future A *financial futures contract in which a currency for forward delivery is bought or sold at a particular exchange rate.

currency option A contract giving the right either to buy or to sell a specified currency at a fixed exchange rate within a given period. The price agreed is called the *exercise price or strike price. This is the price at which the buyer has the right to buy or sell the currency.

currency risk *See* EXCHANGE-RATE EXPOSURE.

currency swap A *swap in which specified amounts of one currency are exchanged for another currency at agreed principles over time. In an ordinary currency swap both currencies bear interest at a fixed rate: if both currencies bear interest at a floating rate the transaction is known as a *basis swap and if one rate is floating and the other fixed it is a *cross-currency interest-rate swap.

current account **1.** An active account at a bank or building society into which deposits can be paid and from which withdrawals can be made by cheque (*see also* CHEQUE ACCOUNT), ATM, standing order, and direct debit. **2.** The part of the *balance of payments account that records non-capital transactions. It includes trade in visibles and invisibles. **3.** An account in which intercompany or interdepartmental balances are recorded. **4.** An account recording the transactions of a partner in a partnership that do not relate directly to his or her capital in the partnership (*see* CAPITAL ACCOUNT).

current assets Assets that form part of the working capital of a business and are turned over frequently in the course of trade. The most common current assets are stock in trade, debtors, and cash. *Compare* CAPITAL ASSET.

current cost accounting (CCA) A method of accounting, recommended by the Sandilands Committee (1975), to deal with the problem of showing the effects of inflation on business profits. Instead of showing assets at their historical cost (i.e. their original purchase price), less depreciation where appropriate, the assets are shown at their current cost at the time of producing the accounts. This method of accounting was used widely in the UK in the late 1970s and early 1980s, when inflation was high; it was not popular, however, and as inflation has reduced it has been largely abandoned.

current liabilities Amounts owed by a business to other organizations and individuals that should be paid within one year from the balance-sheet date. These generally consist of trade creditors, *bills of exchange payable, amounts owed to group and related companies, taxation, social-security creditors, proposed dividends, accruals, deferred income, payments received on account, bank overdrafts, and short-term loans. Any long-term loans repayable within one year from the balance-sheet date should also be included. Current liabilities are distinguished from long-term liabilities on the balance sheet.

current purchasing power accounting (constant purchasing power accounting; CPP accounting) A form of accounting that measures profit after allowing for the maintenance of the purchasing power of the shareholders' capital. The *Retail Price Index is used to adjust for general price changes to ensure that the shareholders' capital maintains the same monetary purchasing power. There is no requirement to allow for the maintenance of the purchasing power of the loan creditors' capital.

current ratio (working-capital ratio) The ratio of the current assets of a business to the current liabilities, expressed as *x*:1 and used as a test of liquidity. For example, if the current assets are £25,000 and the current liabilities are £12,500 the current ratio is 2:1. There is no simple rule of thumb, but a low ratio, e.g. under 1:1, would usually raise concern over the liquidity of the company. Too high a ratio, e.g. in excess of 2:1, may indicate poor management of working capital; this would be established by calculating the *stock turnover ratio and *debtor collection period ratio. Care must be taken when making comparisons between companies to ensure that any industry differences are recognized. The *liquid ratio is regarded as a more rigorous test of liquidity.

current-year basis The basis of assessment for tax purposes in the UK in which tax is charged in a *fiscal year on profits arising in the accounts for the period ending in that tax year.

current yield *See* YIELD.

CUSIP Abbreviation for *Committee on Uniform Securities Identification Procedures.

custodian A person who holds securities on behalf of their owner.

Customs and Excise *See* BOARD OF CUSTOMS AND EXCISE.

customs union A union of two or more states to form a region in which there are no import or export duties between members but goods imported into the region bear the same import duties. The *European Union is an example.

CVM Abbreviation for *Commissão de Valores Mobiliaros.

CVS Abbreviation for *corporate venturing scheme.

***cwmni cyfyngedig cyhoeddus* (c.c.c.)** Welsh for *public limited company.

cyclical stock Shares whose prices rise or fall in line with the *business cycle.

DA **1.** Abbreviation for *deposit account. **2.** Abbreviation for *discretionary account.

D/A Abbreviation for *documents against acceptance.

Daily Official List A publication issued daily by the London Stock Exchange to summarize transactions in listed securities.

daily trading limit *See* INTRADAY LIMIT; LIMIT.

***daimyo* bond** A *bearer bond issued on the Japanese markets and in the *eurobond market by supranational institutions.

daisy chain **1.** Trading activity to create the illusion of volume, in order to attract investors; this may take the form of buying and selling the same items several times over. **2.** A certification process for euromarket transactions, to comply with US law.

dalasi (D) The standard monetary unit of the Gambia, divided into 100 bututs.

damages Compensation, in monetary form, for a loss or injury, breach of contract, tort, or infringement of a right. Damages refers to the compensation awarded, as opposed to damage, which refers to the actual injury or loss suffered. The legal principle is that the award of damages is an attempt, as far as money can, to restore the position of the injured party to what it was before the event in question took place. In general, damages capable of being quantified in monetary terms are known as **liquidated damages**. In particular, liquidated damages include instances in which a genuine pre-estimate can be given of the loss that will be caused to one party if a contract is broken by the other party. However, liquidated damages must be distinguished from a *penalty. Another form of liquidated damages is that expressly made recoverable under a statute. These may also be known as **statutory damages** if they involve a breach of statutory duty or are regulated or limited by statute. **Unliquidated damages** are those fixed by a court rather than those that have been estimated in advance.

Datastream A UK financial information provider.

dated security A stock that has a fixed redemption date. *Compare* UNDATED SECURITY.

dawn raid An attempt by one company or investor to acquire a significant holding in the equity of another company by instructing brokers to buy all the shares available in that company as soon as the stock exchange opens, usually before the target company knows that it is, in fact, a target. The dawn raid may provide a significant stake from which to launch a *takeover bid. The conduct of dawn raids is now restricted by the *City Code on Takeovers and Mergers.

Dax Abbreviation for *Deutsche Aktienindex.

daylight exposure limit A limit set by a bank on its foreign-exchange dealings in a given currency with a particular counterparty.

day order An order to a stockbroker, commodity broker, etc., to buy or sell a specified security or commodity. The order is valid for the day on which it is given and automatically becomes void at the close of trading on that day.

days of grace 1. The period elapsing between a security offer and establishing a *sinking fund or purchase fund. **2.** The period in a loan during which repayment of the principal is not required. **3.** The time given to defaulters to satisfy their obligations. **4.** The extra time allowed for payment of a *bill of exchange or insurance premium after the actual due date. With bills of exchange the usual custom is to allow 3 days of grace (not including Sundays and *Bank Holidays) and 14 days for insurance policies.

day-to-day money (overnight money) Money lent, often by one bank to another, for one trading day and repayable 24 hours later.

DB scheme Abbreviation for *defined-benefit pension scheme.

DCF Abbreviation for *discounted cash flow.

DC scheme Abbreviation for defined-contribution pension scheme. *See* DEFINED-BENEFIT PENSION SCHEME.

dead-cat bounce A temporary recovery on a stock exchange, after a substantial fall. It does not imply a reversal of the downward trend.

dealer 1. A trader of any kind. **2.** A person who deals as a principal on a financial market rather than as a broker or agent.

Dearing Report The report of a committee set up under the chairmanship of Sir Ronald Dearing to examine the setting of accounting standards. The report, published in 1988, led to the establishment of the *Accounting Standards Board and the *Financial Reporting Council in 1990.

dear money (tight money) A monetary policy in which loans are difficult to obtain and only available at high rates of interest. *Compare* CHEAP MONEY.

death duties Taxes levied on a person's estate at the time of death. The principal death duty in the UK is *inheritance tax. Gifts made within the seven years preceding death are also within the scope of this tax.

death-valley curve A curve on a graph showing how the venture capital invested in a new company falls as the company meets its start-up expenses before its income reaches predicted levels. This erosion of cash makes it difficult for the company to interest further investors in providing additional venture capital. *See also* MAXIMUM SLIPPAGE.

debenture 1. The most common form of long-term loan taken by a company. It is usually a loan repayable at a fixed date, although some debentures are *irredeemable securities; these are sometimes called *perpetual debentures. Most debentures also pay a fixed rate of interest, and this interest must be paid before a *dividend is paid to shareholders. Most debentures are also secured on the borrower's assets, although some, known as **naked debentures** or *unsecured loan stock, are not. In the USA debentures are usually unsecured, relying only on the reputation of the borrower. In a *secured debenture, the bond may have a *fixed charge (i.e. a charge over a particular asset) or a *floating charge. If debentures are issued to a large number of people (for example in the form of **debenture stock** or **loan stock**) trustees may be appointed to act on behalf of the debenture holders. There may be a premium on redemption and some debentures are *convertible, i.e.

they can be converted into ordinary shares on a specified date, usually at a specified price. The advantage of debentures to companies is that they carry lower interest rates than, say, overdrafts and are usually repayable a long time into the future. For an investor, they are usually saleable on a stock exchange and involve less risk than *equities. **2.** A *deed under seal setting out the main terms of such a loan. **3.** A form of bank security covering corporate debt, either fixed or floating; in either case the bank ranks as a preferred creditor in the event of liquidation.

debit balance The balance of an account whose total debit entries exceed the total of the *credit entries. Debit balances represent expenditure and *assets.

debit card A plastic card issued by a bank or building society to enable its customers with cheque accounts to pay for goods or services at certain retail outlets by using the telephone network to debit their cheque accounts directly. It is also known as a **payment card**. The retail outlets need to have the necessary computerized input device, into which the card is inserted; the customer may be required to tap in a *personal identification number before entering the amount to be debited. Most debit cards also function as *cheque cards and *cash cards. In the USA these cards are sometimes called **Asset cards**.

debt 1. A sum owed by one party to another. **2.** Any funding instrument other than equity, such as a *bond or *promissory note.

debt adjusting *See* ANCILLARY CREDIT BUSINESS.

debt buy-back A transaction that enables an issuer to repurchase some of its securities, sometimes at a large discount.

debt capacity The ability of a company or other entity to raise loan finance.

debt collection agency An organization that specializes in collecting the outstanding debts of its clients, charging a commission for doing so. Because of the historical stigma attached to the phrase 'debt collection', these agencies prefer to be called **commercial collection agencies**. *See also* ANCILLARY CREDIT BUSINESS.

debt counselling *See* ANCILLARY CREDIT BUSINESS.

debt discounting The purchase of a *debt from a trader, especially an exporter at a discount. *See* DEBT COLLECTION AGENCY; FORFAITING.

debt–equity ratio A ratio used to examine the financial structure or *gearing or *leverage of a business. The long-term debt, normally including *preference shares, of a business is expressed as a percentage of its equity. A business may have entered into an agreement with a bank that it will maintain a certain debt–equity ratio; if it breaches this agreement the loan may have to be repaid. A highly geared company is one in which the debt is higher than the equity, compared to companies in a similar industry. A highly geared company offers higher returns to shareholders when it is performing well but should be regarded as a speculative investment. The debt–equity ratio is now sometimes expressed as the ratio of the debt to the sum of the debt and the equity.

debt-for-equity swap A transaction in which debt is swapped for equity. It often accompanies the reorganization of companies in *financial distress.

debt forgiveness The act of writing off a proportion of debt. A prime example is the writing off by lenders of interest on *sovereign loans to developing countries.

debt instrument A document used to raise non-equity finance consisting of a *promissory note, *bill of exchange, or any other legally binding *bond.

Debt Management and Financial Analysis System (DMFAS) A system produced by the *United Nations Conference on Trade and Development to manage a country's debt owed to the *Group of Ten. The system is computerized in three languages and underwritten by the United Nations. *See also* DEBT RESCHEDULING.

debt market A market in which financial instruments (mainly bonds) dealing in outstanding debts are bought and sold. The New York Bonds Exchange is such a market.

debtor One who owes money to another. In *balance sheets, debtors are those who owe money to the organization and a distinction has to be made between those who are expected to pay their debts during the next accounting period and those who will not pay until later.

debt overhang A situation in which a third-world country cannot afford to service its debt on the original terms and carries forward some or all of its debt on new terms that are within its ability to pay.

debt rescheduling A change in the terms of outstanding loans in which the debtor has repayment difficulties. The rescheduling can take the form of an entirely new loan or an extension of the existing loan repayment period, deferring interest or principal repayments. When debt rescheduling concerns less developed countries, the new agreement may involve a lowering of interest rates or an offer of an aid package of foreign investment to the country to offset some of the existing debt. In the late 1980s the major UK commercial banks wrote off or made provision for nearly £10 billion of debt to less developed countries — often Latin American countries who had simply stopped repaying their earlier loans. In the late 1980s and early 1990s a wide range of rescheduling schemes were adopted, including some in which the debt, or part of it, is converted into internal aid programmes.

debt restructuring The adjustment of a debt, either as a result of legal action or by agreement between the interested parties, to give the debtor a more feasible arrangement with the creditors for meeting the financial obligations. The management may also voluntarily restructure debt, for example by replacing long-term debt with short-term debt.

debt security A financial instrument by which borrowing is raised and repaid with interest.

debt service ratio (DSR) The proportion of annual export earnings needed to service a country's external debts, including both interest payments and repayment of principal. The DSR is an important statistic, indicating the severity of a country's indebtedness. The effect of *debt rescheduling programmes can be examined by comparing pre- and post-rescheduling DSRs.

debt swap The exchange of an outstanding loan to a third party between one bank and another. The loans are usually to governments of third-world countries and are often expressed in the local currency.

decimal currency A currency system in which the standard unit is subdivided into 100 parts. Following the example of the USA in 1792, most countries have introduced a decimal system. However, it was not until 15 February 1971 that decimalization was introduced in the UK, following the recommendations of the Halesbury Committee of 1961.

decision making The act of deciding between alternative courses of action. In the running of a business, accounting information and financial techniques are used to facilitate decision making, especially by the provision of *decision models, such as *discounted cash flow.

decision model A model that simulates the elements or variables inherent in a business decision, together with their relationships to each other and the constraints under which they operate; the purpose of the model is to enable a solution to be arrived at in keeping with the objectives of the organization. For example, a **linear programming decision model** may arrive at a particular production mix that, having regard to the constraints that exist, either minimizes costs or maximizes the contribution. Other decision models include *decision trees and *discounted cash flow.

decision table A table used to aid decision making. The table shows the problems requiring actions to be considered and estimated probabilities of outcomes. Where probabilities are difficult to estimate, the maximax and maximin criteria are often used, the former leading to the selection of the option with the greatest maximum outcome, the latter to the selection of the action with the greatest minimum outcome.

decision trees Diagrams that illustrate the choices available to a decision maker and the estimated outcomes of each possible decision. Each possible decision is shown as a separate branch of the tree, together with each estimated outcome for each decision and the subjective *probabilities of these outcomes actually occurring. From this information the expected values for each outcome can be determined, which can provide valuable information in decision making. The decision criterion is usually to implement the decision that has the greatest expected monetary value.

declaration day The last day but one of an account on the London Stock Exchange, on which traditional *options must be declared, i.e. the owner of the option must state whether or not the option to purchase (call) or sell (put) the securities concerned will be exercised.

declaration of dividend A statement in which the directors of a company announce that a *dividend of a certain amount is recommended to be paid to the shareholders. The liability should be recognized as soon as the declaration has been made and the appropriate amount is included under *current liabilities on the *balance sheet. The company pays the dividend net of income tax to the shareholders.

declaration of solvency A declaration made by the directors of a company seeking voluntary liquidation that it will be able to pay its debts within a specified period, not exceeding 12 months from the date of the declaration. It must contain a statement of the company's assets and liabilities, and a copy must be sent to the Registrar of Companies. A director who participates in a declaration of solvency without reasonable grounds will be liable to a fine or imprisonment on conviction. *See* MEMBERS' VOLUNTARY LIQUIDATION.

decreasing term assurance A form of *term assurance in which the amount to be paid in the event of the death of the *life assured reduces with the passage of time. These policies are usually arranged in conjunction with a cash loan or mortgage and are designed to repay the loan if the *life assured dies. As the amount of the loan decreases with successive repayments the sum assured reduces at the same rate.

deductions at source A method of tax collection in which a person paying income to another deducts the tax on the income and is responsible for paying it to the authorities. Tax authorities have found that, in general, it is easier to collect tax from the payer rather than the recipient of income, especially if paying the tax is made a condition of the payer's obtaining tax relief for the payment. The payee receives a credit against any tax liability for the tax already suffered. Examples of this in the UK tax system are *PAYE, share dividends, interest on government securities, deeds of covenant, trust income, and sub-contractors in the building industry. Normally, tax is deducted at the basic rate of income tax only, although in certain cases, such as PAYE and payments from discretionary trusts, other rates might be used.

deed A document that has been signed, sealed, and delivered. The seal and the delivery make it different from an ordinary written agreement. The former use of sealing wax and a signet to effect the seal is now usually replaced by using a small paper disc; delivery may now be informal, i.e. by carrying out some act to show that the deed is intended to be operative. Some transactions, such as conveyances of land, must be carried out by deed to be effective.

deed of covenant A former legal document enabling a person to obtain tax relief on regular annual payments to a charity. From 2000 it was replaced by the *gift aid system.

deed of partnership A *partnership agreement drawn up in the form of a deed. It covers the respective *capital contributions of the partners, their entitlement to interest on their capital, their profit-sharing percentages, agreed salary, etc.

deep-discount A loan stock issued at a discount of more than 15% of the amount on redemption or, if less, at a discount of more than ½% for each completed year between issue and redemption. The discount will be treated as income accruing over the life of the stock. For example, a **deep-discount bond** might be a four-year loan stock issued at £95 for every £100 nominal (the discount exceeds ½% per annum) or a 25-year loan stock issued at £75 for every £100 nominal (the discount exceeds 15% in total).

deep-gain security A security issued at a *deep discount or redeemed at a premium. The terms of the issue mean that the amount of discount or premium cannot be allocated evenly over the life of the bond.

deep market A market in which a large number of transactions can take place without moving the price of the underlying commodity, currency, or financial instrument. *Compare* THIN MARKET.

default 1. Failure to do something that is required by law, especially failure to comply with the rules of legal procedure. **2.** Failure to comply with the terms of a contract. **3.** Failure to make required payments.

defeasance The act of a *bond issuer in which assets are placed with a *trustee, who makes use of them to pay interest on the bond and eventually to repay the capital.

defended takeover bid A *takeover bid for a company in which the directors of the target company oppose the bid.

defensive security A stable security that is expected to have relatively good performance in periods of recession or downturn in financial markets.

deferred annuity An *annuity in which payments do not start at once but either at a specified later date or when the policyholder reaches a specified age.

deferred coupon note A bond on which no interest is paid until after a set date. In the USA such bonds are called **deferred interest bonds**.

deferred credit (deferred liability; deferred income) Income received or recorded before it is earned, under the *accruals concept. The income will not be included in the *profit and loss account of the period but will be carried forward on the *balance sheet until it is matched with the period in which it is earned. A common example of a deferred credit is a government grant. The grant is shown as a separate item or under *creditors in the balance sheet, and an annual amount is transferred to the profit and loss account until the deferred credit balance is brought to nil.

deferred debit (deferred asset; deferred DB expense) An item of expenditure incurred in an accounting period but, under the *accruals concept, not matched with the income it will generate. Instead of being treated as an operating cost for that period, it is treated as an *asset with the intention of treating it as an operating cost to be charged against the income it will generate in a future period. An example is rent paid for a period beyond the end of the accounting period.

deferred income *See* DEFERRED CREDIT.

deferred ordinary share **1.** A type of ordinary share, formerly often issued to founder members of a company, in which dividends are only paid after all other types of ordinary share have been paid. They often entitle their owners to a large share of the profit. **2.** A type of share on which little or no dividend is paid for a fixed number of years, after which it ranks with other ordinary shares for dividend.

deferred-payment agreement *See* HIRE PURCHASE.

deferred pricing A situation in which a transaction is agreed upon before the price of the transaction is settled.

deferred swap A *swap in which the payments are deferred.

deferred taxation A sum set aside for tax in the *accounts of an organization that will become payable in a period other than that under review. It arises because of timing differences between tax rules and accounting conventions. The principle of **deferred-tax accounting** is to re-allocate a tax payment to the same period as that in which the relevant amount of income or expenditure is shown. Historically, the most common reason for this timing difference is because the percentages used for the calculation of capital allowances have differed from those used for depreciation.

deficit financing The creation of a government *budget deficit for the purpose of expanding economic activity by fiscal policy.

defined-benefit pension scheme (DB scheme) An occupational pension scheme in which the rules specify the benefits to be received on retirement and the scheme is funded accordingly. The benefits are normally calculated on a formula incorporating years of service and salary levels (*see* FINAL SALARY SCHEME). Accounting for pension costs poses a number of difficulties for accountants; *Statement of Standard Accounting Practice 24 provides the regulations.

In a **defined-contribution pension scheme (DC scheme)**, the contribution is specified, while the amount of pension received will depend on the size of the fund accumulated and the annuity that can be obtained from it at the retirement date.

deflation **1.** A general fall in the level of prices; the opposite of *inflation. *See also*

DISINFLATION. **2.** The adjustment of economic values to eliminate inflationary impacts. **3.** A state of economic *recession.

degearing Lowering the proportion of long-term debt to equity.

deleveraging Reducing a company's level of debt. *See* LEVERAGE.

deliverable That which is delivered at the expiry of a *futures contract.

delivery 1. The completion of the physical operation of transferring goods, mail, etc., to its proper destination. **2.** The goods so transferred. **3.** The transfer of *title to property, assets, etc., from one owner to another. **4.** The final act required to bring a *deed into force.

delivery date 1. The day in the month that commodities on a futures contract have to be delivered. **2.** The maturity date for foreign exchange in a forward exchange contract. **3.** The date that a buyer of securities receives the relevant certificates.

delivery factor An adjustment to the prices of bonds delivered in *futures contracts where a range of securities can be delivered.

delivery month The month in which the *underlying or cash of a futures contract must be handed over to the buyer. A month is specified but usually any day within that month will fulfil the contract obligations.

delta One of a group of measures related to the pricing of options known as *greeks. The delta is a measure of the sensitivity of an option value to a change in the value of the *underlying; formally expressed, it is the partial derivative of the option value with respect to changes in the value of the underlying. *See also* GAMMA.

delta/gamma hedge A *hedge of an options price risk with respect to changes in *delta and *gamma.

delta hedge A *hedge of an options price risk with respect to changes in *delta.

delta neutral Describing a position in which the risk relating to changes in the value of the *underlying has been eliminated.

delta stocks The least liquid stocks on the London Stock Exchange, whose prices did not have to be displayed under the former classification system. This system has now been replaced by *Normal Market Size. *See also* ALPHA STOCKS.

demand deposit An instant-access current account (or check account) in the USA.

demand for money The quantity of money that economic actors wish to hold at a particular point in time. It is influenced by the levels of transactions, wealth, and the interest rate in the economy. The assumption that the function determining the demand for money was stable was a key but questionable assumption of *monetarism.

demand-pull inflation A rise in prices caused by an excess of aggregate demand over aggregate supply in the economy as a whole.

demerger A business strategy in which a large company or group of companies splits up so that its activities are carried on by two or more independent companies. Alternatively, subsidiaries of a group are sold off. Demerging was popular in the late 1980s when large conglomerates became unfashionable. One of the main reasons for demerging is to improve the value of the company's shares, particularly if one part of a group's value can be better reflected by a separate share quotation.

demutualization The act by which a *mutual, such as a building society, changes its status to that of a public limited company. This has been seen in the retail financial services industry worldwide.

denar (MKD) The standard monetary unit of Macedonia, divided into 100 deni.

deni A monetary unit of Macedonia, worth one hundredth of a *denar.

denomination 1. The face value of a security, i.e. the sum to be paid on its redemption. **2.** The act of nominating a currency in which an international transaction is to take place.

Department of Trade and Industry (DTI) The UK government department controlling and advising on UK business and finance.

deposit 1. A sum of money paid by a buyer as part of the sale price of something in order to reserve it. Depending on the terms agreed, the deposit may or may not be returned if the sale is not completed. **2.** A sum of money left with an organization, such as a bank, for safekeeping or to earn interest or with a broker, dealer, etc., as a security to cover any trading losses incurred. **3.** A sum of money paid as the first instalment on a *hire-purchase agreement. It is usually paid when the buyer takes possession of the goods.

deposit account (DA) An *account with a bank from which money cannot be withdrawn without notice and on which interest is paid.

deposit insurance Protection against loss of deposits by a customer, in case a bank or other financial institution fails. In the UK, depositors are protected by the **Deposit Protection Fund** up to a specified percentage of their deposits. In the USA, the *Federal Deposit Insurance Corporation provides similar protection, through the Bank Insurance Fund. *See also* INVESTORS' COMPENSATION SCHEME.

Deposit Insurance National Bank A US institution that manages banks in *financial distress.

deposit note A type of *medium-term note issued by foreign banks in the US market.

Depository Trust and Clearing Corporation (DTCC) The US central depository for stock exchange securities. It is used by option writers as a way of facilitating delivery.

deposit-taking institution An institution whose main function is to take deposits. This is the basis of the legal definition of a bank as laid down in the *Banking Acts 1979 and 1987. In the UK deposit-taking institutions are regulated by the Bank of England.

depreciation 1. An amount charged to the *profit and loss account of an organization to represent the wearing out or diminution in value of an asset. The amount charged is normally based on a percentage of the value of the asset as shown in the books; however, the way in which the percentage is used reflects different views of depreciation. **Straight-line depreciation** allocates a given percentage of the cost of the asset each year, thus suggesting an even spread of the cost of the asset over its useful life. **Reducing-** or **diminishing-balance depreciation** applies a constant percentage reduction first to the cost of the asset and subsequently to the cost as reduced by previous depreciations. In this way reducing amounts are charged periodically to the profit and loss account; by this method the depreciated value of the asset in the balance sheet may approximate more closely to its true value. *See also* ACCUMULATED DEPRECIATION. **2.** A fall in the value of a currency with a *floating exchange rate relative to another. Depreciation can refer both to day-to-day movements and to long-term realignments in value. For currencies with a *fixed exchange rate a *devaluation or *revaluation of currency is required to change the relative value. *Compare* APPRECIATION.

depression (slump) An extended or severe period of *recession. Depressions occur infrequently. The most recent Great Depression occurred in the 1930s; prior to that they occurred in the periods 1873–96, 1844–51, and 1810–17. Depressions are usually associated with falling prices (*see* DEFLATION) and large-scale involuntary unemployment. They are often preceded by major financial crashes, e.g. the Wall Street crash of 1929.

deregulation The removal of controls imposed by governments on the operation of markets. Many economists and politicians believe that during the mid-20th century governments imposed controls over markets that had little or no justification. Since the 1980s many governments have followed a deliberate policy of deregulation. However, most economists still argue that certain markets should be regulated (*see* REGULATION), particularly if market failure is involved.

derivative A financial instrument, the price of which has a strong relationship with an *underlying commodity, currency, economic variable, or financial instrument. The different types of derivatives are *futures contracts, forwards (*see* FORWARD DEALING), *swaps, and *options. They are traded on markets or over the counter (OTC). The market-traded derivatives are standard, while the OTC trades are specific and customized. The main market-traded derivatives are futures and options.

Designated Investment Exchange (DIE) Any investment exchange outside the UK that is acknowledged by the UK *Financial Services Authority (FSA) as operating similarly to UK exchanges approved by the FSA.

designated order turn-around (DOT) An electronic system on the New York Stock Exchange that enables members to place orders to buy or sell stocks within a specified range of prices for automatic execution.

Deutsche Aktienindex (Dax) A share index on the Frankfurt Stock Exchange. Introduced in mid-1988, it was the first real-time German index of 30 leading stocks.

Deutsche Terminbörse A futures and options exchange based in Frankfurt. It opened in 1990 and trades in *financial futures and *options. It is now part of *Eurex.

Deutschmark (DM) Formerly, the standard monetary unit of Germany, divided into 100 Pfennige. It was subsumed into the euro for all purposes other than cash transactions in 1999 and abolished in 2002.

devaluation A fall in the value of a currency relative to gold or to other currencies. Governments engage in devaluation when they feel that their currency has become overvalued, for example through high rates of inflation making exports uncompetitive or because of a substantially adverse *balance of trade. The intention is that devaluation will make exports cheaper and imports dearer, although the loss of confidence in an economy forced to devalue invariably has an adverse effect.

Devaluation is a measure that need only concern governments with a *fixed exchange rate for their currency. With a *floating exchange rate, devaluation or revaluation takes place continuously and automatically (*see* DEPRECIATION; REVALUATION OF CURRENCY).

DIE Abbreviation for *Designated Investment Exchange.

difference clause An agreement to pay net in *swaps and *forward rate agreements.

difference option An *option that pays the difference between the price of two assets. The buyer's profit will depend on how the price differential at the *exercise date compares with the price differential at the time of purchase.

digital option *See* BINARY OPTION.

dilution of equity An increase in the number of ordinary shares in a company without a corresponding increase in its assets or profitability. The result is a fall in the value of the shares as a result of this dilution.

diminishing-balance depreciation *See* DEPRECIATION.

dinar **1.** (DA) The standard monetary unit of Algeria, divided into 100 centimes. **2.** The standard monetary unit of Bahrain (BD), Iraq (ID), Jordan (JD), and Kuwait (KD), divided into 1000 fils. **3.** (TD) The standard monetary unit of Tunisia, divided into 1000 millimes. **4.** (Din.) The standard monetary unit of Serbia, divided into 100 paras. **5.** (LD) The standard monetary unit of Libya, divided into 1000 dirhams. **6.** (SD) The standard monetary unit of Sudan. **7.** A monetary unit of Iran, worth one hundredth of a *rial.

direct costing *See* MARGINAL COSTING.

direct debit A form of *standing order given to a bank by an account holder to pay regular amounts from a cheque account to a third party. Unlike a normal standing order, however, the amount to be paid is not specified; the account holder trusts the third party to claim an appropriate sum from the bank. The amount to be paid can be varied. In the USA this arrangement is known as **reverse wire transfer**.

direct investment An investment in overseas productive facilities.

directive **1.** An instruction to carry out certain money-market operations, particularly instructions given by the US Federal Reserve Open Market Committee. **2.** A legislative decision by the European Union's Council of Ministers and Parliament, which is binding on member states but allows them to decide how to enact the required legislation. *See* BANKING DIRECTIVES; EIGHTH DIRECTIVE; FINANCIAL SERVICES DIRECTIVE; FOURTH DIRECTIVE; INVESTMENT SERVICES DIRECTIVE; MERGER CONTROL DIRECTIVE; SECOND DIRECTIVE; SEVENTH DIRECTIVE; SOLVENCY RATIO DIRECTIVE.

director A person appointed to carry out the day-to-day management of a company. A public company must have at least two directors, a private company at least one. The directors of a company, collectively known as the **board of directors**, usually act together, although power may be conferred (by the *articles of association) on one or more directors to exercise executive powers; in particular there is often a **managing director** with considerable executive power. The first directors of a company are usually named in its articles of association or are appointed by the subscribers; they are required to give a signed undertaking to act in that capacity, which must be sent to the *Registrar of Companies. Subsequent directors are appointed by the company at a general meeting, although in practice they may be appointed by the other directors for ratification by the general meeting. Directors may be discharged from office by an ordinary resolution with special notice at a general meeting, whether or not they have a *service contract in force. They may be disqualified for *fraudulent trading or *wrongful trading or for any conduct that makes them unfit to manage the company.

Directors owe duties of honesty and loyalty to the company (fiduciary duties) and a duty of care; their liability in *negligence depends upon their personal qualifications (e.g. a chartered accountant must exercise more skill than an unqualified man). Directors need no formal qualifications. Directors may not put their own interests before those of the company, may not make contracts (other than service contracts) with the company, and must declare any personal interest in work undertaken by the company. Their formal responsibilities include: presenting to members of the company, at least annually, the *accounts of the company and a *directors' report; keeping a register of directors, a register of directors' shareholdings, and a register of shares; calling an annual general meeting; sending all relevant documents to the Registrar of Companies; and submitting a statement of affairs if the company is wound up (*see* LIQUIDATOR). Directors' remuneration consists of a salary and in some cases **directors' fees**, paid to them for being a director, and an expense allowance to cover their expenses incurred in the service of the company. Directors' remuneration must be disclosed in the company's accounts and shown separately from any pension payments or *compensation for loss of office. *See also* EXECUTIVE DIRECTOR.

directors' interests The interests held by *directors in the shares and debentures of the company of which they are a director. The directors' interests can also include options on shares and debentures of the company. These interests must be disclosed to comply with the Companies Acts.

directors' report An annual report by the directors of a company to its shareholders, which forms part of the company's *accounts required to be filed with the Registrar of Companies under the Companies Act 1985. The information that must be given includes the principal activities of the company, a fair review of the developments and position of the business with likely future developments and any significant post-balance sheet events, details of research and development, significant issues on the sale, purchase, or valuation of assets, recommended dividends, transfers to reserves, names of the directors and their interests in the company during the period, employee consultation policy, creditor payment policy, and any political or charitable gifts made during the period. *See also* MEDIUM-SIZED COMPANY; SMALL COMPANY.

direct placing A *placing of shares in a company direct to investors, without recourse to underwriters to back the deal or to public subscription.

direct quote (reciprocal exchange rate) An exchange rate expressed in terms of the number of units of domestic currency corresponding to one unit of the foreign currency. In EU countries, for example, a direct quote for the US dollar might be €0.63. *Compare* INDIRECT QUOTE.

direct taxation Taxation, the effect of which is intended to be borne by the person or organization that pays it. Economists distinguish between direct taxation and indirect taxation. The former is best illustrated by *income tax, in which the person who receives the income pays the tax and his income is thereby reduced. The latter is illustrated by *value added tax (VAT), in which the tax is paid by traders but the effects are borne by the consumers who buy the trader's goods. In practice these distinctions are rarely clear-cut. Corporation tax is a direct tax but there is evidence that its incidence can be shifted to consumers by higher prices or to employees by lower wages. *Inheritance tax could also be thought of as a direct tax on the deceased, although its incidence falls on the heirs of the estate.

direct write-off method In the USA, the procedure of writing off bad debts as they occur instead of creating a provision for them. Although this practice is unacceptable for financial reporting purposes, as it ignores the matching concept and *prudence concept, it is the only method allowed for tax purposes.

dirham **1.** (DH) The standard monetary unit of Morocco, divided into 100 centimes. **2.** (Dh) The standard monetary unit of the United Arab Emirates, divided into 100 fils. **3.** A Qatari monetary unit, worth 10 dinars and one hundredth of a *riyal. **4.** A Libyan monetary unit, worth one thousandth of a *dinar. **5.** A Kuwaiti monetary unit, worth one tenth of a *dinar.

dirty float A technique for managing the exchange rate in which a government intervenes in the foreign-exchange markets at its own discretion to influence the exchange rate of its own currency. This technique was widely used after the collapse of the Bretton Woods fixed exchange rate system in the early 1970s as governments were unable to agree programmes of explicitly managed floating, but were not prepared to accept fully floating rates.

dirty money *See* BLACK MONEY.

dirty price The price of a bond or other *debt instrument with the addition of the interest that has not yet been paid (*see* ACCRUED INTEREST).

disbursement **1.** A payment by a bank under a facility or other agreement. **2.** A payment made by an agent, often a professional, on behalf of a client.

discharge To release a person from a binding legal obligation by agreement, by the performance of an obligation, or by law. For example, the payment of a debt discharges the debt; similarly, a judicial decision that a contract is frustrated discharges the parties from performing it.

disclaimer A clause in a contract that reduces potential liability. For instance, a liquidator of a company may disclaim its lease to avoid liability for the rent.

discontinuity risk The *risk arising from sudden jumps in the prices of financial obligations.

discount **1.** A deduction from a *bill of exchange when it is purchased before its maturity date. The party that purchases (discounts) the bill pays less than its face value and therefore makes a profit when it matures. The amount of the discount consists of interest calculated at the *bill rate for the length of time that the bill has to run. *See* DISCOUNT MARKET. **2.** A reduction in the price of goods below list price, for buyers who pay cash (**cash discount**), for members of the trade (**trade discount**), for buying in bulk (**bulk** or **quantity discount**), for retailers who advertise a manufacturer's product (**promotional discount**), etc. **3.** The amount by which the market price of a security is below its *par value. A £100 par value loan stock with a market price of £95 is said to be at a 5% discount. **4.** To change a *future value into a *present value.

discount broker *See* BILL BROKER.

discounted cash flow (DCF) A method used in *capital budgeting, *capital expenditure appraisal, and decision appraisal that predicts the future stream of cash flows, both inflows and outflows, over time and discounts them, using a *cost of capital rate or *hurdle rate, to calculate *present values or discounted values in order to determine whether the project or decision is likely to be financially sensible. A number of appraisal approaches use the DCF principle, namely the *net present value, the *internal rate of return, and the *profitability index. Most computer spreadsheet programs now include a DCF appraisal routine.

discounted margin A measure of the excess return of a *floating-rate note relative to a *benchmark rate.

discount factor (present-value factor) A factor that, when multiplied by a particular year's predicted cash flow, brings the cash flow to a *present value. The factor takes into consideration the number of years from the inception of the project and the *hurdle rate that the project is expected to earn before it can be regarded as feasible. The factor is computed using the formula:

discount factor $= 1/(1 + r)^t$,

where r is the hurdle rate required and t is the number of years from project inception.

In practice there is little necessity to compute discount factors when carrying out appraisal calculations as they are readily available in discount tables. Most computer spreadsheet programs now include a *discounted cash flow routine, which also obviates the need for using discount factors.

discount house A company or bank on the *discount market that specializes in discounting *bills of exchange, especially *Treasury bills.

discounting back Reducing a future payment or receipt to its present equivalent by taking account of the interest, which when added to the present equivalent for the relevant number of years would equate to the future payment or receipt. *See also* DISCOUNTED CASH FLOW.

discount market In the UK, the part of the *money market consisting of banks, *discount houses, and *bill brokers. By borrowing money at short notice from commercial banks or discount houses, bill brokers are able to *discount bills of exchange, especially Treasury bills, and make a profit. The loans are secured on unmatured bills.

discount market deposit A short-term deposit made with a *discount house, usually by a *clearing bank, earning a rate of interest known as the **discount market deposit rate**. These deposits provide the discount houses with their main source of funds.

discount rate 1. The *hurdle rate of interest or *cost of capital rate applied to the *discount factors used in a *discounted cash flow appraisal calculation. The discount rate may be based on the cost-of-capital rate adjusted by a risk factor based on the risk characteristics of the proposed investment or decision in order to create a hurdle rate that the project must earn before being worthy of consideration. Alternatively, the discount rate may be the interest rate that the funds used for the project could earn elsewhere. **2.** *See* BILL RATE. **3.** The interest rate charged by the US Federal Reserve Banks when lending to other banks.

discount window A method by which a central bank supplies a banking system with short-term funds, either by purchasing *Treasury bills or by making secured loans. The term arose in the USA when banks with insufficient funds sent a cashier to the counter window of the Federal Reserve Bank to ask for additional money.

discrepancy Any significant difference between the real and expected values of a transaction, the terms of a *letter of credit and the documents presented against it, etc.

discretionary account (DA) An account placed with a stockbroker, securities house, commodity broker or other authorized investment manager in which they are empowered to carry out transactions on this account without referring back for approval to the principal. Principals normally set parameters for their accounts, but with a discretionary account the broker has more discretion, only reporting back on purchases, sales, profits and losses, and the value of the portfolio.

discretionary order 1. An order given to a stockbroker, commodity broker, etc., to buy or sell a stated quantity of specified securities or commodities, leaving the broker discretion to deal at the best price. **2.** A similar order given to a stockbroker in which the sum of money is specified but the broker has discretion as to which security to buy for his client.

discretionary trust 1. A trust in which the shares of each beneficiary are not fixed by the settlor in the trust deed but may be varied at the discretion of some person or persons (often the trustees). In an **exhaustive discretionary trust** all the income arising in any year must be paid out during that year, although no beneficiary has a right to any specific sum. In a **nonexhaustive discretionary trust** (or **accumulation trust**), income may be carried forward to subsequent years and no beneficiary need receive anything. Such trusts are useful when the needs of the beneficiaries are likely to change, for example when they are children. **2.** In the USA, an investment trust in which the managers can decide what investment to make.

dishonour 1. To fail to accept (*see* ACCEPTANCE) a *bill of exchange (**dishonour by non-acceptance**) or to fail to pay a bill of exchange (**dishonour by non-payment**). A dishonoured foreign bill must be protested (*see* PROTEST). **2.** To fail to pay a cheque when the account of the drawer does not have sufficient funds to cover it. When a bank dishonours a cheque it marks it "refer to drawer" and returns it to the payee through his bank. **3.** To fail to honour any other financial obligation.

disinflation A fall in the rate of *inflation.

disintermediation The elimination of financial intermediaries, such as brokers and bankers, from transactions between borrowers and lenders or buyers and sellers in financial markets. Disintermediation has been a consequence of improved technology and *deregulation (*see also* GLOBALIZATION). Disintermediation allows both parties to a financial transaction to reduce costs by eliminating payments of commissions and fees. Disintermediation also often occurs when governments attempt to impose direct controls on the banking system, such as reserve asset ratios and lending ceilings. In response, the market develops new instruments and institutions that are not covered by the direct controls. When these controls are relaxed, funds may return to the normal banking system, i.e. there may be **reintermediation**.

disinvestment The reducing of investment in an activity, asset, or location.

disposable income 1. The income a person has available to spend after payment of taxes, National Insurance contributions, and other deductions, such as pension contributions. **2.** In *national income accounts, the total value of income of individuals and households available for consumer expenditure and savings, after deducting income tax, National Insurance contributions, and remittances overseas.

distributable profits (**distributable reserves**) The profits of a company that are legally available for distribution as *dividends. They consist of a company's accumulated *realized profits after deducting all realized losses, except for any part of these net realized profits that have been previously distributed or capitalized. *Public companies, however, may not distribute profits to such an extent that their net assets are reduced to less than the sum of their called-up capital (*see* SHARE CAPITAL) and their undistributable reserves (*see* CAPITAL RESERVES).

distribution 1. A payment by a company from its *distributable profits, usually by means of a *dividend. **2.** The allocation of goods to consumers by means of wholesalers and retailers. **3.** The division of property and assets according to law, e.g. of a bankrupt person or a deceased person. *See also* QUALIFYING DISTRIBUTION.

distribution to owners In the USA, a payment of a *dividend to shareholders (stockholders).

diversification 1. The spreading of an investment portfolio over a wide range of companies to avoid serious losses if a recession is localized to one sector of the market. **2.** The movement of a manufacturer, trader, etc., into a wider field of products or services.

dividend The distribution of part of the earnings of a company to its shareholders. The dividend is normally expressed as an amount per share on the *par value of the share. Thus a 15% dividend on a £1 share will pay 15p. However, investors are usually more interested in the **dividend yield**, i.e. the dividend expressed as a percentage of the share value; thus if the market value of these £1 shares is now £5, the dividend yield would be $1/5 \times 15\% = 3\%$. The size of the dividend payment is determined by the board of directors of a company, who must decide how much to pay out to shareholders and how much to retain in the business; these amounts may vary from year to year. In the UK it is usual for companies to pay a dividend every six months, the largest portion (the **final dividend**) being announced at the company's AGM together with the annual financial results. A smaller **interim dividend** usually accompanies the interim statement of the company's affairs, six months before the AGM. Dividends are paid by *dividend warrant. In the USA dividends are usually paid quarterly by **dividend check**. *See also* DIVIDEND COVER; YIELD.

Interest payments on *gilt-edged securities are also sometimes called dividends although they are fixed.

dividend check *See* DIVIDEND.

dividend cover The number of times a company's *dividends to ordinary shareholders could be paid out of its *net profits after tax in the same period. For example, a net dividend of £400,000 paid by a company showing a net profit of £1M is said to be covered 2½ times. Dividend cover is a measure of the probability that dividend payments will be sustained (low cover might make it difficult to pay the same level of dividends in a bad year's trading) and of a company's commitment to investment and growth (high cover implies that the company retains its earnings for investment in the business). Negative dividend cover is unusual, and may be a sign that a company is in difficulties although a company may maintain its dividend in spite of temporary problems. In the USA, the dividend cover is expressed as the **pay-out ratio**, the total dividends paid as a percentage of the net profit. *See also* PRICE–DIVIDEND RATIO.

dividend mandate A document in which a shareholder of a company notifies the company to whom dividends are to be paid.

dividend stripping (bond washing) The practice of buying *gilt-edged securities after they have gone ex-dividend (*see* EX-) and selling them cum-dividend just before the next dividend is due. This procedure enables the investor to avoid receiving dividends, which in the UK are taxable as income, and to make a tax-free *capital gain. This activity has mainly been indulged in by high-rate taxpayers but has now become of little interest since the rules regulating the taxation of accrued interest were changed.

dividend waiver A decision by a major shareholder in a company not to take a dividend, usually because the company cannot afford to pay it.

dividend warrant The cheque issued by a company to its shareholders when paying *dividends. It states the tax deducted and the net amount paid. This document must be sent by non-taxpayers to the Inland Revenue when claiming back the tax.

dividend yield The dividend per share divided by the share price.

DJIA Abbreviation for *Dow Jones Industrial Average.

DMFAS Abbreviation for *Debt Management and Financial Analysis System.

dobra (Db) The standard monetary unit of São Tomé e Príncipe, divided into 100 centavos.

documentary bill A *bill of exchange attached to the shipping documents of a parcel of goods. These documents include the bill of lading, insurance policy, dock warrant, invoice, etc.

documentary credit *See* LETTER OF CREDIT.

documentation fee A charge levied by a lender to cover the cost of the documentation involved. *See* FRONT-END FEE.

documents against acceptance (D/A) A method of payment for goods that have been exported in which the exporter sends the shipping documents with a *bill of exchange to a bank or agent at the port of destination. The bank or agent releases the goods when the bill has been accepted by the consignee. *Compare* CASH AGAINST DOCUMENTS.

documents against presentation (D/P) *See* CASH AGAINST DOCUMENTS.

dog *See* BOSTON MATRIX.

dollar The standard monetary unit of American Samoa (US$), Antigua and Barbuda (EC$), Australia ($A), the Bahamas (B$), Barbados (BDS$), Belau (US$), Belize (BZ$), Bermuda (Bd$), the British Virgin Islands (US$), Brunei (B$), Canada (Can$), the Cayman Islands (CI$), Dominica (EC$), East Timor (US$), Ecuador (US$), El Salvador (US$), Fiji (F$), Grenada (EC$), Guam (US$), Guatemala (US$), Guyana (G$), Hong Kong (HK$), Jamaica (J$), Kiribati ($A), Liberia (L$), Malaysia (M$; called a ringgit), the Marshall Islands (US$), Micronesia (US$), Namibia (N$), Nauru ($A), New Zealand ($NZ), Puerto Rico (US$), Saint Kitts and Nevis (EC$), Saint Lucia (EC$), Saint Vincent and the Grenadines (EC$), Singapore (S$), the Solomon Islands (SI$), Taiwan (NT$), Trinidad and Tobago (TT$), Tuvalu ($A), the USA (US$), the Virgin Islands (US$), and Zimbabwe (Z$), in all cases divided into 100 cents.

dollar-cost averaging *See* CONSTANT-DOLLAR PLAN.

dollarization The adoption by a country of the US dollar in place of its own currency, usually as a means of controlling inflation and interest-rate volatility. Partial dollarization is said to occur when a country gives the US dollar equal status to its own currency or pegs its currency one-to-one with the dollar.

dollar pool The fund of dollars and other currencies held to enable UK residents to buy foreign securities, domestic property, etc. It was abolished in 1979 when UK exchange control was abandoned.

dollar stocks US or Canadian securities.

domicile (domicil) 1. The country or place of a person's permanent home, which may differ from that person's nationality or place where they are a *resident. Domicile is determined by both the physical fact of residence and the continued intention of remaining there. For example, a citizen of a foreign country who is resident in the UK is not necessarily domiciled there unless there is a clear intention to make the UK a permanent home. Whether a person is domiciled in the UK may affect their liability to UK taxation. Under the common law, it is domicile and not residence or nationality that determines a person's civil status, including the capacity to marry. A corporation may also have a domicile, which is determined by its place of registration. **2.** In banking, an account is said to be domiciled at a particular branch and the customer treats that branch as his or her main banking contact. Customers may be charged for using other branches as if they were their own. Computer technology, however, now allows customers to use many branches as if their account was domiciled there.

dông (D) The standard monetary unit of Vietnam, divided into 10 hào.

DOT Abbreviation for *designated order turn-around.

double auction An *auction in which bids and offers are competitive. An important example is an open outcry market, in which buyers and sellers shout out the prices at which they are willing to trade. If a buyer and a seller shout out the same price a deal is concluded and subsequently confirmed by written contract.

double bottom In *chartist analysis, the situation in which the prices of a security fall, then rise, then fall again to the same level, producing a 'W' pattern on a graph. This pattern is thought to indicate that the security has much support at the price at the bottom of the W. *Compare* DOUBLE TOP. *See* SUPPORT LEVEL.

double option A combination of a put *option and a call option. It is less flexible, since the put and call cannot be separated.

double taxation Taxation that falls on more than one base, for example on the same source of income in more than one country. Taxation is normally levied on a person's worldwide income in the country of residence but, in addition, most countries also levy a charge on income that arises within that country whether it is from interest or a business. As a result a large number of treaties (**double-taxation agreements**) have been concluded between countries to ensure that their own residents are not doubly taxed. The agreements also attempt to cover fiscal evasion. As a result there are several different kinds of relief from double taxation available: (1) relief by agreement, providing for exemption, in whole or in part, of certain categories of income; (2) credit agreement, in which tax charged in one country is allowed as a credit in the other; (3) deduction agreement, in which the overseas income is reduced by the foreign tax paid on it; (4) if there is no agreement the UK tax authorities will allow the foreign tax paid as a credit up to the amount of the corresponding UK liability. *See* UNILATERAL RELIEF.

double top In technical analysis, a pattern of fluctuation in the price of a security, seen on a *chartist's graph, in which a rise is followed by a fall, then a second rise to the same level. This pattern is thought to indicate that the security is meeting resistance to a move to a higher level. *Compare* DOUBLE BOTTOM. *See also* ASCENDING TOPS; RESISTANCE LEVEL.

Dow Jones Industrial Average (DJIA) An index of security prices issued by Dow Jones & Co. (a US firm providing financial information), used on the New York Stock Exchange. It is a narrowly based index, having 30 constituent companies. The index was founded in 1884, based then on 11 stocks (mostly in railways), but was reorganized in 1928 when it was given the value of 100. Its lowest point was on 2 July 1932, when it reached 41. In 2004 it exceeded 10,000. Dow Jones also publishes other indices, and the DJIA is now just one of a number of US stock price indices.

downside A downward price movement or loss. *Compare* UPSIDE.

downsizing A reduction in the size of an organization, often associated with *process engineering, to save costs and increase the flexibility and adaptability of the organization. In some instances this can be disadvantageous; it has been suggested that an organization can lose its business memory and experience a major decline in its morale if too many of its most experienced staff have taken early retirement or been made redundant as part of a continuing policy of downsizing. *See also* CORPORATE ANOREXIA; RIGHTSIZING.

downstream 1. To borrow funds for use by a subsidiary company at the better rates appropriate to the parent company, which would not have been available to the subsidiary company. *Compare* UPSTREAM. **2.** Denoting the respondent bank (**downstream bank**) in an arrangement with a *correspondent bank. **3.** Denoting a later stage in the production process or value chain.

drachma (Dr) Formerly, the standard monetary unit of Greece, divided into 100 lepta. It was subsumed into the *euro for all purposes except cash transactions in 2001 and abolished in 2002.

draft 1. *See* BANK DRAFT. **2.** Any order in writing to pay a specified sum, e.g. a *bill of exchange. **3.** A preliminary version of a document, before it has been finalized.

dragon bond A foreign *bond issued in the Asian bond markets.

dragon markets A colloquial name for those markets and economies in the Pacific basin that developed rapidly in the 1980s and early 1990s, notably Indonesia, Malaysia, the Philippines, and Thailand. They enjoyed dynamic growth and high savings ratios until 1997, when the region suffered a severe financial and economic crisis.

dram (AMD) The standard monetary unit of Armenia, divided into 100 louma.

drawdown 1. The drawing of funds against a *credit line. *See also* FLEXIBLE DRAWDOWN. **2.** The movement of a customer's funds from one account to another account, which may be in another bank.

drawee 1. The person on whom a *bill of exchange is drawn (i.e. to whom it is addressed). The drawee will accept it (*see* ACCEPTANCE) and pay it on maturity. **2.** The bank on whom a cheque is drawn, i.e. the bank holding the account of the individual or company that wrote it. **3.** The bank named in a *bank draft. *Compare* DRAWER.

drawer 1. A person who signs a *bill of exchange ordering the *drawee to pay the specified sum at the specified time. **2.** A person who signs a cheque ordering the drawee bank to pay a specified sum of money on demand.

drawing rights *See* SPECIAL DRAWING RIGHTS.

drip-feed To fund a new company in stages rather than by making a large capital sum available at the start.

drop-dead fee A fee paid by an individual or company that is bidding for another company to the organization lending the money required to finance the bid. The fee is only paid if the bid fails and the loan is not required. Thus, for the price of the drop-dead fee, the bidder ensures that the interest charges are only incurred if the money is required. It is sometimes called a **termination fee**.

drop lock A bond initially issued with a variable rate of interest which becomes a fixed-rate bond if the index or rate falls below a trigger at a coupon reset date.

DSR Abbreviation for *debt service ratio.

DTB Abbreviation for *Deutsche Terminbörse.

DTCC Abbreviation for *Depository Trust and Clearing Corporation.

dual-capacity system A system of trading on a stock exchange in which the functions of *stockjobber and *stockbroker are carried out by separate firms. In a **single-capacity system** the two functions can be combined by firms known as *market makers. Dual capacity existed on the *London Stock Exchange prior to October 1986 (*see* BIG BANG), since when a single-capacity system has been introduced, bringing London into line with most foreign international stock markets. The major advantage of single capacity is that it cuts down on the costs to the investor, although it can also create more opportunity for unfair dealing (*see* CHINESE WALL).

dual currency bond A bond denominated in one currency that pays interest and/or principal at a fixed rate of exchange in another currency.

due date The date on which a debt is due to be settled, such as the maturity date of a *bill of exchange.

due diligence 1. An internal analysis by a lender, such as a bank, of existing debts owed by a borrower in order to identify or re-evaluate the risk. **2.** An independent analysis of the current financial state and future prospects of a company in anticipation of a major investment of venture capital or a stock-exchange flotation.

duration (modified duration) A measure of the sensitivity of bond prices to changes in yield. *See also* CONVEXITY.

Dutch auction *See* AUCTION.

duty A government-imposed tax on certain goods or services. *See* EXCISE DUTY; IMPORT DUTY.

EAGGF Abbreviation for *European Agricultural Guidance and Guarantee Fund.

E & O Abbreviation for *errors and omissions.

E & OE Abbreviation for errors and omissions excepted. This abbreviation was frequently printed on invoice forms to protect the sender from the consequences of any clerical or accounting errors in the preparation of the invoice. This practice has now, however, largely fallen into disuse.

early bargains *See* AFTER-HOURS TRADING.

EARN Abbreviation for *Euro Area Reference Note.

earned income Income generally acquired by the personal exertion of the taxpayer as distinct from such passive income as dividends from investments. It is often thought by tax theorists that earned income should be taxed at a lower rate than unearned income, since the latter accrues without the expenditure of the taxpayer's time and effort. This has been reflected in different ways in the UK over the years, with such measures as earned-income relief, wife's earned-income relief, and investment-income surcharge. Earned income consists primarily of wages and salaries, business profits, royalties, and some pensions. There are currently no differences in the UK between the rates of taxation for earned and unearned income. *See* INCOME-TAX ALLOWANCES.

earnings before interest and tax *See* EBIT; EBITDA.

earnings per share (eps) The *profit in pence attributable to each *ordinary share in a company, based on the consolidated profit for the period, after tax and after deducting *minority interests and *preference share dividends. This profit figure is divided by the number of equity shares in issue that rank for dividend in respect of the period. The eps may be calculated on a **net basis** or a **nil basis**. Using the net basis, the tax charge includes any unrelieved overseas tax arising from the payment or proposed payment of dividends (*see* OVERSEAS-INCOME TAXATION). The nil basis excludes both these items from the tax charge. The eps should be shown on the face of the *profit and loss account on the net basis, both for the period under review and for the corresponding previous period. The basis of calculating the earnings per share should be disclosed on the face of the profit and loss account or in the notes to the accounts. *See also* FULLY DILUTED EARNINGS PER SHARE.

earnings retained The *profit of a company after the distribution of *dividends; the earnings retained in the business are used to fund future operations.

earnings yield *See* YIELD.

earn-out agreement (contingent contract) An agreement to purchase a company in which the purchaser pays a lump sum at the time of the acquisition, with a promise to pay more (a **contingent consideration**) if certain criteria, usually specified earnings levels, are met for a specified number of years. This method of acquisition has been popular in 'people' businesses, in particular advertising agencies. The agreement provides a means of retaining the previous owners in the business, with a motivation to maintain the company's profitability.

easy money *See* CHEAP MONEY.

e-banking Abbreviation for *electronic banking.

EBIT Abbreviation for earnings before interest and tax, the *profit of a company as shown on the *profit and loss account, before deducting the variables of interest and tax. This figure, which is used in calculating many ratios, enables better comparisons to be made with other companies.

EBITDA Abbreviation for earnings before interest, taxation, depreciation, and amortization. This figure is frequently cited by investment analysts since it represents a *cash-flow vision of shareholders' return.

EBRD Abbreviation for *European Bank for Reconstruction and Development.

EC Abbreviation for European Community. *See* EUROPEAN ECONOMIC COMMUNITY; EUROPEAN UNION.

ECB Abbreviation for *European Central Bank.

ECGD Abbreviation for *Export Credits Guarantee Department.

economic appraisal A method of *capital budgeting that makes use of *discounted cash flow techniques to determine a preferred investment. However, instead of using annual projected cash flows in the analysis, the technique discounts over the project's life the expected annual *economic costs and *economic benefits. It is mainly used in the assessment of governmental or quasi-governmental projects, such as road, railway, and port developments.

economic benefits The projected benefits revealed by an *economic appraisal. Economic benefits are usually gains that can be expressed in financial terms as the result of an improvement in facilities provided by a government, local authority, etc. For example, the economic benefits arising from the construction of a new or improved road might include lower vehicle operating costs, time savings for the road users, and lower accident costs as a result of fewer accidents. In each case the savings would be in economic terms, that is, excluding the effect of taxes and subsidies within the economy. *See also* ECONOMIC COSTS.

economic costs **1.** *See* OPPORTUNITY COST. **2.** The projected costs revealed by an *economic appraisal. Economic costs differ from financial costs in that they exclude the transfer payments within the economy, which arise when an investment is made. In the construction of a road, for example, the economic costs exclude taxes and import duties on the materials and plant used in its construction, while any subsidies made are added back to the costs.

economic environment Factors that affect the buying power and spending patterns of consumers. These factors include income distribution, changes in purchasing power as a result of inflation, the state of the country's economy, etc. While the economic environment can be influenced extensively by government activity, companies need to monitor these changes in order to predict their sales estimates.

economic exposure **1.** The possible impact of macroeconomic variables on the performance of a business. **2.** The exposure of a business selling goods abroad or buying goods from abroad to the risks resulting from changes in exchange rates. *See* EXCHANGE-RATE EXPOSURE.

economic value The *present value of expected future *cash flows. For example, the economic value of a fixed *asset would be the present value of any future revenues it is expected to generate, less the present value of any future costs related to it.

Economic Value Added (EVA) A proprietary measure of the addition to value by a firm's activity in a given time period; it was developed by the economist Stern Stewart III and outlined in his book *The Quest for Value*. The measure is adjusted profits with a deduction for a capital charge.

economies of scale *See* SCALE EFFECT.

economies of scope *See* SCOPE ECONOMIES.

ECP Abbreviation for *euro-commercial paper.

ECU Abbreviation for *European Currency Unit.

EDF Abbreviation for *European Development Fund.

Edge Act A US law, passed in 1919, that first allowed US banks to set up subsidiaries (Edge Act Corporations) to carry out international banking and investment activities.

EDI Abbreviation for *electronic data interchange.

EDSP Abbreviation for Exchange Delivery Settlement Price. *See* SETTLEMENT PRICE.

EEA Abbreviation for *European Economic Area.

EEC Abbreviation for *European Economic Community.

effective annual rate The total interest paid or earned in a year expressed as a percentage of the principal amount at the beginning of the year.

effective exchange rate The effective *rate of exchange between the currencies of trading partners. It is a weighted index in which the weights are based on levels of trade.

effective tax rate The average tax rate that is applicable in a given circumstance. In many cases the actual rate of tax applying to an amount of income or to a gift may not, for various reasons, be the published rate of the tax; these reasons include the necessity to gross up, the complex effects of some reliefs, and peculiarities in scales of rates. The effective rate is therefore found by dividing the additional tax payable as a result of the transaction by the amount of the income, gift, or whatever else is involved in the transaction.

effective yield *See* GROSS REDEMPTION YIELD.

efficient markets hypothesis A central theory of modern finance holding that transactors in financial markets cannot make *abnormal returns on the basis of exploiting information, since market prices incorporate all available information. Eugene Fama defined three categories of market efficiency: *weak-form efficiency, in which only historical information is incorporated into the market prices; *semi-strong-form efficiency, in which all publicly available information, past or present, is incorporated; and *strong-form efficiency, in which all public or private information is incorporated. *See also* ACTIVE MANAGEMENT; ANOMALY.

EFRAG Abbreviation for *European Financial Reporting Advisory Group.

EFTA Abbreviation for *European Free Trade Association.

EFTPOS Abbreviation for *electronic funds transfer at point of sale.

EIB Abbreviation for *European Investment Bank.

Eighth Directive An EU directive on the role of auditors and company financial statements.

EIS Abbreviation for *enterprise investment scheme.

electronic banking The facility to operate a bank account by remote instructions using a computer and telephone line. *See* HOME BANKING.

electronic data interchange (EDI) The use of electronic data-transmission networks to move information. For example, EDI can be used for orders, invoices, and payments to suppliers, customers, banks, etc., without recourse to hard copy. EDI is dependent on users having compatible technology and systems that are transparent to the other members of the network.

electronic funds transfer at point of sale (EFTPOS) The automatic debiting of a purchase price from the customer's bank or credit-card account by a computer link between the checkout till and the bank or credit-card company. The system depends on a customer's plastic card which is 'swiped' through a terminal reader machine at the point of sale. This gives authorization and prints a voucher for the customer to sign. For added security, the transactions may also be ratified by the use of a *personal identification number (PIN). Transfer of funds to the retailer can take place within 48 hours.

electronic transfer of funds (ETF) The transfer of money from one bank account to another by means of computers and communications links. Banks routinely transfer funds between accounts using computers. *See also* ELECTRONIC FUNDS TRANSFER AT POINT OF SALE.

eligibility Criteria that determine which bills the Bank of England will discount, as *lender of last resort. Such bills, known as *eligible paper, include Treasury bills, short-dated gilts, and first-class trade bills.

eligible list A listing of the names of banks entitled to discount acceptances at the Bank of England.

eligible paper **1.** Treasury bills, short-dated gilts, and any first-class security, accepted by a British bank or an accepting house and thus acceptable by the Bank of England for rediscounting, or as security for loans to discount houses. The Bank of England's classification of eligible paper influences portfolios because of the ability to turn them into quick cash, and thus reinforces the Bank's role as *lender of last resort. **2.** Acceptances by US banks available for rediscounting by the *Federal Reserve System.

eligible reserves Cash held in a US bank plus the money held in its name at its local Federal Reserve Bank.

EMA Abbreviation for *European Monetary Agreement.

emalengeni The plural of *lilangeni.

EMCOF Abbreviation for *European Monetary Cooperation Fund.

emerging markets 1. Financial markets in the early stages of development, as in developing countries or former communist countries in Eastern Europe or Asia. **2.** Developing countries showing signs of economic growth.

EMI Abbreviation for *European Monetary Institute.

emoluments Amounts received from an office or employment including all salaries, fees, wages, perquisites, and other profits as well as certain expenses and benefits paid or provided by the employer, which are deemed to be emoluments.

employee buy-out The acquisition of a controlling interest in the equity of a company by its employees. This may occur if the company is threatened with closure and the employees wish to secure their jobs. By obtaining financial backing, the employees acting as a group of individuals, or by means of a trust, can acquire a majority of the shares.

employee participation 1. The encouragement of motivation in a workforce by giving shares in the company to employees. Employee shareholding (*see* EMPLOYEE SHARE OWNERSHIP PLAN) is now an important factor in improving industrial relations. **2.** The appointment to a board of directors of a representative of the employees of a company, to enable the employees to take part in the direction of the company.

Employee Retirement Income Security Act 1974 (ERISA) US legislation setting guidelines for the running of private pension plans and employee profit-sharing schemes. The act also set up an insurance fund, the Pension Benefit Guaranty Corporation, to protect employees' contributions if the scheme failed or ended before its term.

employee share ownership plan (ESOP) A method of giving employees shares in the business for which they work. Various such plans came into existence in the UK after their announcement in 1989; in 1990, in order to encourage their growth, company owners were given *roll-over relief from capital gains tax for sales of shares through ESOPs.

employee share ownership trust (ESOT) A trust set up by a UK company, under the provisions introduced in 1989, to acquire shares in the company and distribute them to the employees. The company's payments to the trust are tax-deductible. The trust deed sets out the specified period of employment and all those employees who fulfil the requirements must be included in the class of beneficiaries of the trust. *See also* EMPLOYEE SHARE OWNERSHIP PLAN.

EMS Abbreviation for *European Monetary System.

EMU Abbreviation for European Monetary Union. *See* EUROPEAN MONETARY SYSTEM.

end-of-day sweep An automatic transfer of funds from one bank account held by a company to another of its bank accounts, usually one that pays interest on deposits. The sweep takes place at the end of every day, or at the end of the day when certain conditions are met.

endorsement (indorsement) 1. A signature on the back of a *bill of exchange or cheque, making it payable to the person who signed it. A bill can be endorsed any number of times, the presumption being that the endorsements were made in the order in which they appear, the last named being the holder to receive payment. If the bill is **blank endorsed**, i.e. no endorsee is named, it is payable to the bearer. In the case of a **restrictive endorsement** of the form "Pay X only", it ceases to be a *negotiable instrument. A **special endorsement**, when the endorsee is specified, becomes payable **to order**, which is short for 'in obedience to the order of'. **2.** A signature required on a document to make it valid in law. **3.** An amendment to an *insurance policy or cover note, recording a change in the conditions of the insurance. **4.** Another term for a guarantee.

endowment assurance An assurance policy that pays a specified amount of money on an agreed date or on the death of the *life assured, whichever is the earlier. As these policies guarantee to make a payment (either to the policyholder or his or her dependants) they offer both life cover and a reasonable investment. A *with-profits policy will also provide bonuses in addition to the sum assured. These policies are often used in the repayment of an *endowment mortgage or as a form of saving.

endowment mortgage A *mortgage in which repayment of the principal is made principally by means of an *endowment assurance policy. In the UK in the 1980s and 1990s, many first-time home buyers were encouraged to take out this form of mortgage (which earns the mortgagor's agent an immediate commission from the life cover provider). However, with the subsequent poor performance of investments on the stock exchange, many endowment mortagees, rather than looking forward to a profit from the life fund once the principal has been repaid, are facing a shortfall in the principal at the end of the mortgage's life. *Compare* REPAYMENT MORTGAGE.

enterprise investment scheme (EIS) An investment scheme in the UK that replaced the business expansion scheme (BES) on 1 January 1994. Relief is available under the scheme when eligible shares in a qualifying company (a company unquoted on a stock exchange that has been trading in qualifying activity for three years) are issued to an individual on subscription. The company issuing the shares must be engaged in the qualifying activity (basically trading rather than investment) and the money raised through the EIS must be used wholly for that purpose. The tax relief available on a qualifying EIS investment is 20% of the amount subscribed. This contrasts with the relief given under the BES, in which a higher-rate taxpayer received full tax relief. *See also* CORPORATE VENTURING SCHEME.

enterprise zone An area, designated as such by the government, in which its aim is to restore private-sector activity by removing certain tax burdens and by relaxing certain statutory controls. Benefits, which are available for a 10-year period, include: exemption from rates on industrial and commercial property; 100% allowances for corporation- and income-tax purposes for capital expenditure on industrial and commercial buildings; exemption from industrial training levies; and a simplified planning regime.

entrepreneur An individual who undertakes (from the French *entreprendre* to undertake) to supply a good or service to the market for profit. The entrepreneur will usually invest capital in the business and take on the risks associated with the investment. In most modern capitalist economies the initiative of entrepreneurs is regarded as an important element in creating a society's wealth; governments are therefore encouraged to establish conditions in which they will thrive.

environmental audit (green audit) An *audit of the impact of the activities of an organization on the environment. Its purpose is usually to ensure that the organization has clear environmental policies, that its operations comply with the stated environmental policies, and that its policies are subject to regular review. Environmental audits may be conducted internally or externally by environmental consultants. Areas covered by a green audit include energy usage, wastage and recycling procedures, conservation of raw materials, and adopting cleaner technologies.

EOE Abbreviation for *European Options Exchange.

eps Abbreviation for *earnings per share.

EPU Abbreviation for *European Payments Union.

equitable interest An interest in, or ownership of, property that is recognized by equity but not by the common law. A beneficiary under a trust has an equitable interest. Any disposal of an equitable interest (e.g. a sale) must be in writing. Some equitable interests in land must be registered or they will be lost if the legal title to the land is sold. Similarly, equitable interests in other property will be lost if the legal title is sold to a bona fide purchaser for value who has no notice of the equitable interest. In such circumstances the owner of the equitable interest may claim damages from the person who sold the legal title.

Equitas An insurance vehicle used to cap long-term liabilities of Lloyd's of London on underwriting losses prior to 1993, notably in relation to regulations in the USA concerning asbestos and pollution.

equities The ordinary shares of a company, especially those of a publicly owned quoted company. In the event of a liquidation, the ordinary shareholders are entitled to share out the asssets remaining after all other creditors (including holders of *preference shares) have been paid out. Investment in equities on a stock exchange represents the best opportunity for capital growth, although there is a high element of risk as only a small proportion (if any) of the investment is secured. Although equities pay relatively low profit-related dividends, unlike *fixed-interest securities, they are popular in times of low interest rates or inflation, as they tend to rise in value as the value of money falls.

equity **1.** A beneficial interest in an asset. For example, a person having a house worth £250,000 with a mortgage of £100,000 may be said to have an equity of £150,000 in the house. **2.** The net assets of a company after all creditors (including the holders of *preference shares) have been paid off. **3.** The amount of money returned to a borrower in a mortgage or hire-purchase agreement, after the sale of the specified asset and the full repayment of the lender of the money. **4.** The ordinary share capital of a company (*see* EQUITIES; EQUITY CAPITAL). **5.** The market value of outstanding shares. **6.** The *risk capital of a company.

equity accounting The practice of showing in a company's accounts a share of the undistributed profits and a share of the net assets of another company in which it holds a share of the *equity (usually a share of between 20% and 50%). The share of profit shown by the equity-holding company is usually equal to its share of the equity in the other company. Although none of the profit may actually be paid over, the company has a right to this share of the undistributed profit.

equity approach to bank valuation The valuation of a bank on the basis of free cash flows to equity holders discounted at the required return on equity.

equity capital **1.** The part of the share capital of a company owned by ordinary shareholders, although for certain purposes, such as *pre-emption rights, other classes of shareholders may be deemed to share in the equity capital and therefore be entitled to share in the profits of the company or any surplus assets on winding up. *See also* A SHARES. **2.** The market value of outstanding shares.

equity dilution A reduction in the percentage of the *equity owned by a shareholder as a result of a new issue of shares in the company, which rank equally with the existing voting shares.

equity dividend cover A ratio that shows how many times the *dividend to ordinary shareholders can be paid out of the profits of a company available for distribution. The higher the cover, the greater the certainty that dividends will be paid in the future.

equity finance Finance raised from shareholders in the form of *ordinary shares and reserves, as opposed to *non-equity shares and to borrowing.

equity gearing *See* GEARING.

equity kicker An option to buy ordinary shares at a preferential rate that is used as a sweetener in high-risk funding deals. *See* KICKER.

equity-linked notes Financial instruments that involve a guarantee of principal and a return based on the performance of a basket of equities.

equity-linked policy An insurance or assurance policy in which a proportion of the premiums paid are invested in equities. The surrender value of the policy is therefore the selling price of the equities purchased; as more premiums are paid the portfolio gets larger. Although investment returns may be considerably better on this type of policy than on a traditional endowment policy, the risk is greater, as the price of equities can fall dramatically reducing the value of the policy. With *unit-linked policies, a much wider range of investments can be achieved and the risk is correspondingly reduced.

equity multiplier The ratio of total bank equity to total assets.

equity share capital The *share capital of a company that consists of its equity shares as opposed to its *non-equity shares.

equity swap A type of *interest-rate swap in which one party's payment is related to a stock index, while the other's is a fixed or floating rate.

equity warrant A tradable call option on the shares of a company. *See* WARRANT.

equivalent bond yield A metric used to compare yields on bonds and money-market instruments with the same maturity.

ERDF Abbreviation for *European Regional Development Fund.

ERISA Abbreviation for *Employee Retirement Income Security Act 1974.

ERM Abbreviation for Exchange Rate Mechanism. *See* EUROPEAN MONETARY SYSTEM.

errors and omissions (E & O) Errors or omissions arising as a result of incorrect records or accounting. Specialist insurance cover can be obtained to guard against the consequences of E & O.

errors and omissions excepted *See* E & OE.

escalation of commitment Increasing the resources available to an unsuccessful venture in the hope of recovering past losses. This is sometimes called a **creeping commitment**. This policy is often adopted in new product development when the company continues to pour in funds, irrespective of the likelihood of success, in an attempt to recover some of its investment. It is known colloquially as throwing good money after bad.

ESCB Abbreviation for European System of Central Banks. *See* EUROPEAN CENTRAL BANK.

escrow A *deed that has been signed and sealed but is delivered on the condition that it will not become operative until some stated event happens. It will become effective as soon as that event occurs and it cannot be revoked in the meantime. Banks often hold escrow accounts, in which funds accumulate to pay taxes, insurance on mortgaged property, etc.

escudo **1.** The standard monetary unit of Cape Verde (CV Esc), divided into 100 centavos. **2.** The former monetary unit of Portugal and Madeira, divided into 100 centavos. It was subsumed into the *euro for all purposes other than cash transactions in 1999 and abolished in 2002.

ESOP Abbreviation for *employee share ownership plan (or, in the USA, employee stock option plan).

ESOT Abbreviation for *employee share ownership trust.

establishment fee A charge levied by a lender to establish a loan. *See* FRONT-END FEE.

estate **1.** The sum total of a person's assets less liabilities (usually as calculated at death for the purposes of *inheritance tax). **2.** A substantial piece of land, usually attached to a large house.

estate duty *See* INHERITANCE TAX.

estoppel **1.** A rule of evidence by which a person is prevented from denying that a certain state of affairs exists, having previously asserted that it does. **2. (promissory estoppel)** The rule that if a person has declared that the strict legal rights under a contract will not be insisted upon, they cannot be insisted upon later if the other party has relied on that declaration. The strict legal rights may, however, be enforced on giving reasonable notice, if this would not be inequitable. **3. (proprietary estoppel)** The rule that if one person allows or encourages another person to act to his or her detriment in respect of land, he or she will not later be able to refuse to grant something that he or she allowed the other person to expect. For example, if A encourages B to build a garage, which can only be reached by driving over A's land, saying that a right of way will be granted, A will not later be able to refuse to do so.

ETF Abbreviation for *electronic transfer of funds.

ethical dilemmas The moral quandaries that can occur in running a business. While not confronting the law, most of these dilemmas arise as a result of conflict between what the businessperson sees as necessary in the interests of the business and his or her personal ethical values. These dilemmas may be related to entrepreneurial activities (Does the product or service offered conflict with one's social responsibility?), to one's behaviour to competitors (Have the claims for the superiority of one's product or service overstepped the limits of fair competition?), to one's shareholders (Are they earning a fair return on their capital?), and most of all, perhaps, to one's customers (Does the product or service offer fair value for money?).

ethical investment (socially responsible investment) An investment made in a company not engaged in an activity that the investor considers to be unethical, such as armaments or tobacco, or an investment in a company of which the investor approves on ethical grounds, e.g. one having a good environmental employment record.

ETL Abbreviation for *expected tail losses.

EU *See* EUROPEAN UNION.

Eurex An electronic derivatives exchange formed by a merger of the *Deutsche Terminbörse and the *Swiss Options and Financial Futures Exchange in 1998. The electronic system on which trading occurs is accessible in 700 locations worldwide.

Euribor Abbreviation for *Euro Inter Bank Offered Rate.

euro The currency unit of the European Monetary Union, divided into 100 cents (*see* EUROPEAN MONETARY SYSTEM). In January 1999 it was adopted for all purposes except cash transactions by Austria, Belgium, Finland, France, Germany, Ireland, Italy, Luxembourg, The Netherlands, Portugal, and Spain; Greece followed suit in 2001. Euro-denominated notes and coins were issued in January 2002 and the national currencies were withdrawn after a short period of dual circulation. The EU countries that adopted the euro have become known collectively as the *eurozone. The euro is also used by Andorra, Bosnia and Hercegovina, French Guiana, Guadeloupe, Kosovo, Madeira, Martinique, Mayotte, Monaco, Montenegro, Réunion, San Marino, and the Vatican City.

Euro Area Reference Note (EARN) A euro-denominated bond first issued by the *European Investment Bank in 1999 to establish a market in euro-denominated securities.

eurobanks Financial intermediaries that deal in the *eurocurrency market.

eurobond A *bond issued in a *eurocurrency, which is now one of the largest markets for raising money (it is much larger than the UK stock exchange). The reason for the popularity of the eurobond market is that *secondary market investors can remain anonymous, usually for the purpose of avoiding tax. For this reason it is difficult to ascertain the exact size and scope of operation of the market. Issues of new eurobonds normally take place in London, largely through syndicates of US and Japanese investment banks; they are *bearer securities, unlike the shares registered in most stock exchanges, and interest payments are free of any *withholding taxes. There are various kinds of eurobonds. An ordinary bond, called a **straight**, is a fixed-interest loan of 3 to 8 years duration; others include **floating-rate notes**, which carry a variable interest rate based on the *London Inter Bank Offered Rate; and perpetuals, which are never redeemed. Some carry *warrants and some are *convertible. Eurobonds in British pounds are referred to as **eurosterling bonds**. *See also* CENTRALE DE LIVRAISON DE VALEURS MOBILIÈRES; EUROCLEAR; NOTE ISSUANCE (OR PURCHASE) FACILITY; SWAP; ZERO-COUPON BOND.

euro certificate of deposit (Euro CD) A *certificate of deposit denominated in a *eurocurrency. London is the main issuing centre.

eurocheque A cheque drawn on a European bank, which can be cashed at any bank or bureau de change in the world that displays the European Union sign (of which there are some 200 000). It can also be used to pay for goods and services in shops, hotels, restaurants, garages, etc., that display the EU sign (over 4 million). The cheques are blank and are made out for any amount as required, usually in euros or the local currency. They have to be used with a **Eurocheque Card**, which guarantees cheques for up to a stated limit. In most cases, a commission of 1.25% is added to the foreign currency value of the cheque before it is converted to sterling and there is a cheque charge (for cheques drawn on UK banks).

Euroclear One of two settlement houses for the clearance of *eurobonds. Based in Brussels, it was set up in 1968 by a number of banks. The other settlement house is *Centrale de Livraison de Valeurs Mobilières.

euro-commercial paper (ECP) *Commercial paper issued in a *eurocurrency, the market for which is centred in London. It provides a quick way of obtaining same-day funds by the issue of unsecured notes, for example in Europe for use in New York.

eurocredit A loan in a *eurocurrency.

eurocurrency A currency held in a country other than its country of origin. For example, dollars deposited in a bank in Switzerland are *eurodollars, yen deposited in Germany are **euroyen**, etc. Eurocurrency is used for lending and borrowing; the **eurocurrency market** often provides a cheap and convenient form of liquidity for the financing of international trade and investment. The main borrowers and lenders are the commercial banks, large companies, and the central banks. By raising funds in eurocurrencies it is possible to secure more favourable terms and rates of interest, and sometimes to avoid domestic regulations and taxation. The deposits and loans were initially on a short-term basis but increasing use is being made of medium-term and long-term loans, particularly through the raising of *eurobonds. This has to some extent replaced the syndicated loan market, in which banks lent money as a group in order to share the risk. *Euromarkets emerged in the 1950s.

eurocurrency market *See* EUROCURRENCY.

eurodeposit A deposit using the currency of another country, i.e. a transaction in the *eurocurrency market.

eurodollars Dollars deposited in financial institutions outside the USA. The eurodollar market evolved in London in the late 1950s when the growing demand for dollars to finance international trade and investment coincided with a greater supply of dollars. The prefix 'euro' indicates the origin of the practice but it now refers to all dollar deposits made anywhere outside the USA. *See also* EUROCURRENCY.

euroequity A capital issue in a country foreign to that of the issuing company and in a different currency to that of the location of the market in which it is traded.

Euro Inter Bank Offered Rate (Euribor) The *Inter Bank Offered Rate for loans denominated in euros.

euromarket 1. A market that emerged in the 1950s for financing international trade. Its principal participants are *commercial banks, large companies, the *central banks of members of the EU, and (from 1999) the European Central Bank. Its main business is in *eurobonds, *euro-commercial paper, *euronotes, and *euroequities issued in *eurocurrencies. The largest euromarket is in London, but there are smaller ones in Paris, Brussels, and Frankfurt. **2.** The European Union, regarded as one large market for goods.

Euronext NV A holding company, set up in September 2000, incorporating the Amsterdam, Brussels, and Paris futures and options exchanges. It acquired the *London International Financial Futures and Options Exchange (LIFFE) and the Bolsa de Valores de Lisboa e Porto in 2002. It provides a market and clearing system for traded derivatives.

euronote A form of *euro-commercial paper consisting of short-term negotiable *bearer *notes. They may be in any currency but are usually in dollars or euros. The **euronote facility** is a form of *note issuance facility set up by a syndicate of banks, which underwrites the notes.

European Agricultural Guidance and Guarantee Fund (EAGGF) A fund set up under the *Common Agricultural Policy to buy produce from farmers in EU member states at pre-arranged minimum prices and to sell when prices have risen. It also provides money for agricultural improvement in the European Union. Criticism of the uses of the fund to create the 'butter mountain' and 'wine lake' of the 1970s led to the imposition of production quotas in the 1980s.

European Bank for Reconstruction and Development (EBRD) An intergovernmental bank set up in April 1991 to finance industrial and commercial projects in the countries of central and Eastern Europe. Membership includes all the countries of the *European Union (EU) and the *Organization for Economic Cooperation and Development, as well as the central and Eastern European countries, the USA, and Japan. The EU provided 51% of the initial capital.

European Central Bank (ECB) A central bank, created under the terms of the *Maastricht Treaty, which was established in 1998 and became fully operational on 1 January 1999. From that date it superseded the *European Monetary Institute and the *European Monetary Cooperation Fund. It is responsible for *eurozone monetary policy and in particular the setting of interest rates. It is independent of national governments but works with the central banks of the individual eurozone countries. It is based in Frankfurt-am-Main, Germany.

European Commission The single executive body formed in 1967 (as the Commission of the European Communities) from the three separate executive bodies of the European Coal and Steel Community, the European Atomic Energy Community, and the *European Economic Community. It now consists of 30 Commissioners: two each from France, Germany, Italy, Spain, and the UK; and one each from Austria, Belgium, Cyprus, the Czech Republic, Denmark, Estonia, Finland, Greece, Hungary, Ireland, Latvia, Lithuania, Luxembourg, Malta, The Netherlands, Poland, Portugal, Slovakia, Slovenia, and Sweden. Under the proposed EU Constitution membership will be reduced to one Commissioner per country, with further reductions planned from 2009. The Commissioners accept joint responsibility for their decisions, which are taken on the basis of a majority vote. The Commission initiates and implements EU legislation and mediates between member governments. The Commissioners are backed by a staff of some 20 000 civil servants.

European Community *See* EUROPEAN ECONOMIC COMMUNITY; EUROPEAN UNION.

European Currency Unit (ECU) A currency medium and unit of account created in 1979 to act as the reserve asset and accounting unit of the *European Monetary System (EMS). The value of the ECU was calculated as a weighted average of a basket of specified amounts of *European Union currencies; its value was reviewed periodically as currencies changed in importance and membership of the EU expanded. Fluctuations in the value of the ECU in terms of the currencies of the member states were controlled by the EMS. The ECU also acted as the unit of account for all EU transactions. ECU reserves were not allocated to individual countries but held in the *European Monetary Cooperation Fund. With the introduction of the *euro in January 1999 the ECU ceased to exist. The initial value of the euro against other currencies was set at one ECU.

European Development Fund (EDF) A fund administered by the European Union; it gives grant aid and makes loans to developing countries for specific infrastructure projects.

European Economic Area (EEA) The organization formed in 1992 between members of the European Community (later the *European Union) and all the members of the *European Free Trade Association (EFTA) except Switzerland. The EEA was intended to come into force in 1993, with the single market of the EU, but owing to Swiss objections, this was delayed until 1994. The EEA is controlled by a committee of EU and EFTA members and meetings of ministers.

European Economic Community (EEC; Common Market) The European common market set up in 1957 by the six member states of the European Coal and Steel Community (ECSC); i.e. Belgium, France, West Germany, Italy, Luxembourg, and The Netherlands. At the same time the European Atomic Energy Community (Euratom) was set up. The European Parliament and the European Court of Justice were formed in accordance with the Treaty of Rome in 1957. The treaty aimed to forge a closer union between the countries of Europe by removing the economic effects of their frontiers. This included the elimination of customs duties and quotas between members, a common trade policy to outside countries, the abolition of restrictions on the movement of people and capital between member states, and a *Common Agricultural Policy. In addition to these trading policies, the treaty envisaged a harmonization of social and economic legislation to enable the Common Market to work (*see also* EUROPEAN INVESTMENT BANK). The **European Community** (EC) was created in 1967, when the controlling bodies of the EEC, ECSC, and Euratom were merged to form the Commission of European Communities (*see* EUROPEAN COMMISSION) and the Council of European Communities. The UK, Ireland, and Denmark joined the EC in 1973, Greece joined in 1979, and Portugal and Spain became members in 1986. In 1992, following implementation of the *Maastricht Treaty, the European Community became the *European Union. *See also* EUROPEAN MONETARY SYSTEM.

European Financial Reporting Advisory Group (EFRAG) A group set up in 2001 to advise whether an International Accounting Standard is suitable for the EU.

European Free Trade Association (EFTA) A trade association formed in 1960 between Austria, Denmark, Norway, Portugal, Sweden, Switzerland, and the UK. Finland, Iceland, and Liechtenstein joined later while the UK, Denmark, Portugal, Austria, Finland, and Sweden left on joining the *European Union (or its earlier forms). EFTA is a looser association than the EU, dealing only with trade barriers rather than generally coordinating economic policy. All tariffs between EFTA and EU countries were abolished finally in 1984. EFTA is governed by a council in which each member has one vote; decisions must normally be unanimous and are binding on all member countries. In 1992 the *European Economic Area (EEA) was formed to facilitate the movement of goods, services, capital, and labour between all EU and EFTA countries with the exception of Switzerland. EFTA has also signed economic cooperation treaties with some former eastern bloc countries.

European Investment Bank (EIB) A bank set up under the Treaty of Rome in 1958 to finance capital-investment projects in the *European Economic Community (EEC). It grants long-term loans to private companies and public institutions for projects that further the aims of the Community. The members of the EIB are the 15 member states of the *European Union, all of whom have subscribed to the Bank's capital. Most of the funds lent by the bank are borrowed on the EU and international capital markets. The bank is non-profitmaking and charges interest at a rate that reflects the rate at which it borrows. Its headquarters are in Luxembourg.

European Monetary Agreement (EMA) An agreement made in 1958 by the then members of the *Organization for European Economic Cooperation (now known as *Organization for Economic Cooperation and Development). The agreement enabled currencies of member states to be bought, sold, and exchanged without restriction and allowed for certain credit funds to be established.

European Monetary Cooperation Fund (EMCOF) A fund organized by the *European Monetary System in which members of the *European Union deposited reserves to provide a pool of resources to stabilize exchange rates and to finance *balance of payments support. In return for depositing 20% of their gold and gross dollar reserves, member states were given access to a wide variety of credit facilities, denominated in ECU, from the fund. It ceased operations with the introduction of the *euro in 1999.

European Monetary Institute (EMI) An organization set up by the Maastricht Treaty in 1991 in order to coordinate the economic and monetary policy of members of the *European Union before the introduction of a single European currency in accordance with the objectives of European Monetary Union (EMU; *see* EUROPEAN MONETARY SYSTEM). The members of the EMI council were the governors of the central banks of the EU countries. It was superseded by the *European Central Bank.

European Monetary System (EMS) A system of exchange-rate stabilization involving the countries of the *European Union, which began operations in 1979. There were two elements: the **Exchange Rate Mechanism** (ERM), under which participating countries committed themselves to maintaining the values of their currencies within agreed limits, and a *balance of payments support mechanism, organized through the *European Monetary Cooperation Fund. The ERM operated by giving each currency a value in ECUs and drawing up a **parity grid** giving exchange values in ECUs for each pair of currencies. In practice, however, the Deutschmark replaced the ECU as the anchor currency. If market rates differed from the agreed parity by more than a permitted percentage (2.25% or 6% depending on the currency), the relevant governments had to take action to correct the disparity. Two currencies, the UK pound and the Italian lira, were forced out of the ERM in 1992 and some of the currencies remaining in it were allowed 15% fluctuations. Although some saw the EMS as no more than a mechanism to facilitate monetary cooperation, the view that its ultimate goal should be **European Monetary Union** (EMU), with a single European currency and a *European Central Bank gained ground in the 1980s and 1990s. The decision to create a single currency was part of the *Maastricht Treaty in 1991, provided that the participants fulfilled certain conditions. In June 1998 11 EU countries – all the then member states except Denmark, Greece, Sweden, and the UK – committed themselves to monetary union. Their currencies were locked together irrevocably and the *European Central Bank was established to direct the single monetary policy essential for EMU. The *euro was launched for all purposes except cash transactions in January 1999. Euro bank notes and coins came into circulation from January 2002 and the national currencies were withdrawn after a short transitional period. A new exchange-rate mechanism, known as ERMII, was established in January 1999 to link the currencies of other EU states to the euro (with fluctuation rates of plus or minus 15% as the basic rule). Its initial members were Denmark and Greece; the latter adopted the euro in 2001. In mid-2004 three of the new accession states – Estonia, Lithuania, and Slovenia –

joined ERMII, with others announcing plans to follow suit in due course. Countries must participate in ERMII for a minimum of two years before adopting the euro.

European Monetary Union (EMU) *See* EUROPEAN MONETARY SYSTEM.

European option *See* OPTION.

European Options Exchange (EOE) A market based in Amsterdam that deals in traded *options. It was established in 1978. In January 1987 it merged with the *Amsterdam Stock Exchange to form the Amsterdam Exchanges.

European Payments Union (EPU) The original arm of the *Organization for European Economic Cooperation (OEEC), formed to look after payments for international trade. In 1958 the EPU was replaced by the *European Monetary Agreement.

European Regional Development Fund (ERDF) A fund set up in 1975 by the European Community to allocate money for specific projects in member states for work on the infrastructure, usually in regions of high unemployment or social deprivation. Each country has a quota and has to undertake works approved by the EU before grant aid is given.

European terms The quotation of foreign-exchange rates in terms of how many units of a currency can be exchanged for one US dollar. *Compare* AMERICAN TERMS.

European Union (EU) The 25 nations that have joined together to form an economic community, with some common monetary, political, and social aspirations. The EU was created in 1993 from the European Community, which itself grew from the European Coal and Steel Community, the European Atomic Energy Community, and the *European Economic Community. The 12 nations of the EU were joined by Austria, Sweden, and Finland in 1995 and by (Greek) Cyprus, the Czech Republic, Estonia, Hungary, Latvia, Lithuania, Malta, Poland, Slovakia, and Slovenia in May 2004. Its executive body is the *European Commission, which was formed in 1967 with the Council of the European Communities. EU policy emerges from a dialogue between the Commission, which initiates and implements the policy, and the Council, which takes the major policy decisions. The European Parliament, formed in 1957, exercises democratic control over policy, and the European Court of Justice imposes the rule of law on the EU, as set out in its various treaties. A draft EU Constitution, which proposes the creation of an EU president and foreign minister, was published in 2004. *See also* SINGLE MARKET.

eurosecurities Financial instruments traded on *euromarkets, notably *euro-commercial paper, *euronotes, *eurobonds, and *euroequities.

eurosterling bond *See* EUROBOND.

Euro-Top Index *See* FINANCIAL TIMES SHARE INDEXES.

Eurotrack 100 Index *See* FINANCIAL TIMES SHARE INDEXES.

Eurotrack 200 Index *See* FINANCIAL TIMES SHARE INDEXES.

eurowarrant A *warrant traded on *euromarkets.

euroyen *See* EUROCURRENCY.

eurozone The 12 member countries of the European Union that have adopted the *euro as their currency, namely Austria, Belgium, Finland, France, Germany, Greece,

Ireland, Italy, Luxembourg, The Netherlands, Portugal, and Spain. *See* EUROPEAN MONETARY SYSTEM.

EVA Abbreviation for *Economic Value Added.

even-par swap A *swap involving two bonds of the same *par value.

event An item of new information that could impact on the prices of financial instruments. *See also* MATERIAL NEWS.

event of default A critical clause in a loan agreement, the breaching of which will make the loan repayable immediately. The breaching of any *covenant clause will be an event of default. Events of default also include failure to pay, failure to perform other duties and obligations, false *representation and warranty, *material adverse change, bankruptcy, and alienation of assets.

event risk The *risk associated with the impact of some unexpected event on market prices.

event study An econometric analysis of the impact of new information on financial markets. A major application is the study of the gains and losses associated with mergers and acquisitions.

evergreen credit (evergreen facility) A *revolving credit facility.

evergreen fund A fund that provides capital for new companies and supports their development for a period with regular injections of capital.

ex- (Latin: without) A prefix used to exclude specified benefits when a security is quoted. A share is described as **ex-dividend** (xd or ex-div) when a potential purchaser will no longer be entitled to receive the company's current dividend, the right to which remains with the vendor. Government stocks go ex-dividend 36 days before the interest payment. Similarly, **ex-rights, ex-scrip, ex-coupon, ex-capitalization** (ex-cap), and **ex-bonus** mean that each of these benefits belongs to the vendor rather than the buyer. **Ex-all** means that all benefits belong to the vendor. **Cum-** (Latin: with) has exactly the opposite sense, meaning that the dividend or other benefits belong to the buyer rather than the seller. The price of a share that has gone ex-dividend will usually fall by the amount of the dividend, while one that is **cum-dividend** will usually rise by this amount. However, in practice market forces usually mean that these falls and rises are often slightly less than expected.

ex-all *See* EX-.

ex-ante Describing a desired or forecast level for a variable. *Compare* EX-POST.

ex-bonus *See* EX-.

ex-capitalization (ex-cap) *See* EX-.

exceptional items Costs or income affecting a company's *profit and loss account that arise from the normal activities of the company but are of exceptional magnitude, either large or small. These should be included but disclosed separately in arriving at the profit or loss on ordinary activities. *Compare* EXTRAORDINARY ITEMS.

excess **1.** An initial sum which the holder of an insurance policy must bear before any claim is met by the insurer. It is most often used in car insurance, e.g. the first £50 of any claim has to be borne by the insured party. **2.** A bank or other financial institution's margin of assets over liabilities. *See also* EXCESS RESERVES. **3.** In the USA, a situation in which a bank has greater reserves with the Federal Reserve than is required. **4.** *See* EXCESS SHARES.

excess reserves Higher reserves than required, held by banks. This usually undesirable state occurs as a result of poor demand for loans or high interest rates. Banks often sell excess reserves to one another.

excess return Return above a particular benchmark, which may be the *risk-free rate, the *expected return, or some other level of return. *See also* ABNORMAL RETURNS.

excess shares Shares not taken up by other shareholders in a *rights issue, for which an invitation to purchase is sent to shareholders with their standard letters of *allotment.

exchange 1. The trading of goods, stocks, shares, commodities, paper currencies, or other financial instruments. **2.** The place in which such trading occurs, e.g. a stock exchange or commodities exchange. This may not necessarily have a physical location. **3.** A feature of securities that allows the nature of the obligations to be changed. **4.** An agreement to swap, as in *exchange of contracts.

exchange control Restrictions on the purchase and sale of foreign exchange. It is operated in various forms by many countries, in particular those who experience shortages of *hard currencies; sometimes different regulations apply to transactions that would come under the capital account of the *balance of payments. There has been a gradual movement towards dismantling exchange controls by many countries in recent years. The UK abolished all form of exchange control in 1979.

Exchange Delivery Settlement Price (EDSP) *See* SETTLEMENT PRICE.

exchange equalization account An account set up in 1932 and managed by the Bank of England on behalf of the government. It contains the official gold and foreign-exchange reserves (including *Special Drawing Rights) of the UK and is used to manage the value of sterling. Although all *exchange controls were abolished in 1979, the Bank of England still makes use of this account to help to stabilize rates of exchange.

exchange for physical 1. Exchanging a *futures contract in a currency or commodity for an immediate (spot) delivery of that currency or commodity. This can occur if the holder of the futures contract needs the currency or commodity before the futures contract calls for delivery, or if market differentials make the exchange profitable. **2.** In cash-settled contracts, an agreement between parties to deliver the *underlying.

exchange of contracts A procedure adopted in the sale and purchase of land in which both parties sign their copies of the contract, having satisfied themselves as to the state of the property, etc., and agreed that they wish to be bound. There need be no physical exchange of documents; the parties or their advisers can exchange contracts by agreeing to do so orally (for example, by telephone). From that moment the contract is binding and can normally be enforced by specific performance. Contracts for the sale of land must be in writing.

exchange offer A proposal to debt or equity holders that they should exchange their existing securities for new securities, the terms of which are usually less favourable. It is a mechanism for capital restructuring in situations of *financial distress.

exchange option 1. An *option that allows the holder to exchange one *underlying for another. **2.** *See* EXCHANGE-TRADED OPTION.

exchange rate *See* RATE OF EXCHANGE.

exchange-rate exposure (currency risk; exchange-rate risk; foreign-exchange rate risk) The *risk associated with uncertain exchange rates. The three types of risk are *transaction exposure, *translation exposure, and *economic exposure.

Exchange Rate Mechanism (ERM) *See* EUROPEAN MONETARY SYSTEM.

exchange-rate regimes The *rate of exchange between currencies can be managed in a variety of ways:
Single currency peg – one country's currency is linked to that of another country, with little opportunity for adjustment.
Composite currency peg – one country's currency is linked to a *basket of currencies of its major trading partners. Often a *weighted average is used.
Managed float – this is effectively a single currency peg with more frequent adjustments to the rate permitted.
Independent float – rates of exchange are determined only by market forces.

exchange-rate risk *See* EXCHANGE-RATE EXPOSURE.

exchange-rate spread The difference between the buying and selling rates of exchange of a currency.

exchange-traded Denoting a financial instrument traded on an institutional market.

exchange-traded option (exchange option; listed option) An option traded on one of the institutional markets, such as the *London International Financial Futures and Options Exchange or the *Chicago Board Options Exchange; such options have standard terms and conditions.

exchequer The account held by the *Bank of England for all government funds.

Exchequer stocks *See* GILT-EDGED SECURITY.

excise duty A duty or tax levied on certain goods consumed within a country, such as alcoholic drinks and tobacco products, unlike customs duty, which is levied on imports. In the UK, both excise and customs duties are collected by the *Board of Customs and Excise.

ex-coupon *See* EX-.

ex-dividend *See* EX-.

execution 1. The carrying out of a contract or other obligation. **2.** The final act required to make a document valid. For example, a *deed is executed when it is signed, sealed, and delivered.

execution only A dealing service provided by a broker, e.g. a stockbroker or commodity broker, in which the broker has no responsibility for advising the client on the wisdom of carrying out a particular transaction. The broker's responsibility is limited to executing the transaction on the client's instructions.

execution risk The *risk that a transaction cannot be carried out at the current market price.

executive director (working director) A *director of a company who is also an employee (usually full-time) of that company. An executive director will often have a specified role in the management of the company, such as finance director, marketing director, production director, etc. A **non-executive director** is a member of the board of directors and is therefore involved in planning and policy-making, but not in the day-to-day management of the company. A non-executive director is often employed for prestige (if he is well known), for his experience or contacts, or for his specialist knowledge, which may only be required occasionally.

executive share option scheme An approved share option scheme that entitles a specified class of directors or employees to purchase shares in the company in which they are employed. Strict conditions need to be met in order to receive Inland Revenue approval for such a scheme. Once achieved there are no income tax charges on the grant or exercise of the option or on the growth in value of the shares. The only charge will be to *capital gains tax when the shares are sold.

executor A person named in a will of another person to gather in the assets of that person's estate, paying any outstanding liabilities and distributing any residue to the beneficiaries in accordance with the instructions contained in the will.

exempt gilts In the UK, government *gilt-edged securities that pay interest gross, unlike ordinary gilts, on which tax is deducted from interest payments. These gilts are of particular interest to foreign buyers and others, such as institutions, who do not pay income tax.

exempt securities In the USA, securities that do not require registration under the US *Securities Exchange Act 1934.

exempt supplies Supplies of goods or services in the categories of items that are identified as exempt from *value added tax, as given in the Value Added Tax Act 1994. The main categories are: land (including rent), financial services, postal services, betting, charities (except on their business activities), education (non-profitmaking), health services, burial and cremation.

exempt transfers Transfers resulting in no liability to *inheritance tax. These are:
• the first £3000 transferred in any tax year,
• gifts to a spouse,
• normal expenditure out of income,
• small gifts, up to £250, to any number of individuals,
• marriage gifts, up to £5000 for each parent of the parties to the marriage and up to £2500 for each grandparent but limited to £1000 for other gifts in consideration of marriage,
• gifts to charities,
• gifts for national purposes,
• gifts for public benefit,
• gifts to political parties,
• certain transfers to employee trusts.
See also POTENTIALLY EXEMPT TRANSFER.

exempt unit trust A *unit trust in which only institutional investors who are not subject to taxation are allowed to invest, i.e. it is restricted to charities and pension funds.

exercise To make use of the right to carry out a transaction on previously agreed terms, mainly in the *options market.

exercise date The date on which the holder of an *option can exercise the right to implement the option contract. It is normally after three, six, or nine months.

exercise limit A limit imposed by *exchange-traded options markets on the number of options that one party can exercise in a given period.

exercise notice Formal notification from the owner of an *option to the person or the firm that has written it that the owner wishes to exercise the option to buy (for a call option) or sell (for a put option) at the *exercise price on the *exercise date.

exercise premium The difference between the current market price and the *exercise price of an *equity warrant.

exercise price (strike price; striking price) The price per share at which a traded *option entitles the owner to buy the *underlying in a call option or to sell it in a put option. *See also* EXERCISE NOTICE.

ex gratia (Latin: as of grace) Denoting a payment made out of gratitude, moral obligation, kindness, etc., rather than to fulfil a legal obligation. When an ex gratia payment is made, no legal liability is admitted by the payer.

ex growth (of a share or a company) Having had substantial growth in the past but now not holding out prospects for immediate growth of earnings or value.

exhaust price The price at which a broker will close out a trading position unless his or her client provides additional *margin. *See* MARGIN CALL.

Eximbank *See* EXPORT-IMPORT BANK.

exit 1. The way in which a trader closes out a position. **2.** The way in which a venture capitalist closes out a gain.

exit bond A type of *bond created in the rescheduling of the debts of less-developed countries (LDCs) to enable lenders to reduce their exposure.

exit charge The charge to *inheritance tax made when an asset is taken out of a *discretionary trust. The inheritance tax liability is calculated by taking the rate of inheritance tax charged at the most recent ten-year charge before the asset leaves the trust and applying the fraction:

number of completed quarters since the ten-year charge/40.

exit value The *net realizable value of an asset, i.e. its market price at the date of a balance sheet less the selling expenses. Exit values are effectively *break-up values and are not consistent with the *going-concern concept, which assumes that a business is continuing to trade.

ex-new Describing a share that is offered for sale without the right to take up any *scrip issue or *rights issue. *Compare* CUM-NEW.

exotic options (exotics) Options that have unusual features, particularly in relation to their *exercise price, payoff formula, or *underlying. Examples include *Asian options, *binary options, and *exploding options.

expectations hypothesis In the forecasting of interest and exchange rates, the assumption that the forward rate is determined by expectation of the future spot rate. *See* SPOT CURRENCY MARKET.

expected credit loss The *expected value of the losses associated with a particular class of loan or counterparty. It is used as a key variable for pricing credit-related transactions.

expected return The *expected value of returns in relation to an investment or portfolio.

expected tail losses (ETL) The level of losses that will, on average, be suffered in extreme cases, where the level of losses exceeds the cut-off value used to define the *value-at-risk. It is perceived to be a more reliable calculation of risk than the value-at-risk.

expected value A statistical measure of central tendency analogous to the average. It is the sum of the possible values that a random variable can take multiplied by the probabilities of the possible values.

expected volatility An estimate of the future *standard deviation of the value of a particular financial variable. It is important in the valuation of options, since the higher the volatility of the security or commodity underlying an option, the greater the market price of the option.

expenditure tax (outlay tax) A tax on the expenditure of individuals or households. This form of taxation, of which VAT is an example, is often preferred by tax theorists to income taxes, as it does not distort the incentive to work.

expense account 1. An account, opened in either the cost ledger or the nominal ledger, for each expenditure heading in which the costs of an organization are recorded before being totalled and transferred to the *profit and loss account at the end of an accounting period. **2.** The amount of money that certain staff members are allowed to spend on personal expenses in carrying out their activities for an organization.

expiration cycle (expiry cycle) The temporal pattern of expiry dates for *exchange-traded options and futures.

expiry date 1. The date on which a contract expires. **2.** The last day on which an *option expires. In a European option the option must be taken up or allowed to lapse on this date. In an American option the decision can be taken at any time up to the expiry date.

exploding option An *exotic option in which exercise is automatic if the price of the *underlying reaches the *exercise price.

exponential smoothing An econometric technique in which greater weight is accorded to more recent data in order to identify emerging trends.

Export Credits Guarantee Department (ECGD) A UK government department, responsible to the President of the Board of Trade, that operates under the Export and Investment Guarantees Act 1991. It encourages exports from the UK by making export credit insurance available to exporters and guaranteeing repayment to UK banks that provide finance for exports on credit terms of two years or more. It also insures British private investment overseas against war risk, expropriation, and restrictions on the making of remittances. Some sections of the ECGD were privatized in 1991, including short-term credit insurance.

Export–Import Bank (Eximbank) A US bank established by the US government to foster trade with the USA. It provides export credit guarantees and guarantees loans made by commercial banks to US exporters.

Export–Import Bank of Japan A Japanese bank that funds export credits from a variety of sources, including foreign-exchange loans from commercial banks.

ex-post Describing the outcome value of a variable, which may be different from its *ex-ante level.

exposure The degree of *risk involved in holding a particular trading *position.

expropriation The confiscation of property by government, seen as a risk of certain types of overseas investment. *See* CONFISCATION RISK.

ex-rights *See* EX-; EX-NEW.

ex-scrip *See* EX-; EX-NEW.

extendible bond issue A *bond, the maturity of which can be extended at the option of all the parties.

extendible swap A *swap in which the conditions permit one of the parties to extend the term of the agreement for an agreed time period.

extension risk The *risk associated with an agreement that permits one of the partners to extend its term, so that payments take place later than expected. It is the opposite of *prepayment risk.

external account 1. Another term for the *balance of payments. **2.** A UK bank account held by a customer who is an overseas resident.

external audit An *audit of an organization carried out by an *auditor who is external to, and independent of, the organization. An example would be a *statutory audit carried out on behalf of the shareholders of a limited company. *Compare* INTERNAL AUDIT.

external bond Any *bond denominated in a foreign currency.

external debt (foreign debt) 1. The financial commitments of a company in a foreign country or countries. **2.** The commitments of one government to other governments, banks or to other financial institutions abroad. This is usually expressed in US dollars.

external funds Funds obtained by an organization from an outside source (e.g. by borrowing from a bank).

external growth The means by which a business can grow by merger, takeover, or joint ventures, rather than by growing organically through its own internal development (*see* BUSINESS STRATEGY). External growth is widely used by companies as it can offer greater speed in achieving its corporate objectives than internal development. Typically firms can increase their market share by merging with or taking over a competitor in the same field (horizontal diversification). In mature or declining markets, restructuring of combined operations can lead to cost savings. Alternatively, a company may seek to gain greater control of its supply chain by expanding through merging or taking over a supplier or distributor (vertical integration). Unrelated external expansion may take place when a firm buys into a market in which it has no existing expertise; often the time taken to develop a significant presence on its own account is considered to be too long and risky, compared to buying an established business. Although great benefits may accrue from external growth, it also carries high risks, since the expected gains may often be slow to appear as a result of the restructuring and organizational changes involved as well as the high costs of financing the merger or takeover. Joint ventures, often between rival firms, sometimes between companies from different countries, are becoming a more common form of external growth. In such cases, the parties bring complementary strengths (technology, operations, marketing) and share the risks of the venture, although differences in company and country culture may cause difficulties.

externality A cost or benefit to an economic agent that is not matched by a compensating financial flow. Because externalities give rise to *market failure, they are a principal reason for legal or regulatory intervention, notably in banking.

external member A person (name) investing in *Lloyd's but having no control over the day-to-day activities of the *underwriters.

extraordinary items Costs or income affecting a company's *profit and loss account that do not derive from the ordinary activities of the company and, if undisclosed, would distort the normal trend of profits. They should also be not expected to recur. This requirement and a wider definition of ordinary activities were introduced by Financial Reporting Standard (FRS) 3 'Reporting Financial Performance', with the result that virtually all previously extraordinary items are now treated as *exceptional items.

extraordinary resolution A resolution submitted to a general meeting of a company; 14 days' notice of such a resolution is required, and the notice should state that it is an extraordinary resolution. 75% of those voting must approve the resolution for it to be passed.

extreme value theory In statistical analysis, a theory relating to the occurrence of unlikely events. It has become a key element in the analysis of financial risks, which are often in the extreme *tails of distributions.

eyrir (*plural* **aurar**) A monetary unit of Iceland worth one hundredth of a *króna.

face value **1.** The nominal value (*see* NOMINAL PRICE) printed on the face of a security. This is known also as the *par value. It may be more or less than the market value. **2.** The value printed on a banknote or coin.

facility **1.** An agreement between a bank and a company that grants the company a line of credit with the bank. This can either be a *committed facility or an *uncommitted facility. **2.** An agreement between an issuer of short-term securities and underwriters who commit to buy a security.

factoring The buying of the trade debts of a manufacturer, assuming the task of debt collection and accepting the credit risk, thus providing the manufacturer with working capital. A firm that engages in factoring is called a **factor**. **With service factoring** involves collecting the debts, assuming the credit risk, and passing on the funds as they are paid by the buyer. **With service plus finance factoring** involves paying the manufacturer up to 90% of the invoice value immediately after delivery of the goods, with the balance paid after the money has been collected. This form of factoring is clearly more expensive than with service factoring. In either case the factor, which may be a bank or finance house, has the right to select its debtors.

factor model A model for calculating security returns that analyses their sources in terms of a number of different factors. It is used most notably in *arbitrage pricing theory.

facultative reinsurance A form of *reinsurance in which the terms, conditions, and reinsurance premium are individually negotiated between the insurer and the reinsurer. There is no obligation on the reinsurer to accept the risk or on the insurer to reinsure it if it is not considered necessary. The main differences between facultative reinsurance and *coinsurance is that the policyholder has no indication that reinsurance has been arranged. In coinsurance, the coinsurers and the proportion of the risk they are covering are shown on the policy schedule. Also, coinsurance involves the splitting of the premium charged to the policyholder between the coinsurers, whereas the reinsurers charge entirely separate reinsurance premiums.

fair game An uncertain situation in which the differences between expected and actual outcomes show no systematic relations. This is one of the key characteristics that define an efficient market. *See* EFFICIENT MARKETS HYPOTHESIS.

fair market value (fair value) **1.** The amount of money that a seller will accept in exchange for an asset and that a buyer is willing to pay, it being assumed that both are rational and in possession of sufficiently reliable information. **2.** The value of a *derivative as deduced from an appropriate pricing model.

fair presentation In the USA, the requirement that financial statements should not be misleading.

fair value *See* FAIR MARKET VALUE.

fair-weather trading Trading by transactors who will offer to buy and sell only when the market conditions are favourable.

fall-back rate A rate of interest that can be used if the *reference rate for a contract is unavailable.

fallen angel 1. An institution whose creditworthiness has declined considerably. **2.** A security in the US market that has dropped below its original value; it may be sold for its increased *yield.

false market An inefficient market in which the transactors are not all in possession of sufficiently reliable information.

Fannie Mae Colloquial name in the USA for the *Federal National Mortgage Association (FNMA).

FAPA Abbreviation for Fellow of the Association of Authorized Public Accountants.

FARC Abbreviation for *Federal Agricultural Rural Corporation.

Farmer Mac Colloquial name in the USA for the *Federal Agricultural Rural Corporation.

Farmers Home Administration (FMHA) An agency established by the US Department of Agriculture to provide a variety of credit facilities, including residential mortgages and operating loans, to farmers.

farther out/in Describing the relative expiry dates of options.

FASAC Abbreviation for *Financial Accounting Standards Advisory Council.

FASB Abbreviation for *Financial Advisory Standards Board.

fate Whether or not a cheque or bill has been paid or dishonoured. A bank requested by another bank to *advise fate of a cheque or bill is being asked if it has been paid or not.

FATFML Abbreviation for *Financial Action Task force on Money Laundering.

fat tails In the statistical analysis of probability, a set of risky outcomes in which extreme events are more likely than would be expected if the outcomes in relation to risk could be described by a *normal distribution. *See* TAIL.

FCA Abbreviation for Fellow of the *Institute of Chartered Accountants.

FCCA Abbreviation for Fellow of the Chartered Association of Certified Accountants. *See* CERTIFIED ACCOUNTANT; CHARTERED ACCOUNTANT.

FCIA Abbreviation for *Foreign Credit Insurance Association.

FCII Abbreviation for Fellow of the *Chartered Insurance Institute.

FCT Abbreviation for Fellow of the *Association of Corporate Treasurers.

FDI Abbreviation for *foreign direct investment.

FDIC Abbreviation for *Federal Deposit Insurance Corporation.

FECDBA Abbreviation for the *Foreign Exchange and Currency Deposit Brokers' Association.

Fed Abbreviation for the *Federal Reserve System or the Federal Reserve Board.

federal agencies Institutions founded by the US federal government, which de facto guarantees their debt. The institutions are responsible for providing different types of credit. The key institutions are: *Export–Import Bank; *Farmers Home Administration; *Federal Home Loan Bank System; *Federal Home Loan Mortgage Corporation (Freddie Mac); *Federal National Mortgage Association (Fannie Mae); and *Government National Mortgage Association (Ginnie Mae).

Federal Agricultural Rural Corporation (FARC) A US federal agency set up in 1988 to guarantee farm loans. It is often referred to as **Farmer Mac**.

Federal Deposit Insurance Corporation (FDIC) A corporation that provides *deposit insurance for US banks through the Bank Insurance Fund. It operates throughout the *Federal Reserve System and also for other banks outside it (see STATE BANKS).

federal funds rate The highly volatile and sensitive interest rate charged between member banks of the *Federal Reserve System. As the overnight rate paid on federal funds, it is a key indicator of money-market interest rates. Every transaction can alter the level at which the rate is fixed.

Federal Home Loan Bank System A US federal institution that regulates *savings and loan associations. There are also 12 banks that extend credit to savings and loan institutions.

Federal Home Loan Mortgage Corporation (FHLMC) A corporation established in the USA in 1970 to buy mortgages from *savings and loan associations in order to resell them in the secondary market packaged as securities. The stock of the corporation is held by the *Federal Home Loan Bank System, the regulatory body for the savings and loans associations established in the 1930s to provide reserves for the mortgage lending institutions. The FHLMC is usually referred to in market reports as **Freddie Mac**.

Federal National Mortgage Association (FNMA) A government sponsored privately owned quoted company formed in the USA to trade in *mortgages, guaranteed by the Federal Housing Finance Board (see FEDERAL HOME LOAN BANK SYSTEM). It is the largest source of housing finance in the USA. FNMA is often referred to in market reports as **Fannie Mae**.

Federal Open Market Committee (FOMC) The policy committee of the *Federal Reserve System, which sets the level of money and credit in the US banking system. Its members, the governors of the Federal Reserve Board and the presidents of the 12 *Federal Reserve Banks (seven of whom cannot vote on policy), meet monthly and regulate the money supply by instructing the federal banks to buy or sell securities.

Federal Reserve Bank Any of the 12 banks that together form the *Federal Reserve System in the USA; they are situated in Boston, New York, Philadelphia, Cleveland, Richmond, Atlanta, Chicago, St Louis, Minneapolis, Kansas City, Dallas, and San Francisco. They provide *central bank services and are involved with the Federal Reserve Board of Governors in developing and enacting monetary policy, as well as regulating local commercial and savings banks. Each Federal Reserve Bank is owned by the local banks in its district.

federal reserve float Fictitious money created when a *Federal Reserve Bank credits an account in another bank with the value of a cheque before it has collected payment from the paying bank. A float is not created when the transaction involves a paying bank in the same city as the Federal Reserve Bank. Processing and transport delays cause the creation of most floats.

Federal Reserve System (Fed) The organization, consisting of the 12 *Federal Reserve Banks, that functions as the *central bank of the USA. Created by the Federal Reserve Act 1913, the system controls monetary policy, regulates the cost of money and the money supply to local banks, and supervises international banking by means of its agreement with the central banks of other countries. The system is administered centrally by the **Federal Reserve Board**, based in Washington DC.

Fédération Internationale des Bourses de Valeurs (FIBV) A world federation of stock exchanges, formed in 1961 by a number of stock markets as a means of exchanging information and opinions.

Fed funds (Federal funds) Non-interest-bearing deposits held at the US *Federal Reserve System that are traded between member banks.

fedwire A high-speed electronic link in the USA between the 12 *Federal Reserve Banks and the Treasury, used to move large sums of money for themselves and their customers. The transactions are often completed within minutes of being initiated.

fen A monetary unit of China worth one hundredth of a *yuan.

FHLMC Abbreviation for *Federal Home Loan Mortgage Corporation.

FIA Abbreviation for Fellow of the *Institute of Actuaries.

fiat money Money that a government has declared to be legal tender, although it has no intrinsic value and is not backed by reserves. Most of the world's paper money is now fiat money.

FIBV Abbreviation for *Fédération Internationale des Bourses de Valeurs.

fictitious asset An asset, usually as shown in a balance sheet, that does not exist. The reasons for showing it may be fraudulent, the asset may have ceased to exist but has not been taken out of the accounts, or it may be an asset, such as goodwill, that no longer has any value. *Compare* INTANGIBLE ASSET.

fidelity guarantee An insurance policy covering employers for any financial losses they may sustain as a result of the dishonesty of employees. Policies can be arranged to cover all employees or specific named persons. Because of the nature of the cover, insurers require full details of the procedure adopted by the organization in recruiting and vetting new employees and they usually reserve the right to refuse to cover a particular person without giving a reason.

fiduciary Denoting a person who holds property in trust or as an executor. Persons acting in a fiduciary capacity do so not for their own profit but to safeguard the interests of some other person or persons.

fiduciary deposit Funds deposited in a bank and managed for the benefit of the depositor by the bank.

fiduciary issue Banknotes issued by a central bank without backing in gold, the value of the issues relying entirely on the reputation of the issuing bank.

fiduciary loan A loan that is made on trust, rather than against some security.

fiduciary risk The *risk of loss arising from actions undertaken on behalf of clients.

FIFO Abbreviation for *first in, first out.

fill and kill Denoting a situation in which a client's order to a broker is either executed ('filled') immediately or not at all.

fillér A monetary unit of Hungary worth one hundredth of a *forint.

fils 1. A monetary unit of the United Arab Emirates, worth one hundredth of a *dirham. **2.** A monetary unit of Bahrain, Iraq, Jordan, and Kuwait, worth one thousandth of a *dinar. **3.** A monetary unit of Yemen, worth one hundredth of a *riyal.

filter (filter rule) Any rule or set of rules regulating when to buy and sell securities.

FIMBRA Abbreviation for *Financial Intermediaries, Managers and Brokers Regulatory Association Ltd.

final accounts The accounts for a company produced at the end of its financial year (*see* ANNUAL ACCOUNTS), as opposed to any **interim accounts** produced during the year, often after six months. Interim accounts are for the guidance of management and are often not audited, whereas final accounts must be audited and are open for inspection by the public.

final dividend *See* DIVIDEND.

final salary scheme An occupational pension scheme in which payments are determined by the employee's final salary. *See* DEFINED-BENEFIT PENSION SCHEME.

final trading day The last day for trading a financial obligation with a specified expiry or delivery date.

finance 1. The practice of manipulating and managing money. **2.** The capital involved in a project, especially the capital that has to be raised to start a new business. **3.** A loan of money for a particular purpose, especially by a *finance house. **4.** An academic discipline within the general field of economics dealing with funding, financial markets, and the funding implications for managing businesses.

Finance Act The annual UK Act of Parliament that changes the law relating to taxation, giving the rates of income tax, corporation tax, etc., proposed in the preceding *Budget.

Finance and Leasing Association (FLA) A trade association of *finance houses formed in 1992, which incorporates the former *Finance Houses Association. It negotiates with the government and the *European Commission on acceptable terms and conditions for *hire purchase and other forms of asset finance. Its members control the majority of asset finance in the UK.

finance bill A *bill of exchange used for short-term credit. It cannot be sold on to another party in the same way as a *banker's acceptance.

finance house An organization, many of which are owned by *commercial banks, that provides finance for *hire-purchase or *leasing agreements. A consumer, who buys an expensive item (such as a car) from a trader and does not wish to pay cash, enters into a hire-purchase contract with the finance house, who collects the deposit and instalments. The finance house pays the trader the cash price in full, borrowing from the commercial banks in order to do so. The finance house's profit is the difference between the low rate of interest it pays to the commercial banks to borrow and the high rate it charges the consumer. Most finance houses are members of the *Finance Houses Association.

finance-house base rate The rate of interest charged by a *finance house for *hire purchase, *leasing, and other borrowings. It is based on the *London Inter Bank Offered Rate plus a margin.

finance-house deposit A deposit by a major lender, such as a bank, with a *finance house.

Finance Houses Association A former UK organization of *finance houses, set up in 1945 to regulate the trade of hire purchase and to negotiate with the government on acceptable terms and conditions. Its members controlled most UK hire-purchase agreements. The Finance Houses Association was incorporated into the *Finance and Leasing Association in 1992.

finance lease A lease in which the lessee acquires all the financial benefits and risks attaching to ownership of whatever is being leased. In accounting, it is as if the business owned the assets. *Compare* OPERATING LEASE.

finance vehicle 1. A business set up by a company to obtain some financial benefit. The setting up of overseas companies to lower tax liabilities is a prime example of a finance vehicle. **2.** An amalgam of financial products to produce a sophisticated payoff structure.

financial accounting The branch of accounting concerned with classifying, measuring, and recording the transactions of a business. At the end of a period, usually a year but sometimes less, a *profit and loss account, a *balance sheet and statement of true recognized gains and losses, and a cash-flow statement are prepared to show the performance and position of the business. Financial accounting is primarily concerned with providing a *true and fair view of the activities of a business to parties external to it. To ensure that this is done correctly considerable attention will be paid to *accounting concepts and to any requirements of legislation, accounting standards, and (where appropriate) the regulations of the *stock exchange. Financial accounting can be separated into a number of specific activities, such as conducting *audits, *taxation, book-keeping, and *insolvency. **Financial accountants** need not be qualified, in that they need not belong to an accountancy body, although the majority of those working in public practice will be. *Compare* MANAGEMENT ACCOUNTING.

Financial Accounting Standards Advisory Council (FASAC) In the USA, a council that advises the *Financial Accounting Standards Board as to its agenda and accounting standards.

Financial Accounting Standards Board (FASB) The US body that sets accounting standards. Owing to its close relationship with the *Securities and Exchange Commission, companies that wish for a market listing have to comply with its standards.

Financial Action Task Force on Money Laundering (FATFML) An organization founded in 1989 by the *Organization for Economic Cooperation and Development to curtail the practice of *laundering money, chiefly by persuading individual governments to legislate against it.

financial adviser 1. Anyone who offers financial advice to someone else, especially one who advises on *investments. *See also* INDEPENDENT FINANCIAL ADVISER. **2.** An organization, usually a merchant bank, that advises the board of a company during a takeover (*see* TAKEOVER BID).

financial analysis The use of *financial statements and the calculation of ratios, to monitor and evaluate the financial performance and position of a business.

financial appraisal The use of financial evaluation techniques to determine which of a range of possible alternatives is preferred. Financial appraisal usually refers to the use of *discounted cash flow techniques but it may also be applied to any other approaches used to assess a business problem in financial terms, such as *ratio analysis, *profitability index, and risk analysis.

financial control (financial management) The actions of the management of an organization taken to ensure that the costs incurred and revenue generated are at acceptable levels. Financial control is assisted by the provision of financial information to management by the accountant and by the use of such techniques as *budgetary control and *standard costing, which highlight and analyse any variances.

financial crisis A collapse in the price of financial obligations, which may lead to a collapse in the economy. The major financial crisis in the history of world finance took place after the Wall Street Crash of 1929. This crisis led to a widespread failure in the US banking system and the interwar recession. Recent years have seen a number of financial crises, notably in Russia, South-East Asia, and Latin America. These crises have had major impacts on the economies of the countries that suffered them, but the impacts have not spread to the international economy.

financial distress A situation in which the activity of a business is influenced by the possibility of impending insolvency. The costs of distress can be divided into those related to bankruptcy and those incurred without bankruptcy. The costs of bankruptcy are those directly incurred in winding up or restructuring the business. The costs short of bankruptcy are those arising from a sudden change in suppliers' and customers' behaviour, prompted by their concerns over dealing with a potentially insolvent firm. They also include costs engendered by the diversion of managerial focus and conflicts between stakeholders, notably managers, debt holders, and shareholders. As a firm increases the level of its debt or *gearing, so the costs of financial distress will rise (and hence the cost of funding). The costs of financial distress are an important factor in determining the firm's level of gearing.

financial futures A *futures contract in currencies or interest rates (*see* INTEREST-RATE FUTURES) to purchase a specific amount of a financial asset at a particular price on a particular date. The contract is a standard one, which is exchange-traded. Until about 1970 trading in financial futures did not exist, although futures and options were dealt in widely on *commodity markets. However, instantaneous trading across the world coupled with accelerated international capital flows combined to produce great volatility in interest rates, stock-market prices, and currency exchanges. The result has been an environment in which organizations and individuals responsible for managing large sums need a financial futures and options market both to manage risks effectively and as a source of additional profit. In the UK financial futures and options are traded on the *London International Financial Futures and Options Exchange (LIFFE). *See also* HEDGE; INDEX FUTURES; PORTFOLIO INSURANCE.

financial gearing *See* GEARING; DEBT–EQUITY RATIO.

financial institution An organization whose core activity is to provide financial services or advice in relation to financial products. Financial institutions include state bodies, such as central banks, and private companies, such as banks, savings and loan associations, and also financial markets.

financial instrument A contract involving a financial obligation. Examples are stocks, bonds, loans, and derivatives. *See* INSTRUMENT; NEGOTIABLE INSTRUMENT.

Financial Intermediaries, Managers and Brokers Regulatory Association Ltd (FIMBRA) A former *Self-Regulating Organization that regulated organizations marketing and managing securities, unit trusts, and unit-linked life assurance policies, as well as independent financial advisers. Most of its business was transferred to the *Personal Investment Authority in 1993 and it was subsequently absorbed into the *Financial Services Authority.

financial intermediary **1.** An institution, be it a bank, building society, finance house, insurance company, investment trust, etc., that holds funds borrowed from lenders in order to make loans to borrowers. **2.** In the *Financial Services Act 1986, a person or organization that sells insurance but is not directly employed by an insurance company (e.g. a broker, insurance agent, bank). *See also* INDEPENDENT INTERMEDIARY.

financial investment *See* INVESTMENT.

financial leverage A US term for *gearing.

financial management **1.** The branch of financial economics that is concerned with questions of business funding and the management of a business in the interests of shareholders. **2.** *See* FINANCIAL CONTROL.

financial modelling The construction and use of planning and decision models based on financial data to simulate actual circumstances in order to facilitate decision making within an organization. The financial models used include *discounted cash flow, *decision trees, and *budgetary control.

Financial Ombudsman Service (FOS) A UK body set up to deal with complaints in relation to financial services and products. It was established by the *Financial Services and Markets Act 2000 to replace a number of separate complaint schemes: the Banking Ombudsman; Building Societies Ombudsman; Insurance Ombudsman; Investment Ombudsman; and Pensions Ombudsman.

financial planning The formulation of short-term and long-term plans in financial terms for the purposes of establishing goals for an organization to achieve, against which its actual performance can be measured.

financial product Any good or service provided by a financial institution. Financial products include loans, mortgages, insurance policies, advice, derivatives, etc.

financial ratios *See* FINANCIAL ANALYSIS.

financial report The *financial statements of a company.

Financial Reporting Council (FRC) A UK company limited by guarantee, set up in 1989 to oversee and support the work of the *Accounting Standards Board and the *Financial Reporting Review Panel to encourage good financial reporting generally.

Financial Reporting Release (FRR) In the USA, a pronouncement on financial reporting policy issued by the *Securities and Exchange Commission.

Financial Reporting Review Panel (FRRP) A UK company limited by guarantee; it is a subsidiary of the *Financial Reporting Council, which acts as its sole director. The panel investigates departures from the accounting requirements of the

Companies Acts and is empowered to take legal action to remedy any such departures. Its remit covers the financial reports of public companies and large private companies. All other companies are subject to scrutiny by the Department of Trade and Industry. The panel does not look at all company accounts but has doubtful cases drawn to its attention.

Financial Reporting Standard (FRS) Any of a series of standards issued by the *Accounting Standards Board. They are:
 1. Cash Flow Statements, issued 1991, revised 1996
 2. Accounting for Subsidiary Undertakings, issued 1992
 3. Reporting Financial Performance, issued 1992
 4. Capital Instruments, issued 1993
 5. Reporting the Substance of Transactions, issued 1994, amended 1998, 2003
 6. Acquisitions and Mergers, issued 1994
 7. Fair Values in Acquisition Accounting, issued 1994
 8. Related Party Transactions, issued 1995
 9. Associates and Joint Ventures, issued 1997
10. Goodwill and Intangible Assets, issued 1997
11. Impairment of Fixed Assets and Goodwill, issued 1998
12. Provisions, Contingent Liabilities, and Contingent Assets, issued 1998
13. Derivatives and Other Financial Instruments: Disclosures, issued 1998
14. Earnings Per Share, issued 1998, now superseded by FRS 22 below
15. Tangible Fixed Assets, issued 1999
16. Current Tax, issued 1999
17. Retirement Benefits, issued 2000, revised 2002
18. Accounting Policies, issued 2000
19. Deferred Tax, issued 2000
20. Share-Based Payment, issued 2004
21. Events After the Balance Sheet Date, issued 2004
22. Earnings Per Share, issued 2004
23. The Effects of Change in Foreign Exchange Rates, issued 2004
24. Financial Reporting in Hyperinflationary Economies, issued 2004
25. Financial Instruments: Disclosure and Presentation, issued 2004
26. Financial Instruments: Measurement, issued 2004
27. Life Assurance, issued 2004

financial risk The *risk that a firm will not be able to meet its monetary commitments, notably any debt-related payments.

financials A shorthand term for a firm's *financial statements.

Financial Services Act 1986 A UK Act of Parliament that came into force in April 1988. Its main objectives were to regulate investment business, providing investors with greater protection, and to promote greater competition in the industry. These objectives were to be achieved by means of the *Securities and Investment Board and its *Self-Regulating Organizations. It provided legislation for many of the recommendations of the *Gower Report. The act's provisions and framework were amended by the *Financial Services and Markets Act 2000.

Financial Services and Markets Act 2000 Legislation, implemented in November 2001, establishing a regulatory framework for UK banking, insurance, and investment. Under the terms of the Act, the *Financial Services Authority became the key regulator, taking over functions from the Bank of England, the Building Societies Commission, and the Treasury. However, the Bank of England still retains a regulatory interest where *systemic risk to the UK financial system is concerned. *See also* FINANCIAL OMBUDSMAN SERVICE.

Financial Services Authority (FSA) The financial services regulatory body in the UK. Formed in 1997, this independent body was charged with four statutory duties under the *Financial Services and Markets Act 2000: to maintain market confidence; to ensure a satisfactory level of customer protection; to reduce financial crime; and to increase public knowledge of the finance system. In the early 2000s, the FSA was criticized for its failure to intervene on behalf of small investors who were missold financial services, notably pensions and *endowment mortgages.

Financial Services Compensation Scheme A body established under the UK Financial Services and Markets Act 2000 to provide compensation to customers of insolvent businesses or to those who have incurred losses as a result of bad financial advice.

Financial Services Directive An EU directive on the regulation of financial services. It is based on the principle that a firm authorized to undertake business in one EU state should be able to conduct business in any other member state.

Financial Services Modernization Act 1999 (Gramm–Leach–Bliley Act) Legislation enacted in the USA that removed the restrictions on banks undertaking securities business that had been imposed by the *Glass–Steagal Act 1933. It also empowered companies to set up financial holding companies to supply banking, insurance, and investment services.

financial-statement analysis Analysis of the *financial statements of companies, mainly in terms of ratios. The standard analysis will consider the business from the perspectives of managerial performance, liquidity, and stock-exchange performance.

Financial Statement and Budget Report (FSBR) The document published by the Chancellor of the Exchequer on Budget Day. It summarizes the provisions of the Budget as given in the Chancellor's speech to the House of Commons. It is sometimes known as the **Red Book**.

financial statements The annual statements summarizing a company's activities over the last year. They consist of the *profit and loss account, *balance sheet, statement of total recognized gains and losses, and, if required, the *cash-flow statement, together with supporting notes.

Financial Statistics A monthly publication of the UK *Office for National Statistics giving a full account of financial statistics.

Financial Times Share Indexes A number of share indexes published by the *Financial Times* as a barometer of share prices on the London Stock Exchange. The **Financial Times Actuaries Share Indexes** are calculated by the Institute of Actuaries and the Faculty of Actuaries as weighted arithmetic averages for 54 sectors of the market (capital goods, consumer goods, etc.) and divided into various industries. They are widely used by investors and portfolio managers. The widest measure of the market comes from the **FTA All-Share Index** of some 800 shares and fixed-interest stocks (increased from 657 in October 1992), which includes a selection from the financial sector. Calculated after the end of daily business, it covers 98% of the market and 90% of turnover by value. The **FTA World Share Index** was introduced in 1987 and is based on 2400 share prices from 24 countries. The **Financial Times Industrial Ordinary Share Index** (or FT-30) represents the movements of shares in 30 leading industrial and commercial shares, chosen to be representative of British industry rather than of the Stock Exchange as a whole; it therefore excludes banks, insurance companies, and government stocks. The index is an unweighted geometric average, calculated hourly during the day and closing at 4.30 pm. The index started from a base of 100 in 1935 and for many years was the main day-to-day market barometer. It continues to be published but it has been superseded as the main index by the **Financial Times-Stock Exchange 100 Share Index** (FT-SE 100 or **FOOTSIE**), a weighted arithmetic index representing the price of 100 securities with a base of 1000 on 3 January 1984. This index is calculated minute-by-minute and its constituents, whose membership is by market capitalization, above £1 billion, are reviewed quarterly. The index was created to help to support a UK equity-market base for a futures contract. In 1992 the index series was extended to create two further real-time indexes, the **FT-SE Mid 250**, comprising companies capitalized between £150 million and £1 billion, and the **FT-SE Actuaries 350**, both based on 31 December 1985. These indexes are further broken down into Industry Baskets, comprising all the shares of the industrial sectors, to provide an instant view of industry performance across the market, and corresponding roughly to sectors defined by markets in New York and Tokyo. A **FT-SE Small Cap Index** covers 500–600 companies capitalized between £20 million and £150 million, calculated at the end of the day's business, both including and excluding investment trusts. The **Financial Times Government Securities Index** measures the movements of Government stocks (gilts). The newest indexes measure the performance of securities throughout the European market. The **Financial Times-Stock Exchange Eurotrack 100 Index** (FT-SE Eurotrack 100) is a weighted average of 100 stocks in Europe, which started on 29 October 1990, with a base of 1000 at the close of business on 26 October 1990. Quoted in euros, the index combines prices from *SEAQ and SEAQ International with up-to-date currency exchange rates. On 25 February 1991 the **Financial Times-Stock Exchange Eurotrack 200 Index** was first quoted, with the same base as the Eurotrack 100 to combine the constituents of the FT-SE 100 and the Eurotrack 100. New global sector indexes were introduced in 2001, including the **Euro-Top Index** of the 100 largest European companies. There is also a **Euro-Top 300 Index**.

financial year 1. Any year connected with finance, such as a company's accounting period or a year for which budgets are made up. **2.** In the UK, a specific period relating to *corporation tax, i.e. the 12 months beginning 1 April in one year and ending on 31 March in the next (the year beginning 1 April 2005 is the financial year 2005). Corporation-tax rates are fixed for specific financial years by the Chancellor in the Budget; if a company's accounting period falls into two financial years the profits have to be apportioned to the relevant financial years to find the rates of tax applicable. *Compare* FISCAL YEAR.

financier A person who finances a business deal or venture or who makes arrangements for such a deal or venture to be financed by a merchant bank or other *financial institution. The term often implies a hands-on approach, in addition to providing finance.

financing gap The difference between a country's foreign exchange requirements, for imports and the servicing of its debts, and what it has available from export receipts and overseas earnings. This gap must be filled either by raising further foreign exchange (donor aid, loans, etc.) or by cutting back the requirements, either by reducing imports or rescheduling the repayment of debts. Forecasting the financing gap and negotiating means of bridging it are major elements in helping countries with balance of payments problems.

fine paper *See* FIRST-CLASS PAPER.

fine trade bill A *bill of exchange that is acceptable to the Bank of England as security, when acting as *lender of last resort. It will be backed by a first-class bank or finance house.

fine tuning The implementation of economic policy, in particular monetary and fiscal policy, by means of small, incremental policy changes. Doubt has been cast on any real possibility of fine-tuning economies, given their lack of short-term forecastability. Critics argue that, if an economy is impossible to forecast in detail, then it follows that it is also impossible to determine appropriate short-term incremental policies.

FINEX 1. The financial futures division of the *New York Cotton Exchange. **2.** The name for certain Brazilian export finance programmes.

firewall In a financial conglomerate, a barrier created between the organization, funding, and ownership of one business entity and those of other entities in the group, so that problems experienced by the one do not affect others. The creation of subsidiaries with superior credit ratings to the parent company in order to indulge in derivatives business is a prime example of a firewall strategy.

firm commitment 1. An undertaking by a bank to lend up to a maximum sum over a period at a specified rate; a *commitment fee usually has to be paid by the borrower, which is not returned if the loan is not taken up. **2.** An agreement in which an underwriter of a flotation in the USA assumes the risk that not all the securities issued will be sold, by guaranteeing to buy all the excess securities at the offer price. **3.** A binding commitment to enter into an agreement.

firm order An order to a broker (for securities, commodities, currencies, etc.) that remains firm for a stated period or until cancelled. A broker who has a firm order from a principal does not have to refer back if the terms of the order can be executed in the stated period.

firm price A guaranteed price for a specified period offered by a trader.

firm surveillance The authority of the *International Monetary Fund to oversee the exchange-rate policies of member states.

first call date The earliest date on which the issuer of a bond can exercise a *call provision.

first-class paper (fine paper) A money-market instrument that is backed by a bank with a high credit rating.

first in, first out (FIFO) A method of charging homogeneous items of stock to production when the cost of the items has changed. It is assumed, both for costing and stock valuation purposes, that the earliest items taken into stock are those used in production, although this may not necessarily correspond with the physical movement of the stock items. *Compare* LAST IN, FIRST OUT.

first-line reserves Liquid reserves held by a central bank for intervention in the currency market.

first-loss guarantee An agreement to guarantee losses in order to enhance the credit of a security.

first-loss policy A property insurance policy in which the policyholder arranges cover for an amount below the full value of the items insured and the insurer agrees not to penalize the policyholder for under-insurance. The main use of these policies is in circumstances in which a total loss is virtually impossible. For example, a large warehouse may contain £2.5M worth of wines and spirits but the owner may feel that no more than £500,000 worth could be stolen at any one time. The solution is a first-loss policy that deals with all claims up to £500,000 but pays no more than this figure if more is stolen. First-loss policies differ from coinsurance agreements with the policyholders because the insured is not involved in claims below the first-loss level and the premiums are not calculated proportionally. In the above example, the premium might be as much as 80–90% of the premium on the full value.

first mortgage debenture A *debenture with the first charge over property owned by a company. Such debentures are most commonly issued by property companies.

first notice day **1.** The date on which a seller in a futures market contract gives notice of an intention to deliver according to the terms of a particular *futures contract. **2.** The date on which the buyer is notified of such an arrangement.

first of exchange *See* BILLS IN A SET.

first preferred stock In the USA, *preferred stock with prior rights where dividends are concerned or in the event of liquidation.

first-tier stock market The main market on which the equity of large companies is traded. There is customarily a high level of regulation and supervision in such markets.

first-year allowance In the UK, a special *capital allowance against *corporation tax that is granted in the year of purchase of an asset in place of the standard *writing-down allowance of 25%. Various first-year allowances have been made available at various times. In 2000–03, for example, small businesses that invested in computer and Internet technology were able to claim 100% first-year allowances.

fiscal agent **1.** A third party who acts on behalf of a bond issuer to pay subscribers to the issue and generally assist the issuer. **2.** An agent for one of the national *financial institutions in the USA who acts as an adviser, for example, to the National Mortgage Association for its debt securities. **3.** In the USA, an agent empowered to collect taxes, revenues, and duties on behalf of the government. For example, the *Federal Reserve Banks perform this function for the US Treasury.

fiscal drag The deflationary impact on a country's economy of a steady increase in tax revenues. Because most developed countries have progressive rates of taxation, the proportion of national income paid in taxes rises as national income grows.

fiscal policy The use of government spending and taxation to influence macroeconomic conditions. Fiscal policy was actively pursued to sustain full employment in the post-war years; however, monetarists and others have claimed that this set off the inflation of the 1970s. Fiscal policy has remained generally 'tight' in most Western countries since the 1980s.

fiscal year In the UK, the 12-month period beginning on 6 April in one year and ending on 5 April in the next (the fiscal year 2005–06 runs from 6 April 2005 to 5 April 2006). Income tax, capital gains tax, and annual allowances for inheritance tax are calculated for fiscal years, and the UK Budget estimates refer to the fiscal year. In the USA the fiscal year now runs from 1 October to the following 30 September. The fiscal year is sometimes called the **tax year** or the **year of assessment**. *Compare* FINANCIAL YEAR.

Fisher effect A hypothesis advanced by the economist Irving Fisher that the *nominal interest rate will rise in direct proportion to a rise in the rate of expected inflation. *See also* INTERNATIONAL FISHER EFFECT.

Fitch's Investors' Service A US credit *rating agency.

fixed asset *See* CAPITAL ASSET.

fixed capital The amount of capital tied up in the *capital assets of an organization.

fixed capital formation An investment over a given period, as used in the *national income accounts. It consists primarily of investment in manufacturing and housing. **Gross fixed capital formation** is the total amount of expenditure on investment, while **net fixed capital formation** includes a deduction for the *depreciation of existing capital.

fixed charge (specific charge) A *charge in which a creditor has the right to have a specific asset sold and applied to the repayment of a debt if the debtor defaults on any payments. The debtor is not at liberty to deal with the asset without the charge-holder's consent. *Compare* FLOATING CHARGE.

fixed debenture A *debenture that has a *fixed charge as security. *Compare* FLOATING DEBENTURE.

fixed exchange rate A *rate of exchange between one currency and another that is fixed by government and maintained by that government's economic policy and its buying or selling its currency to support or depress it. *Compare* FLOATING EXCHANGE RATE.

fixed-for-fixed Denoting a *currency swap in which both parties pay a fixed rate of interest.

fixed-for-floating Denoting an *interest-rate swap or *cross-currency interest-rate swap in which one party pays a fixed rate, while the other pays a floating rate.

fixed-interest security A type of *security that gives a fixed stated interest payment. They include *gilt-edged securities, *bonds, *preference shares, and *debentures; as they entail less risk than *equities they offer less scope for capital appreciation. They do, however, often give a better *yield than equities. The prices of fixed-interest securities tend to move inversely with the general level of interest rates, reflecting changes in the value of their fixed yield relative to the market. Fixed-interest securities tend to be particularly poor investments at times of high and increasing inflation as their value does not adjust to changes in the price level. To overcome this problem some gilts now give index-linked interest payments.

fixed-price tender A bid to undertake an activity for a given price.

fixed-price tender offer A tender process in which the price is fixed and buyers and sellers may choose the amount they wish to trade. It is often used by central banks in carrying out *open-market operations.

fixed rate A rate of interest that remains the same throughout the life of a contract.

fixed-rate loan A loan on which the interest rate is fixed at the start of the loan.

fixed-rate mortgage A *mortgage in which the rate of interest paid by the borrower is fixed, usually for the first few years of the loan.

fixing 1. The determination of a market price, interest rate, exchange rate, security or commodity price. **2.** An agreement by traders on the price of a commodity being traded between them. **3.** A UK term for *short selling.

FLA Abbreviation for *Finance and Leasing Association.

flag A roughly rectangular (i.e. flag-shaped) pattern on a chart produced by price fluctuations within a defined range. A *chartist will try to identify a *breakout from this range signalling a definite movement of prices in a particular direction. *Compare* PENNANT.

flash On an exchange, an information system that displays up-to-the-minute prices for the most heavily traded securities at regular intervals.

flat bond A bond traded excluding interest, either because none is due or because the interest due has been defaulted upon.

flat-rate forward A *futures contract or forward contract with a constant *contango throughout the life of the contract.

flat yield *See* YIELD.

flat yield curve A graphic representation of the situation in which the yield from securities of the same credit rating is at the same level whatever their maturity date. *See* YIELD CURVE.

flexible budget A budget in which values for income and expenditure depend on the level of volume achieved in the business.

flexible drawdown The *drawdown in stages of funds available under a credit agreement.

flexible future A *futures contract that can be changed by buyers and sellers. It has some of the advantages of a forward contract (*see* FORWARD DEALING) with none of the *credit risk.

flexible swap An *interest-rate swap in which the party paying a floating rate undertakes to pay a floor rate if the *reference rate of interest should fall below a certain threshold rate.

flex option An *exchange-traded option in which financial institutions can vary the standard terms of the option contract.

flight to quality A movement of investors into safer assets in times of uncertainty. Government securities, *blue-chip stocks, short-term government debt, gold, and US investments all typify the type of assets that are bought at such times.

flip-flop FRN 1. A term in a financial instrument that allows the holder to change between sets of payments and obligations. **2.** A perpetual *floating-rate note (i.e. one without redemption), which can be converted into a short-term note of up to four years' maturity and back again into a perpetual FRN.

float 1. In the USA, the proportion of a corporation's stocks that are held by the public rather than the corporation. **2.** Money created as a result of a delay in processing cheques, e.g. when one account is credited before the paying bank's account has been debited. *See* FEDERAL RESERVE FLOAT. **3.** Money set aside as a contingency fund or an advance to be reimbursed. **4.** *See* FLOTATION. **5.** The amount of money that a bank holds with a central bank.

floater A colloquial name for a *floating-rate note.

floating capital Funds available for carrying on a business, including funds employed in marketable investments.

floating charge A *charge over the assets of a company; it is not a legal charge over its fixed assets but floats over the charged assets until crystallized by some predetermined event. For example, a floating charge may be created over all the assets of a company, including its trading stock. The assets may be freely dealt with until a crystallizing event occurs, such as the company going into liquidation. Thereafter no further dealing may take place but the debt may be satisfied from the charged assets. Such a charge ranks in priority after legal charges and after preferred creditors in the event of a winding-up. It must be registered (*see* REGISTER OF CHARGES).

floating debenture A *debenture that has a *floating charge as security. *Compare* FIXED DEBENTURE.

floating debt **1.** The part of the *national debt that consists primarily of short-term *Treasury bills. *See also* FUNDING OPERATIONS. **2.** Short-term borrowing (i.e. for less than one year). **3.** Debt with a floating rate of interest.

floating exchange rate A *rate of exchange between one currency and others that is permitted to change according to market forces. Most major currencies and countries now have floating exchange rates but governments and central banks intervene, buying or selling currencies when rates become too high or too low. *Compare* FIXED EXCHANGE RATE.

floating interest rate A rate of interest that rises and falls in relation to some indicator, such as the *London Inter Bank Offered Rate (LIBOR).

floating policy An insurance policy that has only one sum insured although it may cover many items. No division of the total is shown on the policy and the policyholder is often able to add or remove items from the cover without reference to the insurers, provided that the total sum insured is not exceeded.

floating-rate certificate of deposit (FRCD) A certificate of deposit with a variable interest rate, normally for interbank lending purposes. Commonly bearing a one-year maturity, these certificates have interest rates that may be adjusted (e.g. every 90 days); they are usually expressed in eurodollars at a rate linked to LIBOR.

floating-rate credit-rate-sensitive note A *floating-rate note in which the margin to the *reference rate is determined by the issuer's credit rating.

floating-rate interest An *interest rate on certain bonds, certificates of deposit, etc., that changes with the market rate in a predetermined manner, usually in relation to the *base rate.

floating-rate loan A loan that does not have a fixed interest rate throughout its life. Floating-rate loans can take various forms but they are all tied to a short-term market indicator; in the UK this is usually the *London Inter Bank Offered Rate.

floating-rate note (FRN) A *eurobond with a *floating-rate interest, usually based on the *London Inter Bank Offered Rate. They first appeared in the 1970s and have a maturity of between 7 and 15 years. They are usually issued as negotiable *bearer bonds. A **perpetual FRN** has no *redemption. *See also* FLIP-FLOP FRN.

floating spread A variable margin on a floating rate of interest.

floating supply The proportion of a share issue held by investors who wish to sell.

floating warranty A guarantee given by one person to another that induces this other person to enter into a contract with a third party. For example, a car dealer may induce a customer to enter into a hire-purchase contract with a finance company. If the car does not comply with the dealer's guarantee, the customer may recover damages from the dealer, on the basis of the hire-purchase contract, even though the dealer is not a party to that contract.

floor 1. The room in a financial market in which dealing takes place. Dealings are invariably restricted to *floor traders. With the increased use of computers floor trading is becoming less frequent. **2.** The minimum interest rate on a financial obligation. *Compare* CAP. *See also* COLLAR. **3.** A hedge against downside movements of the *underlying.

floor broker A person who deals on the *floor of an exchange for a third party.

floor–ceiling swap An *interest-rate swap in which the variable rate is subject to a minimum payment ('floor') and a maximum payment ('ceiling').

floored put A put *option with a limit on the gain if there is a fall in the value of the *underlying.

floor official A market official who settles disputes on a financial trading floor.

floortion (floption) The option of buying an interest-rate floor (*see* COLLAR).

floor trader A member of a stock exchange, commodity market, Lloyd's, etc., who is permitted to enter the dealing room of these institutions and deal with other traders, brokers, underwriters, etc. Each institution has its own rules of exclusivity, but in many, computer dealing has replaced face-to-face floor trading.

floption *See* FLOORTION.

florin (Af) The standard monetary unit of Aruba, divided into 100 cents.

flotation The process of launching a public company for the first time by inviting the public to subscribe in its shares (also known as 'going public'). It applies both to private and to previously nationalized share issues, and can be carried out by means of an *introduction, *issue by tender, *offer for sale, *placing, or *public issue. After flotation the shares can be traded on a stock exchange. Flotation allows the owners of the business to raise new capital or to realize their investments.

flotation cost The total cost incurred by a company in offering its securities to the public.

flowback The resale on the domestic market of shares initially sold to overseas investors.

flower bond A US Treasury bond that can be used to pay death duties at a par value if held by the deceased.

flow of funds account Statistics generated by the US Federal Reserve relating to the demand and supply of short-term funds in the US market.

flurry A burst of activity on a speculative market, especially on a financial market.

FMHA Abbreviation for *Farmers Home Administration.

FNMA Abbreviation for *Federal National Mortgage Association.

focused strategy A business strategy in which firms seek to divest themselves of all but their core activities, using the funds so raised to enhance their core skills. This strategy is a reaction to the trend towards *diversification and the development of *conglomerates.

FOMC Abbreviation for *Federal Open Market Committee.

FOOTSIE Colloquial name for the Financial Times-Stock Exchange 100 Share Index. *See* FINANCIAL TIMES SHARE INDEXES.

forbearance **1.** The position taken by a lender who chooses not to exercise his or her legal right of *foreclosure when a borrower defaults. Instead, the lender may renegotiate the terms of the loan. **2.** Tolerance granted by the regulators to banks with low levels of *capital adequacy.

forced conversion The exercise of a *convertible security as a result of the issuer being able to force conversion.

forced sale A sale that has to take place because it has been ordered by a court or because it is necessary to raise funds to avoid bankruptcy or liquidation.

forced saving A government measure imposed on an economy with a view to increasing savings and reducing expenditure on consumer goods. It is usually implemented by raising taxes, increasing interest rates, or raising prices.

force majeure (French: superior force) An event outside the control of either party to a contract (such as a strike, riot, war, act of God) that may excuse either party from fulfilling his contractual obligations in certain circumstances, provided that the contract contains a *force majeure* clause. If one party invokes the *force majeure* clause the other may either accept that it is applicable or challenge the interpretation. In the latter case an arbitration would be involved.

foreclosure The legal right of a lender of money if the borrower fails to repay the money or part of it on the due date. The lender must apply to a court to be permitted to sell the property that has been held as security for the debt. The court will order a new date for payment in an order called a **foreclosure nisi**. If the borrower again fails to pay, the lender may sell the property. This procedure can occur when the security is the house in which the mortgagor lives and the mortgagor fails to pay the mortgagee (bank, building society, etc.) the mortgage instalments. The bank, etc., then forecloses the mortgage, dispossessing the mortgagor.

Foreign Bank Supervision Enhancement Act A US act passed in 1991, giving the *Federal Reserve System increased powers to supervise foreign banks operating in the USA. Any bank wishing to open branches in the USA must seek permission to do so and all foreign banks in the USA are inspected at least annually by the Federal Reserve.

foreign bill *See* INLAND BILL.

foreign bond A bond held by a resident of one country that is denominated in the currency of another country and issued by a non-domestic creditor. *See* BULLDOG BOND; YANKEE BOND.

Foreign Corrupt Practices Amendment Legislation enacted (1997) in the USA outlawing bribery and corruption by US companies in their overseas operations.

Foreign Credit Insurance Association (FCIA) A consortium operated on voluntary lines by 50 US insurance companies to underwrite export credits for US exporters. It is run under the aegis of the *Export-Import Bank.

foreign currency bill A bill in a different currency to that of the country in which it is issued.

foreign currency bond **1.** A *bond that pays interest in a different currency to its denomination. It is sometimes referred to as a **dual currency bond**. **2.** A bond in a different currency to that of the country in which it was issued.

foreign currency cross-rate A mechanism whereby an exchange rate can be calculated between two currencies for which no direct *rate of exchange exists. The US dollar, which is customarily used as the vehicle currency in foreign-exchange trading, is the common denominator of such calculations. Thus, there may not be a direct rate between, say, the Barbados dollar and the Argentine peso. A cross-rate is calculated by dividing the $US rate for the peso by the $US rate for the Barbados dollar, showing how many Barbados dollars are needed to purchase one peso.

foreign debt *See* EXTERNAL DEBT.

foreign desk The section of the Reserve Bank of New York that undertakes intervention on the foreign-exchange markets at the behest of the US Treasury.

foreign direct investment External investment in assets or businesses, as opposed to financial obligations.

foreign exchange (FX; FOREX) The currencies of foreign countries. Foreign exchange is bought and sold in *foreign-exchange markets. Firms or organizations require foreign exchange to purchase goods from abroad or for purposes of investment or speculation.

Foreign Exchange and Currency Deposit Brokers' Association (FECDBA) The UK trade association for brokers dealing in *foreign exchange.

Foreign Exchange and Trade Central Law A Japanese law, enacted in 1949, regulating import controls; owing to Western pressure, it has subsequently been relaxed, particularly since Japan joined the *Organization for Economic Cooperation and Development.

foreign-exchange broker A *broker who specializes in arranging deals in foreign currencies on the *foreign-exchange markets. Most transactions are between commercial banks and governments. Foreign-exchange brokers do not normally deal direct with the public or with firms requiring foreign currencies for buying goods abroad (who buy from commercial banks). Foreign-exchange brokers earn their living from the *brokerage paid on each deal.

foreign-exchange dealer A person who buys and sells *foreign exchange on a *foreign-exchange market, usually as an employee of a *commercial bank. Banks charge fees or commissions for buying and selling foreign exchange on behalf of their customers; dealers may also be authorized to speculate in forward exchange rates.

foreign-exchange market An international market in which foreign currencies are traded. It consists primarily of foreign-exchange dealers employed by *commercial banks (acting as principals) and *foreign-exchange brokers (acting as intermediaries). Although tight *exchange controls have been abandoned by many governments, including the UK government, the market is not entirely free in that it is to some extent manipulated by governments. Currency dealing has a *spot currency market for delivery of foreign exchange within two days and a forward-exchange market (*see* FORWARD-EXCHANGE CONTRACT) in which transactions are made for foreign currencies to be delivered at agreed dates in the future. This enables dealers, and their customers who require foreign exchange in the future, to hedge their purchases and sales. Options and futures on forward-exchange rates can also be traded on various world markets, both *over-the-counter (OTC) and on exchanges.

foreign-exchange rate risk *See* EXCHANGE-RATE EXPOSURE.

foreign-exchange trading line A facility that enables a *counterparty to trade in foreign exchange up to a given limit.

foreign-exchange transactions date The date on which the terms of a foreign-exchange contract are agreed.

foreign-exchange value date The date on which a foreign-exchange transaction is settled.

foreign financing Borrowing by a company in the financial markets of another country in the currency of that country. An example would be a British company borrowing francs in France.

foreign investment Investment in the domestic economy by foreign individuals or companies. Foreign investment takes the form of either direct investment in productive enterprises or investment in financial *instruments, such as a portfolio of shares. Countries receiving foreign investment tend to have a mixed attitude towards it. While the creation of jobs and wealth is welcome, there is frequently antagonism on the grounds that the country is being 'bought by foreigners'. Similarly, there is frequently resentment in the country whose nationals invest overseas, especially if there is domestic unemployment. Nevertheless, foreign investment is increasingly important in the economy of the modern world.

foreign sector The part of a country's economy that is concerned with external trade (imports and exports) and capital flows (inward and outward).

foreign trade multiplier The mutually beneficial effect on national income that occurs when one country buys another's exports. The rise in employment and income levels in the exporting country will enable workers there to spend more on products from the other country. *See* MULTIPLIER.

forensic accounting **1.** Accounting undertaken in relation to proceedings in a court of law. In such circumstances accountants may be called on to provide expert evidence. **2.** Accounting that sets out to determine the nature of past business activity, often on the basis of partial documentation.

FOREX Abbreviation for *foreign exchange.

forfaiting A form of *debt discounting for exporters in which a forfaiter accepts at a discount, and without recourse, a *promissory note, *bill of exchange, *letter of credit, etc., received from a foreign buyer by an exporter. Maturities are normally from one to three years. Thus the exporter receives payment without risk at the cost of the discount.

forfeited share A partly paid share in a company that the shareholder has to forfeit because of a failure to pay a subsequent part or final payment. Such shares must be sold or cancelled by a public *company but a private company is not regulated in this respect.

forgery The legal offence of making a false instrument in order that it may be accepted as genuine, thereby causing harm to others. Under the Forgery and Counterfeiting Act 1981, an instrument may be a document or any device (e.g. magnetic tape) on which information is recorded. An instrument is considered false, for example, if it purports to have been made or altered by someone who did not do so, on a date or at a place when it was not, or by someone who does not exist. It is also an offence to copy or use a false instrument knowing it to be false or to make or possess any material meant to be used to produce such specified false instruments as money, cheques, share certificates, cheque cards, credit cards, passports, or registration certificates.

for information only Denoting a quotation given to provide a client with a guide to current market prices. It cannot be treated as a firm offer either to buy or to sell at the quoted price.

forint (Ft) The standard monetary unit of Hungary, divided into 100 fillér.

Form 3 A US *Securities and Exchange Commission (SEC) form requiring disclosure of the shareholdings of a firm's officers and major shareholders.

Form 13-D A notification to the market of trading by a US shareholder who holds more than 5% of the equity in a company.

Form F1 A document that must be filed with the US *Securities and Exchange Commission (SEC) whenever a share issue is made available to the public.

Form 8-K A US *Securities and Exchange Commission (SEC) form that must be filed by companies giving details of any material *event that may affect their financial state or share price. The report must be filed within 30 days of the event.

Form 10-K An annual report supplied to the US *Securities and Exchange Commission (SEC) by companies listed on the national stock exchanges, detailing financial and other information on the operations of the business. The form must be filed within 90 days of the end of a company's financial year.

Form 10-Q A quarterly submission by publicly quoted companies to the US *Securities and Exchange Commission (SEC). The information it required is less detailed than that on *Form 10-K and does not have to be audited.

Forum of European Securities Commissions A body, set up in 1997, representing securities regulators in the European Union.

forwardation A situation in a *commodity market in which spot goods can be bought more cheaply than goods for forward delivery, enabling a dealer to buy spot goods and carry them forward to deliver them against a forward contract. *Compare* BACKWARDATION.

forward cover A *hedge for a known future foreign-currency receipt or payment created by buying or selling on the forward currency markets. *See* FORWARD-EXCHANGE CONTRACT.

forward currency swap A *currency swap whose start date is deferred.

forward curve A graphic representation of the situation in which the *yield from securities of the same credit rating increases with the length of time they have to run to maturity. *See* YIELD CURVE.

forward-dated *See* POST-DATE.

forward dealing Dealing in commodities, securities, currencies, freight, etc., for delivery at some future date at a price agreed at the time the contract (called a **forward contract**) is made. This form of trading enables dealers and manufacturers to cover their future requirements by hedging their more immediate purchases (*see* HEDGE). Strictly, a forward contract differs from a *futures contract in that the former cannot be closed out by a matching transaction, whereas a futures contract can, and often is. However, this distinction is not always adhered to and the two words are sometimes used synonymously.

forward delivery Terms of a contract in which goods are purchased for delivery at some time in the future (*compare* SPOT GOODS). Commodities may be sold for forward delivery up to one year or more ahead, often involving shipment from their port of origin. *See also* FORWARD DEALING.

forward differential *See* FORWARD POINTS.

forward-exchange contract An agreement to purchase *foreign exchange at a specified date in the future at an agreed exchange rate. In international trade, with floating rates of exchange, the forward-exchange market provides an important way of eliminating risk on future transactions that will require foreign exchange. *See* FINANCIAL FUTURES; FOREIGN-EXCHANGE MARKET.

forward Fed funds *Fed funds traded on a forward basis for future delivery.

forward–forward Describing an exchange-rate *swap in which the start date is deferred until some point in the future.

forward intervention Central bank intervention in the forward currency markets.

forward margin *See* FORWARD POINTS.

forward points (forward differential; forward margin) The amount to be added to or deducted from the spot foreign-exchange rate to calculate the forward exchange rate.

forward price The fixed price at which a given amount of a commodity, currency, or a financial instrument is to be delivered on a fixed date in the future. A forward contract differs from a *futures contract in that each forward deal stands alone.

forward rate agreement (FRA) An agreement in which one party agrees to pay a fixed interest rate and the other a variable interest rate on contracts of usually two years. The net payment is the difference between these two rates. In such transactions the parties take a risk on the difference between what they expect the interest rates will be in the period and what they actually are.

forward regular dates Regular intervals established for transactions in forward foreign-exchange markets. The regular periods are 1, 2, 3, 6, 9, and 12 months in advance.

forward spread agreement A financial instrument in which the *spread between two interest rates denominated in different currencies drives gains or losses. It is a way of hedging or speculating on the interest-rate differentials.

forward start An agreement to start an agreed-terms contract at a point in time beyond the normal settlement date for that particular market.

forward swap A *swap in which the start date for payments is deferred. *See also* FORWARD CURRENCY SWAP; FORWARD–FORWARD.

FOS Abbreviation for *Financial Ombudsman Service.

founders' shares Shares issued to the founders of a company. They often have special rights to dividends. *See also* DEFERRED ORDINARY SHARE.

Fourth Directive An EU directive concerning the harmonization of company law and accounting practices in member states (*see* ACCOUNTING CONCEPTS).

FRA Abbreviation for *forward rate agreement.

fractional banking A banking practice that some governments impose on their banks, calling for a fixed fraction between cash reserves and total liabilities. If governments increase the ratio of reserves to deposits, this indicates a tighter credit policy.

franc **1.** (F) The standard monetary unit of various former French colonies and some French dependencies: Benin (Communauté Financière Africaine franc; CFAF), Burkina-Faso (CFAF), Burundi (FBu), Cameroon (CFAF), the Central African Republic (CFAF), Chad (CFAF), Comoros (CF), Congo-Brazzaville (CFAF), the Democratic Republic of Congo (CoF), Côte d'Ivoire, (CFAF), Djibouti (DF), Equatorial Guinea (CFAF), French Polynesia (FPF), Gabon (CFAF), Guinea (GF), Guinea-Bissau (CFAF), Madagascar (FMG), Mali (CFAF), New Caledonia (FPF), Niger (CFAF), Rwanda (RF), Senegal (CFAF), and Togo (CFAF). In all countries it is divided into 100 centimes. **2. (Swiss franc)** the standard monetary unit of Switzerland and Liechtenstein, divided into 100 centimes. **3.** The former standard monetary unit of France, most French dependencies, Monaco, and (with the peseta) Andorra (**French franc**); of Belgium (**Belgian franc**); and of Luxembourg (**Luxembourg franc**). In each case it was subsumed into the euro for all purposes other than cash transactions in January 1999 and abolished in 2002.

franked investment income Formerly, dividends and other distributions from UK companies received by other companies. The principle of the *imputation system of taxation was that once one company has paid corporation tax, any dividends it paid could pass through any number of other companies without carrying a further corporation-tax charge, hence the term 'franked'.

Frankfurt Stock Exchange (Frankfurt Wertpapierbörse) The oldest and largest of eight regional stock exchanges in Germany, accounting for more than 75% of equity trading in Germany. It first recorded trading in 1820 (of shares in the Austrian National bank) and was subsequently recognized as a centre for dealing in bonds. Trading is now on four markets; the *Amlichter Handel* for Government bonds and major companies, the *Geregelter Markt* for smaller companies, the *Freiverkehr*, or third market, and the *Neuer Markt*, launched in 1997 for companies involved in Internet trading. Prices are determined on an auction basis by the official brokers (*Kursmakler*) and free brokers (*Freimakler*), who base them on buying and selling orders from the banks. The main market indicator is the *Deutsche Aktienindex (Dax index).

fraption An option on a *forward rate agreement.

fraud A false representation by means of a statement or conduct, in order to gain a material advantage. A contract obtained by fraud is voidable on the grounds of fraudulent *misrepresentation. If a person uses fraud to induce someone to part with money that he or she would not otherwise have parted with, this may amount to theft. *See also* FRAUDULENT CONVEYANCE; FRAUDULENT PREFERENCE; FRAUDULENT TRADING.

fraudulent conveyance The transfer of property to another person for the purposes of putting it beyond the reach of creditors. For example, if a man transfers his house into the name of his wife because he realizes that his business is about to become insolvent, the transaction may be set aside by the court under the provisions of the Insolvency Act 1986.

fraudulent preference Paying money to a creditor of a company, or otherwise improving a creditor's position, at a time when the company is unable to pay its debts. If this occurs because of an act of the company within six months of winding-up (or two years if the preference is given to a person connected with the company), an application to the court may be made to cancel the transaction. The court may make any order that it thinks fit, but no order may prejudice the rights of a third party who has acquired property for value without notice of the preference.

fraudulent trading The carrying on of the business of a company with intent to defraud creditors or for any other fraudulent purpose. This includes accepting money from customers when the company is unable to pay its debts and cannot meet its obligations under the contract. The liquidator of a company may apply to the court for an order against any person who has been a party to fraudulent trading to make such contributions to the assets of the company as the court thinks fit. Thus an officer of the company may be made personally liable for some of its debts. 'Fraudulent' in this context implies actual dishonesty or real moral blame; this definition has limited the usefulness of the remedy as fraud is notoriously difficult to prove. *See* WRONGFUL TRADING.

FRC Abbreviation for *Financial Reporting Council.

FRCD Abbreviation for *floating-rate certificate of deposit.

Freddie Mac Colloquial name in the USA for the *Federal Home Loan Mortgage Corporation.

free asset ratio The ratio of the market value of an insurance company's assets to its liabilities.

free capital **1.** Capital in the form of cash. *See also* LIQUID ASSETS. **2.** The shares in a public company that are available to the general public, i.e. those not held by controlling shareholders. In the USA it is known as the **free float**.

free cash flow **1.** Cash in excess of that required for all of a company's positive *net present value activities. **2.** The positive *cash flows in relation to a decision under consideration. **3.** In certain forms of business analysis, earnings plus depreciation minus dividends.

free depreciation A method of granting tax relief to organizations by allowing them to charge the cost of fixed assets against taxable profits in whatever proportions and over whatever period they choose. This gives businesses considerable flexibility, enabling them to choose the best method of depreciation depending on their anticipated cash flow, profit estimates, and taxation expectations.

free float *See* FREE CAPITAL.

free issue *See* SCRIP ISSUE.

free lunch Economists' jargon for a nonexistent benefit. It derives from a 19th-century tavern that advertised free food, it being clearly understood that anyone attempting to exploit this offer without buying a drink would be thrown out. The phrase is now used to reflect the economist's belief that wherever there appears to be a free benefit, someone, somewhere, always pays for it.

freely callable Describing a bond that the issuer may choose to redeem at any time from the issue date (i.e. the issuer has a *call provision that applies immediately). *See* CALLABLE BONDS; INSTANT CALL BOND.

free market 1. A market that is free from government interference, prices rising and falling in accordance with supply and demand. **2.** A security that is widely traded on a stock exchange, there being sufficient stock on offer for the price to be uninfluenced by availability. **3.** A *foreign-exchange market that is free from influence on rates by governments, rates being free to rise and fall in accordance with supply and demand.

free port (free zone) An area in which imports and resulting re-exports are exempt from tax – more particularly import or export duties – provided products are not resold on the domestic market.

free reserves Reserves of a bank or insurance company in excess of those required by its regulator.

free ride The situation in which an economic agent benefits from the expenditure of others without making a contribution. A free ride is a type of *externality and a source of market imperfection. An important example of free riding is when small investors benefit from the monitoring of firms carried out by institutional investors.

free trade agreement An agreement to abolish tariffs between two or more countries. The most notable examples are the agreement to set up the *European Free Trade Association (EFTA) in 1960 and the *North American Free Trade Agreement (NAFTA), concluded in 1994 between the USA, Canada, and Mexico.

freeze-out Pressure applied to minority shareholders of a company that has been taken over, to sell their stock to the new owners.

freezing injunction An order of the court preventing the defendant from dealing with specified assets. Such an order will be granted in cases in which the plaintiff can show that there will be a substantial risk that any judgment given against the defendant will be worthless, because the defendant will sell assets to avoid paying it. It is usually granted to prevent assets leaving the jurisdiction of the English courts, but may in exceptional circumstances extend to assets abroad. It was formerly called a **Mareva injunction**, after the 1975 case *Mareva Compania Naviera SA* v *International Bulkcarriers SA*.

frequency In statistics, a measurement of the likelihood of a particular event occurring.

frequency–density function In statistical analysis, a function that maps events to their frequency.

Friendly Society A non-profit-making mutual organization in the UK. Friendly Societies provide a range of personal assurance and insurance benefits relating to sickness, pensions, and unemployment. *See* MUTUAL LIFE-ASSURANCE COMPANY.

fringe benefits 1. Non-monetary benefits offered to the employees of a company in addition to their wages or salaries. They include company cars, expense accounts, the opportunity to buy company products at reduced prices, private health plans, canteens with subsidized meals, luncheon vouchers, cheap loans, social clubs, etc. Some of these benefits, such as company cars, do not escape the tax net. **2.** Benefits, other than dividends, provided by a company for its shareholders. They include reduced prices for the company's products or services, Christmas gifts, and special travel facilities.

FRN Abbreviation for *floating-rate note.

frogs US *floating-rate notes that have a coupon dependent on a 30-year US Treasury bond.

front-door method *See* BACK DOOR.

front-end fee **1.** A payment at the beginning of a financial arrangement. **2.** A charge levied by a lender when a loan is set up or when the first payment of the loan is taken. It may be a *commitment fee, an *establishment fee, or a *documentation fee.

front-end load The initial charge made by a unit trust, life-assurance company, or other investment fund to pay for administration and commission for any introducing agent. The investment made on behalf of the investor is, therefore, the total initial payment less the front-end load. *Compare* BACK-END LOAD.

front office The sections of a financial firm that deal with clients, investors, financial markets, and the public. *Compare* BACK OFFICE; MIDDLE OFFICE.

front running The generally illegal practice by brokers or intermediaries of dealing on advance information provided by their brokers and investment analysis department, before their clients have been given the information. *See also* CHINESE WALL.

frozen assets Assets that for one reason or another cannot be used or realized. This may happen when a government refuses to allow certain assets to be exported. An example of this was the block on the use of Iraqi accounts in the period 1990–91, during that country's invasion of Kuwait.

FRR Abbreviation for *Financial Reporting Release.

FRRP Abbreviation for *Financial Reporting Review Panel.

FRS Abbreviation for *Financial Reporting Standard.

FSA Abbreviation for *Financial Services Authority.

FSBR Abbreviation for *Financial Statement and Budget Report.

FT-SE 100 *See* FINANCIAL TIMES SHARE INDEXES.

FT-SE Eurotrack Indexes *See* FINANCIAL TIMES SHARE INDEXES.

FT Share Indexes *See* FINANCIAL TIMES SHARE INDEXES.

fuefuki A Japanese term for a short halt in trading.

full consolidation A method of accounting in which the whole impact of subsidiaries is incorporated into group accounts.

full listing A description of a company whose shares appear on the *Official List of the *main market of the *London Stock Exchange. *See* LISTING REQUIREMENTS.

fully diluted earnings per share The *earnings per share for a company that takes into account the number of shares in actual issue as well as those that may be issued as a result of such factors as convertible loans and options or warranties.

fully paid share A *share in a company in which all calls for payment have been paid. The total paid will be the *par value plus any premium.

fully paid share capital *See* SHARE CAPITAL.

functions of money In economics, money fulfils the functions of acting as a *medium of exchange, a *unit of account, and a store of value. None of the functions occur in an economy based on barter.

fund 1. A resource managed on behalf of a client by a *financial institution. **2.** A separate pool of monetary and other resources used to support designated activities.

fundamental analysis Analysis of financial market instruments based on their underlying economics. It may, for example, involve the use of accounting information for company valuation or inflation and interest rates to understand exchange rate movements. It is a contrasting approach to technical analysis (*see* CHARTIST), which uses past prices and trading to forecast future prices. *See* INVESTMENT ANALYST.

funded debt 1. The part of the *national debt that the government is under no obligation to repay by a specified date. This consists mostly of *Consols. *See also* FUNDING OPERATIONS. **2.** Borrowing with a maturity in excess of a year.

funded pension scheme A pension scheme that pays benefits to retired people from a *pension fund invested in securities. The profits produced by such a fund are paid out as pensions to the members of the scheme.

funding Paying short-term debt by arranging long-term borrowing. *See* FUNDING OPERATIONS.

funding operations 1. The replacement of short-term fixed-interest debt (*floating debt) by long-term fixed-interest debt (*funded debt). This is normally associated with the government's handling of the *national debt through the operations of the Bank of England. The bank buys Treasury bills and replaces them with an equal amount of longer-term government bonds, thus lengthening the average maturity of government debt. This has the effect of tightening the monetary system, as Treasury bills are regarded by the commercial banks as liquid assets while bonds are not. *See also* OVERFUNDING. **2.** A change in the capital *gearing of a company, in which short-term debts, such as overdrafts, are replaced by longer-term debts, such as *debentures.

fund manager (investment manager) An employee of one of the larger institutions, such as an insurance company, *investment trust, or *pension fund, who manages its investment fund. The fund manager decides which investments the fund shall hold, in accordance with the specified aims of the fund, e.g. high income, maximum growth, etc.

fund of funds A *unit trust belonging to an institution in which most of its funds are invested in a selection of other unit trusts owned by that institution. It is designed to give maximum security to the small investor by spreading the investments across a wide range.

funds broker In the USA, a broker who arranges short-term loans between banks.

fund supermarket An Internet facility that provides private investors with a range of advice and investment opportunities.

fungible issue 1. A security that is interchangeable with another of the same class. **2.** A *bond issued on the same terms and conditions as a bond previously issued by the same company. It has the advantage of having paperwork consistent with the previous bond and of increasing the depth of the market of that particular bond (*see* DEEP MARKET; THIN MARKET). The *gross redemption yield on the fungible issue will probably be different from that of the original issue, which is achieved by issuing the bond at a discount or a premium.

fungibles 1. Interchangeable goods, securities, etc., that allow one to be replaced by another without loss of value. Bearer bonds and banknotes are examples. **2.** Perishable goods the quantity of which can be estimated by number or weight.

FUTOP Abbreviation for *Guarantee Fund for Danish Options and Futures.

futures *See* FUTURES CONTRACT.

Futures and Options Exchange (London Fox) The principal European exchange for soft commodities. A successor to the *London Commodity Exchange, which it replaced in 1987, it merged in 1996 with the *London International Financial Futures and Options Exchange, becoming a separate department within this exchange (**LIFFE Commodity Products**).

futures contract An agreement to buy or sell a fixed quantity of a particular commodity, currency, or security for delivery at a fixed date in the future at a fixed price. Unlike an *option, a futures contract involves a definite purchase or sale and not an option to buy or sell; it therefore may entail a potentially unlimited loss. However, **futures** provide an opportunity for those who wish to *hedge against changes in price. In London, futures are traded in a variety of markets. Financial futures are traded on the *London International Financial Futures and Options Exchange; the *London Commodity Exchange, which incorporates the Baltic International Freight Futures Exchange, deals with shipping and cocoa, coffee, and other foodstuffs; the *London Metal Exchange with metals; and the International Petroleum Exchange with oil. In these **futures markets**, in many cases actual goods (*see* ACTUALS) do not pass between dealers, a bought contract being cancelled out by an equivalent sale contract, and vice versa; money differences arising as a result are usually settled through a *clearing house (*see also* LONDON CLEARING HOUSE). In some futures markets only brokers are allowed to trade; in others, both dealers and brokers are permitted to do so. *See also* FORWARD-EXCHANGE CONTRACT.

futures-driven Describing a market in which trading in the futures market is driving prices on the spot markets.

futures market *See* FUTURES CONTRACT.

future value The value that a sum of money (the **present value**) invested at compound interest will have in the future. If the future value is F, and the present value is P, at an annual rate of interest r, compounded annually for n years, $F = P(1 + r)^n$. Thus a sum with a present value of £1000 will have a future value of £1973.82 at 12% p.a., after six years.

FX Abbreviation for *foreign exchange.

G3; G5; G7; G8; G10; G11; G77 Abbreviations for *Group of Three; *Group of Five; *Group of Seven; *Group of Eight; *Group of Ten; *Group of Eleven; *Group of Seventy Seven.

GAAP Abbreviation for *generally accepted accounting principles.

GAB Abbreviation for *general arrangements to borrow.

GAFTA Abbreviation for *Grain and Feed Trade Association.

gai atsu Foreign pressure on Japan to bring its trade and financial policies more in line with those of the rest of the developed world.

gaijin A foreign investor on the Japanese Stock Market.

game theory A mathematical theory, developed by J. von Neumann (1903–57) and O. Morgenstern (1902–77) in 1944, concerned with predicting the outcome of games of strategy (rather than games of chance) in which the participants have incomplete information about the others' intentions. Under perfect competition there is no scope for game theory, as individual actions are assumed not to influence others significantly; under oligopoly, however, this is not the case. Game theory has been increasingly applied to economics in recent years, particularly in the theory of industrial organizations. The theory was further elucidated by the economists John Nash, John Harsanyi, and Reinhard Selten, who received the Nobel Prize for Economics in 1994.

gaming contract A contract involving the playing of a game of chance by any number of people for money. A **wagering contract** involves only two people. In general, both gaming contracts and wagering contracts are by statute null and void and no action can be brought to recover money paid or won under them.

gamma One of a group of measures related to the pricing of *options that are known as *greeks. Expressed in formal terms, the gamma is the second partial derivative of the option price with respect to the value of the *underlying: that is, it measures how rapidly the relationship between the option price and the value of the underlying will change with changes in the value of the underlying. Whereas the *delta of an option expresses how much an option price will change with a change in the value of the underlying, the gamma expresses how much the delta will change with a change in the underlying. The value of the gamma is highest for an *at-the-money option.

gamma distribution A frequency distribution often used to characterize the distribution of financial returns. It differs from a *normal distribution in its *skewness (lack of symmetry). *Compare* LEPTOKURTIC DISTRIBUTION.

gamma-neutral portfolio An options portfolio in which the *gamma is zero. This means the portfolio has a constant *delta or relation between the value of the portfolio and the value of the *underlying.

gamma stocks Formerly, stocks in relatively small companies in which trade was infrequent. The term was used in the former classification system on the London Stock Exchange, but this has now been replaced by the *Normal Market Size system. *See also* ALPHA STOCKS.

Gann analysis In technical analysis (*see* INVESTMENT ANALYST), a method used to predict price cycles in financial markets.

Gantt chart A chart presenting a planned activity as a series of horizontal bands against a series of vertical lines representing dates. It can also be used to compare planned production in a specified period to actual production. It was invented by Henry A. Gantt in 1917.

GAO Abbreviation for *General Accounting Office.

gap **1.** A measure of *interest-rate risk used in banking. It comprises the difference between rate-sensitive assets and rate-sensitive liabilities within a particular range of repricing time periods. If short-term rate-sensitive assets are greater than short-term liabilities, the gap will lead to an *asset-sensitive situation in which an interest-rate fall will lower the profitability and value of a bank. *See* ASSET–LIABILITY GAP; MATURITY GAP. **2.** A sudden rise or fall in the price of a stock or a commodity, such that its opening price on an exchange is outside the range of the previous day's trading.

gap analysis (gap management) The management of a bank's *interest-rate risk by monitoring and controlling *gaps between rate-sensitive assets and liabilities. *See also* ASSET–LIABILITY MANAGEMENT.

gapping The use of *gaps to speculate in relation to expected interest-rate movements.

gap ratio The value of a bank's interest-rate assets (i.e. loans) divided by the value of its interest-rate liabilities (i.e. deposits). A value of the gap ratio of greater than one means that when interest rates rise, the profitability and value of a bank are likely to rise. *See* GAP.

garage **1.** To transfer assets and liabilities internationally in order to benefit from tax advantages. **2.** An annex to the main floor of the New York Stock Exchange.

GARCH Abbreviation for *general autoregressive conditional heteroscedasticity model.

Garman–Kohlhagen option-pricing model A modification of the *Black–Scholes option-pricing model to European-style currency options.

garnishee order An order made by a judge on behalf of a *judgment creditor restraining a third party (often a bank), called a **garnishee**, from paying money to the judgment debtor until sanctioned to do so by the court. The order may also specify that the garnishee must pay a stated sum to the judgment creditor, or to the court, from the funds belonging to the judgment debtor.

Garn–St Germain Act 1982 US legislation that enabled banks to compete for customers on equal terms with other money-market funds, allowed *savings and loans associations to make business loans and increase their consumer lending, gave the federal authorities powers to allow for mergers and acquisitions of failed banks and savings institutions, and increased the lending limits for national banks.

gatekeeper A manager in a large company who controls the flow of information.

It is the gatekeeper who decides what information shall be passed upwards to a parent company and downwards to a subsidiary.

gather in the stops To influence the price of a security by triggering *stop orders.

GATT Abbreviation for *General Agreement on Tariffs and Trade.

Gaussian distribution *See* NORMAL DISTRIBUTION.

gazump To raise the price of, or accept a higher offer for, land, buildings, etc., on which a sale price has been agreed but before the *exchange of contracts has taken place. The intending purchaser with whom the sale price had been verbally agreed has no remedy, even though he or she may have incurred expenditure on legal fees, surveys, etc. Proposals to reform the law in this respect have been put forward but not enacted.

gazunder To reduce an offer on a house, flat, etc., immediately before exchanging contracts, having previously agreed a higher price. In a market in which house prices are falling, the unscrupulous buyer is aware that the seller will be extremely anxious to sell, having incurred legal expenses and perhaps having bought another property.

GDP Abbreviation for *gross domestic product.

GDP deflator The factor by which the value of GDP (*see* GROSS DOMESTIC PRODUCT) at current prices must be reduced (deflated) to express GDP in terms of the prices of some base year (e.g. 1980). The GDP deflator is thus a measure of *inflation.

geared-equity capital unit (GECU) A *unit trust that provides a geared return on equity by investing in options.

geared futures and options fund (GFOF) A *unit trust that invests in futures and options.

geared investment trust An *investment trust that raises debt to increase its investment in equities. The shares of a geared investment trust tend to rise faster in rising markets and fall faster in falling markets than ungeared trusts.

gearing (capital gearing; equity gearing; financial gearing; leverage) The ratio of long-term debt funding to all long-term funding, or more rarely the ratio of long-term debt funding to equity funding. Increased gearing raises the risk to all funders, since it raises the probability of *financial distress. The US word **leverage** is increasingly used in the UK. *See also* OPERATIONAL GEARING.

gearing adjustment In *current cost accounting, an adjustment that reduces the charge to the owners for the effect of price changes on *depreciation, *stock, and *working capital. It is justified on the grounds that a proportion of the extra financing is supplied by the *loan capital of the business.

gearing effect 1. The way in which the capital *gearing of a company affects its shareholders' dividends and earnings per share. **2.** The impact of a change in the price of the *underlying on a portfolio payoff where the portfolio contains derivative products.

gearing ratios (leverage ratios) Ratios that express a company's capital *gearing. There are a number of different ratios that can be calculated from either the *balance sheet or the *profit and loss account. Ratios based on the balance sheet usually express *debt as a percentage of *equity, or as a percentage of debt plus equity. **Income gearing** is normally calculated by dividing the *profit before interest and tax by the gross interest payable to give the *interest cover.

GECU Abbreviation for *geared-equity capital unit.

geisha bond *See* SHOGUN BOND.

GEMU Abbreviation for *German Economic and Monetary Union.

General Accounting Office (GAO) The investigation and audit department of the US Congress.

General Agreement on Tariffs and Trade (GATT) A trade treaty that operated from 1948 until 1995, when it was replaced by the *World Trade Organization (WTO). GATT was supported by 95 nations and a further 28 nations applied its rules de facto. Its objectives were to expand world trade and to provide a permanent forum for international trade problems. GATT was especially interested in extending free trade, which it achieved in eight 'rounds': Geneva (1947), Annecy (1948), Torquay (1950), Geneva (1956), Dillon (1960–61), Kennedy (1964–67), Tokyo (1973–79), and Uruguay (1986–94).

general arrangements to borrow (GAB) The special arrangements made by the *Group of Ten (G10) to enable the *International Monetary Fund to increase its lending to members of G10. They came into effect in 1962 and were augmented in 1983 when Switzerland, though not a member of the IMF, joined the GAB, enabling it to extend its loan facilities to non-members.

general autoregressive conditional heteroscedasticity model (GARCH) In statistics, a generalized model of autoregressive conditional heteroscedasticity models, which are used in finance as a way of estimating volatility. These are complicated time-series econometric models, in which the past value of a variable is used to predict its future value. *See* HETEROSCEDASTIC.

general average loss A loss incurred for the common good and shared by all the parties to a venture.

General Commissioners An unpaid local body of persons of good standing appointed by the Lord Chancellor or, in Scotland, by the Secretary of State for Scotland, to hear appeals against income tax, corporation tax, and capital gains tax assessments or matters of dispute arising from them. General Commissioners can appoint their own clerk, often a lawyer, who can advise them on procedure and legal matters. *Compare* SPECIAL COMMISSIONERS.

general crossing *See* CHEQUE.

general insurance *Insurance cover against the occurrence of certain specified events. The most common examples of general insurance relate to the risks of fire, automobile damage or loss, and theft.

General Insurance Standards Council A UK regulatory body set up to oversee the insurance industry in 2000 but wound up in 2002 as a result of the *Financial Services Authority taking over the regulatory role in this sector in December 2001.

generally accepted accounting principles (GAAP) Standards followed by US accountants in measuring, recording, and reporting transactions. In the USA there is a requirement to state whether financial statements conform with GAAP. In the UK the concept is more loosely used but is normally taken to mean accounting standards and the requirements of company legislation and the stock exchange. *See*

ACCOUNTING CONCEPTS; FINANCIAL REPORTING STANDARD; INTERNATIONAL
ACCOUNTING STANDARDS BOARD; STATEMENT OF FINANCIAL ACCOUNTING STANDARDS;
STATEMENT OF STANDARD ACCOUNTING PRACTICE.

general obligation bond In the USA, a security in which the municipal
department with the authority to levy taxes has unconditionally promised payment.

general partner See PARTNERSHIP.

general power of investment A power, introduced by the Trustee Act 2000,
that allows a trustee to make any kind of investment that he could make if he were
absolutely entitled to the assets of the trust fund. Previously, trustees were only
permitted to make certain *authorized investments. This much wider general
power of investment may be expressly excluded in the trust instrument. There are
still some restrictions on investments in land. In exercising the general power of
investment, the trustees are required by the Act to consider criteria relating to the
suitability of the proposed investment to the trust and the need for diversification of
investment within the unique circumstances of the trust. Trustees are also required
by the Act to review the investments from time to time with the same standard
criteria in mind. Before investing, the trustee must obtain and consider proper
advice, unless he reasonably considers it unnecessary or inappropriate to do so.

general price level An index that gives a measure of the purchasing power of
money. In the UK, the best-known measure is the *Retail Price Index; in the USA it
is the consumer price index.

general undertaking The undertaking given by the directors of a UK company
setting out their obligations to the London Stock Exchange when their shares are to
be traded on the *unlisted securities market. It is equivalent to the listing
agreement (see LISTING REQUIREMENTS) of the *main market.

Gensaki The market for the resale and repurchase of medium- and long-term
government securities to provide a money market substitute in Japan.

geometric mean An average obtained by calculating the nth root of a set of n
numbers multiplied together. For example the geometric mean of 7, 100, and 107 is
$\sqrt[3]{74\,900} = 42.15$, which is considerably less than the *arithmetic mean of 71.3.

German Economic and Monetary Union (GEMU) The integration of the
economy and currency of the former East Germany (DDR) into the reunified state of
Germany in 1990.

German Futures and Options Market See DEUTSCHE TERMINBÖRSE.

German stock exchanges Stock exchanges in Berlin, Bremen, Dusseldorf,
Frankfurt, Hamburg, Hanover, Munich, and Stuttgart. Frankfurt is the largest
exchange, handling more than 75% of German equity trading (see FRANKFURT STOCK
EXCHANGE).

Gesellschaft The German name for a limited company. See AKTIENGESELLSCHAFT;
GESELLSCHAFT MIT BESCHRÄNKTER HAFTUNG.

Gesellschaft mit beschränkter Haftung (GmbH) The German name for a
private limited company. The letters GmbH after the name of a company is
equivalent to Ltd in the UK. Compare AKTIENGESELLSCHAFT.

GFOF Abbreviation for *geared futures and options fund.

gift The transfer of an asset from one person to another for no consideration. Gifts have importance for tax purposes; if they are sufficiently large they may give rise to charges under *inheritance tax if given within seven years prior to death. *See* POTENTIALLY EXEMPT TRANSFER.

gift aid A system enabling individuals and companies to donate money to charities and for the charities to recover the tax paid on these donations (thus increasing the value of the donation by 28% in 2004–05). The taxpayer must make a **gift aid declaration** to the charity, stating that the payment is to be treated as gift aid. This system was first introduced in 1990, but tax relief was subject to the donation being of a minimum value. From April 2000, however, the system was extended to gifts of any value, including regular and one-off payments. It replaced the *deed of covenant in favour of charities from that date, although existing covenants remain valid.

gift tax A US federal tax on property given away, levied on the donor.

gift with reservation A gift in which the donor retains some benefit (e.g. the gift of a house in which the donor continues to reside). In general, the donor is treated as not having parted with the asset until any reservation has been removed.

gilt-edged dealer *See* PRIMARY DEALER.

gilt-edged market makers (**gilts primary dealers**) The *market makers approved and supervised by the Bank of England for dealing directly with the Bank of England in gilt-edged securities. They have to some extent taken over the role of the *government broker.

gilt-edged security (**gilt**) A *fixed-interest security or stock issued by the British government in the form of **Exchequer stocks** or **Treasury stocks**. Gilts are among the safest of all investments, as the government is unlikely to default on interest or on principal repayments. They may be irredeemable (*see* CONSOLS) or redeemable. **Redeemable gilts** are classified as: **long-dated gilts** or **longs** (not redeemable for 15 years or more), **medium-dated gilts** or **mediums** (redeemable in 5 to 15 years), or **short-dated gilts** or **shorts** (redeemable in less than 5 years). Like most fixed-interest securities, gilts are sensitive not only to interest rates but also inflation rates. This led the government to introduce **index-linked gilts** in the 1970s, with interest payments moving in a specified way relative to inflation. Most gilts are issued in units of £100. If they pay a high rate of interest (i.e. higher than the current rate) a £100 unit may be worth more than £100 for a period of its life, even though it will only pay £100 on *redemption.

gilt repos market A market in the sale and repurchase of *gilt-edged securities set up by the Bank of England in 1996. Its size relative to the money market has made it an attractive market for the implementation of monetary policy with regard to the liquidity of the banking system.

gilts primary dealers *See* GILT-EDGED MARKET MAKERS.

gilt strip A discount UK government stock that has been issued by the Bank of England since 1996. A bond can be divided into a set of payments, which are made by the state and sold at a discount.

gilt unit trust A *unit trust that invests in *gilt-edged securities only.

Ginnie Mae **1.** Colloquial US name for the *Government National Mortgage Association (GNMA). **2.** Colloquial US name for a mortgage-supported bond issued by the Government National Mortgage Association. A **Ginnie Mae pass-through** is a bond backed by mortgages guaranteed by the GNMA, entitling the buyer to part of a pool of residential mortgages. These securities are called *pass-throughs because the investor receives both the principal and interest from the bank or originating mortgage supplier, who retains no margin or profit.

giro 1. A banking arrangement for clearing and settling small payments that has been used in Europe for many years. In 1968 the Post Office set up the UK **National Girobank** (now **Girobank plc**) based on a central office in Bootle, Merseyside. Originally a system for settling debts between people who did not have bank accounts, it now offers many of the services provided by *commercial banks, with the advantage that there are more post offices, at which Girobank services are provided, than there are bank branches. Also the post offices are open for longer hours than banks. Girobank also offers banking services to businesses, including an **automatic debit transfer** system, enabling businesses to collect money from a large number of customers at regular intervals for a small charge. **Bank Giro** is a giro system operated in the UK, independently of Girobank, by the clearing banks. It has no central organization, being run by bank branches. The service enables customers to make payments from their accounts by *credit transfer to others who may or may not have bank accounts. **Bancogiro** is a giro system in operation in Europe, enabling customers of the same bank to make payments to each other by immediate book entry. **2.** A colloquial name for a payment made by the UK Department of Social Security to a person in need of financial support.

Giscard bond A French gold-linked bond.

glamour stock A fashionable investment stock.

Glass–Steagall Act 1933 US legislation that separated commercial banking and securities operations by banks. It was introduced in the aftermath of the great stock-market crash of 1929 to lessen the likelihood of such panics occurring again. It has been extensively modified in recent years, most notably by the *Financial Services Modernization Act 1999.

global asset allocation The allocation of assets and financial obligations in a portfolio on a global basis.

global bond 1. A bond traded in a number of different markets. **2.** A single bond for the total amount of a new issue of bonds, issued on a temporary basis to the bank (normally the *paying agent) that has responsibility for distributing the actual bonds to investors. In due course the global bond, sometimes referred to as a **global bearer bond**, is exchanged for the actual bonds.

global custody Safekeeping, usually by banks, of securities held on behalf of clients. It can include full portfolio services, with valuation and reporting, settlement of trades, registration of ownership, use of specialized nominee companies, collection of domestic and foreign income, and tax accounting. These services span markets and securities in a number of countries.

globalization 1. The process that has enabled investment in financial markets to be carried out on an international basis. It has come about as a result of improvements in technology and *deregulation; with globalization, for example, investors in London can buy shares or bonds directly from Japanese brokers in Tokyo rather than passing through intermediaries. *See also* DISINTERMEDIATION. **2.** The process by which the world economy has become dominated by powerful *multinational enterprises operating across national and geographical barriers. The emergence since the 1980s of a single world market in which companies can easily move their operations from one country to another to take advantage of factors such as lower labour costs has affected the ability of national governments to order their own economic affairs. The benefits and drawbacks of this process, and the extent to which it may be controlled or influenced, are the subject of much controversy. **3.** The internationalization of products and services by large firms, so that the same product can be marketed in many different countries, usually with the same brand name and imagery. **4.** The consideration of business in terms of an international *value chain.

global medium-term note A *medium-term note issued on US markets and *euromarkets.

global offering A security offered in a number of different markets at the same time.

global risk management Overall *risk management, generally with an international perspective.

Globex A global round-the-clock futures and options trading system introduced by the *Chicago Mercantile Exchange, the Chicago Board of Trade, *Marché à Terme Internationale de France, and *Reuters.

GmbH Abbreviation for *Gesellschaft mit beschränkter Haftung. Compare AG.

GNMA Abbreviation for *Government National Mortgage Association, often referred to colloquially as *Ginnie Mae.

gnomes de l'ombre (shadowy gnomes) A pejorative phrase originally coined in 1995 by the French prime minister, Alain Jupé, to characterize international dealers who were speculating against the French government's view of the value of the franc.

gnomes of Zürich An unflattering term applied to Swiss bankers and financiers, alluding to their secrecy and speculative activity. It was popularized by the Labour politician George Brown during the sterling crisis of 1964.

GNP Abbreviation for *gross national product.

go-around The soliciting by the US Federal Reserve of quotes from primary securities dealers in relation to *repurchase agreements.

godfather offer A *tender offer pitched so high that the management of the target company is unable to discourage shareholders from accepting it.

go-go fund A mutual investment fund that attempts to obtain high capital gains.

going ahead The unethical practice in which a broker/dealer trades on his or her own account before trading for clients. See also BACKING AWAY.

going away The situation of an asset that is being withdrawn from the market, as a result of its having been bought by a retail customer, who is more likely to hold it than trade it.

going-concern concept A principle of accounting practice that assumes businesses to be going concerns, unless circumstances indicate otherwise. It assumes that an enterprise will continue in operation for the foreseeable future, i.e. that the accounts assume no intention or necessity to liquidate or significantly curtail the scale of the enterprise's operation. The implication of this principle is that assets are shown at cost, or at cost less depreciation, and not at their break-up values; it also assumes that liabilities applicable only on liquidation are not shown. The **going-concern value** of a business is higher than the value that would be achieved by disposing of its individual assets, since it is assumed that the business has a continuing potential to earn profits. The concept is assumed in the preparation of *financial statements. If an *auditor thinks otherwise the *auditors' report should be qualified.

going long Adopting a *long position in a financial instrument.

going short Adopting a *short position in a financial instrument.

gold card A *credit card or charge card that entitles its holder to various benefits (e.g. an unsecured overdraft, some insurance cover, a higher limit, lower interest rates) in addition to those offered to standard card holders. The cards are available only to those on higher-than-average incomes.

gold certificate A statement certifying ownership of current gold holdings, issued by the US Treasury Department to Federal Reserve Banks.

gold clause A clause in a loan agreement between governments stipulating that repayments must be made in the gold equivalent of the currency involved at the time either the agreement or the loan was made. The purpose is to protect the lender against a fall in the borrower's currency, especially in countries suffering high rates of inflation.

gold coins In the UK, coins made of gold ceased to circulate after World War I. At one time it was illegal to hold more than four post-1837 gold coins and there have been various restrictions on dealing in and exporting gold coins at various times. Since 1979 (Exchange Control, Gold Coins Exemption, Order) gold coins may be imported and exported without restriction, except that gold coins more than 50 years old with a value in excess of £8000 cannot be exported without authorization from the Department of Trade and Industry. *See also* BRITANNIA COINS; KRUGERRAND.

gold convertible A certificate that can be converted into gold.

golden handcuffs Financial incentives offered to key staff to persuade them to remain with an organization.

golden handshake *See* COMPENSATION FOR LOSS OF OFFICE.

golden hello A payment made to induce an employee to take up employment. The tax treatment depends on the nature of the payment; in some cases the taxpayer has successfully argued that the payment should be tax-free. However, in 1991 the House of Lords ruled that a payment made to a well-known footballer by a football club, as an inducement to join a new club, was taxable.

golden parachute A clause in an employment contract, usually of a senior executive, that provides for financial and other benefits if this person is sacked or decides to leave as the result of a takeover or change of ownership.

golden share A share in a company that controls at least 51% of the voting rights. A golden share has been retained by the UK government in some *privatization issues to ensure that the company does not fall into foreign or other unacceptable hands.

gold forward-rate agreement A *forward-exchange contract based on determining a price for gold.

gold future A *futures contract for the delivery of gold.

Goldilocks economy A colloquial term for an economy that combines low inflation with steady economic growth. Such an economy is "not too hot, not too cold, but just right"—like the porridge in the story of *Goldilocks and the Three Bears*.

Gold Institute The trade association of North American gold producers.

gold market The market for buying and selling gold, which can be traded as *bullion, as coins, or in the futures and forward markets.

gold pool An organization of eight countries (Belgium, France, Italy, Netherlands, Switzerland, UK, USA, and West Germany) that between 1961 and 1968 joined together in an attempt to stabilize the price of gold.

gold reserves Reserves held in the form of gold by a country for intervention on foreign-exchange markets.

gold shares Shares in gold-mining companies.

gold standard A former monetary system in which a country's currency unit was fixed in terms of gold. In this system a currency was freely convertible into gold and free import and export of gold was permitted. It formed the basis for stable prices, since it linked the money supply to the quantity of gold reserves in a country. The UK was on the gold standard from the early 19th century until it finally withdrew in 1931. Most other countries withdrew soon after. *See also* INTERNATIONAL MONETARY FUND.

gold tranche *See* RESERVE TRANCHE.

gold warrant A specialized *derivative that gives the holder an *option to buy or sell in gold at a *maturity date in excess of one year.

good A *commodity or *service regarded by economists as satisfying a human need. An **economic good** is one that is both needed and sufficiently scarce to command a price.

good delivery Delivery on the terms specified by the contract.

good for the day A broker's instruction that is valid for a single day.

Goodhart's law An economic theory stating that if a definition of the *money supply were to be used as the basis for monetary policy, the stability of its statistical relationship with spending on the economy would break down and the policy would prove ineffective. The law is now used more widely to highlight the difficulty of regulators focusing on the value of any specific variable.

goodwill The difference between the value of the separable net *assets of a business and the total value of the business. Purchased goodwill is the difference between the fair value of the price paid for a business and the aggregate of the fair values of its separable net assets. It may be written off to *reserves or recognized as an *intangible asset in the balance sheet and written off by *amortization to the *profit and loss account over its useful economic life. Internally generated goodwill should not be recognized in the financial statements of an organization.

gopik A monetary unit of Azerbaijan worth one hundredth of a *manat.

go private To take a company into private ownership, thus removing its shares from the stock exchange. *Compare* GO PUBLIC.

go public To apply to a stock exchange to become a *public limited company. *Compare* GO PRIVATE. *See* FLOTATION.

Gordon growth model A model used to value businesses or shares based on applying a *present-value formula to future dividends. It assumes that the value of shares is the present value of future dividends, which will grow at a fixed rate g, and is expressed in the formula:

$P_t = D_{i+1}/(r - g)$,

where P_t is the value of a share or business in time period t; D_{i+1} is the value of the dividend in time period t plus one time period; r is the appropriate present value discount rate; and g is the growth rate of dividends per time period. The formula will only work if r is greater than g, which will be the case for mature companies.

gourde (G) The standard monetary unit of Haiti, divided into 100 centimes.

Government Accounting Standards Board In the USA, the organization responsible for accounting standards for government units. It is under the control of the Financial Accounting Foundation.

government broker The stockbroker formerly appointed by the government to sell government securities on the London Stock Exchange, under the instructions of the Bank of England. The government broker is also the broker to the National Debt Commissioners (*see* NATIONAL DEBT). Until October 1986 (*see* BIG BANG) the government broker was traditionally the senior partner of Mullins & Co. Since then, when the Bank of England started its own gilt-edged dealing room, the government broker has been appointed from the gilt-edged division of the Bank of England, although some of the functions formerly carried out by the government broker are now undertaken by the *gilt-edged market makers.

government grant An amount paid to an organization to assist it to pursue activities considered socially or economically desirable.

Government National Mortgage Association (GNMA) A US government agency that guarantees payment on securities backed by mortgages granted by such national organizations as the Federal Housing Association. *See also* GINNIE MAE.

government security (government stock) *See* GILT-EDGED SECURITY.

Government Statistical Service (GSS) *See* OFFICE FOR NATIONAL STATISTICS.

government stock Stocks issued by a government, e.g. US Treasury bonds or UK Treasury stock and Exchequer stock (*see* GILT-EDGED SECURITY).

Gower Report A report on the protection of investors delivered to the UK government in 1984 by Professor J. Gower. Many of its recommendations were adopted in the subsequent *Financial Services Act 1986.

GPW Abbreviation for *gross premium written.

grace and notice provision The provision in a loan agreement that a borrower who fails on the due date to meet either an interest obligation or capital repayment obligation or who fails to comply with an undertaking is not initially in default. The grace and notice provision is inserted into a loan agreement to avoid problems arising because of administrative mistakes, such as payments not being made on the correct day.

grace period 1. The interval between the establishment of a loan and the first due date for repayment. **2.** Extra time granted for payment after a due date. *See*

DAYS OF GRACE. **3.** The period between a debt or security being offered and the initiation of its purchase or sinking fund.

grading 1. One of several recognized standards of a product traded on a commodity exchange. **2.** One of several different categories recognized by a system of *credit rating or credit scoring.

graduated payments mortgage A type of *mortgage in which the payments increase over time.

Grain and Feed Trade Association (GAFTA) A commodity association that provides contracts for transaction in grain, rice, and animal feeds. It no longer provides a futures or options market, which has now moved to the *Futures and Options Exchange.

Gramm–Leach–Bliley Act *See* FINANCIAL SERVICES MODERNIZATION ACT 1999.

Gramm–Rudman Act 1985 US legislation requiring the federal budget to balance.

grandfathered activity A transaction or practice that may be continued by those already engaged in it, but that is forbidden to new participants by changes in the legal or regulatory framework.

granny bond An index-linked savings certificate (*see* NATIONAL SAVINGS). They were formerly only available to persons over retirement age, hence the name.

grant anticipation note In the USA, a *municipal bond issued in anticipation of receipt of a federal grant.

grant date 1. The initial date for a deferred-start option. **2.** The date of receipt of an employee option.

granter *See* GRANTOR.

grant-in-aid Any grant from central government to a local authority for particular services, other than the rate-support grant.

grant of probate An order from the High Court in the UK authorizing the executors of a will to deal with and distribute the property of the deceased person. If the person died intestate or did not appoint executors, the administrator of the estate has to obtain *letters of administration.

grantor (granter) The seller of an *option.

grantor trust A US trust in which tax is levied on individual rather than trust income.

grantor underwritten note An agreement according to which a group of banks buy fixed-rate notes from investors and sell them on by auction.

graveyard market A market in which securities are rarely traded.

greeks Measures of the sensitivity of the value of an *option to the different determinants of option value. They may be the partial derivatives of an option-pricing formula with respect to such right-hand side terms as the *exercise price, the price of the *underlying, the risk-free interest rate, and the time to maturity. Individual greeks include *delta, *gamma, *kappa, *lambda, *rho, *tau, *theta, and *vega.

green audit *See* ENVIRONMENTAL AUDIT.

greenback A colloquial name for a US currency note, especially a dollar bill.

Greenbury Committee A *Confederation of British Industry (CBI) committee that investigated and reported on executive remuneration. Its report was published in 1995.

green-field project A project that starts from scratch, e.g. building a factory on a virgin site in the country.

greenmail (greymail) The purchase of a large block of shares in a company, which are then sold back to the company at a premium over the market price in return for a promise not to launch a bid for the company. This practice is not uncommon in the USA, where companies are much freer than in the UK to buy their own shares.

greenshoe (greenshoe option) An option given by an issuer of securities to an underwriter entitling the latter to buy and sell extra shares in an issue if there is high public demand. The term derives from the first company to provide such an arrangement, the Green Shoe Manufacturing Co.

Gresham's law The maxim named after the 16th-century adviser to the royal court, Sir Thomas Gresham, that "bad money drives out good money, but that good money does not drive out bad". It arose from the once widespread practice of 'clipping' gold and silver coins (i.e. removing shavings from the edges of the coins) or of counterfeiting gold and silver coins. The bad coins (clipped or counterfeit coins) tended to be passed on quickly, whereas the good coins were retained or hoarded.

Grey Book Regulations issued by the Bank of England to the UK banking sector.

grey-hair investment *See* GREY WAVE.

grey knight In a takeover battle, a counterbidder whose ultimate intentions are undeclared. The original unwelcome bidder is the *black knight, the welcome counterbidder for the target company is the *white knight. The grey knight is an ambiguous intervener whose appearance is unwelcome to all.

greymail *See* GREENMAIL.

grey market **1.** Any market for goods that are in short supply. It differs from a black market in being legal. **2.** A market in shares that have not been issued, although they are due to be issued in a short time. Market makers will often deal with investors or speculators who are willing to trade in anticipation of receiving an allotment of these shares or are willing to cover their deals after flotation. This type of grey market provides an indication of the market price (and premium, if any) after flotation. An investor who does not receive the anticipated allocation has to buy the shares on the open market, often at a loss.

grey money *See* BLACK MONEY.

grey wave (grey-hair investment) A company that is thought to be potentially profitable and ultimately a good investment, but that is unlikely to fulfil expectations in the near future. The fruits of an investment in the present should be available when the investor has grey hair.

Groschen **1.** A former monetary unit of Austria, worth one hundredth of a *Schilling (until 2002). **2.** A former German coin, worth 10 Pfennige (until 2002).

gross domestic product (GDP) The monetary value of all the goods and services produced by an economy over a specified period. It is measured in three ways:
(1) on the basis of expenditure, i.e. the value of all goods and services bought, including consumption, capital expenditure, increase in the value of stocks, government expenditure, and exports less imports;
(2) on the basis of income, i.e. income arising from employment, self-employment, rent, company profits (public and private), and stock appreciation;
(3) on the basis of the value added by industry, i.e. the value of sales less the costs of raw materials.
In the UK, statistics for GDP are published monthly by the government on all three bases, although there are large discrepancies between each measure. Economists are usually interested in the real rate of change of GDP to measure the performance of an economy, rather than the absolute level of GDP. *See also* GDP DEFLATOR; GROSS NATIONAL PRODUCT; NET NATIONAL PRODUCT.

gross income 1. The income of a person or an organization before the deduction of the expenses incurred in earning it. **2.** Income that is liable to tax but from which the tax has not been deducted. For many types of income, tax may be deducted at source (*see* DEDUCTIONS AT SOURCE) leaving the taxpayer with a net amount.

grossing up Converting a net return into the equivalent gross amount.

gross interest The amount of interest applicable to a particular loan or deposit before tax is deducted. Interest rates may be quoted gross or net. The gross interest less the tax deducted at the basic rate of income tax gives the net interest. Any tax suffered is usually, but not always, available as a credit against tax liabilities. Since 1991 low wage-earners and non-taxpayers have been able to apply to have interest on bank and building-society accounts paid gross.

gross investment *See* NET INVESTMENT.

gross national product (GNP) The *gross domestic product (GDP) with the addition of interest, profits, and dividends received from abroad by UK residents and with those payments made from the UK to overseas residents deducted. The GNP better reflects the welfare of the population in monetary terms, although it is not as accurate a guide as to the productive performance of the economy as the GDP. *See also* NET NATIONAL PRODUCT.

gross premium written (GPW) The total insurance premium written minus costs and reinsurance premiums paid.

gross profit (gross margin) The total sales revenue of an organization, less the cost of the goods sold. The cost of the goods sold includes their purchase price and costs of bringing them to a state to be sold but not the costs of distribution, general administration, or finance costs.

gross receipts The total amount of money received by a business in a specified period before any deductions for costs, raw materials, taxation, etc. *Compare* NET RECEIPTS.

gross redemption yield (effective yield; yield to maturity) The internal rate of return of a bond bought at a specified price and held until maturity; it therefore includes all the income and all the capital payments due on the bond. The tax payable on the interest and the capital repayments are ignored.

gross settlement An *interest-rate swap in which the two payments are made in total and not netted off against each other.

gross spread A proportion of the underwriting proceeds paid to managers and underwriters.

gross yield The *yield on a security calculated before tax is deducted. This yield is often quoted for the purpose of comparison even on ordinary shares, where dividends have tax deducted before they are paid. The yield after tax is paid is called the **net yield**.

grosz (*plural* **groszy**) A monetary unit of Poland worth one hundredth of a *zloty.

group A parent undertaking and its subsidiary or subsidiaries. *See* CONSOLIDATION; CONSOLIDATED FINANCIAL STATEMENTS.

group accounts (group financial statements) *See* CONSOLIDATED FINANCIAL STATEMENTS.

group life assurance A life-assurance policy that covers a number of people, usually a group of employees or the members of a particular club or association. Often a single policy is issued and premiums are deducted from salaries or club-membership fees. In return for an agreement that all employees or members join the scheme, insurers are prepared to ask only a few basic questions about the health of a person joining. However, with the advent of AIDS insurers are no longer prepared to waive all health enquiries.

Group of Eight (G8) The *Group of Seven plus Russia. Russia was admitted as a full member of this economic summit grouping in June 2002.

Group of Eleven (G11) The eleven main debtor countries of Latin America. The group, set up in 1984, consists of Argentina, Bolivia, Brazil, Chile, Colombia, the Dominican Republic, Ecuador, Mexico, Peru, Uruguay, and Venezuela.

Group of Five (G5) Formerly, the five countries France, Japan, UK, USA, and Germany who agreed to stabilize their exchange rates by acting together to overcome adverse market forces. The agreement, made at the Plaza Hotel, New York, in 1985 was known as the **Plaza Agreement**.

Group of Forty An international association of medium-sized banks.

Group of Seven (G7) The seven leading industrial nations excluding Russia and China: namely, the USA, Japan, Germany, France, UK, Italy, and Canada. This group evolved from the first economic summit held in 1976 and now holds an annual meeting attended by heads of state. The original aim was to discuss economic coordination but the agenda has since broadened to include political issues. Since the 1980s increasing enthusiasm for international economic cooperation has sometimes led to collective action, for example on exchange rates as a result of meetings of G7 finance ministers. Since 1991 Russia has attended G7 meetings, initially as an observer but from 2002 as a full participant. *See* GROUP OF EIGHT.

Group of Seventy Seven (G77) A group of developing countries set up in 1964 to enhance their bargaining power with the developed nations and to offset the influence of the *Group of Ten. The **Group of Twenty Four** (G24) is a subset of this group. The name G77 is misleading as there are now some 120 members of the group.

Group of Ten (G10; The Paris Club) The ten relatively prosperous industrial nations that agreed in 1962 to lend money to the *International Monetary Fund (IMF). They are Belgium, Canada, France, Italy, Japan, The Netherlands, Sweden, Germany, UK, and the USA. They inaugurated *Special Drawing Rights. Switzerland, although not a member of the IMF, is a party to the *general arrangements to borrow, which the G10 countries established to provide additional credit facilities. Luxembourg is also an associate member.

Group of Thirty A group of economic experts comprising individuals from central and commercial banks and finance ministries, as well as academic economists. The group was founded in 1979 by the Rockefeller Foundation to carry out research into international economic issues.

Group of Three (G3) The three largest industrialized economies, i.e. the USA, Germany, and Japan.

Group of Twenty An organization of twenty large international banks.

Group of Twenty Four (G24) *See* GROUP OF SEVENTY SEVEN.

group relief Relief available to companies within a 75% group as a result of which *qualifying losses can be transferred to other group companies. The losses transferred are available to set against the other group members' profits chargeable to corporation tax, thus reducing the overall tax liability for the group. A 75% group, for group relief, exists if one company holds 75% or more of:
• the ordinary share capital, and
• the distributable income rights, and
• the rights to the net assets in a winding-up.

growth **1.** An increase in the value of an asset. If growth is sought in an investment, it is an increase in its capital value that is required. *See also* GROWTH STOCKS. **2.** The expansion of an economy, usually expressed in terms of an increase of national income.

growth curve A curve on a graph in which a variable is plotted as a function of time. The curve thus illustrates the growth of the variable. This may be used to show the growth of a population, sales of a product, price of a security, etc. If the log of the variable is plotted against time, a straight line upwards represents a fixed level of growth.

growth fund A managed fund holding assets that are expected to grow in value and provide capital gains. In general, these funds are supposed to provide higher returns but with greater risks.

growth industry Any industry that is expected to grow faster than GDP.

growth rate **1.** The amount of change over a period in some of the financial characteristics of a company, such as sales revenue or profits. It is normally measured in percentage terms and can be compared to the *Retail Price Index, or some other measure of inflation, to assess the real performance of the company. **2.** The change in the value of a variable divided by its initial level, or the natural log of the final value of a variable divided by its initial level.

growth stocks Securities that are expected to offer the investor sustained *capital growth. Investors and investment managers often distinguish between growth stocks and income stocks. The former are expected to provide *capital gains; the latter, high income. The investor will usually expect a growth stock to be an ordinary share in a company whose products are selling well and whose sales are expected to expand, whose capital expenditure on new plant and equipment is high, whose earnings are growing, and whose management is strong, resourceful, and investing in product development and long-term research. Growth stocks are likely to be high *beta stocks, since they will rise more rapidly when the overall market rises.

GSS Abbreviation for Government Statistical Service. *See* OFFICE FOR NATIONAL STATISTICS.

guaraní (₡) The standard monetary unit of Paraguay, divided into 100 céntimos.

guarantee **1.** *See* WARRANTY. **2.** A promise made by a third party (**guarantor**), who is not a party to a contract between two others, that the guarantor will be liable if one of the parties fails to fulfil the contractual obligations. For example, a bank may make a loan to a person, provided that a guarantor is prepared to repay the loan if the borrower fails to do so. The banker may require the guarantor to provide some *security to support the guarantee. *See also* BANK GUARANTEE.

guaranteed bond (**guaranteed stock**) A *bond in which payments of principal or interest are guaranteed by a third party other than the issuer. In the USA this is often a state.

guaranteed coupon reinvestment bond A *bond entitling an investor to receive additional bonds at par instead of coupon payments.

guaranteed equity bond A *bond in which the return is related to the equity-market index but the principal is guaranteed.

guaranteed-income bond A bond issued by a life-assurance company that guarantees the purchaser a fixed income for a specified period as well as a guaranteed return of capital at the end of the term or on prior death. *See also* SINGLE-PREMIUM ASSURANCE.

guaranteed investment contract A US insurance contract in which the holder is guaranteed a rate of return.

guaranteed minimum pension The earnings-related component of a state pension that a person would have been entitled to as an employee of a company, had that person not contracted out of the *State Earnings-Related Pension Scheme (SERPS). Any private pension contract must pay at least the guaranteed minimum pension if it is to be an acceptable replacement of a SERPS pension.

guaranteed return structure A property of a security that enables it to preserve the initial investment while allowing participation in gains.

guaranteed share A share in which interest or return is guaranteed by another company.

guaranteed stock *See* GUARANTEED BOND.

guaranteed warrant In the USA, a *warrant that offers exposure to a stock index.

guarantee fund An *offshore fund in which the investor's initial investment is guaranteed.

Guarantee Fund for Danish Options and Futures (**FUTOP**) An options and futures exchange, based in Copenhagen, that opened in September 1988 and trades as an exchange in Danish government bond futures, options, and mortgage credits.

guarantor A person who guarantees to pay a debt incurred by someone else if that person fails to repay it. A person who acts as a guarantor for a bank loan, for example, must repay the loan if the borrower fails to repay it when it becomes due.

guilder **1.** The standard monetary unit of the Netherlands Antilles (NAf) and Surinam (Sf), divided into 100 cents. **2.** The former standard monetary unit of The Netherlands, divided into 100 cents. It was subsumed into the euro for all purposes other than cash transactions in January 1999 and abolished in 2002.

gun jumping A colloquial term for *insider dealing.

g

haircut **1.** *See* MARGIN. **2.** A fee or commission.

haircut finance Borrowing against pledged collateral, usually in the form of securities.

halal Acceptable under Islamic law. The term is applied to those forms of banking and finance that avoid the religious prohibition against taking interest payments. *Compare* HARAAM. *See* ISLAMIC FINANCE.

halala A monetary unit of Saudi Arabia worth one hundredth of a *riyal.

haler (*plural* **haleru** or **halers**) A monetary unit of the Czech Republic and Slovakia, worth one hundredth of a *koruna.

half-commission man A person who is not a member of a stock exchange but works for a *stockbroker, introducing clients in return for half, or some other agreed share, of the commission.

half-life The period of time before half of the principal of a bond is redeemed.

hammering An announcement on the *London Stock Exchange that a broker is unable to meet his or her obligations. It was formerly (until 1970) introduced by three blows of a hammer by a waiter and followed by the broker's name.

Hammersmith and Fulham swaps *Swaps entered into by the London borough of Hammersmith and Fulham although it had no legal authority to do so. The swaps were declared *ultra vires* by the House of Lords in 1992.

handle The whole number associated with a bid or offer. Because the market moves by small amounts, bids and offers are often expressed as the fractions or decimals added to known whole numbers.

hand signals In *open outcry markets, signals used to communicate between *floor traders in the dealing process.

Hang Seng Index An arithmetically weighted index based on the capital value of 33 stocks on the Hong Kong Stock Exchange. It was first quoted in 1964 and takes its name from the Hang Seng Bank. The number of stocks, 33, was chosen because the bank was founded in 1933 and 33 is a lucky number in Chinese astrology.

hao A monetary unit of Vietnam worth one tenth of a *đông.

haraam Forbidden by Islamic law. In financial contexts, this applies chiefly to lending or borrowing money at interest. Various schemes enable Muslims to take out loans, notably mortgages, without violating this principle of faith. *Compare* HALAL. *See* ISLAMIC FINANCE.

hara-kiri swap A *swap made on terms less favourable than those currently offered on the market. Such a swap may be offered as a loss-leader in order to attract business. The term derives from the Japanese word for ritual suicide.

hard Describing markets that are expected to rise due to an excess of demand.

hard commodity A *commodity that is not perishable, excluding precious metals and energy products. The key hard commodities are copper, zinc, mercury, tin, aluminium, and lead.

hard currency A currency that is commonly accepted throughout the world; they are usually those of the western industrialized countries although other currencies have achieved this status, especially within regional trading blocs. Holdings of hard currency are valued because of their universal purchasing power. Countries with *soft currencies go to great lengths to obtain and maintain stocks of hard currencies, often imposing strict restrictions on their use by the private citizen.

hard dollars A fee paid to a US stockbroker, investment adviser, etc., for research, analysis, or advice, as opposed to **soft dollars**, which refers to the commission earned on purchases made.

harvesting strategy Making a short-term profit from a particular product shortly before withdrawing it from the market. This is often achieved by reducing the marketing support it enjoys, such as advertising, on the assumption that the effects of earlier advertising will still be felt and the product will continue to sell.

head and shoulders The *chartist theory that a graph of a financial market price against time that begins to resemble a human head and shoulders indicates an imminent major market fall before the second arm is reached.

Heath–Jarrow–Morton option-pricing model A binomial model for pricing bond options that is based on the mean reversion properties of interest rates. *See* BINOMIAL PROCESS.

heaven-and-hell bond A *bond in which the redemption amount is linked to a spot rate of exchange (*see* SPOT CURRENCY MARKET) at maturity.

heavy share **1.** A share that has a high price relative to the average price of shares on the market. As investors tend to prefer to buy larger numbers of low-priced shares, heavy shares are often split, i.e. the par value is divided by two or four, which has the same effect on the market price. **2.** A share with greater relative voting rights.

hedge A transaction or position designed to mitigate the risk of other financial exposures. For example, a manufacturer may contract to sell a large quantity of a product for delivery over the next six months. If the product depends on a raw material that fluctuates in price, and if the manufacturer does not have sufficient raw material in stock, an open position will result. This open position can be hedged by buying the raw material required on a *futures contract; if it has to be paid for in a foreign currency the manufacturer's currency needs can be hedged by buying that foreign currency forward or on an *option. Operations of this type do not offer total protection because the prices of *spot goods and futures do not always move together, but it is possible to reduce the vulnerability of an open position substantially by hedging.

Buying futures or options as a hedge is only one kind of hedging; it is known as **long hedging**. In **short hedging**, something is sold to cover a risk. For example, a fund manager may have a large holding of long-term fixed income investments and is worried that an anticipated rise in interest rates will reduce the value of the *portfolio. This risk can be hedged by selling interest-rate futures on a *financial futures market. If interest rates rise the loss in the value of the portfolio will be offset by the profit made in covering the futures sale at a lower price.

hedged fund A unit trust that is subject to minimum regulation, typically a partnership or mutual fund that attempts to obtain gains by exploiting market anomalies. These funds, however, are often high-return and are regarded as speculative. The hedged fund **Long Term Capital Management** got into trouble in 1998, raising concerns over the stability of the whole international financial system.

hedge ratio The amount of a *hedge that needs to be bought in order to cover one unit of the position to be hedged.

hedging against inflation Protecting one's cash flow, income, or capital against inflation by buying *equities or making other investments that are likely to rise with the general level of prices.

hedging effectiveness The degree to which a *hedge adequately matches the movements in the position to be hedged. It can be measured by the *R-squared of the regression of the value of the initial position to that of the value of the hedge.

Herstatt risk. *See* SETTLEMENT RISK.

heteroscedastic In statistics, describing the errors in a *regression analysis that are not constant for different values of the independent variable. *Compare* HOMOSCEDASTIC. *See* GENERAL AUTOREGRESSIVE CONDITIONAL HETEROSCEDASTICITY MODEL.

hidden reserve Funds held in reserve but not disclosed on the balance sheet (they are also known as **off-balance-sheet reserves** or **secret reserves**). They arise when an asset is deliberately either undisclosed or undervalued. Such hidden reserves are permitted for some banking institutions but are not permitted for limited companies as they reduce profits and therefore the corporation tax liability of the company.

hidden tax (stealth tax) A tax, the incidence of which may be hidden from the person who is suffering it. An example could be a tax levied on goods at the wholesale level, which increases the retail price in such a way that the final customer cannot detect either that it has happened or the amount of the extra cost.

high-coupon bond refunding A situation in which a funder replaces high-coupon bonds with low-coupon bonds to reduce funding costs when interest rates fall.

higher rate of income tax A rate of *income tax that is higher than the *basic rate of income tax. For 2004–05 higher rate tax is payable on taxable income, after *personal allowances and other allowances, of over £31,400. The rate of tax is 40%.

high/low method A form of *chartist analysis in which a price on a financial market is charted against time. Each day is represented by a vertical bar denoting the range between the day's highest and lowest price and has a small horizontal bar across it at the day's closing price.

High-Street bank *See* COMMERCIAL BANK.

high yielder A stock or share that gives a high yield but is more speculative than most, i.e. its price may fluctuate.

hire purchase (HP) A method of buying goods in which the purchaser takes possession of them as soon as an initial instalment of the price (a **deposit**) has been paid; ownership is obtained when all the agreed number of subsequent instalments have been completed. A **hire-purchase agreement** differs from a **credit-sale**

agreement and **sale by instalments** (or a **deferred payment agreement**) because in these transactions ownership passes when the contract is signed. It also differs from a contract of hire, because in this case ownership never passes. Hire-purchase agreements in the UK were formerly controlled by government regulations stipulating the minimum deposit and the length of the repayment period. These controls were removed in 1982. Hire-purchase agreements were also formerly controlled by the Hire Purchase Act 1965, but most are now regulated by the Consumer Credit Act 1974. In this Act a hire-purchase agreement is regarded as one in which goods are bailed in return for periodical payments by the bailee; ownership passes to the bailee if the terms of the agreement are complied with and the option to purchase is exercised. A hire-purchase agreement often involves a *finance company as a third party. The seller of the goods sells them outright to the finance company, which enters into a hire-purchase agreement with the hirer.

historical cost A method of valuing units of stock or other assets based on the original cost incurred by the organization. For example, the issue of stock using *first-in, first-out cost or *average cost charge the original cost against profits. Similarly, the charging of depreciation to the *profit and loss account, based on the original cost of an asset, is writing off the historical cost of the asset against profits. An alternative approach is the use of *current cost accounting.

historical cost accounting A system of accounting based primarily on the original costs incurred in a transaction. It is relaxed to some extent by such practices as the valuation of *stock at the lower of cost and *net realizable value and, in the UK, revaluation of *capital assets. The advantages of historical cost accounting are that it is relatively objective, easy to apply, difficult to falsely manipulate, and suitable for audit verification. In times of high inflation, however, the results of historical cost accounting can be misleading as profit can be overstated, assets understated in terms of current values, and *capital maintenance is only concerned with the nominal amount of the capital invested rather than its purchasing power. Because of these defects it is argued that historical cost accounting is of little use for decision making, but attempts to replace it with such other methods as *current cost accounting have failed. Company legislation sets out the rules for the application of historical cost accounting to *financial statements. Companies may also choose to use alternative accounting rules based on current cost accounting.

historical rate rollover An extension of a foreign currency *forward-exchange contract at the original rate.

historical summary A voluntary statement appearing in the *annual accounts and report of some companies in which the main financial results are given for the previous five to ten years.

historic volatility The past value of the *standard deviation of the price of, or return on, a financial obligation. *See* VOLATILE.

holder The purchaser of a financial obligation, i.e. a dealer who has a *long position in this obligation.

holding company (parent company) A company in a *group that holds shares in other companies (usually, but not necessarily, its subsidiaries).

holding cost The cost of maintaining a particular financial *position.

holding period The time period over which a dealer or investor expects to hold a particular *position.

holdout A situation in which creditors refuse to agree to a particular reorganization proposal for a firm in *financial distress.

Ho–Lee option-pricing model A binomial option-pricing model based on the term structure of interest rates. *See* BINOMIAL PROCESS.

home banking Carrying out banking transactions by means of a home computer linked to a bank's computer via the Internet (**e-banking**) or by means of a telephone link to a call centre or a computerized system (**telephone banking**). This enables the account-holder to carry out certain operations – most commonly checking the balance held or transferring sums between accounts – at any time of the day or night without leaving the home or office. Although regular transfers, such as direct debits, can be arranged, paying in or drawing cheques is not possible in home banking (although it is using a *postal account). In the UK these services are now offered by all the High-Street banks but only a minority of account-holders make regular use of them. Home banking is, however, a growing trend among business customers.

home service assurance *See* INDUSTRIAL LIFE ASSURANCE.

homoscedastic In statistics, describing errors in a *regression analysis that are constant for different values of the independent variable. *Compare* HETEROSCEDASTIC.

Hong Kong Commodities Exchange Ltd A commodity exchange in Hong Kong founded in 1977. It deals in sugar futures and other commodities.

Hong Kong stock exchanges Two exchanges were established in 1891 and 1921, which were merged into the Hong Kong Stock Exchange in 1947. This took over the Far East Stock Exchange (founded 1969), the Kam Ngam Stock Exchange (founded 1971), and the Kowloon Stock Exchange (founded 1972) to become the **Stock Exchange of Hong Kong** in April 1986. *See also* HANG SENG INDEX.

horizontal integration *See* INTEGRATION.

horizontal spread A combination of *options with different expiry dates, such as a long put option combined with a short put option.

host bond A *bond with a *warrant attached.

hostile bid A *takeover bid that is unwelcome either to the board of directors of the target company or to its shareholders.

hot money **1.** Money that moves at short notice from one financial centre to another in search of the highest short-term interest rates, for the purposes of *arbitrage, or because its owners are apprehensive of some political intervention in the money market, such as a *devaluation. Hot money can influence a country's *balance of payments. **2.** Money that has been acquired dishonestly and must therefore be untraceable.

HP Abbreviation for *hire purchase.

hryvna (hryvnya) The standard monetary unit of Ukraine, divided into 100 kopiykas.

Hull–White option-pricing model A trinomial model for pricing interest-rate-based options. *See* TRINOMIAL TREE.

human capital The skills, general or specific, acquired by an individual in the course of training and work experience. The concept was introduced by Gary Becker in the 1960s in order to point out that wages reflect in part a return on human capital. This theory has been used to explain large variations in wages for apparently similar jobs and why even in a recession a firm may retain its workers on relatively high wages, in spite of involuntary unemployment.

hurdle rate The rate of interest in a *capital budgeting study that a proposed project must exceed before it can be regarded worthy of consideration. The hurdle rate is often based on the *cost of capital or the *weighted average cost of capital, adjusted by a factor to represent the risk characteristics of the projects under consideration.

hybrid A synthetic financial instrument formed by combining two or more individual financial instruments, such as a bond with a warrant attached.

hyperinflation A situation in which levels of *inflation are so high that money becomes virtually worthless and monetary exchange breaks down, to be replaced by a system of barter.

hypothecation **1.** An authority given to a banker, usually as a **letter of hypothecation**, to enable the bank to sell goods that have been pledged (*see* PLEDGE) to them as security for a loan. It applies when the bank is unable to obtain the goods themselves. The goods have often been pledged as security in relation to a documentary bill, the banker being entitled to sell the goods if the bill is dishonoured by non-acceptance or non-payment. **2.** A mortgage granted by a ship's master to secure the repayment with interest, on the safe arrival of the ship at her destination, of money borrowed during a voyage as a matter of necessity (e.g. to pay for urgent repairs). The hypothecation of a ship itself, with or without cargo, is called **bottomry** and is effected by a **bottomry bond**; that of its cargo alone is **respondentia** and requires a **respondentia bond**. The bondholder is entitled to a maritime *lien. **3.** The linking of certain taxes or government revenue to particular expenditures. **4.** The practice of reserving the revenue from a tax or duty for spending on a particular stated purpose; for example dedicating revenues received from the tax on tobacco products to health spending.

IBBR Abbreviation for Inter Bank Bid Rate. *See* LONDON INTER BANK BID RATE.

IBCA Abbreviation for *International Banking Credit Agency.

IBEL Abbreviation for *interest-bearing eligible liabilities.

IBF Abbreviation for *international banking facility.

IBMBR Abbreviation for Inter Bank Market Bid Rate. *See* LONDON INTER BANK BID RATE.

IBNR claims reserve A reserve held by an insurance company for claims 'incurred but not yet reported'.

IBOR Abbreviation for *Inter Bank Offered Rate.

IBRC Abbreviation for *Insurance Brokers Registration Council.

IBRD Abbreviation for *International Bank for Reconstruction and Development.

ICC Abbreviation for *International Chamber of Commerce.

ICCH Abbreviation for International Commodities Clearing House. *See* LONDON CLEARING HOUSE.

ICSA Abbreviation for *Institute of Chartered Secretaries and Administrators.

ICSID Abbreviation for *International Centre for the Settlement of Investment Disputes.

IDA Abbreviation for *International Development Association.

IDR Abbreviation for *International Depository Receipt.

IFA Abbreviation for *independent financial adviser.

IFAD Abbreviation for *International Fund for Agricultural Development.

IFC Abbreviation for *International Finance Corporation.

Ifox Abbreviation for *Irish Futures and Options Exchange.

IGC Abbreviation for Inter-Government Conference. *See* MAASTRICHT TREATY.

IHT Abbreviation for *inheritance tax.

ijarah *See* ISLAMIC FINANCE.

ijarawa-iktina *See* ISLAMIC FINANCE.

illegal contract A contract prohibited by statute (e.g. one between traders providing for minimum resale prices) or illegal at common law on the grounds of *public policy. An illegal contract is totally void, but neither party (unless innocent of the illegality) can recover any money paid or property transferred under it, according to the maxim *ex turpi causa non oritur actio* (a right of action does not arise out of an evil cause). Related transactions may also be affected. A related transaction between the same parties (e.g. if X gives Y a promissory note for money due under an illegal contract) is equally tainted with the illegality and is therefore void. The same is true of a related transaction with a third party (e.g. if Z lends X the money to pay Y) if the original illegality is known to the third party.

illegal partnership A partnership formed for an illegal purpose and therefore disallowed by law. A partnership of more than 20 partners is illegal, except in the case of certain professionals, e.g. accountants, solicitors, and stockbrokers.

illiquid 1. Denoting an asset that cannot readily be converted into cash. **2.** Denoting a person or an organization lacking in cash or in assets readily convertible into cash.

ILU Abbreviation for *Institute of London Underwriters.

IMF Abbreviation for *International Monetary Fund.

immediate annuity An *annuity contract that begins to make payments as soon as the contract has come into force.

immediate holding company A company that has a *controlling interest in another company, even though it is itself controlled by a third company, which is the *holding company of both companies.

immigrant remittances Money sent by immigrants from the country in which they work to their families in their native countries. These sums can be a valuable source of foreign exchange for the native countries.

immunization A technique for eliminating *interest-rate risk in bond and fixed-interest portfolios by making the *duration of the assets and liabilities equal.

impact day The first day on which a *new issue may be traded.

imperfect hedge A *hedge that does not entirely eliminate *market risk. Changes in the underlying position are not entirely reflected by changes in the hedge. This may be owing to timing issues or to the use of hedging instruments that are not entirely correlated to the underlying position. *Compare* PERFECT HEDGE.

implicit interest A benefit accruing to a bank customer in lieu of an actual interest payment. For example, implicit interest may be in the form of free services or zero transaction charges.

implied forward interest rate The implied interest rate for some period of time in the future, as derived from current interest rates. It is part of the *term structure of interest rates, and can be calculated using the rates on a series of *zero-coupon bonds that incorporate the time period under consideration.

implied future rate The implied interest rate for some period of time in the future, as derived from the price of *interest-rate futures contracts.

implied term A provision of a contract not agreed to by the parties in words but either regarded by the courts as necessary to give effect to their presumed intentions or introduced into the contract by statute (as in the case of contracts for the sale of goods). An implied term may constitute either a condition of the contract or a *warranty; if it is introduced by statute it often cannot be expressly excluded.

implied volatility The expected *standard deviation in the price of the *underlying in an options contract. It is calculated by using the market price of the option to solve an option-pricing formula in which the volatility of the underlying is the only unknown. *See* BLACK–SCHOLES OPTION-PRICING MODEL.

implied yield A yield calculated on the basis of the current *term structure of interest rates, working from the assumption that the *yield curve is an unbiased estimate of the bond's return.

import duty A tax on imported goods; it can either be a fixed amount or a percentage of the value of the goods (*see* AD VALOREM). Import duties have been used to protect domestic producers against foreign competition and as a source of revenue.

imprest account A means of controlling petty-cash expenditure in which a person is given a certain sum of money (float or imprest). When some of it has been spent that person provides the appropriate vouchers for the amounts spent and is then reimbursed so that the float is restored. Thus at any given time the person should have either vouchers or cash to a total of the amount of the float.

imputation system Formerly, the UK system in which the *advance corporation tax paid by a company making *qualifying distributions was available to set against the gross *corporation tax for the company. The shareholder receiving the *dividend was treated as having suffered tax on the dividend and the *tax credit was available to set against his or her own liability to tax. Advance corporation tax was abolished in 1999.

IMRO Abbreviation for Investment Management Regulatory Organization. *See* SELF-REGULATING ORGANIZATION.

in-arrears swap An *interest-rate swap in which the floating-rate element of the swap is set at the end of the time period.

in-barrier option An *option that is eliminated if the price of the *underlying fails to pass a certain level. In such cases the premium paid for the option is partly reimbursed. *Compare* OUT-BARRIER OPTION.

incentive-compatible contract A contract designed to ensure mutually beneficial behaviour by the parties. So, for example, the employment contracts of a company's managers might incorporate a bonus system to make sure that their interests and those of the shareholders are congruent. *See* AGENCY PROBLEM.

incentive compensation (incentive bonus) The provision to employees of rewards for the delivery of economic value (e.g. in the form of rising share value deriving from greater productivity).

incentive stock option In the USA, the right given to employees to purchase a specified number of company shares at a specified price during a specified period. Only when the stock is sold by employees is it subject to tax.

incentive trade An agreement by which a broker receives a higher payment if he or she obtains a more favourable rate for a transaction.

incestuous share dealing The buying and selling of shares in companies that belong to the same group, in order to obtain an advantage of some kind, usually a tax advantage. The legality of the transaction will depend on its nature.

inchoate instrument A *negotiable instrument in which not all the particulars are given. The drawer of an inchoate instrument can authorize a third party to fill in a specified missing particular.

incidence of taxation The impact of a tax on those who bear its burden, rather than those who pay it. For example, *value added tax (VAT) is paid by traders, but part of the ultimate burden of it falls on the consumer of the trader's goods or services. Again, a company may pay corporation tax but if it then raises its prices or reduces its employees' wages to recoup some or all of the tax, it may be said to have shifted the incidence.

income The return, measured over a given time period, for the use of factors of production. It may take the form of payments for labour, rent, dividends, interest, or profit. *See also* GROSS INCOME.

income and expenditure account An account, similar to a *profit and loss account, prepared by an organization whose main purpose is not the generation of profit (e.g. a charity). It records the income and expenditure of the organization and results in either a surplus of income over expenditure or of expenditure over income.

income bond **1. (National Savings Income Bond)** A type of bond introduced by the Department for *National Savings in 1982. They offer monthly interest payments on investments between £2000 and £250,000. Interest is taxable but not deducted at source. The bonds have a guaranteed life of 10 years. **2.** *See* GUARANTEED-INCOME BOND. **3.** A US bond with guaranteed principal but in which the interest payments depend on the earnings of the issuer.

income distribution **1.** The proportions of income paid to different sections of a community. **2.** The payment by a *unit trust of its half-yearly income to unit holders, in proportion to their holdings. The income distributed is the total income less the manager's service charge and income tax at the standard rate.

income shares *See* INVESTMENT TRUST.

income smoothing The manipulation by companies of certain items in their *financial statements so that they eliminate large movements in profit and are able to report a smooth trend over a number of years. The practice is pursued because of the belief that investors have greater confidence in companies that are reporting a steady increase in profits year by year. It is doubtful if any regulations can totally prevent this form of *creative accounting.

incomes policy A government policy aimed at controlling inflation and maintaining full employment by holding down increases in wages and other forms of income and prices by means of statute or *moral suasion.

income statement In the USA, the equivalent of a UK *profit and loss account.

income stock A stock or share bought primarily for the steady and relatively high income that it can be expected to produce. This may be a fixed-interest gilt-edged security or an ordinary share with a good dividend *yield record.

income tax (IT) A tax based on an individual's income. In general individuals can earn income without paying tax up to a threshold, with subsequent income giving rise to tax liabilities, usually at increasing rates as income increases (progressive taxation). In UK tax legislation income is not defined; amounts received are classified under various headings or *schedules and these schedules are subdivided into cases. In order to be classed as income an amount received must fall into one of these schedules. There are some specific occasions when the legislation requires capital receipts to be treated as income for taxation purposes, e.g. when a landlord receives a lump sum on the granting of a lease. In the UK the importance of the distinction between income and capital has diminished since income and capital have been charged at the same rate. Prior to 6 April 1988 capital was charged at 30%, whereas the top rate of income tax was 60%. The tax is calculated on the taxpayer's taxable income, i.e. gross income less any *income-tax allowances and deductions. If the allowances and deductions exceed the gross income in a *fiscal year, no income tax is payable. In the UK, there are three tax-rate bands: a *starting rate of income tax of 10% on taxable earnings up to £2020, a *basic rate of income tax of 22% on taxable earnings between £2020 and £31,400, and a *higher rate of income tax at 40% on taxable earnings over £31,400 (2004–05 figures). *See also* PAYE.

income-tax allowances Allowances that may be deducted from a taxpayer's gross income before calculating the liability to *income tax. Every individual who is a UK resident is entitled to a *personal allowance, the level of which will depend on the age of the individual. After 5 April 2000 the former married couple's allowance was discontinued for all couples in which the elder spouse was under 65 on that date: it has since been replaced by a series of tax credits for families with children under 16. If one spouse was born before 6 April 1935, the married couple's allowance is £5725 for 2004–05. This increases to £5795 if one spouse is aged 75 and over. A blind person's allowance is £1560.

income-tax year *See* FISCAL YEAR.

income warrant A *warrant that pays interest before it is exercised.

inconvertible currency A currency that cannot be legally converted into other currencies. It is often the case that currencies are inconvertible for certain purposes, such as overseas investment. Currencies are most likely to be inconvertible where the underlying economy is weak or underdeveloped.

inconvertible paper money Paper money that cannot be converted into gold. Most paper money now falls into this category, although until 1931, in the UK, the Bank of England had an obligation to supply any holder of a bank note with the appropriate quantity of gold.

incorporated company *See* COMPANY.

increasing capital An increase in the number or value of the shares in a company to augment its authorized *share capital. If the articles of association of the company do not permit this to be done (with the agreement of the members), the articles will need to be changed. A company cannot increase its share capital unless authorized to do so by its articles of association.

increasing rate note A *junk bond in which the interest rate is set with an increasing margin to a reference rate over time.

increasing rate preference share (increasing rate preferred stock) A *preference share in which the coupon rate rises over time.

incremental cash flow The net changes to *cash flow that will result from a new decision or activity by a company. Incremental cash flow is a key factor in appraising new projects or investments and the capital expenditure they will require; these are evaluated according to the total nature of their impact on cash flow, calculated on a *present value basis. *See also* DISCOUNTED CASH FLOW.

incremental cost of capital The overall cost of raising extra finance. For example, if extra debt is incurred, this increases the risk to equity and debt funders, who will in turn demand a higher rate of return on their investment. The concept is also applied to funding raised to implement specific decisions, and should reflect the risks involved in the activity.

indemnity 1. An agreement by one party to make good the losses suffered by another, usually by payment of money, repair, replacement, or reinstatement. **2.** An undertaking by a bank's client, who has lost a document (such as a share certificate or bill of lading), that the bank will be held harmless against any consequences of the document's absence if it proceeds to service the documents that have not been mislaid. The bank usually requires a *letter of indemnity to make sure that it suffers no loss.

indemnity insurance Any insurance designed to compensate a policyholder for a loss suffered, by the payment of money, repair, replacement, or reinstatement. In every case the policyholder is entitled to be restored to the same financial position as that immediately before the loss-causing event occurred. There must be no element of profit to the policyholder nor any element of loss. Most – but not all – insurance policies are *indemnity contracts. For example, personal accident and life-assurance policies are not contracts of indemnity as it is impossible to calculate the value of a lost life or limb (as the value of a car or other property can be calculated).

indenture 1. A *deed, especially one creating or transferring an estate in land. It derives its name from the former practice of writing the two parts of a two-part deed on one piece of parchment and separating the two parts by an irregular wavy line. The two parts of the indenture were known to belong together if the indented edges fitted together. **2.** A document establishing the terms and conditions of a securities issue.

independent broker A member of the *New York Stock Exchange who acts for other members in a transaction.

independent financial adviser (IFA) A UK person or firm defined under the *Financial Services Act 1986 as an adviser who is not committed to the products of any one company or organization. Such a person is licensed to operate by one of the *Self-Regulating Organizations or *Recognized Professional Bodies replaced by the *Financial Services Authority in the *Financial Services and Markets Act 2000. With no loyalties except to the customer, the IFA must offer **best advice** from the whole market place. Eight categories of IFA exist, grouped into four main areas: advising on investments; arranging and transacting life assurance, pensions, and unit trusts; arranging and transacting other types of investments; and management of investments. All licensed independent financial advisers contribute to a compensation fund for the protection of their customers.

independent intermediary A person who acts as a representative of a prospective policyholder in the arrangement of an insurance or assurance policy. In *life assurance and *pensions it is a person who represents more than one insurer and is legally bound to offer advice to clients on the type of assurance or investment contracts best suited to their needs. In general insurance the independent intermediary can represent more than six insurers and is responsible for advising clients on policies that best suit their needs. They must, themselves, have *professional-indemnity insurance to cover any errors that they may make. Although, in both cases, intermediaries are the servants of the policyholder (and the insurer is therefore not responsible for their errors), they are paid by the insurer in the form of a commission, being an agreed percentage of the first or renewal premium paid by the policyholder.

independent taxation A system of personal taxation introduced in the UK in the fiscal year 1990–91 in which a husband and wife are treated as completely separate and independent taxpayers for both *income tax and *capital gains tax. The change affects a number of reliefs, primarily the personal allowance, to which every taxpayer is entitled: it also introduced a new married couples allowance. Moreover under this system each spouse is entitled to their own capital gains tax exemption and wives will pay tax on their own income, including their share arising from jointly held property.

index-allocated principal collateralized mortgage A form of home loan in which the repayment rate is determined by changes in an index.

index-amortizing rate swap A *swap in which the notional principal changes according to the movements in an index. If, for example, interest rates fall then the notional principal may be deemed to fall.

index arbitrage The practice of simultaneously buying *index futures and selling the stocks that underlie them (or vice versa), in order to exploit any anomalies between their prices. *See* ARBITRAGE.

indexation 1. The policy of connecting such economic variables as wages, taxes, social-security payments, annuities, or pensions to rises in the general price level (*see* INFLATION) This policy is often advocated by economists in the belief that it mitigates the effects of inflation. In practice, complete indexation is rarely possible, so that inflation usually leaves somebody worse off (e.g. lenders, savers) and somebody better off (borrowers). *See* RETAIL PRICE INDEX. **2.** Formerly, an adjustment to take account of the rise in the *Retail Price Index over the period of ownership of an asset. Indexation was applied to the cost, or 31 March 1982 value, of an asset. The indexed cost, or indexed 31 March 1982 value, was deducted from the proceeds of sale on disposal of the asset, in order to establish the *chargeable gain for *capital gains tax purposes. Indexation was introduced to eliminate the part of the gain arising from inflation. This system was effectively abolished from 5 April 1998. However, for assets acquired before that date, the indexation allowance is calculated to 5 April 1998 and this figure is used to calculate the chargeable gain in any subsequent disposal. For all other disposals made after 5 April 1998 the indexation allowance is replaced by *taper relief.

indexed principal swap A *swap in which the notional principal changes according to some index rate.

indexed security 1. A *security that has its coupon payment or redemption value adjusted for inflation. **2.** A security in which the coupon or the principal is related to the performance of an index.

index fund (tracker fund) A portfolio of investments weighted in the same proportions as a leading financial market index, such as FT-SE 100 (*see* FINANCIAL TIMES SHARE INDEXES). This ensures that the fund does not do worse than that particular index. The process of linking a portfolio in this way to a specific share index is called *index tracking.

index futures A *futures contract on a *financial futures market, such as the *London International Financial Futures and Options Exchange, which offers facilities for trading in futures and *options on a financial index as for example the FT-SE 100 Index and the FT-SE Eurotrack 100 Index (*see* FINANCIAL TIMES SHARE INDEXES). On the FT-SE 100 Index the trading unit is £25 per index point; thus if a futures contract is purchased when the index stands at 2400, say, the buyer is covering an equivalent purchase of equities of £60,000 (£25 × 2400). If the index rises 100 points the purchaser can sell a matching futures contract at this level, making a profit of £2500 (£25 × 100). On the FT-SE Eurotrack 100 Index the trading unit is DM100 per index point. *See also* PORTFOLIO INSURANCE.

indexing *See* INDEX FUND.

index-linked annuity *See* INDEXATION.

index-linked gilts *See* GILT-EDGED SECURITY; INDEXATION.

index-linked savings certificates *See* INDEXATION; NATIONAL SAVINGS.

index number A number used to represent the changes in a set of values between a *base year and the present. If the index reflects fluctuations in a single variable, such as the price of a commodity, the index number can be calculated using the formula:

$$100(p_n/p_0),$$

where p_0 represents the price in the base year and p_n represents the price in the current year. In practice many indices reflect variations in a combination of variables, such as the raw materials required to manufacture a product. In this situation it is necessary to produce an index that weights the important variables; these are known as **weighted aggregate indices**. If both costs and quantities have varied over a period, it is further necessary to find a way of using the same quantities for the numerator and denominator of the index. When the calculation uses base-year quantities as the fixed point, the resultant index is a **base-weighted** (or **Laspeyres'**) **index**, i.e.:

100(total cost of base year quantities at current prices/total cost of base year quantities at base year prices),

or

$$100(\Sigma p_n q_0/\Sigma p_0 q_0),$$

where p represents the price and q represents the quantity. When the calculation uses current year quantities, it is known as **current-weighted** (or **Paasche's**) **index**, i.e.:

100(total cost of current quantities at current prices/total cost of base year quantities at current prices),

or

$$100(\Sigma p_n q_n/\Sigma p_0 q_n).$$

See also FINANCIAL TIMES SHARE INDEXES; RETAIL PRICE INDEX.

index tracking 1. Setting up a portfolio or investment product in such a way that it will provide the same returns as a particular market index. *See* INDEX FUND. **2.** Comparing the performance of an investment portfolio with a *benchmark index.

index warrant A *warrant exercisable for cash based on a stock index.

indication of interest A mechanism whereby investors give indications of their possible reactions to the pricing of new share issues. This information is then used in establishing the issue price.

indicative prices On a financial market, prices quoted as indicators of the likely prices at which market makers or dealers will trade. However, they are not explicit commitments to deal at those prices.

indicator A measurable variable that gives information regarding economic performance or prospects. Examples of economic indicators are price, money supply, income, imports, and exports.

indirect quote The expression of an exchange rate in terms of the number of units of a foreign currency corresponding to a single unit of the domestic currency. For example, in the UK an indirect quote for the dollar might be $1.8 = £1. *Compare* DIRECT QUOTE.

indirect taxation Taxation that is intended to be borne by persons or organizations other than those who pay the tax (*compare* DIRECT TAXATION). The principal indirect tax in the UK is *value added tax (VAT), which is paid by traders as goods or services enter into the chain of production, but which is ultimately borne by the consumer of the goods or services. One of the advantages of indirect taxes is that they can be collected from comparatively few sources while their economic effects can be widespread.

individual retirement account (IRA) A US pension plan that allows annual sums to be set aside from earnings free of tax and accumulated in a fund, which pays interest. Basic-rate tax is payable once the saver starts to withdraw from the account, which must be done no later than the participant's 70th birthday. The concession is not available to employees in a company-pension scheme or profit-sharing scheme.

Individual Savings Account (ISA) A savings portfolio for small investors introduced in the UK in 1999. It replaced *personal equity plans (PEPs) and *Tax Exempt Special Savings Accounts (TESSAs); ISAs entitle individuals to save up to £7000 per year free of tax. The savings may be in the form of cash, shares, or life-assurance policies. ISAs are available in two main forms: **maxi-ISAs**, which must include shares, either exclusively or together with cash or assurance policies (or both), and the whole package must be supplied by one provider; and **mini-ISAs**, in which each component can be supplied by different providers, the maximum holding of shares being £3000, of cash £3000, and of assurance policies £1000. Savers can invest in either one maxi-ISA or up to three mini-ISAs in one year but not both. ISAs can be cashed in at any time without loss of the tax relief which includes exemption from personal income tax and capital gains tax. *See also* ISA MORTGAGE.

industrial bank **1.** A relatively small *finance house that specializes in *hire purchase, obtaining its own funds by accepting long-term deposits, largely from the general public. **2.** A US bank that specializes in industrial leasing.

industrial life assurance A life-assurance policy, usually for a small amount, the premiums for which are paid on a regular basis (weekly or monthly) and collected by an agent of the assurance company, who calls at the policyholder's home. Records of the premium payments are kept in a book, which – together with the policy document – has to be produced to make a claim. This type of assurance began in industrial areas (hence its name), where small weekly policies were purchased to help pay the funeral expenses of the policyholder. The company official, who calls to collect the premium is called an agent or, in certain areas, a tally man (*see also* AGENCY). This type of insurance is now more widely known as **home service assurance**. However, it is becoming obsolete, due to its high costs and low revenues.

industrials Stocks in industrial companies.

ineligible bill A *bill of exchange that is not acceptable for discounting at the relevant central bank.

inflation A general increase in prices in an economy and consequent fall in the purchasing value of money. *See also* RETAIL PRICE INDEX.

inflation accounting A method of accounting that, unlike *historical cost accounting, attempts to take account of the fact that a monetary unit (e.g. the pound sterling) does not have a constant value; because of the effects of inflation, successive accounts expressed in that unit do not necessarily give a fair view of the trend of profits. The principal methods of dealing with inflation have been *current cost accounting and *current purchasing power accounting.

inflationary gap The difference between the total spending in an economy (both private and public) and the total spending that would be needed to maintain full employment in a given time period.

inflationary spiral A description of the inflationary process, in which price rises stimulate wage rises, which in turn lead to further price rises.

inflation proofing Increasing the value of an asset, such as a pension, in line with increases in a cost-of-living index, such as the *Retail Price Index. In the USA an index-linked security is known as an **inflation-proof security**.

inheritance tax (IHT) A tax introduced in the Budget of 1986 to replace *capital transfer tax (which in turn replaced **estate duty**). Inheritance tax is chargeable on the death of an individual domiciled in the UK on all property, wherever it is situated. It is also charged on *potentially exempt transfers made within seven years of death. A non-UK domiciled individual is charged on death to inheritance tax on all UK property. Inheritance tax arises on lifetime *chargeable transfers at a lifetime rate, which is half the death rate of inheritance tax (*see also* EXEMPT TRANSFERS). In 2004 the threshold at which inheritance tax takes effect was set at £263,000. No tax is payable if the cumulative total of all chargeable transfers is less than the threshold. Above this amount, tax is payable on the excess at a single rate of 40%.

initial charge The charge paid to the managers of a *unit trust by an investor when units are first purchased. For most trusts the initial charge ranges between 5% and 6%, as laid down in the trust deed. *Money-market unit trusts and *exempt unit trusts have lower initial charges and in some cases no initial charge.

initial margin A payment that must be deposited in a brokerage account on the initial purchase or sale of an *exchange-traded future or option to cover the risks involved in the transaction. *See* MARGIN.

initial public offering (IPO) The US name for a *flotation.

initial yield The gross initial annual income from an asset divided by the initial cost of that asset. *Compare* GROSS REDEMPTION YIELD.

injunction An order by a court that a person shall do, or refrain from doing, a particular act. This is an equitable remedy that may be granted by the High Court wherever 'just and convenient'. The county court also has a limited jurisdiction to grant injunctions. An **interlocutory injunction** lasts only until the main action is heard. **Interim injunctions**, lasting a short time only, may be granted on the application of one party without the other being present (an **ex parte interim injunction**) if there is great urgency. **Prohibitory injunctions** forbid the doing of a particular act; **mandatory injunctions** order a person to do some act. Failure to obey an injunction is contempt of court and punishable by a fine or imprisonment.

inland bill (agency bill) A *bill of exchange that is both drawn and payable in the UK. Any other bill is classed as a **foreign bill**.

Inland Revenue *See* BOARD OF INLAND REVENUE.

input tax *Value added tax paid by a *taxable person on purchasing goods or services from a VAT-registered trader. The input tax, excluding irrecoverable input VAT, is set against the *output tax in order to establish the amount of VAT to be paid to the tax authorities.

inscribed stock (registered stock) Shares in loan stock, for which the names of the holders are kept in a register rather than by the issue of a certificate of ownership. On a transfer, a new name has to be registered, which makes them cumbersome and unpopular in practice.

insider dealing (insider trading) Dealing in company securities with a view to making a profit or avoiding a loss while in possession of information that, if generally known, would affect their price (*see* INSIDER INFORMATION). Under the UK Companies Securities (Insider Dealing) Act 1985 those who are or have been connected with a company (e.g. the directors, the company secretary, employees, and professional advisers) are prohibited from such dealing on or, in certain circumstances, off the stock exchange if they acquired the information by virtue of their connection and in confidence. The prohibition extends to certain unconnected persons to whom the information has been conveyed. Similar laws on insider dealing now operate in most developed countries.

insider information Price-sensitive information held by officers of a company or their advisers. In most developed countries, it is illegal to trade on the basis of this knowledge. *See* INSIDER DEALING.

insolvency The inability to pay one's debts when they fall due. In the case of individuals this may lead to *bankruptcy and in the case of companies to *liquidation. In both of these cases the normal procedure is for a specialist, a trustee in bankruptcy or a liquidator, to be appointed to gather and dispose of the assets of the insolvent and to pay the creditors. Insolvency does not always lead to bankruptcy and liquidation, although it often does. An insolvent person may have valuable assets that are not immediately realizable.

insolvency practitioner A person authorized to undertake insolvency administration as a *liquidator, provisional liquidator, *administrator, *administrative receiver, or nominee or supervisor under a *voluntary arrangement. Insolvency practitioners are members of the Insolvency Practitioners Association.

Insolvency Practitioners Association A professional body whose members act as *liquidators, receivers, and trustees in *insolvency and are identified by the letters MIPA (membership) or FIPA (fellowship).

insolvency risk 1. The *risk that a borrower may be unable to repay a debt. **2.** The risk that a *counterparty may be unable to honour a contract owing to insolvency. *See* COUNTERPARTY RISK.

insolvency test A test of the ability of a company to continue trading. Under UK legislation directors may be liable if a company continues to trade while insolvent.

inspection and investigation of a company An inquiry into the running of a company made by inspectors appointed by the Department of Trade and Industry. Such an inquiry may be held to supply company members with information or to investigate fraud, unfair prejudice, nominee shareholdings, or *insider dealing. The inspectors' report is usually published.

Inspector of Taxes A civil servant responsible to the *Board of Inland Revenue for issuing tax returns and assessments, the conduct of appeals, and agreeing tax liabilities with taxpayers.

instalment One of a series of payments, especially when buying goods on *hire purchase, settling a debt, or buying a new issue of shares.

instalment credit A consumer credit loan in which the rate of interest is fixed at the outset; the principal and the interest are repaid in equal (usually monthly) instalments.

instalment option An *option in which the premium is settled in a number of payments.

instalment sale In the USA, the equivalent of a UK retail sale by *hire purchase.

instant call bond or **note** A bond or note that is *freely callable, i.e. one in which the issuer has an immediate *call provision.

Institute of Actuaries One of the two professional bodies in the UK to which actuaries belong. To become an actuary it is necessary to qualify as a fellow of one or the other. The roots of the profession go back to 1756, when a Fellow of the Royal Society, James Dodson, produced the first table of premiums for life assurance, after having been turned down for an assurance policy on the grounds of his age. The Institute is in London; the other organization, the **Faculty of Actuaries**, is based in Edinburgh.

Institute of Certified Public Accountants A body of accountants established in 1903 and amalgamated in 1932 with the Central Association of Accountants; in 1941 this body amalgamated with the Chartered Association of Certified Accountants (*see* CERTIFIED ACCOUNTANT).

Institute of Chartered Accountants Any of the three professional accountancy bodies in the UK, the **Institute of Chartered Accountants in England and Wales**, the **Institute of Chartered Accountants of Scotland**, and the **Institute of Chartered Accountants in Ireland**. The institutes are separate but recognize similar codes of practice. The largest is the England and Wales institute, with some 90 000 members, who are identified by the letters ACA or FCA (as are members of the Ireland institute; in Scotland members use the letters CA). The institutes ensure high standards of education and training in accountancy, provide qualification by examination, and supervise professional conduct in the service of clients and of the public. They are members of the Consultative Committee of Accountancy Bodies, whose Accounting Standards Committee is responsible for drafting accounting standards. *See also* CHARTERED ACCOUNTANT.

Institute of Chartered Secretaries and Administrators (ICSA) A professional body for secretaries and administrators in the UK. Founded in 1891 and granted a Royal Charter in 1902, the institute represents members' interests to government bodies on such matters as company law; publishes journals, reports, pamphlets, and papers; promotes the professional standing of members; and conducts the education and examination of members.

Institute of London Underwriters (ILU) An association of UK insurance companies that cooperate with each other in providing a market for marine insurance and aviation insurance. Although Lloyd's underwriters are not members of the institute, the two organizations work closely with each other. The ILU appoints agents to settle claims, provides certificates of insurance for cargo shippers insured by members, and is responsible for drawing up its own insurance contracts for the use of members; it also draws up the Institute cargo clauses widely used in many marine and aviation policies.

Institute of Management Accountants (IMA) A US accountancy body established in 1919 as the National Association of Cost Accountants.

institutional broker A securities firm or broker dealing with financial institutions.

institutional investor (institution) A large organization, such as an insurance company, unit trust, bank, trade union, or a pension fund of a large company, that has substantial sums of money to invest on a stock exchange. Institutions usually employ their own investment analysts and advisors; they are usually able to influence stock exchange sentiment more profoundly than private investors and their policies can often affect share prices. Because institutions can build up significant holdings in companies, they can also influence company policy, usually by making their opinions known at shareholders' meetings, especially during *takeover-bid negotiations.

instrument 1. A formal legal document. *See also* NEGOTIABLE INSTRUMENT. **2.** A tool that is used by a government in achieving its macroeconomic targets. For example, interest rates and the *money supply may be considered instruments in the pursuit of stable prices, while government expenditure and taxation may be considered instruments in the pursuit of full employment. **3.** A financial services product.

insurable interest The legal right to enter into an insurance contract. A person is said to have an insurable interest if the event insured against could cause that person a financial loss. For example, anyone may insure their own property as they would incur a loss if an item was lost, destroyed, or damaged. If no financial loss would occur, no insurance can be arranged. For example, a person cannot insure a next-door neighbour's property. The limit of an insurable interest is the value of the item concerned, although there is no limit on the amount of life assurance a person can take out, because the financial effects of death cannot be accurately measured.

Insurable interest was made a condition of all insurance by the UK Life Assurance Act 1774. Without an insurable interest, an insured person is unable to enforce an insurance contract (or life-assurance contract) as it is the insurable interest that distinguishes insurance from a bet or wager. A marine insurance policy requires that the insurable interest must exist at the time of the loss. Other general forms of insurance require that the insurable interest exists both at the time of contracting and at the time of loss.

insurable risk The possibility of suffering some form of loss or damage that can be described sufficiently accurately for a calculation to be made of the probability of its happening, on the basis of past records. Fire, theft, accident, etc., are all insurable risks because underwriters can assess the probability of having to pay out a claim and can therefore calculate a reasonable *premium. If the risk is met so infrequently that no way of calculating the probability of the event exists, no underwriter will insure against it and it is therefore an **uninsurable risk**. *See also* ACTUARY; PERIL.

insurance 1. A legal contract in which an *insurer promises to pay a specified amount to another party, the *insured, if a particular event (known as the *peril), happens and the insured suffers a financial loss as a result. The insured's part of the contract is to promise to pay an amount of money, known as the **premium**, either once or at regular intervals. In order for an insurance contract to be valid, the insured must have an *insurable interest. It is usual to use the word 'insurance' to cover events (such as a fire) that may or may not happen, whereas *assurance refers to an event (such as death) that must occur at some time (*see also* LIFE ASSURANCE). *See also* REINSURANCE. **2.** The hedging of financial market risks (*see* HEDGE).

insurance broker A person who offers advice on all insurance matters and arranges cover, on behalf of the client, with an *insurer. Insurance brokers act as intermediaries and their income comes from commission paid to them by insurers, usually in the form of an agreed percentage of the first premium or on subsequent premiums. Insurance brokers are regulated by the *Financial Services Authority. *See also* LLOYD'S.

Insurance Brokers Registration Council (**IBRC**) A statutory body established under the Insurance Brokers Registration Act 1977. It is responsible for the registration and training of insurance brokers and for laying down rules relating to such matters as accounting practice, staff qualifications, advertising, and the orderly conduct and discipline of broking businesses.

insurance futures A *futures contract on an index of insurance losses.

Insurance Ombudsman *See* FINANCIAL OMBUDSMAN SERVICE.

insurance option 1. An over-the-counter *option on an insurance index. *See* OVER-THE-COUNTER MARKET. **2.** An option on an *insurance futures contract.

insurance policy A document that sets out the terms and conditions of an insurance contract, stating the benefits payable and the *premium required. *See also* LIFE ASSURANCE.

insurance premium *See* INSURANCE; PREMIUM.

insurance premium tax A UK tax on insurance premiums, introduced in 1994. It is levied on travel, motor vehicle, household, and other general insurance but not on aircraft, marine, and life insurance or on other specialized commercial insurance and reinsurance.

insurance tied agent An agent who represents a particular insurance company or companies. In life and pensions insurance, a tied agent represents only one insurer and is only able to advise the public on the policies offered by that one company. In general insurance (motor, household, holiday, etc.), a tied agent represents no more than six insurers, who are jointly responsible for the financial consequences of any failure or mistake the agent makes. In both cases the agent receives a commission for each policy that is sold and a further commission on each subsequent renewal of the policy. The commission is calculated as an agreed percentage of the total premium paid by the policyholder. The distinction between the two forms of insurance tied agent was a consequence of the Financial Services Act 1986 and the General Insurance Selling Code 1989 of the *Association of British Insurers.

insured A person or company covered by an *insurance policy. In some policies that cover death, the alternative word *assured may be used for the person who receives the payment in the event of the assured's death.

insurer A person, company, syndicate, or other organization that underwrites an insurance risk.

intangible asset (invisible asset) An asset that can neither be seen nor touched. The most common of these are competencies, *market power, *goodwill, *patents, *trademarks, and copyrights. Goodwill is probably the most intangible and invisible of all assets as no document provides evidence of its existence and its commercial value is difficult to determine. However, it frequently does have very substantial value as the capitalized value of future profits, not attributable purely to the return on *tangible assets. While goodwill is called either an intangible asset or an invisible asset, such items as insurance policies and less tangible overseas investments are usually called invisible assets. Intangible assets are increasingly seen as the key to competitive advantage and the market value of a firm. *Compare* FICTITIOUS ASSET.

integration The combination of two or more companies under the same control for their mutual benefit, by reducing competition, saving costs by reducing overheads, capturing a larger market share, pooling resources, cooperating on research and development, enhancing competitive advantage, etc. In **horizontal** (or **lateral**) **integration** the businesses carry out the same stage in the *value chain or produce similar products or services; they are therefore competitors. In a monopoly, horizontal integration is complete, while in an oligopoly there is considerable horizontal integration. In **vertical integration** a company obtains control of its suppliers (sometimes called **backward integration**) or of the concerns that buy its products or services (**forward integration**). Conglomerate integration takes place between firms in different value chains.

intellectual property An *intangible asset, such as a copyright, *patent, *trademark, or design right. *See also* ROYALTY.

interbank deposit A wholesale money-market deposit.

interbank market The wholesale market for short-term money and foreign exchange in which banks, companies, and other organizations trade.

Inter Bank Offered Rate (IBOR) The rate of interest at which banks lend to one another. Many of the world's financial centres have such a rate, for example London has the *London Inter Bank Offered Rate (LIBOR).

inter-commodity spread The holding of options in two different but related commodities with the same delivery date.

inter-dealer broker A member of the *London Stock Exchange who is only permitted to deal with *market makers, rather than the public.

interdict An *injunction in Scottish law.

interest 1. The charge made for borrowing a sum of money. The *interest rate is the charge made, expressed as a percentage of the total sum loaned, for a stated period of time (usually one year). Thus, a rate of interest of 15% per annum means that for every £100 borrowed for one year, the borrower has to pay a charge of £15, or a charge in proportion for longer or shorter periods. In **simple interest**, the charge is calculated on the sum loaned only, thus $I = Prt$, where I is the interest, P is the principal sum, r is the rate of interest, and t is the period. In **compound interest**, the charge is calculated on the sum loaned plus any interest that has acrued in previous periods. In this case $I = P\left[(1 + r)^n - 1\right]$, where n is the number of periods for which interest is separately calculated. Thus, if £500 is loaned for two years at a rate of 12% per annum, compounded quarterly, the value of n will be $4 \times 2 = 8$ and the value of r

will be 12/4 = 3%. Thus, $I = 500 [(1.03)^8 - 1] = £133.38$, whereas on a simple-interest basis it would be only £120. These calculations of interest apply equally to deposits that attract income in the form of interest. In general, rates of interest depend on the money supply, the demand for loans, government policy, the risk of nonrepayment as assessed by the lender, the period of the loan, and relative levels of foreign-exchange rates into other currencies. **2.** An indication to buy or sell. **3.** A share of ownership.

interest arbitrage Transactions between financial centres in foreign currencies that take advantage of differentials in interest rates between the two centres and the difference between the forward and spot exchange rates. In some circumstances it is possible to make a profit by borrowing money on domestic markets at fixed rates, buying a foreign currency, lending the foreign currency at fixed rates, and entering into a forward contract to buy domestic currency. In general, however, this is not possible; the relation imposed on interest rates and exchange rates both spot and forward is described as the *covered interest-rate parity.

interest-basis conversion A term in a bond issue that provides for a change in the mechanism for computing the rate of interest.

interest-bearing eligible liabilities (IBEL) Liabilities recognized by the Bank of England as being held by UK banks, e.g. net deposits. In times of strict monetary control the Bank of England requires other UK banks to deposit a percentage of these liabilities with it.

interest cover (fixed-charge–coverage ratio) A ratio showing the number of times interest charges are covered by earnings before interest and tax (*see* EBIT). For example, a company with interest charges of £12 million and earnings before interest and tax of £36 million would have its interest covered three times. The ratio is one way of analysing *gearing and reflects the vulnerability of a company to changes in interest rates or profit fluctuations. A highly geared company, which has a low interest cover, may find that an increase in the interest rate will mean that it has no earnings after interest charges with which to provide a dividend to shareholders.

interest-in-possession trust A type of fixed-interest *trust in which there is an entitlement to the income generated by the trust assets. The *beneficiaries of an interest-in-possession trust, the life tenants, are entitled to the income arising for a fixed period or until their death. The capital in the trust then passes absolutely to the recipient known as the remainderman.

interest-only mortgage A *mortgage on which interest is paid and the capital is paid off at the termination of the mortgage.

interest-only yield *See* YIELD.

interest rate The amount charged or paid for a loan, usually expressed as a percentage of the sum borrowed. Conversely, the amount paid by a bank, building society, etc., to a depositor on funds deposited, again expressed as a percentage of the sum deposited. *See* ANNUAL PERCENTAGE RATE; BASE RATE; LONDON INTER BANK BID RATE; LONDON INTER BANK OFFERED RATE.

interest-rate cap or **ceiling** *See* CAP.

interest-rate collar *See* COLLAR.

interest-rate cycle The notion that the movement of interest rates is cyclical and related to the *business cycle. Historically, the variable path of inflation has modified any cyclical pattern in rates.

interest-rate differential The difference between two interest rates.

interest-rate exposure *See* INTEREST-RATE RISK.

interest-rate floor *See* FLOOR.

interest-rate futures A form of *financial futures that enables investors, *portfolio managers, borrowers, etc., to obtain protection or speculate against future movements in interest rates. Interest-rate futures also enable dealers to speculate on these movements. In the UK, interest-rate futures are dealt in on the *London International Financial Futures and Options Exchange, using contracts for three-month sterling, eurodollars, euros, etc., in the short term and long gilts, US Treasury bonds, euro bonds, etc., in the long term. For long gilts, for example, the standard contract is for £50,000 of nominal value and the *tick size is 0.01% of the nominal value. *See* HEDGE.

interest-rate guarantee An indemnity sold by a bank, or similar financial institution, that protects the purchaser against the effect of future movements in interest rates. It is similar to a *forward rate agreement, but the terms are specified by the customer.

interest-rate margin **1.** The difference between the rate at which banks lend and the rate they pay for liabilities. It is likely to be a major indicator of banks' profitability. **2.** The amount charged to borrowers over and above a transfer-price interest rate. This margin is the bank's profit on the transaction but has to take account of risk of loss or default by the borrower. **3.** The difference between a transfer-price interest rate and the interest cost of funds. **4.** The difference between the rate on a debt security and a *reference rate.

interest-rate option A form of *option enabling traders and speculators to *hedge themselves against future changes in interest rates. It is an option to purchase a specific debt instrument.

interest-rate parity theory An economic model associated with exchange-rate forecasting. The **covered interest-rate parity theory** identifies a relationship between the interest rates in two currencies and the spot and forward exchange rates (*see* COVERED INTEREST-RATE PARITY). The **uncovered interest-rate parity theory** substitutes the expected actual spot rate for the forward rate and provides an estimate of future currency movements and their relationship to interest rates in the different currencies. *See* FORWARD DEALING; SPOT CURRENCY MARKET.

interest-rate policy The policy by which governments or central banks influence *interest rates. Higher rates of interest will reduce the *demand for money, giving a downward impetus to output, employment and prices. Lower interest rates will have the opposite effect. Responsibility for interest-rate policy was restored to the Bank of England by the UK government in 1997.

interest-rate risk (interest-rate exposure) The *risk arising from changes in interest rates. In recent decades the different forms of interest-rate risk have been the subject of much analysis, monitoring, and scrutiny. In the 1980s, for example, the *Savings and Loan Associations in the USA faced a major crisis as a result of continuing to offer fixed-rate loans despite a steadily climbing interest rate; this meant that their interest revenues remained at a constant level while their interest costs rose. The main forms of interest-rate risk are: the risk that interest-rate changes will impact on the value of fixed-interest assets and liabilities; the risk of mismatches in terms of the repricing of interest on assets and liabilities (as illustrated by the S & L example); *prepayment risk, in which assets may be redeemed by the holder of a loan exercising a *call provision (as in the case of fixed-rate mortgages redeemed early in a situation of falling interest rates); the risk that reinvestment may take place at lower rates; and the risk that, as rates rise, repayments will take longer than expected. *See* GAP.

interest-rate risk management The identification, modification, and mitigation of *interest-rate risk, most notably in a financial institution. *See also* ASSET–LIABILITY MANAGEMENT; GAP ANALYSIS.

interest-rate spread The difference between the average rate of interest on assets and that on liabilities. This mechanism is commonly used as an indicator of bank performance.

interest-rate swap A form of dealing between banks, security houses, and companies in which institutions exchange interest-rate payments on a notional capital value. *Swaps can be in the same currency or cross-currency (*see* CROSS-CURRENCY INTEREST-RATE SWAP). If a swap is in the same currency it will usually involve a fixed interest payment in exchange for a floating interest payment; a swap involving two different floating rates is called a *basis swap. *See also* RATE ANTICIPATION SWAP.

interest-sensitive Denoting an activity that is sensitive to changes in the general level of interest rates. For example, the demand for consumer goods usually bought on some form of *hire-purchase basis is interest-sensitive because they cost more as interest rates rise.

interest yield (current yield) The coupon payment on a percentage of the current market price.

interim accounts *See* INTERIM FINANCIAL STATEMENTS.

interim dividend A *dividend paid during a *financial year.

interim financial statements (interim accounts; interim report) *Financial statements issued for a period of less than a financial year. Although there are provisions under the Companies Act 1985 that refer to interim accounts in certain circumstances relating to the distribution of *dividends, there are no legal requirements obliging companies to produce interim accounts on a regular basis. However, *listed companies on the *London Stock Exchange are required to prepare a half-yearly report on their activities and a *profit and loss account during the first six months of each financial year. The interim financial statement must be either sent to the holders of the company's listed *securities or advertised in at least one national newspaper not later than four months after the end of the period to which it relates. A copy of the interim financial statements must also be sent to the Company Announcements Office and to the competent authority of each other state in which the company's shares are listed. The vast majority of companies choose to send the interim statement to shareholders with a brief announcement of the headline figures reported in the press. There is no requirement for the interim statements to be audited. Although the stock-exchange regulations require mainly profit information, there is a trend for the larger companies to also provide *balance sheet and *cash-flow statements. In the UK, the requirements only call for six-monthly financial statements, but some of the larger companies with interests in the USA follow the US practice of issuing reports quarterly.

intermarket spread swap Swapping securities in the hope of improving the spread between the yields of the securities.

Intermarket Trading System *See* NATIONAL MARKET SYSTEM.

intermediary Any person or organization that acts as an agent, (*see* AGENCY), facilitator, or *broker between the parties to a transaction. *See also* FINANCIAL INTERMEDIARY; INDEPENDENT INTERMEDIARY.

intermediate-term *See* MEDIUM-TERM.

intermediation The activity of a bank, similar financial institution, broker, etc., in acting as an *intermediary between the two parties to a transaction; the intermediary can accept all or part of the credit risk or the other commercial risks. *Compare* DISINTERMEDIATION.

internal audit An *audit that an organization carries out on its own behalf, normally to ensure that its own internal controls are operating satisfactorily. Whereas an external audit is almost always concerned with financial matters, this may not necessarily be the case with an internal audit; internal auditors may also concern themselves with such matters as the observation of the safety and health at work regulations or of the equal opportunities legislation. It may also be used to detect any theft or fraud (*see also* INTERNAL CONTROL).

internal capital generation rate The rate at which an organization creates equity in its balance sheet by retained earnings.

internal control The measures an organization employs to ensure that opportunities for fraud or misfeasance are minimized. Examples range from requiring more than one signature on certain documents, security arrangements for stock-handling, division of tasks, keeping of control accounts, use of special passwords, handling of computer files, etc. It is one of the principal concerns of an *internal audit to ensure that internal controls are working properly so that the external auditors can have faith in the accounts produced by the organization. Internal control should also reassure management of the integrity of its operations.

internal growth (organic growth) The means by which a business can grow using its own resources (*see* BUSINESS STRATEGY). A business will grow by increased *market penetration at the expense of its competitors, by new product development, and by market development through seeking new applications and markets for existing products or services. All these means utilize a firm's core competencies and while some may have a relatively short lead time (e.g. market penetration) others, notably product development, can involve significant lead times and development costs. Firms that have a successful record of innovation are usually more successful at internal growth, whereas others favour greater reliance on *external growth.

internal rate of return (IRR) An interest rate that gives a *net present value of zero when applied to a projected cash flow of an asset, liability, or financial decision. This interest rate, where the *present values of the cash inflows and outflows are equal, is the internal rate of return for a project under consideration, and the decision to adopt the project would depend on its size compared with the *cost of capital. The approximate IRR can be computed manually by interpolation but most computer spreadsheet programs now include a routine enabling the IRR to be computed quickly and accurately. The IRR technique suffers from the possibility of multiple solution rates in some circumstances. If it suggests a different decision to that obtained from *net present value the decision should not be taken, because net present value is a superior decision tool.

Internal Revenue Code The federal tax law of the USA, which comprises the regulations applied to taxpayers.

Internal Revenue Service (IRS) In the USA, the branch of federal government responsible for collecting most types of taxes. The IRS administers the *Internal Revenue Code, investigates tax abuses, and makes criminal prosecution for tax fraud through the US tax court.

International Accounting Standards Board (IASB) A body established in 2001 to take responsibility for setting **International Financial Reporting Standards** (IFRSs). It replaced the earlier International Accounting Standards Committee. Some of the advantages claimed for international standards are that *financial statements prepared in different countries will be more comparable, multinational companies will find preparation of their accounts easier, listing on different stock exchanges can be achieved more simply, and financial statements will be of greater use to users. However, others argue that some international standards permit such a degree of flexibility in accounting treatments that comparability is impaired. Although the IASB has no authority to impose its standards, a growing number of countries require that the financial statements of public companies are prepared in accordance with IFRSs. These include the USA, Japan, Australia, and (from January 2005) all member states of the EU.

International Bank for Reconstruction and Development (IBRD) A specialized agency established by the *Bretton Woods Conference of 1944 to help finance post-war reconstruction and to help raise standards of living in developing countries, by making loans to governments or guaranteeing outside loans. It lends on broadly commercial terms, either for specific projects or for more general social purposes; funds are raised on the international capital markets. The Bank and its affiliates, the *International Development Association and the *International Finance Corporation, are often known as the **World Bank**; it is owned by the governments of 183 (2002) countries. Members must also be members of the Bank's sister organization, the *International Monetary Fund. The headquarters of the Bank are in Washington, with a European office in Paris and a Tokyo office.

International Banking Credit Agency (IBCA) Formerly, a credit *rating agency based in London and focusing its activities on those institutions that traded in the City. It merged with the US rating agency Fitch in 1997.

international banking facility (IBF) A banking facility in the USA that is authorized by the *Federal Reserve System to participate in *eurocurrency lending. Such facilities are exempt from *reserve requirement and may have many other advantages usually associated with offshore banking.

international bond A *bond issued outside the country of the issuer. It may be in the form of a *foreign bond or a *eurobond.

International Centre for the Settlement of Investment Disputes (ICSID) An office of the *International Bank for Reconstruction and Development (World Bank) that resolves investment disputes between member states.

International Chamber of Commerce (ICC) An international business organization that represents business interests in international affairs. Its office is in Paris.

International Commodities Clearing House (ICCH) *See* LONDON CLEARING HOUSE.

international commodity agreements Agreements between governments that aim to stabilize the price of commodities. This is often important for producing nations, for whom the revenue from commodity sales may make a major contribution to the national income. Methods tried include government-financed buffer stocks and the imposition of price limits between which the price of the commodity is allowed to fluctuate. Among the commodities for which agreements have been made are coffee, sugar, wheat, cocoa, and tin.

International Depository Receipt (IDR) A certificate of ownership of stock that is held outside the country from which the stock derives. The stock, or other securities, will be held by the issuing bank.

International Development Association (IDA) An affiliate of the *International Bank for Reconstruction and Development (IBRD) established in 1960 to provide assistance for poorer developing countries. With the IBRD it is known as the **World Bank**. It is funded by subscription and transfers from the net earnings of IBRD. The headquarters of the IDA are in Washington, with offices in Paris and Tokyo, administered by IBRD staff.

International Finance Corporation (IFC) An affiliate of the *International Bank for Reconstruction and Development (IBRD) established in 1956 to provide assistance for private investment projects. Although the IFC and IBRD are separate entities, both legally and financially, the IFC is able to borrow from the IBRD and reloan to private investors. The headquarters of the IFC are in Washington. Its importance increased in the 1980s after the emergence of the debt crisis and the subsequent reliance on the private sector.

international Fisher effect The hypothesis, first advanced by the economist Irving Fisher, that the difference between the nominal interest rates in two different currencies is equal to the difference between the expected rates of inflation in the two countries. *See* FISHER EFFECT.

International Fund for Agricultural Development (IFAD) A fund, proposed by the 1974 World Food Conference, that began operations in 1977 with the purpose of providing additional funds for agricultural and rural development in developing countries. It has some 158 member states. The headquarters of the IFAD are in Rome.

international futures *Futures contracts in an *underlying based in a different country.

International Monetary Fund (IMF) An international organization set up by the *Bretton Woods Conference and established in 1947. Its remit is to enhance stability and convertibility in the international monetary system. The Fund assists members by supplying the amount of foreign currency it wishes to purchase in exchange for the equivalent amount of its own currency. The member repays this amount by buying back its own currency in a currency acceptable to the Fund, usually within three to five years. High levels of borrowing are conditional on the implementation of IMF suggested policies for a country. The Fund is financed by subscriptions from its members, the amount determined by an estimate of their means. International liquidity was enhanced by its creation of *special drawing rights in 1970. Voting power is related to the amount of the subscription – the higher the contribution the higher the voting rights. The head office of the IMF is in Washington. *See also* CONDITIONALITY.

International Monetary Market Part of the *Chicago Mercantile Exchange that trades in futures and options, treasury bills, eurodollar deposits, and currencies.

international mutual fund A *unit trust (mutual fund) that invests on a global basis.

International Organization for Securities Commissions (IOSCO) A body formed in 1987 with the objective of establishing internationally agreed accounting standards to aid in multinational share offering by companies. Formerly critical of Accounting Standards issued by the International Accounting Standards Committee, it is now actively cooperating in the improvement of these standards.

International Petroleum Exchange (IPE) An exchange, founded in London in 1980, that deals in *futures contracts and *options (including traded options) in oil (gas oil, Brent crude oil, and heavy fuel oil) with facilities for making an exchange of futures for physicals (*see* ACTUALS). The exchange is located in St Katharine Dock and is shared with the *London Commodity Exchange.

International Securities Market Association (ISMA) The *eurobond market's trade association. It was formerly called the Association of International Bond Dealers (AIBD).

international security identification number (ISIN) An identification system for all securities issues on the international market.

International Stock Exchange in London *See* LONDON STOCK EXCHANGE.

International Swaps and Derivatives Association (ISDA) The trade association for international traders in *derivatives. Established in 1985, it focuses on the *over-the-counter market (OTC) and seeks to establish codes of behaviour for the market. Most OTC derivative agreements now conform to ISDA standards. Over 200 of the leading institutions in the market are members.

International Union of Credit and Investment Insurers *See* BERNE UNION.

intervention mechanism Formerly, the action by central banks and governments to stabilize exchange rates of currencies in the *European Monetary System by buying or selling currencies on the open market or by initiating *currency swaps. Such action was rendered unnecessary by the creation of the *euro.

intervention price *See* COMMON AGRICULTURAL POLICY.

intestacy The state of a person who has died without having left a valid will. Such a person is said to have died **intestate**. Intestacy can be either total (if no will is left at all) or partial (if not all the deceased's property is left by will). The Administration of Estates Act contains a table showing the destination of the property in an intestacy.

in-the-money option An *option that would generate a gain if currently exercised. *See* INTRINSIC VALUE.

intraday limit **1.** The maximum price movement in a single day's trading that is permitted by the rules of a particular financial market. **2.** The limit placed on a given trader's *exposure in a single day.

intrinsic value The difference between the market value of the underlying security in a traded *option and the *exercise price when the option is in the money. Otherwise the intrinsic value is zero.

introduction A method of issuing shares on the *London Stock Exchange in which a broker or issuing house takes small quantities of the company's shares and issues them to clients at opportune moments. It is also used by existing public companies that wish to issue additional shares. *Compare* ISSUE BY TENDER; OFFER FOR SALE; PLACING; PUBLIC ISSUE.

inverse floater swap An *interest-rate swap in which the variable interest rate payment rises when overall interest rates fall.

inverse floating-rate note *See* REVERSE FLOATING-RATE NOTE.

inverse yield curve *See* NEGATIVE YIELD CURVE.

inverted market A futures market in which the months closer to delivery are selling at higher prices than those further in the future. *See* FUTURES CONTRACT.

investment 1. The purchase of capital goods, such as plant and machinery in a factory in order to produce goods for future consumption. This is known as **capital investment**; the higher the level of capital investment in an economy, the faster it will grow. **2.** The purchase of assets, such as securities, works of art, bank and building-society deposits, etc., with a primary view to their financial return, either as income or capital gain. This form of **financial investment** represents a means of saving. The level of financial investment in an economy will be related to such factors as the rate of interest, the extent to which investments are likely to prove profitable, and the general climate of business confidence.

investment analyst A person employed by stockbrokers, banks, insurance companies, unit trusts, pension funds, etc., to give advice on the making of investments, especially investments in securities, commodities, etc. Many pay special attention to the study of *equities in the hope of being able to advise their employers to make profitable purchases of ordinary shares. To do this they use a variety of techniques, including a comparison of a company's present profits with its future trading prospects; this enables the analyst to single out the companies likely to outperform the general level of the market. This form of **technical analysis** is often contrasted with **fundamental analysis**, in which predicted future market movements are related to the underlying state of an economy and its expected trends. Analysts who rely on past movements to predict the future are called *chartists.

investment bank A US bank that fulfils many of the functions of a UK *merchant bank. It is usually one that advises on mergers and acquisitions and provides finance for industrial corporations by buying shares in a company and selling them in relatively small lots to investors. Capital provided to companies is usually long-term and based on fixed assets. In the USA, commercial banks were excluded from selling securities for many years but the law was relaxed in the late 1980s, when certain safeguards were introduced, including a ceiling on the value of transactions.

investment bond A single-premium life-assurance policy in which an investment of a fixed amount is made (usually over £1000) in an *asset-backed fund. Interest is paid at an agreed rate and at the end of the period the investment is returned with any growth. Investment bonds confer attractive tax benefits in some circumstances. *See also* SINGLE-PREMIUM ASSURANCE; TOP SLICING.

investment climate The factors influencing the confidence of investors. The investors may be individuals, companies, or governments; the investments may be in domestic or foreign projects or companies. Many aspects of government policy, the economic situation, international politics, etc., combine to create the investment climate.

investment club A group of investors who, by pooling their resources, are able to make more frequent and larger investments on a stock exchange, often being able to reduce brokerage and to spread the risk of serious loss. The popularity of investment clubs has waxed and waned with the developments of investment vehicles and the value of stocks.

investment company *See* INVESTMENT TRUST.

investment-grade Describing a bond that has been given a relatively high credit rating by a major *rating agency, namely Baa and above by Moody's or BBB and above by Standard & Poor's or Fitch's. Lower-rated bonds may promise a higher yield but are inherently more speculative.

investment horizon The time period over which an investor wishes to retain a particular position.

investment income **1.** A person's income derived from investments. **2.** The income of a business derived from its outside investments rather than from its trading activities.

Investment Management Regulatory Organization (IMRO) A former *Self-Regulating Organization whose functions are now exercised by the *Financial Services Authority, into which it was absorbed in 1997.

investment manager *See* FUND MANAGER.

Investment Ombudsman *See* FINANCIAL OMBUDSMAN SERVICE.

investment portfolio *See* PORTFOLIO.

investment properties Properties owned by a company that holds investments as part of its business, such as an *investment trust or a property-investment company. Investment properties may also include properties owned by a company whose main business is not the holding of investments. Such properties are strictly defined by *Statement of Standard Accounting Practice 19, 'Accounting for Investment Properties', as being an interest in land and/or buildings:
(1) in respect of which construction work and development have been completed; and
(2) that is held for its investment potential, any rental income being negotiated at arm's length.
   However, a property owned and occupied by a company for its own purposes is not an investment property, and a property let to and occupied by another company in the same group is not an investment property for the purposes of its own accounts or the *group accounts. Investment properties should not be depreciated annually unless they are held on a lease. If they are leased they should be depreciated on the basis set out in *Statement of Standard Accounting Practice 12, 'Accounting for Depreciation', at least over the period, when the unexpired term is 20 years or less. Investment properties should be included in the *balance sheet at their open-market value, movements being taken to the *investment revaluation reserve unless it is insufficient to cover a deficit, in which case it should be taken to the *profit and loss account.

investment revaluation reserve A *reserve created by a company with *investment properties, if these properties are included in the *balance sheet at open-market value. Changes in the value of investment properties should be disclosed as movements on the investment revaluation reserve, unless the total of the investment revaluation reserve is insufficient to cover a deficit, in which case the amount by which the deficit exceeds the amount in the investment revaluation reserve should be charged to the *profit and loss account. In the case of investment *trust companies and property *unit trusts it may not be appropriate to deal with these deficits in the profit and loss account; in these circumstances they should be shown prominently in the *financial statements.

Investment Services Directive An EU directive providing a regulatory framework for securities dealing. It proposes that securities firms should be admitted by their domestic regulator before they are allowed to operate at a European level.

investment trust (**investment company**) A company that invests the funds provided by shareholders in a wide variety of securities. It makes its profits from the income and capital gains provided by these securities. The investments made are usually restricted to securities quoted on a stock exchange, but some will invest in unquoted companies. The advantages for shareholders are much the same as those with *unit trusts, i.e. spreading the risk of investment and making use of professional managers. Investment trusts, which are not usually *trusts in the usual sense, but private or public limited companies, differ from unit trusts in that in the latter the investors buy units in the fund but are not shareholders. Some investment trusts aim for high capital growth (**capital shares**), others for high income (**income shares**). *See also* ACCUMULATION UNIT; GEARED INVESTMENT TRUST; SPLIT-CAPITAL INVESTMENT TRUST; UNITIZATION.

Investors' Compensation Scheme A scheme set up in 1988 under the *Financial Services Act 1986 to provide compensation for private investors who stand to lose money as a result of the default or bankruptcy of an investment firm that is authorized under the *Financial Services Act.

invisible asset *See* INTANGIBLE ASSET.

invisible balance The *balance of payments between countries that arises as a result of transactions involving services, such as insurance, banking, shipping, and tourism (often known as **invisibles**), rather than the sale and purchase of goods. Invisibles can play an important part in a nation's current account, although they are often difficult to quantify. The UK relies on a substantial invisible balance in its balance of payments.

invisibles *See* INVISIBLE BALANCE.

IOSCO Abbreviation for *International Organization for Securities Commissions.

IOU A written document providing evidence of a debt, usually in the form "I owe you…". It is not a *negotiable instrument or a *promissory note and requires no stamp (unless it does include a promise to pay). It can, however, be used as legal evidence of a debt.

IPE Abbreviation for *International Petroleum Exchange.

IPO Abbreviation for *initial public offering.

IRA Abbreviation for *individual retirement account.

Irish Futures and Options Exchange (Ifox) An exchange that opened in Dublin in 1989; it trades principally in short-term and long-term Irish gilt futures in conjunction with the Irish Stock Exchange.

IRR Abbreviation for *internal rate of return.

irredeemable securities (irredeemables) Securities, such as some government loan stock (*see* CONSOLS) and some *debentures, on which there is no date given for the redemption of the capital sum. The price of fixed-interest irredeemables on the open market varies inversely with the level of interest rates.

irrevocable documentary acceptance credit A form of irrevocable confirmed *letter of credit in which a foreign importer of UK goods opens a credit with a UK bank or the UK office of a local bank. The bank then issues an irrevocable letter of credit to the exporter, guaranteeing to accept *bills of exchange drawn on it on presentation of the shipping documents. Once the letter of credit has been drawn up, the importer has to 'accept' that he or she will pay, by signing the acceptance.

irrevocable letter of credit *See* LETTER OF CREDIT.

IRS Abbreviation for *Internal Revenue Service.

ISA Abbreviation for *Individual Savings Account.

ISA mortgage A *mortgage in which the borrower repays only the interest on the loan to the lender, but at the same time puts regular sums into an *Individual Savings Account (ISA). When the ISA matures it is used to repay the capital. An ISA mortgage is similar to an endowment mortgage, except that it does not provide any life-assurance cover and that ISA funds are untaxed.

ISDA Abbreviation for *International Swaps and Derivatives Association.

ISE Abbreviation for International Stock Exchange. *See* LONDON STOCK EXCHANGE.

ISIN Abbreviation for *international security identification number.

Islamic finance A system of finance that is bound by religious laws that prevent the taking of interest payments (*see* HALAL; HARAAM). Joint ventures in which the funder and the borrower share profits and risks are, however, acceptable. There are a number of different techniques by which this takes place. **Murabaha** is a good vehicle for temporary idle funds, which are used to purchase goods from a supplier for immediate sale and delivery to the buyer, who pays a predetermined margin over cost on a deferred payment date. The term can be as short as seven days. **Musharaka transactions** involve participation with other parties in trade financing, leasing, real estate, and industrial projects. Net profits are shared in proportions agreed at the outset. **Shirkah** is a partnership between a bank and a customer to share the risks and gains of a project. **Muqarada** is a joint venture by finance providers. **Ijarah** involves profit from rental income on real estate. **Ijarawa-iktina** is leasing of large capital items, such as property or plant and machinery. Leasing is achieved by the equivalent of monthly rental payments, and at the expiry the lessee purchases the equipment.

ISMA Abbreviation for *International Securities Market Association.

issue 1. The number of shares or the amount of stock on offer to the public at a particular time. *See also* NEW ISSUE; RIGHTS ISSUE; SCRIP ISSUE. **2.** The number of banknotes distributed by the Bank of England at a particular time.

issue by tender (sale by tender) A method of issuing shares on the *London Stock

Exchange in which an *issuing house asks investors to *tender for them. The stocks or shares are then allocated to the highest bidders. It is usual for the tender documents to state the lowest price acceptable. This method may be used for a *new issue or for loan stock (*see* DEBENTURE), but is not frequently employed. *Compare* INTRODUCTION; OFFER FOR SALE; PLACING; PUBLIC ISSUE.

issue date The date from which interest accrued on a security is calculated.

issued share A *share that has been allotted by the directors of a company to an applicant and paid for in full by that applicant.

issued share capital *See* SHARE CAPITAL.

issue price The price at which a *new issue of shares is sold to the public. Once the issue has been made the securities will have a market price, which may be above (at a premium on) or below (at a discount on) the issue price (*see also* STAG). In an *introduction, *offer for sale, or *public issue, the issue price is fixed by the company on the advice of its stockbrokers and bankers; in an *issue by tender the issue price is fixed by the highest bidder; in a *placing the issue price is negotiated by the *issuing house or broker involved.

issuing house A financial institution, usually a *merchant bank or *investment bank, that specializes in the *flotation of private companies on a *stock exchange. In some cases the issuing house will itself purchase the whole issue (*see* UNDERWRITER), thus ensuring that there is no uncertainty in the amount of money the company will raise by flotation. It will then sell the shares to the public, usually by an *offer for sale, *introduction, *issue by tender, or *placing.

Istanbul Menkul Kiymetter Borsasi The stock exchange of Turkey.

IT 1. Abbreviation for *income tax. **2.** Abbreviation for information technology.

itayose The Japanese concept for stock-exchange dealing in which all orders that arrive at a broker's or dealer's office before the exchange has opened are treated as having arrived at the same time, i.e. the time the exchange opened.

ITS Abbreviation for Intermarket Trading System. *See* NATIONAL MARKET SYSTEM.

Jakarta Stock Exchange A stock exchange in Indonesia that originally opened in 1912 but was closed during World War II and from 1958 to 1977, when the modern market reopened.

J-curve The shape of a graph in which the balance of payments is plotted against time immediately after a devaluation of the currency. Initially the balance of payments gets worse, since imports are more highly priced and their demand in the short term is inelastic. The balance of payments improves with time as imports fall and exports rise due to a change in relative competitiveness. Over a longer period these impacts may be nullified by the effects of inflation.

jiao A monetary unit of China worth one tenth of a *yuan.

jobber **1.** A former dealer in stocks and shares, who had no contact with the general public, except through a *stockbroker. Jobbers were replaced by *market makers on the *London Stock Exchange in the Big Bang of October 1986. **2.** A dealer who buys and sells commodities, etc., for his or her own account.

jobber's turn The difference between the price at which a former jobber on the London Stock Exchange was prepared to buy and the price at which the jobber was prepared to sell. *See also* SPREAD.

jobbing backwards (jobbing back) Looking back on a transaction or event and thinking about how one might have acted differently, had one known then what one knows now.

job lot A collection of diverse things, such as stocks or shares, sold together as one lot at one all-inclusive price.

Johannesburg Stock Exchange (JSE) The principal stock exchange of South Africa.

joint account **1.** A bank account or a building-society account held in the names of two or more people, often husband and wife. On the death of one party the balance in the account goes to the survivor(s), except in the case of partnerships, executors' accounts, or trustees' accounts. It is usual for any of the holders of a joint account to operate it alone. **2.** In the USA, a syndicate of *investment banks acting together in an underwriting venture.

joint and several liability A liability that is entered into by a group, on the understanding that if any of the group fail in their undertaking the liability must be shared by the remainder. Thus, if two people enter into a joint and several guarantee for a bank loan, if one becomes bankrupt the other is liable for repayment of the whole loan.

joint bond A *bond issue in which more than one party may be liable for its cash flows.

joint investment A security purchased by more than one person. The certificate will bear the names of all the parties, but only the first named will receive notices. To dispose of the holding all the parties must sign the *transfer deed.

joint-life and last-survivor annuities Annuities that involve two people (usually husband and wife). A joint-life annuity begins payment on a specified date and continues until both persons have died. A last-survivor annuity only begins payment on the death of one of the two people and pays until the death of the other. *Compare* SINGLE-LIFE PENSION.

joint-stock bank A UK bank that is a *public limited company rather than a private bank (which is a partnership). During the 19th century many private banks failed; the joint-stock banks became stronger, however, largely as a result of amalgamations and careful investment. In the 20th century, they became known as *commercial banks or High-Street banks.

joint-stock company A *company in which the members pool their stock and trade on the basis of their joint stock. This differs from the earliest type of company, the merchant corporations or regulated companies of the 14th century, in which members traded with their own stock, subject to the rules of the company. Joint-stock companies originated in the 17th century; they are now rare.

joint venture 1. A commercial undertaking entered into by two or more parties, usually in the short term. Joint ventures are generally governed by the Partnership Act 1890 but they differ from *partnerships in that they are limited by time or by activity. Separate books are not usually kept and the joint venturers will have a profit- or loss-sharing ratio for the purpose of the joint venture only. Joint venturers often carry on their principal businesses independently of, and at the same time as, the joint venture. Joint ventures are becoming increasingly common as companies cooperate with each other in international markets, in order to share costs, exploit new technologies, or gain access to new markets. 2. A company owned by a number of other companies.

joint venturing In international marketing, an arrangement between a domestic company and a foreign host company to set up production and marketing facilities in the foreign market.

JSE Abbreviation for *Johannesburg Stock Exchange.

judgment creditor The person in whose favour a court decides, ordering the **judgment debtor** to pay the sum owed. If the judgment debtor fails to pay, the judgment creditor must return to the court asking for the judgment to be enforced.

judgment debtor *See* JUDGMENT CREDITOR.

jump A discontinuous movement of a price on a financial market.

jump process A statistical process that includes jumps in value. It is often used to characterize changes in the prices of financial obligations on financial markets.

junior debt The colloquial name for a *subordinated debt.

junk bond A *bond that offers a high rate of interest because it carries a higher than usual probability of default. The issuing of junk bonds to finance the takeover of large companies in the USA is a practice that developed in the 1970s and subsequently spread elsewhere. *See* LEVERAGED BUY-OUT.

juristic person *See* LEGAL PERSON.

kaffirs An informal name for shares in South African gold-mining companies on the London Stock Exchange.

kamikaze pricing The practice of offering loans and transactions at exceptionally low rates to capture a larger share of the corporate banking market. It is used pejoratively to describe the practice of some Japanese banks and stockbrokers, and is named after the Japanese suicide pilots of World War II.

kangaroos An informal name for Australian shares, especially in mining, land, and tobacco companies, on the London Stock Exchange.

Kansas City Board of Trade A US grain market in Kansas City that also trades in futures and options.

kappa One of a group of measures related to the pricing of *options that are known as *greeks. Formally expressed, the kappa is the partial derivative of the price of an option with respect to changes in the volatility of the price of the *underlying. It is a measure of the sensitivity of an option price to the volatility in the price of the underlying.

Kassenobligation A German term for a medium-term financial obligation, most notably in the form of three- to five-year federal government securities.

keepwell An indication by a parent or *holding company that its subsidiary will fulfil certain conditions.

Keidanren The Japanese name for the Federation of Economic Organizations, which is the most powerful of the Japanese business organizations. It functions as the headquarters of the business community; its members are the major trade associations and the prominent companies.

keiretsu In Japan, a group of companies that have interlocking *cross-holdings. These are usually minor shareholdings to cement relationships and typically involve at least one financial institution. The *keiretsu* is now the main form of business organization in Japan. *Compare* ZAIBATSU.

Keogh plan A US savings scheme to create a pension plan for self-employed people or employees of small and unincorporated businesses, in which tax is deferred until withdrawals are made. It can be held at the same time as a corporate pension or *individual retirement account. Keogh plans originated with the Self-Employment Individuals Retirement Act 1982.

kerb market **1.** The former practice of trading on the street after the formal close of business of the London Stock Exchange. **2.** Any informal market, such as one for dealing in securities not listed on a stock exchange.

key-person assurance An assurance policy on the life of a key employee of a company, especially the life of a senior executive in a small company, whose death would be a serious loss to the company. In the event of the key person dying, the benefit is paid to the company. In order that there should be an *insurable interest, a loss of profit must be the direct result of the death of the key person.

khoum A monetary unit of Mauritania worth one fifth of an *ouguiya.

KIBOR Abbreviation for *Kuwait Inter Bank Offered Rate.

kickback A colloquial term for an illegal payment made to secure favourable treatment in the award of a contract.

kicker An additional feature attached to a security to make it more attractive, for example an option or warrant. *See also* EQUITY KICKER.

killer bee A banker who assists a business in resisting predatory takeover bids by making the target company appear a less attractive proposition.

kina (k) The standard monetary unit of Papua New Guinea, divided into 100 toea.

kip (KN) The standard monetary unit of Laos, divided into 100 at.

KISS Abbreviation for *Kurs Information Service System.

kite An informal name for an *accommodation bill. **Kite-flying** or **kiting** is the discounting of a kite (accommodation bill) at a bank, knowing that the person on whom it is drawn will dishonour it.

kiting **1.** *See* KITE. **2.** An informal US name for the dishonest practice of improving the apparent cash position in a company's accounts by paying a large cheque on the last day of the accounting period from one of its current accounts into a second current account. Because the first account will not have been debited, but the second account will have been credited, the overall cash position is temporarily overstated. **3.** The act of changing a cheque illegally by altering the amount to be drawn. **4.** The practice of artificially driving up the market price of a share.

KLSE Abbreviation for *Kuala Lumpur Stock Exchange.

knock-in option A type of *barrier option that becomes activated if the price of the *underlying passes through a trigger price. An option that becomes deactivated in the same circumstances is known as a **knock-out option**.

kobo A monetary unit of Nigeria worth one hundredth of a *naira.

Kondratieff cycle A hypothesis, first suggested by the economist Nikolai Kondratieff, that the international economy is characterized by 50-year price cycles. The term has also been used more generally to support the notion that there are 50-year cycles in economic activity. *See* BUSINESS CYCLE.

kopeck A monetary unit of Russia and Belarus worth one hundredth of a *rouble.

kopiyka A monetary unit of Ukraine worth one hundredth of a *hryvna.

Korea Stock Exchange A securities trading market in Seoul that dates from 1911; the present system was set up in 1956 and the exchange is now one of Asia's largest and most modern.

koruna (Kčs) The standard monetary unit of the Czech Republic and Slovakia, divided into 100 haleru.

krona (Skr) The standard monetary unit of Sweden, divided into 100 öre.

króna (*plural* **krónor**; ISk) The standard monetary unit of Iceland, divided into 100 aurar.

krone (*plural* **kroner**) The standard monetary unit of Denmark (Dkr), the Faeroe Islands (Fkr), Greenland (Dkr), and Norway (Nkr), divided into 100 øre.

kroon (*plural* **krooni**; EEK) The standard monetary unit of Estonia, divided into 100 sents.

Krugerrand A South African coin containing 1 troy ounce of gold, minted since 1967 for investment purposes.

Kuala Lumpur Commodity Exchange A commodity market trading in rubber and palm oil in Malaysia. It provides hedging facilities for consumers and traders in natural rubber.

Kuala Lumpur Stock Exchange (KLSE) The stock exchange of Malaysia.

kuna (*plural* **kune**) The standard monetary unit of Croatia, divided into 100 lipas.

Kurs Information Service System (KISS) The share information system on the *Frankfurt Stock Exchange. Among other uses, it provides information for the *Deutsche Aktienindex.

kurtosis In statistics, the degree of sharpness (i.e. concentration about the mean) of a particular distribution curve. *See* LEPTOKURTIC DISTRIBUTION; MOMENTS.

kuru (*plural* **kuruş**) A monetary unit of Turkey, worth one hundredth of a *lira.

Kuwait Inter Bank Offered Rate (KIBOR) The rate at which banks lend to each other in the Kuwait interbank market.

kwacha **1.** (Mk) The standard monetary unit of Malawi, divided into 100 tambala. **2.** (k) The standard monetary unit of Zambia, divided into 100 ngwee.

kwanza (Nkz) The standard monetary unit of Angola, divided into 100 lwei.

kyat (k) The standard monetary unit of Myanmar (Burma), divided into 100 pyas.

laari A monetary unit of the Maldives worth one hundredth of a *rufiyaa.

labour-intensive Denoting a production process, project, or investment that relies heavily on the use of labour. *Compare* CAPITAL-INTENSIVE.

laches (Norman French *lasches*: negligence) Neglect and unreasonable delay in enforcing an equitable right. If a plaintiff with full knowledge of the facts takes an unnecessarily long time to bring an action (e.g. to set aside a contract obtained by fraud) the court will be of no assistance; hence the maxim "the law will not help those who sleep on their rights". No set period is given but if the action is covered by limitation-of-actions legislation, the period given will not be shortened. Otherwise the time allowed depends on the circumstances.

laddered portfolio A portfolio holding a range of fixed-interest bonds or other securities with fixed values in different maturities. *See also* BARBELL.

ladder option An *option in which the holder receives a payment every time the value of the *underlying passes a given level, irrespective of the final value of the underlying.

Lady Macbeth strategy A strategy used in takeover battles in which a third party makes a bid that the target company would favour, i.e. it appears to act as a *white knight, but subsequently changes allegiance and joins the original bidder.

lagged reserve requirement (LRR) A requirement of the US Federal Reserve Banks from the 1960s to the mid-1980s in which local banks had to leave with them deposits reflecting the local banks' own deposits two weeks earlier. This was a crude method of monetary control, which has now been superseded by the system of contemporaneous reserves (excluding time deposits, which are still subject to the two-week lag).

lambda A measure of the relationship between the value of an *option and the rate of interest. *See* GREEKS.

land bank **1.** The amount of land a developer owns that is awaiting development. **2.** *See* AGRICULTURAL BANK.

Landesbank A bank that acts primarily as a quasi-central bank for a group of German regional banks but which can, in some cases, also offer many of the services of a conventional bank.

lapping In the USA, the fraudulent practice of concealing a shortage of cash by delaying the recording of cash receipts. In the UK it is referred to as **teeming and lading**. There are a number of variations, but essentially the cashier conceals the theft of cash received from the first customer by recording the cash received from the second customer as attributable to the first, and so on with subsequent customers. The cashier hopes to be in a position to replace the cash before the dishonesty is discovered. As such hopes are frequently based on attempts at gambling, the deception is often discovered.

lapsed option An *option that has reached its expiry date without being exercised.

lari The standard monetary unit of Georgia, divided into 100 tetri.

last in, first out (LIFO) A method of charging homogeneous items of stock to production when the cost of the items has changed. It is assumed, both for costing and stock valuation purposes, that the latest items taken into stock are those used in production although this may not necessarily correspond with the physical movement of the goods. *Compare* FIRST IN, FIRST OUT.

last sale (last trade) The most recent transaction in a particular security. On some markets, the nature of the last trade may affect what trades are permitted to follow.

last-survivor policy 1. An assurance policy on the lives of two or more people, the sum assured being paid on the death of the last to die. *See also* JOINT-LIFE AND LAST-SURVIVOR ANNUITIES. **2.** A contract (formerly called a **tontine**) in which assurance is arranged by a group of people, who all pay premiums into a fund while they are alive. No payment is made until only one person from the group is left alive. At that point the survivor receives all the policy proceeds. Contracts of this kind are not available in the UK because of the temptation they provide to members to murder their fellows, in order to be the last survivor.

last trading day The last day on which a futures contract can be traded for a particular delivery period.

lats (*plural* **lati**) The standard monetary unit of Latvia, divided into 100 santimes.

launch date The date on which a *eurobond underwriter is invited to participate in a new issue.

laundering money Processing money acquired illegally (as by theft, drug dealing, etc.) so that it appears to have come from a legitimate source. This may be achieved by paying the illegal cash into a foreign bank and transferring its equivalent to a bank with a good name in a hard-currency area. There are now stringent controls on this activity.

LAUTRO Abbreviation for *Life Assurance and Unit Trust Regulatory Organization.

law of one price A law stating that, if two sets of financial obligations provide the same cash flow, then they have the same price.

LBO Abbreviation for *leveraged buy-out.

LCE Abbreviation for *London Commodity Exchange.

LCH Abbreviation for *London Clearing House.

LDP Abbreviation for *London daily prices.

lead The first named underwriting syndicate on a Lloyd's insurance policy. When a broker seeks to cover a risk he will first try to get a large syndicate to act as lead, which encourages smaller syndicates to cover a share of the risk. The premium rate is calculated by the lead; if others wish to join in the risk they have to insure at that rate. On a collective policy the lead insurer is the first insurer on the schedule of insurers; he issues the policy, collects the premiums, and distributes the proportions to the coinsurers.

lead banks *See* LEAD MANAGERS.

leading and lagging **1.** Techniques often used at the end of a financial year to enhance a cash position and reduce borrowing. This is achieved by arranging for the settlement of outstanding obligations to be accelerated (leading) or delayed (lagging). **2.** The use of similar techniques to benefit from the expected change in a currency value.

lead managers (lead banks) Banks that launch a new issue or *syndicated loan facility. They are usually chosen either because they have a close relationship with the borrower or because they have been successful in a competitive bought deal contest. They are the main organizer of the transactions.

leakage **1.** The acquisition by particular individuals of information before it is generally known in the market. *See* INSIDER INFORMATION. **2.** Cash flows that do not go to the buyer of a financial obligation (e.g. dividends when shares are bought ex-dividend). **3.** In a basic Keynesian economic model, income that is not consumed but used to finance the payment of taxes, savings, or exports.

lean back A period of cautious inaction by a government agency or regulator before intervening in a market. For example, a central bank might allow a lean-back period to elapse to allow exchange rates to stabilize, before intervening in the foreign-exchange market.

LEAPS Abbreviation for *long-term equity anticipation securities.

leaseback (renting back) An arrangement in which the owner of an *asset (such as land or buildings) sells it to another party but immediately enters into a lease agreement with the purchaser to obtain the right to use the asset. Such a transaction is a method for raising funds and can affect the *financial statements of a company, depending on whether a *finance lease or an *operating lease is entered into.

lease obligation bond (LOB) A US *municipal bond in which the security is a lease.

lease-purchase agreement A lease in which the payments go towards the purchase of the asset. *See also* HIRE PURCHASE.

leasing Hiring equipment, such as a car or a piece of machinery, to avoid the capital cost involved in owning it. In some companies it is advantageous to use capital for other purposes and to lease some equipment, paying for the hire out of income. The equipment is then an asset of the leasing company rather than the lessor. Sometimes a case can be made for leasing rather than purchasing, on the grounds that some equipment quickly becomes obsolete.

leg One element in a complex set of transactions. *See* BREAKING A LEG; STRADDLE.

legal capital In the USA, the amount of *stockholders' equity, which cannot be reduced by the payment of dividends. This is the value of a company's shares in the balance sheet.

legal owner A person in whose name an asset is held, who can legally transfer the asset to another person. The legal owner is not, however, the owner in every sense and might be holding the asset as a *nominee or a *trustee. *See also* BENEFICIAL OWNER.

legal person A human being (a natural person) or a **juristic person**. A juristic person is an entity, such as a corporation, that is recognized as having a legal personality, i.e. capable of enjoying and being subject to legal rights and duties.

legal reserve The minimum amount of money that building societies, insurance companies, etc., are bound by law to hold as security for the benefit of their customers.

legal risk In a financial transaction, the possibility of adverse impacts flowing from the legal or regulatory system.

legal tender Money that must be accepted in discharge of a debt. It may be **limited legal tender**, i.e. it must be accepted but only up to specified limits of payment; or **unlimited legal tender**, i.e. acceptable in settlement of debts of any amount. Bank of England notes and the £2 and £1 coins are unlimited legal tender in the UK. Other Royal Mint coins are limited legal tender; i.e. debts up to £10 can be paid in 50p and 20p coins; up to £5 by 10p and 5p coins; and up to 20p by bronze coins.

lek (Lk) The standard monetary unit of Albania, divided into 100 qindars.

lempira (L) The standard monetary unit of Honduras, divided into 100 centavos.

lender liability The liability of a lender for the actions of a borrower.

lender of last resort A country's central bank with responsibility for controlling its banking system. In the UK, the Bank of England fulfils this role, lending to *discount houses, either by repurchasing *Treasury bills, lending on other paper assets, or granting direct loans, charging the *base rate of interest. *Commercial banks do not go directly to the Bank of England; they borrow from the discount houses.

lending multiple 1. The ratio of bank deposits to highly liquid assets. **2.** In the UK housing market, a multiple of the borrower's income used to calculate the maximum amount that will be lent on a mortgage.

lending security A security borrowed by a *market maker, usually to cover a *short position.

leone (Le) The standard monetary unit of Sierra Leone, divided into 100 cents.

leptokurtic distribution In statistics, a distribution that is more sharply peaked (i.e. more concentrated about the mean) than a *normal distribution. *See* KURTOSIS. *Compare* GAMMA DISTRIBUTION.

lepton (*plural* **lepta**) A former monetary unit of Greece, worth one hundredth of a *drachma (until 2002).

lessee The party to a lease contract who uses the asset and makes the lease payments.

lessor The party to a lease contract who provides the asset and receives the lease payments.

letter bond (letter stock) A private placement of bonds or stocks.

letter of allotment *See* ALLOTMENT.

letter of comfort 1. A letter to a bank from the parent company of a subsidiary that is trying to borrow money from the bank. The letter gives no guarantee for the repayment of the projected loan but offers the bank the comfort of knowing that the subsidiary has made the parent company aware of its intention to borrow; the parent also usually supports the application, giving, at least, an assurance that it intends that the subsidiary should remain in business and that it will give notice of any relevant change of ownership. **2.** A letter by one party to a bank indicating a relationship that will make a second party more likely to repay a bank loan.

letter of credit (documentary credit) A letter from one banker to another authorizing the payment of a specified sum to the person named in the letter on certain specified conditions (*see* LETTER OF INDICATION). Commercially, letters of credit are widely used in the international import and export trade as a means of payment. In an export contract, the exporter may require the foreign importer to open a letter of credit at the importer's local bank (the issuing bank) for the amount of the goods. This will state that it is to be negotiable at a bank (the negotiating bank) in the exporter's country in favour of the exporter; often, the exporter (who is called the beneficiary of the credit) will give the name of the negotiating bank. On presentation of the shipping documents (which are listed in the letter of credit) the beneficiary will receive payment from the negotiating bank.

An **irrevocable letter of credit** cannot be cancelled by the person who opens it or by the issuing bank without the beneficiary's consent, whereas a **revocable letter of credit** can. In a **confirmed letter of credit** the negotiating bank guarantees to pay the beneficiary, even if the issuing bank fails to honour its commitments (in an **unconfirmed letter of credit** this guarantee is not given). A confirmed irrevocable letter of credit therefore provides the most reliable means of being paid for exported goods. However, all letters of credit have an expiry date, after which they can only be negotiated by the consent of all the parties. A **circular letter of credit** is an instruction from a bank to its correspondent banks to pay the beneficiary a stated sum on presentation of a means of identification. It has now been replaced by *traveller's cheques.

Although the term 'letter of credit' is still widely used, in 1983 the International Chamber of Commerce recommended **documentary credit** as the preferred term for these instruments.

letter of hypothecation *See* HYPOTHECATION.

letter of indemnity 1. A letter stating that the organization issuing it will compensate the person to whom it is addressed for a specified loss. *See also* INDEMNITY. **2.** A letter written to a company registrar asking for a replacement for a lost share certificate and indemnifying the company against any loss that it might incur in so doing. It may be required to be countersigned by a bank.

letter of indication (letter of identification) A letter issued by a bank to a customer to whom a *letter of credit has been supplied. The letter has to be produced with the letter of credit at the negotiating bank; it provides evidence of the bearer's identity and signature. It is used particularly with a circular letter of credit carried by travellers, although *traveller's cheques are now more widely used.

letter of intent A letter in which a person formally sets out an intention to do something, such as signing a contract in certain circumstances, which is often specified in detail in the letter. The letter does not constitute either a contract or a promise to do anything, but it does indicate the writer's serious wish to pursue a particular course.

letter of licence A letter from a creditor to a debtor, who is having trouble raising the money to settle the debt. The letter states that the creditor will allow the debtor a stated time to pay and will not initiate proceedings against the debtor before that time. *See also* ARRANGEMENT.

letter of regret A letter from a company, or its bankers, stating that an application for an allotment from a *new issue of shares has been unsuccessful.

letter of renunciation 1. A form, often attached to an *allotment letter, on which a person who has been allotted shares in a *new issue renounces the rights to them, either absolutely or in favour of someone else (during the **renunciation period**). **2.** A form on the reverse of some unit-trust certificates, which the holder completes when wishing to dispose of the holding. The completed certificate is sent to the trust managers.

letters of administration An order authorizing the person named (the *administrator) to distribute the property of a deceased person, who has not appointed anyone else to do so. The distribution must be in accordance with the deceased's will, or the rules of *intestacy in the absence of a will.

letter stock *See* LETTER BOND.

leu (*plural* **lei**) The standard monetary unit of Romania (ROL) and Moldova (MLD), divided into 100 bani.

lev (*plural* **leva**; BGL) The standard monetary unit of Bulgaria, divided into 100 stotinki.

level yield *See* YIELD.

leverage 1. The US word for *gearing. **2.** The use by a company of its limited assets to guarantee substantial loans to finance its business. **3.** A *position (usually a derivatives position) in which the principal is small relative to the market risks.

leverage–capital ratio The ratio of a bank's *tier 1 capital (as defined by the *Basle Concordat) to its average total assets over an accounting period.

leveraged buy-out (LBO) The acquisition of one company by another through the use of borrowed funds. The intention is that the loans will be repaid from the cash flow of the acquired company. In the 1980s many takeovers in the USA were financed by the issue of *junk bonds in highly leveraged buyouts.

leveraged capped floating-rate note A *floating-rate note in which the *coupon rate is leveraged on an interest rate with a maximum rate.

leveraged lease A lease in which the lessor borrows as part of the finance of the asset to be leased.

leveraged reverse floating-rate note *See* REVERSE FLOATING-RATE NOTE.

leveraged securities Securities partly bought on a *margin account (i.e. with borrowed finance).

leveraged swap A *swap in which changes in interest rates lead to larger changes in the structure of payments.

leverage factor The change in the value of a *derivative resulting from a change in the value of the *underlying.

leverage ratios *See* GEARING RATIOS.

liability 1. The funding of a business debt. *See* CURRENT LIABILITIES; DEFERRED CREDIT; LONG-TERM LIABILITY; SECURED LIABILITY. **2.** An obligation to make a financial payment. *See* CONTINGENT LIABILITY. **3.** The acceptance of an insurance risk.

liability insurance A form of insurance policy that promises to pay any compensation and court costs the policyholder becomes legally liable to pay because of claims for injury to other people or damage to their property as a result of the policyholder's negligence. Policies often define the areas in which they will deal with liability, e.g. personal liability or employers' liability.

liability management The management of an organization's (especially a bank's) funding. The key purposes are to lower funding cost, control *interest-rate risk, and manage liquidity. *See also* ASSET–LIABILITY MANAGEMENT.

liability swap A *swap that is used to *hedge liabilities.

LIBID Abbreviation for *London Inter Bank Bid Rate.

LIBOR Abbreviation for *London Inter Bank Offered Rate.

licence 1. Official permission to do something that is forbidden without a licence (e.g. sell alcohol or own a TV or a firearm). Licences may be required for social reasons or simply to enable revenue to be collected. Since the Consumer Credit Act 1974 all businesses involved with giving credit to purchasers of goods must be licensed by the Office of Fair Trading. **2.** Formal permission to enter or occupy land. Such licenses are of three kinds. (a) The simplest gives the licensee the permission of the landowner to be on land (e.g. the right of a visitor to enter a house). It may be revoked at any time as long as the licensee is given time to leave. (b) **Contractual licences** are permissions to be on land in the furtherance of some contractual right (e.g. the right of the holder of a cinema ticket to be in the cinema). This type of licence has been used to get round the Rent Acts (which apply to leases only): a licence to occupy a flat or house may be granted, which is said to be revocable at any time. It has been held that if the licence gives the licensee exclusive possession of the property, it is in fact a lease, despite the fact that it is called a licence. The exact state of the law in this area is uncertain. It is also unclear whether a contractual licence can be made irrevocable and binding on those who were not a party to the contract (e.g. purchasers of the land). It was originally held that a licence could always be revoked, although damages might be payable. Recent cases have cast doubt on this proposition. (c) Licences coupled with an interest are those that go with a recognizable interest in the land of another. Such licences are irrevocable and assignable. They bind successors in title in the same way as the interest in land to which they relate.

licensed dealer A dealer licensed under the *Financial Services Act 1986 to provide investment advice and deal in securities, either as an agent or principal. Licensed dealers are not members of the *London Stock Exchange and are not covered by its compensation fund.

licensed deposit taker A category of financial institutions as defined by the Banking Act 1979, which divided banking into recognized banks, licensed deposit takers, and exempt institutions. To qualify for authorization, the licensed deposit taker had to satisfy the Bank of England that it conducted its business in a prudent manner. The aim of the Act was to bring more institutions under the supervision of the Bank of England. As the Banking Act 1987 established a single category of authorized institutions eligible to carry out banking business the distinction has now disappeared.

lien The right of one person to retain possession of goods owned by another until the possessor's claims against the owner have been satisfied. The lien may be **general**, when the goods are held as security for all outstanding debts of the owner, or **particular**, when only the claims of the possessor in respect of the goods held must be satisfied. A **banker's lien** applies to certain financial documents held by a bank on behalf of a customer who owes money to the bank.

life annuity An *annuity that ceases to be paid on the death of a specified person, which may or may not be the *annuitant.

life assurance An *insurance policy that pays a specified amount of money on the death of the *life assured or, in the case of an *endowment assurance policy, on the death of the life assured or at the end of an agreed period, whichever is the earlier. Life assurance grew from a humble means of providing funeral expenses to a means of saving for oneself or one's dependants, with certain tax advantages. *With-profits policies provide sums of money in excess of the sum assured by the addition of *bonuses. *Unit-linked policies invest the premiums in funds of assets, by means of buying units in the funds. *See also* WHOLE (OF) LIFE POLICY.

Life Assurance and Unit Trust Regulatory Organization (LAUTRO) A former *Self-Regulating Organization that regulated institutions offering life assurance and unit trusts as principals. Most of its business was taken over by the *Personal Investment Authority in 1994 and LAUTRO was wound up in 1995.

life assured The person upon whose death a life-assurance policy makes an agreed payment. The life assured need not be the owner of the policy.

lifeboat 1. A fund set up to rescue dealers on an exchange or banks in the event of a market collapse and the ensuing insolvencies. **2.** The rescue of a company that is in financial difficulty by new or restructured loans from its group of bankers.

life-cycle costing The approach to determining the total costs of a fixed asset that takes into account all the costs likely to be incurred both in acquiring it and in operating it over its effective life. For example, the initial cost to an airline of an aircraft is only part of the costs relevant to the decision to purchase it. The operating costs over its effective life are also relevant and would therefore be part of the decision-making data.

life of contract The period of trading to expiry of a contract, most notably on traded derivative markets.

life office A company that provides *life assurance.

lifestyle business A small business run by owners with a personal interest in the product. The business reflects their lifestyles and provides them with a comfortable income, but is not a growth venture.

lifetime transfers *See* POTENTIALLY EXEMPT TRANSFER.

LIFFE Abbreviation for *London International Financial Futures and Options Exchange.

LIFO Abbreviation for *last in, first out.

lift 1. Any favourable transaction. **2.** A rise in the market on favourable news.

lifting a leg *See* BREAKING A LEG.

lilangeni (*plural* **emalangeni**; E) The standard monetary unit of Swaziland, divided into 100 cents.

LIMEAN Abbreviation for *London Inter Bank Mean Rate.

limit 1. An order given by an investor to a broker restricting a particular purchase to a stated maximum price or a particular sale to a stated minimum price. Such a **limit order** will also be restricted as to time; it may be given firm for a stated period or firm until cancelled. **2.** The *maximum fluctuations (up or down) allowed in certain markets over a stated period (usually one day's trading; *see* INTRADAY LIMIT). In some volatile circumstances the market moves the limit up (or down). The movement of prices on the *Tokyo Stock Exchange is limited in this way as it is on certain US commodity markets. In some markets, if the limit is reached trading is stopped for the day or for a cooling-off period. *See* LIMIT MOVE; LIMIT UP/DOWN. **3.** A restriction on a derivatives or commodity exchange on the number of contracts or positions one party can hold. **4.** A risk limit in relation to, for example, the credit exposure to a particular counterparty.

limited by guarantee *See* LIMITED COMPANY.

limited company A *company in which the liability of the members in respect of the company's debts is limited. It may be **limited by shares**, in which case the liability of the members on a winding-up is limited to the amount (if any) unpaid on their shares. This is by far the most common type of registered company. The liability of the members may alternatively be **limited by guarantee**; in this case the liability of members is limited by the memorandum to a certain amount, which the members undertake to contribute on winding-up. These are usually societies, clubs, or trade associations. Since 1980 it has not been possible for such a company to be formed with a share capital, or converted to a company limited by guarantee with a share capital. *See also* PUBLIC LIMITED COMPANY.

limited liability *See* LIMITED COMPANY.

limited market 1. A market that is illiquid. **2.** A market with restricted numbers of buyers.

limited recourse financing 1. Recourse to a project sponsor attached to a specific project finance undertaking. **2.** A loan made to a company specifically set up by a developer to manage a particular property. In case of default, the lender has no recourse to the other assets of the developer.

limit move The maximum possible price movement on a derivatives exchange; if it is reached, trading will be stopped for the session. *See* LIMIT.

limit order *See* LIMIT.

limit up/down The maximum upward or downward price on a derivatives exchange; if it is reached, trading will be stopped for the session.

line 1. The acceptance of a risk by an insurance *underwriter. **2.** A large quantity of something, such as a block of shares. *See also* CREDIT LINE. **3.** A particular item in a set of financial accounts.

line of credit *See* CREDIT LINE.

lipa A monetary unit of Croatia worth one hundredth of a *kuna.

liquid assets (liquid capital; quick assets; realizable assets) Assets held in cash or in something that can be readily turned into cash with minimal capital loss (e.g. deposits in a bank current account, trade debts, marketable investments). The ratio of these assets to current liabilities provides an assessment of an organization's *liquidity or solvency. *See also* LIQUID RATIO; MANDATORY LIQUID ASSETS.

liquidate To wind up or dissolve a *limited company. This may be undertaken by either the directors or the shareholders. If the company is solvent, i.e. its assets exceed its liabilities, the assets will be distributed to the shareholders. *See* LIQUIDATION; LIQUIDATOR.

liquidated damages *See* DAMAGES.

liquidation (winding-up) The distribution of a company's assets among its creditors and members prior to its dissolution. This brings the life of the company to an end. The liquidation may be voluntary (*see* CREDITORS' VOLUNTARY LIQUIDATION; MEMBERS' VOLUNTARY LIQUIDATION) or by the court (*see* COMPULSORY LIQUIDATION). *See also* LIQUIDATE; LIQUIDATOR.

liquidation committee A committee set up by the creditors of a company being wound up in order to consent to the *liquidator exercising certain powers. When the company is unable to pay its debts, the committee is usually composed of creditors only; otherwise it consists of creditors and *contributories.

liquidator A person appointed by a court, or by the members of a company or its creditors, to regularize the company's affairs on a *liquidation (winding-up). In the case of a *members' voluntary liquidation, it is the members of the company who appoint the liquidator. In a *creditors' voluntary liquidation, the liquidator may be appointed by company members before the **meeting of creditors** or by the creditors themselves at the meeting; in the former case the liquidator can only exercise his or her powers with the consent of the court. If two liquidators are appointed, the court resolves which one is to act. In a *compulsory liquidation, the court appoints a *provisional liquidator after the winding-up petition has been presented; after the order has been granted, the court appoints the *official receiver as liquidator, until or unless another officer is appointed.

The liquidator is in a relationship of trust with the company and the creditors as a body; a liquidator appointed in a compulsory liquidation is an officer of the court, is under statutory obligations, and may not profit from the position. A liquidator must be a qualified **insolvency practitioner**, according to the Insolvency Act 1986. Under this Act, insolvency practitioners must meet certain statutory requirements, including membership of an approved professional body (such as the Insolvency Practitioners' Association or the Institute of Chartered Accountants). On appointment, the liquidator assumes control of the company, collects the assets, pays the debts, and distributes any surplus to company members according to their rights. In the case of a compulsory liquidation, the liquidator is supervised by the court, the *liquidation committee, and the Department of Trade and Industry. The liquidator receives a *statement of affairs from the company officers and must report on these to the court.

liquid capital *See* LIQUID ASSETS.

liquid instrument A *negotiable instrument that the purchaser is able to sell before maturity.

liquidity The extent to which an organization's assets are liquid (*see* LIQUID ASSETS), enabling it to pay its debts when they fall due and also to move into new investment opportunities.

liquidity index A measure of a company's liquidity assessed by calculating the number of days it would take for current assets to be converted into cash.

liquidity premium The relative advantage of holding assets in liquid form.

Investors are prepared to receive lower returns on *liquid assets, because they can easily be transferred into cash with little capital loss. Liquid assets are thus to some extent a hedge against uncertainty.

liquidity ratio *See* CASH RATIO.

liquidity risk 1. The *risk, in lending operations, that an investment cannot be liquidated during its life without significant costs. **2.** The risk that markets will not exist for certain transactions or that they can only be executed with delay and wide margins.

liquidity trap A situation in which investors hold on to cash because they are worried about the likelihood of a fall in the price of financial assets. J. M. Keynes argued that in these circumstances monetary policy becomes ineffective, because monetary expansion will not lower interest rates.

liquid market A market in which *spreads are narrow, there are many buyers and sellers, and large transactions do not have a marked impact on the market price.

liquid ratio (acid-test ratio; quick ratio) A ratio used for assessing the *liquidity of a company; it is the ratio of the *liquid assets to the *current liabilities. The answer is expressed either as a percentage or as x:1. For example, a company with current assets of £25,000 including stock of £15,000 and liabilities of £12,000 will have a liquid ratio of:

$$(£25,000 - £15,000)/£12,000 = 0.83,$$

i.e. 83% or 0.83:1. This may be interpreted as the company having 83 pence of liquid or current assets for every £1 of current liabilities. If, for some reason, the company is obliged to repay the current liabilities immediately there would be insufficient liquid assets to allow it to do so. The company may therefore be forced into a hurried sale of stock at a discount to raise finance. Although there is no rule of thumb, and there are industry differences, a liquid ratio significantly below 1:1 will give rise to concern. The liquid ratio is regarded as an acid test of its solvency and is therefore sometimes called the acid-test ratio.

lira 1. (IT) The standard monetary unit of Turkey, divided into 100 kuruş. **2.** (Lm) The standard monetary unit of Malta, divided into 100 cents and 1000 mils. **3.** (l; lit) Formerly, the standard monetary unit of Italy and San Marino, divided into 100 centesimi. It was subsumed into the *euro for all purposes except cash transactions in January 1999 and abolished in 2002.

LIRMA Abbreviation for London International Insurance and Reinsurance Market Association. *See* LONDON UNDERWRITING CENTRE.

Lisbon Stock Exchange Portugal's main stock exchange, regulated by Portugal's central bank, the Bank of Portugal.

lisente A monetary unit of Lesotho worth one hundredth of a *loti.

listed company A company that has a **listing agreement** (*see* LISTING REQUIREMENTS) on a major stock exchange and whose shares therefore have a *quotation. These companies were formerly called **quoted companies**.

listed option *See* EXCHANGE-TRADED OPTION.

listed security 1. In general, a security that has a *quotation on a recognized *stock exchange. **2.** On the *London Stock Exchange, a security that has a quotation in the Official List of Securities of the *main market. *See also* ALTERNATIVE INVESTMENT MARKET; FLOTATION; LISTING REQUIREMENTS; YELLOW BOOK.

listing requirements The conditions that must be satisifed before a security can be traded on a stock exchange. To achieve a quotation in the Official List of Securities of the *main market of the *London Stock Exchange, the requirements contained in a **listing agreement** must be signed by the company seeking quotation. The two main requirements of such a listing are usually: (i) that the value of the company's assets should exceed a certain value; (ii) that the company publish specific financial information, both at the time of *flotation and regularly thereafter (*see* ACCOUNTS; DIRECTORS' REPORT).

The listing requirements are set out in the *Yellow Book.

lists closed The closing of the application lists for a *new issue on the London Stock Exchange, after a specified time or after the issue has been fully subscribed.

litas (*plural* **litai**) The standard monetary unit of Lithuania, divided into 100 centai.

litigation **1.** The taking of legal action. The person who takes it is called a **litigant**. **2.** The activity of a solicitor when dealing with proceedings in a court of law.

Little Board The colloquial name for the *American Stock Exchange, the New York market for smaller company stocks and bonds. *Compare* BIG BOARD.

Liverpool Cotton Association A major world market in cotton, set up originally in 1841. It now trades in both actuals and futures.

living dead A company that has received venture capital funding but is unlikely to meet its growth targets or provide the required rate of return on the investment.

Lloyd's A corporation of underwriters (**Lloyd's underwriters**) and insurance brokers (**Lloyd's brokers**) that developed from a coffee shop in Tavern Street in the City of London in 1689. It takes its name from the proprietor of the coffee shop, Edward Lloyd. By 1774 it was established in the Royal Exchange and in 1871 was incorporated by act of parliament. It now occupies a building in Lime Street (built in 1986 by Richard Rogers). As a corporation, Lloyd's itself does not underwrite insurance business; all its business comes to it from Lloyd's brokers, who are in touch with the public, and is underwritten by *syndicates of Lloyd's underwriters, who are approached by the brokers and who do not, themselves, contact the public.

The 20 000 or so Lloyd's underwriters must each deposit a substantial sum of money with the corporation and accept unlimited liability before they can become members. They are grouped into syndicates, run by a syndicate manager or agent, but most of the members of syndicates are **names**, underwriting members of Lloyd's who take no part in organizing the underwriting business, but who share in the profits or losses of the syndicate and provide the risk capital. Lloyd's has long specialized in marine insurance but now covers almost all insurance risks. In the period 1988 to 1994 Lloyd's lost some £8 billion. This brought severe hardship to many names and a number of changes to the way in which the organization is run, including allowing limited liability companies to become underwriters.

Lloyd's adviser A person who negotiates membership of individual syndicates and presents analyses on behalf of corporate members of *Lloyd's.

Lloyd's broker *See* LLOYD'S.

Lloyd's Register of Shipping A society formed by *Lloyd's in 1760 to inspect and classify all ocean-going vessels in excess of 100 tonnes. Ships are periodically surveyed by **Lloyd's surveyors** and classified according to the condition of their hulls, engines, and trappings. The society also provides a technical advice service. Its annual publication is called *Lloyd's Register of British and Foreign Shipping*. The Register enables underwriters to have instant access to the information they need to underwrite marine risks, even when the vessels may be thousands of miles away.

Lloyd's underwriter *See* LLOYD'S.

LME Abbreviation for *London Metal Exchange.

loading 1. The addition of a charge to cover incidental expenses, administrative costs, profit, etc., on an insurance policy, bank account, or purchases of unit trusts. **2.** The charging of interest and fees on an account. **3.** The charges and premia on unit trusts to cover administrative expenses.

loan Money lent on condition that it is repaid, either in instalments or all at once, on agreed dates and usually that the borrower pays the lender an agreed rate of interest (unless it is an **interest-free loan**). *See also* BALLOON; BANK LOAN; BRIDGING LOAN; BULLET; LOCAL LOAN; PERSONAL LOAN.

loan account An account opened by a bank in the name of a customer to whom it has granted a loan, rather than an *overdraft facility. The amount of the loan is debited to this account and any repayments are credited; interest is charged on the full amount of the loan less any repayments. The customer's current account may be credited with the amount of the loan. With an overdraft facility, interest is only charged on the amount of the overdraft, which may be less than the full amount of the loan.

loanback An arrangement in which an individual can borrow from the accumulated funds of his or her pension scheme. Usually a commercial rate of interest has to be credited to fund for the use of the capital. Some life assurance companies offer loan facilities on this basis of up to fifteen times the annual pension premium.

loan-backed Describing an *asset-backed security in which the assets are portfolios of loans. For example, credit-card portfolios or portfolios of unsecured personal loans are loan-backed securities.

loan capital (borrowed capital; debt capital) Capital used to finance an organization that is subject to payment of interest over the life of the loan, at the end of which the loan is normally repaid. There are different categories of loan capital: *mortgage debentures are secured on specific assets of the organization, while convertible debentures may be converted into equity according to the terms of the issue.

loan creditor A person or institution that has lent money to a business. For example, when a bank loan is obtained the bank becomes a loan creditor.

Loan Guarantee Scheme A UK government scheme introduced in 1980 that guarantees 70% of a company's overdraft for a 3% premium. The bank must accept the risk for the balance of 30%. Its purpose is to support small businesses.

loan note A form of loan stock (*see* DEBENTURE) in which an investor takes a note rather than cash as the result of a share offer to defer tax liability. The yield is often variable and may be linked to the *London Inter Bank Offered Rate. Loan notes are not usually marketable but are usually repayable on demand.

loan–price ratio The ratio of the value of a loan to the value of any *collateral. This formula is often used to judge the risk exposure for mortgages.

loan quality A measure of the likelihood of the lender making a loss on a loan. It will be determined in part by the creditworthiness of the counterparty and the *collateral on the loan.

loan review A review of problem loans in terms of *loan quality and of any actions that may need to be undertaken.

loan selling The sale of bank loans by one bank to another. For example, Third World debt may be sold at a discount to the market value in order to reduce the burden of the debt on a particular bank. Loans to individuals may also be sold in this way, from one financial institution to another, often without the borrower knowing that the lender has changed. *See also* EUROBOND.

loan stock *See* DEBENTURE.

LOB Abbreviation for *lease obligation bond.

local A person who has a seat on a financial market and who deals for his or her own account.

local authority bill A *bill of exchange drawn on a UK local government authority.

local authority stock A bond issued by a UK local government authority.

local loan A loan issued by a UK local government authority for financing capital expenditure.

local taxation A form of taxation levied by a local government authority rather than by a central government. It can take various forms, including a local sales tax, local income tax, a property tax (e.g. UK rates), or a poll tax (e.g. the former UK community charge).

lockbox In the USA, a Postal Service box used for the collection of customer payments. The recipient's bank will arrange collection from these boxes throughout the day, deposit the funds, and provide a computer listing of the payments with the daily total. This method is effective for small number of payments with a high value as the bank's charges per item are relatively high.

locked in 1. Describing a financial *position that cannot be unwound. *See* UNWINDING. **2.** Describing a contract with a fixed rate of interest.

lock-up An investment in an asset that is not readily realizable or one that is specifically intended to be held for a long period (e.g. over ten years).

loco The location in which a particular commodity has been traded, e.g. a contract in rubber futures may have been traded "loco KL" (in Kuala Lumpur).

Lombard rate 1. The rate of interest at which the German central bank, the *Bundesbank, lends to German commercial banks, usually ½% above the *discount rate. **2.** The interest rate charged by a European commercial bank lending against security.

Lombard Street The street in the City of London that is the centre of the money market. Many commercial banks have offices in or near Lombard Street, as do many bill brokers and discount houses. The Bank of England is nearby.

Lomé Convention The convention which, in 1976, set up the *European Development Fund to aid developing countries outside the European Community.

London acceptance credit A method of providing immediate cash for a UK exporter of goods. On shipment of the goods the exporter draws a *bill of exchange on the foreign buyer. The accepted bill is then pledged to a *merchant bank in London, which accepts an *accommodation bill drawn by the exporter. The acceptance can be discounted on the bank's reputation, to provide the exporter with immediate finance, whereas the foreign buyer's acceptance would be difficult, or impossible, to discount in London.

London and New Zealand Futures Association A UK commodity market in Bradford, established in 1953 to trade in New Zealand wool.

London approach The approach adopted by London banks to customers facing a cash-flow crisis. The key feature is that the banks remain supportive for as long as possible, decisions are made collectively, and all information and any money paid is shared between the lending banks on an equitable basis.

London Bankers' Clearing House The organization that daily sets off all cheques drawn for and against the *clearing banks in the UK. It has been housed in 10 Lombard Street, in the City of London, since the 1770s. *See also* ASSOCIATION FOR PAYMENT CLEARING SERVICES.

London Bullion Market The world's largest market for gold. Prices are fixed for gold twice daily by five fixing members meeting at Rothschild's bank. Prices are given in US dollars. Trading is now carried out on screen between market members. Silver is also traded on the London Bullion Market.

London Chamber of Commerce and Industry The largest chamber of commerce in the UK. It provides the normal services of a chamber of commerce and in addition runs courses and examinations in business subjects.

London Clearing House (LCH) A *clearing house established in 1888 (known before 1991 as the International Commodities Clearing House and originally as the London Produce Clearing House). LCH is an independent body, owned by six major UK commercial banks. It provides futures and options markets with netting and settlement services as well as becoming a counterparty (*see* COUNTERPARTY RISK) to every transaction between its members. In this capacity LCH takes the risk of its members defaulting, which it covers by collecting *margins from members; it also provides an independent guarantee of £200 million from its shareholders and from the insurance market. Exchanges making use of LCH facilities include the *London International Financial Futures and Options Exchange, the *London Metal Exchange, the *International Petroleum Exchange, and *Tradepoint Investment Exchange.

London Club A group of commercial banks formed in the 1980s to reschedule debts (*see* MULTI-YEAR RESCHEDULING AGREEMENT), especially from developing countries.

London Cocoa Terminal Market A former market now incorporated into the *London Commodity Exchange.

London code of conduct A code, issued by the Bank of England, that is applicable to all wholesale dealings not regulated by the rules of a recognized exchange. It is considered the best practice for company treasurers by the *Association of Corporate Treasurers.

London Commodity Exchange (LCE) A commodity exchange, which emerged in 1954 as a successor to the London Commercial Sale Rooms. It merged with the Soft Commodity Futures Trade Association to form a single *Recognized Investment Exchange under the Financial Services Act 1986. In 1987 it became the *Futures and Options Exchange (London FOX), Europe's leading market for trading in *futures contracts and *options in cocoa, coffee, white sugar, wheat, barley, and potatoes. It took over the Baltic International Freight Futures Exchange (BIFFEX), on which futures in dry cargo freight are traded, in 1991 and merged with the *London International Financial Futures and Options Exchange (LIFFE) in 1996. LIFFE is now part of *Euronext NV.

London daily prices (LDP) The price fixed each day for trading in white sugar.

London FOX Abbreviation for the London *Futures and Options Exchange.

London Inter Bank Bid Rate (LIBID) The rate of interest at which banks bid for funds to borrow from each other. *See* LONDON INTER BANK OFFERED RATE.

London Inter Bank Currency Options Market A London-based *over-the-counter market in currency options.

London Inter Bank Mean Rate (LIMEAN) The median average between the London Inter Bank Offered Rate (LIBOR) and the London Inter Bank Bid Rate (LIBID).

London Inter Bank Offered Rate (LIBOR) The rate of interest in the short-term wholesale market (*see* INTERBANK MARKET) in which banks offer to lend money to each other. The loans are for a minimum of £250,000 for periods from overnight up to five years. The importance of the market is that it allows individual banks to adjust their liquidity positions quickly, covering shortages by borrowing from banks with surpluses. This reduces the need for each bank to hold large quantities of liquid assets, thus releasing funds for more profitable lending transactions. LIBOR is the most significant interest rate for international banks. It is officially fixed at 11 a.m. each day by five major London banks, but fluctuates during the day. It is also used as a benchmark for lending to bank customers. It is also a reference rate for many derivatives. *See also* LONDON INTER BANK BID RATE.

London International Financial Futures and Options Exchange (LIFFE) A *financial futures market opened in 1982, in London's Royal Exchange, to provide facilities within the European time zone for dealing in options and futures contracts, including those in government bonds, stock-and-share indexes, foreign currencies, and interest rates. In 1991 LIFFE moved into its own premises in the City of London. A client wishing to buy or sell options or futures telephones a LIFFE broker, who instructs the booth run by that broker on the floor of the exchange. The booth clerk hands a slip to the broker's trader in the *pit of the market who executes the transaction with another trader. The bargain details are passed to the *London Clearing House, which acts as guarantor. Automated (electronic) pit trading was introduced in 1989, though this only operates after the close of live pit trading. The London Traded Options Market merged with LIFFE in 1992, when the words 'and Options' was added to its name, although the acronym remains unchanged. In 1996 LIFFE merged with the *London Commodity Exchange, making it the only exchange in the world to provide futures and options contracts on financial, equity, and commodity products and equity indices. Since 2001, it has become part of the European derivatives business *Euronext NV, with markets in Amsterdam, Brussels, Lisbon, and Paris.

London International Insurance and Reinsurance Market Association
(LIRMA) *See* LONDON UNDERWRITING CENTRE.

London Metal Exchange (LME) A central market for non-ferrous metals,
established in London in 1877 to supply a central market for the import of large
quantities of metal from abroad. The Exchange deals in copper, lead, zinc,
aluminium, tin, and nickel. The official prices of the LME are used by producers and
consumers worldwide for their long-term contracts. Dealings on the LME include
*options and *futures contracts. Bargains are guaranteed by the *London Clearing
House.

London rules A set of guidelines, approved by the Bank of England, relating to
the treatment of distressed borrowers.

London Securities and Derivatives Exchange (OMLX) An exchange set up in
1990 to trade in *futures contracts and *options in Swedish equities. Originating as
a way of reducing liability to Swedish tax, it has remained in London after the tax it
was set up to avoid was rescinded.

London Stock Exchange The market in London that deals in securities. Dealings
in securities began in London in the 17th century. The name Stock Exchange was
first used for New Jonathan's Coffee House in 1773, although it was not formally
constituted until 1802. The development of the industrial revolution encouraged
many other share markets to flourish throughout the UK, all the remnants of which
amalgamated in 1973 to form the Stock Exchange of Great Britain and Ireland. After
the *Big Bang in 1986 this organization became the **International Stock Exchange of
the UK and Republic of Ireland Ltd**. Its major reforms included:
(i) allowing banks, insurance companies, and overseas securities houses to become
members and to buy existing member firms;
(ii) abolishing scales of commissions, allowing commissions to be negotiated;
(iii) abolishing the division of members into jobbers and brokers, enabling a
member firm to deal with the public, to buy and sell shares for their own account,
and to act as *market makers;
(iv) the introduction of *SEAQ, a computerized dealing system that has abolished
face-to-face dealing on the floor of exchange.
   In merging with members of the international broking community in London, the
International Stock Exchange became a registered investment exchange. The
International Stock Exchange provides two markets for companies: the *main
market for *listed companies and the *Alternative Investment Market (AIM). The
International Stock Exchange formerly provided a market in traded options but this
has now moved to the *London International Financial Futures and Options
Exchange.

London Sugar Futures Market A former market now incorporated into the
*Futures and Options Exchange.

London Traded Options Market (LTOM) A former subsidiary company of the
London Stock Exchange. In 1992 this market, dealing in traded options in equities,
merged with the *London International Financial Futures and Options Exchange.

London Underwriting Centre (LUC) A centre for the London company
insurance and *reinsurance market specializing in non-marine insurance. Unlike
*Lloyd's the LUC is not a market association; it is essentially a place in which
leading underwriting companies active in the London insurance market can have
their offices and be visited by brokers. It also houses the London International
Insurance and Reinsurance Market Association (LIRMA), the organization that

represents the interests of companies active in the London international non-marine insurance and reinsurance market.

long-dated forward A foreign exchange contract with a maturity in excess of one year.

long-dated gilt *See* GILT-EDGED SECURITY.

long-funded Describing a situation in which the time to maturity of a bank's liabilities is greater than that of its assets. *See* MISMATCH.

long hedging *See* HEDGE.

long position A *position held in derivatives, securities, commodities, or currencies, etc., such that a rise in the market increases the value of the position. *Compare* SHORT POSITION.

longs **1.** *See* GILT-EDGED SECURITY. **2.** Securities, commodities, currencies, etc., held in a *long position.

long-term bond A bond that does not mature in less than one year.

long-term contract A contract that falls into two or more accounting periods before being completed. Such a contract may be for the design, manufacture, or construction of a single substantial asset, for example in the construction or civil engineering industries. From an accounting point of view, there is a problem in determining how much profit can be reasonably allocated to each accounting period, although the contract is not complete. *Statement of Standard Accounting Practice 9, 'Stocks and Long Term Contracts', requires contracts to be assessed on an individual basis and shown in the *profit and loss account by recording turnover and related activity as the contract progresses. Where the outcome of the contract can be assessed with reasonable certainty, even though it is not complete, the part of the profit that can be attributed to the work performed by an accounting date may be recognized in the profit and loss account. Attributable profit is that part of the total profit currently estimated to arise over the duration of the contract, after allowing for estimated remedial costs, maintenance costs, and increases in costs not recoverable under the contract agreement.

long-term debt Loans and debentures that are not due for repayment for at least ten years.

long-term equity anticipation securities **(LEAPS)** A type of long-dated market-traded index or equity option.

long-term liability A sum owed that does not have to be repaid within the next accounting period of a business. In some contexts a long-term liability may be regarded as one not due for repayment within the next three, or possibly ten, years.

long-term prime rate A long-term Japanese reference interest rate used for lending contracts.

long-term rate risk The *interest-rate risk resulting from changes in long-term interest rates.

lookback option An *option in which the *exercise price is determined by the path of the price of the *underlying throughout the life of the option.

loss adjuster A person appointed by an insurer to negotiate an insurance claim. The loss adjuster, who is independent of the insurer, discusses the claim with both the insurer and the policyholder, producing a report recommending the basis on which the claim should be settled. The insurer pays a fee for this service based on the amount of work involved for the loss adjuster, not on the size of the settlement. *Compare* LOSS ASSESSOR.

loss assessor A person who acts on behalf of the policyholder in handling a claim. A fee is charged for this service, which is usually a percentage of the amount received by the policyholder. *Compare* LOSS ADJUSTER.

loss-of-profits policy *See* BUSINESS-INTERRUPTION POLICY.

loss ratio The total of the claims paid out by an insurance company, underwriting *syndicate, etc., expressed as a percentage of the amount of premiums coming in during the same period. For example, if claims total £2M and premiums total £4M, the result is a 50% loss ratio. Insurers use this figure as a guide to the profitability of their business when they are reconsidering premium rates for a particular risk.

loss reliefs Relief available to sole traders, partnerships, and companies making losses, as adjusted for tax purposes. *Capital allowances can create a trading loss or can enhance it. Trading losses can be carried forward to set against future trading profits. For sole traders and partnerships, trading losses can be set against other income for the year of the loss and for the previous year. Partners can decide individually how to use their share of the losses. Special rules apply to trading losses in the early years of a trade. These losses can be carried back three years to a period before the trade commenced. From 1991–92 it has been possible to set trading losses against capital gains if the loss cannot be used first by setting against other income during the year. **Terminal-loss relief** is available when a trade is permanently discontinued and a loss is made during the last 12 months. For companies, a trading loss can be set off against profits of the three previous accounting periods, provided the company was carrying on the same trade during that period. *Capital losses can be set against capital gains in the same period. Any surplus capital loss that cannot be utilized during the current year must be carried forward to set against future capital gains. Capital losses cannot be set against other income, unlike trading losses.

lot 1. The minimum quantity that can be bought or sold on a commodity market, security market, etc. **2.** A group of items offered as a single item in an auction sale.

loti (*plural* **maloti**; MI) The standard monetary unit of Lesotho, divided into 100 lisente.

lottery A random method of allocating a new share issue that is oversubscribed.

lower of cost or market (LCM) A method of valuing a current asset of an organization in which the value taken is either its purchase (or production) price or the cost of replacing it (by purchase or manufacture), whichever is the lower. The Companies Act 1985 requires that a current asset be valued at either its purchase (or production) price or its *net realizable value, whichever is the lower.

lower rate of income tax In the UK, a former rate of income tax below the *basic rate of income tax. It was re-introduced in 1992–93 at 20%; in 1999 it was replaced with the *starting rate of income tax.

loyalty bonus An inducement offered to the subscribers of a *privatization share issue, to retain the shares they have acquired beyond a specified date. The bonus may be paid in cash or in free additional shares.

LRR Abbreviation for *lagged reserve requirement.

Ltd The usual abbreviation for *limited*. This (or the Welsh equivalent) must appear in the name of a private *limited company. *Compare* PLC.

LTOM Abbreviation for London Traded Options Market. *See* LONDON INTERNATIONAL FINANCIAL FUTURES AND OPTIONS EXCHANGE.

LUC Abbreviation for *London Underwriting Centre.

luma A monetary unit of Armenia worth one hundredth of a *dram.

lump sum 1. A sum of money paid all at once, rather than in instalments. **2.** An insurance benefit, such as a sum of money paid on retirement or redundancy or to the beneficiaries on the death of an insured person. Retirement *pensions can consist of a lump sum plus a reduced pension. **3.** A form of *damages; a **lump-sum award** is given in tort cases.

Lutine Bell A bell that hangs in the underwriting room at *Lloyd's and is rung for ceremonial occasions and, rarely, to draw the attention of underwriters to an important announcement. It was formerly rung once if a ship sank and twice for good news. It was recovered from the *Lutine*, a ship that was insured by Lloyd's and sank in the North Sea in 1799, with a cargo of bullion (£1.4M value), most of which was lost.

Luxembourg Stock Exchange A small stock exchange in Luxembourg; it functions as a settlement centre for trading in *eurobonds.

lwei A monetary unit of Angola worth one hundredth of a *kwanza.

M0; M1; M2; M3; M4; M5 *See* MONEY SUPPLY.

Maastricht Treaty Legislation, signed in 1992, creating the *European Union (EU) from the existing 12 member countries of the *European Economic Community (EC). In the main financial provisions of the treaty, the states agreed to a process of European Monetary Union (EMU; *see* EUROPEAN MONETARY SYSTEM), with the creation of a single European currency (the *euro) as its ultimate goal. The Treaty, named after the Dutch town in which it was agreed and signed, came into force in 1993. European Monetary Union was designed to be achieved in three stages, starting with participation in the Exchange Rate Mechanism (ERM). The second stage created the *European Monetary Institute (EMI) to set qualifying conditions for a move towards the establishment of a single currency. It also provided for the creation of the *European Central Bank. The third stage, achieved by January 1999, locked member states into a fixed exchange rate and activated the European Central Bank as the governor of economic and monetary policy throughout the European Union. The euro was fully adopted in nine EU countries (all the then members with the exception of Denmark, Sweden, and the UK) in January 2002.

macroeconomics The branch of economics that deals with economies as a whole rather than the behaviour of particular individuals or firms. The division of the subject into *microeconomics and macroeconomics derives mainly from the work of J.M. Keynes. In recent years the distinction between macroeconomics and microeconomics has become less clear-cut.

macroenvironment The broad sweep of the environment that creates the forces that shape every business and non-profit marketer. The physical environment, social and cultural forces, demographic make-up, economic climate, prevailing political beliefs, and current legal infrastructure are components of the macroenvironment. Generally, most companies have no control over these factors.

macrohedge A *hedge designed to cover the net or overall risks of an entire portfolio. *Compare* MICROHEDGE.

Madrid Stock Exchange The largest of four stock exchanges in Spain, the others being in Barcelona, Bilbao, and Valencia. They all now use a centralized settlement system, with the markets modelled on the London system (after the *Big Bang). The markets are overseen by a national securities commission, the Comisión del Mercado de Valores (CNMV).

magnetic ink character recognition (MICR) A type of magnetic ink used on cheques and other documents to enable them to be automatically sorted and the characters to be read and fed into a computer.

main market The premier market for the trading of *equities on the *London Stock Exchange. For this market the *listing requirements are the most stringent and the liquidity of the market is greater than in the *Alternative Investment Market. A company wishing to enter this market must have audited trading figures covering at least five years and must place 25% of its shares in public hands. The main market currently deals in over 2600 securities.

mainstream corporation tax (MCT) Formerly, the liability for *corporation tax of a company for an accounting period after the relevant *advance corporation tax was deducted. Advance corporation tax was abolished in 1999. *See also* IMPUTATION SYSTEM.

maintenance margin The minimum *margin required in a brokerage account by a particular exchange or brokerage firm.

maintenance period The period, usually two weeks, in which a US local bank must have lodged sufficient cash to activate its *reserve requirement with the *Federal Reserve System.

making a book Buying shares, commodities, etc., long (i.e. without having sold them) or selling them short (i.e. without having bought them) for one's own account. Making a book is therefore a speculative activity in which market makers and dealers, but not brokers, indulge. A dealer will often have a complicated *book, with many transactions open (*see* OPEN POSITION). Whether the overall position is long or short will depend on the dealer's view of the market.

making a price On the *London Stock Exchange, the quoting by a *market maker of a selling price and a buying price for a particular security, usually without knowing whether the broker or other person asking for a price wishes to buy or sell. Having made a price, the market maker is bound to buy or sell at the prices quoted, though the quantity may be limited if the broker stipulates the quantity at the time of making the price. *See* BACKING AWAY.

making-up price The price at which securities that have not been paid for on *account day (on the London Stock Exchange) are carried forward to the next account.

malpractice insurance In the USA, liability insurance taken out by an *accountant against legal action in connection with professional services. There have been a number of very high awards made to plaintiffs and this has greatly increased the cost to the accountant of obtaining insurance cover. One solution to this may be for accountants to form corporate bodies rather than *partnerships, thus reducing their exposure to personal liability.

managed currency (managed floating) A currency in which the government influences the exchange rate. This control is exerted by the central bank buying and selling in the foreign-exchange market and by its overall economic policy. *See also* CLEAN FLOATING.

managed fund A fund, made up of investments in a wide range of financial obligations, that is actively managed by a life-assurance company to provide low risk investments for the smaller investor, usually in the form of *investment bonds, *unit trusts, or unit-linked saving plans (*see* UNIT-LINKED POLICY). The *fund managers will have a stated investment policy favouring a specific category of investments.

managed PEP *See* PERSONAL EQUITY PLAN.

managed unit trust *See* MANAGED FUND.

management accounting The techniques used to collect, process, and present financial and quantitative data within an organization to help effective performance measurement, cost control, planning, pricing, and decision making to take place.

The major professional body of **management accountants** in the UK is the Chartered Institute of Management Accountants (CIMA).

management audit An independent review of the management of an organization, carried out by a firm of *management consultants specializing in this type of review. The review will cover all aspects of running the organization, including the control of production, marketing, sales, finance, personnel, warehousing, etc.

management buy-in The acquisition of a company by an outside team of managers, usually specially formed for the purpose, often backed by a venture-capital organization. Their normal target is the small family-owned company, which the owners wish to sell, or occasionally an unwanted subsidiary of a public company.

management buy-out (MBO) The acquisition of a company or a subsidiary by the existing management. It is frequently used as a means of divestment by companies seeking to focus on their core activities. The new owner-managers of the buy-out frequently improve its performance as they usually are well aware of any remedial action required and have a serious incentive in the form of their equity stake. Additional capital is provided by financial institutions and venture capitalists and also in many cases by allowing other employees to buy shares. In a few instances, all employees have participated in a buy-out; these are sometimes called **employee buy-outs**. Some very large companies have been bought out by management, but many of these have suffered from unrealistically high levels of debt (in the form of loan capital), which has restricted their successful recovery and longer-term viability.

management company A company that manages *unit trusts. Its fees, known as **management charges**, are usually stated in the agreement setting up the trust; they are paid by the unit holders.

management consultant A professional adviser who specializes in giving advice to organizations on ways for improving their efficiency and hence their profitability.

management contracting The practice in which a domestic firm supplies the management know-how to a foreign company that provides the capital in order to create a *joint venture: the domestic firm exports management services rather than products.

manat 1. (AZM) The standard monetary unit of Azerbaijan, divided into 100 gopik. **2.** (TMM) The standard monetary unit of Turkmenistan, divided into 100 tenesi.

M and A Abbreviation for mergers and acquisitions. *See* MERGER.

mandate 1. A written authority given by one person (the **mandator**) to another (the **mandatory**) giving the mandatory the power to act on behalf of the mandator. It comes to an end on the death, mental illness, or bankruptcy of the mandator. **2.** A document instructing a bank to open an account in the name of the mandator (customer), giving details of the way it is to be run, and providing specimen signatures of those authorized to sign cheques, etc.

mandatory bid A bid that must be made according to the *City Code on Takeovers and Mergers if a potential buyer has acquired 30% or more of the equity of a target company on the open market.

mandatory liquid assets Certain *liquid assets, the structure and nature of which is defined by regulatory requirement, that a bank is required to maintain on its balance sheet. It may be implemented as an instrument of monetary control or as a protection against 'runs' on particular banks. The regulatory trend is away from this type of control, since it often gives a market advantage to short-term government debt, which is a major part of the specified assets.

mandatory quote period The period between Monday and Friday when all *market makers registered in a security on the *London Stock Exchange must display their prices. For *SEAQ the period is 8.30 a.m. to 4.30 p.m., and on SEAQ International 9.30 a.m. to 4.00 p.m.

Manila Stock Exchange (MSE) One of three stock exchanges in the Philippines. Manila Stock Exchange dates from 1927 and was modelled on the New York Stock Exchange; the other two are the Makati Stock Exchange (1965) and the Metropolitan Stock Exchange (1974), which is now inactive.

Marché à Terme Internationale de France (MATIF) The French international *financial futures exchange. It opened in 1986 (as the Marché à Terme des Instruments Financiers), became involved in the *Globex system in 1993, and is now part of the *Euronext NV group of markets.

Marché des Options Négotiables de Paris (MONEP) The French traded *options market, founded in 1987.

Mareva injunction *See* FREEZING INJUNCTION.

margin (haircut) 1. The difference between the sales revenue and the cost of goods or services expressed as a percentage of revenue. *See* GROSS PROFIT; NET PROFIT; PROFIT MARGIN. **2.** The difference between the prices at which a *market maker or commodity dealer will buy and sell. This is also referred to as the *bid–offer spread. **3.** The difference between the rate of interest on funds lent and funds borrowed by a bank. **4.** In commodity and currency dealing, the amount advanced by a speculator or investor to a broker or dealer, when buying futures or other derivatives. **5.** Money or securities deposited with a stockbroker to cover any possible losses a client may make. *See* MAINTENANCE MARGIN; MARGIN CALL.

margin account 1. An account in the name of an investor held by a broker on which only a percentage of the price of securities, commodities, etc., is paid, the balance being borrowed. Companies often borrow from banks to buy their own company shares, paying the broker only a part of the shares' market value. Effectively, therefore, the investor is buying on credit. Margin trading is not without its risks, especially in a falling market. **2.** A brokerage account relating to exchange-traded derivatives.

marginal cost The additional cost incurred as a result of the production of one additional unit of production. In accounting, it usually equates to the variable costs per unit of production. The variable costs are usually regarded as the direct costs plus the variable overheads.

marginal costing (direct costing; variable costing) A costing and decision-making technique that charges only the *marginal costs to the cost units and treats the fixed costs as a lump sum to be deducted from the total contribution, in obtaining the profit or loss for the period. In some cases, inventory valuation is also at marginal cost, although this approach does not conform to Statement of Standard Accounting Practice 9 and is used for internal reporting purposes only. *Compare* ABSORPTION COSTING.

marginal relief (small companies relief) In the UK, relief available when the profits chargeable to *corporation tax of a company fall between the upper and lower limits for the *financial year (currently between £300,000 and £1,500,000). Since 1999 marginal relief has also been available for very small companies whose total profits fall between £10,000 (currently the upper limit for the starting rate of corporation tax) and £50,000.

margin call A call to a client from a commodity broker, financial futures broker, or stockbroker to increase the *margin, i.e. the amount of money or securities deposited with the broker as a safeguard. This usually happens if the client has an *open position in a market that is moving adversely for this position.

margin of safety The difference between the breakeven volume and the forecast volume in a *break-even analysis.

margin trading The buying of securities on credit in order to make short-term gains. *See* MARGIN ACCOUNT.

marker crude A standard oil price based on one barrel of Saudi Arabian oil or some other internationally recognized oil (e.g. North Sea Brent crude). It sets standard prices for oil in the rest of the world.

market 1. An arena in which buyers and sellers exchange goods and services, usually for money. It does not have to have a physical location. **2.** An organized gathering for trading in financial obligations. **3.** The demand for a particular product or service, often measured by sales during a specified period.

marketable security A security (stock, share, bond, etc.) that can be bought or sold on a *stock exchange. *See also* LONDON STOCK EXCHANGE. *Compare* NON-MARKETABLE SECURITIES.

market access The ability of an organization to raise funds in a particular securities market.

market analysis An analysis of the investment value of the assets held in a portfolio based on a consideration of the market in its entirety, rather than a consideration of individual securities or sectors.

market capitalization (market valuation) The value of a company obtained by multiplying the number of its issued shares by their *market price.

market economy An economic system in which the main decisions regarding production, distribution, and exchange are made by the market, i.e. by the forces of supply and demand. The opposite is a **controlled** (or **command**) **economy**, as in the former communist countries, in which supply was controlled and prices were fixed by governments. In a **mixed economy** *capitalism is encouraged but the government intervenes to control an unbridled market economy, using legal safeguards to protect the poor, sick, elderly, etc., from exploitation and to protect consumers from exploitation by monopolies.

market failure A situation in which a market does not operate efficiently. Factors that may cause market failure include the possession of *market power by transactors, *externalities, or information problems. *See also* EFFICIENT MARKETS HYPOTHESIS.

market forces The forces of supply and demand that in a *free market determine the quantity available of a particular product or service and the price at which it is offered.

market instrument A *negotiable instrument used for short-term debt.

market maker **1.** An intermediary who creates a market for a financial obligation. **2.** A dealer in securities on the *London Stock Exchange who undertakes to buy and sell securities as a principal and is therefore obliged to announce buying and selling prices for a particular security at a particular time. Before October 1986 (*see* BIG BANG) this function was performed by a *stockjobber, who was then obliged to deal with the public through a *stockbroker. However since October 1986, when the rules changed, market makers attempt to make a profit by dealing in securities as principals (selling at a higher price than that at which they buy; *see* MARGIN) as well as acting as agents, working for a commission. While this dual role may create a conflict of interest for market makers (*see* CHINESE WALL; FRONT RUNNING), it avoids the restrictive trade practice of the former system and reduces the cost of dealing in the market.

market order An instruction to a broker to make a transaction at the prevailing *market price. *Compare* LIMIT ORDER (*see* LIMIT).

market overhang The situation in which sellers, worried by falling prices, prefer to postpone their sales until there is greater market demand. By reducing transactions, this behaviour can itself delay the hoped for recovery.

market portfolio *See* MARKOWITZ MODEL.

market power The ability of a transactor to influence market prices, owing to the very large share of the demand or supply in a particular market that this transactor controls. The major UK supermarkets are often said to possess market power of this kind.

market price The price of a raw material, product, service, security, etc., in an open market. In formal markets, such as a stock exchange, commodity market, foreign-exchange market, etc., there is often a *margin between the buying and selling price; there are, therefore, two market prices. In these circumstances the market prices often quoted are the average of the buying and selling price (*see* MIDDLE PRICE).

market profile A form of technical analysis in which an *investment analyst considers the movements of market prices during short periods within a particular day.

market rate of discount *See* BILL RATE.

market risk The *risk inherent in dealing on a market where prices may change. The obvious market risks are buying on a market that subsequently falls and selling on a market that rises; these risks can be reduced by hedging (*see* HEDGE), especially by means of *futures contracts or *options, but they can never be eliminated. These forms of market risk are the obverse of the market opportunities that provide speculators with the chance of making a profit. *Exchange-rate exposure may be an element of the market risk. For example, a buyer of US securities in London, paying in sterling, faces not only the risk that the price of the securities will fall in the USA, but also the risk that there will be an unfavourable change in the rate of exchange between dollars and pounds. *See also* SYSTEMATIC RISK; VALUE-AT-RISK.

Market Risk Amendment *See* BASLE MARKET RISK AMENDMENT.

market-risk premium *See* RISK PREMIUM.

market segmentation theory **1.** A theory that explains the *yield curve in terms of different levels of demand for different maturities. **2.** The hypothesis that transactors on a financial market specialize in certain parts of the market. **3.** In marketing, any approach that seeks to divide markets according to demographic factors or the requirements of particular groups of customers.

market sentiment An optimistic feeling that will push up the general level of prices on a financial market, commodity market, etc., or a pessimistic view that will depress the general level of prices. Financial market sentiment can be triggered by bad results or profit warnings from leading companies, apprehension regarding government policy, interest rates and general economic data, or market rises or falls on other exchanges.

market timing An investment strategy based on the forecasting of changes in the direction of market prices. However, there is little evidence to suggest that investors can apply such a strategy systematically and even if it were possible, it would violate the *efficient markets hypothesis.

market-to-book ratio The ratio of the market value of a company's equity to the accounting value of that company's equity.

market valuation *See* MARKET CAPITALIZATION.

market value The value of an asset if it were to be sold on the open market at its current *market price. When land is involved it may be necessary to distinguish between the market value in its present use and that in some alternative use; for example, a factory site may have a market value as a factory site, and be so valued in the company's accounts, which may be less than its market value as building land.

marking down Lowering the prices of a security by *market makers in anticipation of a lower demand or greater supply.

markings The official number of bargains that have taken place during a working day on the *London Stock Exchange.

marking to market The valuation of financial obligations according to current *market prices.

marking to model The valuation of financial obligations according to pricing models. This occurs when there is not a current market price for the obligation, for example in relation to derivatives sold on the *over-the-counter market.

marking up The raising of the price of a security by *market makers in anticipation of an increased demand or reduced supply.

markka (Fmk) The former standard monetary unit of Finland, divided into 100 penniä. It was absorbed into the euro for all purposes other than cash transactions in January 1999 and abolished in 2002.

Markowitz model A method of selecting the optimum investment *portfolio, devised by H. M. Markowitz (1927–) and for which he received the Nobel prize in Economics in 1990. It assumes that investors are interested in the average return on a risky investment and the standard deviation of those returns. Investors are risk-averse, which means they like higher returns and dislike higher standard deviations of returns. It concludes that investors should diversify as widely as possible and decide the level of risk and return they choose by the proportions they borrow, lend, and invest in risky assets.

Marshall Plan A plan put forward by the US Secretary of State George Marshall

(1880–1959) to rebuild the economies of European countries after World War II. *See also* BRETTON WOODS CONFERENCE.

master agreement An overall contract within the terms of which individual transactions take place.

master trust 1. A name sometimes used by unit-trust managers for their *fund of funds. **2.** A pool of assets held to support *asset-backed securities.

match A purchase contract and a sales contract that cancel each other out.

matched bargain A transaction in which a sale of a particular quantity of stock is matched with a purchase of the same quantity of the same stock. Transactions of this kind are carried out on the *London Stock Exchange by **matching brokers**.

matched sale–purchase agreement (MSP) A device used by the US Federal Reserve in which it sells money-market instruments for immediate effect and couples the sale with the forward purchase of the same instrument, to facilitate the distribution of reserves of the banking system.

matched swap A *swap that is used to change the nature of the cash flows from an existing asset or liability. For example, a swap may be used to change the interest payments arising from an asset from fixed to variable.

matching The striking of a balance by a bank between its assets and its liabilities, taking risk factors into account.

material adverse change A clause in a loan agreement or bank facility stating that the loan will become repayable if there should a material change in the borrower's credit standing. The clause can be contentious because it is not always clear what constitutes a material change.

material facts Information pertinent to an insurance policy or claim that an insured person is obliged to provide for the insurer. The policy can be declared invalid if material facts are shown to have been deliberately withheld or incorrectly stated.

material information *See* MATERIAL NEWS.

materiality The extent to which an item of accounting information is material. Information is considered material if its omission from or misstatement in a *financial statement could influence the decision making of its users. Materiality is therefore not an absolute concept but is dependent on the size and nature of an item and the particular circumstances in which it arises.

material news (material information) Information that may affect a company's share price, such as a *profit warning or news of a proposed merger or acquisition. *See also* EVENT.

MATIF Abbreviation for *Marché à Terme Internationale de France.

maturity balance The combination of securities, both federal and national, held by the US Federal Reserve.

maturity bucket One of various time periods elapsing before the maturity or repricing of assets and liabilities. *See* MATURITY GAP; MATURITY LADDER.

maturity date The date on which a document, such as a *bond, *bill of exchange, or insurance policy, becomes due for payment. The **original maturity** is the length of time from the opening agreement to the final repayment date. The **residual maturity** is the term of the agreement remaining from a particular date to the final repayment date. In some cases, especially for redeemable government stocks, the maturity date is known as the **redemption date**. *See also* REDEMPTION.

maturity gap The value of assets in a particular *maturity bucket minus the value of liabilities in that time bucket. Banks in particular use this measure to assess *interest-rate risk. *See* GAP.

maturity guarantee A guarantee on *asset-backed securities that there will be sufficient funds at redemption.

maturity ladder A type of report frequently used in banking, in which the value of the bank's assets and liabilities are compared in all its *maturity buckets.

maturity mismatch risk The *interest-rate risk and *liquidity risk arising from positive or negative *maturity gaps in particular periods of time. *See* GAP; GAP ANALYSIS; MISMATCH.

maturity yield *See* YIELD.

maximum fluctuation The maximum daily price fluctuation that is permitted in some markets. *See* LIMIT; LIMIT MOVE.

maximum investment plan (MIP) A unit-linked endowment policy marketed by a life-assurance company that is designed to produce maximum profit rather than life-assurance protection. It calls for regular premiums, usually over ten years, with options to continue. These policies normally enable a tax-free fund to be built up over ten years and, because of the regular premiums, *pound cost averaging can be used, linked to a number of markets. Such investment products are now largely obsolete, since there is now a general preference for separating the life assurance and investment elements of products.

maximum slippage The period between the date on which a new company expects to start earning income and the date up to which it can survive on its venture capital. After this date has passed, the company would be unable to raise further funds and would sink into insolvency. *See also* DEATH-VALLEY CURVE.

MBO Abbreviation for *management buy-out.

MCT 1. Abbreviation for Member of the *Association of Corporate Treasurers. **2.** Abbreviation for *mainstream corporation tax.

mean *See* ARITHMETIC MEAN; GEOMETRIC MEAN. *Compare* MEDIAN. *See also* MOMENTS.

mean deviation In statistics, the *arithmetic mean of the deviations (all taken as positive numbers) of all the numbers in a set of numbers from their arithmetic mean. For example, the arithmetic mean of 5, 8, 9, and 10 is 8, and therefore the deviations from this mean are 3, 0, 1, and 2, giving a mean deviation of 1.5. *Compare* STANDARD DEVIATION.

mean price *See* MIDDLE PRICE.

median A typical value that is identified by arranging a set of numbers in an ascending or descending scale and selecting the middle number (if there are an odd number in the set) or the arithmetic mean of the middle two numbers (if there are an even number). This can give a more representative average in some circumstances than an *arithmetic mean or a *geometric mean.

medium-dated gilt *See* GILT-EDGED SECURITY.

medium of exchange A substance or article that may have little intrinsic value that is used to pay for goods or services. In primitive economies various articles, such as sea shells, have been used for this purpose but *money is now used universally.

mediums *See* GILT-EDGED SECURITY.

medium-sized company A company that may claim certain filing exemptions if it meets two out of three of the following criteria for the current and preceding year, or the two preceding financial years:
• the *balance-sheet total (total assets) should not exceed £11,400,000;
• the *turnover should not exceed £22,800,000;
• the average number of employees should not exceed 250.
In a company's first *financial year it need only meet the conditions for that year; in its second financial year it may claim the filing exemptions of a medium-sized company if it met the conditions in its first financial year. A public *company, a banking or insurance company, an authorized person under the Financial Services Act 1986, or a member of an ineligible group may not claim medium-sized company filing exemptions. A medium-sized company must prepare full audited *financial statements for distribution to its shareholders but it may file abbreviated accounts instead of full accounts with the *Registrar of Companies. *Compare* SMALL COMPANY.

medium-term (intermediate-term) Denoting a time period of medium duration, the extent of which will differ according to context. For example, in accounting "medium-term" describes liabilities of between one and ten years, in money markets it means maturities of greater than a year, in bond markets a period of five to ten years, and in *eurobond markets one of two to seven years.

medium-term financial assistance (MTFA) A loan available to member states of the European Union experiencing balance of payments difficulties. The donor countries may attach conditions on granting these loans, which usually have a term of two to five years. *Compare* SHORT-TERM MONETARY SUPPORT.

medium-term liabilities Liabilities falling due in, say, more than one but less than ten years.

medium-term note (MTN) An unsecured *note issued in a eurocurrency with a maturity of about three to six years.

meeting of creditors *See* BANKRUPTCY; CREDITORS' VOLUNTARY LIQUIDATION; LIQUIDATOR.

MEFF Renta Fija (MEFF RF) A *financial futures and *options exchange in Barcelona. Until December 1991, when it merged with MOFEX, the Madrid options exchange, it was known as MEFF (Mercado de Futuros Financieros) and dealt exclusively in financial futures (both fixed income and variable income). Since the merger MEFF RF deals in fixed income products (interest-rate and currency futures and options), while the Madrid exchange, known as **MEFF Renta Variable** (MEFF RV), handles variable income derivatives (equity and stock index futures and options).

MEFF Renta Variable (MEFF RV) *See* MEFF RENTA FIJA.

meltdown A disastrous and uncontrolled fall in share prices. *Black Monday has also been called Meltdown Monday, for example. The expression is, of course, derived from the disaster that results when the core of a nuclear reactor melts uncontrollably.

member bank A bank that belongs to a central banking or clearing system. In the UK a member bank is a *commercial bank that is a member of the *Association for Payment Clearing Services. In the USA it is a commercial bank that is a member of the *Federal Reserve System.

member firm A firm of brokers or *market makers that is a member of the *London Stock Exchange (International Stock Exchange). Banks, insurance companies, and overseas securities houses can now become corporate members.

member of a company A shareholder of a company whose name is entered in the *register of members. Founder members (*see* FOUNDERS' SHARES) are those who sign the memorandum of association; anyone subsequently coming into possession of the company's shares becomes a member.

members' voluntary liquidation (members' voluntary winding-up) The winding-up of a company by a special resolution of the members in circumstances in which the company is solvent. Before making the winding-up resolution, the directors must make a *declaration of solvency. It is a criminal offence to make such a declaration without reasonable grounds for believing that it is true. When the resolution has been passed, a *liquidator is appointed; if, during the course of the winding-up, the liquidator believes that the company will not be able to pay its debts, a meeting of creditors must be called and the winding-up is treated as a members' *compulsory liquidation.

memorandum of association An official document setting out the details of a *company's existence. It must be signed by the first *subscribers and must contain the following information (as it applies to the company in question): the company name; a statement that the company is a public company; the address of the registered office; the objects of the company (called the **objects clause**); a statement of limited liability; the amount of the guarantee; and the amount of authorized share capital and its division.

memorandum of satisfaction A document stating that a mortgage or charge on property has been repaid. It has to be signed by all the parties concerned and a copy sent to the *Registrar of Companies, if the mortgage or charge was made by a company.

Mercado de Valores de Buenos Aires *See* BUENOS AIRES STOCK EXCHANGE.

merchant bank A bank that formerly specialized in financing foreign trade, an activity that often grew out of its own merchanting business. This led them into accepting *bills of exchange and functioning as accepting houses. More recently they have tended to diversify into the field of *hire-purchase finance, the granting of long-term loans (especially to companies), providing venture capital, advising companies on flotations and *takeover bids, underwriting new issues, and managing investment portfolios and unit trusts. Many of them are old-established and some offer a limited banking service. Their knowledge of international trade makes them specialists in dealing with the large multinational companies. They are most common in Europe, but some merchant banks operate in the USA: the US equivalent in terms of current activity is known as an *investment bank. Several UK merchant banks were taken over in the 1990s either by the commercial banks or by large overseas banks.

merger A combination of two or more businesses on relatively equal footing that results in the creation of a new reporting entity formed from the combining businesses. The shareholders of the combining entities mutually share the risks and rewards of the new entity and no one party to the merger obtains control over another. Under Financial Reporting Standard 6, 'Acquisitions and Mergers', to qualify as a merger (*see* MERGER ACCOUNTING) a combination must satisfy five criteria:
• no party is the acquirer or acquired;
• all parties to the combination participate in establishing the management structure of the new entity;
• the combining entities are relatively equal in terms of size;
• the consideration received by the equity shareholders of each party consists primarily of equity shares in the combined entity, any other consideration received being relatively immaterial;
• no equity shareholder of any of the combining entities may retain an interest in only part of the combined entity.
In the UK, approval of the *Monopolies and Mergers Commission may be required and the merger must be conducted on lines sanctioned by the City Code on Takeovers and Mergers.

When one business takes control of another this is known as an **acquisition** (*see* ACQUISITION ACCOUNTING). Investment banks and other financial institutions often have mergers and acquisitions (**M and A**) departments, to provide financial and other forms of support for these activities.

merger accounting A method of accounting that treats two or more businesses as combining on an equal footing. It is usually applied without any restatement of *net assets to fair value and includes the results of each of the combined entities for the whole of the *accounting period, as if they had always been combined. It does not reflect the issue of shares as an application of resources at fair value. The difference that arises on *consolidation does not represent *goodwill but is deducted from, or added to, *reserves. *Compare* ACQUISITION ACCOUNTING.

Merger Control Directive An EU directive on the regulation of mergers and acquisitions.

merger relief Relief from adding to, or setting up, a *share premium account when issuing shares at a premium if an issuing company has secured at least a 90% equity holding in another company. This relief applies if the issuing company is providing for the allotment of equity shares in the issuing company in exchange for the equity shares (or non-equity shares) in the other company or by the cancellation of any such shares not held by the issuing company. This relief is given under section 131 of the Companies Act 1985. *See* MERGER RESERVE.

merger reserve (merger capital reserve) A *reserve credited in place of a *share premium account when *merger relief is made use of. *Goodwill on consolidation may be written off against a merger reserve (unlike the share premium account).

mergers task force An office of the *European Commission that oversees the regulation of mergers.

method of advice The means used to send documents by a *collecting bank to the bank from which a collection order has been received. *See* BILL OF EXCHANGE.

METI The Japanese Ministry for Economy, Trade and Industry, formerly known as MITI (Ministry for International Trade and Industry). This government body played a vital role in Japan's postwar economic boom.

metical (*plural* **meticais**; Mt) The standard monetary unit of Mozambique, divided into 100 centavos.

Mexican Stock Exchange (**Bolsa Mexicana de Valores**) The largest Latin American stock exchange, which opened in 1894.

mezzanine finance 1. Finance, usually provided by specialist financial institutions, that is neither pure equity nor pure debt. It can take many different forms and can be secured or unsecured; it usually earns a higher rate of return than pure debt but less than equity. Conversely, it carries a higher risk than pure debt, although less than equity. It is often used in *management buy-outs. **2.** A form of finance used by venture capitalists after *seed capital has been provided.

MFR Abbreviation for *minimum funding requirement.

MICR Abbreviation for *magnetic ink character recognition.

microcredit The lending of small sums of money on very low security, especially to small businesses or to small producers in the developing world.

microeconomics The branch of economics that deals with the behaviour of individual market participants, mainly individual firms or consumers. *Compare* MACROECONOMICS.

microenvironment The environment close to a company, which affects its ability to serve its customers. This includes the company itself, firms in its market channel, customer markets, and competitors.

microhedge A *hedge relating to an individual financial obligation. *Compare* MACROHEDGE.

Mid-America Commodity Exchange An exchange in Chicago that deals in *options and *futures contracts in a variety of commodities as well as in *financial futures.

middleman A person or organization that makes a profit by trading in goods as an intermediary between the producer and the consumer. Middlemen include agents, brokers, dealers, merchants, factors, wholesalers, distributors, and retailers. They earn their profit by providing a variety of different services, including finance, bulk buying, holding stocks, breaking bulk, risk sharing, making a market and stabilizing prices, providing information about products (to consumers) and about markets (to producers), providing a distribution network, and introducing buyers to sellers.

middle office The section of a financial trading organization that customarily provides systems support and derivatives pricing to the *front office. *See also* BACK OFFICE.

middle price (**mean price**) The average of the *offer price of a security, commodity, currency, etc., and the *bid price. It is the middle price that is often quoted in the financial press.

MIGA Abbreviation for *Multilateral Investment Guarantee Agency.

mil A monetary unit of Malta worth one thousandth of a *lira.

Milan Stock Exchange A relatively small stock exchange in Italy. As Italian banks undertake a great deal of share trading, the stock exchange is not as central to business as in many other countries. The Milan exchange is due for *deregulation.

millième A monetary unit of Egypt worth one thousandth of a *pound.

millime A Tunisian monetary unit worth one thousandth of a *dinar.

minimum funding requirement (MFR) In the UK, the legal requirement that the assets of an occupational pension should represent at least 90% of its liabilities at any time. Since the liabilities and assets of a fund relate to future obligations and returns, both depend on certain actuarial assumptions about the future and thus may fluctuate from year to year. The MFR was introduced as a provision of the Pensions Act 1995 and came into force in 1997.

minimum lending rate (MLR) The successor, between 1971 and 1981, of the *bank rate. In this decade it was the minimum rate at which the Bank of England would lend to the *discount houses. This was a published figure; the present more informal *base rate does not have the same status. When the government suspended MLR in 1981 it reserved the right to reintroduce it at any time, which it did for one day in January 1985.

minimum subscription 1. The minimum sum of money, stated in the *prospectus of a new company, that the directors consider must be raised if the company is to be viable. **2.** The smallest bid required in terms of the number of new securities at issue.

minimum variance hedge ratio The ratio of futures contracts to the *underlying, giving the minimum *hedge value variance.

minority interest The interest of individual shareholders in a company more than 50% of which is owned by a holding company. For example, if 60% of the ordinary shares in a company are owned by a holding company, the remaining 40% will represent a minority interest. These shareholders will receive their full share of profits in the form of dividends although they will be unable to influence company policy as they will always be outvoted by the majority interest held by the holding company.

minority protection Remedies evolved to safeguard a minority of company members from the abuse of majority rule. They include just and equitable winding-up, applying for relief on the basis of unfair prejudice, bringing a derivative or representative action, and seeking an inspection and investigation of the company.

mint par of exchange (mint parity) The rate of exchange between two currencies that were on the *gold standard. The rate was then determined by the gold content of the basic coin.

MIP 1. Abbreviation for *maximum investment plan. **2.** Abbreviation for monthly investment plan.

MIRAS Abbreviation for *mortgage interest relief at source.

mirror swap *See* OFFSETTING SWAP.

misdeclaration penalty A penalty of 15% of the *value added tax lost in understating the VAT liability or overstating the VAT refund due on the VAT return, when the amounts involved are material. The penalty will apply if the inaccuracy equals the lesser of £1 million and 30% of the total amount of tax due for the period of the VAT return. The penalty can be avoided if the *taxable person can show that there was reasonable excuse, that there had been a voluntary disclosure, or that the taxable person had reason to believe that their VAT affairs were under investigation by Customs and Excise.

misfeasance 1. The negligent or otherwise improper performance of a lawful act. **2.** An act by an officer of a company in the nature of a breach of trust or breach of duty, particularly if it relates to the company's assets.

misfeasance summons An application to the court by a creditor, contributory, liquidator, or the official receiver during the course of winding up a company. The court is asked to examine the conduct of a company officer and order restitution to be made if the officer is found guilty of breach of trust or duty.

mismatch 1. Any *position that is not perfectly *offset. **2.** A *floating-rate note in which the coupon is paid monthly but the interest rate paid is that applicable to a note of longer maturity. **3.** The state of the typical books of a bank that borrows short-term and lends long-term, creating a condition in which assets and liabilities are not matched. This is usually acceptable as long as deposits keep coming in. *See* ASSET–LIABILITY MANAGEMENT; GAP; MATURITY MISMATCH RISK.

misrepresentation An untrue statement of fact, made by one party to the other in the course of negotiating a contract, that induces the other party to enter into the contract. The person making the misrepresentation is called the **representor**, and the person to whom it is made is the **representee**. A false statement of law, opinion, or intention does not constitute a misrepresentation; nor does a statement of fact known by the representee to be untrue. Moreover, unless the representee relies on the statement so that it becomes an inducement to enter into the contract, it is not a misrepresentation. The remedies for misrepresentation vary according to the degree of culpability of the representor. If the representor is guilty of **fraudulent misrepresentation** (i.e. not honestly believing in the truth of any statement made) the representee may, subject to certain limitations, set the contract aside and may also sue for *damages. If the representor is guilty of **negligent misrepresentation** (i.e. believing a statement made without reasonable grounds for doing so) the representee may also rescind (*see* RESCISSION) the contract and sue for damages. If the representor has committed merely an **innocent misrepresentation** (reasonably believing a statement to be true) the representee is restricted to rescinding the contract.

mission statement A statement that encapsulates the overriding purpose and objectives of an organization. It is used to communicate this purpose to all stakeholder groups, both internal and external, and to guide employees in their contribution towards achieving it. *See also* STRATEGIC INTENT.

mitigation of damage Minimizing the loss incurred by the person who suffered a loss and is claiming *damages as a result of it. The injured party has a duty to take all reasonable steps to mitigate any loss and the courts will not, therefore, award damages to compensate for a loss that could have been avoided by reasonable action.

mixed credit An aid-to-trade agreement with a developing country, in which government finance and trade finance are jointly arranged to subsidize the sale of exported goods.

mixed economy *See* MARKET ECONOMY.

MLR Abbreviation for *minimum lending rate.

MMC Abbreviation for *Monopolies and Mergers Commission.

MMDA Abbreviation for *money-market deposit account.

MM hypothesis The hypothesis, advanced by the economists Franco Modigliani and Merton Millar, that in a world with no market imperfections, costs of *financial distress, or taxation, differences in the level of a company's *gearing would not lead to any gains to shareholders.

MNE Abbreviation for *multinational enterprise.

mock auction An *auction during which a lot is sold to someone at a price lower than the highest bid, part of the price is repaid or credited to the bidder, the right to bid is restricted to those who have bought or agreed to buy one or more articles, or articles are given away or offered as gifts. Under the Mock Auction Act 1961 it is an offence to promote or conduct a mock auction.

model risk The *risk that derives from problems in financial modelling, for example that the model may not accurately price a derivative on the *over-the-counter market or that the hedging based on a model will not anticipate risks that subsequently become financially significant.

modified duration *See* DURATION.

modified pass-through A securitized mortgage vehicle that pays interest to the security holder whether or not it is received by the security agent from the mortgages, but only pays the principal when it is received from the mortgages. *See* GINNIE MAE; PASS-THROUGH.

moments Statistical measures of a distribution of outcomes. The main moments used are the *mean, *variance, third moment, and fourth moment. The mean is a measure of the centre or average outcome. The variance is a measure of the spread of outcomes. The third moment measures the *skewness (asymmetry) of a distribution. The fourth moment measures the *kurtosis (sharpness or flatness) of the distribution. Moments are often used in considering the distribution of the returns on investment.

momentum strategy An investment analysis strategy based on the anticipation of a market trend.

MONEP Abbreviation for *Marché des Options Négotiables de Paris.

monetarism A school of thought in economics that places money at the centre of macroeconomic policy. Based on the *quantity theory of money, it relates the price level to the quantity of money in the economy. It claims that monetary factors are a major influence on the economy and that, in particular, government expansion of the money supply will tend to generate inflation rather than employment. This view is now associated with Milton Friedman (1912–) of Chicago University. Monetarism is also associated with the idea that relying on the market is more efficient than relying on state-sponsored activity.

monetarist A person who supports *monetarism.

monetary aggregate Any of several measures of the *money supply from the narrow M0 to the broad M5.

monetary assets and liabilities Amounts receivable (assets) or payable (liabilities) that appear in a company's accounts as specific sums of money, e.g. cash and bank balances, loans, debtors, and creditors. These are to be distinguished from such non-monetary items as plant and machinery, stock in trade, or equity investments, which, although they are also expressed in accounts at a value (frequently cost), are not necessarily realizable at that value.

monetary base In the UK, total bank deposits and all the notes and coins in circulation, plus *clearing banks' deposits and other bank deposits lodged with the *Bank of England. This is equivalent to M0 of the *money supply. In the USA, it is the total bank deposits plus the notes and coins in circulation.

monetary control The use of the *central bank of a country by its government to control the *money supply. In the UK, the Bank of England acted in this way prior to 1997 but, as with the Federal Reserve Bank in the USA, it is now largely independent of government policy.

Monetary Control Act 1980 The US legislation that made all US banks members of the *Federal Reserve System.

monetary inflation The theory that *inflation is related to the expansion of the *money supply. *See* MONETARY POLICY; QUANTITY THEORY OF MONEY.

monetary policy A means by which central banks try to affect macroeconomic conditions by influencing the supply of money. Four main options are available: (i) printing more money (now rarely used in practice); (ii) direct controls over money held by the monetary sector; (iii) *open-market operations; and (iv) influencing the interest rate. The traditional Keynesian view has been that monetary policy is at best a blunt instrument, while *monetarism expresses the opposite view. In practice, governments have tended to employ 'tight' monetary policies, in the belief that this restrains inflation. *Compare* FISCAL POLICY.

Monetary Policy Committee (MPC) The committee of Bank of England officials and outside economic experts that has been responsible for setting interest rates in the UK since 1997. Prior to this date, interest rates were set by the Treasury.

monetary reform The revision of a country's currency by the introduction of a new currency unit or a substantial change to an existing system. Examples include decimalization of the UK currency (1971), the change from the austral to the peso in Argentina (1992), and the introduction of the *euro (1999–2002).

monetary stock *See* MONEY SUPPLY.

monetary system **1.** The system used by a country to provide the economy with money for internal use and to control the exchange of its own currency with those of foreign countries. It also includes the system used by a country for implementing its *monetary policy. **2.** A system used to control the exchange rate of a group of countries. *See* EUROPEAN MONETARY SYSTEM.

monetary theory Any theory concerned with the influence of money in an economic system. *See* MONETARY POLICY; QUANTITY THEORY OF MONEY.

monetary union A group of countries using a single currency. *See* EUROPEAN MONETARY SYSTEM; MAASTRICHT TREATY.

monetary unit The standard unit of currency in a country. The monetary unit of each country is related to those of other countries by a *foreign exchange rate.

monetization The sale of *Treasury bills to banks by the UK government to finance a budgetary deficit.

money A *medium of exchange that functions as a unit of account, a store of value, and a means for deferred payment. Originally money enhanced economic development by enabling goods to be bought and sold without the need for barter. However, throughout history money has been beset by the problem of its debasement as a store of value as a result of *inflation. Now that the supply of money is a monopoly of the state, most governments are committed in principle to stable prices. The word 'money' is derived from the Latin *moneta*, which was one of the names of Juno, the Roman goddess whose temple was used as a mint.

money at call and short notice One of the assets that appears in the balance sheet of a bank. It includes funds lent to discount houses, money brokers, the stock exchange, bullion brokers, corporate customers, and increasingly to other banks. 'At call' money is repayable on demand, whereas 'short notice' money implies that notice of repayment of up to 14 days will be given. After cash, money at call and short notice are the banks' most liquid assets. They are usually interest-earning secured loans but their importance lies in providing the banks with an opportunity to use their surplus funds and to adjust their cash and liquidity requirements.

money broker In the UK, a broker who arranges short-term loans in the *money market, i.e. between banks, discount houses, and dealers in government securities. Money brokers do not themselves lend or borrow money; they work for a commission arranging loans on a day-to-day and overnight basis. Money brokers also operate in the eurobond markets.

money-centre banks The major *clearing banks in an economy.

money laundering *See* LAUNDERING MONEY.

moneylender A person whose business it is to lend money, other than pawnbrokers, friendly or building societies, corporate bodies with special powers to lend money, banks, or insurance companies. The Consumer Credit Act 1974 replaces the earlier Moneylenders Acts and requires all moneylenders to be registered, to obtain an annual licence to lend money, and to state the true *annual percentage rate (APR) of interest at which a loan is made.

money market **1.** The market for short-term loans and debt instruments. In the UK, *money brokers arrange for loans between the banks, the government, the *discount houses, and the *accepting houses, with the Bank of England acting as *lender of last resort. The main instruments are *bills of exchange, Treasury bills, and trade bills. The market takes place in and around Lombard Street in the City of London. Private investors, through their banks, can place deposits in the money market at a higher rate of interest than bank deposit accounts. **2.** The foreign-exchange market and the bullion market in addition to the short-term loan market.

money-market basis The method of calculating *accrued interest on money-market instruments. It is based on a 365-day year in the UK and on a 360-day year in the USA.

money-market deposit account (MMDA) A high-yielding savings account introduced in the USA in 1982 to allow deposit-taking institutions to compete for savers' funds with the money markets. As long as the account has a balance of more than $1000 there is no regulatory limit on the account. Balances below $1000 attract a lower rate of interest. Restrictions on the account apply to withdrawals (three a month) and transfers for bill payment (three a month).

money-market instruments Financial products, usually with a short-term life, such as *certificates of deposit, that are traded on the *money markets.

money-market mutual fund A US *open-end trust that invests in short-term debt instruments and sells its shares to investors.

money-market unit trust (cash unit trust) A *unit trust that invests in money-market instruments in order to provide investors with a risk-free income.

money-purchase pension scheme A defined-contribution pension scheme as opposed to a *defined-benefit pension scheme.

money supply (monetary stock) The quantity of money issued by a country's monetary authorities (usually the central bank). If the demand for money is stable, the widely accepted *quantity theory of money implies that increases in the money supply will lead directly to an increase in the price level, i.e. to inflation. Since the 1970s most western governments have attempted to reduce inflation by controlling the money supply. This raises two issues:
(i) how to measure the money supply;
(ii) how to control the money supply (*see* INTEREST-RATE POLICY).

In the UK various measures of the money supply have been used, from the very narrow M0 to the very broad M5. They are usually defined as:
M0 — notes and coins in circulation plus the banks' till money and the banks' balances with the Bank of England;
M1 — notes and coins in circulation plus private-sector current accounts and deposit accounts that can be transferred by cheque;
M2 — notes and coins in circulation plus non-interest-bearing bank deposits plus building society deposits plus National Savings accounts;
M3 — M1 plus all other private-sector bank deposits plus certificates of deposit;
M3c — M3 plus foreign currency bank deposits;
M4 — M1 plus most private-sector bank deposits plus holdings of money-market instruments (e.g. Treasury bills);
M5 — M4 plus building society deposits.

In some contexts the amount of money existing in an economy is called the **monetary stock**. To obtain the money supply the monetary stock has to be multiplied by the *velocity of circulation.

money-supply rules A policy in which a government states in advance the extent to which it intends to expand the *money supply. It is based on the belief that *fiscal policy and *monetary policy cannot affect the real variables in an economic situation but that uncertainty concerning government intentions can destabilize markets. In these circumstances a stable-policy rule is the best a government can achieve.

möngö A Mongolian monetary unit worth one hundredth of a *tugrik.

Monopolies and Mergers Commission (MMC) *See* COMPETITION COMMISSION.

monopoly A market in which there is only one seller (or producer). Governments usually try to eliminate monopolies as being against the public interest. In recent decades some of the services formerly regarded as natural monopolies, such as electricity and water supply, have been privatized to encourage competition and eliminate the monopolistic element. *See also* CARTEL.

Monte Carlo simulation A *simulation in which random data are generated from specified distributions and used as an input into predictive or other models. Such simulations are used to price complicated derivatives and portfolios and provide the basis for many financial risk-management systems. Firms also employ them in their decision and capital-appraisal models. *See also* RANDOM NUMBER GENERATOR.

Monthly Digest of Statistics A monthly publication of the UK *Office for

National Statistics providing statistical information on industry, national income, and the UK population.

moonlighting Having two jobs, one a full-time daytime job, the other a part-time evening job. Often the second job is undertaken on a self-employed basis and income is not returned for tax purposes.

moral hazard The situation in which a person has no incentive to act honestly or with due prudence in the absence of penalties. The term is mainly used in the insurance world, where a typical example of a person exposed to moral hazard would be the owner of an insured car, who has little or no incentive to guard against theft. Moral hazard is closely associated with the concept of *adverse selection, as when a person purchasing health insurance declines to reveal his or her greater likelihood to need health treatment than the average.

moral suasion A regulatory body's use of argument and persuasion, rather than coercion or legislation, to influence the activities of those within its purview. The term is often applied to the efforts of the Federal Reserve Board (*see* FEDERAL RESERVE SYSTEM) to persuade its members to comply with its policies.

moratorium **1.** An agreement between a creditor and a debtor to allow additional time for the settlement of a debt. **2.** A period during which one government permits a government of a foreign country to suspend repayments of a debt. **3.** A period during which all the trading debts in a particular market are suspended as a result of some exceptional crisis in the market. In these circumstances, not to call a moratorium would probably lead to more insolvencies than the market could stand. The intention of such a moratorium is, first, that firms should be given a breathing space to find out exactly what their liabilities are and, secondly, that they should be given time to make the necessary financial arrangements to settle their liabilities.

mortality rate (death rate) The crude death rate, i.e. the number of deaths per 1000 of the average population in a given year. It can be subdivided into different rates for different age groups of the population and for different regions.

mortality table (life table) An actuarial table prepared on the basis of mortality (death) rates for people in different occupations in different regions of a country. It provides life-assurance companies with the information they require to quote for life-assurance policies, annuities, etc.

mortgage An interest in property created as a security for a loan or payment of a debt and terminated on payment of the loan or debt. The borrower, who offers the security, is the **mortgagor**; the lender, who provides the money, is the **mortgagee**. *Building societies and banks are the usual mortgagees for house purchasers. In either case the mortgage is repaid by instalments over a fixed period (often 25 years), either of capital and interest (**repayment mortgage**) or of interest only, with other arrangements being made to repay the capital, for example by means of an *endowment assurance policy (this is known as an **endowment mortgage**). Business uses of the mortgage include using property to secure a loan to start a business. Virtually any property may be mortgaged (though land is the most common).

Under the Law of Property Act 1925, which governs mortgage regulations in the UK, there are two types of mortgage, legal and equitable. A **legal mortgage** confers a legal estate on the mortgagee; the only valid mortgages are (a) a lease granted for a stated number of years, which terminates on repayment of the loan at or before the end of that period; and (b) a deed expressed to be a *charge by way of legal mortgage. An **equitable mortgage** can be created if the mortgagee has only an equitable interest in the property (for example, being a beneficiary under a trust of the property). Provided that this is done by *deed, the rights of the parties are very similar to those under a legal mortgage. An equitable mortgage can also be created of a legal or equitable interest by an informal agreement, e.g. the mortgagor hands the title deeds to the mortgagee as security for a loan. Such a mortgagee has the remedies of possession and foreclosure only (see below). A *second mortgage or subsequent mortgage may be taken out on the same property, provided that the value of the property is greater than the amount of the previous mortgage(s) and permission is granted by the previous mortgagee(s). All mortgage of registered land are noted in the charges register at the Land Registry on application by the mortgagee, to whom a charge certificate is issued. When mortgaged land is unregistered, a first legal mortgagee keeps the title deeds. A subsequent legal mortgagee and any equitable mortgagee who does not have the title deeds should protect their interests by registration.

Under the **equity of redemption**, the mortgagor is allowed to redeem the property at any time on payment of the loan together with interest and costs, which may include a penalty for early redemption; any provisions in a mortgage deed to prevent redemption (known as **clogs**) are void.

In theory, the mortgagee always has the right to take possession of mortgaged property even if there has been no default. This right is usually excluded by building-society mortgages until default, and its exclusion may be implied in any instalment mortgage. Where residential property is concerned, the court has power to delay the recovery of possession if there is a realistic possibility that the default will be remedied in a reasonable time. In case of default, the mortgagor has a statutory right to sell the property, but this will normally be exercised after obtaining possession first. Any surplus after the debt and the mortgagee's expenses have been met must be paid to the mortgagor. The mortgagee also has a statutory right to appoint a *receiver to manage mortgaged property in the event of default; this power is useful where business property is concerned. As a final resort, a mortgage may be brought to an end by *foreclosure, in which the court orders the transfer of the property to the mortgagee. This is not common in times of rising property prices, as the mortgagor would lose more than the value of the debt, so the court will not order foreclosure where a sale would be more appropriate.

mortgage-backed security A security in which cash flows derive from an underlying pool of mortgages. They are very widely used in the USA.

mortgage bond In the USA, a bond in which a debt is secured by a real *asset. **Senior mortgage bonds** have first claim on assets and **junior mortgage bonds** are subordinate. A mortgage bond may have a closed-end provision, which prevents an organization issuing further bonds of a similar nature on the same asset or open-end provision, which permits further issues with the same status.

mortgage debenture A loan made to a company by an investor, secured on the real property of the company. *See* DEBENTURE.

mortgagee A lender who provides a *mortgage.

mortgagee in possession A *mortgagee who has exercised the right to take possession of the mortgaged property; this may happen at any time, even if there has been no default by the mortgagor. However, the mortgage deed may contain an agreement not to do this unless there is default and a court order will be needed to obtain possession in the case of a dwelling house. The court may adjourn the hearing to allow the mortgagor time to pay. The mortgagee will either receive the rents and profits if the property has been let or will manage the property. The mortgagee will be liable to account strictly for any actions and is not entitled to reap any personal benefit beyond repayment of the interest and the principal debt. The mortgagee must carry out reasonable repairs and must not damage the property.

mortgage interest relief at source (MIRAS) Formerly, an arrangement allowing income tax relief to be given to a mortgagor on the first £30,000 of a loan taken out to purchase a main residence. Introduced in 1982 to stimulate home ownership, MIRAS was progressively restricted from 1994 and abolished in 2000.

mortgagor A borrower who takes out a *mortgage.

mountain A surplus of agricultural produce that is created by price supports, most notoriously as a result of the EU's *Common Agricultural Policy.

moving average A series of *arithmetic means calculated from data in a time series, which reduces the effects of temporary seasonal variations. For example, a moving average of the monthly sales figures for an organization might be calculated by averaging the 12 months from January to December for the December figure, the 12 months from February to January for the January figure, and so on.

MPC Abbreviation for *Monetary Policy Committee.

MSP Abbreviation for *matched sale–purchase agreement.

MTFA Abbreviation for *medium-term financial assistance.

MTN Abbreviation for *medium-term note.

multibuyer policy An insurance policy covering a range of buyers on a US exporter's order book. The policy covers the solvency of the buyers and is usually only available from the *Export–Import Bank.

multi-component euronote facility A *euronote issued in a variety of currencies.

multifunctional card A plastic card issued by a bank or building society to its customers to function as a *cheque card, *debit card, and *cash card. Multifunctional cards operate in conjunction with a *personal identification number.

multilateral development bank A multinational financial institution that operates in a range of countries, such as the *World Bank or the *European Bank for Reconstruction and Development.

Multilateral Investment Guarantee Agency (MIGA) An affiliate of the *International Bank for Reconstruction and Development (IBRD) established in 1988 to encourage foreign investment in developing countries by providing investors with guarantees and developing countries with an advisory service.

multilateral netting 1. The centralizing of international payments of a group of companies so that payments and receipts in different currencies can be offset, thus reducing transaction and hedging costs. **2.** A method of reducing bank charges in which the subsidiaries of a group offset their receipts and payments with each other, usually monthly, resulting in a single net intercompany payment or receipt made by each subsidiary to cover the period concerned. This saves both on transaction costs and paperwork. *See also* BILATERAL NETTING; NETTING.

multinational enterprise (MNE) A corporation that has production operations in more than one country for various reasons, including securing supplies of raw materials, utilizing cheap labour sources, servicing local markets taking advantage of tax differences, and bypassing protectionist barriers. Multinationals may be seen as an efficient form of organization, making effective use of the world's resources and transferring technology between countries. On the other hand, some have excessive power, are beyond the control of governments (especially weak governments), and are able to exploit host countries, especially in the developing world, where they are able to operate with low safety levels and inadequate control of pollution. *See* GLOBALIZATION.

multi-option facility A mixture of various financial instruments (e.g. *euronotes, *commercial paper) to support a short-term loan. Only part of the credit is usually offered, the balance being payable on notice.

multiple *See* PRICE–EARNINGS RATIO.

multiple application The submission of more than one application form for a new issue of shares that is likely to be oversubscribed (*see* ALLOTMENT). In many countries it is illegal to do so either if the applications are made in the same name or if false names are used.

multiple exchange rate An exchange rate quoted by a country that has more than one value, depending on the use to which the currency is put. For example, some countries have quoted a specially favourable rate for tourists or for importers of desirable goods.

multiple taxation Taxation of the same income by more than two countries. *Compare* DOUBLE TAXATION.

multiplier The feedback effect generated by a change in an economic variable. For example, an increase in total *investment will raise national income by an amount equal to its monetary value, but in addition it will have a wider positive feedback effect by stimulating other parts of the economy, thus creating new jobs and additional demand for goods. *See* FOREIGN TRADE MULTIPLIER.

Multi-Year Rescheduling Agreement (MYRA) Agreements made in the 1980s in which outstanding loans from developing countries were rescheduled by clearing banks throughout the world in order to ease the financial burden on the developing nations and to avoid the banks having to write off the loans as bad debts. Deals often involved interest-only payments, even part-interest-only payments, or transferable bonds in other currencies. Some developing countries stopped servicing their debts altogether, but by the mid-1990s most had begun to make some form of repayment. In the UK, the clearing banks were heavily exposed and were forced to make provisions or complete write-offs of the debts in their balance sheets. This had a major impact on shareholders' dividends. *See also* LONDON CLUB.

municipal bond A bond issued by a local government authority, especially one in the USA.

muqarada *See* ISLAMIC FINANCE.

murabaha *See* ISLAMIC FINANCE.

musharaka *See* ISLAMIC FINANCE.

mutual 1. A company that is owned by its members or depositors. *Building societies in the UK used to have this structure, but most have now demutualized, becoming *public limited companies. *See also* MUTUAL LIFE-ASSURANCE COMPANY; MUTUAL SAVINGS BANKS. **2.** In the USA, an *open-ended investment company.

mutual fund The US name for a *unit trust.

mutual life-assurance company A type of life-assurance company that grew out of the Friendly Societies; there are no shareholders and apart from benefits and running expenses there are no other withdrawals from the fund; thus any profits are distributed to policyholders.

mutually exclusive projects A number of alternative projects being considered for appraisal, in which no one project can be pursued in conjunction with any of the other projects. For example, a parcel of land may be used to build a factory, an office block, or a mixture of the two. Each alternative is mutually exclusive because the choice of one alternative automatically excludes the others. Mutually exclusive projects arise when there is a scarce resource, in this case land.

mutual savings banks US institutions that take deposits and make domestic mortgage loans. They are owned by the depositors but do not have shareholders. *See also* THRIFTS.

MYRA Abbreviation for *Multi-Year Rescheduling Agreement.

m

NAFTA Abbreviation for *North American Free Trade Agreement.

naira (₦) The standard monetary unit of Nigeria, divided into 100 kobo.

Nakasone bond A bond issued by the Japanese government in a foreign currency. It is named after the prime minister in office when it was introduced (1982).

naked call writing Selling (writing) a call *option on equities that one does not own. A person may do this if he or she expects the price of a particular share to fall or remain unchanged. It is, however, a dangerous strategy because if the price rises the shares will have to be purchased at the market price in order to deliver them, thus involving an unlimited risk. *Compare* COVERED CALL WRITING.

naked debenture An unsecured *debenture.

naked position *See* OPEN POSITION.

naked swap A *swap for which the purchaser does not have an offsetting structure of cash flows.

nakfa The standard monetary unit of Eritrea.

name *See* LLOYD'S; SYNDICATE.

narrow market 1. A commodities or securities market in which few trades take place. **2.** A market for shares in a company for which there are not a large number of shares available. Favourable news about such a company's prospects would dramatically increase the value of its shares, because the number available is small and buyers would outnumber sellers.

narrow money An informal name for M0, or sometimes M1: the part of the *money supply that can directly perform the function of a *medium of exchange. *Compare* BROAD MONEY.

narrow-range securities *See* TRUSTEE INVESTMENTS.

NASD Abbreviation for *National Association of Securities Dealers Inc.

NASDAQ Abbreviation for *National Association of Securities Dealers Automated Quotation System.

NASDAQ index The price index of the *National Association of Securities Dealers Automated Quotation System for over-the-counter trading. The index is market-value-weighted. There are six indexes covering different sectors of the market, all of which were based on 5 February 1971. Two newer indexes are the NASDAQ-100 and the NASDAQ-Financial, operating from 1 February 1985, valued at 250.

NASDAQ International An international service based on NASDAQ that came into operation in January 1992. It provides a screen-based quotation system to support market-making in US registered equities from 8.30 am until 2 pm London time (i.e. between 3.30 am and 9 am Eastern Standard Time) on US business days. Most US and Canadian equity securities are available on the system.

NASDIM Abbreviation for *National Association of Securities Dealers and Investment Managers.

National Association of Securities Dealers and Investment Managers (NASDIM) A former association of some 800 licensed securities dealers. It was formed in 1979 from the Association of Licensed Dealers and disbanded in 1987 on the establishment of the statutory *Self-Regulating Organizations. System

National Association of Securities Dealers Automated Quotation System (NASDAQ) A US computer system for trading in over-the-counter securities that began operations on 8 February 1971, when it was the first screen-based trading system with no market floor. It is the largest stock market in the USA, listing more than 5000 companies. In the early 2000s, NASDAQ had over 500 market makers and some 180,000 terminals, of which 25,000 were operating outside the USA (*see also* NASDAQ INTERNATIONAL). NASDAQ provided the basis for the *SEAQ system on the *London Stock Exchange.

National Association of Securities Dealers Inc. (NASD) A US self-regulating organization of the securities industry responsible for operating and regulating the NASDAQ and over-the-counter securities markets. It is based in Washington, DC.

national banks US commercial banks established by federal charter (approved by the *Comptroller of the Currency), which requires them to be members of the *Federal Reserve System. They were created by the National Bank Act 1863 and formerly issued their own banknotes.

national debt The debts of a central government, both internal and overseas. Net government borrowing each year is added to the national debt. The non-sterling debt is important because interest on it adversely affects the *balance of payments. Management of the national debt, which can be an important aspect of government monetary policy, is in the hands of the **National Debt Commissioners** of the Bank of England.

national income accounts Accounts that measure the income generated by factors of production owned by residents of a country or factors located in a country. They are calculated by measuring the expenditure, income, and output of the economy.

National Insurance contribution (NIC) Payments made by those with earned income that contribute to the National Insurance Fund, from which benefits are paid. These benefits include retirement pensions, unemployment pay, widow's benefits, invalidity benefit, and certain sickness and maternity benefits. There are six different classes of National Insurance contributions; the class applicable to a person depends on the type of earned income received by that person. Class 1 is paid by those with earnings from employment. There are two parts to class 1, primary contributions paid by the employee and secondary contributions paid by the employer. The rates of contributions depend on the level of earnings and also whether or not the employee is a member of a contracted-out occupational, personal, or stakeholder pension scheme; for employees the standard rate is 11% on weekly earnings between £91 and £610 and 1% on weekly earnings thereafter (2004–05 figures). Class 2 is a flat-rate contribution of £2.05 paid by the self-employed. Class 3 is voluntary, and is also at a flat rate (£7.15 per week in 2004–05). It is paid by those wishing to maintain their contribution record even though they may be unemployed or their level of earnings is below that for mandatory contributions. Class 4 is paid by the self-employed at a rate of 8% on income between a lower limit of £4745 per year and an upper limit of £31,720 per year and

1% on yearly income thereafter. Class 1A was introduced in 1991 and is payable by employers who provide cars for private as well as business use for their employees. The level of payment depends on the cost and age of the car and the number of business miles travelled. It is based on the list price of the vehicle, on the day it was first registered as brand new. Class 1B is payable by employers in value of any items included in a PAYE settlement with the Inland Revenue.

nationalization The process of bringing the assets of a business into the ownership of the state. Examples of industries nationalized in the past in the UK include the National Coal Board and British Rail. Historically, nationalization has been achieved through compulsory purchase, although this need not necessarily be the case. Nationalization has often been pursued as much for political as economic ends and the economic justifications themselves are varied. One argument for nationalization is that if a company possesses a natural monopoly, then it should, for reasons of economic welfare, be run at a loss. Another argument might be that particular industries are strategically important for the nation and therefore cannot be entrusted to private enterprise. In the 1980s and 1990s Conservative governments reversed Labour's nationalization of the 1950s, 1960s, and 1970s with a series of *privatization measures, on the grounds that competition should in theory increase efficiency and reduce prices. However, even where this has not proved to be the case in practice – notably the privatization of the UK rail network – Labour administrations since 1997 have been reluctant to take the utility back into public ownership.

National Market System (NMS) A system linking the US stock exchanges together, providing information on the price and volume of securities. It was instituted in 1975 to increase competition among the stock exchanges. Its **Intermarket Trading System** (ITS) displays current bid and offer prices of securities across all markets in the system.

national plan An economic plan formulated by a government as a blueprint for its economic development over a stated period, usually five or ten years.

National Savings The UK Department for National Savings was established in 1969, having previously been known as the Post Office Savings Department. It is responsible for administering a wide range of schemes for personal savers, including *premium bonds, *income bonds, and *capital bonds. In addition the department has offered a range of **National Savings Certificates** on which the income is tax-free and the element of capital gain is free of capital gains tax. Since April 1999 the Department has also offered *Individual Savings Accounts (ISAs). *See also* NATIONAL SAVINGS BANK; NATIONAL SAVINGS STOCK REGISTER.

National Savings Bank (NSB) A savings bank founded in 1861, now operated by the Department for *National Savings through the agency of the Post Office (it was formerly called the Post Office Savings Bank).

National Savings Certificates *See* NATIONAL SAVINGS.

National Savings Stock Register An organization run by the Department for *National Savings from the Bonds and Stock Office in Blackpool. It enables members of the public to buy certain Treasury stocks and other *gilt-edged securities without going through a stockbroker; it thus provides an alternative to the main Bank of England Stock Register. Purchases and sales are made by post and the interest paid is taxable, but is paid before deduction of tax (unlike the Bank of England Register). Because transactions are carried out by post, this method does not provide the maximum flexibility in a moving market.

National Securities Clearing Corporation (NSCC) A US securities *clearing house formed in 1977 by the merger of the National Clearing Corporation, owned by the *National Association of Securities Dealers Inc., and the clearing facilities of the *New York Stock Exchange (NYSE) and the *American Stock Exchange (AMEX). Purchases and sales in both markets are settled through the NSCC.

National Stock Exchange *See* US STOCK EXCHANGES.

natural option A transaction that has an implicit or embedded *option as part of the package of elements.

NAV Abbreviation for *net asset value.

NBV Abbreviation for *net book value.

NCI Abbreviation for *New Community Instrument.

NDP Abbreviation for *net domestic product.

near money (quasi money) An asset that is immediately transferable and may be used to settle some but not all debts, although it is not as liquid as banknotes and coins. *Bills of exchange are examples of near money. Near money is not included in the *money supply definitions.

negative cash flow A *cash flow in which the outflows exceed the inflows.

negative equity **1.** An asset that has a market value below the sum of money borrowed to purchase it. **2.** The state of holding such an asset, especially a house bought at a time of high prices that now has a current market value below the sum still outstanding on the *mortgage. *Compare* NEGATIVE NET WORTH.

negative income tax (NIT) A system designed to target social security benefits to those most in need. After submitting an income-tax return showing an income level below a set minimum, an individual then receives a direct subsidy from the tax authorities bringing income up to that level.

negative interest A charge made by a bank or other deposit taker for looking after a sum of money for a given period.

negative net worth The value of an organization that has liabilities in excess of its assets.

negative pledge A *covenant in a loan agreement in which a borrower promises that no secured borrowings will be made during the life of the loan or will ensure that the loan is secured equally and ratably with any new borrowings as specifically defined.

negative yield curve (inverse yield curve) A curve on a graph in which interest rates for deposits or securities are plotted against different maturities, when short-term interest rates are higher than longer rates. The curve starts at a high value and falls downwards. *See* YIELD CURVE.

negligence A tort in which a breach of a **duty of care** results in damage to the person to whom the duty is owed. Such a duty is owed by manufacturers to the consumers who buy their products, by professional persons to their clients, by a director of a company to its shareholders, etc. A person who has suffered loss or injury as a result of a breach of the duty of care can claim damages in tort.

negotiability The ability of a document to change hands thereby entitling its owner to some benefit, so that legal ownership of the benefit passes by delivery or endorsement of the document. For a document to be negotiable it must also entitle the holder to bring an action in law if necessary. *See* NEGOTIABLE INSTRUMENT.

negotiable instrument A document of title that can be freely negotiated (*see* NEGOTIABILITY). Such documents are *cheques and *bills of exchange, in which the stated payee of the instrument can negotiate the instrument by either inserting the name of a different payee or by making the document 'open' by endorsing it (signing one's name), usually on the reverse. Holders of negotiable instruments cannot pass on a better title than they possess. Bills of exchange, including cheques, in which the payee is named or that bear a restrictive endorsement, such as "not negotiable", are **non-negotiable instruments**.

negotiable order of withdrawal (NOW) A type of cheque used in US savings accounts that are interest-bearing and from which sums can be withdrawn. If no interest is paid the account is called a **NINOW**.

negotiate **1.** To confer with a view to arriving at mutually acceptable terms for a contract or agreement. **2.** To transfer a *bill of exchange or cheque to another for consideration (*see* NEGOTIABILITY; NEGOTIABLE INSTRUMENT).

net assets The assets of an organization less its *current liabilities. The resultant figure is equal to the *capital of the organization. Opinion varies as to whether long-term liabilities should be treated as part of the capital and are therefore not deductible in arriving at net assets, or whether they are part of the liabilities and therefore deductible. The latter view is probably technically preferable and is more common. A further practice is to split long-term liabilities and to treat those described as the 'finance element' as part of the capital. *See also* NET CURRENT ASSETS.

net asset value (NAV) The value of a share in a company calculated by dividing the amount for the *net assets of the company by the number of shares in issue. The net asset value is frequently below the *market price of a share because *financial statements do not reflect the present values of all assets because of the monetary measurement convention and the *historical cost accounting convention, whereas the market price may reflect them.

net book value (NBV) The value at which an asset appears in the books of an organization (usually as at the date of the last balance sheet). This value is the purchase cost or latest revaluation less any depreciation applied since purchase or revaluation.

net borrowed reserves The amount that a US bank has borrowed from the *Federal Reserve System less the reserves they hold in excess of the required minimum. It is used as an indicator of interest-rate tendencies. If the banks have more money on loan than is covered by their reserves, interest rates will tend to rise.

net capital rule A requirement set by the US *Securities and Exchange Commission that dealers and brokers maintain a maximum ratio of indebtedness to realizable assets of 15:1.

net current assets *Current assets less *current liabilities. The resultant figure is also known as *working capital, as it represents the amount of the organization's capital that is constantly being turned over in the course of its trade. *See also* NET ASSETS.

net dividend The dividend paid by a company to its shareholders, after excluding the *tax credit received by the shareholders.

net domestic product (NDP) The *gross domestic product of a country less *capital consumption (i.e. depreciation).

net income **1.** The income of a person or organization after the deduction of the appropriate expenses incurred in earning it. **2.** *Gross income from which tax has been deducted.

net interest Interest paid into a savings or current account at a UK bank or building society after the deduction of tax at source. Interest on bank and building society accounts is taxed at the basic rate, currently 20%.

net interest income (NII) The interest income of a bank minus its interest costs.

net interest income margin (NIIM) The *net interest income of a bank divided by the value of its earning assets, i.e. its loans.

net investment The addition to the stock of capital goods in an economy during a particular period (the **gross investment**) less *capital consumption (i.e. depreciation).

net lease A lease in which the lessee pays the operating costs on the asset.

net liquid funds The cash available to an organization (including investments shown as *current assets) less any overdrafts or short-term loans.

net national product (NNP) The *gross national product less *capital consumption (i.e. depreciation) during the period. NNP is therefore equal to the national income, i.e. the amount of money available in the economy for expenditure on goods and services. However, NNP cannot be considered a very accurate measure, as it is difficult to calculate depreciation reliably.

net position The difference between an investor's long and short *positions in the same security or market.

net premium The annual payment received by an insurance company for an insurance policy after any charges (e.g. commission, brokerage, etc.) have been deducted.

net present value (NPV) In *discounted cash flows, the difference between the *present values of the cash outflows and the present values of the cash inflows. The NPV is the result of the application of *discount factors, based on a required rate of return to each year's projected cash flow, both in and out, so that the cash flows are discounted to *present values. If NPV is positive, the return will be greater than that required by the capital markets (making the project viable), whereas if the NPV is negative, the return will be less than that required by the capital markets, calling the wisdom of the venture into question.

net price The price a buyer pays for goods or services after all discounts have been deducted.

net profit **1. (net profit before taxation)** The profit of an organization when all receipts and expenses have been taken into account. In trading organizations, net profit is arrived at by deducting from the *gross profit all the expenses not already taken into account in arriving at the gross profit. **2. (net profit after taxation)** The final profit of an organization, after all appropriate taxes have been deducted from the net profit before taxation. *See also* PROFIT AND LOSS ACCOUNT.

net-profit ratio The proportion that *net profit bears to the total sales of an organization. This ratio is used in analysing the profitability of organizations and is an indicator of the extent to which sales have been profitable.

net realizable value (NRV) The sales value of the stock of an organization less the additional costs likely to be incurred in getting the stocks into the hands of the customer.

net receipts The total amount of money received by a business in a specified period after deducting costs, raw materials, taxation, etc. *Compare* GROSS RECEIPTS.

net relevant earnings A person's non-pensionable earned income before personal allowances have been deducted but after deduction of expenses, capital allowances, losses, or any stock relief agreed with the Inland Revenue. It forms income from which any tax relief on pension contributions can be calculated.

net residual value (disposal value) The expected proceeds from the sale of an asset, net of the costs of sale, at the end of its estimated useful life. It is used for computing the straight-line method and reducing-balance method of *depreciation, and also for inclusion in the final year's cash inflow in a *discounted cash flow appraisal.

net return The profit made on an investment after the deduction of all expenses, either before or after deduction of *capital gains tax.

net settlement A situation in which payments are offset and the net amount is paid. *See* SETTLEMENT.

net tangible assets The *tangible assets of an organization less its current liabilities. In analysing the affairs of an organization the net tangible assets indicate its financial strength in terms of being solvent, without having to resort to such nebulous (and less easy-to-value) assets as *goodwill. *See also* PRICE–NET TANGIBLE ASSETS RATIO.

netting The process of setting off matching sales and purchases against each other, especially sales and purchases of futures, options, and forward foreign exchange. This service is usually provided for an exchange or market by a *clearing house. It also provides a means by which a firm can deal with its risks, notably *exchange-rate risk exposure. *See also* NOVATION.

net worth The value of an organization or individual when its liabilities have been deducted from the value of its assets. For businesses, it is often taken to be synonymous with *net asset value (i.e. the total assets as shown by the balance sheet less the current liabilities), net worth so defined can be misleading in that balance sheets rarely show the real value of assets; in order to arrive at the true net worth it would normally be necessary to assess the true market values of the assets rather than their *book values. It would also be necessary to value *goodwill, which may not even appear in the balance sheet. *See also* NEGATIVE NET WORTH; NET TANGIBLE ASSETS.

net yield *See* GROSS YIELD.

neural network A mathematical technique for recognizing patterns in data that is supposed to be based on the structure and function of the human brain. In finance, it is used to model the behaviour of financial variables.

neutral hedge A *hedge that works well for small variations in variables or risk factors.

NEWCO An insurance company set up to reinsure debts from the *Old Years at *Lloyd's.

New Community Instrument (NCI) Loans to the *European Commission which are lent on to public and private bodies in the European Union.

new for old The basis for household insurance policies in which payments of claims are not subject to a deduction for wear and tear. As a result, a claim for an old and worn-out table would be met by the payment of the price of a new table of a similar type.

new issue The issue of a new security, be it an equity, a *debt instrument, or a *money-market instrument.

new-issue market *See* PRIMARY MARKET.

new shares Shares that have been newly issued by a company on the *primary market of a stock exchange.

new sol (S/.) The standard monetary unit of Peru, divided into 100 céntimos.

new time The purchase or sale of securities on the *London Stock Exchange during the last two dealing days of an account, for settlement during the following account. When making a bargain for new time this must be clearly understood between investor, broker, and market maker.

New York Clearing House Association A US *clearing house for bankers in New York City. Founded in 1853, it is the oldest bank clearing house association in the USA.

New York Cotton Exchange The oldest commodity exchange in New York (founded in 1870) and the world's premier market for cotton futures and options trading. Since 1966 it has expanded into frozen concentrated orange juice (fcoj) through the Citrus Associates of the New York Cotton Exchange Inc. It also created FINEX, the Financial Instrument Exchange, which trades in US dollar index futures and options, five-year Treasury note futures and options, two-year US Treasury note futures, and ECU futures. The Cotton Exchange also houses the trading operations of the New York Futures Exchange.

New York Futures Exchange (NYFE) A wholly owned subsidiary of the *New York Cotton Exchange. It was set up in 1979 to deal in futures in equities, etc., and was acquired from the New York Stock Exchange in 1993.

New York Mercantile Exchange (NYMEX) A futures exchange in New York dealing in oil products and some rare metals.

New York Stock Exchange (NYSE) The main US stock exchange, though no longer the only one (*see* AMERICAN STOCK EXCHANGE; NATIONAL ASSOCIATION OF SECURITIES DEALERS AUTOMATED QUOTATION SYSTEM). It was founded in 1792 under the Buttonwood Agreement (the name of the tree under which 24 merchants agreed to give each other preference in their dealings); it moved to Wall Street in 1793. The New York Stock & Exchange Board was formally established in 1817; it was renamed the New York Stock Exchange in 1983.

ngultrum (Nu) The standard monetary unit of Bhutan, divided into 100 chetrum.

ngwee A monetary unit of Zambia worth one hundredth of a *kwacha.

niche player *See* BOUTIQUE.

NIF Abbreviation for *note issuance facility.

NII Abbreviation for *net interest income.

NIIM Abbreviation for *net interest income margin.

Nikkei Dow Jones Index *See* NIKKEI STOCK AVERAGE.

Nikkei Stock Average (Nikkei Index) An index of prices on the *Tokyo Stock Exchange. It was originally known as the **Nikkei Dow Jones Index** and first calculated on 16 May 1949, based at 176.21. The Nikkei Stock Average is a price-weighted index of 225 Japanese companies representing 19% of first section issues, and accounting for about 51% of market value. It was restructured for the first time in its history in late 1991 by its administrator, the Nihon Keizai Shimbun (Japan Economic Journal) financial newspaper group, to try to reduce the impact of futures-related trading on the index (Nikkei is a shortening of the full name of the newspaper group). Membership of the index is now reviewed annually, when up to six members can be replaced if their shares become illiquid or unrepresentative. Previous changes only occurred when companies were taken over or liquidated.

nil paid Denoting a share issue that has been made without payment, usually as a result of a *rights issue.

NINOW *See* NEGOTIABLE ORDER OF WITHDRAWAL.

NIT Abbreviation for *negative income tax.

NL Abbreviation for no liability. It appears after the name of an Australian company, being equivalent to the British abbreviation *plc (denoting a public limited company).

NMS **1.** Abbreviation for *Normal Market Size. **2.** Abbreviation for *National Market System.

N/N Abbreviation for 'not to be noted', which may be written on a *bill of exchange to indicate that the collecting bank should not incur the expense of *noting it, if it is dishonoured.

NNP Abbreviation for *net national product.

no-arbitrage condition *See* ARBITRAGE-FREE CONDITION.

no-claim bonus A reward, in the form of a premium discount, given to policyholders if they complete a year or more without making a claim. The system is most commonly used in motor insurance. In every case, the bonus is allowed for remaining claim-free and is not dependent on blame for a particular accident. So, for example, a no-claim bonus is lost if a vehicle is stolen through no fault of the insured.

noise In statistics, random fluctuations in data.

nominal capital (authorized capital) *See* SHARE CAPITAL.

nominal interest rate **1.** An interest rate not adjusted for inflation. **2.** The interest rate on a fixed-interest security calculated as a percentage of its par value rather than its market price.

nominal partner *See* PARTNERSHIP.

nominal price **1.** A minimal price fixed for the sake of having some consideration for a transaction. It need bear no relation to the market value of the item. **2.** The price given to a security when it is issued, also called the **face value**, **nominal value**, or *par value. For example, XYZ plc 25p ordinary shares have a nominal price of 25p, although the market value may be quite different. The nominal value of a share is the maximum amount the holder can be required to contribute to the company. **3.** An estimated price for a time period in which the security under consideration is not traded.

nominal principal A notional valuation of the principal in derivatives contracts. For example, in an ordinary option it would be the value of the *underlying involved in the contract.

nominal value *See* PAR VALUE.

nominal yield *See* YIELD.

nomination The person to whom the proceeds of a life-assurance policy should be paid as specified by the policyholder. *See* ASSIGNMENT OF LIFE POLICIES.

nominee A person named by another (the **nominator**) to act on his or her behalf, often to conceal the identity of the nominator. *See* NOMINEE SHAREHOLDING.

nominee shareholding A shareholding held in the name of a bank, stockbroker, company, individual, etc., that is not the name of the beneficial owner of the shares. A shareholding may be in the name of nominees to facilitate dealing or to conceal the identity of the true owner. Although this cover was formerly used in the early stages of a takeover, to enable the bidder clandestinely to build up a substantial holding in the target company, this is now prevented by the Companies Act 1981, which makes it mandatory for anyone holding 5% or more of the shares in a public company to declare that interest to the company. The earlier Companies Act 1967 made it mandatory for directors to openly declare their holdings, and those of their families, in the companies of which they are directors.

non-acceptance The failure by the person on whom a *bill of exchange is drawn to accept it on presentation.

non-amortizing mortgage *See* BALLOON MORTGAGE.

non-assented stock *See* ASSENTED STOCK.

non-borrowed reserves The reserves that a US bank has acquired by banking business and not through borrowing from the Federal Reserve.

non-business days *See* BANK HOLIDAYS.

noncallable bonds Bonds that cannot be redeemed by the issuer before their maturity date. *Compare* CALLABLE BONDS.

non-competitive bid A method of buying US Treasury securities that does not require the bidder to compete with others in the usual Dutch auction. The bids, which are submitted by smaller investors, are allocated at the average price paid by successful bidders in the competitive auction.

non-contributory pension A *pension in which the full premium is paid by an employer or the state and the pensioner makes no contribution. *Compare* CONTRIBUTORY PENSION.

non-cumulative preference share A *preference share that does not have the right to *dividends unpaid in previous years. *Compare* CUMULATIVE PREFERENCE SHARE.

non-domiciled Denoting a person whose country of *domicile is not the same as his or her country of residence for tax purposes.

non-equity share A *share in a company having any of the following characteristics:
• any of the rights of the share to receive payments are for a limited amount that is not calculated by reference to the company's assets or profits or the dividends on any class of equity share;
• any of the rights of the share to participate in a surplus on *liquidation are limited to a specific amount that is not calculated by reference to the company's assets or profits;
• the share is redeemable either according to its terms or because the holder, or any party other than the issuer, can require its redemption.

non-executive director A director of a company who is not involved in the day-to-day management of the business but who is appointed to bring independent judgment on issues of strategy, performance, resources, and standards of conduct. The Cadbury Report on corporate governance recommended the appointment of non-executive directors.

nonlinearity A property of *options, expressing the fact that there is no linear relationship between their value and the value of the *underlying.

non-marketable securities Securities that are not sold on financial markets, notably (in the UK) savings bonds and National Savings Certificates.

non-monetary benefits and costs Those aspects of an employment that are not connected with its financial remuneration. They include the employees' subjective opinion of their working environment, the stimulation or boredom of the work itself, the companionship or isolation experienced in their place of work, the distance travelled to reach work, etc. These aspects of an employment, together with the salary, bonuses, commission, and fringe benefits, make employees decide either to stay in their present jobs or seek another.

non-negotiable instruments *See* NEGOTIABLE INSTRUMENT.

non-obligatory expenditure Expenditure that has been initiated by the European Parliament as an amendment to European Union budgets; it does not derive from the treaty obligations of the Union. *Compare* OBLIGATORY EXPENDITURE.

non-participating preference share A *preference share that does not carry a right to participate in the profits of a company beyond a fixed rate of *dividend. This is the most common type of preference share.

non-performing loan **1.** A loan on which the interest payments or capital are overdue. **2.** In the USA, as defined by the regulators, a category of loan more than 90 days in arrears. **3.** Third World debts to clearing banks on which interest payments ceased in the 1980s.

non-recourse finance A bank loan in which the lending bank is only entitled to repayment from the profits of the project the loan is funding and not from other resources of the borrower.

non-resident The status of an individual who has never lived in a particular country for fiscal purposes or who has moved to another country, either for employment or permanently. This person's liability to tax in the first country is restricted to income from sources within that country. Interest on all British government stocks is exempt from UK tax for non-residents. *See also* RESIDENT; DOUBLE TAXATION.

non-revolving bank facility A loan from a bank to a company in which the company has a period (often several years) in which to make its *drawdowns, as well as flexibility with regard to the amount and timing of the drawdowns, but once drawn an amount takes on the characteristics of a *term loan. *Compare* REVOLVING BANK FACILITY.

non-statutory accounts Any *balance sheet or *profit and loss account dealing with a financial period of a company that does not form part of the *statutory accounts. An example is the early announcement of annual results. Prior to the Companies Act 1989 non-statutory accounts were known as abridged accounts.

non-systematic risk *See* SPECIFIC RISK.

non-taxable income Income that is specifically exempt from tax. This includes interest from *Individual Savings Accounts, the increase in value of National Savings Certificates, premium bond prizes, the capital part of the yearly amount received from a purchased life annuity, some social security benefits, prizes and betting winnings (including the National Lottery), *savings related share option scheme (SAYE) account bonuses, shares allotted by an employer under an approved profit-sharing scheme, and statutory redundancy pay.

non-underwritten Denoting an issue (particularly of *euronotes) that is not underwritten, but rather is subject to best efforts to sell. Non-underwritten issues are common in money markets. *See* UNDERWRITER.

no-par-value Denoting a share issued by a company that has no *par value (*see also* NOMINAL PRICE). Dividends on such shares are quoted as an amount of money per share rather than as a percentage of the nominal price. No-par-value shares are not allowed by UK law but they are issued by some US and Canadian companies.

normal distribution (Gaussian distribution) The symmetrical bell-shaped frequency curve formed when the frequency of a range of values is plotted on the vertical axis against the value of a random variable. The bell shape indicates that extreme values (both large and small) occur infrequently, while the more frequent occurrences are clustered around the *arithmetic mean value, which in a normal distribution is also equal to the *median and the mode (the value that occurs most frequently).

A wide variety of natural, social, and economic phenomena fall approximately into a normal distribution, which is therefore an important concept in determining the probability of uncertain events. For a normal distribution, one *standard deviation (SD) either side of the mean covers 68% (34% + 34%) of observed values (or the area under the curve); for two SDs it covers 95% and for three SDs it covers 99%. *Compare* GAMMA DISTRIBUTION; LEPTOKURTIC DISTRIBUTION.

Normal Market Size (NMS) A classification system for trading in securities, which replaced the alpha, beta, gamma, and delta classification used on the *London Stock Exchange in January 1991. The old system had developed in a way that, contrary to the original intention, had made it a measure of corporate virility. NMS is the minimum size of the package of shares in a company traded in normal-sized market transactions; there are 12 categories. The main purpose of the system is to fix the size of transactions in which *market makers are obliged to deal, and to set a basis on which the bargains should be published.

normal retirement age The age of an individual when he or she retires. At present this is normally 65 for a man and 60 for a woman in the UK. It is at these ages that state pensions begin. However, other policies can nominate other pre-agreed dates, which the Inland Revenue will accept in certain cases. The inequality between a man's normal retirement age and a woman's retirement age in the UK will be ended in 2010, when both sexes will qualify for state pensions at 65.

normal yield curve A *yield curve in which the yield rises in proportion to the length of time the security has to run until maturity.

North American Free Trade Agreement (NAFTA) A trade agreement between the USA, Canada, and Mexico that removes all trade *tariffs between them for a 10-year period. It was concluded between the USA and Canada in 1988, with Mexico joining in 1992. There are currently negotiations to include Chile.

nostro account A bank account conducted by a UK bank with a bank in another country, usually in the currency of that country. *Compare* VOSTRO ACCOUNT.

notary public A legal practitioner, usually a solicitor, who is empowered to attest deeds and other documents and notes (*see* NOTING) dishonoured *bills of exchange.

note 1. A *promissory note. **2.** A negotiable record of an unsecured loan (*see* COMMERCIAL PAPER). The word 'note' is now used in preference to *bond when the principal sum is repayable in less than five years. **3.** A *banknote. **4.** An inscription on an unpaid *bill of exchange (*see* NOTING) made by a *notary public.

note issuance (or **purchase**) **facility (NIF)** A means of enabling short-term borrowers in the *eurocurrency markets to issue euronotes, with maturities of less than one year, when the need arises rather than having to arrange a separate issue of euronotes each time they need to borrow. A **revolving underwriting facility (RUF)** achieves the same objective.

notes to the accounts (notes to financial statements) Information supporting that given on the face of a company's *financial statements. Many notes are required to be given by law, including those detailing *capital assets, investments, *share capital, *debentures, and *reserves. Other information may be required by accounting standards or be given to facilitate the users' understanding of the company and its current and future performance; social and environmental information, for example, falls into this category.

notice day The day on which notice must be given that goods will be supplied to fulfil a commodity-market contract, rather than having it cancelled out by a matching contract.

notice in lieu of distringas *See* STOP NOTICE.

noting The procedure adopted if a *bill of exchange has been dishonoured by non-acceptance or by non-payment. Not later than the next business day after the day on which it was dishonoured, the holder has to hand it to a *notary public to be noted. The notary re-presents the bill; if it is still unaccepted or unpaid, the notary notes the circumstances in a register and also on a **notarial ticket**, which has to be attached to the bill. The noting can then, if necessary, be extended to a *protest.

notional income Income that is not received although it might be deemed to be properly chargeable to income tax.

not negotiable Words marked on a *bill of exchange indicating that it ceases to be a *negotiable instrument, i.e. although it can still be negotiated, the holder cannot obtain a better title to it than the person from whom it was obtained, thus providing a safeguard if it is stolen. A cheque is the only form of bill that can be crossed 'not negotiable'; other forms must have it inscribed on their faces.

novation The replacement of one legal agreement by a new obligation, with the agreement of all the parties. For example, on exchanges using the *London Clearing House (LCH), transactions between members are novated by the LCH, so that one contract is created between the buyer and LCH while a matching contract is created between the seller and LCH (*see* COUNTERPARTY RISK).

NOW Abbreviation for *negotiable order of withdrawal.

NPV Abbreviation for *net present value.

NRV Abbreviation for *net realizable value.

NSB Abbreviation for *National Savings Bank.

NSC Abbreviation for National Savings Certificates. *See* NATIONAL SAVINGS.

NSCC Abbreviation for *National Securities Clearing Corporation.

nudum pactum (Latin: nude contract) An agreement that is unenforceable in British law because no consideration is mentioned. *See* CONTRACT.

numbered account A bank account identified only by a number. This service, offered by some Swiss banks at one time, encouraged funds that had been obtained illegally to find their way to Switzerland. A numbered account is now more frequently used to ensure legitimate privacy.

NV Abbreviation for *Naamloze Vennootschap*. It appears after the name of a Dutch company, being equivalent to the British abbreviation plc (denoting a public limited company). *Compare* BV.

NYFE Abbreviation for *New York Futures Exchange.

NYMEX Abbreviation for *New York Mercantile Exchange.

NYSE Abbreviation for *New York Stock Exchange.

objectivity An accounting concept attempting to ensure that any subjective actions taken by the preparer of *accounts are minimized. The aim of the rules and regulations required to achieve objectivity is that users should be able to compare *financial statements for different companies over a period with some confidence that the statements have been prepared on the same basis. One of the major advantages claimed for *historical cost accounting is that it is objective, but necessarily some subjective decisions will have been made.

obligation **1.** The duty of a borrower to repay a loan and that of the lender to ensure that repayment is made. **2.** A bond or other promise to pay a sum of money.

obligatory expenditure The spending of the European Union, governed by such treaties as the Common Agricultural Policy and the European Regional Development Fund. The European Parliament can add to the amount spent but if it wishes to reduce it, it must obtain the agreement of the Council of Ministers, or reject the whole of the Union Budget in that year.

OBSF Abbreviation for *off-balance-sheet finance.

occupational pension scheme A pension scheme open to employees within a certain trade or profession or working for a particular firm. An occupational pension scheme can either be insured or self-administered. If it is insured, an insurance company pays the benefits under the scheme in return for having the premiums to invest. In a self-administered scheme, the pension-fund trustees are responsible for investing the contributions themselves. In order to run an occupational pension scheme, an organization must satisfy the Occupational Pension Board that the scheme complies with the conditions allowing employers to contract out of the *State Earnings-Related Pension Scheme (SERPS). Since 1997 it has not been possible to accrue any SERPS while being a member of a contracted-out occupational or *personal pension scheme. *See also* DEFINED-BENEFIT PENSION SCHEME.

odd lot *See* ROUND LOT.

OECD Abbreviation for *Organization for Economic Cooperation and Development.

off-balance-sheet finance (OBSF) A method of financing a company's activities so that some or all of the finance and the corresponding assets do not appear on the *balance sheet of the company. By making use of OBSF a company can enhance its accounting ratios, such as the *gearing ratio and *return on capital employed, and also avoid breaking any agreements it has made with the banks in respect of the total amount it may borrow. It has been possible for companies, by drawing up complex legal agreements, to conduct off-balance-sheet finance and thus mislead the user of the accounts. The accounting profession has attempted to counter these practices by emphasizing that accounting should reflect the commercial reality of transactions and not simply their legal form. Financial Reporting Standard 5, 'Reporting the Substance of Transactions' introduced a general requirement that the financial statements should reflect the substance of transactions. In addition to this general requirement it provides specific guidance for certain transactions, such as

*factoring and consignment stock, for which companies have previously used off-balance-sheet finance.

off-balance-sheet instrument A *derivative that does not have to be disclosed on a firm's *balance sheet.

off-balance-sheet reserve *See* HIDDEN RESERVE.

offer The price at which a seller makes it known that he is willing to sell something. If there is an *acceptance of the offer a legally binding *contract has been entered into. In law, an offer is distinguished from an **invitation to treat**, which is an invitation by one person or firm to others to make an offer. An example of an invitation to treat is to display goods in a shop window. *See also* OFFER PRICE; QUOTATION.

offer by prospectus An offer to the public of a new issue of shares or debentures made directly by means of a *prospectus, a document giving a detailed account of the aims, objects, and capital structure of the company, as well as its past history. The prospectus must conform to the provisions of the Companies Act 1985. *Compare* OFFER FOR SALE.

offer document A document sent to the shareholders of a company that is the subject of a *takeover bid. It gives details of the offer being made and usually provides shareholders with reasons for accepting the terms of the offer.

offer for sale An invitation to the general public to purchase the stock of a company through an intermediary, such as an *issuing house or *merchant bank (*compare* OFFER BY PROSPECTUS); it is one of the most frequently used means of *flotation. An offer for sale can be in one of two forms: at a fixed price (the more usual), which requires some form of balloting or rationing if the demand for the shares exceeds supply; or an *issue by tender, in which case individuals offer to purchase a fixed quantity of stock at or above some minimum price and the stock is allocated to the highest bidders. In the USA an offer for sale is called a **public offering**. *Compare* INTRODUCTION; PLACING; PUBLIC ISSUE.

offering memorandum A document outlining the terms of an offer to sell securities privately.

offer price The price at which a security is offered for sale by a *market maker and also the price at which an institution will sell units in a unit trust. *Compare* BID.

offer to purchase *See* TAKEOVER BID.

Office for National Statistics The UK government's statistical unit, formed by a merger of the **Central Statistical Office** and the Office of Population Censuses and Surveys in 1996. It is an executive agency of the Treasury responsible for collecting economic statistics for the government. Among its publications are the **Monthly Digest of Statistics*, **Financial Statistics* (monthly), *Economic Trends* (monthly), **UK National Accounts* (the *Blue Book*; annual), **UK Balance of Payments* (the *Pink Book*; annual), and the *Annual Abstract of Statistics*.

Office of Fair Trading (OFT) A government department that, under the Director General of Fair Trading, reviews commercial activities in the UK and aims to protect the consumer against unfair practices. Established in 1973, its responsibilities include the Fair Trading Act 1973, the Consumer Credit Act 1974, the Restrictive Trade Practices Act 1976, the Estate Agents Act 1979, the Competition Act 1980, the Control of Misleading Advertisements Regulations 1988, and the Broadcasting Act

1990. It is also the UK authority responsible for the application of the competition rules of the European Commission. Its five main areas of activity are: consumer affairs, consumer credit, monopolies and mergers, restrictive trade practices, and anti-competitive practices.

Office of Thrift Supervision (OTS) An agency of the US Treasury, founded in 1989, that supervises the country's *Savings and Loan associations.

officer of a company A person who acts in an official capacity in a company. Company officers include the directors, managers, the company secretary, and in some circumstances the company's auditors and solicitors. The Companies Act 1985 empowers a court dealing with a *liquidation to investigate the conduct of the company's officers with a view to recovering any money they may have obtained illegally or incorrectly.

Official List **1.** A list of all the securities traded on the *main market of the *London Stock Exchange. *See* LISTED SECURITY; LISTING REQUIREMENTS; YELLOW BOOK. **2.** A list prepared daily by the London Stock Exchange, recording all the bargains that have been transacted in listed securities during the day. It also gives dividend dates, rights issues, prices, and other information.

official rate The rate of exchange given to a currency by a government. If the official rate differs from the market rate, the government has to be prepared to support its official rate by buying or selling in the open market to make the two rates coincide.

official receiver (OR) A person appointed by the Secretary of State for Trade and Industry to act as a *receiver in *bankruptcy and winding-up cases. The High Court and each county court that has jurisdiction over insolvency matters has an official receiver, who is an officer of the court. Deputy official receivers may also be appointed. The official receiver commonly acts as the *liquidator of a company being wound up by the court.

off-market Describing a transaction on terms that are different from those prevailing on the market.

offset **1.** The right that enables a bank to seize any bank-account balances of a guarantor or debtor if a loan has been defaulted upon (*see also* GARNISHEE ORDER). **2.** A code on the magnetic strip of a plastic card that, together with the *personal identification number (PIN), verifies that the user of the card is entitled to use it. **3.** To cancel a futures contract or options contract by entering into a reverse agreement.

offsetting swap (mirror swap) A *swap in which cash flows exactly offset those of an existing swap.

offsetting transaction A transaction on futures or options markets to close out a previous transaction.

offshore banking The practice of offering financial services in locations that have attractive tax or regulatory advantages to non-residents. Offshore banking centres are based in many European countries, e.g. France, Switzerland, the Isle of Man, and Jersey, as well as the Middle East, the Caribbean, and Asia. These locations are often described as *tax havens because they can reduce customers' tax liabilities in entirely legal ways. *See* OFFSHORE FINANCIAL CENTRES.

offshore company **1.** A company not registered in the same country as that in which the persons investing in the company are resident. **2.** A company set up in a foreign country or *tax haven by a financial institution with the object of benefiting from tax laws or regulations in that country.

offshore financial centres Centres that provide advantageous deposit and lending rates to non-residents because of low taxation, liberal exchange controls, and low reserve requirements for banks. Some countries have made a lucrative business out of *offshore banking; the Cayman Islands is currently one of the world's largest offshore centres. In Europe, the Channel Islands and the Isle of Man are very popular. The USA and Japan have both established domestic offshore facilities enabling non-residents to conduct their business under more liberal regulations than domestic transactions. Their objective is to stop funds moving outside the country.

offshore fund 1. A fund that is based in a tax haven (offshore tax haven) outside the UK to avoid UK taxation. Offshore funds operate in the same way as *unit trusts but are not supervised by the Department of Trade and Industry. **2.** A fund held outside the country of residence of the holder. *See* OFFSHORE BANKING; OFFSHORE FINANCIAL CENTRES.

off-the-run issues Bonds that were issued some time ago. The market for such bonds is less active than that in new issues and they are likely to trade at wider spreads.

off-the-shelf company A company that is registered with the *Registrar of Companies although it does not trade and has no directors. It can, however, be sold and reformed into a new company with the minimum of formality and expense. Such companies are easily purchased from specialist brokers.

OFT Abbreviation for *Office of Fair Trading.

Old Lady of Threadneedle Street An affectionate name for the *Bank of England, coined by the English politician and dramatist R. B. Sheridan (1751–1816). The street in which the Bank stands (since 1734 in a Renaissance building by George Sampson) probably takes its name from the thread and needle used by the Merchant Taylors, a guild whose hall is in the same street.

Old Years The business years at *Lloyd's up to and including 1985, when heavy losses were made, largely as a result of national disasters as well as asbestosis and pollution claims from the USA (some going back for 40 years). *See also* NEWCO.

OM Abbreviation for the Swedish Options Market, which is based in Stockholm and London; it opened in 1985.

Ombudsman *See* FINANCIAL OMBUDSMAN SERVICE.

OMLX *See* LONDON SECURITIES AND DERIVATIVES EXCHANGE.

omnibus account An account held by one *financial intermediary in the name of another; it will be made up of numerous accounts of individual clients of the second intermediary.

OMV Abbreviation for *open-market value.

on-balance-sheet Denoting assets and liabilities that have to be reported on a firm's *balance sheet. *Compare* OFF-BALANCE-SHEET FINANCE; OFF-BALANCE-SHEET INSTRUMENT. *See also* HIDDEN RESERVE.

on demand Denoting any liability that may be subject to immediate repayment.

one-month money Money placed on the *money market for one month, i.e. it cannot be withdrawn without penalty during this period.

one-off A single transaction that is unlikely to be repeated and may in some cases be custom-made, for example a derivatives contract on the *over-the-counter market.

one-sided Describing a situation in which a price quote is only made in one direction, either bid or offer. It is a sign of an *illiquid market.

one-year money Money placed on the *money market for one year, i.e. it cannot be withdrawn without penalty for one year.

on stream Denoting that a specified investment or asset is providing the expected revenues.

on-the-run Describing *certificates of deposit issued by different banks that are nevertheless considered as identical, in order to make the market for them wider and more liquid.

OPEC Abbreviation for *Organization of Petroleum Exporting Countries.

open auction An *auction in which each participant is aware of the value of the others' bids.

open cheque *See* CHEQUE.

open contract A futures or traded option contract that has not been closed out. *See* OPEN INTEREST.

open credit Unlimited credit offered by a supplier to a trusted client.

open economy An economy in which a significant percentage of its goods and services are traded internationally. The degree of openness of an economy usually depends on the amount of overseas trade in which the country is involved or the political policies of its government. Thus the UK economy is relatively open, as the economy is significantly dependent on foreign trade, while the US economy is relatively closed as overseas trade is not as important to its economy.

open-end credit The US name for a *revolving credit.

open-ended investment company An investment business that operates an *open-end trust. It sells or buys unit trusts to meet market demand, the size of the fund depending on the number of units sold.

open-end trust (open-end fund; mutual fund) A form of *unit trust in which the managers of the trust may vary the investments held without notifying the unit holders. Open-end trusts are used in the USA.

opening bank The bank that opens a *letter of credit on the instructions of an importer in order to pay the exporter in another country.

opening prices The bid prices and offer prices made at the opening of a day's trading on any security or commodity market. The opening prices may not always be identical to the previous evening's *closing prices, especially if any significant events or movements in markets in another time zone have taken place during the intervening period.

opening stock The stock held by an organization at the beginning of an accounting period as raw materials, *work in progress, or finished goods. The closing stocks of one period become the opening stocks of the succeeding period and it is necessary to establish the level of closing stocks so that the cost of their creation is not charged against the profits of that period but brought forward as opening stocks to be charged against the profits of the succeeding period.

open interest 1. The total number of options contracts on a particular *underlying that are still open (i.e. they have not been exercised, offset, or permitted to expire). **2.** The total number of futures contracts on an underlying that are still outstanding (i.e. they have not reached their delivery date or been offset by other transactions).

open-market desk The part of the *Federal Reserve System that conducts *open-market operations under the supervision of the Open Market Committee.

open-market operations The purchase or sale by a central bank of bonds (gilt-edged securities) in exchange for money, with the aim of influencing monetary policy. Buying debt provides liquidity and selling debt reduces liquidity in the private banking sector.

open-market value (OMV) The value of an asset equal to the amount that a willing purchaser would be prepared to pay a willing vendor.

open-mouth operations The use of public statements by economic spokespersons (e.g. of the US Federal Reserve) to try to influence markets and the economy.

open outcry Quoting prices, making offers, bids, and acceptances, and concluding transactions by word of mouth in a *commodity market or *financial futures exchange, usually in a trading *pit. *See also* CALLOVER.

open position (naked position) A trading position that is unhedged (*see* HEDGE) against the underlying risk factors. *Compare* COVERED POSITION.

open years The first and second years in the normal three-year business cycle of syndicates at *Lloyd's. On this three-year cycle accounts are not closed until after the end of the third year to allow for late claims on the open years.

operating budget A forecast of the financial requirements for the future trading of an organization, including its planned sales, production, cash flow, etc. An operating budget is normally designed for a fixed period, usually one year, and forms the plan for that period's trading activities. Any divergences from it are usually monitored and, if appropriate, changes can then be made to it as the period progresses.

operating lease A lease under which an asset is hired out to a lessee or lessees for a period that is substantially shorter than its useful economic life. Under an operating lease, some of the risks and rewards of the ownership of the leased asset remain with the lessor. *Statement of Standard Accounting Practice 21, 'Accounting for Leases and Hire Purchase Contracts', defines an operating lease as a lease other than a *finance lease.

operating profit/loss The profit or loss made by a company as a result of its principal trading activity. This is arrived at by deducting its **operating expenses** from its *trading profit, or adding its operating expenses to its trading loss; in either case this is before taking into account any extraordinary items.

operating statement A financial and quantitative statement provided for the management of an organization to record the performance achieved by that area of the operation for which the management is responsible, for a selected budget period. An operating statement may include production levels, costs incurred, and (where appropriate) revenue generated, all compared with budgeted amounts and the performance in previous periods.

operating target The total of the reserves, non-borrowed reserves, and Federal funds rate that govern the open-market operation of the *Federal Reserve System of the USA.

operational gearing (operational leverage) The ratio of a company's fixed costs to its total costs. The higher the level of operational gearing, the greater the risk, since fixed costs have to be covered before a profit can be recorded.

operational risk The *risk of direct or indirect loss resulting from inadequate or failed internal processes and systems, or from a wide variety of external events. The control of operational risk has been the object of much attention in recent years, for example in the *Basle Two accord concerning the *capital adequacy of banks and in the *Turnbull Report in the UK. It has also led to changes in the regulation of financial institutions and the requirements for the listing of public companies (*see* LISTING REQUIREMENTS).

OPIC Abbreviation for *Overseas Private Investment Corporation.

opportunity cost The economic cost of an action measured in terms of the benefit foregone by not pursuing the best alternative course of action. The cost of funds, for example, must be measured in terms of the returns they could earn in the capital markets for taking the same degree of risk. Opportunity cost is an important factor in decision making (*see* COST-BENEFIT ANALYSIS), although it represents costs that are not recorded in the accounts of the relevant organization.

option The right to buy or sell a fixed quantity of a commodity, currency, or security at a particular date at a particular price (the *exercise price). Unlike futures, the purchaser of an option is not obliged to buy or sell at the exercise price and will only do so if it is profitable; if the option is allowed to lapse, the purchaser loses only the initial purchase price of the option (the *option money).

An option to buy is known as a **call option** and is usually purchased in the expectation of a rising price; an option to sell is called a **put option** and is bought in the expectation of a falling price or to protect a profit on an investment. Options, like futures, allow individuals and firms to *hedge against the risk of wide fluctuations in prices; they also allow speculators to gamble for large profits with limited initial payments. Professional traders in options make use of a large range of potential strategies, often purchasing combinations of options that reflect particular expectations or cover several contingencies (*see* BUTTERFLY; STRADDLE).

In a **European option** the buyer can only exercise the right to take up the option or let it lapse on the *expiry date, whereas with an **American option** this right can be exercised at any time up to the expiry date. European options are therefore cheaper than American options. *See also* EXERCISE NOTICE; INTRINSIC VALUE; OPTION TO DOUBLE; TIME VALUE; TRADED OPTIONS.

option-adjusted analysis A technique for valuing a security with an embedded option.

option-adjusted duration A technique for calculating the *duration of a security with an embedded option.

option-adjusted spread A technique for valuing an embedded option in terms of a rate of interest.

option class A category of *traded options consisting of options of the same type (i.e. call or put) based on the same *underlying.

option dealer A dealer who buys and sells either *traded options or traditional options.

option money The price paid for an *option. The cost of a call option is often known as the **call money** and that for a put option as the **put money**. In traded options the option money is usually called the *premium.

option period The time during which an option remains open, i.e. before the final choice as to exercise has to be made.

option strategies The trading of *options with varying exercise prices and maturities to obtain different payoff profiles on the same *underlying.

option to double 1. An *option by a seller to sell double the quantity of securities for which an option has been sold, if so desired. In some markets this is called a **put-of-more option**. **2.** An option by a buyer to buy double the quantity of securities for which an option has been bought, if so desired. In some markets this is called a **call-of-more option**.

option to purchase 1. A right given to shareholders to buy shares in certain companies in certain circumstances at a reduced price. **2.** A right purchased or given to a person to buy something at a specified price on or before a specified date. Until the specified date has passed, the seller undertakes not to sell the property to anyone else and not to withdraw it from sale.

option writer The individual or organization selling an *option.

OR Abbreviation for *official receiver.

order *See* LIMIT; MARKET ORDER; STOP-LOSS ORDER.

order cheque *See* CHEQUE.

order-driven Denoting a market in which prices are determined by the publication of orders to buy or sell shares, with the objective of attracting a counterparty. *See* SETS. *Compare* QUOTE-DRIVEN.

ordinary resolution A resolution that is valid if passed by a majority of the votes cast at a general meeting of a British company. No notice that the resolution is to be proposed is required.

ordinary share A fixed unit of the *share capital of a company. Shares in publicly owned *listed companies are usually traded on *stock exchanges and represent one of the most important types of security for investors. Shares yield dividends, representing a proportion of the profits of a company (*compare* FIXED-INTEREST SECURITY; PREFERENCE SHARE). In the long term, ordinary shares, by means of *capital growth, yield higher rewards, on average, than most alternative forms of securities, which compensates for the greater element of risk they entail. *See also* CONVERTIBLE; GROWTH STOCKS.

ordinary share capital The total *share capital of a company consisting of *ordinary shares.

öre A monetary unit of Sweden worth one hundredth of a *krona.

øre A monetary unit of Denmark, the Faeroe Islands, Greenland, and Norway. It is worth one hundredth of a *krone.

organic growth *See* INTERNAL GROWTH.

organizational culture The values, customs, rituals, and norms shared by all the members of an organization, which have to be learnt and accepted by new members of the organization. It is argued that there are at least three different types of organizational culture. In an **integrative culture** the objective is to obtain a consensus regarding the values and basic assumptions of the organization and to produce consistent actions. This integration brings unity, predictability, and clarity to work experiences. In a **differentiated culture**, subcultures develop that have internal consensus about values and basic assumptions but differ greatly between each subculture; this produces inconsistencies throughout the organization. In a **fragmentation culture** there are multiple interpretations of values and assumptions, which produce great ambiguity. This ambiguity can arise from fast changes within the organization, the growing diversity of the workforce, and the increasingly global environment with which organizations are faced.

organization chart A chart illustrating the structure of an organization; in particular it will show for which function of the business each manager is responsible and the chain of responsibility throughout the organization. Some organization charts include managers by name; others show the management positions in the structure.

Organization for Economic Cooperation and Development (OECD) An organization formed in 1961, replacing the *Organization for European Economic Cooperation (OEEC), to promote cooperation among industralized member countries on economic and social policies. Its objectives are to assist member countries in formulating policies designed to achieve high economic growth while maintaining financial stability, contributing to world trade on a multilateral basis, and stimulating members' aid to developing countries. Members are Australia, Austria, Belgium, Canada, the Czech Republic, Denmark, Finland, France, Germany, Greece, Hungary, Iceland, Ireland, Italy, Japan, South Korea, Luxembourg, Mexico, The Netherlands, New Zealand, Norway, Poland, Portugal, Slovakia, Spain, Sweden, Switzerland, Turkey, UK, and the USA. Its headquarters are in Paris.

Organization for European Economic Cooperation (OEEC) An organization set up after World War II to administer the US Marshall Plan for funding the rebuilding of war-ravaged Europe. Its major achievement was the European Recovery Programme. It became the *Organization for Economic Cooperation and Development (OECD) in 1961.

Organization of Petroleum Exporting Countries (OPEC) An organization created in 1960 to unify and coordinate the petroleum policies of member countries and to protect their interests, individually and collectively. In the 1970s OPEC was responsible for two major rises in the price of oil. Its influence then waned due to the development of non-OPEC oil fields. Its current members are Algeria, Indonesia, Iran, Iraq, Kuwait, Libya, Nigeria, Qatar, Saudi Arabia, the United Arab Emirates, and Venezuela.

organized market A formal market in a specific place in which buyers and sellers meet to trade according to agreed rules and procedures. Stock exchanges, *financial futures exchanges, and commodity markets are examples of organized markets.

origin 1. The country from which a commodity originates. **Shipment from origin** denotes goods that are shipped directly from their country of origin, rather than from stocks in some other place. **2.** The country from which a person comes. A person's country of origin is not necessarily that person's country of *domicile or the country in which he or she is *resident.

original maturity *See* MATURITY DATE.

originating exchange The exchange in which an option was first purchased, as opposed to the exchange in which it is closed out.

OTC market Abbreviation for *over-the-counter market.

OTOB Abbreviation for the Austrian Futures and Options Exchange, which opened in 1991. Its prices are given in the Austrian Traded Index (ATX).

OTS Abbreviation for *Office of Thrift Supervision.

ouguiya (UM) The standard monetary unit of Mauritania, divided into 5 khoums.

out-barrier option An *option that is eliminated when the value of the *underlying reaches a certain level, at which point the initial premium is partly refunded. *Compare* IN-BARRIER OPTION.

outcry *See* CALLOVER.

out-of-the-money option *See* INTRINSIC VALUE.

output tax The VAT that a trader adds to the price of the goods or services supplied. The trader must account for this output tax to HM Customs and Excise, having first deducted the *input tax.

outright forward A contract to buy or sell a currency at a fixed price in the future, without a corresponding offsetting transaction.

outside broker A stockbroker who is not a member of a stock exchange but acts as an intermediary between the public and a stockbroker who is a member.

outside director In the USA, a person who is a member of the board of directors of a company but is not an employee of the company and has no executive responsibilities. Such directors are appointed because they offer either wide business experience or specialist knowledge not available from the *executive directors.

outside purchase/sale The buying/selling of Treasury bills and other government financial instruments to increase/reduce the US banking system's reserves.

overall return The total profit on a transaction before taxation. For example, the overall return on an investment in shares could consist of *dividends received plus any profit realized on selling the shares.

overborrowed *See* OVERGEARED.

overbought 1. Having purchased more of a good than one needs or has orders for. **2.** Having purchased more securities or commodities than are covered by margins deposited with a broker or dealer. In a falling market, for example, a bull speculator can become overbought without having made a fresh purchase.

3. Denoting a market that has been pushed up by excessive buying. An overbought market is likely to fall if unsupported. *Compare* OVERSOLD.

overcapitalization A condition in which an organization has too much *capital for the needs of its business. If a business has more capital than it needs it is likely to be overburdened by interest charges or by the need to spread profits too thinly by way of dividends to shareholders. Businesses can now reduce overcapitalization by repaying long-term debts or by buying their own shares.

over-collateralized Denoting an *asset-backed security in which the level of *credit enhancement is such that the collateral is greater than the principal.

overdraft A loan made to a customer with a cheque account at a bank or building society, in which the account is allowed to go into debit, usually up to a specified limit (the **overdraft limit**). Interest is charged on the daily debit balance. This is a less costly way of borrowing than taking a *bank loan at the same interest rate as, with an overdraft, credits are taken into account.

overfunding A policy available to the UK government in which it sells more government securities than it needs to pay for public spending. The objective of the policy is to absorb surplus money and so curb *inflation.

overgeared (overborrowed) Denoting a company with excessively high capital *gearing, i.e. one in which fixed interest loan stock and preference shares far outweigh its ordinary share capital.

overhanging Denoting the shares left in the hands of *underwriters when a *new issue of shares has not been fully absorbed by the market. *See also* MARKET OVERHANG.

overhead A fixed, indirect cost of doing business, i.e. one that does not vary with the volume of goods produced or services supplied. Major business overheads include rent, rates, depreciation, and costs arising from maintenance and administration.

overheating The state of an economy during a boom, with increasing aggregate demand leading to rising prices rather than higher output. Overheating reflects the inability of some firms to increase output as fast as demand; they therefore profit from the excess demand by raising prices.

overinsurance The practice of insuring an item for a greater amount than its value. This is pointless as insurers are only obliged to pay the full value (usually the replacement value) of an insured item and no more, even if the sum insured exceeds this value. If insurers find a policyholder has overinsured an item, the premium for the cover above the true value is returned.

overinvestment Excessive investment of capital, especially in the manufacturing industry towards the end of a boom as a result of over-optimistic expectations of future demand. When the boom begins to fade, the manufacturer is left with surplus capacity and can therefore make no further capital investments, which itself creates unemployment and fuels the imminent recession. It is often seen with new technology investment booms.

overlay portfolio management An investment strategy in which the overall allocation of a *portfolio is undertaken by a strategic manager, while the asset allocation is made by individual market specialists.

overnight money *See* DAY-TO-DAY MONEY.

overnight position An *open position held overnight.

overnight repo A method of overcoming a short-term shortage of funds on the *money market using *repurchase agreements (repos) on an overnight basis. Their use was developed in the USA but they are now used elsewhere.

overseas company A company incorporated outside the UK that has a branch or a subsidiary company in the UK. Overseas companies with a place of business in the UK have to make a return to the Registrar of Companies, giving particulars of their memorandum of association, directors, and secretary as well as providing an annual balance sheet and profit and loss account.

overseas-income taxation Income that has been subject to taxation outside the jurisdiction of the UK tax authorities. When the same income is subject to taxation in more than one country, relief for the double tax is given either under the provisions of the *double taxation agreement with the country concerned or unilaterally.

overseas investment Investment by the government, industry, or members of the public of a country in the industry of another country. For members of the public this is often achieved by investing through foreign stock exchanges.

overseas joint ownership A *joint venture in which a company joins investors in a foreign market to create a local business in which the company shares ownership and control.

Overseas Private Investment Corporation (OPIC) A US government organization that lends to developing nations and underwrites loan guarantees. It was formed in 1961 to support private investment in developing countries. *See also* RUSSIAN COUNTRY FUND.

overshooting A jump in the value of an asset followed by a slow adjustment to equilibrium. Overshooting has been used as an explanation of exchange-rate movements arising from adjustment problems in economies.

oversold 1. Having sold more of a product or service than one can produce or purchase. **2.** Denoting a market that has fallen too fast as a result of excessive selling. It may therefore be expected to have an upward reaction.

oversubscription A situation that arises when there are more applications for a *new issue of securities than there are securities available. In these circumstances, applications have to be scaled down according to a set of rules devised by the company issuing the shares or their advisors. Alternatively some companies prefer to allocate the shares by ballot (*see* ALLOTMENT). Oversubscription usually occurs because of the difficulty in arriving at an issue price that will be low enough to attract sufficient investors to take up the whole issue and yet will give the company the maximum capital. Speculative purchases by *stags also make it difficult to price a new issue so that it is neither oversubscribed nor undersubscribed. In the case of **undersubscription**, which is rare, the *underwriter has to take up that part of the issue that has not been bought by the public. Undersubscription can occur if some unexpected event occurs after the announcement of the issue price but before the issue date.

over-the-counter market (OTC market) A market in which financial obligations are bought and sold outside the jurisdiction of a recognized financial market; it was originally so named in the 1870s, from the practice of buying shares over bank counters in the USA. OTC markets are used for trading in specific tailor-made derivative products. The world's largest OTC market is the US *National Association of Securities Dealers Automated Quotation System (NASDAQ).

overtrading Trading by an organization beyond the resources provided by its existing capital. Overtrading tends to lead to *liquidity problems as too much stock is bought on credit and too much credit is extended to customers, so that ultimately there is not sufficient cash available to pay the debts as they arise. The solution is either to cut back on trading or to raise further permanent capital.

own-account transaction A transaction undertaken by a broker/dealer for his or her own benefit rather than that of a client.

owners' equity The funds of an organization that have been provided by its owners, i.e. its total assets less its total liabilities. The balance-sheet value of the owners' equity is unlikely to be equal to its market value.

ownership Rights over property, including rights of possession, exclusive enjoyment, destruction, etc. In UK common law, land cannot be owned outright, as all land belongs to the Crown and is held in tenure by the 'owner'. However, an owner of an estate in land in fee simple is to all intents and purposes an outright owner (*see* TITLE). In general, ownership can be split between different persons. For example, a trustee has the legal ownership of trust property but the beneficiary has the equitable or beneficial ownership. If goods are stolen, the owner still has ownership but not possession. Similarly, if goods are hired or pledged, the owner has ownership but no immediate right to possession.

own resources The funds owned outright by the European Union, rather than those contributed by its member states, e.g. 1% of VAT revenues within Europe go direct to the Union's funds.

own shares purchase The purchase or redemption of its own shares by a company; this is permitted subject to certain legal restrictions. For example, in the UK redeemable shares may only be redeemed if they are fully paid. If the redemption or purchase of a company's own shares would lead to a reduction of its capital, a *capital redemption reserve will need to be created. In certain cases private companies may reduce their capital in this way (*see* PERMISSIBLE CAPITAL PAYMENT).

PA **1.** Abbreviation for personal account, used to denote a transaction made by a professional investment advisor for his or her own account rather than for the firm for which he or she works. **2.** Abbreviation for *power of attorney.

pa'anga (T$) The standard monetary unit of Tonga, divided into 100 seniti.

Pacific Stock Exchange (PSE) The only stock market in the USA operating west of the Mississippi; it has trading floors in San Francisco and Los Angeles. It signed a cooperation deal in 1990 with the Taiwan Stock Exchange, seeing its future in linking with other exchanges bordering on the Pacific.

package deal An agreement that encompasses several different parts, all of which must be accepted. A package deal may have involved either or both parties in making concessions on specific aspects of the package in order to arrive at a compromise arrangement.

paid-up policy An *endowment assurance policy in which the assured has decided to stop paying premiums before the end of the policy term. This results in a *surrender value, which instead of being returned in cash to the assured is used to purchase a single-premium *whole (of) life policy. In this way the life assurance protection continues (for a reduced amount), while the policyholder is relieved of the need to pay further premiums. If the original policy was a *with-profits policy, the bonuses paid up to the time the premiums ceased would be included in the surrender value. If it is a unit-linked policy, capital units actually allocated would be allowed to appreciate to the end of the term.

paid-up share A share the par value of which has been paid in full. *See* SHARE CAPITAL.

paid-up share capital (fully paid capital) The total amount of money that the shareholders of a company have paid to the company for their fully paid shares. *See* SHARE CAPITAL.

paisa (*plural* **paise**) A monetary unit of Bangladesh, Bhutan, India, Nepal, and Pakistan, worth one hundredth of a *rupee.

P & L account *See* PROFIT AND LOSS ACCOUNT.

Panel on Takeovers and Mergers *See* CITY CODE ON TAKEOVERS AND MERGERS.

paper An informal name for securities that can be bought and sold or held as an investment. It is used particularly on the *money market for *debt instruments maturing in less than 90 days. *See* COMMERCIAL PAPER; EURO-COMMERCIAL PAPER.

paper bid A *bid in which a company offers its own shares in exchange for those of the company it is trying to acquire.

paper gold *See* SPECIAL DRAWING RIGHTS.

paper money 1. Legal tender in the form of banknotes. **2.** Banknotes and any form of paper that can be used as money, such as cheques, *bills of exchange, promissory notes, etc., even though they are not legal tender.

paper profit A profit shown by the books or accounts of an organization, which may not be a *realized profit because the value of an asset has fallen below its book value, because the asset, although nominally showing a profit, has not actually been sold, or because some technicality of book-keeping might show an activity to be profitable when it is not. For example, a share that has risen in value since its purchase might show a paper profit but this would not be a real profit since the value of the share might fall again before it is sold.

paper trail *See* AUDIT TRAIL.

par *See* PAR VALUE; PAR OF EXCHANGE.

para A monetary unit of Serbia worth one hundredth of a *dinar.

parallel hedge A *hedge in which exposure to fluctuation in one foreign currency is matched by a purchase or sale of another currency, which is expected to move in sympathy with the first currency.

parallel money markets *Money markets in which banks, companies, and local government bodies can borrow or lend to each other without using traditional *discount houses. The primary parallel money market is the *interbank market.

parallel shift A vertical shift in the *yield curve, with the result that the new curve runs parallel to the old one.

par banking The US practice of one bank paying the full face value of a cheque drawn on another bank, without imposing a charge for encashment. Members of the *Federal Reserve System are obliged to comply with the rules of par banking.

par bond A security or financial instrument that is bought and sold at its face value, rather than at a discount or premium.

parent company (parent undertaking) *See* HOLDING COMPANY.

parenting The way in which the directors of the main holding company of a large group manage their relationships with the subsidiary companies or business units. The method by which control is exercised varies, with some firms concentrating on financial control and others on the broader strategic targets.

Pareto's Rule (80/20 rule) A rule originally applied by the economist Vilfredo Pareto (1848–1923) to income distribution, i.e. 80% of a nation's income is earned by 20% of the population. It can be widely extended; for example: 80% of value is locked up in 20% of inventory; 80% of car breakdowns can be fixed by 20% of the spare parts range; 80% of a company's profits will come from 20% of its product range; and 80% of system failures will be caused by 20% of possible causes. The rule can be used as a guide to managers: in deciding how to spend limited funds, priority should be given to the most significant 20% of problems. Once they are eliminated the 80/20 rule will again apply to the remainder.

pari passu (Latin: with equal step) Ranking equally. When a new issue of shares is said to rank *pari passu* with existing shares, the new shares carry the same dividend rights and winding-up rights as the existing shares. A *pari passu* bank loan is a new loan that ranks on level par with older loans.

Paris Bourse From January 1991, the only stock exchange in France, incorporating the six provincial stock exchanges in Bordeaux, Lille, Lyons, Marseilles, Nancy, and Nantes. The merger recognized the dominance of the Paris Bourse, which accounted for 95% of all trading in French securities. The **CAC** (Cotation Assistée en Continue) electronic trading system was introduced in 1988 and the Relit five-day rolling settlement system was launched in 1990, based on delivery against payment. Trading is carried out through 45 broker members of the exchange; the market's indicator is the **CAC General Index**, based on the prices of 250 shares, with a subsidiary CAC-40 developed for an *index futures contract.

Paris Club *See* GROUP OF TEN.

Paris Inter Bank Offered Rate (**PIBOR**) The French equivalent of the *London Inter Bank Offered Rate (LIBOR).

parity **1.** An equality between prices of commodities, currencies, or securities on separate markets. **2.** A fixed exchange rate. **3.** Another term for *par value.

parity grid *See* EUROPEAN MONETARY SYSTEM.

parking **1.** Putting company shares that one owns in the name of someone else or of nominees in order to hide their real ownership. This is often illegal. *See also* WAREHOUSING. **2.** Holding assets in a short-term riskless form pending an investment decision.

par of exchange The theoretical *rate of exchange between two currencies in which there is equilibrium between the supply and demand for each currency. The par value lies between the market buying and selling rates. *See also* MINT PAR OF EXCHANGE.

par priced Denoting a security that is trading at its *par value.

parquet A colloquial name for the *Paris Bourse.

partial delivery A delivery in part of a commodity or security in order to reduce potential liability.

partial loss *See* AVERAGE.

participated loan (**participation financing**) A large loan, exceeding the lending limit of an individual bank, that is shared among a group of lenders.

participating call/put An *option in which the holder receives only part of any favourable move in the value of the *underlying.

participating cap An interest-rate *cap in which the protection afforded to the lender is considered inadequate from a *risk-management perspective.

participating interest An interest held by one organization in the shares of another organization, provided these shares are held on a long-term basis for the purpose of exercising some measure of control over the organization's activities. Options to buy shares are normally treated as an interest in these shares.

participating preference share *See* PREFERENCE SHARE.

participation financing *See* PARTICIPATED LOAN.

participator Any person having an interest in the capital or income of a company, e.g. a shareholder, loan creditor, or any person entitled to participate in the *distributions of the company.

partly paid shares Shares on which the full nominal or *par value has not been paid. Formerly, partly paid shares were issued by some banks and insurance companies to inspire confidence, i.e. because they could always call on their shareholders for further funds if necessary. Shareholders, however, did not like the liability of being called upon to pay out further sums for their shares and the practice largely died out. It has been revived for large new share issues, especially in *privatizations, in which shareholders pay an initial sum for their shares and subsequently pay one or more *calls on specified dates (*see also* SHARE CAPITAL).

partnership An association of two or more people formed for the purpose of carrying on a business. Partnerships are governed by the Partnership Act 1890. Unlike an incorporated *company, a partnership does not have a legal personality of its own and therefore partners are liable for the debts of the firm. **General partners** are fully liable for these debts, **limited partners** only to the extent of their investment. A **limited partnership** is one consisting of both general and limited partners and is governed by the Limited Partnership Act 1907. A **partnership-at-will** is one for which no fixed term has been agreed. Any partner may end the partnership at any time provided that notice is given of the intention to do so to all the other partners. **Nominal partners** are those who allow their names to be used for the benefit of the partnership, usually for a reward but not for a share of the profits. They are not legal partners.

Partnerships are usually governed by a *partnership agreement.

partnership accounts The accounts kept by a *partnership. They include an *appropriation account in which the *profit of a *partnership is shared between the partners in accordance with the *partnership agreement. This may be in the form of salaries, interest on capital, and a share of the profit in the appropriate *profit-sharing ratio. Each partner also has a *capital account and a *current account. The former is used to account for capital contributions, *goodwill, and revaluations; the latter for all other transactions, such as appropriations of profit and drawings.

partnership agreement (articles of partnership) An agreement made between the partners of a *partnership. In the absence of either an express or an implied agreement the provisions of the Partnership Act 1890 apply. These provisions are also applicable if an agreement is silent on a particular point. The provisions are:
- partners share equally in the *profits or losses of the partnership;
- partners are not entitled to receive salaries;
- partners are not entitled to interest on their capital;
- partners may receive interest at 5% per annum on any advances over and above their agreed capital;
- a new partner may not be introduced unless all the existing partners consent;
- a retiring partner is entitled to receive interest at 5% per annum on his or her share of the partnership assets retained in the partnership after his or her retirement;
- on dissolution of the partnership the assets of the firm must be used first to repay outside creditors, secondly to repay partners' advances, and thirdly to repay partners' capital. Any residue on dissolution should be distributed to the partners in the *profit-sharing ratio.

The Limited Liability Partnerships Act 2000 provides for businesses to combine a partnership with the advantage of limited liability (*see* LIMITED COMPANY).

par value (face value; nominal value) The *nominal price of a share or other security. If the market value of a security exceeds the nominal price it is said to be above par; if it falls below the nominal price it is **below par**. Gilt-edged securities are always repayed **at par** (usually £100), i.e. at the par value.

passing a name The disclosure by a firm of brokers of the name of the principal for whom they are acting. In some commodity trades, if brokers disclose the names of their buyers to the sellers, they do not guarantee the buyers' solvency, although they may do so in some circumstances. However, if brokers do not pass their principals' names, it is usual for them to guarantee their solvency. Thus, to remain anonymous, a buyer may have to pay an additional brokerage.

passing off Conducting a business in a manner that misleads the public into thinking that one's goods or services are those of another business. The commonest form of passing off is marketing goods with a design, packaging, or trade name that is very similar to that of someone else's goods. It is not necessary to prove an intention to deceive; innocent passing off is actionable.

passing the book Transferring the management of a financial position from one office of a business to another in a different time zone to take advantage of *twenty-four-hour trading.

passive management A style of *portfolio management that involves holding assets over the long term and, in many cases, tracking a market index. *Compare* ACTIVE MANAGEMENT.

pass-through A type of asset securitization in which payments on the underlying asset are 'passed-through' to the holders of the security. *See* GINNIE MAE.

past-due loan A banking loan on which the interest is more than 90 days overdue. After this *grace period has elapsed, the borrower becomes liable for late charges.

pataca (MOP) The standard monetary unit of Macao, divided into 100 avos.

patent The grant of an exclusive right to exploit an invention. In the UK patents are granted by the Crown through the *Patent Office, which is part of the Department of Trade and Industry. An applicant for a patent (usually the inventor or the inventor's employer) must show that the invention is new, is not obvious, and is capable of industrial application. An expert known as a **patent agent** often prepares the application, which must describe the invention in considerable detail. The Patent Office publishes these details if it grants a patent. A patent remains valid for 20 years from the date of application (the **priority date**) provided that the person to whom it has been granted (the **patentee**) continues to pay the appropriate fees. During this time, the patentee may assign the patent or grant licences to use it. Such transactions are registered in a public register at the Patent Office. If anyone infringes the patentee's monopoly, the patentee may sue for an *injunction and *damages or an account of profits. However, a patent from the Patent Office gives exclusive rights in the UK only: the inventor must obtain a patent from the European Patent Office in Munich and patents in other foreign countries to protect the invention elsewhere.

Patent Office A UK government office that administers the Patent Acts, the Registered Designs Act, and the Trade Marks Act. It also deals with questions relating to the Copyright Acts and provides an information service about *patent specifications.

path-dependent option An *exotic option in which the payoff is determined by the path taken by the value of the *underlying. An example of such an option is a so-called *Asian option, in which the payoff is the average value of the underlying over a period of time.

pathfinder prospectus An outline prospectus concerning the flotation of a new company in the UK; it includes enough details to test the market reaction to the new company but not its main financial details or the price of its shares. Pathfinder prospectuses are known in the USA as **red herrings**.

pawnbroker A person who lends money against the security of valuable goods used as collateral. Borrowers can reclaim their goods by repaying the loan and interest within a stated period. However, if the borrower defaults, the pawnbroker is free to sell the goods. The operation of pawnbrokers is governed by the Consumer Credit Act 1974.

payable to bearer Describing a *bill of exchange in which neither the payee or endorsee are named. A holder, by adding his or her name, can make the bill *payable to order.

payable to order Describing a *bill of exchange in which the payee is named and on which there are no restrictions or endorsements; it can therefore be paid to the endorsee.

pay and file A former procedure for paying *corporation tax introduced in the UK for *accounting periods ended after 30 September 1993. Corporation tax is due nine months after the end of the accounting period. Under the pay-and-file system, the company had to file a detailed return within twelve months of the end of the accounting period. Previously, estimated assessments were issued by the Inland Revenue if the finalized computations were not available. Since 1999 pay and file has been replaced by *self-assessment, which was extended to companies in June of that year.

pay-as-you-earn *See* PAYE.

payback period The period required for a project to repay its initial outlay. This is usually projected on the assumption that any further recoveries are then pure profit. This is a relatively unsophisticated method of appraising a capital project (*compare* DISCOUNTED CASH FLOW; NET PRESENT VALUE), although it is frequently used in industry. *See also* INTERNAL RATE OF RETURN.

payback period method A method of *capital budgeting in which the time required before the projected cash inflows for a project equal the investment expenditure is calculated; this time is compared to a required *payback period to determine whether or not the project should be considered for approval. If the projected cash inflows are constant annual sums, after an initial capital investment the following formula may be used:

payback (years) = initial capital investment/annual cash inflow.

Otherwise, the annual cash inflows are accumulated and the year determined when the cumulative inflows equal the investment expenditure. The method is sometimes seen as a measure of the risk involved in the project.

PAYE Pay-as-you-earn. This means of collecting tax arose under Schedule E of the UK income-tax legislation on wages and salaries. Because it is often difficult to collect tax at the end of the year from wage and salary earners, the onus is placed on employers to collect the tax from their employees as payments are made to them. There is an elaborate system of administration to ensure that broadly the correct amount of tax is deducted week by week or month by month and that the employer remits the tax collected to the Inland Revenue very quickly. Although technically called pay-as-you-earn, the system would be better called pay-as-you-get-paid.

payee A person or organization to be paid. In the case of a cheque payment, the payee is the person or organization to whom the cheque is made payable.

payer A person or organization who makes a payment.

paying agent An organization that makes payments either of capital or interest to bond-holders. Banks performing this function charge a fee.

paying banker The bank on which a *bill of exchange (including a cheque) has been drawn and which is responsible for paying it if it is correctly drawn and correctly endorsed (if necessary).

paying-in book A book of slips used to pay cash, cheques, etc., into a bank account. The counterfoil of the slip is stamped by the bank if the money is paid in over the counter.

pay-later option An *exotic option in which the payment of the premium is a contingent event.

payment date The date on which payments for securities are actually made.

payment for honour *See* ACCEPTANCE SUPRA PROTEST.

payment in advance (prepayment) Payment for goods or services before they have been received. In company accounts, this often refers to rates or rents paid for periods that carry over into the next accounting period.

payment in due course The payment of a *bill of exchange when it matures (becomes due).

payment in kind A payment that is not made in cash but in goods or services. It is often in the form of a discount or an allowance, e.g. cheap fares for British Airways employees, staff prices for food at supermarkets, etc. Now regarded as a bonus or *fringe benefit, payment in kind in the 19th century was widespread; the Truck Acts 1831 were passed to discourage employers who insisted on paying their employees in goods instead of cash (as often the cash value of goods bought in bulk by the employer was much less than their value to the employee).

payment on account **1.** A payment made for goods or services before the goods or services are finally billed. *See also* DEPOSIT. **2.** A payment towards meeting a liability that is not the full amount of the liability. The sum paid will be credited to the account of the payer in the books of the payee as a part-payment of the ultimate liability.

payment supra protest *See* ACCEPTANCE SUPRA PROTEST.

payment terms The agreed way in which a buyer pays the seller for goods. The commonest are cash with order or cash on delivery; prompt cash (i.e. within 14 days of delivery); cash in 30, 60, or 90 days from date of invoice; *letter of credit; *cash against documents; *documents against acceptance; or *acceptance credit.

payoff The value of a portfolio or a single financial obligation at a particular date or at the expiry of an instrument. The value is sometimes calculated in absolute terms and sometimes in terms of the gain made over a given time period.

pay-out ratio *See* DIVIDEND COVER.

payroll tax A tax based on the total of an organization's payroll. The main function of such a tax would be to discourage high wages or over-employment.

pay-through bond (cash-flow bond) A mortgage-backed security in which the cash flows of the underlying asset are paid to the bond holders.

PBGC Abbreviation for *Pension Benefit Guaranty Corporation.

PCP Abbreviation for *permissible capital payment.

PDR (P/D ratio) Abbreviations for *price–dividend ratio.

PEFCO Abbreviation for *Private Export Funding Corporation.

pegging 1. (pegging the exchange) The fixing of the value of a country's currency on foreign exchange markets. *See* CRAWLING PEG; FIXED EXCHANGE RATE. **2. (pegging wages)** The fixing of wages at existing levels by government order to prevent them rising during a period of *inflation. The same restraint may be applied to prices (**pegging prices**) in order to control inflation.

penalty An arbitrary pre-arranged sum that becomes payable if one party breaches a contract or undertaking. It is usually expressly stated in a **penalty clause** of the contract. Unlike liquidated *damages, a penalty will be disregarded by the courts and treated as being void. Liquidated damages will generally be treated as a penalty if the amount payable is extravagant and unconscionable compared with the maximum loss that could result from the breach. However, use of the terms 'penalty' or 'liquidated damages' is inconclusive as the legal position depends on the interpretation by the courts of the clause in which they appear.

pennant In *chartist analysis, a situation in which the highs and lows in the price of a financial instrument move closer together over time. The pattern that this trend makes on a chart resembles a pointed *flag.

penni (*plural* **penniä**) A former monetary unit of Finland, worth one hundredth of a *markka (until 2002).

penny (p) **1.** A monetary unit of the UK worth one hundredth of a *pound. **2.** A former monetary unit of the Republic of Ireland, worth one hundredth of a *punt (until 2002).

penny shares Securities with a very low market price (although they may not be as low as one penny) traded on a stock exchange. They are popular with small investors, who can acquire a significant holding in a company for a very low cost. Moreover, a rise of a few pence in a low-priced share can represent a high percentage profit. However, they are usually shares in companies that have fallen on hard times and may, indeed, be close to bankruptcy. The investor in this type of share is hoping for a rapid recovery or a takeover.

pension A specified sum paid regularly to a person who has reached a certain age or retired from employment. It is normally paid from the date of reaching the specified age or the retirement date until death. A widow may also receive a pension from the date of her husband's death.

In the UK, contributory **retirement pensions** are usually paid by the state from the normal retirement age (currently 65 for men and 60 for women, adjusting after 2010 to 65 for both) irrespective of whether or not the pensioners have retired from full-time employment. A non-working wife or widow also receives a state pension based on her husband's contributions. Self-employed people are also required to contribute towards their pensions.

Since 1978 state pensions have been augmented by the *State Earnings-Related Pension Scheme (SERPS); this is now gradually being replaced by a non-earnings-related scheme. Employers can contract out of this second state pension scheme provided that they replace it with an *occupational pension scheme that complies with the Social Security Act 1986. Employees may also contract out by starting their own approved *personal pension scheme or, from 2001, a *stakeholder pension scheme.

The private sector of the insurance industry also provides a wide variety of pensions, *annuities, and *endowment assurances. Financial analysts predict a major pensions crisis in the mid-21st century, since demographic trends will produce an ever-growing number of people beyond retirement age drawing on insufficient state and personal provision. *See also* DEFINED-BENEFIT PENSION SCHEME.

pensionable earnings The part of an employee's salary that is used to calculate the final pension entitlement. Unless otherwise stated, overtime, commission, and bonuses are normally excluded in the UK.

pension age The age at which a *pension becomes payable, irrespective of whether or not the pensioner has retired.

Pension Benefit Guaranty Corporation (PBGC) A US federal agency that insures *defined-benefit pension schemes of companies.

pensioneer trustee A person authorized to oversee the management of a *pension fund in accordance with the provisions of the Pension Trust Deed.

pension funds State and private pension contributions invested to give as high a return as possible to provide the funds from which pensions are paid. In the UK, pension funds managed by individual organizations work closely with insurance companies and investment trusts, being together the *institutional investors that have a dominant influence on many securities traded on the London Stock Exchange. An enormous amount of money is accumulated by these pension funds, which grows by weekly and monthly contributions; real estate and works of art are often purchased for investment by pension funds in addition to stock-exchange securities. *See also* PENSIONEER TRUSTEE; UNFUNDED PENSION SCHEME.

pension mortgage A *mortgage in which the borrower repays interest only and also contributes to a pension plan designed to provide an eventual tax-free lump sum, part of which is used to pay off the capital at the end of the mortgage term and the rest to provide a pension for the borrower's retirement.

pension scheme Any arrangement the main purpose of which is to provide a defined class of individuals (called members of the scheme) with *pensions. A pension scheme may include benefits other than a pension and may provide a pension for dependants of deceased members. *See also* OCCUPATIONAL PENSION SCHEME; PERSONAL ANNUITY SCHEME; PERSONAL PENSION SCHEME; STAKEHOLDER PENSION SCHEME.

Pensions Ombudsman *See* FINANCIAL OMBUDSMAN SERVICE.

PEP Abbreviation for *personal equity plan.

PEP mortgage A *mortgage in which the borrower repays only the interest on the loan to the lender, but at the same time puts regular sums into a *personal equity plan (PEP). When the PEPs mature they are used to repay the capital. The PEP mortgage is similar to an endowment mortgage, except that the PEP mortgage does not provide any life-assurance cover and that PEP funds are untaxed.

P/E ratio Abbreviation for *price–earnings ratio.

per capita income The average income of a group, obtained by dividing the group's total income by its number of members. The **national per capita income** is the ratio of the national income to the population.

per diem (Latin: per day) Denoting a fee charged by a professional person who is paid a specified fee for each day of employment.

perfect hedge A *hedge whose movements eliminate the risk associated with the underlying instrument. *Compare* IMPERFECT HEDGE.

perfecting the sight *See* BILL OF SIGHT.

performance The difference between a *benchmark and the actual return on a portfolio.

performance bond A bank guarantee given to a third party that a customer of the bank will complete a specified contract and will fulfil all its terms. It is often used to support a contract with an overseas firm; for example, a US importer may require such a bond from the bankers of a UK exporter.

performance fund An investment that expects to pay high returns in the long run, although this will involve a higher risk. Some performance funds hope to achieve a high capital gain rather than a regular income.

peril An event that can cause a financial loss, against which an *insurance contract provides cover. An **excepted peril** is one that is not normally covered by an insurance policy. *See also* INSURABLE RISK.

period bill (term bill) A *bill of exchange payable on a specified date rather than on demand.

period of grace The time, usually three days, allowed for payment of a *bill of exchange (except those payable at sight or on demand) after it matures.

perks An informal word for **perquisites**, the benefits arising as a result of employment, in addition to regular renumeration. Perks are privileges that are expected mainly by senior employees (e.g. a company car, private health insurance, an executive dining room). *See* BENEFITS IN KIND.

permanent health insurance (PHI) A form of health insurance that provides an income up to normal retirement age (or *pension age) to replace an income lost by prolonged illness or disability in which the insured is unable to perform any part of his or her normal duties. Premiums are related to age and occupation. *Compare* SICKNESS AND ACCIDENT INSURANCE.

permanent interest bearing share (PIBS) A fixed-interest non-redeemable security, issued by building societies, that pays interest at a fixed rate. However, these shares carry the risks associated with fixed-interest securities, being the last to be paid out should an issuing building society go into liquidation.

per mille (per mill; per mil) (Latin: per thousand) Denoting that the premium on an insurance policy is the stated figure per £1000 of insured value. Per mille is also used to mean 0.1% in relation to interest rates.

permissible capital payment (PCP) A payment made out of *capital when a company is redeeming or purchasing its own *shares and has used all available distributable profits as well as the proceeds of any new issue of shares. *See* OWN SHARES PURCHASE.

permission to deal Permission by the *London Stock Exchange to deal in the shares of a newly floated company. It must be sought three days after the issue of a *prospectus.

perpetual annuity The receipt or payment of a constant annual amount in perpetuity. Although the word annuity refers to an annual sum, in practice the constant sum may be for periods of less than a year. The *present value of an annuity is obtained from the formula:

$P = (a \times 100)/i$,

where P is the present value, a is the annual sum, and i is the interest rate.

perpetual debenture 1. A bond or *debenture that can never be redeemed. *See* IRREDEEMABLE SECURITIES. **2.** A bond or debenture that cannot be redeemed on demand.

perpetual FRN A *floating-rate note that is never redeemed. *See also* FLIP-FLOP FRN.

perpetual succession The continued existence of a corporation until it is legally dissolved. A corporation, being a separate legal person, is unaffected by the death or other departure of any member but continues in existence no matter how many changes in membership occur.

perpetuity A security that makes a fixed-value payment in every time period forever. Its value is the fixed payment divided by the appropriate interest rate for that time period. If the time period is a year, its value will be the annual rate of interest paid on securities of that level of risk.

per pro (per proc; p.p.) Abbreviations for *per procurationem* (Latin: by procuration): denoting an act by an agent, acting on the authority of a principal. The abbreviation is often used when signing letters on behalf of a firm or someone else, if formally authorized to do so. The firm or person giving the authority accepts responsibility for documents so signed.

perquisites *See* PERKS.

personal accident and sickness insurance *See* SICKNESS AND ACCIDENT INSURANCE.

personal account 1. An *account in a ledger that bears the name of an individual or of an organization; it records the state of indebtedness of the named person to the organization keeping the account or vice versa. Personal accounts are normally kept in the sales (or total debtors) ledger and the purchases (or total creditors) ledger. **2.** *See* PA.

personal allowances Sums deductible from *taxable income under an income-tax system to allow for personal circumstances. In the UK, the basic personal allowance, to which everyone is entitled, is £4745 (2004–05). For those aged between 65 and 74 this increases to £6830, and for those aged 75 or more it is £6950. Additional allowances include a range of tax credits for families with children under 16 and people with disabilities. The former married couples' tax allowance was discontinued from 5 April 2000, except for those couples in which the senior spouse was 65 or over on that date.

personal annuity scheme A contributory *pension scheme designed for people who are self-employed or not covered by an *occupational pension scheme. *See also* PENSION.

personal equity plan (PEP) A UK government scheme introduced by the Finance Act 1986 to encourage individuals to invest in company shares and equity-based unit and investment trusts, offering investors certain tax benefits. PEPs were superseded in 1999 by *Individual Savings Accounts (ISAs), but arrangements for existing PEPs continue unaltered. The investment is administered by an authorized plan manager. **General PEPs** invest in the shares of more than one company. They may be **managed PEPs**, in which the plan manager makes the investment decisions; **self-select PEPs**, in which the investor makes the decisions; or **advisory PEPs**, in which the plan manager (usually a stockbroker) advises the investor about investment decisions. Investors may put in a lump sum or regular monthly amounts. Re-invested dividends are free of *income tax and *capital gains tax is not incurred, as long as the investment is retained in the plan for at least a complete calendar year. There is currently a limit of £6000 on the amount an individual can invest in a general PEP in any year. However, an additional £3000 may be invested in a **single-company PEP** (containing the shares of only one, EU-based company), which may be a self-select PEP or a **corporate PEP**, sponsored by the company issuing the shares. A few corporate PEPs are general PEPs, with an investment limit of £6000.

personal financial planning Financial planning for individuals, which involves analysing their current financial position, predicting their short-term and long-term needs, and recommending a financial strategy. This may involve advice on pensions, the provision of independent school fees, mortgages, life assurance, and investments.

personal identification number (PIN) A number memorized by the holder of a *cash card, *credit card, or *multifunctional card and used in *automated teller machines and *electronic funds transfer at point of sale to identify the card owner. The number is given to the cardholder in secret and is memorized so that if the card is stolen it cannot be used. The number is unique to the cardholder. Banks will not reimburse *phantom withdrawals if it can be shown that the PIN number was known to a party other than the customer to whom it was allocated.

Personal Investment Authority (PIA) A *Self-Regulating Organization that since 1993 has regulated the activities of investment business carried out mainly with or for private investors. The PIA took over many of the responsibilities of the *Financial Intermediaries, Managers and Brokers Regulatory Association Ltd (FIMBRA) and the *Life Assurance and Unit Trust Regulatory Organization (LAUTRO) and some of the activities of IMRO. It has been absorbed into the *Financial Services Authority.

personal loan A loan to a private person by a bank or building society for domestic purposes, buying a car, etc. There is usually no security required and consequently a high rate of interest is charged. Repayment is usually by monthly instalments over a fixed period. This is a more expensive way of borrowing from a bank than by means of an *overdraft.

personal pension scheme An arrangement in which an individual contributes part of his or her salary to a pension provider, such as an insurance company or a bank. The pension provider invests the money in a *pension fund so that at retirement a lump sum is available to the pensioner. This is used to purchase an *annuity to provide regular pension payments. In the UK the system is that an employee who chooses a personal pension instead of SERPS, or their employer's pension scheme, must pay National Insurance contributions at the full ordinary rate and the employer's share must be paid at the same rate. The state pays the difference between the lower contracted-out rate and the full ordinary rate direct to the personal pension scheme. The administration of pensions is scrutinized by the *Financial Ombudsman Service, which is empowered to deal with complaints relating to personal pension schemes. *See also* STAKEHOLDER PENSION SCHEME.

personal property (personalty) Any property other than *real property (realty). This distinction is especially used in distinguishing property for *inheritance tax. Personal property includes money, shares, chattels, etc.

personal representative A person whose duty is to gather in the assets of the estate of a deceased person, to pay any liabilities, and to distribute the residue. Personal representatives of a person dying testate are known as *executors; those of a person dying intestate are known as *administrators.

peseta (Pta) Formerly, the standard monetary unit of Spain and one of the two standard monetary units of Andorra (*see also* FRANC), divided into 100 céntimos. It was subsumed into the *euro for all purposes other than cash transactions in January 1999 and abolished in 2002.

pesewa A monetary unit of Ghana, worth one hundredth of a *cedi.

peso 1. The standard monetary unit of Argentina ($), Chile (Ch$), Colombia (Col$), Cuba (CUP), the Dominican Republic (RD$), Mexico (Mex$), and the Philippines; it is divided into 100 centavos. **2.** (NUr$) The standard monetary unit of Uruguay, divided into 100 centésimos.

PET Abbreviation for *potentially exempt transfer.

petrodollars Reserves of US dollars deposited with banks as a result of the steep rises in the price of oil in the 1970s. The export revenues of the oil-exporting nations increased rapidly in this period, leading to large current-account surpluses, which had an important impact on the world's financial system.

petroleum revenue tax (PRT) A tax on the profits from oil exploration and mining occurring under the authority of licences granted in accordance with the Petroleum (Production) Act 1934 or the Petroleum (Production) Act (Northern Ireland) 1964. This tax was the principal means enabling the UK government to obtain a share in the profits made from oil in the North Sea.

petty cash The amount of cash that an organization keeps in notes or coins on its premises to pay small items of expense. This is to be distinguished from cash, which normally refers to amounts held at banks. Petty-cash transactions are normally recorded in a **petty-cash book**, the balance of which should agree with the amounts of petty cash held at any given time.

Pfennig (*plural* **Pfennige**) A former monetary unit of Germany, worth one hundredth of a *Deutschmark (until 2002).

phantom withdrawals The removal of funds from bank accounts through *automated teller machines (ATMs) by unauthorized means and without the knowledge or consent of the account holder. Banks have maintained that such withdrawals are not possible without the collusion, intended or unintended, of account holders by divulging their *personal identification numbers (PINs) to a third party or lending their ATM card to someone else.

PHI **1.** Abbreviation for *permanent health insurance. **2.** Abbreviation for *private health insurance.

Philadelphia Stock Exchange *See* US STOCK EXCHANGES.

Philippines stock exchanges *See* MANILA STOCK EXCHANGE.

physical capital Items such as plant and machinery, buildings, and land that can be used to produce goods and services. It is compared to financial capital, i.e. money, and *human capital.

physical controls Direct measures used by a government to regulate an economy, compared to indirect controls, which influence the price mechanism. For example, the imposition of a quota on a specific import would be a physical control, whereas a surcharge on that import would be an indirect control.

physical delivery The settlement of an option or futures contract by the delivery of the *underlying rather than an equivalent cash settlement.

physical price The price of a commodity that is available for delivery. In most forward contracts (*see* FORWARD DEALING) and *futures contracts the goods are never actually delivered because sales and purchases are set off against each other.

physicals *See* ACTUALS.

PIA Abbreviation for *Personal Investment Authority.

piastre A monetary unit of Egypt, Lebanon, and Syria worth one hundredth of a *pound.

PIBOR Abbreviation for *Paris Inter Bank Offered Rate.

PIBS Abbreviation for *permanent interest bearing share.

PIN Abbreviation for *personal identification number.

PINC Abbreviation for *property income certificate.

Pink Book *See* UK BALANCE OF PAYMENTS.

pink form (preferential form) An *application form in a flotation that is printed on pink paper and usually distributed to employees of the company to give them preference in the allocation of shares. Up to 10% of a share issue can be set aside under London Stock Exchange rules for applications from employees or from shareholders in a parent company that is floating a subsidiary.

pink sheets The US National Quotation Bureau publications listing the bid and offer prices of the securities available on the *over-the-counter markets. *Compare* YELLOW SHEETS.

Pink 'Un The colloquial name for the *Financial Times*, the London business newspaper, which is published on pink newsprint.

pin risk The *market risk to an *at-the-money option shortly before expiry.

pip The minimum price movement in a financial market, for example a *basis point (0.01%) on foreign-exchange markets.

pit (trading pit; pitch) An area of a stock market, financial futures and options exchange, or commodity exchange in which a particular stock, financial future, or commodity is traded, especially one in which dealings take place by *open outcry (*see* LONDON INTERNATIONAL FINANCIAL FUTURES AND OPTIONS EXCHANGE; CALLOVER). A member who is allowed to trade on the floor but wishes to conceal his or her identity may use a **pit broker** to carry out transactions. Dealers in these markets are called **pit traders**.

placement *See* PLACING; PRIVATE PLACING.

placing The sale of shares by a company to a selected group of individuals or institutions. Placings can be used either as a means of *flotation or to raise additional capital for a quoted company (*see also* PRE-EMPTION RIGHTS; RIGHTS ISSUE). Placings are usually the cheapest way of raising capital on a *stock exchange and they also allow the directors of a company to influence the selection of shareholders. The success of a placing usually depends on the placing power of the company's stockbroker. Placings of *public companies are sometimes called **public placings** (*compare* PRIVATE PLACING). In the USA a placing is called a **placement**. *Compare* INTRODUCTION; ISSUE BY TENDER; OFFER FOR SALE; PUBLIC ISSUE.

plain vanilla A colloquial name for a financial instrument in its simplest form.

planning blight Difficulty in selling or developing a site, building, etc., because it is affected by a government or local-authority development plan. Planning blight may be ended by a compulsory purchase by the government or local authority, but it may continue indefinitely if the government plans fail to mature or if the site itself is not required by the development but is rendered unsaleable or less valuable by its proximity to a development.

plastic money A colloquial name for a *credit card, *cash card, or *multifunctional card. It is often shortened to **plastic**.

playing the yield curve An investment strategy designed to take advantage of differences in yield for different terms, for example by funding short term and investing longer term on a *normal yield curve.

Plaza Agreement *See* GROUP OF FIVE.

plc Abbreviation for *public limited company. This (or its Welsh equivalent *c.c.c.) must appear in the name of a UK public limited company. *Compare* LTD.

pledge An article given by a borrower (**pledgor**) to a lender (**pledgee**) as a security for a debt. It remains in the ownership of the pledgor although it is in the possession of the pledgee until the debt is repaid. *See also* PAWNBROKER.

ploughed-back profits *See* RETAINED EARNINGS.

PMT Abbreviation for *post-market trading.

point *See* TICK.

point and figure chart A chart used in technical analysis, on which price rises are marked by a column of Xs and price falls by a column of Os. It indicates whether a security has shown an upward or downward momentum in price over a set time period.

poison pill A tactic used by a company that fears an unwanted takeover by ensuring that a successful takeover bid will trigger some event that substantially reduces the value of the company. Examples of such tactics include the sale of some prized asset to a friendly company or bank or the issue of securities with a conversion option enabling the bidder's shares to be bought at a reduced price if the bid is successful. Poison pills are used all over the world but were developed in the USA. *See also* PORCUPINE PROVISIONS; STAGGERED DIRECTORSHIPS.

polarization The regulation in the *Financial Services Act 1986 that stipulates that financial intermediaries, such as banks and building societies, must either act as advisers who may not offer their own financial products for sale, or as agents selling their own products; they cannot, as they previously could, do both.

policy *See* INSURANCE POLICY.

policy mix A combination of fiscal, monetary, and other policies employed by a government to achieve an economic objective.

policy proof of interest (PPI) An insurance policy (usually marine insurance) in which the insurers agree that they will not insist on the usual requirement that the insured must prove an *insurable interest existed in the subject matter before a claim is paid. The possession of the policy is all that is required. These policies are a matter of trust between insurer and insured as they are not legally enforceable.

political credit risk The *credit risk that arises as a result of actions by a foreign government, which may affect the management of a foreign business, control of its assets, and its ability to make payments to its creditors. *Compare* TRANSFER RISK.

poll tax A tax that is the same for each individual, i.e. a lump sum per head (from Middle Low German *polle*: head). The benefits of such taxes are that they do not distort choices, being an equal levy from everyone's resources whatever their circumstances; however, poll taxes are sometimes criticized as being regressive in that they do not take account of persons' ability to pay. The **community charge**, an alternative to rates, was a poll tax introduced in the UK by the Conservative government in 1990 (1989 in Scotland) and replaced by a *council tax in 1993.

Ponzi scheme A type of banking fraud named after Charles Ponzi, who operated such a scheme in the USA in 1920. Depositors are offered unsustainably high rates of interest (e.g. 50% p.a.) and are initially paid their interest from a fund consisting of new deposits. When the deposits dry up, the bank collapses. Ponzi managed to fool enough depositors to amass a fund of $8M before the police caught up with him. Depositors lost every cent. The term is now used generally for schemes of this sort, based on chain letters.

pool **1. (residual pool)** That portion of the total financing of a *syndicated bank facility retained by the *lead manager as a fee for arranging and managing the loan. **2.** The combination of financial instruments in a security. **3.** An aggregation of accounts. **4.** To join together as a group to increase the resources for investment.

porcupine provisions (shark repellents) Provisions made by a company to deter *takeover bids. They include *poison pills, *staggered directorships, etc.

portable pension A *pension entitlement that can be moved from one *pension scheme to another without loss, as when a person changes jobs.

PORTAL market A market in the USA operated by the *National Association of Securities Dealers Inc. (NASD) since June 1990 for qualified investors to trade privately in unregistered international securities.

portfolio **1.** The set of holdings in securities owned by an investor or institution. The choice of portfolio will depend on the mix of income and capital growth its owner expects, some investments providing good income prospects while others provide good prospects for capital growth. **2.** A list of the loans made by an organization. Banks, for example, attempt to balance their portfolio of loans to limit the risks.

portfolio insurance (portfolio protection) The use of a *financial futures and *options market to protect the value of a portfolio of investments. For example, a fund manager may expect the general level of prices to fall on the stock exchange. The manager could protect the portfolio by selling the appropriate number of *index futures, which could then be bought back at a profit if the market falls. Alternately, the manager could establish the value of the portfolio at current prices by buying put options, which would provide the opportunity to benefit if there was a rise in the general level of prices.

portfolio theory The theory developed by H. M. Markowitz that rational investors are averse to taking increased risk unless they are compensated by an adequate increase in expected return. The theory also assumes that for any given expected return, most rational investors will prefer a lower level of risk and for any given level of risk they will prefer a higher return than a lower return. A set of efficient *portfolios can be calculated from which the investor will choose the one most appropriate for their risk profile. The practical conclusions of the theory are that investors should diversify widely and determine their levels of risk by lending a proportion of their assets or borrowing to buy more risky assets. See also MARKOWITZ MODEL; PORTFOLIO INSURANCE.

position The extent to which an investor, dealer, or speculator has made a commitment in the market by buying or selling securities, currencies, commodities, or any financial obligation. See LONG POSITION; OPEN POSITION; SHORT POSITION.

position limit **1.** A limit placed by an exchange on the *exposure that any single transactor may undertake. **2.** An internal risk-management limit imposed on *positions to be held by traders, desks, etc. within an organization. See also INTRADAY LIMIT; LIMIT.

position trading The holding of an *open position for a long period of time with an eye to achieving long-term profits from calculated risks.

postal account A savings account with a bank or a building society that can only be operated by letter or (sometimes) by automated teller machine: amounts paid into the account or withdrawn from it cannot be dealt with over the counter or by telephone or over the Internet. Postal accounts usually pay a higher rate of interest than those that can be operated in person because of their cost structure. In some postal accounts the bank will draw a cheque on a saver's account in response to written instructions.

post-Bang Denoting the method of operation of the *London Stock Exchange after the *Big Bang of October 1986. It also refers to the widening of all the activities of the London security markets as a result of these changes.

post-date To insert a date on a document that is later than the date on which it is signed, thus making it effective only from the later date. A **post-dated** (or **forward-dated**) **cheque** cannot be negotiated before the date written on it, irrespective of when it was signed. Compare ANTE-DATE.

posted price The price at which a financial obligation may be traded.

post-market trading (PMT) An automated trading system on screens, operated by the *Chicago Mercantile Exchange.

potentially exempt transfer (PET) A lifetime gift made by an individual to another individual, or into an *interest-in-possession trust that does not attract a liability to *inheritance tax at the date of the gift. No charge occurs if the donor survives seven years after the date of the gift. If death occurs within seven years of the gift, the total lifetime gifts in the seven years preceding death are added back into the estate of the deceased for the purpose of levying duty. The gifts are taken in chronological order with the first £215,000 worth of gifts being covered by the nil-rate band. Gifts in excess of this sum are charged at a flat rate of 40% with graduated relief for gifts made between three and seven years before death. *See also* EXEMPT TRANSFERS.

pound 1. (£) The standard monetary unit of the UK, divided into 100 pence. It dates back to the 8th century AD when Offa, King of Mercia, coined 240 pennyweights of silver from 1 pound of silver. When *sterling was decimalized in 1971 it was divided into 100 newly defined pence. The pound is also the currency unit of the Falkland Islands (Fk£), Gibraltar (Gib£), the Channel Islands, and the Isle of Man. *See also* PUNT. **2.** The standard monetary unit of Egypt (LE), Lebanon (LL), and Syria (LS), divided into 100 piastres. **3.** (£C) The standard monetary unit of Cyprus, divided into 100 cents.

poundage *See* RATES.

pound cost averaging A method of accumulating capital by investing a fixed sum of money in a particular share every month (or other period). When prices fall the fixed sum will buy correspondingly more shares and when prices rise fewer shares are bought. The result is that the average purchase price over a period is lower than the arithmetic average of the market prices at each purchase date (because more shares are bought at lower prices and fewer at higher prices).

poverty trap A situation in which an increase in the income of a low-earning household causes either a loss of state benefits or an increase in taxation that is equal to or greater than the increase in earnings, i.e. the household faces a marginal tax rate of 100% (in some instances the marginal tax rate can exceed 100%). The poverty trap creates a disincentive to earning and is often demoralizing for those caught in it. Most tax and benefit systems create poverty traps and policies for removing them are difficult to find.

power of attorney (PA) A formal document giving one person the right to act for another. A power to execute a *deed must itself be given by a deed. An attorney may not delegate these powers unless specifically authorized to do so.

p.p. Abbreviation for *per procurationem*. *See* PER PRO.

PPI 1. Abbreviation for *policy proof of interest. **2.** Abbreviation for *producer price index.

PPP Abbreviation for *purchasing power parity.

preacquisition profit The retained profit of one company before it is taken over by another company. Preacquisition profits should not be distributed to the shareholders of the acquiring company by way of dividend, as such profits do not constitute income to the parent company but a partial repayment of its capital outlay on the acquisition of the shares.

preceding-year basis (PYB) A basis for assessing profits or income in which the assessment in any given *fiscal year is based on the accounts that ended during the previous tax year. For example, in the system used in the UK, in an ongoing business with accounts drawn up to 30 April, the profits assessed in 2004–05 will be based on the profits as set out in the accounts for the year ended 30 April 2003 (the accounts ending in the previous tax year, 6 April 2003 to 5 April 2004).

precept A command by the Commissioners of Inland Revenue to a taxpayer to make certain relevant documents available, usually by a specified date.

pre-emption First refusal: the right of a person to be the first to be asked to enter into an agreement at a specified price; for example, the right to be offered a house at a price acceptable to the vendor before it is put on the open market.

pre-emption rights A principle, established in company law, according to which any new shares issued by a company must first be offered to the existing shareholders as the legitimate owners of the company. To satisfy this principle a company must write to every shareholder (see RIGHTS ISSUE), involving an expensive and lengthy procedure. Newer methods of issuing shares, such as *vendor placings or *bought deals, are much cheaper and easier to effect, although they violate pre-emption rights. In the USA pre-emption rights have now been largely abandoned but controversy is still widespread in the UK.

preference share A share in a company yielding a fixed rate of interest rather than a variable dividend. A preference share is an intermediate form of security between an *ordinary share and a *debenture. Preference shares, like ordinary shares but unlike debentures, usually confer some degree of ownership of the company. However, in the event of liquidation, they are paid off after *debt capital but before ordinary share capital. Preference shares may be redeemable (see REDEEMABLE SHARES) at a fixed or variable date; alternatively they may be undated. Sometimes they are *convertible. The rights of preference shareholders vary from company to company and are set out in the *articles of association. Voting rights are normally restricted, often only being available if the interest payments are in arrears.

   Participating preference shares carry additional rights to dividends, such as a further share in the profits of the company, after the ordinary shareholders have received a stated percentage. See also PREFERRED ORDINARY SHARE.

preference share capital *Share capital consisting of *preference shares. Under Financial Reporting Standard 4, 'Capital Instruments', preference share capital should be classified as *non-equity share capital. The amount attributable to non-equity shares in the analysis of shareholders' funds and the allocation of finance costs should be disclosed separately in the *financial statements.

preferential creditor A creditor whose debt will be met in preference to those of other creditors and who thus has the best chance of being paid in full on the bankruptcy of an individual or the winding-up of a company. In the UK preferential creditors, who are usually paid in full after *secured debts and before ordinary creditors, include: the Inland Revenue in respect of PAYE, Customs and Excise in respect of VAT and car tax, the DSS in respect of Social Security contributions, the trustees of occupational pensions schemes, and employees in respect of any remuneration outstanding.

preferential debt A debt that will be repaid in preference to other debts. See PREFERENTIAL CREDITOR.

preferential form See PINK FORM.

preferential payment A payment made to a *preferential creditor.

preferred habitat theory A theory that attempts to explain the shape of the *yield curve in terms of investors wishing to invest in certain preferred maturities.

preferred ordinary share A share issued by some companies that ranks between a *preference share and an *ordinary share in the payment of dividends.

preferred stock The US name for a *preference share.

preliminary announcement An early announcement of their profit or loss for the year that *listed companies are required to make under *London Stock Exchange Regulations. The minimum information is a summarized *profit and loss account, although there has been a trend for companies to provide other information, such as *balance sheets. Companies must lodge their preliminary announcement with the Stock Exchange, but there is no requirement to send the information to shareholders. A number of companies publish some of the information in national newspapers and provide *investment analysts and journalists with substantial information, which receives considerable comment in the press.

preliminary expenses Expenses involved in the formation of a company. They include the cost of producing a *prospectus, issuing shares, and advertising the flotation.

pre-market Denoting any trading that takes place before the official opening of a market.

premium **1.** The consideration payable for a contract of *insurance or life assurance. **2.** An amount in excess of the nominal value of a share, bond, or other security. **3.** An amount in excess of the issue price of a share or other security. When dealings open for a new issue of shares, for instance, it may be said that the market price will be at a premium over the issue price (*see* STAG). **4.** The price paid by a buyer of an *option contract to the seller for the right to exercise the option. In general, the premium asked for an option consists of two components, its *intrinsic value and its *time value. **5.** The difference between the spot price for a commodity or currency and the forward price. **6.** A bonus given to bank customers as an inducement to open an account.

premium bonds **1.** Bonds that trade above *par value. **2.** UK government securities first issued in 1956 and now administered by the Department for *National Savings. No regular income or capital gain is offered but bonds enter weekly and monthly draws for tax-free prizes.

premium currency Of two currencies, the one whose exchange rate is higher in the forward market.

premium income The total income of an insurance company from insurance policy *premiums.

Premium Trust Fund The primary business fund of *Lloyd's, into which all insurance premiums are paid and from which all claims are paid.

pre-packaged bankruptcy Bankruptcy proceedings that incorporate in advance an already agreed reorganization plan.

prepayment The settlement of a debt before it is due, for example by the early repayment of a mortgage.

prepayment risk The *risk associated with early payments of obligations. A prime example is the risk that a borrower will repay a fixed-rate mortgage early at a time when interest rates are falling, leaving the lender with a lower interest income than anticipated. To offset this risk, lenders sometimes impose a **prepayment penalty** on loans.

presenting bank Any bank seeking payment of a bill of exchange, cheque, draft, or other financial instrument by submitting it to the *drawee's bank.

present value (discounted value) The result arrived at in a *discounted cash flow calculation by multiplying a projected annual cash flow figure by a *discount factor derived from a *hurdle rate of interest and a time period.

pre-tax profit The profit of a company before deduction of corporation tax.

pre-trading Trading on the London Stock Exchange between 8 a.m. and 8.30 a.m., when the market officially opens. Some *market makers are willing to deal in this half hour on a limited range of stocks and shares. This tends to be speculative *pre-market trading as the prices may change after the official opening.

price control Restrictions by a government on the prices of consumer goods, usually imposed on a short-term basis as a measure to control inflation. *See also* PRICES AND INCOME POLICY.

price–dividend ratio (PDR; P/D ratio) The current market price of a company share divided by the dividend per share for the previous year. It is a measure of the investment value of the share.

price–earnings ratio (P/E ratio) The current market price of a company share divided by the *earnings per share (eps) of the company. The P/E ratio usually refers to the annual eps and is expressed as a number (e.g. 5 or 10), often called the **multiple** of the company. Loosely, it can be thought of as the number of years it would take the company to earn an amount equal to its market value. High multiples, usually associated with low *yields, indicate that the company is likely to grow rapidly, while a low multiple is associated with dull no-growth stocks. The P/E ratio is one of the main indicators used by fundamental analysts to decide whether the shares in a company are expensive or cheap, relative to the market.

price index *See* RETAIL PRICE INDEX.

price level The average level of prices of goods and services in an economy, usually calculated as a figure on a price index. *See* RETAIL PRICE INDEX.

price limit The degree of price change that is permitted on a financial market before trading is suspended. *See also* LIMIT; LIMIT MOVE.

price–net tangible assets ratio The current market price of a company share divided by its *net tangible assets. The higher the ratio, the more attractive the share as an investment.

price range The difference between the highest and lowest price of a financial obligation over a particular time period.

prices and income policy A government policy to curb *inflation by directly imposing wage restraint and *price controls. Less interventionist governments prefer indirect methods using fiscal and monetary policies.

price-sensitive information Information (usually unpublished) about a company that is likely to cause its share prices to move. *See* INSIDER INFORMATION.

price support A government policy of providing support for certain basic, usually agricultural, products to stop the price falling below an agreed level. Support prices can be administered in various ways: the government can purchase and stockpile surplus produce to support the price or it can pay producers a cash payment as a *subsidy to raise the price they obtain through normal market channels. *See also* COMMON AGRICULTURAL POLICY.

primary dealer 1. A dealer in government (gilt-edged) stocks; they have been established in London markets since the *Big Bang in October 1986. They deal direct with the Bank of England, by whom they are supervised, and can bid for *tap stocks when required, as well as having an obligation to maintain a market in all government stocks. There were 27 primary dealers in 1986, but only 21 in 1997. They have taken over the role of the *government broker. They are also known as **gilt-edged dealers. 2.** *See* REPORTING DEALER.

primary earnings per share In the USA, a calculation for assessing the performance of companies with complex capital instruments. The net income available to holders of *common stock is divided by the weighted average of the common stock outstanding plus common-stock equivalents; common-stock equivalents are securities that can be converted into common stock. The figure is shown on the face of the income statement.

primary market The market into which a new issue of securities is launched. *Compare* SECONDARY MARKET.

prime cost The total of the direct costs incurred in making a product. These include material costs, direct labour costs, and direct expenses. The prime cost may be expressed per product or per year (or other period). The total production cost will also include an item for the indirect overhead costs.

prime rate The rate of interest at which US banks lend money to first-class borrowers. It is similar in operation to the *base rate in the UK. Competitive markets have forced many banks, both in the USA and the UK, to offer business customers credit at below prime rates. The main difference between US and UK practice is that the US prime rate is approximately equal to the dollar three-month *London Inter Bank Offered Rate (LIBOR) plus 1%, whereas the UK base rate is approximately equivalent to the sterling three-month LIBOR.

principal 1. A person on whose behalf an agent or broker acts. **2.** A sum of money on which *interest is earned.

principles of taxation A set of criteria, largely determined by the economist Adam Smith (1723–90), for determining whether a given tax or system of taxation is efficient. The main principles are that taxes should be equitable and certain. Subsidiary principles are that they should distort choices that would otherwise be made as little as possible and that the cost of collection should be as low as possible. Some economists argue that a further principle might be that the tax should be effective in redistributing income.

priority percentage (prior charge) The proportion of any profit that must be paid to holders of fixed-interest capital (*preference shares and loan stock; *see* DEBENTURE) before arriving at the sums to be distributed to holders of *ordinary shares. These percentages help to assess the security of the income of ordinary shareholders and are related to the *gearing of the company's capital.

prior-period adjustments Material adjustments applicable to prior financial periods arising from changes in accounting policies or from the correction of fundamental errors. They do not include normal recurring adjustments or corrections of accounting estimates made in prior periods. Under Financial Reporting Standard 3, if prior-period adjustments fall within these definitions, the *financial statements for the current period should not be distorted, but the prior periods should be restated with an adjustment to the opening balance of the retained *profit.

private bank **1.** A *commercial bank owned by one person or a partnership (*compare* JOINT-STOCK BANK). Popular in 19th-century Britain, they have been superseded by joint-stock banks. They still exist in the USA. **2.** A bank that is not a member of a *clearing house and therefore has to use a clearing bank as an agent. **3.** A bank that is not owned by the state.

Private Export Funding Corporation (PEFCO) A private company, formed in 1970 and owned by a consortium of US banks and industries, that funds US exports in collaboration with the *Export-Import Bank. It aims to arrange funds for companies and organizations in the rest of the world that wish to purchase US goods or services.

private health insurance (PHI) A form of insurance that covers all the normal costs associated with private medical treatment. PHI enables those who wish to do so to choose their own consultants, choose when and where they are hospitalized, and to have private rooms (with private telephones) in hospitals. Because these facilities are often important for managers and executives, businesses often offer PHI to senior employees as a fringe benefit. Many companies offer group schemes at discounted premiums.

private limited company Any *limited company that is not a *public limited company. Such a company is not permitted to offer its shares for sale to the public and it is free from the rules that apply to public limited companies.

private placing The selling of shares in a company direct to investors, often without the intermediary of a stockbroker. In the USA it is called a **private placement**. *See also* PLACING.

private sector The part of an economy that is not under government control. In a mixed economy most commercial and industrial firms are in the private sector, run by private enterprise. *Compare* PUBLIC SECTOR.

private-sector liquidity *See* MONEY SUPPLY.

private trading system A screen-based automated trading system run by a private company in the USA. It is offered to brokers, dealers, and investors who may not, for any reason, wish to use the official markets.

private treaty Any contract made by personal arrangement between the buyer and seller or their agents, i.e. not by public auction.

privatization (denationalization) The process of selling a publicly owned company or asset (*see* NATIONALIZATION) to the private sector. Privatization may be pursued for political as well as economic reasons. The economic justification for privatization is that a company will be more efficient as a result of competition. Politically, privatization in the form of share offers to the general public is seen as a means of widening the share-owning public and thus increasing the commitment of working people to the capitalist system.

privatization voucher A coupon redeemable against a share in one of the recently privatized companies in Russia. From 1992 all Russian citizens were issued with such vouchers.

probability The likelihood that an event or a particular result will occur. It can be represented on a scale by a number between 0 (zero probability of the event happening, i.e. it is certain not to) and 1 (certainty that it will occur). It is treated mathematically on this basis in statistics.

probate A certificate issued by the Family Division of the High Court, on the application of *executors appointed by a will, to the effect that the will is valid and that the executors are authorized to administer the deceased's estate. When there is no apparent doubt about the will's validity, probate is granted in **common form** on the executors filing an affidavit. Probate granted in common form can be revoked by the court at any time on the application of an interested party who proves that the will is invalid. When the will is disputed, probate in **solemn form** is granted, but only if the court decides that the will is valid after hearing the evidence on the disputed issues in a **probate action**.

probate price The price of shares or other securities used for *inheritance-tax purposes on the death of the owner.

probate value The value of the assets at the time of a person's death, agreed with the Inland Revenue for the purposes of calculating *inheritance tax.

problem children See BOSTON MATRIX.

process engineering (**process innovation; process re-engineering**) An approach to the restructuring of organizations that aims to achieve lower costs and improved quality of output. It involves the analysis of an organization in terms of its core processes, followed by a fundamental redesign of these processes through the application of enhanced information technology.

procuration See PER PRO.

produce See COMMODITY.

produce broker See COMMODITY BROKER.

producer price index (**PPI**) A measure of the rate of *inflation among goods purchased and manufactured by UK industry (replacing the former **wholesale price index**). It measures the movements in prices of about 10 000 goods relative to the same base year. Compare RETAIL PRICE INDEX.

productive expenditure Money spent by a government on public services, schools, hospitals, etc., i.e. for benefits in the future as opposed to the immediate benefits that follow from current consumption.

products-guarantee insurance An insurance policy covering financial loss as a consequence of a fault occurring in a company's product. A product-guarantee claim would be made, for example, to pay for the cost of recalling and repairing cars that are found to have a defective component. This type of policy would not pay compensation to customers or members of the public injured as a result of the defect. Such claims would be met by a *products-liability insurance.

products-liability insurance An insurance policy that pays any compensation the insured is legally liable to pay to customers who are killed, injured, or have property damaged as a result of a defect in a product that they have manufactured or supplied. Costs incurred as a consequence of the defect that are not legal *damages would not be covered by a policy of this kind. A *products-guarantee insurance is intended to cover these costs.

professional-indemnity insurance A form of third-party insurance that covers a professional person, such as a solicitor, surveyor, accountant, business manager, etc., against paying compensation in the event of being sued for professional negligence. This can include giving defective advice if the person professes to be an expert in a given field. *See also* PUBLIC-LIABILITY INSURANCE.

professional valuation An assessment of the value of an asset (share, property, stock, etc.) in the balance sheet or prospectus of a company, by a person professionally qualified to give such a valuation. The professional qualification necessary will depend on the asset; for example, a qualified surveyor may be needed to value property, whereas unquoted shares might best be valued by a qualified accountant.

profit **1.** For a single transaction, the excess of the selling price of the article or service being sold over the costs of providing it. **2.** For a period of trading, the surplus of net assets at the end of a period over the net assets at the start of that period, adjusted where relevant for amounts of capital injected or withdrawn by the proprietors. As profit is notoriously hard to define, it is not always possible to derive one single figure of profit for an organization from an accepted set of data.

profitability The capacity or potential of a project or an organization to make a *profit. Measures of profitability include return on capital employed, and the ratio of net profit to sales.

profitability index (PI) A method used in *discounted cash flow for ranking a range of projects under consideration in which *standard cash flow patterns are projected. It is based on the ratio:

total present values of cash inflows/initial investment,

the value of which is compared for each project.

The projects with a PI of less than 1 are not expected to earn the required *rate of return and are rejected. The projects with a PI in excess of 1 are ranked according to the magnitude of the PI.

profit and loss account (P & L account) **1.** An *account in the books of an organization showing the profits (or losses) made on its business activities with the deduction of the appropriate expenses. **2.** A statement of the profit (or loss) of an organization derived from the account in the books. It is one of the statutory accounts that, for most limited companies, has to be filed annually with the UK Registrar of Companies. The profit and loss account usually consists of three parts. The first is a trading account, showing the total sales income less the costs of production, etc., and any changes in the value of stock or work in progress from the last accounting period. This gives the *gross profit (or loss). The second part gives any other income and lists administrative and other costs to arrive at a *net profit (or loss). From this net profit before taxation the appropriate corporation tax is deducted to give the net profit after taxation. In the third part, the net profit after tax is appropriated to dividends or to reserves.

profiteer A person who makes excessive profits by charging inflated prices for a commodity that is in short supply, especially during a war or national disaster.

profit forecast A forecast by the directors of a public company of the profits to be expected in a stated period. If a new flotation is involved, the profit forecast must be reported on by the reporting accountants and the sponsor to the share issue. An existing company is not required to make a profit forecast with its *accounts, but if it does it must be reported on by the company's auditors.

profit margin The ratio of the net profit of an organization to its turnover.

profits available for distribution *See* DISTRIBUTABLE PROFITS.

profit-sharing ratio (PSR) The ratio in which the profits or losses of a business are shared. For a partnership, the profit-sharing ratios will be set out in the partnership agreement. This will show the amount, usually given as a percentage of the total profits, attributable to each partner. In some agreements there is a first charge on profits, which is an allocation of the first slice of the profits for the year. The remainder will then be split in the profit-sharing ratios as specified in the agreement. The profit-sharing ratios can also apply to the capital of the partnership, but this does not always follow. The partnership agreement can specify a different capital-sharing ratio. If no specific agreement has been made, profits and losses will be shared equally in accordance with the Partnership Act 1890.

profit-sharing scheme A scheme by which employees share in the profits of a business, usually through some type of share ownership.

profits tax Any tax on the profits of a company. *Corporation tax in the UK is a form of profits tax.

profit taking Selling financial obligations at a profit, either after a market rise or because they show a profit at current levels but will not do so if an expected fall in prices occurs. .

profit warning An announcement by a company that its future profits will be significantly lower than previously announced or forecast.

program trading Trading on financial markets using computer programs. The programs used trigger trading automatically once certain limits are reached. It was said to account for some 10% of the daily turnover on the New York Stock Exchange in the late 1980s and has been partly blamed for the market crash in October 1987. Subsequently the New York Stock Exchange imposed limits on program trading.

progressive tax A tax in which the rate of tax increases with increases in the tax base. The most common of these is *income tax but progressive rates are also applied to National Insurance contributions, *inheritance tax, and to a limited extent *corporation tax. Such taxes are generally linked to the ability-to-pay principle. *Compare* PROPORTIONAL TAX.

progress payment An instalment of a total payment made to a contractor, when a specified stage of the operation has been completed.

project finance Money or loans put up for a particular project (e.g. a property development), which are usually secured on that project rather than forming part of the general borrowing of the company carrying out the development.

promissory note A *negotiable instrument that contains a promise to pay a certain sum of money to a named person, to that person's order, or to the bearer at a specified time in the future. It must be unconditional, signed by the maker, and delivered to the payee or bearer. They are widely used in the USA but are not common in the UK. A promissory note cannot be reissued, unless the promise is made by a banker and is payable to the bearer, i.e. unless it is a *banknote.

promoter A person involved in setting up and funding a new company, including preparing its articles and memorandum of association, registering the company, finding directors, and raising subscriptions. The promoter is in a position of trust with regard to the new company and may not make an undisclosed profit or benefit at its expense. A promoter may be personally liable for the fulfilment of a contract entered into by, or on behalf of, the new company before it has been formed.

prompt cash Payment terms for goods or services in which payment is due within a few days (usually not more than 14) of delivery of the goods or the rendering of the service.

prompt day (prompt date) 1. The day (date) on which payment is due for the purchase of goods. In some commodity spot markets it is the day payment is due and delivery of the goods may be effected. **2.** The date on which a contract on a commodity exchange, such as the *London Metal Exchange, matures.

property Something capable of being owned (*see* PERSONAL PROPERTY; REAL PROPERTY). It may be tangible, such as a building or work of art, or intangible, such as a right of way or an *intellectual property, such as a copyright.

property bond A bond issued by a life-assurance company, the premiums for which are invested in a fund that invests in property.

property income certificate (PINC) A certificate giving the bearer a share in the value of a particular property and a share of the income from it. PINCs can be bought and sold.

property insurance Insurance covering loss, damage, or destruction of any form of item from personal jewellery to industrial plant and machinery. Property-insurance policies are a form of *indemnity in which the insurer undertakes to make good the loss suffered by the insured. The policy may state the specific compensation payable in the event of loss or damage; if it does not, the policy will normally pay the intrinsic value of the insured object, taking into account any appreciation or depreciation on the original cost. Such policies usually have a maximum sum for which the insurers are liable.

property tax A tax based on the value of property owned by the taxpayer.

proportional tax A tax in which the amount of tax paid is proportional to the size of the tax base, i.e. a tax with a single rate. *Compare* PROGRESSIVE TAX.

proportional treaty (quota share reinsurance treaty) A *reinsurance agreement in which the risks are transferred in direct proportion to the premiums paid over.

proprietary company *See* PTY.

proprietary network A network of *automated teller machines (ATMs) available for use only by the customers of a specific bank or financial institution or some other limited group. Proprietary networks have been supplanted by ATM networks that allow the customers of a bank to use free of charge the withdrawal facilities of several other banks with which it has entered a reciprocal agreement.

prospect theory A theory, developed by the economists Daniel Kahneman and Amos Tversky, that seeks to explain how individuals make decisions when faced with uncertainty. It is central to the growing new area of research known as behavioural finance, which posits that psychology plays a major part in financial decision making. In essence, prospect theory has three components, which concern the role played by decision frames, mistakes in relation to evaluating probabilities, and a *risk preference structure. To help them make a decision individuals use a framework, which has a strong influence on the decision made. Individuals believe that improbable events are more likely to occur than they are in practice, and conversely that probable events are less likely to occur than they are in practice. Moreover, they define outcomes in terms of gains and losses, with the latter having a more important impact on their welfare than the former. *See also* UTILITY THEORY.

prospectus A document that gives details about a new issue of shares and invites the public to buy shares or debentures in the company. A copy must be filed with the Registrar of Companies. The prospectus must conform to the provisions of the Companies Act 1985, describe the aims, capital structure, and any past history of the venture, and may contain future *profit forecasts. There are heavy penalties for knowingly making false statements in a prospectus.

protected bear *See* COVERED BEAR.

protest A certificate signed by a *notary public at the request of the holder of a *bill of exchange that has been refused payment or acceptance. It is a legal requirement after *noting the bill (*see also* ACCEPTANCE SUPRA PROTEST). The same procedure can also be used for a *promissory note that has been dishonoured.

provision An amount set aside out of profits in the accounts of an organization for a known liability (even though the specific amount might not be known) or for the diminution in value of an asset. Common examples include *provision for bad debts, *provision for depreciation, and also provision for accrued liabilities.

provisional liquidator A person appointed by a court after the presentation of a winding-up petition on a company (*see* COMPULSORY LIQUIDATION). The provisional liquidator, whose powers are limited, has to protect the interests of all the parties involved until the winding-up order is made. The *official receiver is normally appointed to this post. *See also* LIQUIDATOR.

provision for bad debts A provision calculated to cover the debts during an *accounting period that are not expected to be paid. A **general provision**, e.g. 2% of debtors, is not allowed as a deduction for tax purposes. A **specific provision**, in which specific debts are identified, is allowed if there is documentary evidence to indicate that these debts are unlikely to be paid. A **provision for doubtful debts** (or **allowance for doubtful accounts**) is treated in the same way for tax purposes.

provision for depreciation A sum credited to an *account in the books of an organization to allow for the *depreciation of a fixed asset. The aggregate amounts set aside from year to year are deducted from the value of the asset in the balance sheet to give its *net book value.

proximate cause The dominant and effective cause of an event or chain of events that results in a claim on an insurance policy. The loss must be caused directly, or as a result of a chain of events initiated, by an insured peril. For example, a policy covering storm damage would also pay for items in a freezer that deteriorate because of a power cut caused by the storm, which is the proximate cause of the loss of the frozen food.

proxy A person who acts in the place of a member of a company at a company meeting at which one or more votes are taken. The proxy need not be a member of the company but it is quite common for directors to offer themselves as proxies for shareholders who cannot attend a meeting. Notices calling meetings must state that a member may appoint a proxy and the appointment of a proxy is usually done on a form provided by the company with the notice of the meeting; it must be returned to the company not less than 48 hours before the meeting. A **two-way proxy form** is printed so that the member can state whether the proxy should vote for or against a particular resolution. A **special proxy** is empowered to act at one specified meeting; a **general proxy** is authorized to vote at any meeting.

PRT Abbreviation for *petroleum revenue tax.

prudence concept The accounting concept that insists on a realistic view of business activity and stresses that anticipated revenues and profits have no place in a *profit and loss account until they have been realized in the form of cash or other assets for which the ultimate cash value can be assessed with reasonable certainty. Moreover, provision should be made for all known expenses and losses whether the amount of these is known with certainty or is a best estimate in the context of the information available.

prudential ratios *Capital adequacy ratios for a bank or other financial institution that show restraint, not because the bank needs to protect its assets or because the money supply needs to be controlled, but because the bank wishes to exercise caution.

prudent insurer A theoretical insurer who needs to know all the *material facts before entering into a contract of insurance. The insured must not conceal any information that a prudent insurer would need to know in assessing a risk.

prudent-man rule A US criterion for managing investments, especially in relation to pensions, that is designed to avoid reckless speculation. It requires that a *fiduciary behave as a notional prudent man or woman would when making an investment.

PSBR Abbreviation for *Public Sector Borrowing Requirement.

PSL Abbreviation for private-sector liquidity, a concept formerly used as a measure of the *money supply.

PSR Abbreviation for *profit-sharing ratio.

Pty Abbreviation for proprietary company, the name given to a *private limited company in Australia and the Republic of South Africa. The abbreviation Pty is used after the name of the company as Ltd is used in the UK. It is also used in the USA for an insurance company owned by outside shareholders.

public company A company whose shares are available to the public through a stock exchange. *See* PUBLIC LIMITED COMPANY.

public corporation A state-owned organization that provides a national service (such as the British Broadcasting Corporation) or runs a nationalized industry. The chairman and members of the board of a public corporation are usually appointed by the appropriate government minister, who retains overall control and accountability to parliament. The public corporation attempts to reconcile public accountability for the use of public finance, freedom of commercial operation on a day-to-day basis, and maximum benefits for the community.

public debts The debts of the *public sector of the economy, including the *national debt.

public deposits The balances to the credit of government departments held at the Bank of England.

public examination *See* BANKRUPTCY.

public finance **1.** The financing of the goods and services provided by national and local government through taxation or other means. **2.** The economic study of the issues involved in raising and spending money for the public benefit.

public finance accountant A member of the Chartered Institute of Public Finance and Accountancy. The principal function of the members of this body is to prepare the financial accounts and act as management accountants for government agencies, local authorities, nationalized industries, and such bodies as publicly owned health and water authorities. As many of these bodies are non-profitmaking and are governed by special statutes, the skills required of public sector accountants differ from those required in the private sector.

public issue A method of making a *new issue of shares, loan stock, etc., in which the public are invited, through advertisements in the national press, to apply for shares at a price fixed by the company. *Compare* INTRODUCTION; ISSUE BY TENDER; OFFER FOR SALE; PLACING.

public-liability insurance An insurance policy that pays compensation to a member of the public and court costs in the event of the policyholder being successfully sued for causing death, injury, or damage to property by failing to take reasonable care in his or her actions or those of any employees. A business whose work brings it into contact with the public must have a public-liability policy. *See also* PROFESSIONAL-INDEMNITY INSURANCE.

public limited company (plc) A company registered under the Companies Act 1985 as a public company. Its name must end with the initials 'plc'. It must have an authorized share capital of at least £50,000 of which at least £12,500 must be paid up. The company's memorandum must comply with the format in Table F of the Companies Regulations 1985. It may offer shares and securities to the public. The regulation of such companies is stricter than that of private companies. Most public companies are converted from private companies, under the re-registration procedure in the Companies Act. *See also* C.C.C.

public offering The US name for an *offer for sale.

public placing *See* PLACING.

public policy The interests of the community. If a contract is (on common-law principles) contrary to public policy, this will normally make it an *illegal contract. In a few cases, however, such a contract is void but not illegal, and is treated slightly more leniently (for example, by severance). Contracts that are illegal because they contravene public policy include any contract to commit a crime or a tort or to defraud the revenue, any contract that prejudices national safety or the administration of justice, and any immoral contract. Contracts that are merely void include contracts in restraint of trade.

public sector The part of an economy in a mixed economy (*see* MARKET ECONOMY) that covers the activities of the government and local authorities. This includes education, the health and social services, the police, local public services, etc., as well as state-owned industries and *public corporations. *Compare* PRIVATE SECTOR.

Public Sector Borrowing Requirement (PSBR) The amount by which UK government expenditure exceeds its income (i.e. the **public sector deficit**); this must be financed by borrowing (e.g. by selling gilt-edged securities) or by printing money. As an indicator of government fiscal policy the PSBR has acquired increased status since the late 1970s. By that time many economists had come to accept that a high PSBR is inflationary or leads to the crowding out of private expenditure; this remains a widely held view. While printing money simply causes prices to rise, selling gilts has the effect of raising interest rates, reducing private investment, and curbing private expenditure.

public sector deficit *See* PUBLIC SECTOR BORROWING REQUIREMENT.

public works Construction work by government, local authority, or public corporation, especially that undertaken during a *recession or a depression on such activities as house building or road building. It is aimed at increasing the level of employment and aggregate demand. *See also* PUMP PRIMING; REFLATION.

published accounts Accounts of organizations published according to UK law. The accounts comprise the *balance sheet, the *profit and loss account, the statement of *source and application of funds, the *directors' report, and the *auditors' report. In the case of *groups of companies, consolidated accounts are also required. *Small companies and *medium-sized companies, as defined by the Act, need not file some of these documents.

puisne mortgage A legal *mortgage of unregistered land that is not protected by the deposit of title deeds. It should instead be protected by registration.

pul (*plural* **puli**) A monetary unit of Afghanistan worth one hundredth of an *afghani.

pula (P) The standard monetary unit of Botswana, divided into 100 thebe.

pull to redemption The increase in the redemption *yield of a fixed-interest dated stock as the redemption date approaches.

pumping The colloquial name for the injection of money into the US banking system by the *Federal Reserve Bank to force down interest rates.

pump priming An addition to aggregate demand generated by a government in order to set off the *multiplier process. It usually involves allowing government expenditure to exceed receipts, creating a *budget deficit. Pump priming was widely used by governments in the post-war era in order to maintain full employment; however, it became discredited in the 1970s when it failed to halt rising unemployment and was held to be responsible for *inflation.

punt (Ir£) The Irish pound: formerly the standard monetary unit of the Republic of Ireland, divided into 100 pence. It was subsumed into the *euro for all purposes except cash transactions in January 1999 and abolished in 2002.

punter A speculator on a financial market, especially one who hopes to make quick profits.

purchased goodwill *Goodwill acquired when a business is purchased as opposed to that which has been internally generated.

purchased life annuity An *annuity in which a single premium purchases an income to be paid from a specified date for the rest of the policyholder's life.

purchase fund A fund used to purchase bonds that have fallen below *par value.

purchasing power The ability to purchase goods and services. In times of inflation a loss of purchasing power occurs when *monetary assets are held because of the decline in the purchasing power of the currency. If a company has monetary liabilities, a purchasing power gain will arise because the absolute sum of the loans will be repaid with currency with less purchasing power.

purchasing power parity (PPP) The theory that when adjusting for the exchange rate, the cost of a good should be the same in all countries. This is never actually the case, although over the long term exchange rates do appear to adjust to differences in national inflation. This latter proposition is referred to as the **relative purchasing power parity theory**.

pure endowment assurance An assurance policy that promises to pay an agreed amount if the policyholder is alive on a specified future date. If the policyholder dies before the specified date no payment is made and the premium payments cease. The use of the word 'assurance' for this type of contract is questionable as there is no element of life-assurance cover.

pure play A company that is dedicated to a single narrowly defined activity, as opposed to one that has diverse interests. Investing in a pure play is therefore much the same as investing in the commodity or product that the company deals in.

pure risk An insurance risk that will lead to loss if certain events occur; it is therefore one that can be calculated and have premiums calculated for it. *See* INSURABLE RISK.

put–call parity A relationship between the put and call prices of European *options provided that the *arbitrage-free condition holds. It is expressed by the following formula:

$$E + C = U + P,$$

where E is the present value of the *exercise price, C is the value of a call, U is the value of the *underlying, and P is the value of the put. The formula assumes that the put and call have the same exercise price and the same time period to expiry.

put–call ratio A ratio arrived at by dividing the *open interest in a put option by the open interest in the equivalent call. It gives some idea of the mood of the market on which way the *underlying is expected to move in the future.

put-of-more option *See* OPTION TO DOUBLE.

put option *See* OPTION.

puttable bonds Bonds issued with a provision that the holder is entitled to redeem the bond before the final maturity date. *Compare* CALLABLE BONDS.

put-through Two deals made simultaneously by a *market maker on the London Stock Exchange, in which a large quantity of shares is sold by one client and bought by another, the market maker taking a very small turn.

pya A monetary unit of Myanmar (Burma) worth one hundredth of a *kyat.

PYB Abbreviation for *preceding-year basis.

pyramiding The snowballing effect that derives from a holding company acquiring a number of subsidiary companies.

qindar (*plural* **qindarka**) A monetary unit of Albania, worth one hundredth of a *lek.

Q ratio (Tobin's Q) A ratio devised by the economic analyst James Tobin of Yale University to measure the impact of *intangible assets on business value. It is the ratio of the market value of a business to the *replacement cost of its assets.

qualified acceptance An *acceptance of a *bill of exchange that varies the effect of the bill as drawn. If the holder refuses to take a qualified acceptance, the drawer and any endorsers must be notified or they will no longer be liable. If the holder takes a qualified acceptance, all previous signatories who did not assent from liability are released.

qualified audit report An *auditors' report in which some qualification of the *financial statements is required because the *auditor feels there is a limitation on the scope of the audit examination or because the auditor disagrees with the treatment or disclosure of a matter in the financial statements. The type of qualification used will depend upon the degree of *materiality of the limitation or disagreement. If the limitation of scope is very material, a disclaimer of opinion will be issued; if it is less material the 'except for the limitation of scope' form of qualification will be issued in the report. If the auditor disagrees with the accounting treatment or disclosure in the financial statements and feels the effect is material and potentially misleading, an *adverse opinion will be expressed. If the disagreement is not so material, a qualified opinion will be given using the 'except for the effects of disagreement' form of qualification.

qualified stock option In the USA, an agreement giving employees the right to purchase company *stock at a later date at a specified option price, which is normally lower than the market price. It meets the requirements of the *Internal Revenue Service (IRS).

qualifying distribution Formerly, a distribution from a company resulting in *advance corporation tax being paid. Qualifying distributions included dividends and distributions from any company assets to shareholders (except for capital repayments). In the UK, the requirement for payment of Advance Corporation Tax was abolished in 1999.

qualifying loss A trading loss arising in a current accounting period as a result of computing the profits and losses of an organization in accordance with accepted *corporation-tax principles.

quality The creditworthiness or *credit rating of a securities issue.

quality spread The difference in yield between two securities with the same maturities but different levels of creditworthiness.

quango Acronym for quasi-autonomous non-governmental organization. Such bodies, some members of which are likely to be civil servants and some not, are appointed by a minister to perform some public function at the public expense.

While not actually government agencies, they are not independent and are usually answerable to a government minister.

quantity theory of money A theory, first proposed by the philosopher David Hume (1711–76), stating that the price level is proportional to the quantity of money in the economy. Formally, it is usually stated in the equation $MV = PT$, where M is the quantity of money, V is its velocity of circulation, P is the price level, and T the number of transactions in the period. Milton Friedman (1912–   ) made this equation the central pivot of *monetarism, with the additional assumption that V is predictable; thus, for a given number of transactions, the relationship between M and P is direct. This implies that any increase in the *money supply will lead to an increase in the price level, i.e. to inflation. *See* DEMAND FOR MONEY; MONETARY POLICY.

quarter days Four days traditionally taken as the beginning or end of the four quarters of the year, often for purposes of charging rent. In England, Wales, and Northern Ireland they are Lady Day (25 March), Midsummer Day (24 June), Michaelmas (29 September), and Christmas Day (25 December). In Scotland they are Candlemas (2 February), Whitsuntide (15 May), Lammas (1 August), and Martinmas (11 November).

quarterly report In the USA, a financial report issued by a company every three months. The usual contents are an income statement, *balance sheet, statement of changes in financial position, and a narrative overview of business operations.

quarter up The means of arriving at the *probate price of a share or other security.

quasi-contract A legally binding obligation that one party has to another, as determined by a court, although no formal contract exists between them.

quasi-loan An arrangement between two parties in which one party agrees to settle a financial obligation of the other party on condition that a reimbursement will follow.

quasi money *See* NEAR MONEY.

quasi-subsidiary A company, trust, partnership, or other arrangement that does not fulfil the definition of a *subsidiary undertaking but is directly or indirectly controlled by the reporting entity and gives rise to benefits for that entity that are in substance no different from those that would arise if it was a subsidiary. This definition is based on that given in Financial Reporting Standard 5, 'Reporting on the Substance of Transactions'. If a reporting entity has a quasi-subsidiary, the substance of the transactions entered into by the quasi-subsidiary should be reported in *consolidated financial statements.

question mark *See* BOSTON MATRIX.

quetzal (*plural* **quetzales**; Q) The standard monetary unit of Guatemala, divided into 100 centavos.

quick assets *See* LIQUID ASSETS.

quick ratio *See* LIQUID RATIO.

quid pro quo (Latin: something for something) Something given as compensation for something received. *Contracts require a quid pro quo; without a *consideration they would become unilateral agreements.

quorum The smallest number of persons required to attend a meeting in order that its proceedings may be regarded as valid. For a company, the quorum for a meeting is laid down in the articles of association.

quota **1.** A share of a whole that must not be exceeded. **2.** A fixed amount of a product or commodity that may be imported into or exported from a country as laid down by a government in an attempt to control the market in that product or commodity. **3.** A fixed amount of funds allocated by the *International Monetary Fund to its participating member countries. **4.** A maximum amount that may be bought or sold.

quota share reinsurance treaty *See* PROPORTIONAL TREATY.

quotation **1.** The representation of a security on a recognized *stock exchange (*see* LISTED COMPANY). A quotation allows the shares of a company to be traded on the stock exchange and enables the company to raise new capital if it needs to do so (*see* FLOTATION; LISTING REQUIREMENTS; RIGHTS ISSUE). **2.** An indication of the price at which a seller might be willing to offer goods for sale. A quotation does not, however, have the status of a firm *offer. **3.** A bid and offer price indicated by a dealer.

quoted company *See* LISTED COMPANY.

quoted price The last price at which a security was traded. On the London Stock Exchange, quoted prices are given daily in the *Official List. Quoted prices of commodities are given by the relevant markets and recorded in the financial press.

quote-driven Denoting a market in which prices are determined by the quotations made by *market makers or dealers. The London *Stock Exchange Automated Quotations System and the US *National Association of Securities Dealers Automated Quotation System use quote-driven arrangements. *Compare* ORDER-DRIVEN.

qursh A monetary unit of Saudi Arabia worth one twentieth of a *riyal.

q

RAFT Abbreviation for *revolving acceptance facility by tender.

raider An individual or organization that specializes in exploiting companies with undervalued assets by initiating hostile *takeover bids.

rainbow option An *exotic option in which the payoff is based on the performance of a number of *underlyings.

rally A rise in prices in a financial market, after a fall. This is usually brought about by a change of *market sentiment. However, if the change has occurred because there are more buyers than sellers, it is known as a **technical rally**. For example, unfavourable sentiment might cause a market to fall, in turn causing sellers to withdraw at the lower prices. The market will then be sensitive to the presence of very few buyers, who, if they show their hand, may bring about a technical rally.

ramping The practice of trying to boost the image of a security and the company behind it by buying the securities in the market with the object of raising demand; if the price rises, the ramper may be able to make a quick profit by selling.

rand (R) The standard monetary unit of South Africa, divided into 100 cents.

random number generator A computer programme that produces numbers by a random process. It is often used to provide an input to financial *simulation models, notably those using a *Monte Carlo simulation.

random-walk theory The theory that prices on a financial market move, for whatever reason, without any memory of past movements and that the movements therefore follow no pattern. This theory is used to dispute the predictions of *chartists, who do rely on past patterns of movements to predict present and future prices.

ranking The prioritization of liabilities in the *liquidation of a business.

RAROC Abbreviation for *risk-adjusted return on capital.

ratchet effect An irreversible change to an economic variable, such as prices, wages, exchange rates, etc. For example, once a price or wage has been forced up by some temporary economic pressure, it is unlikely to fall back when the pressure is reduced. This rise may be reflected in parallel sympathetic rises throughout the economy, thus fuelling *inflation.

rate **1.** To assess the creditworthiness of an individual, financial instrument, or organization. *See* CREDIT RATING; RATING AGENCY. **2.** *See* RATES. **3.** *See* INTEREST RATE.

rateable value *See* RATES.

rate anticipation swap An *interest-rate swap in which the swap is related to predicted interest-rate changes. *See also* SWAP.

rate capping *See* RATES.

rate of exchange (exchange rate) The price of one currency in terms of another.

It is usually expressed in terms of how many units of the home country's currency are needed to buy one unit of the foreign currency. However, in some cases, notably in the UK, it is expressed as the number of units of foreign currency that one unit of the home currency will buy. Two rates are usually given, the buying and selling rate; the difference is the profit or commission charged by the organization carrying out the exchange.

rate of interest *See* INTEREST RATE.

rate of return The annual amount of income from an investment, expressed as a percentage of the original investment. This rate is very important in assessing the relative merits of different investments. It is therefore important to note whether a quoted rate is before or after tax, since with most investments, the after-tax rate of return is most relevant. Also, because some rates are payable more frequently than annually, it may be important, in order to make true comparisons, to consider the *annual percentage rate (APR), which most investment institutions are required to state by law. *See also* RISK-FREE RATE.

rate of turnover The frequency, expressed in annual terms, with which some part of the assets of an organization is turned over. The total sales revenue is often referred to as *turnover and in order to see how frequently stock is turned over, the sales revenue (or if a more accurate estimate is needed the cost of goods sold) is divided by the average value of the stock to give the number of times the stock is turned over. This provides a reasonable measure in terms of stock. However, some accountants divide the sales figure by the value of the fixed assets to arrive at turnover of fixed assets. This is less realistic, although it does express the relationship of sales to the fixed assets of the organization, which in some organizations could be significant.

rate order A statement by US utility regulators setting a maximum price.

rates A local-authority tax calculated as a poundage on the rateable value of property in the area of the rating authority. The **poundage** is fixed annually by the rating authority as the number of pence that must be paid for each pound of rateable value. Under the Rates Act 1984, the Secretary of State for the Environment is empowered to limit the rates a local council can charge ratepayers (a process known as **rate capping**). The **rateable value** (or **net annual rentable value**) is determined by the Board of Inland Revenue for each property by deducting, from the rack rent that the property would earn, certain allowable costs. Domestic rates were replaced in the UK by the community charge (*see* POLL TAX), which, in turn, was replaced by the *council tax. *See also* UNIFORM BUSINESS RATE.

rate support grant Central government funding in the UK of local government authorities to supplement income from local taxes. The grant helps local authorities to maintain services and taxes at levels comparable to other authorities.

rating agency An organization that monitors the credit backing of institutions and of bond issues and other forms of public borrowings. It may also give a rating of the risks involved in holding specific stocks. The two best known are Standard & Poor and Moody, both of which have been in existence for over 100 years. *See also* CREDIT RATING.

ratio analysis The use of ratios to evaluate a company's operating performance and financial stability. Ratios, such as *return on capital employed, can be used to assess *profitability. The *current ratio can be used to examine solvency and *gearing ratios to examine the financial structure of the company. In conducting an analysis comparisons will be made with other companies and with industry averages over a period of time. The analysis of ratios indicates how well a company is run, the risks of financial insolvency, and the financial returns provided.

ratio covenant A form of *covenant in a loan agreement that includes conditions relating to such ratios as the *gearing ratio and *interest cover. Breaching such a covenant could indicate significant deterioration in the company's business or a major change in its nature; this will usually empower the lender to request repayment of any of the loan then outstanding, and the loan then becomes null and void.

rational expectations The theory, developed by the economist John Muth, that economic transactors make unbiased forecasts on the basis of all the information available. They thus do not make systematic forecasting errors.

rationalization A reorganization of a firm, group, or industry to increase its efficiency and profitability. This may include closing some units and expanding others (horizontal *integration), merging different stages of the production process (vertical integration), merging support units, closing units that are duplicating effort of others, etc. A firm may also rationalize its product range to reflect changes in demand, concentrating its sales and marketing effort on its best sellers. *See also* DOWNSIZING; RIGHTSIZING.

reaction A reversal in a market trend as a result of overselling on a falling market (when some buyers are attracted by the low prices) or overbuying on a rising market (when some buyers are willing to take profits).

real (cruzeiro real; R$) The standard monetary unit of Brazil, divided into 100 centavos.

real estate The US name for *real property.

real-estate investment trust (REIT) In the USA, a company that invests in property, earning profits for its shareholders through *closed-end funds.

real interest rate The actual interest rate less the current rate of inflation. For example, if a building society is paying 5% interest and the rate of inflation is 3%, the real growth of a deposit held for a year in the building society is 2% – this is the real rate of interest. Real interest rates are used to calculate more accurate pre-tax returns on investment, i.e. by discounting inflation.

real investment Investment in capital equipment, such as a factory, plant and machinery, etc., or valuable social assets, such as a school, a dam, etc., rather than in such paper assets as securities, debentures, etc.

realizable account An account drawn up on the dissolution of a *partnership. The account is debited with the assets of the partnership and any expenses on realization; it is credited with the proceeds of any sales made. The difference between the total debits and credits is either a *profit or loss on realization and must be shared between the partners in the *profit-sharing ratio.

realizable asset *See* LIQUID ASSETS.

realization account An *account used to record the disposal of an asset or assets and to determine the profit or loss on the disposal. The principle of realization accounts are that they are debited with the book value of the asset and credited with the sale price of the asset. Any balance therefore represents the profit or loss on disposal.

realized profit/loss A profit or loss that has arisen from a completed transaction (usually the sale of goods or services or other assets). In accounting terms, a profit is normally regarded as having been realized when an asset has been legally disposed of and not when the cash is received, since if an asset is sold on credit the asset being disposed of is exchanged for another asset, a debtor. The debt may or may not prove good but that is regarded as a separate transaction.

realized yield The total return obtained on a security, including that from the investment of any interest paid.

real market A view of the market based on the prices at which transactions actually occur, rather than the bid and offer prices.

real option An *option that occurs as a by-product of business activities rather than one traded in financial markets. A common example of a real option is early investment in a technology, which will enable a firm to exploit the new technology should it prove successful.

real property (realty) Any property consisting of land or buildings as distinct from *personal property (personalty).

real terms A representation of the value of a good or service in terms of money, taking into account fluctuations in the price level. Economists are usually interested in the relationship between the prices of goods in real terms, i.e. by adjusting prices according to a price index or some other measure of inflation.

real terms accounting A system of accounting in which the effects of changing prices are measured by their effect on a company's financial capital (i.e. *shareholders' equity) to see if its value is maintained in real terms. *Assets are measured at current cost. Profit is defined as any surplus remaining after the shareholders' equity (determined by reference to the current cost of *net assets) have been maintained in real terms. The unit of measurement may be either the nominal pound or the unit of constant purchasing power.

real-time operation A computer operation in which time is significant. Either it is essential that the computer coordinates its activities with external events (e.g. in the control of industrial processes) or any delay in response should be minimal (e.g. in such point of sale terminals as airline reservation systems).

realtor The US name for an estate agent or land agent.

realty *See* REAL PROPERTY.

real value A monetary value expressed in *real terms.

real-yield security A security whose yield is adjusted to take account of the rate of inflation.

reasonable care The care expected of a bank when dealing with *bills of exchange, *letters of credit, etc., to ensure that all the relevant documents called for are produced and are authentic before payment is authorized. This legal requirement includes a responsibility on the part of the bank to inform the parties concerned if the documents are not produced or are not in order.

rebalancing 1. The adjustment of a *hedge in order to improve its effectiveness as circumstances change. **2.** The adjustment of a portfolio over time to better reflect its underlying strategy. For example, a market-tracking hedge will require changes over time in order to reflect the differing importance of particular securities.

rebate   1. A discount offered on the price of a good or service, often one that is paid back to the payer, e.g. a tax rebate is a refund to the taxpayer. **2.** A discount allowed on a *bill of exchange that is paid before it matures.

recapitalization   In the USA, the process of changing the balance of *debt and *equity financing of a company without changing the total amount of *capital. Recapitalization is often required as part of reorganization of a company under bankruptcy legislation.

receivables   Sums of money due to a business from persons or businesses to whom it has supplied goods or services in the normal course of trade.

receiver   A person exercising any form of *receivership. In *bankruptcy, the *official receiver becomes receiver and manager of the bankrupt's estate. Where there is a *floating charge over the whole of a company's property and a crystallizing event has occurred, an **administrative receiver** may be appointed to manage the whole of the company's business. The administrative receiver will have wide powers under the Insolvency Act to carry on the business of the company, take possession of its property, commence *liquidation, etc. A receiver appointed in respect of a *fixed charge can deal with the property covered by the charge only, and has no power to manage the company's business.

receivership   A situation in which a lender holds a mortgage or charge (especially a *floating charge) over a company's property and, in consequence of a default by the company, a receiver is appointed to realize the assets charged in order to repay the debt.

receiving order   Formerly, an order made during the course of bankruptcy or insolvency. It is now called a bankruptcy order (*see* BANKRUPTCY).

recession   A slowdown or fall in economic growth rate. A recession is defined by the US National Bureau of Economic Research as a decline in *Gross Domestic Product in two successive quarters. A severe recession is called a *depression. Recession is associated with falling levels of *investment, rising unemployment, and sometimes falling prices. *See also* BUSINESS CYCLE.

reciprocal exchange rate   *See* DIRECT QUOTE.

reciprocity   A form of negotiation in which one party agrees to make a concession in return for a reciprocal, or broadly equivalent, action by the other. Most international economic negotiations take this form. For example, agreements to lower protectionist barriers over markets are nearly always made on a reciprocal basis. Economists often argue that this is inefficient, since unilateral action is frequently beneficial by itself.

reclamation   The recovery of losses incurred as a result of unsatisfactory *delivery.

Recognized Investment Exchange (RIE)   A body authorized in the UK under the Financial Services Act 1986 to sell financial instruments, with the approval of the *Financial Services Authority. The *London Stock Exchange, *London International Financial Futures and Options Exchange (LIFFE), *International Petroleum Exchange, *London Commodity Exchange, *London Metal Exchange, *London Securities and Derivatives Exchange, and *Tradepoint Investment Exchange are RIEs.

Recognized Professional Body (RPB)   An organization registered with the *Financial Services Authority as having statutory recognition for regulating their professions; the RPBs are the Chartered Association of Certified Accountants (ACCA),

Institute of Actuaries, Institute of Chartered Accountants in England and Wales, Institute of Chartered Accountants in Ireland, Institute of Chartered Accountants for Scotland, the Insurance Brokers Registration Council (IBRC), the Law Society, the Law Society of Northern Ireland, and the Law Society of Scotland.

Recognized Supervisory Body A body recognized in the UK by the Secretary of State for Trade and Industry as supervising and maintaining the conduct and technical standards of *auditors performing statutory *audits. Currently the Institute of Chartered Accountants in England and Wales, the Institute of Chartered Accountants of Scotland, and the Institute of Chartered Accountants in Ireland are recognized, together with the Chartered Association of Certified Accountants; in principle, the Association of Authorized Public Accountants is also recognized.

recontracting The renegotiation of contracts between a company in *financial distress and its creditors.

recourse The right of redress should the terms of a contract not be fulfilled. *See* WITH RECOURSE; WITHOUT RECOURSE.

recourse agreement An agreement between a hire-purchase company and a retailer, in which the retailer undertakes to repossess the goods if the buyer fails to pay the regular instalments.

recoverable advance corporation tax Formerly, *advance corporation tax (ACT) that could be set off in full against the current year's gross corporation tax liability or set back against gross corporation tax for accounting periods beginning six years preceding the current accounting period. In the UK, this system no longer pertains since the abolition of ACT in 1999.

recoverable amount The value of an *asset treated as the greater of its *net realizable value and its *net present value. The value of an asset to a business can be regarded as the lower of the recoverable amount and the current *replacement cost.

recovery stock A share that has fallen in price but is believed to have the potential of climbing back to its original level.

recycling of deposits A situation that can occur when there is a *run on a bank, i.e. when depositors clamour to withdraw their deposits from a bank thought to be in trouble. In these circumstances other banks and financial institutions may be persuaded to come to the aid of the ailing bank by lending it their own surplus deposits to prevent the collapse of the troubled bank.

Red Book The UK Treasury's financial statement and report, which is issued on Budget Day.

Red Clause An amendment to a *letter of credit granting full payment to the exporter, often before the goods being bought have been delivered.

redeemable gilts *See* GILT-EDGED SECURITY.

redeemable shares *Shares (either *ordinary shares or *preference shares) in a company that the issuing company has the right to redeem, under terms specified on issue. Redemption may be funded from *distributable profits or from a fresh issue of shares.

redemption The repayment at maturity of *shares, *stocks, *debentures, or *bonds. The amount payable on redemption is usually specified on issue. The

redemption date, or dates, may or may not be specified on issue. *See also* GILT-EDGED SECURITY; MATURITY DATE.

redemption date *See* REDEMPTION.

redemption premium *See* CALL PREMIUM.

redemption price *See* CALL PRICE.

redemption yield *See* GROSS REDEMPTION YIELD; YIELD.

red herring A colloquial name in the USA for a *pathfinder prospectus.

rediscounting The discounting of a *bill of exchange or *promissory note that has already been discounted by someone else, usually by a *discount house. A *central bank, acting as *lender of last resort, may be said to be rediscounting securities submitted to it by brokers in the money market, as the securities will have already been discounted in the market. In some cases the US *Federal Reserve Bank will rediscount a financial instrument that has already been discounted by a local bank.

reducing-balance depreciation *See* DEPRECIATION.

reduction of capital A reduction in the *issued share capital of a company. The Companies Act states that, subject to confirmation by the court, a company may, if authorized by its *articles of association, pass a special *resolution to reduce its issued share capital. It may (a) cancel any paid-up capital that is lost or no longer represented by available assets, (b) extinguish or reduce the liability on any of its shares in respect of share capital not paid up, (c) pay off any paid-up share capital that is in excess of its *warrants.

redundancy **1.** The loss of a job by an employee because the job has ceased to exist or because there is no longer work available. It involves dismissal by the employer, with or without notice, for any reason other than a breach of the contract of employment by the employee, provided that no reasonable alternative employment has been offered by the same employer. In the UK in these circumstances, and if the employee has been continuously employed in the business for at least two years, a **redundancy payment** must be made by the employer according to the Employment Rights Act 1996, the amount of which will depend on the employee's age, length of service, and rate of pay. **2.** *See* COMPENSATION FOR LOSS OF OFFICE.

referee **1.** A person who will, if asked, provide a **reference** for an applicant for a job. An approach to a referee can be in writing or by telephone and the referee should be given a brief job description of the job the applicant is trying to secure. **2.** A person appointed by two arbitrators who cannot agree on the award to be made in a dispute to be settled by arbitration. The procedure for appointing a referee in these circumstances is usually laid down in the terms of arbitration. **3.** A person or organization named on some *bills of exchange as a **referee** (or **reference**) **in case of need**. If the bill is dishonoured its holder may take it to the referee for payment.

reference *See* BANKER'S REFERENCE; REFEREE.

reference bank A bank nominated under the terms of a loan agreement to provide the marker rates for the purposes of fixing interest charges on a variable-rate loan.

reference index A price index against which a derivative payment is determined.

reference rate 1. An interest rate relative to which a bank prices its products, sometimes referred to as its *base rate. **2.** An interest rate relative to which financial markets price their products, for example the *London Inter Bank Offered Rate (LIBOR). **3.** A foreign-exchange rate that a country wishes to maintain.

refer to drawer Words written on a cheque that is being dishonoured by a bank, usually because the account of the person who drew it has insufficient funds to cover it and the manager of the bank is unwilling to allow the account to be overdrawn or further overdrawn. Other reasons for referring to the drawer are that the drawer has been made bankrupt, that there is a garnishee order against the drawer, that the drawer has stopped it, or that something in the cheque itself is incorrect (e.g. it is wrongly dated, words and figures don't agree, etc.). The words 'please re-present' may often be added, indicating that the bank may honour the cheque at a second attempt.

refinance bill *See* THIRD-COUNTRY ACCEPTANCE.

refinance credit A credit facility enabling a foreign buyer to obtain credit for a purchase when the exporter does not wish to provide it. The buyer opens a credit at a branch or agent of his or her bank in the exporting country, the exporter being paid by sight draft on the buyer's credit. The bank in the exporting country accepts a *bill of exchange drawn on the buyer, which is discounted and the proceeds sent to the bank issuing the credit. The buyer only has to pay when the bill on the bank in the exporting country matures.

refinancing The process of repaying some or all of the loan capital of a firm by obtaining fresh loans, usually at a lower rate of interest.

reflation A policy aimed at expanding the level of output of the economy by government stimulus, either fiscal or monetary policy. This could involve increasing the money supply and government expenditure on investment, public works, subsidies, etc., or reducing taxation and interest rates.

refugee capital *Hot money belonging to a foreign government, company, or individual that is invested in the country offering the highest interest rate, usually on a short-term basis.

refunding The issuing of new debt to replace debt that has been redeemed. It may be used to lower the rate on funding if current interest rates are lower than those on the funding to be replaced.

regional bank 1. A US bank that operates in one state or several states but in a limited geographical region. Bank holding companies of significant size with subsidiary banks in separate US states covering a wider region are often known as **super-regional banks. 2.** A local Japanese bank.

regional stock exchanges Stock exchanges established in regional financial centres, whose importance varies with the importance of the main market of the country. Founded in the formative years of capitalism to raise money for local projects, many have succumbed to the *globalization of the markets. However, some, especially in the USA, Japan, and Germany, have survived. In the UK subsidiary exchanges exist in Birmingham, Bristol, Leeds, Manchester, Glasgow, and Belfast; all of these were originally independent but are now branch offices of the *London Stock Exchange. None still have trading floors (the last to close was Birmingham in 1989).

registered capital *See* AUTHORIZED SHARE CAPITAL.

registered company A company incorporated in the UK by the Registrar of Companies in accordance with the Companies Act. It may be a public limited company or a private limited or unlimited company.

registered land certificate The document that has replaced title deeds for registered land. It provides proof of ownership of the land and will be in the possession of the land owner unless the land is subject to a mortgage, in which case it will be retained by the Land Registry.

registered name The name in which a UK company is registered. The name, without which a company cannot be incorporated, will be stated in the memorandum of association. Some names are prohibited by law and will not be registered; these include names already registered and names that in the opinion of the Secretary of State for Trade and Industry are offensive. The name may be changed by special resolution of the company and the Secretary of State may order a company to change a misleading name. The name must be displayed at each place of business, on stationery, and on bills of exchange, etc., or the company and its officers will be liable to a fine.

registered office The official address of a company, to which all correspondence can be sent. Statutory registers are kept at the registered office, the address of which must be disclosed on stationery and in the company's annual return. In the UK, any change of company address must be notified to the Registrar of Companies within 14 days and published in the London Gazette.

registered stock *See* INSCRIBED STOCK.

register of charges **1.** The register maintained by the Registrar of Companies on which certain charges must be registered by companies. A charge is created when a company gives a creditor the right to recover a debt from specific assets. The types of charge that must be registered in this way, and the details that must be given, are set out in the Companies Act 1985. Failure to register the charge within 21 days of its creation renders it void, so that it cannot be enforced against a liquidator or creditor of the company. The underlying debt remains valid, however, but ranks only as an unsecured debt. **2.** A list of charges that a company must maintain at its registered address or principal place of business. Failure to do so may render the directors and company officers liable to a fine. This register must be available for inspection by other persons during normal business hours.

register of companies *See* COMPANY; REGISTERED COMPANY; REGISTRAR OF COMPANIES.

register of debenture-holders A list of the holders of *debentures in a UK company. There is no legal requirement for such a register to be kept but if one exists it must be kept at the company's registered office or at a place notified to the Registrar of Companies. It must be available for inspection, to debenture-holders and shareholders free of charge and to the public for a small fee.

register of directors and secretaries A register listing the directors and the secretary of a UK company, which must be kept at its *registered office. It must state the full names of the directors and the company secretary, their residential addresses, the nationality of directors, particulars of other directorships held, the occupation of directors, and in the case of a public company, their dates of birth. If the function of director or secretary is performed by another company, the name and registered office of that company must be given. The register must be available for inspection by members of the company free of charge and it may be inspected by the public for a small fee.

register of directors' interests A statutory book in which a company must detail the interests of its *directors in the *shares and *debentures of the company. The register must be available for inspection during the annual general meeting of the company.

register of members (share register) A list of the *members of a company, which all UK companies must keep at their *registered office or where the register is made up, provided that this address is notified to the Registrar of Companies. It contains the names and addresses of the members, the dates on which they were registered as members and the dates on which any ceased to be members. If the company has a share capital, the register must state the number and class of the shares held by each member and the amount paid for the shares. As legal, rather than beneficial, ownership is registered, it is not always possible to discover from the register who controls the shares. The register must be available for inspection by members free of charge for at least two normal office hours per working day. Others may inspect it on payment of a small fee. The register may be rectified by the court if it is incorrect.

registrar The appointed agent of a company whose task is to keep a register of share and stock holders of that company. The functions of registrar are often performed by a subsidiary company of a bank.

Registrar of Companies An official charged with the duty of registering all the companies in the UK. There is one registrar for England and Wales and one for Scotland. The registrar is responsible for carrying out a wide variety of administrative duties connected with registered companies, including maintaining the **register of companies** and the *register of charges, issuing certificates of incorporation, and receiving annual returns.

registration fee A small fee charged by a company whose shares are quoted on a stock exchange when it is requested to register the name of a new owner of shares.

registration for value added tax An obligation on a person making taxable supplies to register for *value added tax if at the end of any month the amount of taxable supplies in the period of 12 months ending in that month exceeds the **registration threshold** of £58,000 (2004–05).

registration statement In the USA, a lengthy document that has to be lodged with the *Securities and Exchange Commission. It contains all the information relevant to a new *securities issue that will enable an investor to make an informed decision whether or not to purchase the security.

regression analysis A statistical technique that attempts to measure the extent to which one variable is related to two or more other variables, often with the aim of predicting future values of the dependent variable. It is used extensively in financial economics and marketing theory. *See also* CORRELATION COEFFICIENT; R SQUARED.

regressive tax A tax in which the rate of tax decreases as income or the tax base increases. Indirect taxes fall into this category. Regressive taxes are said to fall more heavily on the poor than on the rich; for example, the poor spend a higher proportion of their incomes on VAT than the rich.

regulated company *See* COMPANY.

regulation The imposition by a government of controls over the decisions of individuals or firms. It often refers to the control of industries in which there is monopoly or oligopoly, in order to prevent firms from exploiting their market power at the expense of the public. Regulation may be seen as an alternative to *nationalization. For example, the types of industries that were formerly nationalized in the UK have usually been regulated in the USA. The main vehicle for regulation in the UK is the *Competition Commission (formerly the Monopolies and Mergers Commission). Regulation is especially important in the financial services industry. *See also* DEREGULATION.

Regulation Q A limitation imposed by the US Federal Reserve on the rate of interest that could be offered by banks on current accounts. It was phased out by 1986.

Regulation S A US *Securities and Exchange Commission regulation governing *euromarket issues.

regulatory arbitrage The setting up of organizations and transactions to avoid the impacts of regulation.

Regulatory News Service (RNS) A screen-based service operated by the *London Stock Exchange for publishing electronically company results, share issues, changes of senior company directorships, and other items relevant to the price of shares. RNS requires companies to notify them of many of these items before publicizing them elsewhere. Price-sensitive information can be given confidentially to the RNS overnight, for publication when the market opens the following day.

rehypothecation The use of securities held in brokers' client accounts as collateral for buying further securities. *See* HYPOTHECATION.

reinstatement of the sum insured The payment of an additional premium to return the sum insured to its full level, after a claim has reduced it. Insurance policies are, in effect, a promise to pay money if a particular event occurs. If a claim is paid, the insurance is reduced by the claim amount (or if a total loss is paid, the policy is exhausted). If the policyholder wishes to return the cover to its full value, a premium representing the amount of cover used by the claim must be paid. In the case of a total loss the whole premium must be paid again.

reinsurance The passing of all or part of an insurance risk that has been covered by an insurer to another insurer in return for a premium. The contract between the parties is usually known as a **reinsurance treaty**. The policyholder is usually not aware that reinsurance has been arranged as no mention is made of it on the policy. Reinsurance is a similar process to the bookmaker's practice of laying off bets with other bookmakers when too much money is placed on a particular horse. Very often an insurer will only accept a risk with a high payout if a total loss occurs (e.g. for a jumbo jet) in the sure knowledge that the potential loss can be reduced by reinsurance. *See also* FACULTATIVE REINSURANCE.

reinsurance to close (RITC) The practice of *syndicates at *Lloyd's of London by which future liabilities for policies are carried over to a new year. Syndicates of investors at Lloyd's have to renew their legal status every year by reforming as a new syndicate (usually with the same members). Before the end of each year syndicates must cover any future liabilities for policies written during that year. They therefore reinsure such outstanding policies by means of a premium with the newly formed syndicate; this practice is known as reinsurance to close.

reintermediation *See* DISINTERMEDIATION.

reinvestment rate The interest rate at which an investor is able to reinvest income earned on an existing investment.

reinvestment risk The *risk that interest paid on investments will be not reinvested at the initial rate of return, owing to falling rates.

REIT Abbreviation for *real-estate investment trust.

related party An individual, partnership, or company that has the ability to control, or exercise significant influence over, another organization.

related-party transaction A transfer of resources or obligations between *related parties, regardless of whether a price is charged.

relationship banking The establishment of a long-term relationship between a bank and its customers. The main advantage is that it enables the bank to develop in-depth knowledge of a customer's business, which improves its ability to make informed decisions regarding loans to the customer. The customer expects to benefit by increased support during difficult times. *See also* BILATERAL BANK FACILITY; SYNDICATED BANK FACILITY.

relative strength The performance of a particular investment or portfolio relative to a wider *benchmark.

relative value-at-risk The average return on a portfolio minus the *value-at-risk cut-off value. It is the value-at-risk relative to the average return.

releveraging Increasing the level of debt in the capital structure of a business. *See* LEVERAGE.

remainderman A person who is a residual *beneficiary of a trust.

remitting bank The bank to which a person requiring payment of a cheque or other financial document has presented the cheque or other document for payment. In the UK this is often known as the **collecting bank**.

remuneration **1.** A sum of money paid for a service given. *See* AUDIT FEE; DIRECTOR (for directors' remuneration). **2.** A salary.

remuneration committee In UK public companies, a committee of non-executive directors who decide the pay of executive directors. Many such bodies were set up as a result of the *Greenbury Committee recommendations of 1995.

renounceable documents Documents that provide evidence of ownership, for a limited period, of unregistered shares. A letter of *allotment sent to shareholders when a new issue is floated is an example. Ownership of the shares can be passed to someone else by *renunciation at this stage.

rent A payment for the use of land, usually under a lease. The most usual kinds are ground rent and **rack rent**. Rack rent is paid when no capital payment (premium) has been made for the lease and the rent therefore represents the full value of the land and buildings. The amount of rent may be regulated by statute in certain cases.

rentes Non-redeemable government bonds issued by several European governments, notably France. The interest, which is paid annually, for ever, is called **rente**.

rentier A person who lives on income from *rentes or on receiving rent from land.

The meaning is sometimes extended to include anyone who lives on income derived from assets rather than a wage or salary.

renting back *See* LEASEBACK.

renunciation **1.** The surrender to someone else of rights to shares in a rights issue. The person to whom the shares are allotted by letter of *allotment fills in the **renunciation form** (usually attached) in favour of the person to whom the rights are renounced. **2.** The disposal of a unit-trust holding by completing the renunciation form on the reverse of the certificate and sending it to the trust managers.

reopen an issue To sell more of an existing bond issue in order to make the offering more liquid.

reorganization **1.** The process of restructuring a US company that is in financial difficulties. Protection against creditors can be sought under *chapter 11 of the Bankruptcy Reform Act 1978 while such a reorganization back to profitability is being undertaken. If creditors cannot agree on a plan, the company's assets are liquidated and the proceeds distributed by the Bankruptcy Court. **2.** The restructuring of a larger organization without the formation of a new company.

repackaged security A new security issue that uses an existing security as its backing.

repatriation **1.** The return of a person to his or her country of origin. **2.** The return of capital from a foreign investment to investment in the country from which it originally came.

repayment mortgage A *mortgage in which the borrower's regular payments consist of both capital repayments and interest.

repayment supplement A tax-free payment of interest by the UK Inland Revenue on delayed income tax or capital gains tax refunds.

replacement cost The cost of replacing an *asset, either in its present physical form or as the cost of obtaining equivalent services. If the latter is lower in amount than the former, the conclusion is that the assets currently used by the company are not those it would choose to acquire in the market place. Replacement cost may be used to value tangible fixed assets and in some circumstances such *working capital as stock.

replacement cycle The period over which a product or fixed asset will need to be replaced due to obsolescence.

replication In *portfolio management, the use of a hedging strategy to replicate the payoff structure of a financial obligation. *See* HEDGE.

repo Short for repurchase agreement. *See* REPURCHASE.

reporting accountants A firm of accountants who report on the financial information provided in a *prospectus. They may or may not be the company's own auditors. It is usual for reporting accountants to have had previous experience of new issues and the preparation of prospectuses.

reporting deadline The deadline for reporting a transaction to an exchange information system on a financial market.

reporting dealer A dealer with whom the US *Federal Reserve Bank does daily business in buying or selling government securities in *open-market operations. A reporting dealer is also known as a **primary dealer**.

reporting partner The partner in a firm of *auditors who forms an *audit opinion on the *financial statements of a client company and signs and dates the *auditors' report after the financial statements have been formally approved by the directors of the company.

report of the auditor(s) *See* AUDITORS' REPORT.

report of the directors *See* DIRECTORS' REPORT.

repossession The taking back of something purchased, for nonpayment of the instalments due under a *hire-purchase agreement. Foreclosing a mortgage on a house is sometimes also referred to as repossessing the house (*see* FORECLOSURE).

representation and warranty A clause in a loan agreement in which the borrower gives a contractual undertaking confirming certain fundamental facts. These will include the borrower's power to borrow and to give guarantees, as well as confirmation that it is not involved in any major litigation.

representations 1. Information given by a person wishing to arrange insurance about the nature of the risk that is to be covered. If it contains a material fact it must be true to the best knowledge and belief of the person wishing to be insured. *See* UTMOST GOOD FAITH. **2.** Information given by one party in furtherance of a deal.

repudiation The refusal of one party to pay or honour a contract. It can refer to the refusal by the government of a country to settle a national debt incurred by a previous government.

repurchase 1. The purchase from an investor of a unit-trust holding by the trust managers. **2.** (repurchase agreement; repo) An agreement (in full a **sale–repurchase agreement**) in which a security is sold and later bought back at an agreed price. The seller is paid in full and makes the agreement to raise ready money without losing the holding. The buyer negotiates a suitable repurchase price to enable a profit to be earned equivalent to interest on the money involved. Repurchase agreements originated in arrangements between the US *Federal Reserve Bank and the *money market, but are now widely used by large companies in the USA and also in Europe. Repos may have a term of only a few days – or even overnight. *See also* OVERNIGHT REPO; RETAIL REPO.

repurchase of own debt The buying back by a company of its own *debt at an amount different from the amount of the liability shown in the *balance sheet.

repurchase transaction A form of discounting in which a corporation raises funds from a bank by selling negotiable paper to it with an undertaking to buy the paper when it matures (*see* NEGOTIABLE INSTRUMENT).

reputational capital The value of an institution's good name and standing.

required reserves The amounts that US banks are obliged to hold against their liabilities. It is a specified proportion of the deposits and other liabilities.

rescheduling The revising of the terms of an existing debt in order to assist the borrower by spreading repayments, and sometimes interest payments, over a longer period. It has been undertaken by a number of sovereign borrowers. *See also* MULTI-YEAR RESCHEDULING AGREEMENT; RESTRUCTURING.

rescission The right of a party to a contract to have it set aside and to be restored to the position he or she was in before the contract was made. This is an equitable remedy, available at the discretion of the court. The usual grounds for rescission are mistake, misrepresentation, undue influence, and unconscionable bargains (i.e. those in which the terms are very unfair). No rescission will be allowed where the party seeking it has taken a benefit under the contract (affirmation), or where it is not possible to restore the parties to their former position (restitutio in integrum), or where third parties have already acquired rights under the contract.

reserve Part of the *capital of a company, other than the share capital, largely arising from retained profit or from the issue of share capital at more than its nominal value. Reserves are distinguished from *provisions in that for the latter there is a known diminution in value of an asset or a known liability, whereas reserves are surpluses not yet distributed and, in some cases (e.g. share premium account or capital redemption reserve), not distributable. The directors of a company may choose to earmark part of these funds for a special purpose (e.g. a **reserve for obsolescence** of plant). However, reserves should not be seen as specific sums of money put aside for special purposes as they are represented by the general net assets of the company. Reserves are subdivided into *retained earnings (revenue reserves), which are available to be distributed to the shareholders by way of dividends, and *undistributable reserves, which for various reasons are not distributable as dividends, although they may be converted into permanent share capital by way of a bonus issue.

reserve asset ratio A former requirement that UK banks had to keep reserves in proportion to their total assets. Abandoned in 1981, it was used in the previous decade as a crude means of monetary control.

reserve assets 1. Gold and foreign currency held by a central bank for intervention in foreign-exchange markets. **2.** A bank's holdings of funds at a central bank.

Reserve Bank *See* FEDERAL RESERVE BANK.

reserve capital (uncalled capital) That part of the issued *capital of a company that is held in reserve and is intended only to be called up if the company is wound up.

reserve currency A foreign currency that is held by a government because it has confidence in its stability and intends to use it to settle international debts. The US dollar and the pound sterling fulfilled this role for many years but the Japanese yen and the euro are now widely used.

reserve for loan losses Money set aside by a bank against potential future losses arising from its loan portfolios.

reserve for obsolescence *See* RESERVE.

reserve price The lowest price a seller is willing to accept for an article offered for sale by public *auction. If the reserve price is not reached by the bidding, the auctioneer is instructed to withdraw the article from sale.

reserve requirement The *cash ratio of a bank: the percentage of its assets that must be held in cash.

reserves 1. In the UK, the amount of gold and convertible currencies held at the *Bank of England, together with credits at the *International Monetary Fund. **2.** In other countries, similar assets held by a government-controlled *central bank.

reserves market The dealings of the *Federal Open Market Committee with other US banks.

reserves multiplier The method used in the US *Federal Reserve System to calculate the level of reserves the banks need to support their liabilities.

reserve tranche The 25% of its quota to which a member of the *International Monetary Fund has unconditional access, for which it pays no charges, and for which there is no obligation to repay the funds. The reserve tranche corresponds to the 25% of quota that was paid not in the member's domestic currency but in *Special Drawing Rights (SDRs) or currencies of other IMF members. It counts as part of the member's foreign reserves. As before 1978 it was paid in gold, it was known as the **gold tranche**. Like all IMF facilities it is available only to avert balance of payments problems, although for the reserve tranche the IMF has no power either to challenge the member's assessment of need or to impose a corrective policy. Further funds are available through credit tranches but these are subject to certain conditions (*see* CONDITIONALITY).

resident A person living or based in the UK to whom one of the following applies for a given tax year:
• the person is present in the UK for 183 days or more during that year;
• the person pays substantial visits to the UK, averaging 90 days or more for four or more consecutive years;
• the person has accommodation available for use in the UK and one visit is made during the year. This does not apply if the taxpayer is working abroad full-time nor to individuals who come to the UK for a temporary purpose only.
Since 15 March 1988 companies incorporated in the UK have been regarded as resident in the UK for corporation-tax purposes, irrespective of where the management and control of the company is exercised. Prior to 15 March 1988 a company was regarded as resident in the UK if its management and control were in the UK.

residual maturity *See* MATURITY DATE.

residual pool *See* POOL.

residual risk **1.** In derivatives, the risk connected with differences between the behaviour of the *underlying and that of any *hedge. **2.** *See* SYSTEMATIC RISK.

resistance level In technical analysis, a level of prices for a security or commodity that is repeatedly reached but not exceeded. Any move beyond this ceiling (*see* BREAKOUT) is regarded as signalling a significant shift to higher prices. *Compare* SUPPORT LEVEL. *See also* DOUBLE TOP.

resolution A binding decision made by the members of a company. If a motion is put before the members of a company at a general meeting and the required majority vote in favour of it, the motion is passed and becomes a resolution. A resolution may also be passed by unanimous informal consent of the members. An **ordinary resolution** may be passed by a bare majority of the members. The UK Companies Act prescribes this type of resolution for certain actions, such as the removal of a director. Normally, no particular length of notice is required for an ordinary resolution to be proposed, beyond the notice needed to call the meeting. However, ordinary resolutions of the company require **special notice** if a director or an auditor is to be removed or if a director who is over the statutory retirement age is to be appointed or permitted to remain in office. An **extraordinary resolution** is one for which 14 days' notice is required. The notice should state that it is an extraordinary resolution and for such a resolution 75% of those voting must approve it if it is to be passed. A **special resolution** requires 21 days' notice to the shareholders and a 75% majority to be effective. The type of resolution required to make a particular decision may be prescribed by the Companies Acts or by the company's articles. For example, an extraordinary resolution is required to wind up a company voluntarily, while a special resolution is required to change the company's articles of association.

respondentia bond *See* HYPOTHECATION.

restitution The legal principle that a person who has been unjustly enriched at the expense of another should make restitution, e.g. by returning property or money. This principle is not yet fully developed in English law but has a predominant place in the law of Scotland and the USA.

restricted surplus *See* UNDISTRIBUTABLE RESERVES.

restrictive covenant 1. A clause in a contract that restricts the freedom of one of the parties in some way. Employment contracts, for example, sometimes include a clause in which an employee agrees not to compete with the employer for a specified period after leaving the employment. Such clauses may not be enforceable in law. **2.** A clause in a contract affecting the use of land. *See* COVENANT.

restrictive endorsement An endorsement on a *bill of exchange that restricts the freedom of the endorsee to negotiate it.

restructuring *Rescheduling a debt, often also involving changes to the internal workings of the borrowing organization, its contracts, or even its products. Restructuring is usually undertaken voluntarily by the borrower, whereas rescheduling is often imposed by the lender to ensure that the debt is serviced.

retail banking Mass-market banking in which the customers are private individuals and small business customers. It typically offers a wide range of such services as personal loans, mortgages, pensions, and insurance as well as providing *current accounts and savings accounts. Cash cards and credit cards are also provided. In most nationwide banking systems it is still the most profitable part of a bank's activities.

Retail Price Index (RPI) An index of the prices of goods and services in retail shops purchased by average households, expressed in percentage terms relative to a base year, which is taken as 100. For example, if 1987 is taken as the base year for the UK (i.e. average prices in January 1987 = 100), then in 1946 the RPI stood at 7.4 and in September 2004 at 188.1. The RPI is compiled on a monthly basis and is based on 600 or so items in 11 groups. The prices of the goods are checked every month and individual items and groups are weighted to reflect their relative importance. Weightings are regularly updated by the Family Expenditure Survey. The RPI can be used to calculate the real change in earnings and expenditure by deflating financial data, and is one of the standard measures of the rate of *inflation. In the USA and some other countries the RPI is known as the **consumer price index**.

retail repo A *repurchase agreement involving a loan to a bank rather than to a company or an individual.

retail tender An application to buy a substantial number of shares in a privatization offer. The application is made through a **retail tender broker**. Usually the investor either decides on the price to bid for the shares (which may or may not be successful) or bids on a 'strike price only' basis, in which case shares will be allocated to the investor at the price paid by like institutions. Generally a retail tender will not attract the special incentives available to purchasers using a *share shop. Retail tender brokers are often also share shops.

retained earnings (retained profits; ploughed-back profits; retentions) The *net profit available for *distribution, less any distributions made, i.e. the amount kept within the company. Retained earnings are recorded in the profit and loss reserve.

retirement pension See PENSION.

retirement relief Formerly, a relief from *capital gains tax given to persons disposing of business assets at or over 50 years of age, or earlier if retiring due to ill-health. In 1999–2003 it was phased out in favour of *taper relief.

retiring a bill The act of withdrawing a *bill of exchange from circulation when it has been paid on or before its due date.

return The income from an investment, frequently expressed as a percentage of its cost. *See also* RETURN ON CAPITAL EMPLOYED.

returned cheque A cheque on which payment has been refused and which has been returned to the bank on which it was drawn. If the reason is lack of funds, the bank will mark it *refer to drawer; if the bank wishes to give the customer an opportunity to pay in sufficient funds to cover it, they will also mark it "please represent". The collecting bank will then present it for payment again, after letting his customer know that the cheque has been dishonoured.

return on assets An accounting ratio expressing the amount of *profit for a *financial year as a percentage of the *assets of a company.

return on capital employed (ROCE) An accounting ratio expressing the *profit of an organization for a *financial year as a percentage of the capital employed. It is probably one of the most frequently used ratios for assessing the performance of organizations. In making the calculation, however, there are a number of differing definitions of the terms used. Profit is usually taken as profit before interest and tax, while capital employed refers to fixed assets plus *working capital minus *current liabilities.

Sometimes the expression **return on investment** (ROI) is used, in which case even greater care must be used in understanding the calculation of the separate items. Management may consider that profit before interest and tax, expressed as a percentage of total assets, is a useful measure of performance. Shareholders, however, may be more interested in taking profit after interest and comparing this to total assets less all liabilities. The ratio can be further analysed by calculating *profit margins and *capital turnover ratios.

return on equity (ROE) The net income of an organization expressed as a percentage of its equity capital.

return on investment (ROI) See RETURN ON CAPITAL EMPLOYED.

Reuters A worldwide agency dealing in news, financial information, and trading services. It was founded in 1851 as a subscription information service for newspapers. It now provides a wide range of financial prices and dealing services.

revalorization of currency The replacement of one currency unit by another. A government often takes this step if a nation's currency has been devalued frequently or by a large amount. The practice is usually associated with high rates of inflation. *Compare* REVALUATION OF CURRENCY.

revaluation account In a *partnership to which a new partner is admitted or if an existing partner dies or retires, assets and liabilities must be revalued to their current market value. The differences between historical values and the revaluations are debited or credited to the revaluation account. The balance on the revaluation account will represent a profit or loss on revaluation, which must be shared between the partners in the *profit-sharing ratio.

revaluation of assets A revaluation of the assets of a company, either because they have increased in value since they were acquired or because *inflation has made the balance-sheet values unrealistic. The Companies Act 1985 makes it obligatory for the directors of a company to state in the directors' report if they believe the value of land differs materially from the value in the balance sheet. The Companies Act 1980 lays down the procedures to adopt when fixed assets are revalued. The difference between the net book value of a company's assets before and after revaluation is shown in a **revaluation reserve account** or, more commonly in the USA, an **appraisal-surplus account** (if the value of the assets has increased).

revaluation of currency An increase in the value of a currency in terms of gold or other currencies. It is usually made by a government that has a persistent balance of payments surplus. It has the effect of making imports cheaper but exports become dearer and therefore less competitive in other countries; revaluation is therefore unpopular with governments. *Compare* DEVALUATION; REVALORIZATION OF CURRENCY.

revaluation reserve account *See* REVALUATION OF ASSETS.

revenue 1. Any form of income. **2.** Cost and income items that are either charged or credited to the *profit and loss account for an accounting period.

revenue account 1. An *account recording the income from trading operations or the expenses incurred in these operations. **2.** A budgeted amount that can be spent for day-to-day operational expenses, especially in public-sector budgeting. *Compare* CAPITAL ACCOUNT.

reverse auction A method of redeeming bonds in which holders express a price at which they will sell the bonds. This system is used by the Bank of England to buy back bonds that it has issued.

reverse floating-rate note **(inverse floating-rate note)** A *floating-rate note on which the payment rises when the *reference rate falls and vice versa. In a **leveraged reverse floating-rate note** the changes in the payments are greater than the changes in the interest rate.

reverse takeover 1. The buying of a larger company by a smaller company. **2.** The purchasing of a public company by a private company. This may be the cheapest way that a private company can obtain a listing on a stock exchange, as it avoids the expenses of a *flotation and it may be that the assets of the public company can be purchased at a discount. However, on the *London Stock Exchange there are regulations stipulating that the nature of the target company's business must be compatible with that of the private company. Usually the name of the public company is changed to that of the private company, who takes over the listing.

reverse yield gap 1. The situation in which the yield on securities is greater than the dividend yield on equities. *See* YIELD GAP. **2.** A downward-sloping yield curve.

reversionary annuity *See* CONTINGENT ANNUITY.

reversionary bonus A sum added to the amount payable on death or maturity of a *with-profits policy for life assurance. The bonus is added if the life-assurance company has a surplus or has a profit on the investment of its life funds. Once a reversionary bonus has been declared it cannot be withdrawn if the policy runs to maturity or to the death of the insured. However, if the policy is cashed, the bonus is usually reduced by an amount that depends on the length of time the policy has to run.

revocable letter of credit See LETTER OF CREDIT.

revolving acceptance facility by tender (RAFT) An underwritten facility from a bank to place sterling *acceptance credits through the medium of a tender panel of eligible banks.

revolving bank facility (standby revolving credit) A loan from a bank or group of banks to a company in which the company has flexibility with regard to the timing and the number of *drawdowns and repayments; any loan repaid can be reborrowed subject to fulfilment of the conditions of the *committed facility. The facility can be a *bilateral bank facility or a *syndicated bank facility.

revolving credit A bank credit that is negotiated for a specified period; it allows for *drawdown and repayment within that period. Repaid amounts can be redrawn up to the agreed limit of the credit. At the end of the loan period there is a *bullet repayment of the principal and any outstanding interest; alternatively, a repayment schedule is negotiated for the outstanding principal and interest. In the USA a revolving credit is called an **open-end credit**. See also CONVERTIBLE REVOLVING CREDIT.

revolving underwriting facility (RUF) See NOTE ISSUANCE (OR PURCHASE) FACILITY.

rho A *greek expressing the relationship between option value and the risk-free interest rate.

rial 1. (Rls) The standard monetary unit of Iran. **2.** (RO) The standard monetary unit of Oman, divided into 1000 baizas.

RIE Abbreviation for *Recognized Investment Exchange.

Riegle–Neale Act 1994 A key act of the US Congress in deregulating interstate banking.

riel (KHR) The standard monetary unit of Cambodia, divided into 100 sen.

rigging a market An attempt to make a profit on a market, usually a security or commodity market, by overriding the normal market forces. This often involves taking a *long position or a *short position in the market that is sufficiently substantial to influence price levels, and then supporting or depressing the market by further purchases or sales.

rights issue A method by which quoted companies on a stock exchange raise new capital, in exchange for new shares. The name arises from the principle of *pre-emption rights, according to which existing shareholders must be offered the new shares in proportion to their holding of old shares (a **rights offer**). For example in a 1 for 4 rights issue, shareholders would be asked to buy one new share for every four they already hold. As rights are usually issued at a discount to the market price of existing shares, those not wishing to take up their rights can sell them in the market (see RIGHTS LETTER; RENUNCIATION). See also EXCESS SHARES. Compare BOUGHT DEAL; VENDOR PLACING; SCRIP ISSUE.

rightsizing The restructuring and *rationalization of an organization to improve effectiveness and cut costs, without involving a full *downsizing operation, which can often be overdone and result in *corporate anorexia. Rightsizing could include increasing the size of an organization to meet increased demand (say), but it is more often used as a euphemism for moderate and controlled downsizing.

rights letter A document sent to an existing shareholder of a company offering shares in a *rights issue on advantageous terms. If the recipient does not wish to take advantage of the offer, the letter and the attendant rights may be sold on a stock exchange (*see* RENUNCIATION).

rights offer *See* RIGHTS ISSUE.

Riksbanken Sweden's *central bank.

ring **1.** A group of dealers or speculators who seek to monopolize a segment of a market in order to push prices up or down. Rings in *commodity markets have frequently been formed. **2.** A trading session in a commodity exchange, usually by *open outcry. *See* CALLOVER. **3.** The trading floor of a commodity exchange.

ring-fence **1.** To allow one part of a company or group to go into receivership or bankruptcy without affecting the viability of the rest of the company or group. **2.** To assign a sum of money to a particular purpose so that it does not become part of the general resources of an organization.

ringgit (M$) The Malaysian dollar: the standard monetary unit of Malaysia, divided into 100 sen.

ring trading *See* CALLOVER; RING; OPEN OUTCRY.

rising bottoms A pattern in which the price lows within market fluctuations display a steady upward trend over time. In *chartist analysis such a pattern is seen as a sign of a *bull market. *Compare* ASCENDING TOPS.

risk **1.** The possibility of loss in absolute terms or relative to expectations. There are a number of different types of risk, some of the major categories being *market risk, *credit risk, *liquidity risk, and *operational risk. Market risk arises from changes in prices in financial markets. Credit risk relates to non-payment of obligations or credit impairment. Liquidity risk is that of running out of cash or problems with asset enhancement. Operational risk is a catch-all category which covers a firm's internal systems and processes, as well as external *events. *See also* COUNTERPARTY RISK; EXCHANGE-RATE EXPOSURE; INTEREST-RATE RISK; SPECIFIC RISK; SYSTEMATIC RISK. **2.** *See* INSURABLE RISK.

risk-adjusted assets The assets, shown on the balance sheet of a bank, that have had a risk weighting applied to them. Since 1922 banks have been required to hold *capital adequacy ratios that take account of the different weights of risk attached to loans, foreign exchange, government securities, cross-border loans, and mortgages. The system also takes account of assets that are held off the balance sheet, such as letters of credit, interest-rate swaps, and currency options, which also have to have risk weightings applied to them. Major changes were brought about in 1992 through the *Bank for International Settlements; these are likely to affect the calculation and measurement of a bank's capital adequacy position when fully formulated. The system has been altered by the *Basle Market Risk Amendment and *Basle Two but risk-adjusted assets are still an important element in banking regulation.

risk-adjusted discount rate In capital budgeting and portfolio management, the *discount rate used in calculations of *present value; it will reflect the level of risk embodied in the cash flows being considered.

risk-adjusted return on capital (RAROC) A measure of the performance of units within a bank or financial organization, be they managerial units, products, distributional units, or such treasury-based units as trading desks. It was developed by Bankers' Trust and the Bank of America in the 1980s. In its most common form RAROC allocates *capital at risk to a unit and divides that into the return obtained from the unit. The capital is allocated in terms of a *value-at-risk methodology. A refinement of this system is known as **RAROC 2020**.

risk analysis The consideration of *risk in a business, project, or decision. It involves the identification of risk, the classification of risks in regard to their impact and likelihood, and a consideration of how they might best be managed.

risk-averse Describing a *risk preference in which an investor's attraction to a potential investment rises with higher average returns and falls with greater *standard deviations of returns. *Compare* RISK-NEUTRAL; RISK-SEEKING. *See also* PORTFOLIO THEORY; UTILITY THEORY.

risk capital (venture capital) Capital invested in a project in which there is a substantial element of risk, especially money invested in a new venture or an expanding business in exchange for shares in the business. It is also commonly used in employee or *management buy-outs. Risk capital is normally invested in the equity of the company; it is not a loan.

risk-free rate The *rate of return on an investment that has no risk. The return on US and UK Treasury bills is often regarded as a very close approximation to this rate. The risk-free rate is an important concept in the *capital asset pricing model.

risk management The control of an individual's or company's chances of losing on an investment. Managing the risk can involve taking out insurance against a loss, hedging a loan against interest-rate rises, and protecting an investment against a fall in interest rates (*see* FINANCIAL FUTURES). A bank will always try to manage the risks involved in lending by adjusting the level of charges and interest rates to compensate for a percentage of losses.

risk matrix A method of *risk analysis customized for businesses from a basic framework developed by the US military in the identification of *operational risk. It is in essence a brainstorming technique. When applied to a business, the two dimensions of the matrix relate to those assets at risk in the business and how these assets are at risk. When considering what is at risk, the assets of the business are defined as widely as possible, including both *tangible assets and such *intangible assets as reputation and branding.

RiskMetrics A *risk analysis and measurement system produced by J. P. Morgan Chase; it is based on the concept of *value-at-risk. *See also* CREDITMETRICS.

risk-neutral Describing a *risk preference in which the investor makes decisions on the average return on an investment and is not interested in the *standard deviation of returns. *Compare* RISK-AVERSE; RISK-SEEKING.

risk-neutral valuation A valuation method, often used for derivatives pricing, which relies on the *risk-free rate of return.

risk preference The attitude of an investor to risks. *See* RISK-AVERSE; RISK-NEUTRAL; RISK-SEEKING.

risk premium (**market-risk premium**) **1.** The difference between the expected *rate of return on an investment and the *risk-free rate of return over the same period. If there is any risk element at all, the rate of return should be higher than if no risk were involved. *See* CAPITAL ASSET PRICING MODEL. **2.** An addition to the normal price of a transaction to reflect any extra risk involved.

risk-seeking Describing a *risk preference in which the investor's attraction to an investment rises with higher average returns and a higher *standard deviation of returns. *Compare* RISK-AVERSE; RISK-NEUTRAL.

RITC Abbreviation for *reinsurance to close.

riyal **1.** (SRls) The standard monetary unit of Saudi Arabia, divided into 20 qurush and 100 halala. **2.** (QR) The standard monetary unit of Qatar, divided into 100 dirhams. **3.** (YRls) The standard monetary unit of Yemen, divided into 100 fils.

RNS Abbreviation for *Regulatory News Service.

ROCE Abbreviation for *return on capital employed.

ROE Abbreviation for *return on equity.

ROI Abbreviation for return on investment. *See* RETURN ON CAPITAL EMPLOYED.

rolled-up coupon **1.** A certificate of interest (*see* COUPON) on a bond or other security, in which the interest is ploughed back to increase the capital value of the original bond, rather than being drawn as cash. **2.** Loan arrears added to the principal.

rolling position A financial *position that is maintained, although the instruments comprising the position are changed over time.

rolling settlement The practice on many stock markets of settling a transaction a fixed number of days after the trade is agreed. On the London Stock Exchange the practice was to have two- or three-week accounts for dealings with a fixed day for settlement after the close of the account. This was replaced in 1994 by a rolling settlement system in which settlement has to be made within a specified number of days of a transaction.

rollover **1.** The resetting of an interest rate in a loan or swap. **2.** The sale of a position and redeployment of the funds to invest in a similar position. **3.** The extension of the period to maturity of a debt.

roll-over CD A *certificate of deposit in which the maturity is divided into short periods to make it easier to sell on the secondary market. They are sometimes known as **roly-poly CDs**. The interest rate changes at roll-over dates.

roll-over credit A medium- or long-term bank loan in which the rate of interest varies with short-term money-market rates (such as LIBOR) because the bank has raised the loan by short-term money-market or *interbank market borrowing.

roll-over relief (**replacement of business asset relief**) A relief from *capital gains tax on certain disposals. A gain arising on the disposal of a business asset may be rolled over in full, resulting in no payment of capital gains tax on its disposal. This can only occur if all the proceeds received from the disposal of the asset are reinvested in a new business asset. Both the old and new asset must both be business assets, which are defined as:

- land or buildings,
- fixed plant and machinery,
- ships, aircraft, and hovercraft,
- goodwill,
- satellites, space stations, and spacecraft,
- milk and potato quotas,
- premium quotas for ewes and suckler cows.

The old asset and the new asset do not have to belong to the same category. The proceeds on disposal of land (the old asset) could be rolled over into the acquisition of a milk quota (the new asset). Full roll-over relief would be available if all the proceeds from the land were used to acquire the milk quota.

roll-up funds An offshore investment fund using securities with *rolled-up coupons designed to avoid *income tax. However, these funds are now assessed for income tax as if the coupons were paid in cash.

roly-poly CD *See* ROLL-OVER CD.

rotation of directors Under the articles of association of most UK companies, one third of the directors are obliged to retire each year (normally at the annual general meeting), so that each director retires by rotation every three years. Retiring directors may be re-elected.

rouble (Rub) **1.** The standard monetary unit of Russia and Belarus, divided into 100 kopeks. **2.** The standard monetary unit of Tajikistan, divided into 100 tanga.

round lot A round number of shares or a round amount of stock for which market makers will sometimes offer better prices than for **odd lots**.

roundtripping A transaction that enables a company to borrow money from one source and lend it at a profit to another, by taking advantage of a short-term rise in interest rates or regulatory anomaly.

Royal Mint The organization in the UK that has had the sole right to manufacture English coins since the 16th century. Controlled by the Chancellor of the Exchequer, it was formerly situated in the City of London but moved to Llantrisant in Wales in 1968. It also makes banknotes, UK medals, and increasing quantities of foreign coins (now about 65% of the Mint's total output).

royalty A payment made for the right to use the property of another person for gain. This may be an *intellectual property, such as a copyright (e.g. in a book) or a *patent (e.g. in an invention). It may also be paid to a landowner, who has granted mineral rights to someone else, on sales of minerals that have been extracted from his land. A royalty is regarded as a wasting asset as copyrights, patents, and mines have limited lives.

RPB Abbreviation for *Recognized Professional Body.

RPI Abbreviation for *Retail Price Index.

R squared In *regression analysis, a measure of the degree to which variations in the dependent variable can be explained in terms of variations in the independent variables. Its value is between 0 and 1. If the regression model exactly explains the data it is 1 and if it explains none of the data it is 0.

RUF Abbreviation for revolving underwriting facility. *See* NOTE ISSUANCE (OR PURCHASE) FACILITY.

rufiyaa (Rf) The standard monetary unit of the Maldives, divided into 100 laari.

run 1. The hasty and simultaneous withdrawal of funds by a large number of depositors, who have lost confidence in a bank or other financial institution. A financial institution on which there is a run can be pushed into collapse by the increasing loss of confidence and panic it creates. **2.** Lack of confidence in a particular currency, causing investors and speculators to sell their holding of that currency, e.g. a run on the pound. **3.** A dealer's list of prices for securities.

running-account credit A personal credit agreement that enables a person to receive loans from time to time from a bank or other lender provided that a specified credit limit is not exceeded. Interest is charged on the amount loaned during any period.

running broker A bill broker who does not himself discount *bills of exchange but acts between bill owners and discount houses or banks for a commission.

running yield *See* YIELD.

run to settlement Denoting a *futures contract in a commodity that has run to its settlement day without being set off by a corresponding sales or purchase contract so that delivery of the physical goods must be made or taken.

rupee 1. The standard monetary unit of India (Re, *plural* Rs), Pakistan (PRs), Nepal (NRs), and Bhutan (BRs), divided into 100 paisa. **2.** The standard monetary unit of Sri Lanka (SLRs), Mauritius (Mau Re; *plural* Mau Rs), and the Seychelles (SR), divided into 100 cents.

rupiah (Rp) The standard monetary unit of Indonesia, divided into 100 sen.

Russian Country Fund A US government scheme, operated through the *Overseas Private Investment Corporation (OPIC), aimed at stimulating private investment in the Russian economy. It is supported by OPIC loans or guarantees. This *closed-end fund set a target of $100M. Its priority is generating new business and funding privatization.

r

SA **1.** Abbreviation for *société anonyme*. It appears after the name of a French, Belgian, or Luxembourg company, being equivalent to the British abbreviation plc (i.e. denoting a public limited company). **2.** Abbreviation for **sociedad anónima*. It appears after the name of a Spanish public company. **3.** Abbreviation for **sociedade anónima*. It appears after the name of a Portuguese public company. *Compare* SARL.

sacrifice Loss of welfare as a result of paying a tax. One of the principles of taxation is that a tax should be formulated so that it involves **equality of sacrifice** on the part of the taxpayers. It is assumed that taxpayers with equal incomes will sacrifice equal amounts of welfare by paying identical taxes.

SAEF Abbreviation for *Stock Exchange Automatic Execution Facility.

safe custody A service offered by most UK commercial banks, in which the bank holds valuable items belonging to its customers in its strong room. These items are usually documents, such as house deeds and bearer bonds, but they may also include jewellery, etc. The bank is a bailee for these items and its liability will depend on whether or not it has charged the customer for the service and the terms of the customer's own insurance (in the case of jewellery, etc.). In a **safe deposit** the customer hires a small lockable box from the bank or safe-deposit company, to which access is provided during normal banking hours. The customer keeps the key to the box.

saitori Members of the *Tokyo Stock Exchange who act as intermediaries between brokers. They cannot deal on their own account or for non-members of the exchange; they may only be allowed to deal in a limited number of stocks.

salaried partner A partner in a *partnership who by agreement draws a regular salary.

salary A regular payment, usually monthly, made by an employer, under a contract of employment, to an employee.

sale and leaseback *See* LEASEBACK.

sale by instalments *See* HIRE PURCHASE.

sale by tender *See* ISSUE BY TENDER.

sale–repurchase agreement *See* REPURCHASE.

sales tax A tax based on the selling price of goods. Such taxes are not now generally favoured, since they have a cascade effect, i.e. if goods are sold on from one trader to another the amount of sales tax borne by the ultimate buyer becomes too great. *Value added tax was largely designed to meet this objection.

salvage value The disposal value of a capital asset.

Samurai bond A *bond issued in Japan by a foreign institution. It is denominated in yen and can be bought by non-residents of Japan.

sandbag A stalling tactic used by an unwilling target company in a takeover bid.

The management of the target company agrees to have talks with the unwelcome bidder, which it protracts for as long as possible in the hope that a *white knight will appear and make a more acceptable bid.

S & L Abbreviation for *savings and loan association.

S & P 500 Abbreviation for *Standard and Poor's 500 Stock Index.

sandwich spread An option strategy in which gains are made if the volatility or movement in the value of the *underlying is relatively small.

Sanmekai The Japanese group of *City Banks that sets short-term interest rates.

sans recours *See* WITHOUT RECOURSE.

santim (*plural* **santimi**) A monetary unit of Latvia worth one hundredth of a *lats.

São Paulo Stock Exchange The most important of the ten stock exchanges in Brazil, called the Bolsa de Valores de São Paulo (BOVESPA); together with the older Rio de Janeiro market it accounts for 90% of Brazilian equity trading.

Sarl. 1. Abbreviation for *società a responsabilità limitata*. It appears after the name of an Italian company, being equivalent to the British abbreviation Ltd (i.e. denoting a private limited liability company). **2.** Abbreviation for *société à responsabilité limitée*. It appears after the name of a French private limited company. *Compare* SA.

SAS Abbreviation for *Statement of Auditing Standards.

satang A monetary unit of Thailand worth one hundredth of a *baht.

satellite banking The arrangement of a network of banks into smaller and larger branches. The smaller branches are restricted to a narrower range of services than the larger branches. The larger branches also have more senior managers, with a greater power of discretion to make loans.

save-as-you-earn (SAYE) A method of making regular savings (not necessarily linked to earnings), which carries certain tax privileges. This method has been used to encourage tax-free savings in building societies or National Savings and also to encourage employees to acquire shares in their own organizations.

savings Money set aside by individuals, either for some special purpose or to provide an income at some time in the future (often after retirement). Money saved can be placed in a *savings account with a bank or building society or an *Individual Savings Account (ISA), invested in *National Savings, or used to purchase *securities. Savings are also used to buy *pensions, *annuities, and *endowment assurance.

savings account A bank or building-society account designed for the investment of personal savings. There are a wide variety available, offering different terms and conditions and interest rates. The rates tend to be higher than old-fashioned deposit accounts and interest-bearing current accounts. Some accounts offer instant access to funds, while others require that notice be given, typically 30, 60, or 90 days. In general terms, interest rates vary according to the sum invested and the length of the notice period.

savings and loan association (S&L) The US equivalent of a UK *building society. It usually offers loans with a fixed rate of interest and has greater investment flexibility than a UK building society.

savings bank A bank that specializes in setting up *savings accounts for relatively small deposits. In the UK the *National Savings Bank and *building societies perform this function. In the USA, *savings and loan associations do so.

savings bonds *See* NATIONAL SAVINGS.

savings certificate *See* NATIONAL SAVINGS.

savings ratio The ratio of *savings by individuals and households to *disposable income. Variations in the savings ratio reflect the changing preferences of individuals between present and future consumption. Countries, such as Japan, with very high savings ratios have tended to experience faster growth in GDP than countries, such as the USA, with low savings ratios.

SAYE Abbreviation for *save-as-you-earn.

scale 1. A range of quotes for different maturities of government paper. **2.** A range of scores used in *credit rating. **3.** A transaction to be executed in a number of stages.

scale effect (economies of scale) The reduction in the average production cost (and hence unit cost) of a product when output and sales increase. *Compare* SCOPE ECONOMIES.

scalpers Traders who deal very frequently for small gains and may only hold a position for a few minutes.

Schatzwechsel A German government Treasury bill, usually repayable in three months.

schedule 1. The part of legislation that is placed at the end of a UK Act of Parliament and contains subsidiary matter to the main sections of the Act. **2.** One of several schedules of income tax forming part of the original income-tax legislation, now used to classify various sources of income for tax purposes. Some of the schedules are further subdivided into cases. The broad classification is: Schedule A, rents from property in the UK; Schedule D, Case 1, profits from trade; Case II, profits from professions or vocations; Case III, interest not otherwise taxed; Case IV, income from securities outside the UK; Case V, income from possessions outside the UK; Case VI, other annual profits and gains; Schedule E, Cases I, II, and III, emoluments of offices or employments (the cases depending on the residential status of the taxpayer); Schedule F, dividends paid by UK companies. Schedule B, income from commercial woodlands, and Schedule C, interest paid by public bodies, no longer apply. **3.** Working papers submitted with tax returns or tax computations. **4.** Any scale of rates. **5.** A plan for undertaking some enterprise, especially one that details the timing of events.

scheme of arrangement *See* ARRANGEMENT.

Schilling (S) Formerly, the standard monetary unit of Austria, divided into 100 Groschen. It was subsumed into the *euro for all purposes except cash transactions in January 1999 and abolished in 2002.

scope economies (economies of scope) The increases in efficiency and sales that can result from producing, distributing, and marketing a range of products, as opposed to a single product or type of product. *Bancassurance is often seen as an example of scope economies.

scorched earth policy An extreme form of *poison pill in which a company that believes it is to be the target of a *takeover bid makes its balance sheet or profitability less attractive than it really is by a reversible manoeuvre, such as borrowing money at an exorbitant rate of interest.

screen trading Any form of trading that relies on the use of a computer screen rather than personal contact as in *floor trading, *pit trading, ring trading, etc. *See also* AUTOMATED SCREEN TRADING.

scrip The certificates that demonstrate ownership of *stocks, *shares, and *bonds (capital raised by subscription), especially the certificates relating to a *scrip issue.

scrip issue (bonus issue; capitalization issue; free issue) The issue of new share certificates to existing shareholders to reflect the accumulation of profits in the reserves of a company's balance sheet. It is thus a process for converting money from the company's reserves into issued capital. The shareholders do not pay for the new shares and appear to be no better off. However, in a 1 for 3 scrip issue, say, the shareholders receive one new share for every three existing shares they own. This automatically reduces the price of the shares by 25%, catering to the preference of shareholders to hold lower-priced shares rather than *heavy shares; it also encourages them to hope that the price will gradually climb to its former value, which will, of course, make them 25% better off. In the USA this is known as a **stock split**.

SDR-linked deposit A special deposit in a private bank account denominated in *Special Drawing rights.

SDRs Abbreviation for *Special Drawing Rights.

SEAQ Abbreviation for *Stock Exchange Automated Quotations System.

seasonality The seasonal variability of certain economic or financial factors, for example unemployment or commodity prices.

seasoned issue A *new issue that has been mostly sold.

SEATS Abbreviation for *Stock Exchange Alternative Trading Service.

SEC Abbreviation for *Securities and Exchange Commission.

secondary bank **1.** A name sometimes given to *finance houses. **2.** Any organization that offers some banking services, such as making loans, offering secondary mortgages, etc., but that does not offer the usual commercial-bank services of cheque accounts, etc.

secondary market (after market) A market in which existing securities are traded, as opposed to a *primary market, in which securities are sold for the first time. In most cases a *stock exchange largely fulfils the role of a secondary market, with the flotation of *new issues representing only a small proportion of its total business. However, it is the existence of a flourishing secondary market, providing *liquidity and the spreading of *risks, that creates the conditions for a healthy primary market.

Second Directive The most important of the EU directives on banking regulation, introduced in 1989 (*see* BANKING DIRECTIVES). It stipulates *capital adequacy requirements for banks in member states. The directive also regulates the licensing and operation of banks based in one member state in other EU countries.

second mortgage A *mortgage taken out on a property that is already mortgaged. Second and subsequent mortgages can often be used to raise money if the value of the property has increased considerably since the first mortgage was taken out. As the deeds of the property are usually held by the first mortgagee (lender), the second mortgagee undertakes a greater risk and therefore usually demands a higher rate of interest. The second mortgagee usually registers the second mortgage to protect himself against subsequent mortgages. In the UK, the Land Registry will issue a certificate of second charge in the case of registered land.

second of exchange *See* BILLS IN A SET.

second state pension *See* STATE EARNINGS-RELATED PENSION SCHEME.

second-tier market A market for stocks and shares in which *listing requirements for the companies are less stringent than those on a *main market. Although a second-tier market needs to be effectively regulated, conditions of entry and reporting are less expensive. *See also* OVER-THE-COUNTER MARKET.

secret reserve Funds accumulated by a company but not disclosed on the *balance sheet. They can arise when an *asset has been deliberately undervalued or a method has been used to account for a transaction with the intention of not showing the effect on the balance sheet. Financial Reporting Standard 5, 'Reporting the Substance of Transactions', is aimed at *off-balance-sheet finance.

sector 1. A category of assets that shares a particular attribute or attributes, for example *credit rating. **2.** A particular part of the economy, for example the industrial sector.

secular Denoting a long-term trend or development, in contrast to seasonal or cyclical phenomena.

secured 1. Denoting a loan (**secured loan**) in which the lender has an asset to sell if the borrower defaults on the loan repayments. **2.** Denoting a creditor (**secured creditor**) who has a charge on the property of the debtor. *See* FIXED CHARGE; FLOATING CHARGE.

secured debenture A *debenture secured by a charge over the property of a company, such as mortgage debentures (secured on land belonging to the company). Usually a trust deed sets out the powers of the debenture holders to enforce their security in the event of the company defaulting in payment of the principal or the interest. It is usual to appoint a *receiver to realize the security.

secured liability A debt against which the borrower has provided sufficient assets as security to safeguard the lender in case of non-repayment.

Securities Act 1933 The first piece of US legislation regulating financial markets. *See also* SECURITIES EXCHANGE ACT 1934.

Securities and Exchange Commission (SEC) A US government agency established in 1934 to protect investors by regulating behaviour in the securities markets.

Securities and Futures Authority Ltd (SFA) The *Self-Regulating Organization formed from the merger of The Securities Association Ltd (TSA) and the Association of Futures Brokers and Dealers Ltd (AFBD) in April 1991. It was responsible for regulating the conduct of brokers and dealers in securities, *options, and futures, including most of those on the *London Stock Exchange and the *London International Financial Futures and Options Exchange. Its responsibilities were taken over by the *Financial Services Authority in 1997.

Securities and Investment Board (SIB) A regulatory body (now superseded by the *Financial Services Authority) set up by the Financial Services Act 1986 to oversee London's financial markets (e.g. the stock exchange, life assurance, unit trusts). Each market had its own *Self-Regulating Organization (SRO), which reported to the SIB. The prime function of the SIB was to protect investors from fraud and to ensure that the rules of conduct established by the government and the SROs were followed. Some City activities were outside its control; for example, takeovers were under the supervision of the Takeover Panel (*see* CITY CODE ON TAKEOVERS AND MERGERS).

Securities Association Ltd, The (TSA) The former *Self-Regulating Organization responsible for regulating the conduct of brokers and dealers in securities, options, and futures. It included most member firms of the *London Stock Exchange. In April 1991 it merged with the *Association of Futures Brokers and Dealers Ltd to form the *Securities and Futures Authority Ltd (SFA); its role is now performed by the *Financial Services Authority.

Securities Exchange Act 1934 US legislation introducing enforcement provisions for the *Securities Act 1933. The *Securities and Exchange Commission came into being as a result of this Act.

Securities Exchange of Thailand (SET) One of the *dragon markets of the Pacific; its share trading dates from 1962 with the foundation of the Bangkok Stock Exchange. The SET itself was established in 1975 and is regulated by the Thai Ministry of Finance.

securities house A large stockbroker-based financial institution, many of which have grown since the 1980s to provide investors with facilities of all types on a global scale. They encompass the activities of brokers, dealers, market makers, researchers, and traders.

Securities Industry Association (SIA) A US trade association for the brokerage industry.

Securities Industry Automation Corporation (SIAC) The US corporation that provides the *National Securities Clearing Corporation with the data-processing and electronic communications facilities required to act as a *clearing house for both New York's stock exchanges.

Securities Investor Protection Corporation (SIPC) A US corporation to which all members of the *National Association of Securities Dealers Inc. belong; its function is to provide compensation for investors who suffer a loss as a result of the activities of a market maker or dealer.

securities loan 1. The lending of securities by one broker to another as part of a short-sale process. **2.** The use of securities as collateral.

securitization The process of creating a tradeable financial instrument (a *security) from a non-tradeable financial asset, such as a bank loan.

securitized mortgage A *mortgage that has been converted into a marketable security, which can be sold to an investor. One advantage of selling on mortgages and other loans in this way is that it enables banks to move assets from their balance sheets, thus boosting their *capital adequacy ratios. Securitization of mortgages is strictly controlled by the regulating authorities.

securitized paper A financial instrument, such as a bond or note, which results from a borrower and investor agreeing on an exchange of funds by means of *securitization.

security **1.** An asset or assets to which a lender can have recourse if the borrower defaults on any loan repayments. In the case of loans by banks and other moneylenders the security is sometimes referred to as *collateral. **2.** A financial asset, including shares, government stocks, debentures, bonds, unit trusts, and rights to money lent or deposited. It does not, however, include insurance policies. *See also* BEARER SECURITY; DATED SECURITY; FIXED-INTEREST SECURITY; GILT-EDGED SECURITY; LISTED SECURITY; MARKETABLE SECURITY.

security-market line A line plotted on a graph that specifies the required *rate of return obtained by the *capital asset pricing model (CAPM). The graph has average return on the vertical axis and *beta coefficient on the horizontal axis. The security-market line links the *risk-free rate on the horizontal axis to the point representing the market return and a beta of one. If extended, this will provide the required rate of return for all levels of beta.

seed capital The small amount of initial capital required to fund the research and development necessary before a new company is set up. The seed capital should enable a persuasive and accurate *business plan to be drawn up.

seigniorage The profits accruing to the issuer of legal tender, mainly as a result of the difference between the material costs of producing currency and its face value. The term is frequently used in reference to the US Treasury's earnings from producing coins and notes; as the producer of the world's major reserve currency and black market currency, the USA can obtain considerable gains from printing money.

self-assessment A system that enables taxpayers to assess their own *income tax and *capital gains tax liabilities for the year. Major changes to the UK system occurred in the year 1996–97, since when a self-assessment section has been contained in the *tax return, in addition to the part requiring details of *taxable income, *chargeable gains, and claims for *personal allowances. At present the self-assessment is voluntary; if the taxpayer prefers to let the Inland Revenue calculate his or her liability, then the tax return must be submitted by September 30 following the end of the year of assessment, rather than the usual January 31. The introduction of self-assessment was accompanied by the *Board of Inland Revenue being granted extensive audit powers to enquire into any tax return.

self-employed taxpayers Persons who are not employees and who trade on their own account. They are taxed on the profits of their trades rather than by *PAYE and their national-insurance contributions differ from those of employees.

Self-Employment Individuals Retirement Act *See* KEOGH PLAN.

self-financing Denoting a company that is able to finance its capital expenditure from undistributed profits rather than by borrowing.

self-liquidating **1.** Denoting an asset that earns back its original cost out of income over a fixed period. **2.** Denoting a loan in which the money is used to finance a project that will provide sufficient yield to repay the loan and its interest and leave a profit.

Self-Regulating Organization (SRO) One of several organizations set up in the UK under the *Financial Services Act 1986 to regulate the activities of investment businesses and to draw up and enforce specific codes of conduct. The SROs recognized by the *Securities and Investment Board, to whom they reported, were: the *Securities and Futures Authority Ltd (SFA), the **Investment Managers Regulatory Organization** (IMRO), which regulated any institution offering investment management (including Friendly Societies), and the *Personal Investment Authority (PIA), which regulated the activities of investment business carried out mainly with or for the private investor. In 2002 the SROs were replaced by the *Financial Services Authority.

self-select PEP *See* PERSONAL EQUITY PLAN.

self-tender A *tender offer in which a company approaches its shareholders in order to buy back some or all of its shares. There are two circumstances in which this operation can be of use. One is in the case of a hostile bid: the directors may wish to buy back shares in their company in order to reduce the chances of the bidder being able to buy a controlling interest in the company. The other circumstance is that the board may wish to show increased earnings per share; if they are unable to increase their profits it may be appropriate for them to reduce the number of shares in the company.

sellers' market A market in which the demand exceeds the supply, so that sellers can increase prices. At some point, however, buyers will cease to follow the price rises and the sellers will be forced to drop prices in order to make sales, i.e. the supply will have exceeded the demand. *Compare* BUYERS' MARKET.

sellers over A market in commodities, securities, etc., in which buyers have been satisfied but some sellers remain. This is clearly a weak market, with a tendency for prices to fall. *Compare* BUYERS OVER.

selling out 1. The selling of securities, commodities, etc., by a broker because the original buyer is unable to pay for them. This invariably happens after a fall in market price (the buyer would have taken them up and sold them at a profit if the market had risen). The broker sells them at the best price available and the original buyer is responsible for any difference between the price realized and the original selling price, plus the costs of selling out. *Compare* BUYING IN. **2.** Closing a trading position held for a client because a *margin call has not been met. **3.** Selling the whole of a new issue of a security.

selling short *See* SHORT SELLING.

semi-annually compounded yield The annual yield on a security that makes coupon payments twice per calendar year.

semi-strong-form market efficiency One of the three categories of market efficiency defined by Eugene Fama. It is characterized by the inability of an investor to obtain *abnormal returns from the use of publicly available information, whether this is historical or new. *See* EFFICIENT MARKETS HYPOTHESIS. *Compare* STRONG-FORM MARKET EFFICIENCY; WEAK-FORM MARKET EFFICIENCY.

semi-variance A measure of the risk of a *portfolio that only considers outcomes below the average. It is a measure of the spead of a distribution on its most risky side. *See* VARIANCE.

sen 1. A monetary unit of Cambodia worth one hundredth of a *riel. **2. (cent)** A monetary unit of Malaysia worth one hundredth of a *ringgit. **3.** A monetary unit of Indonesia worth one hundredth of a *rupiah. **4.** A former monetary unit of Japan (still used as a unit of account), worth one hundredth of a *yen.

S

sene A monetary unit of Samoa worth one hundredth of a *tala.

senior debt The debt that has precedence over other debts for repayment if the loans made to a company are called in for repayment. Often companies borrow different amounts from different sources; one lender may stipulate that their loan should rank as the senior debt.

seniti A monetary unit of Tonga worth one hundredth of a *pa'anga.

sensitive market A market in commodities, securities, etc., that is sensitive to outside influences because it is basically unstable. For example, a poor crop in a commodity market may make it sensitive, with buyers anxious to cover their requirements but unwilling to show their hand and risk forcing prices up. News of a hurricane in the growing area, say, could cause a sharp price rise in such a sensitive market.

sensitivity analysis A financial modelling technique that attempts to measure the sensitivity of an investment to different variables, for example the *present value of a project or the price of an option.

sent (*plural* **senti**) A monetary unit of Estonia worth one hundredth of a *kroon.

separate assessment Before April 1990, an election that could be made by one party to a marriage in the UK enabling each party to pay his or her own tax. Unlike an election for separate taxation of a wife's earnings, this saved no tax. It merely allocated the total tax payable by the married couple as a single unit to the two parties for payment. Husband and wife are now always subject to separate taxation.

separate-entity concept The accounting concept that the *financial statements of an organization should describe the business as if it were entirely separate from its owners.

separation theorem A key conclusion of *portfolio theory, namely that investors should diversify widely (*see* DIVERSIFICATION) and that the required risk–return combination should be obtained either by lending some proportion of the investor's assets or by borrowing and gearing up the levels of risky assets held.

SEPON Ltd *See* TALISMAN.

serial bond A *bond issue made up of tranches with different maturity dates and coupons.

Serious Fraud Office (SFO) A body established in 1987 to be responsible for investigating and prosecuting serious or complex frauds in England, Wales, and Northern Ireland. The Attorney General appoints and superintends its director. Serious and complex fraud cases can go straight to the Crown Court without committal for trial. That court can hold preparatory hearings to clarify issues for the jury and settle points of law.

SERPS Abbreviation for *State Earnings-Related Pension Scheme.

service An economic *good consisting of labour, advice, managerial skill, etc., rather than a *commodity or physical good. **Services to trade** include banking, insurance, transport, etc. **Professional services** encompass the advice and skill of accountants, lawyers, architects, business consultants, doctors, etc. **Consumer services** include those given by caterers, cleaners, mechanics, plumbers, etc. Industry may be divided into extractive, manufacturing, and service sectors. The

service industries make up an increasing proportion of national income in post-industrial societies.

service contract (**service agreement**) An employment contract between an employer and employee, usually a senior employee, such as a director, executive manager, etc. Service contracts must be kept at the registered office of a company and be open to inspection by members of the company. The Companies Acts 1980 and 1985 prohibit service contracts that give an employee guaranteed employment for more than five years, without the company having an opportunity to break the employment as and when it needs to. This measure prevents directors with long service agreements from suing companies for loss of office in the event of a takeover or reorganization. *See also* COMPENSATION FOR LOSS OF OFFICE; GOLDEN PARACHUTE.

servicing a loan Paying the interest on a loan.

SES Abbreviation for *Stock Exchange of Singapore.

SESDAQ Abbreviation for Stock Exchange of Singapore Dealing and Automated Quotation System. *See* STOCK EXCHANGE OF SINGAPORE.

SESI Abbreviation for Stock Exchange of Singapore Index. *See* STOCK EXCHANGE OF SINGAPORE.

SET Abbreviation for *Securities Exchange of Thailand.

set-off An agreement between the parties involved to set off one debt against another or one loss against a gain. A banker is empowered to set off a credit balance on one account against a debit balance on another if the accounts are in the same name and in the same currency. It is usual, in these circumstances, for the bank to issue a **letter of set-off**, countersigned by the customer.

SETS Abbreviation for Stock Exchange Trading System: the London Stock Exchange *order-driven electronic trading system that came into operation in 1997. It partly replaced the existing *quote-driven system (*see* STOCK EXCHANGE AUTOMATED QUOTATIONS SYSTEM). Buyers and sellers enter their orders, which are matched by computer. It covers the 100 shares of the FT-SE 100 index and other BLUE CHIP securities.

settlement 1. The payment of an outstanding account, invoice, charge, etc. **2.** A disposition of land, or other property, made by deed or will under which a *trust is set up by the settlor. The settlement names the beneficiaries and the terms under which they are to acquire the property. **3.** The document in which such a disposition is made. **4.** The voluntary conclusion of civil litigation or an industrial dispute, as a result of agreement between the parties.

settlement day The day on which trades are cleared by the delivery of the securities or foreign exchange.

settlement price The price at which an *index futures or option contract is settled on the *London International Financial Futures and Options Exchange. Officially known as the **Exchange Delivery Settlement Price** (EDSP), the settlement price is calculated on the last day of the delivery month and forms the basis for the cash settlement.

settlement risk The *risk that a transaction will not be settled as expected (i.e. that an agreed delivery or payment will not be made). It is sometimes referred to as **Herstatt risk** after a bank of that name, which failed to honour its foreign-exchange transactions in 1974. *See also* COUNTERPARTY RISK.

settlor A person declaring or creating a *settlement or *trust. For tax purposes any person providing money or property for a settlement will be regarded as the settlor.

seven-day money Money that has been invested in the *money market for a term of seven days. Special interest rates are quoted for seven-day money.

Seventh Directive An EU directive relating to *consolidated financial statements.

severance payment See COMPENSATION FOR LOSS OF OFFICE; REDUNDANCY.

SFA Abbreviation for *Securities and Futures Authority Ltd.

SFO Abbreviation for *Serious Fraud Office.

shadow director A person in accordance with whose instructions the directors of a company are accustomed to act although that person has not been appointed as a director.

Shanghai Securities Exchange The stock market of the People's Republic of China, situated in Shanghai.

share One of a number of titles of ownership in a company. Most companies are limited by shares, thus an investor can limit his liability if the company fails to the amount paid for (or owing on) the shares. A share confers on its owner a legal right to the part of the company's profits (usually by payment of a *dividend) and to any voting rights attaching to that share (see VOTING SHARES; A SHARES). Companies are obliged to keep a public record of the rights attaching to each class of share. The common classes of shares are: *ordinary shares, which have no guaranteed amount of dividend but carry voting rights; and *preference shares, which receive dividends (and/or repayment of capital on winding-up) before ordinary shares, but which have no voting rights. Shares in public companies may be bought and sold in an open market, such as a stock exchange. Shares in a private company are generally subject to restrictions on sale, such as that they must be offered to existing shareholders first or that the directors' approval must be sought before they are sold elsewhere. See also CUMULATIVE PREFERENCE SHARE; DEFERRED ORDINARY SHARE; FOUNDERS' SHARES; PARTLY PAID SHARES; PREFERRED ORDINARY SHARE; REDEEMABLE SHARES; SUBSCRIPTION SHARES.

share account **1.** In the UK, a building society deposit account with no fixed investment period that confers a share of ownership in the society. It entitles the holder to vote at shareholders' meetings and to an allocation of free shares if the society is demutualized. **2.** In the USA, an account with a *credit union (a non-profit making co-operative institution) that pays dividends rather than interest.

share capital That part of the *capital of a company that arises from the issue of *shares. Every company must commence with some share capital (a minimum of two shares). The **authorized share capital** (**registered capital** or **nominal capital**) of a company is the total amount of capital it is authorized to raise according to its articles of association. The **issued share capital** or **subscribed share capital** is the amount of the authorized capital that shareholders have subscribed. If the shareholders have subscribed the full *par value of the share, this will constitute the **fully paid share capital**. If they have subscribed only a proportion of the issued share capital, this is called the **called-up capital**. Some capital may be subscribed on application or on allotment or as separate calls. The shares do not become fully paid until the last call has been made. See also RESERVE CAPITAL.

share certificate A document that provides evidence of ownership of shares in a company. It states the number and class of shares owned by the shareholder and the serial number of the shares. It is stamped by the common seal of the company and usually signed by at least one director and the company secretary. It is not a negotiable instrument. *See* BEARER SECURITY.

share exchange A service offered by most unit-trust managements and life-assurance companies, in which the trust or company takes over a client's shareholding and invests the proceeds in unit-trust funds, etc., of the client's choice. The client is thereby saved the trouble and expense of disposing of the shares and if the shares are absorbed into the trust's or company's own portfolio the client may receive a better price than would be possible on the market (i.e. the offer price rather than the bid price).

share-for-share offer A *takeover bid in which the directors of one company offer shares in that company as the payment for acquiring the shares in the target company. If the offer is accepted the shareholders of both companies will become the owners of the newly formed combination.

shareholder An owner of shares in a limited company or limited partnership. A shareholder is a member of the company. In the USA, the more usual word is **stockholder**.

shareholders' equity (shareholders' funds) **1.** The *share capital and *reserves of a company. Financial Reporting Standard 4, 'Capital Instruments', requires that share capital be split into *equity shares and *non-equity shares. **2.** The market value of a company's equity shares.

shareholder value An approach to business planning that places the maximization of the value of a shareholder's equity above other business objectives. Normally, shareholder value can be increased in three ways: dividend payments, appreciation in the value of the shares, and cash repayments. However, this focus has been widened by companies buying back shares to increase earnings and the demerging of parts of a group in order to unlock the value of individual components by means of a separate flotation. Shareholder value can also be influenced by maximising *economic value, either by undertaking positive *present-value decisions or by ruining the business in such a way as to create a surplus above the market costs of funding. The shareholder-value objective has been criticized as being too narrow and contrary to the longer-term interests of other stakeholder groups. *See* STAKEHOLDER THEORY.

share index An index formed by selecting a number of prominent shares traded on a *stock exchange and comparing the value of these shares with their value on a stated date in the *base year. The daily value of the shares takes into account the volume of shares traded (*see* WEIGHTED AVERAGE). *See* CHAMBRE AGENT GENERAL INDEX; COMMERZBANK INDEX; DOW JONES INDUSTRIAL AVERAGE; FINANCIAL TIMES SHARE INDEXES; NIKKEI STOCK AVERAGE; HANG SENG INDEX.

share issued at a discount A share issued at a price (the *issue price) below its *par value. The discount is the difference between the par value and the issue price. It is illegal to issue shares at a discount in the UK.

share option 1. A benefit sometimes offered to employees, especially new employees, in which they are given an option to buy shares in the company for which they work at a favourable fixed price or at a stated discount to the market price. **2.** *See* OPTION.

share premium The amount payable for shares in a company and issued by the company itself in excess of their nominal value (*see* NOMINAL PRICE). Share premiums received by a company must be credited to a *share premium account.

share premium account The account to which the premium must be credited for *shares issued at a premium. The balance on the share premium account may be used for specified purposes:
• the issue of *bonus shares;
• the writing-off of preliminary expenses;
• the writing-off of underwriting commissions;
• the provision of a premium to be paid on the *redemption of *debentures;
• the provision of a premium to be paid on the redemption or purchase of *share capital, subject to certain limits.
The share premium account may not be used to write off *goodwill on consolidation. Relief from the creation of a share premium account is given in section 131 of the Companies Act; this is known as *merger relief and is available in specified circumstances.

share register (register of members) The register kept by a limited company in which ownership of shares in that company is kept, together with the full names, addresses, extent of holding, and class of shares for each shareholder. Entry in the register constitutes evidence of ownership. Thus, a shareholder who loses a share certificate can obtain a replacement from the company provided that proof of identity is supplied and that the holding is recorded in the register.

share shop A stockbroker, bank, building society, or other financial intermediary appointed by the government to promote and handle applications for shares in a *privatization issue. The purpose of these share shops is to enable those members of the public who do not usually buy shares to purchase publicly offered shares without difficulty. Share shops act on behalf of members of the public but members of the public pay no commission. Commission is paid to the share shops by the government on successful share applications. Share shops exist only for the duration of the public share offer. *See also* RETAIL TENDER.

share splitting The division of the share capital of a company into smaller units. The effect of a share split is the same as a *scrip issue although the technicalities differ. Share splits are usually carried out when the existing shares reach such a high price (*see* HEAVY SHARE) that trading in them becomes difficult.

share transfer *See* TRANSFER DEED.

share warehousing The practice of building up a holding of the shares of a company that is to be the target for a takeover. The shares are bought in the name of nominees in relatively small lots and 'warehoused' until the purchaser has built up a significant interest in the company.

shark repellents *See* PORCUPINE PROVISIONS.

shark watcher A business consultant who specializes in helping companies to identify raiders and to provide early warning of *share warehousing and other manoeuvres used as preliminaries to takeovers.

Sharpe ratio A risk-adjusted measure of the performance of a portfolio. It is calculated by deducting the *risk-free rate of return from the portfolio return and dividing the result by the *standard deviation of the returns on the portfolio. *Compare* TREYNOR INDEX.

SHEEP Acronym for sky-high earnings expectations possibly: applied to investments that appear to offer an unusually high return but that may prove very unreliable.

shelf registration A measure to allow larger US companies to register advance details of new securities with the *Securities and Exchange Commission (SEC), without specifying a date of issue. When companies need the capital, they issue securities 'off the shelf', without having to wait for SEC clearance of the application.

shell company **1.** A non-trading company, with or without a stock-exchange listing, used as a vehicle for various company manoeuvres or kept dormant for future use in some other capacity. **2.** A company that has ceased to trade and is sold to new owners for a small fee to minimize the cost and trouble of setting up a new company. Some business brokers register such companies with the sole object of selling them to people setting up new businesses. The name and objects of such a company can be changed for a small charge. **3.** A name-plate company set up in a tax haven.

sheqel The standard monetary unit of Israel, divided into 100 agorot.

***Shibosai* bond** A *Samurai bond sold direct by a company to investors, without using a stockbroker.

shilling The standard monetary unit of Kenya (KSh), Somalia (So.Sh.), Tanzania (TSh), and Uganda (USh), divided into 100 cents.

shirkah *See* ISLAMIC FINANCE.

Shogun bond A bond sold on the Japanese market by a foreign institution and denominated in a foreign currency. *Compare* SAMURAI BOND.

short bill A *bill of exchange that is payable at sight, on demand, or within ten days.

short coupon A *coupon period of shorter duration than is normal for the type of issue in question.

short covering The purchasing of goods or securities that have been sold short (*see* SHORT POSITION) so that the open position is closed. A dealer in commodities, securities, or foreign exchanges hopes to cover shorts at below the selling price in order to make a profit. Dealers cover their shorts when they expect the market to turn or when it has already started to move upwards.

short-dated gilt *See* GILT-EDGED SECURITY.

short hedging *See* HEDGE.

shorting Establishing a *short position.

short position A *position that will gain from a fall in the value of the *underlying.

shorts **1.** *See* GILT-EDGED SECURITY. **2.** Securities, commodities, currencies, etc., of which a dealer is short, i.e. has a *short position.

short selling Selling commodities, securities, currencies, etc., that one does not have. A short seller expects prices to fall so that the short sale can be bought in at a profit before delivery has to be made. A short seller is a *bear.

short-term capital Capital raised for a short period to cover an exceptional demand for funds over a short period. A bank loan, rather than a debenture, is an example of short-term capital.

short-term instrument A *negotiable instrument that matures in three months or less.

short-term interest rates Interest rates on short-term financial instruments.

short-termism The adoption by shareholders (both individual and institutional) of too limited a perspective on their investment. This makes them overreact to the short-term results and policies of companies. In turn, this may cause companies to lose the long-term focus that is ultimately in the interests of all stakeholders.

short-term monetary support (STMS) Funds available to a member country of the European Union for three months. These funds are provided by the European Central Bank to offset problems one state may be having in relation to temporary balance of payments deficits. *Compare* MEDIUM-TERM FINANCIAL ASSISTANCE.

show stopper **1.** A *consideration that renders a particular action no longer viable. **2.** A legal action taken by the target firm in an unwelcome takeover bid that seeks a permanent injunction to prevent the bidder from persisting in takeover activities, on the grounds that the bid is legally defective in some way.

shut-down cost The costs to be incurred in closing down some part of an organization's activities.

SIA Abbreviation for *Securities Industry Association.

SIAC Abbreviation for *Securities Industry Automation Corporation.

SIB Abbreviation for *Securities and Investment Board.

sickness and accident insurance A form of health insurance in which the benefits are paid for a fixed time after the onset of an illness or accident that prevents the insured from working. Premiums can increase each year and renewal can be refused if a claim has been made. *Compare* PERMANENT HEALTH INSURANCE.

side deal A private deal between two people, usually for the personal benefit of one of them, as a subsidiary to a transaction between the officials of a company, government, etc. For example, the chairman of a public company may agree to encourage the board to welcome a takeover bid, because of a personal profit agreed in some side deal with the bidder. Side deals are rigorously investigated by the Panel on Takeovers and Mergers (*see* CITY CODE ON TAKEOVERS AND MERGERS).

sight bill *See* AT SIGHT.

sight deposit Money deposited in a bank account that can be withdrawn without notice, e.g. money withdrawn by cheque from a current account. In the USA it is known as a *demand deposit.

sight draft Any *bill of exchange that is payable on sight, i.e. on presentation, irrespective of when it was drawn.

signalling hypothesis In investment strategy, the idea that certain decisions made by firms reveal their actual situation (which may be at variance with public statements). Thus, dividend policy is often interpreted as a signal of management's view of the firm's future prospects. Signalling reflects a mismatch between the information available to shareholders and managers (*see* ASYMMETRIC KNOWLEDGE) and differences between the interests of these parties (*see* AGENCY PROBLEM).

SIMEX Abbreviation for *Singapore International Monetary Exchange.

simple interest *See* INTEREST.

simplified financial statements Simplified versions of the *annual accounts and report intended for readers who do not possess sophisticated financial knowledge. The financial information may be made easier to understand by using simple financial terminology, showing the information in the forms of graphs and diagrams, providing fuller explanations, and reducing the amount of information. One form of simplified financial statement is the employee report, which is intended for employees and not covered by legislation; another form is the *summary financial statement intended for shareholders and subject to legislation.

simulation A financial modelling technique that considers the likely outcomes of different hypothetical circumstances. Uncertainty may be modelled by the use of random numbers, as in a *Monte Carlo simulation, or worst cases by the use of *stress testing.

sine die (Latin: without a day) Denoting an adjournment of an action, arbitration, etc., indefinitely.

Singapore International Monetary Exchange (SIMEX) A commodities futures exchange in Singapore launched in 1984; it is linked with the *Chicago Mercantile Exchange and uses *eurodollars for its main contracts.

Singapore Stock Exchange *See* STOCK EXCHANGE OF SINGAPORE.

single-capacity system *See* DUAL-CAPACITY SYSTEM.

single company PEP *See* PERSONAL EQUITY PLAN.

Single European Act The legislation passed in 1986 in the European Community that committed all member states to an integrated method of trading with no frontiers between countries by 31 December 1992. In practice, some of its terms on harmonization, such as the insurance market, have taken considerably longer to implement. The main creation of the Single European Act is the *Single Market for trading in goods and services within the EU.

single-life pension A pension or *annuity that is paid for the lifetime of the beneficiary only, rather than for the lifetime of a surviving spouse. *Compare* JOINT-LIFE AND LAST-SURVIVOR ANNUITIES.

Single Market The concept that underlies trading in the European Union, as codified in the *Single European Act 1986, which was introduced in 1987 with a target date of 31 December 1992 for completion. The Single Market came into force on 1 January 1993 with between 90% and 95% of the necessary legislation enacted by all member countries. The measures covered by the legislation include:
• the elimination of frontier controls (the full measures have been repeatedly delayed);
• the acceptance throughout the market of professional qualifications;
• the acceptance of national standards for product harmonization;
• open tendering for public supply contracts;
• the free movement of capital between states;
• a reduction of state aid for certain industries;
• the harmonization of VAT and excise duties throughout the market.

single-premium assurance A life-assurance policy in which the insured pays only one capital sum rather than regular premiums. *See also* INVESTMENT BOND.

single property ownership trust (SPOT) A single property trust; shares in the trust entitle their holder to a direct share of the property's income and capital. A form of *securitization, a share in a SPOT is similar to a *property income certificate (PINC).

single-tax system A system of taxation in which there would be only one major tax, usually a *comprehensive income tax, instead of several taxes, such as income tax, capital gains tax, and national insurance, as in the UK. Arguments in favour of such taxes are that they should be less avoidable and should simplify administration. On the other hand the present variety of taxes is designed for a variety of purposes and flexibility may be lost in a single-tax system.

sinking fund A fund set up to replace a *wasting asset at the end of its useful life. Usually a regular annual sum is set aside to enable the fund, taking into account interest at the expected rate, to replace the exhausted asset at a specified date. Some have argued that amounts set aside for *depreciation of an asset should be equal to the annual amounts needed to be placed in a notional sinking fund.

SIPC Abbreviation for *Securities Investor Protection Corporation.

six-month money Money invested on the *money market for a period of six months. If it is withdrawn before the six months have elapsed there may be a heavy penalty, although if the market has moved in favour of the recipient of the funds, this penalty may be negligible.

skewness A measure of the lack of symmetry in a probability distribution. A tendency to produce low numbers is referred to as a **negative skew**. In considering the prices of financial obligations, the degree of negative skew may be a measure of risk. *See also* GAMMA DISTRIBUTION; MOMENTS. *Compare* KURTOSIS.

skip-day The two-day period allowed before payment has to be made for a security purchased on the US *money market.

SL Stockbrokers' shorthand for sold. *Compare* BOT.

sleeping partner A person who has capital in a *partnership but takes no part in its commercial activities. He or she has all the legal benefits and obligations of ownership and shares in the profits of the partnership in accordance with the provisions laid down in the partnership agreement.

sliding peg *See* CRAWLING PEG.

slush fund Money set aside by an organization for discreet payments to influential people for preferential treatment, advance information, or other services for the benefit of the organization. Slush funds are normally used for purposes less blatant than bribes, but sometimes not much less.

small companies rate *See* CORPORATION TAX.

small company Under the UK Companies Act 1985 and its 2004 Amendment, a *private limited company that satisfies at least two of the following criteria regarding the number of employees, its turnover, and its assets:
- its *balance-sheet total does not exceed £2.8 million (i.e. assets before deducting *current liabilities and *long-term liabilities);
- its *turnover does not exceed £5.6 million. This must be proportionally adjusted when the *financial year is longer or shorter than 12 months;
- the average number of employees should not exceed 50.

A company that is in its first financial year may still qualify as a small company if it falls within these limits. Alternatively, if the company has qualified in the two preceding financial years, it may qualify. If a company is a member of a *group containing a public *company, a banking or insurance company, or an authorized person under the Financial Services Act 1986, it is not eligible for the exemptions for small or *medium-sized companies. A small company is exempt from a *statutory audit of its *annual accounts (unless this is required by an external shareholder holding at least 10% of the share capital). It is also entitled to reduce the amount of information in its annual report to members. The exemptions allow a number of combinations of format-heading items in the balance sheet and notes. A small company may also file abbreviated accounts with the *Registrar of Companies.

small group A *group that meets two out of three of the following criteria for the current and preceding year, or the two preceding financial years:
• its *balance-sheet total should not exceed £2.8 million net or £3.36 million gross;
• its *turnover should not exceed £5.6 million net or £6.72 million gross. This must be proportionally adjusted when the financial year is longer or shorter than 12 months;
• the average number of employees should not exceed 50.
If a group is in its first financial year, it may still qualify if it falls within these limits.
    An intermediate *holding company or an ultimate holding company cannot qualify as a small company or a *medium-sized company unless the group headed by it qualifies as a small group or a medium-sized group. A group containing a public *company, a banking or insurance company, or an authorized person under the Financial Services Act 1986 is ineligible for the exemptions for small groups or medium-sized groups.
    Under the Companies Act, a parent company is not required to prepare *group accounts for a financial year in which the group headed by that parent qualifies as a small group. A small group may file abbreviated accounts instead of full accounts with the *Registrar of Companies.

small loan company The US equivalent of a *finance house for private consumers, i.e. one that lends money to consumers to enable them to make purchases on an instalment plan.

Small Order Execution System (SOES) The US *National Association of Securities Dealers Automated Quotation System for executing customers' orders of 1000 or fewer shares in securities traded on NASDAQ.

small print Printed matter on a document, such as a life-assurance policy or hire-purchase agreement, in which the seller sets out the conditions of the sale and the mutual liabilities of buyer and seller. The use of a very small type size and unintelligible jargon is often intended to obscure the legal rights and safeguards from the buyer. This unfair practice has largely been remedied by the various Acts that provide consumer protection. *See also* COOLING-OFF PERIOD.

smart card A plastic card that contains a microprocessor that stores and updates information, typically used in performing financial transactions. Unlike an ordinary *debit card or *cash card a smart card memorizes all transactions in which the card is used. Other uses include storing a person's medical records.

smart money Money invested by experienced and successful people, especially those with inside information about a particular project or investment opportunity.

SMI Abbreviation for Swiss Market Index. *See* SWISS OPTIONS AND FINANCIAL FUTURES EXCHANGE; SWISS STOCK EXCHANGES.

snake A European monetary system adopted in 1972, in which the exchange rate between the participants was restricted by a fluctuation limit of 2¼%. The participants were the Belgian franc, Danish krone, French franc, Irish punt, Dutch guilder, German Deutschmark, and Italian lira, the dominating currency being the Deutschmark. It was originally called a snake-in-the-barrel or -tunnel to indicate that the rates of exchange could 'snake' about within the limits imposed by the barrel (tunnel). Sterling did not participate in this arrangement, which was replaced in 1979 by the *European Monetary System.

socially responsible investment *See* ETHICAL INVESTMENT.

social security A government system for paying allowances to the sick and the unemployed, as well as maternity benefits and retirement pensions. Other low-income members of society are also eligible, such as the disabled and single-parent families. Since 1988 in the UK this has been the responsibility of the Department of Social Security, which also administers the National Insurance scheme that funds the social security payments (*see* NATIONAL INSURANCE CONTRIBUTION).

Social Security Act 1986 UK legislation that laid the foundations for freeing the pensions industry by allowing employees to opt out of *occupational pension schemes run by their employers and create their own *personal pension schemes. It was not completely enacted until 1988 because its consumer-protection clauses were bound up in the later *Financial Services Act 1986. The Social Security Act 1990 went further in introducing consumer protection for pension plans and introduced the pensions Ombudsman.

sociedad anónima *See* SA.

sociedade anónima *See* SA.

società a responsabilità limitata *See* SARL.

società per azioni *See* SPA.

société anonyme *See* SA.

société à responsabilité limitée *See* SARL.

Society for Worldwide Interbank Financial Telecommunications (SWIFT) A communications system that advises member banks to transfer funds from one member to another. Based in Brussels, the SWIFT network of terminals links 1500 banks in Europe, USA, Africa, Asia, Australia, and Latin America. It is not a payment system, but an information and instruction network. It began operations in 1977 and is run by a non-profitmaking organization.

SOFFEX Abbreviation for *Swiss Options and Financial Futures Exchange.

SOFS Abbreviation for *Small Order Execution System.

soft commodities (softs) Commodities, other than metals. They include cocoa, coffee, grains, potatoes, and sugar.

soft currency The currency of a country that has a weak *balance of payments and for which there is relatively little demand. *Compare* HARD CURRENCY.

soft dollars *See* HARD DOLLARS.

soft loan A loan with an artificially low rate of interest. Soft loans are sometimes made to developing nations by industrialized nations for political reasons.

sol *See* NEW SOL.

solicitor's letter A letter written by a solicitor, usually threatening to take a matter to court.

solo (sola) A single *bill of exchange of which no other copies are in circulation.

solvency **1.** The financial state of a person or company that is able to pay all debts as they fall due. **2.** The amount by which the assets of a bank exceed its liabilities.

solvency margin The difference between the assets and the liabilities of an insurance company. This margin is carefully regulated by the insurance industry's supervisory organization LAUTRO (*see* SELF-REGULATING ORGANIZATION).

solvency ratio **1.** The ratio of a bank's own assets to its liabilities. **2.** A ratio used by the UK Department of Trade and Industry to evaluate the stability of insurance companies; it is the ratio of the company's net assets to its non-life premium income.

Solvency Ratio Directive An EU directive on bank *capital adequacy. It was issued in 1993 to refine certain provisions of the *Basle Convergence Accord of 1988.

som (*plural* **somy**; KGS) The standard monetary unit of Kyrgyzstan, divided into 100 tyiyn.

sort code A sequence of numbers on a cheque or a bank card that serves to identify the branch holding the account.

source and application (disposition) of funds A statement showing how an organization has raised finance for a specified period and how that finance has been applied. Sources of funds are typically trading profits, issues of shares or loan stock, sales of fixed assets, and borrowings. Applications are typically trading losses, purchases of fixed assets, dividends paid, and repayment of borrowings. Any balancing figure represents an increase or decrease in *working capital. In UK accountancy practice, it has been replaced by the *cash-flow projection.

South Sea Bubble The collapse of the British market in South Sea Company stocks in 1720. The South Sea Company, a *joint-stock company founded in 1711, traded, mostly in slaves, with Spanish America. In 1720 its offer to take over part of the *national debt was accepted by parliament, causing a rise in the value of its shares from 128 (in January) to 1000 (August). By December the bubble had burst and the shares fell to 124, ruining many investors. A subsequent enquiry implicated three ministers on charges of corruption and touched King George I, first because he had become governor of the company in 1718, and secondly because two of his mistresses were involved in the scandal. The situation was saved by Sir Robert Walpole, who transferred the stocks to the Bank of England and the British India Company. The subsequent legislation, known as the Bubble Act 1720, restricted the formation of joint-stock companies. *See* BUBBLE.

sovereign indemnity (sovereign immunity) The restrictions on taking a state or head of state to court.

sovereign loan A loan made by a bank to a foreign government, often the government of a third-world country. The attendant risk is sometimes called *sovereign risk.

sovereign risk The risk of investment in foreign countries in which the political and economic situation might lead to a government expropriation of private assets.

SpA Abbreviation for *società per azioni*. It appears after the name of a public limited company in Italy, being equivalent to the British abbreviation plc. *Compare* SARL.

special clearing The clearing of a cheque through the UK banking system in less than the normal three days, for a small additional charge. A cheque for which a special clearing has been arranged can usually be passed through the system in one day.

Special Commissioners A body of civil servants who are specialized tax lawyers appointed by the Lord Chancellor to hear appeals against assessments to income tax, corporation tax, and capital gains tax. A taxpayer may choose to appeal to the Special Commissioners, rather than the *General Commissioners, particularly in cases in which legal matters rather than questions of fact are at issue.

special crossing A crossing on a *cheque in which the name of a bank is written between the crossing lines. A cheque so crossed can only be paid into the named bank.

special deposits Deposits that the UK government may instruct the clearing banks to make at the Bank of England, as a means of restricting credit in the economy. The less money the clearing banks have at their disposal, the less they are able to lend to businesses. A similar system has been used by the Federal Reserve System in the USA.

special dividend (extra dividend) A single irregular dividend payment. It is usually made after an especially profitable year but is sometimes associated with the restructuring of companies.

Special Drawing Rights (SDRs) The standard unit of account used by the *International Monetary Fund (IMF). In 1970 members of the IMF were allocated SDRs in proportion to the quotas of currency that they had subscribed to the fund on its formation. There have since been further allocations. SDRs can be used to settle international trade balances and to repay debts to the IMF itself. On the instructions of the IMF a member country must supply its own currency to another member, in exchange for SDRs, unless it already holds more than three times its original allocation. The value of SDRs was originally expressed in terms of gold (hence their former name **paper gold**), but since 1974 they have been valued in terms of their members' currencies. SDRs provide a credit facility for IMF members in addition to their existing credit facilities (hence the name); unlike these existing facilities they do not have to be repaid, thus forming a permanent addition to members' reserves and functioning as an international reserve currency. *Compare* EUROPEAN CURRENCY UNIT.

specialist A dealer on the New York Stock Exchange who has been appointed by the exchange to maintain an orderly market in certain assigned securities. Specialists operate as market makers and are required to perform four functions: to quote prices, execute orders, create liquidity in the market, and match bids and offers by bringing together buyers and sellers.

special manager A person appointed by the court in the liquidation of a company or bankruptcy of an individual to assist the *liquidator or *official receiver to manage the business of the company or individual. The special manager's powers are decided by the court.

special notice *See* RESOLUTION.

special-purpose vehicle A legal entity established for the sake of a single transaction, for example in the *credit enhancement of a *securitization.

special resolution *See* RESOLUTION.

specie Money in the form of coins, rather than banknotes or bullion.

specific bank guarantee An unconditional guarantee from the *Export Credits Guarantee Department to a UK bank enabling that bank to finance an exporter's medium-term credit to an export customer without recourse; the arrangement is known as **supplier credit** in contrast to the buyer credit under which the bank finances the overseas buyer to pay the exporter on cash terms.

specific charge *See* CHARGE; FIXED CHARGE.

specific risk (**non-systematic risk**) The *risk associated with each of the individual assets in a *portfolio, as opposed to the *systematic risk associated with the market as a whole. It can be eliminated by *diversification. *Portfolio theory holds that investors should maintain a diversified portfolio in order to maximize the utility of their investments. Because specific risk can be eliminated in this way, there is no requirement for a *risk premium for taking specific risks. This is an important underlying principle of the *capital asset pricing model and *arbitrage pricing theory. Specific risk is measured by the *alpha coefficient.

speculation The purchase or sale of something for the sole purpose of making a capital gain. For professional speculators the security, commodity, and foreign exchange markets are natural venues as they cater for speculation as well as investment and trading. Indeed, speculators help to make a viable market and thus smooth out price fluctuations. This is particularly true of commodity futures and option markets (*see* LONDON INTERNATIONAL FINANCIAL FUTURES AND OPTIONS EXCHANGE).

speculative bubble *See* BUBBLE.

speculative risk **1.** An insurance risk that cannot be calculated and formulated – and is outside the so-called 'law of large numbers', e.g. outside human control – and is therefore difficult or impossible to assess for insurance cover. **2.** Any risk arising from speculation.

split *See* SHARE SPLITTING.

split-capital investment trust (**split-level trust**; **split trust**) An *investment trust with a limited life in which the equity capital is divided into various classes of income shares and capital shares. Holders of income shares receive all or most of the income earned plus a predetermined capital value on liquidation. Holders of capital shares receive little or no income but are entitled to all of the assets remaining after repayment of the income shares.

sponsor **1.** The initiator of a financial project. **2.** The *issuing house that handles a new issue for a company. It will supervise the preparation of the *prospectus and make sure that the company is aware of the benefits and obligations of being a public company.

SPOT Abbreviation for *single property ownership trust.

spot currency market A market in which currencies are traded for delivery within two days, as opposed to the *forward dealing exchange market in which deliveries are arranged for named months in the future. The rate of exchange for spot currency is the **spot rate**.

spot goods Commodities that are available for immediate delivery, as opposed to futures (*see* FUTURES CONTRACT) in which deliveries are arranged for named months in the future. The price of spot goods, the **spot price**, is usually higher than the forward price, unless there is a glut of that particular commodity but an expected shortage in the future.

spot market A market that deals in commodities or foreign exchange for immediate delivery. Immediate delivery in foreign currencies usually means within two business days. For commodities it usually means within seven days.

spot month The month during which goods bought on a futures contract will become available for delivery.

spot price *See* SPOT GOODS.

spot rate *See* SPOT CURRENCY MARKET.

spread **1.** The difference between the buying and selling price made by a *market maker on the stock exchange. **2.** The diversity of the investments in a *portfolio. The greater the spread of a portfolio the less volatile it will be. **3.** The simultaneous purchase and sale of commodity futures (*see* FUTURES CONTRACT) in the hope that movement in their relative prices will enable a profit to be made. This may include a purchase and sale of the same commodity for the same delivery, but on different commodity exchanges (*see* STRADDLE), or a purchase and sale of the same commodity for different deliveries. **4.** An interest-rate margin.

Square Mile The colloquial name for the commercial district of the City of London, traditionally the square mile north of the Thames between Waterloo Bridge and Tower Bridge. It has been the principal financial district of the UK, with office blocks clustering around the Stock Exchange, the Bank of England, Lloyd's, and the commodity markets. Since the 1980s, City institutions have spread eastwards to the London Docklands redevelopment area and westwards to occupy former newspaper offices in Fleet Street.

square position An *open position that has been covered or hedged.

squeeze **1.** Controls imposed by a government to restrict inflation. An **income (pay) squeeze** limits increases in wage and salaries, a **credit squeeze** limits the amounts that banks and other moneylenders can lend, a **dividend (profits) squeeze** restricts increases in dividends. **2.** Any action on a market that forces buyers to come into the market and prices to rise. In a **bear squeeze**, bears are forced to cover in order to deliver. It may be restricted to a particular commodity or security or a particular delivery month may be squeezed, pushing its price up against the rest of the market.

SRO Abbreviation for *Self-Regulating Organization.

SSAP Abbreviation for *Statement of Standard Accounting Practice.

stabilizers Economic measures used in a free economy to restrict swings in prices, production, employment, etc. Such measures include progressive income tax, control of interest rates, government spending, unemployment benefits, and government retraining schemes.

stag A person who applies for shares in new issues in the hope that the price when trading begins will be higher than the issue price. Often measures will be taken by the issuers to prevent excessive stagging; it is usually illegal for would-be investors to attempt to obtain large numbers of shares by making multiple applications. Issuers will often scale down share applications if an issue is oversubscribed, thus limiting quick profit-taking.

staggered directorships A measure used in the defence against unwanted takeover bids. If the company concerned resolves that the terms of office served by its directors are to be staggered and that no director can be removed from office without due cause, a bidder cannot gain control of the board for some years, even with a controlling interest in the share capital. *See* POISON PILL.

STAGS Abbreviation for Sterling Transferable Accruing Government Securities. These European sterling bonds are backed by a holding of Treasury stock. They are *deep-discount bonds paying no interest.

stakeholder pension scheme A new type of low-cost pension, available from April 2001. Employers with five or more employees have to make a stakeholder pension available to their staff. Stakeholder pensions are also available from authorized financial institutions, such as insurance companies, banks, and building societies. Stakeholder pension providers can only charge a maximum of 1% of the value of the pension fund each year to manage the fund, plus costs and charges (such as stamp duty). Any extra services and any extra charges not provided for by law, such as advice on choosing a pension or life assurance cover, must be optional. All stakeholder schemes will accept contributions of as little as £20, payable weekly, monthly, or at less regular intervals. The scheme must be run by trustees or by an authorized stakeholder manager.

stakeholder theory An approach to business that incorporates all the interests of stakeholders in a business. It widens the view that a firm is responsible only to its owners (*see* SHAREHOLDER VALUE); instead it includes other interested groups, such as its employees, customers, suppliers, and the wider community, which could be affected by environmental issues. It thus attempts to adopt an inclusive rather than a narrow approach to business responsibility.

stale bull A dealer or speculator who has a *long position in something, usually a commodity, which is showing a paper profit but which the dealer cannot realize as there are no buyers at the higher levels. Being fully committed financially and therefore unable to increase the bull position, the dealer may be unable to trade.

stale cheque A cheque that, in the UK, has not been presented for payment within six months of being written. The bank will not honour it, returning it marked 'out of date'.

stamp duty A tax on specific transactions collected by stamping the legal documents giving rise to the transactions. The most common in the UK is the stamp duty on the transfer of land above a value of £60,000. The rate is 1% up to and including £250,000 and 3% over £250,000 but not above £500,000. Above this figure it is 4%. The stamp duty on the transfer of securities was abolished in 1992.

standard amount A normal *lot of a commodity, security, etc. as set by market convention.

Standard and Poor's 500 Stock Index (S&P 500) The widest general-market index of stocks produced by the US *rating agency Standard and Poor; it is made up of 425 shares in US industrial companies and 75 stocks in railway and public-utility corporations. Standard and Poor also rate stocks according to the element of risk involved in holding them. The least risky stocks are rated AAA (triple A) and the most speculative are rated triple D.

standard cash flow pattern The circumstances applying in a *discounted cash flow calculation in which the projected cash flows are made up of an initial cash outflow followed by subsequent cash inflows over the life of the project, there being no net cash outflows in subsequent years.

standard costing A system of cost ascertainment and control in which predetermined **standard costs** and income for products and operations are set and periodically compared with actual costs incurred and income generated in order to establish any variances.

standard deviation A measure of the dispersion of statistical data. For a series of n values x_1, x_2, x_n, it is given by the formula

$$\sqrt{(1/n) \sum_i (x_i - \bar{x})]},$$

where $\bar{x}$ is the average of the n values. The standard deviation of the returns from an investment can be used as a measure of the risk associated with that investment.

standard rate **1.** The rate of *value added tax applied to all items sold by *taxable persons that are not specified as either *exempt supplies, *zero-rated goods and services, or taxable at a special rate. The rate for 2004–05 is 17.5%, which has been the rate since 1 April 1991. Previously the standard rate was 15%. **2.** The marginal rate of tax for most taxpayers. *See* BASIC RATE OF INCOME TAX.

standby agreement **1.** An agreement between the *International Monetary Fund and a member state, enabling the member to arrange for immediate drawing rights in addition to its normal drawing rights in such cases of emergency as a temporary balance of payments crisis. **2.** An underwriting agreement. **3.** A loan agreement that can be taken up in the future.

standby credit A *letter of credit that guarantees a loan or other form of credit facility. The bank that issues it promises to refund the amount borrowed if the borrower defaults on repayment. It calls for a certificate of default by the applicant. In a *note issuance facility a standby credit is a third-party guarantee to honour an issue to an investor who may have a low credit rating. *See also* REVOLVING BANK FACILITY.

standing order An instruction by a customer to a bank (**banker's order**) or building society to pay a specified amount of money on a specified date or dates to a specified payee. Standing orders are widely used for such regular payments as insurance premiums, subscriptions, etc. *See also* CREDIT TRANSFER.

standstill agreement **1.** An agreement between two countries in which a debt owed by one to the other is held in abeyance until a specified date in the future. **2.** An agreement between an unwelcome bidder for a company and the company, in which the bidder agrees to buy no more of the company's shares for a specified period. **3.** An arrangement between banks who have loans to a company in trouble, in which they each agree to maintain their existing credit facilities and not to force the company into receivership by acting alone.

star *See* BOSTON MATRIX.

starting rate of income tax A rate of *income tax below the *basic rate of income tax; it was reintroduced in the UK in 1999 to replace the *lower rate of income tax. The starting rate is currently 10%.

start-up A new business or other project, especially one seeking finance.

start-up costs The initial expenditure incurred in the setting up of an operation or project. The start-up costs may include the capital investment costs plus the initial revenue expenditure prior to the start of operations.

state banks Commercial banks in the USA that were established by state charter rather than federal charter (*compare* NATIONAL BANKS). The rules governing their trading are controlled by state laws and there are therefore differences in practices from state to state. State banks are not compelled to join the *Federal Reserve System, although national banks are. State banks are regulated by state banking departments and by the *Federal Deposit Insurance Corporation (FDIC). Even if they choose not to join the Federal Reserve System, they must abide by its rules, particularly on consumer credit protection.

State Earnings-Related Pension Scheme (SERPS) A scheme, started in 1978, run by the UK government to provide a pension for every employed person in addition to the basic state flat-rate pension. The contributions are paid from part of the National Insurance payments made by employees and employers. Payment of the pension starts at the state retirement age and the amount of pension received is calculated using a formula based on a percentage of the person's earnings. Persons who wish to contract out of SERPS may subscribe to an *occupational pension scheme, a *personal pension scheme, or a *stakeholder pension scheme. From 2003 SERPS will be slowly phased out in favour of the **second state pension**, a flat-rate scheme for those on lower incomes.

statement of affairs A statement showing the assets and liabilities of a person who is bankrupt or of a company in liquidation.

Statement of Auditing Standards (SAS) A statement that lays down accepted US auditing standards. It was issued by the Auditing Standards Board of the American Institute of Certified Public Accountants, members of which have to explain any deviation from the SAS in their audit reports.

statement of changes in financial position The US equivalent of the UK *source and application of funds.

Statement of Financial Accounting Standards (SFAS) In the USA, any of the statements detailing the *financial accounting and reporting requirements of the Financial Accounting Standards Board. These accounting standards are generally accepted accounting principles and should be followed by accountants responsible for the preparation of *financial statements.

statement of movements in shareholders' funds A statement that reconciles changes in the financial position of an organization that are not shown on the *statement of total recognized gains and losses covered by Financial Reporting Standard 3, 'Reporting Financial Performance'.

Statement of Recommended Practice In the UK, a statement on accounting practice that does not have the force of a *Statement of Standard Accounting Practice or a *Financial Reporting Standard. They are often related to the technical problems of a specific industry.

statement of source and application of funds *See* SOURCE AND APPLICATION (DISPOSITION) OF FUNDS.

Statement of Standard Accounting Practice (SSAP) Any of the accounting standards prepared by the Accounting Standards Committee (ASC) and issued by the six members of the Consultative Committee of Accountancy Bodies. Starting in 1971, a total of 25 SSAPs were issued up to 1990, when the ASC was replaced by the *Accounting Standards Board. Before a SSAP was issued a discussion document known as an exposure draft was circulated for comment. The SSAPs issued are given below, although some of these were withdrawn by the ASC, amended, or superseded by the later *Financial Reporting Standards:
1. Accounting for the Results of Associated Companies
2. Disclosure of Accounting Policies
3. Earnings per Share
4. The Accounting Treatment of Government Grants
5. Accounting for Value Added Tax
6. Extraordinary Items and Prior Year Adjustments
7. Accounting for the Changes in the Purchasing Power of Money (provisional)
8. The Treatment of Taxation under the Imputation System
9. Stocks and Work in Progress
10. Statement of Sources and Application of Funds
11. Accounting for Deferred Taxation
12. Accounting for Depreciation
13. Accounting for Research and Development
14. Group Accounts
15. Accounting for Deferred Taxation
16. Current Cost Accounting
17. Accounting for Post Balance Sheet Events
18. Accounting for Contingencies
19. Accounting for Investment Properties
20. Foreign Currency Translation
21. Accounting for Leases and Hire Purchase Contracts
22. Accounting for Goodwill
23. Accounting for Acquisitions and Mergers
24. Accounting for Pension Costs
25. Segmental Reporting.

statement of total recognized gains and losses A primary statement showing the extent to which *shareholders' equity has increased or decreased from all the various gains and losses recognized in the period. It includes profits and losses for the period, together with all other movements on *reserves reflecting recognized gains and losses attributable to shareholders. Such a statement has been required from UK companies since 1993. The statement is dealt with under Financial Reporting Standard 3, 'Reporting Financial Performance'.

static gap The *gap position of a bank at a particular point in time.

static risk An insurance risk the magnitude of which can be assessed because it has a direct natural cause, e.g. fire, theft, or disaster caused by adverse weather.

status enquiry *See* BANKER'S REFERENCE.

statute-barred debt A debt that has not been collected within the period allowed by law.

statutory accounts Accounts required by law, for example by the Companies Act. *See also* STATUTORY BOOKS.

statutory audit An *audit of a company as required by the Companies Act 1985, subject to *small company exemptions. The *auditors are required to report to the company's members on all accounts of the company, copies of which are laid before the company in general meeting. Under the amended regulations passed in 2004, companies with a *balance sheet of not more than £2.8 million and *turnover of not more than £5.6 million may be exempt from the statutory audit.

statutory books The books of account that the Companies Act 1985 requires a company to keep. They must show and explain the company's transactions, disclose with reasonable accuracy the company's financial position at any time, and enable the directors to ensure that any accounts prepared therefrom comply with the provisions of the Act. They must also include entries from day to day of all money received and paid out together with a record of all assets and liabilities and statements of stockholding (where appropriate).

statutory company *See* COMPANY.

statutory damages *See* DAMAGES.

statutory meeting A meeting held in accordance with the Companies Act 1985. This normally refers to the annual general meeting of the shareholders, although it could refer to any other meeting required to be held by statute.

statutory report A report required to be made by statute. This normally refers to the annual report and accounts required to be laid before the members of a company by the Companies Act 1985.

stealth tax *See* HIDDEN TAX.

stepped preference share A *preference share that earns a predetermined income, which rises steadily by a set amount each year to the winding-up date; there is also a predetermined capital growth.

sterilization The process of offsetting the inflationary-deflationary effects that result when a government intervenes in foreign-exchange markets. If a nation's currency is depreciating and its government wishes to intervene to stabilize the exchange rate, it can sell its reserves of foreign currency and buy its own currency. However, buying its own currency will take money out of circulation, which could cause interest rates to rise, followed by recession. Sterilization is the process of expanding the money supply in these circumstances to prevent increases in interest rates and any consequent recession. Conversely, if a government intervenes to prevent a currency from appreciating, sterilization would involve reducing the money supply.

sterling The UK *pound, as distinguished from the pounds of other countries. The name derives from *steorra* (Old English), the small star that appeared on early Norman pennies.

Sterling Transferable Accruing Government Securities *See* STAGS.

Sterling Warrant Into Gilt-edged Stock (SWING) A warrant issued by the Bank of England giving the holder an option to buy or sell a specified *gilt-edged security.

STI Abbreviation for *Straits Times (Industrial) Index.

STMS Abbreviation for *short-term monetary support.

stock 1. In the UK, a fixed-interest security (*see* GILT-EDGED SECURITY) issued by the government, local authority, or a company in fixed units, often of £100 each in the UK and $1,000 in the USA. They usually have a *redemption date on which the *par value of the unit price is repaid in full. They are dealt in on stock exchanges at prices that fluctuate, but depend on such factors as their *yield in relation to current interest rates and the time they have to run before redemption. *See also* TAP STOCK. **2.** The US name for an *ordinary share. **3.** The stock-in-trade of an organization. **4.** Any collection of assets, e.g. the stock of plant and machinery owned by a company.

stockbroker An agent who buys and sells securities on a stock exchange on behalf of clients and receives remuneration for this service in the form of a *commission. Before October 1986 (*see* BIG BANG), stockbrokers on the *London Stock Exchange were not permitted by the rules of the Stock Exchange to act as *principals (*compare* STOCKJOBBER) and they worked for a fixed commission laid down by the Stock Exchange. Since October 1986, however, many London stockbrokers have taken advantage of the new rules, which allow them to buy and sell as principals, in which capacity they are now known as *market makers. This change has been accompanied by the formal abolition of fixed commissions, enabling stockbrokers to vary their commission in competition with each other. Stockbrokers have traditionally offered investment advice, especially for their *institutional investors.

stock exchange (stock market) A market for the sale and purchase of securities, in which the prices are controlled by the laws of supply and demand. The first stock exchange was in Amsterdam, where in 1602 shares in the United East India Company could be traded. UK exchanges date from 1673, with the first daily official price lists being issued in London in 1698. Stock markets have developed hand-in-hand with capitalism, gradually growing in complexity and importance. Their basic function is to allow public companies, governments, local authorities, and other incorporated bodies to raise capital by selling securities to investors. They perform valuable secondary functions in allowing those investors to buy and sell these securities, providing liquidity, and reducing the risks attached to investment. Stock markets were abolished after World War II in communist-dominated states but with the collapse of communism many restarted. The major international stock exchanges are based in London, New York, and Tokyo. Outside English-speaking countries, a stock exchange is usually known as a *bourse.

Stock Exchange Alternative Trading Service (SEATS) A computerized system used on the *London Stock Exchange for trading on the *Alternative Investment Market and for stocks of restricted liquidity (e.g. where there is only one *market maker). A screen-based service showing current prices and orders, it runs alongside the *Stock Exchange Automated Quotations System (SEAQ).

Stock Exchange Automated Quotations System (SEAQ) A computerized system used on the *London Stock Exchange to record the prices at which transactions in securities have been struck, thus establishing the market prices for these securities; these prices are made available to brokers through *TOPIC. When a bargain is concluded, the details must be notified to the central system within certain set periods during the day. **SEAQ International** is the system used on the London Stock Exchange for non-UK equities; it operates on similar lines to SEAQ. *See also* SETS; STOCK EXCHANGE ALTERNATIVE TRADING SERVICE.

Stock Exchange Automatic Execution Facility (SAEF) A computerized system used on the *London Stock Exchange to enable a broker to execute a transaction in a security through an SAEF terminal, which automatically completes the bargain at the best price with a *market maker, whose position is automatically adjusted. The price of the transaction is then automatically recorded on a trading report and also passes into the settlement system. The system has greatly reduced the administrative burden on brokers and market makers but has been criticized for eliminating the personal element between brokers and market makers on the floor of the exchange.

Stock Exchange Daily Official List A record of all the bargains made on the *London Stock Exchange. It also provides details of dividend dates, rights issues, prices, etc., of all *listed companies. It is known as the Official List.

Stock Exchange of Hong Kong *See* HONG KONG STOCK EXCHANGES.

Stock Exchange of Singapore (SES) One of the four *tiger markets of South East Asia whose origin goes back to the early years of the century. In its present form it dates from 1973, after Malaysia's decision to sever its currency link with Singapore. It was further modified after the Malaysian government forced companies to delist from the SES in 1990. Its main indicator is the *Straits Times (Industrial) Index, and there is also the less-used Stock Exchange of Singapore Index (SESI). The Overseas China Banking Corporation also calculates an index. A computerized over-the-counter market, the Central Limit Order Book (CLOB) International, was opened in 1990, a year after the main market had changed to electronic trading. A second-tier market has operated since February 1987 as the **Stock Exchange of Singapore Dealing and Automated Quotation System** (SESDAQ). Regulation is by the central bank and the Monetary Authority of Singapore under the Securities Industry Act 1986, passed after the collapse in 1985 of the Pan-Electric Industries conglomerate.

Stock Exchange Pool Nominees Ltd (SEPON Ltd) *See* TALISMAN.

Stock Exchange Trading System *See* SETS.

stockholder The usual US name for a *shareholder.

Stockholm Stock Exchange (Stockholm Fondbors) The main stock exchange in Sweden, which is regulated by the Bank Inspection Board and the Riksbanken (central bank). Taxation on share trading from 1984 drove much trading to London and New York, with 45% of the turnover in Swedish equities being traded outside Sweden. The non-socialist government elected in 1991 subsequently abolished the tax. The Stockholm Stock Exchange was acquired by the Swedish financial services company OMX in 1998 and merged with the Helsinki Stock Exchange in 2003.

stockjobber (jobber) A *market maker on the *London Stock Exchange prior to the *Big Bang (October, 1986). Stockjobbers were only permitted to deal with the general public through the intermediary of a *stockbroker. This single capacity system was replaced by the *dual-capacity system of market makers after the Big Bang.

stock market 1. *See* STOCK EXCHANGE. **2.** A market in which livestock are bought and sold.

stock of money *See* MONEY SUPPLY.

stock option *See* OPTION.

stock repurchase plan A plan to *repurchase shares in a company approved by shareholders.

stock split *See* SCRIP ISSUE.

stock symbol A short form of the full title of a security, used for quick and convenient identification, especially on screen-based trading systems.

Stock Watch The unit of the New York Stock Exchange that monitors share dealing to identify irregular or illegal behaviour.

stock watering The creation of more new shares in a company than is justified by its tangible assets, even though the company may be making considerable profits. The consequences of this could be that the dividend may not be maintained at the old rate on the new capital and that if the company were to be liquidated its shareholders may not be paid out in full.

stop-loss order An order placed with a broker in a security or commodity market to close an *open position at a specified price in order to limit a loss. It may be used in a volatile market, especially by a speculator, if the market looks as if it might move strongly against the speculator's position.

stop-loss treaty A *reinsurance treaty in which the insurer is refunded by the reinsurer for any claims in excess of a specified proportion of the premiums received.

stop notice A court procedure available to protect those who have an interest in shares but have not been registered as company members. The notice prevents the company from registering a transfer of the shares or paying a dividend upon them without informing the server of the notice. It was formerly known as **notice in lieu of distringas**.

stop order An order placed with a broker in a security or commodity market to buy if prices rise to a specified level or sell if they fall to another specified level.

stotin A monetary unit of Slovenia worth one hundredth of a *tolar.

stotinka (*plural* **stotinki**) A monetary unit of Bulgaria worth one hundredth of a *lev.

straddle A strategy used by dealers in *options or *futures contracts. In the option market it involves simultaneously purchasing put and call options; it is most profitable when the price of the underlying security is very volatile. *Compare* BUTTERFLY. In commodity and currency futures a straddle may involve buying and selling options or both buying and selling the same commodity or currency for delivery in the future, often on different markets. Undoing half the straddle is known as *breaking a leg.

straight *See* EUROBOND.

straight bond A *bond issued in the *primary market that carries no equity or other incentive to attract the investor; its only reward is an annual or biannual interest coupon together with a promise to repay the capital at par on the redemption date.

straight-line method of depreciation *See* DEPRECIATION.

Straits Times (Industrial) Index (STI) The main price indicator on the *Stock Exchange of Singapore; it comprises 30 industrial shares and is issued daily by the Straits Times Newspaper Group.

strap A triple *option on a share or commodity market, consisting of one put option and two call options at the same price and for the same period. *Compare* STRIP.

strategic intent A clearly understood statement of the direction in which a firm intends to develop. It should be both understood and interpreted by each employee in relation to their work and is a crucial element in the strategic management of a firm. *See also* MISSION STATEMENT.

strategic investment appraisal An appraisal of an investment decision based on wider grounds than that provided by a purely financial appraisal. It is also necessary to evaluate possible long-term strategic benefits and any intangible factors that may be relevant to the decision, particularly if advanced manufacturing technology is concerned.

street-name stocks The US name for nominee stocks (*see* NOMINEE SHAREHOLDING).

stress testing A method of *risk analysis in which *simulations are used to estimate the impact of worst-case situations. It is commonly used by regulators, rating agencies, and financial institutions, which base their simulations on both historical and hypothetical crises.

strike price (striking price) **1.** *See* EXERCISE PRICE. **2.** The price fixed by the sellers of a security after receiving bids in a *tender offer (for example, in the sale of gilt-edged securities or a new stock-market issue). Usually, those who bid below the strike price receive nothing, while those who bid at or above it receive some proportion of the amount they have bid for.

strip A triple *option on a share or commodity market, consisting of one call option and two put options at the same price and for the same period. *Compare* STRAP.

stripped bond **1.** A bond in which payments are sold as a set of 300 coupon bonds. **2.** A bond or stock that has been subjected to *dividend stripping.

strong-form market efficiency One of three categories of market efficiency defined by Eugene Fama. In a strong-form efficient market, it is impossible to achieve *abnormal returns from the use of any information available in the market, be it public or available only to a restricted number of market participants. In general, markets are held not to be strong-form efficient, since it appears to be possible to make abnormal returns from *insider dealing. *See* EFFICIENT MARKETS HYPOTHESIS. *Compare* SEMI-STRONG-FORM MARKET EFFICIENCY; WEAK-FORM MARKET EFFICIENCY.

structured finance The creation of debt instruments by *securitization or the addition of derivatives to existing instruments.

subordinated debt A debt that can only be claimed by an unsecured creditor, in the event of a liquidation, after the claims of secured creditors have been met. In **subordinated unsecured loan stocks** loans are issued by such institutions as banks, in which the rights of the holders of the stock are subordinate to the interests of the depositors. Debts involving *junk bonds are always subordinated to debts to banks, irrespective of whether or not they are secured.

subrogation The principle that, having paid a claim, an insurer has the right to take over any other methods the policyholder may have for obtaining compensation for the same event. For example, if a neighbour is responsible for breaking a person's window and an insurance claim is paid for the repair, the insurers may, if they wish, take over the policyholder's legal right to claim the cost of repair from the neighbour.

subscribed share capital *See* SHARE CAPITAL.

subscriber A person who signs the memorandum of association of a new company and who joins with other members in the company in paying for a specified quantity of shares in the company, signing the articles of association, and appointing the first directors of the company.

subscription shares 1. Shares in a building society that are paid for by instalments; they often pay the highest interest rates. **2.** The shares bought by the initial *subscribers to a company.

subsidiary undertaking (group undertaking) An undertaking that is controlled by another undertaking (the parent or holding undertaking). The extent of the control needed to define a subsidiary is given in the Companies Act 1985. The *financial statements of a subsidiary undertaking are normally included in the *consolidated financial statements of the group.

subsidy A payment by a government to producers of certain goods to enable them to sell the goods to the public at a low price, to compete with foreign competition, to avoid making redundancies and creating unemployment, etc. In general, subsidies distort international trade and are unpopular but they are sometimes used by governments to help to establish a new industry in a country. *See also* COMMON AGRICULTURAL POLICY.

sum (*plural* sumy; UKS) The standard monetary unit of Uzbekistan, divided into 100 tyin.

sum insured The maximum amount the insurers will pay in the event of a claim.

summary financial statement An abbreviated form of the *annual accounts and report that, providing certain conditions are met, may be sent by *listed companies to their *shareholders instead of the full report. Summary financial statements were introduced by section 251 of the Companies Act 1985, which took effect from 1 April 1990.

sunk capital The amount of an organization's funds that has been spent and is therefore no longer available to the organization, frequently because it has been spent on either unrealizable or valueless assets.

superannuation An *occupational pension scheme. Contributions are deducted from an employee's salary by the employer and passed to an insurance company or the trustees of a pension fund. After retirement, the employee receives a pension payment from the scheme.

supermajority provisions Provisions in the byelaws of a company that call for more than a simple majority of its members when voting on certain motions, such as the approval of a merger or whether or not to agree to a takeover. In these circumstances the provisions may call for a supermajority of between 70% and 80% of the votes cast.

superregional bank In the USA, a bank that operates in a number of different regions.

supervisory board A non-executive board who appoint and oversee the members of the executive boards of many European companies.

supplementary special deposit scheme *See* CORSET.

supply and demand *See* MARKET FORCES.

supply estimate A request by the UK government for parliament's permission to use a specified sum of money, to be provided by the *Consolidated Fund, for use by a government department or some other body requiring money for public purposes.

supply risk 1. The inherent risk in *limited recourse financing of a construction project that the raw materials necessary for the operation of the plant to be constructed may become unavailable. *Compare* COMPLETION RISK; TECHNOLOGICAL RISK. **2.** The risk of disruption of inputs into a firm.

support level In technical analysis, a floor level of prices for a security or commodity at which the price tends to stop falling and begin to rebound. A fall below this level is regarded as marking a significant shift to lower prices. *Compare* RESISTANCE LEVEL. *See also* DOUBLE BOTTOM.

supra protest *See* ACCEPTANCE SUPRA PROTEST.

surety 1. A guarantor for the actions of someone. **2.** A sum of money held as a *guarantee or as evidence of good faith.

surrender value The sum of money given by an insurance company to the insured on a life policy that is cancelled before it has run its full term. The amount is calculated approximately by deducting from the total value of the premiums paid any costs, administration expenses, and a charge for the life-assurance cover up to the cancellation date. There is little or no surrender value to a life policy in its early years. Not all life policies acquire a surrender value; for example, *term assurance policies have no surrender value.

sushi bond A bond issued by a Japanese-registered company in a currency other than yen but targeted primarily at the Japanese institutional investor market.

suspense account A temporary account in the books of an organization to record balances to correct mistakes or balances that have not yet been finalized (e.g. because a particular deal has not been concluded).

swap The means by which a borrower can exchange the type of funds most easily raised for the type of funds required, usually through the intermediary of a bank. For example, a UK company may find it easy to raise a sterling loan when they really want to borrow euros; a German company may have exactly the opposite problem. A swap will enable them to exchange the currency they possess for the currency they need. This is called a *currency swap. The other common type of swap is an *interest-rate swap, in which borrowers exchange fixed- for floating-interest rates. The essence of a swap is that the parties exchange the net cash flows of different types of borrowing instruments on an *over-the-counter market. *See also* BASIS SWAP; CROSS-CURRENCY INTEREST-RATE SWAP.

swap line A line of credit between two central banks in different countries, when securities of equal value are exchanged but the borrowing bank repays on a forward contract.

swaption An *option to enter into a *swap contract.

sweep facility A service provided by a bank which automatically transfers funds above a certain level from a current account to a higher-interest earning account. The process can work in reverse when funds in the current account fall below a certain level. The purpose is to provide the customer with the greatest amount of interest, with the minimum personal intervention.

SWIFT Abbreviation for *Society for Worldwide Interbank Financial Telecommunications.

SWING Abbreviation for *Sterling Warrant Into Gilt-edged Stock.

swing line A short-term and very short notice credit that can be used to cover shortfalls in other credit arrangements, such as commercial paper.

Swiss Options and Financial Futures Exchange (SOFFEX) A *financial futures exchange based in Zurich. Its contracts include *index futures based on the **Swiss Market Index (SMI)**. It was set up by the stock exchanges in Zurich, Basle, and Geneva, with the help of five banks, in 1988.

Swiss stock exchanges Zurich is the largest of the eight stock exchanges in Switzerland, with Geneva, Basle, and Berne ranking next in importance. Numbers may be reduced with the introduction of full electronic trading in 1993. The price level is given daily by the **Swiss Market Index (SMI)**.

switching 1. Using the cash from the sale of one investment to purchase another. This may, or may not, involve a liability for capital gains tax, depending on the circumstances. **2.** Closing an *open position in a commodity market and opening a similar position in the same commodity but for a different delivery period. For example, a trader may switch a holding of sugar for October delivery FOB to an equal quantity of sugar for March delivery FOB for the next year. **3.** A country's intervention in the international currency market to stop an outflow of its currency. **4.** Exporting and importing through a third nation, where the currency paying for the goods can be easily exchanged into one acceptable to the seller.

switching discount A discount offered to holders of a unit trust who wish to switch to another unit trust managed by the same group.

syndicate 1. A group of bankers, insurers, contractors, etc., who join together to work on a large project. Notable activities undertaken by such a group may include syndicated loans and underwriting (*see also* SYNDICATED BANK FACILITY). **2.** A number of *Lloyd's underwriters who accept insurance risks as a group; each syndicate is run by a syndicate manager or agent. The **names** in the syndicate accept an agreed share of each risk in return for the same proportion of the premium. The names do not take part in organizing the underwriting business but treat their involvement with the syndicate as an investment. Since the reorganization of Lloyd's in the 1990s, limited companies have been allowed to become names. Although a syndicate underwrites as a group, each member is financially responsible for only his or her own share.

syndicated bank facility (syndicated loan) A very large loan made to one borrower by a group of banks headed by one lead bank, which usually takes only a small percentage of the loan itself, syndicating the rest to other banks and financial institutions. The loans are usually made on a small margin. The borrower can reserve the right to know the names of all the members of the syndicate. If the borrower states which banks are to be included, it is known as a **club deal**. A syndicated bank facility is usually a *revolving bank facility. There is only one loan agreement.

synergy The added value created by joining two separate firms, enabling a greater return to be achieved than by their individual contributions as separate entities; i.e. the overall gain in return is greater than the sum of its parts. The synergy is usually anticipated and analysed during merger or takeover activities; for example, one firm's strength in marketing would be complementary to the other firm's versatility in new product development. Although synergy is often optimistically sought, it is often hard to achieve in practice due to resistance to change, particularly after a contested takeover. The corporate culture that each participant may have built up over many years of separate existence may prove too inflexible to enable a productive merger to be achieved without friction. *See* ANERGY. *See also* COUPON STRIPPING.

synthetic security A security created by repackaging an existing asset or combination of assets.

systematic risk (general risk; residual risk; undiversifiable risk) The type of *risk in a portfolio of investments that cannot be reduced by *diversification, since it is common to all securities of the same general class. The compensation that an investor requires for undertaking such risks forms the basis for the *risk-premium calculation of the *capital asset pricing model and *arbitrage pricing theory. Systematic risk is measured by the *beta coefficient.

systemic risk The *risk of a failure in a whole system, such as the *clearing-house system in commodity markets.

S

tactical asset allocation An attempt to increase *portfolio returns in the short term by altering the asset composition of the portfolio. The academic literature is sceptical as to whether this will result in higher returns for any reason other than chance.

tail 1. Part of a probability distribution representing events of low probability. *See* EXTREME VALUE THEORY; FAT TAILS. **2.** Decimals or small fractions following the whole-figure sum in a bond issue bid. **3.** The pool of assets backing an *asset-backed security.

Taiwan Stock Exchange One of the *tiger markets of the Pacific, in which share trading dates from 1962 in Taipei, after the formation of a Securities and Exchange Commission in 1960. Trading is mainly in local stocks. An *over-the-counter market was launched in 1982.

taka (Tk) The standard monetary unit of Bangladesh, divided into 100 oisha.

take delivery 1. In a derivatives market, to take physical *delivery of the *underlying. **2.** In a securities market, to receive the relevant certificates of ownership.

takeover bid (offer to purchase) An offer made to the shareholders of a company by an individual or organization to buy their shares at a specified price in order to gain control of that company. In a welcome takeover bid the directors of the company will advise shareholders to accept the terms of the bid. This is usually known as a *merger. If the bid is unwelcome, or the terms are unacceptable, the board will advise against acceptance (*see* HOSTILE BID). In the ensuing **takeover battle**, the bidder may improve the terms offered and will then usually write to shareholders outlining the advantages that will follow from the successful takeover. In the meantime bids from other sources may be made (*see* GREY KNIGHT; WHITE KNIGHT) or the original bidder may withdraw as a result of measures taken by the board of the *target company (*see* POISON PILL; PORCUPINE PROVISIONS). In an **unconditional bid**, the bidder will pay the offered price irrespective of the number of shares acquired, while the bidder of a **conditional bid** will only pay the price offered if sufficient shares are acquired to provide a controlling interest. Takeovers in the UK are subject to the rules and disciplines of the *City Code on Takeovers and Mergers.

Takeover Panel *See* CITY CODE ON TAKEOVERS AND MERGERS.

taker The buyer of a traded *option. *Compare* WRITER.

tala (WS$) The standard monetary unit of Samoa, divided into 100 sene.

TALISMAN Abbreviation for Transfer Accounting Lodgement for Investors and Stock Management. This was the *London Stock Exchange computerized transfer system, which covered most UK securities; it also covered claims for dividends on shares being transferred. It was operated by a special company set up for the purpose, the Stock Exchange Pool Nominees Ltd, known as SEPON Ltd. It ceased trading in 1997 when the Bank of England *CREST system replaced it.

talon A printed form attached to a *bearer bond that enables the holder to apply for a new sheet of *coupons when the existing coupons have been used up.

tambala A monetary unit of Malawi worth one hundredth of a *kwacha.

tanga A monetary unit of Tajikistan worth one hundredth of a *rouble.

tangible assets Assets that can be touched, i.e. physical objects. However, tangible assets usually also include leases and company shares. They are therefore the fixed assets of an organization as opposed to such *intangible assets as goodwill, patents, and trademarks, which are even more intangible than leases and shares.

***Tanshi* company** A Japanese company that deals on the money markets.

tape A reporting system for stock-market information, primarily prices. It was formerly known as **tickertape**, before the process was computerized.

taper relief A tax relief on *capital gains tax in the UK. It applies to capital gains on the disposal of assets acquired after 5 April 1998. The percentage of the gain considered chargeable is reduced for each whole year of ownership after this date. The reductions are at a rate of 7.5% for each whole year of ownership for non-business assets and 5% for each whole year after the first two years for business assets. The maximum reduction is 75% for non-business assets and 40% for business assets. So, for example, the capital gains tax on a business asset held for 7 years will be levied on 75% of the capital gain. In the case of assets acquired before 5 April 1998, the chargeable gain is calculated according to the former system of *indexation.

tap issue The issue of UK government securities or bills to selected market makers, usually to influence the price of gilts. The government can control their volume and price, like turning a tap on or off.

tap stock A gilt-edged security from an issue that has not been fully subscribed and is released onto the market slowly when its market price reaches predetermined levels. **Short taps** are short-dated stocks and **long taps** are long-dated taps.

target company A company that is subject to a *takeover bid.

target payout ratio The desired long-run ratio of dividends to profits after interest and tax.

target price *See* COMMON AGRICULTURAL POLICY.

tariff 1. Any list of charges for goods or services. **2.** A tax or customs duty payable on imports or exports, or a list detailing such duties. The Customs and Excise issue tariffs stating which goods attract duty and what the rate of duty is. **3.** A list of charges in which the charging rate changes after a fixed amount has been purchased or in which a flat fee is imposed in addition to a quantity-related charge, as in two-part tariffs for gas or telephone services.

tariff office An insurance company that bases its premiums on a tariff arranged with other insurance companies. A **non-tariff office** is free to quote its own premiums.

tau A measure of the sensitivity of an *option price to changes in the volatility of the *underlying. *See* GREEKS.

TAURUS Abbreviation for Transfer and Automated Registration of Uncertified Stock. This was the *London Stock Exchange's computerized system designed to enable stocks and shares to be transferred without the use of contract notes or share certificates. It was abandoned in March 1993 leaving London behind its continental competitors; a new system, *CREST, began operating in July 1996.

taxable income Income liable to taxation, usually by reason of the statutes passed by Parliament. It is calculated by deducting *income-tax allowances from the taxpayer's gross income.

taxable person An individual, partnership, limited company, club, association, or charity as defined by the *value added tax legislaton. Value added tax is charged on taxable supplies made by taxable persons in the course or furtherance of a business.

tax allowance *See* INCOME TAX ALLOWANCES; PERSONAL ALLOWANCES.

tax and price index (TPI) A measure of the increase in taxable income needed to compensate taxpayers for any increase in retail prices. As an index of the rate of *inflation, it is similar to the *Retail Price Index, but in addition to measuring price changes it includes changes in average tax liability; for example, a cut in income tax will cause the TPI to rise by less than the RPI. This indicator now receives only limited attention.

taxation A levy on individuals or corporate bodies by central or local government in order to finance the expenditure of that government and also as a means of implementing its fiscal policy. Payments for specific services rendered to or for the payer are not regarded as taxation. In the UK, an individual's income is taxed by means of an *income tax (*see also* PAYE), while corporations pay a *corporation tax. Increases in individual wealth are taxed by means of *capital gains tax and by *inheritance tax. *See also* DIRECT TAXATION; INDIRECT TAXATION; VALUE ADDED TAX.

taxation brackets Figures between which taxable income or wealth is taxed at a specified rate. For example, in the UK for 2004–05, taxable income up to £2020 attracts tax at 10%, from £2020 to £31,400 the basic rate of 22% applies, and over £31,400 the higher rate of 40% has to be paid. *See also* BRACKET INDEXATION.

tax avoidance Minimizing tax liabilities legally and by means of full disclosure to the tax authorities. *See* TAX PLANNING. *Compare* TAX EVASION.

tax base The specified domain on which a tax is levied, e.g. an individual's income for *income tax, the estate of a deceased person for *inheritance tax, the profits of a company for *corporation tax.

tax break A tax advantage for a particular activity.

tax burden The amount of tax suffered by an individual or organization. This may not be the same as the tax actually paid because of the possibility of shifting tax or the normal *incidence of taxation. As an example of the latter case, *inheritance tax is paid by the personal representatives of the deceased but the tax burden falls on the heirs, since their inheritance is reduced.

tax clearance An assurance, obtained from the UK Inland Revenue, that a proposed transaction, for example the reorganization of a company's share capital, will, if executed, not attract tax.

tax credit 1. The tax allowance associated with the *dividend paid by a company. The shareholder is given allowance for the tax paid at source by the tax credit, at the same rate, 10/90; i.e. a dividend of £90 received by the shareholder has an associated tax credit of £10. For those whose total taxable income does not exceed £31,400 there is no further tax to pay. For those whose income is higher, the excess amount is chargeable at a rate of 32.5%. **2.** Any allowance or payment that can be offset against a tax liability. In the UK such allowances now include income-related benefits for families with children under 16. *Compare* INCOME-TAX ALLOWANCES.

tax credit system A taxation system in which individuals are given tax allowances dependent on their needs; if tax on their income is less than the total of their tax credits, they can be paid the excess credits. *See also* NEGATIVE INCOME TAX.

tax-deductible Denoting an amount that can be deducted from income or profits, in accordance with the tax legislation, before establishing the amount of income or profits that is subject to tax.

tax-deferred Describing a financial instrument in which tax is paid at maturity.

tax deposit certificate A certificate issued by the UK Inland Revenue to a taxpayer who has made an advance payment in anticipation of future income tax, capital gains tax, or corporation tax. The initial payment must not be less than £2000 and has to be made to a tax-collection office. The certificates bear interest, which is liable to tax. The interest rate depends on whether the certificate is withdrawn for cash or surrendered to meet a tax demand. A higher rate is paid on the latter. Interest normally runs to the date of encashment but if the certificate is used to pay tax, it runs only to the due date of payment of the liability, not the actual date of payment.

tax evasion Minimizing tax liabilities illegally, usually by not disclosing that one is liable to tax or by giving false information to the authorities. Evasion is liable to severe penalties. *Compare* TAX AVOIDANCE.

Tax Exempt Special Savings Account (Tessa) A UK savings account with a bank or building society, introduced in January 1991, in which savers were allowed to invest up to £9000 over a five-year period with no tax to pay on their interest, provided that special conditions were met. Savers investing in a Tessa for the first time could deposit up to £3000 in the first year and £1800 in any subsequent year (the maximum of £1800 could only be invested in the fifth year if a reduced amount was invested in one of the previous years). Savers with a matured Tessa could invest all the capital (i.e. up to £9000) from this account in a new Tessa during the first year, provided the new account was opened within six months of the maturity date of the old Tessa. The tax exemption was lost if: (a) capital was withdrawn at any time; (b) withdrawals of interest or bonuses exceeded 80% of the total amount of these credited to the account prior to the withdrawal; (c) the account holders' rights were assigned or used as security for a loan. Tessas were replaced by *Individual Savings Accounts (ISAs) in April 1999; however, existing Tessas were allowed to continue under the same arrangements until their term expired.

tax exile A person with a high income or considerable wealth who chooses to live in a *tax haven to avoid high taxation in his or her own country.

tax-free Denoting a payment, allowance, benefit, etc., on which no tax is payable.

tax haven A country or independent area that has a low rate of tax and therefore offers advantages to retired wealthy individuals or to companies that can arrange their affairs so that their tax liability falls at least partly in the low-tax haven. In the case of individuals, the cost of the tax saving is usually residence in the tax haven for a major part of the year (*see* TAX EXILE). For multinational companies, an office in the tax haven, with some real or contrived business passing through it, is required. Monaco, Liechtenstein, the Bahamas, and the Cayman Islands are examples of tax havens.

tax holiday A period during which a company, in certain countries, is excused from paying corporation tax or profits tax (or pays them on only part of its profits) as an export incentive or an incentive to start up a new industry.

tax loss A loss made by an organization in one period, that can be carried forward to another period to reduce the tax payable by that organization in the subsequent period.

tax planning The arrangement of a taxpayer's affairs, in accordance with the requirements of the tax legislation, in order to reduce the overall charge to tax. *See* TAX AVOIDANCE.

tax rebate A repayment of tax paid.

Tax Reform Act 1986 A major US tax reform that abolished many sources of tax deductability (e.g. state and local sales taxes), reduced tax rates, and made income, corporation, and capital gains tax more consistent. It also lowered the top rate of corporation tax from 46% to 34%.

tax relief A deduction from a taxable amount, usually given by statute. In the UK, income-tax reliefs are given in respect of income from tax-exempt sources (e.g. ISAs), as well as tax-deductible expenses, personal allowances, tax credits, and *gift aid. *See* INCOME-TAX ALLOWANCES.
   The reliefs against *capital gains tax include an annual exemption, exemption from the proceeds of the sale of an only or a principal private residence, and retirement relief. For *inheritance tax there is an annual relief as well as relief in respect of gifts between spouses and gifts to political parties and charities; agricultural and business reliefs are also available.

tax return A form upon which a taxpayer makes an annual statement of income and personal circumstances enabling claims to be made for personal allowances. In the UK an income tax return also requires details of *capital gains in the year. The onus is on the taxpayer to give the Inland Revenue the appropriate information even if the taxpayer receives no tax return. Categories of tax payer who can expect to receive a tax return include the self-employed, company directors, people with a high investment income, and those acting as trustees or personal representatives. Since 1996–97 income tax returns have included a section for *self-assessment, in which the tax payer calculates his or her own liability for income tax. Separate returns are required for *inheritance tax purposes and in respect of VAT and excise duties.

tax shelter Any financial arrangement made in order to avoid or minimize taxes.

tax shield A deduction (such as a charitable contribution) that lowers a person's or company's tax liabilities.

tax treaty An agreement between two countries, identifying the treatment of income, profits, or gains that are subject to tax in both countries. The amount of *double taxation relief will be specified in the treaty.

tax year *See* FISCAL YEAR.

teaser rate A low introductory rate of interest on an asset product (i.e. a loan) or a high introductory rate of interest on a liability product (i.e. a deposit) to attract customers.

technical analysis *See* INVESTMENT ANALYST.

technical rally *See* RALLY.

technical reserves The assets held by an insurance company against future claims or losses.

technological risk The *risk to a business from changing technology.

telegraphic transfer (TT) A method of transmitting money overseas by means of a transfer between banks by cable or telephone. The transfer is usually made in the currency of the payee and may be credited to the payee's account at a specified bank or paid in cash to the payee on application and identification.

telephone banking A *home banking facility enabling customers to use banking services by means of a telephone link.

Telerate A US financial news and information service, partly owned and operated by the Dow Jones Corporation. It is also available in some other countries.

Teletext Output Price Information Computer *See* TOPIC.

teller The US name for a bank or building society cashier, i.e. someone who accepts deposits and pays out cash over the counter to customers.

temporal method A method of converting a foreign currency involved in a transaction in which the local currency is translated at the exchange rate in operation on the date on which the transaction occurred. If rates do not fluctuate significantly, an average for the period may be used as an approximation. Any exchange gain or loss on translation is taken to the *profit and loss account. This contrasts with the closing rate or *net-investment method of translation, which uses the exchange rate ruling at the *balance-sheet date for translation and takes exchange differences to *reserves. *Statement of Standard Accounting Practice 20, 'Foreign Currency Translation', allows either method to be adopted.

temporary assurance *See* TERM ASSURANCE.

tender **1.** A written offer to purchase. **2.** A means of auctioning an item of value to the highest bidder. Tenders are used in many circumstances, e.g. for allocating valuable construction contracts, for selling shares on a stock market (*see* OFFER FOR SALE; ISSUE BY TENDER), or for the sale of government securities (*see* GILT-EDGED SECURITY).

tender offer A US practice of offering securities to the public by inviting them to tender a price; the securities are then sold to the highest bidder.

tender panel A group of banks who are asked to subscribe as a *syndicate for the issue of *euronote facilities.

tenesi A monetary unit of Turkmenistan worth one hundredth of a *manat.

tenge (T) The standard monetary unit of Kazakhstan, divided into 100 tiyn.

tenor The time period elapsing between the issue of a security (such as a *bill of exchange) and its maturity.

Ten Windows Ten institutions in the People's Republic of China that are authorized to borrow abroad.

term 1. The period of time before a security expires or is redeemed. **2.** *See* TERM ASSURANCE. **3.** A clause in a contract that refers to a particular obligation between the contracting parties.

term assurance (temporary assurance; term insurance) A life-assurance policy that provides a payment on death within a specified period of time (the term). No benefit is paid if the insured person dies outside the term. This form of insurance is often used to cover the period of a loan, mortgage, etc. *See also* DECREASING TERM ASSURANCE.

term bill *See* PERIOD BILL.

terminable annuity *See* CERTAIN ANNUITY.

terminal bonus An additional amount of money added to payments made on the maturity of an insurance policy or on the death of an insured person, because the investments of the insurer have produced a profit or surplus. Bonuses of this kind are paid at the discretion of the life office and usually take the form of a percentage of the sum assured.

terminal date The date on which a *futures contract expires.

terminal loss-relief *See* LOSS RELIEFS.

terminal market A commodity market in a trading centre, such as London or New York, rather than a market in a producing centre, such as Calcutta or Singapore. The trade in terminal markets is predominantly in *futures contracts, but *spot goods may also be bought and sold.

terminal value (TV) The value of an investment at the end of an investment period taking into account a specified rate of interest over the period. The formula is the same as that for compound *interest, i.e.

$$TV = P(1 + r)^t,$$

where *TV* is the final amount at the end of period, *P* is the principal amount invested, *r* is the interest rate, and *t* is the time in years for which the investment takes place.

term insurance *See* TERM ASSURANCE.

term loan A fixed-period loan, usually for one to ten years, that is paid back by the borrower in regular (often monthly) instalments with interest. This is the most common form of business loan; it may be secured or unsecured.

terms of trade A measure of the trading prospects of a country expressed as an index of export prices divided by an index of import prices. A country's terms of trade improve if this ratio rises, because it can purchase more imports for a particular volume of exports.

term structure of interest rates A set of discount rates for each year to maturity, applied to fixed-rate securities such as government bonds. The term structure of interest rates is related to the *yield curve, but differs from this in that it gives a discount rate appropriate for individual years to maturity, rather than the discount rate for all years on a bond to maturity.

Tessa Abbreviation for *Tax Exempt Special Savings Account.

testacy The state of a person who has died leaving a valid will. Such a person is said to have died **testate**.

testator A person who makes a will. The feminine form is **testatrix**.

tetri A monetary unit of Georgia worth one hundredth of a *lari.

Texas hedge The opposite of a *hedge, which is intended to reduce risk. In a Texas hedge risk is increased, e.g. by buying more than one financial instrument of the same kind.

Thailand Stock Market *See* SECURITIES EXCHANGE OF THAILAND.

thebe A monetary unit of Botswana worth one hundredth of a *pula.

theta A measure of the sensitivity of an option value to time. As the time to expiry of an option declines, its *time value will also decline, since there is less likelihood of a significant improvement in the value of the *underlying. *See* GREEKS.

thin capitalization A form of company capitalization in which the capital of a company consists of too few shares and too much loan stock in the view of the tax authority. Some countries reserve the right in such cases to treat some of the interest on the loan stock as if it were a dividend, thus denying the right to a tax deduction on the interest payment.

thin market A market in which the price of the underlying commodity, currency, or financial instrument may change if sizable transactions are carried out. *Compare* DEEP MARKET.

third-country acceptance (refinance bill) An international trade *time draft drawn on a country other than that of the importer or exporter. *See also* BANKER'S ACCEPTANCE.

third market A market established by the London Stock Exchange in January 1987 for the trading of shares unsuited either to the *main market or the *Unlisted Securities Market (USM). The market was abolished on 31 December 1990 and combined with a reorganized USM. It had the object of specifying less stringent listing standards than either the main or unlisted markets, in order to attract the formerly unregulated *over-the-counter market, which was outside the jurisdiction of the London Stock Exchange. Investment in the third market was generally much more risky, because much less information was available on the companies.

threshold price *See* COMMON AGRICULTURAL POLICY.

thrifts (thrift institutions) US non-banking savings institutions that also gave mortgage finance to home buyers. In the late 1980s the US government had to inject millions of dollars to shore up these institutions, which had found themselves in trouble by relying on short-term deposits to finance long-term lending. They include *savings and loan associations and savings banks.

TIBOR Abbreviation for *Tokyo Inter Bank Offered Rate.

tick (point) The smallest upward or downward price movement of a security on a financial market.

tickertape *See* TAPE.

tied loan A loan made by one nation to another on condition that the money loaned is spent buying goods or services in the lending nation. It thus helps the lending nation, by providing employment, as well as the borrowing nation.

Tier 1 capital *Equity capital held by a bank against its risks. According to the *Basle Convergence Accord on capital adequacy, its value should be at least 4% of the bank's risk-adjusted assets.

Tier 2 capital In *capital adequacy assessments, specific types of debt that may be considered part of a bank's capital. Together with Tier 1 capital it should comprise at least 8% of the bank's risk-adjusted assets.

tiger markets The colloquial name for the four most important markets in the Pacific Basin after Japan. They are Hong Kong, South Korea, Singapore, and Taiwan. *Compare* DRAGON MARKETS.

Tigers *See* TIGR.

tight money *See* DEAR MONEY.

TIGR Abbreviation for Treasury Investors Growth Receipt. These *zero-coupon bonds are linked to US Treasury bonds. They are denominated in dollars and are usually referred to as **Tigers**.

till money The banknotes and coins held by a UK bank. In the USA this is known as **vault money**.

time bargain A contract in which securities have to be delivered at some date in the future.

time decay The loss in value of an option as it moves towards expiry. *See* THETA; TIME VALUE.

time deposit A deposit of money in an interest-bearing account for a specified period. In the USA, a time deposit requires at least 30 days' notice of withdrawal.

time draft A *bill of exchange drawn on and accepted by a US bank. *See also* BANKER'S ACCEPTANCE.

time-series forecasting The use of data from successive time periods to forecast future values for variables.

time value The market value of an *option over and above its *intrinsic value. Thus the time value represents the value of the possibility that the option will be worth exercising before it expires. Clearly, an option's value declines with the passage of time, and its value at expiry will be nil if it is not in the money. At expiry the value of an option, if any, consists solely of its intrinsic value. *See also* THETA.

time value of money The concept, used as the basis for *discounted cash flow calculations, that cash received earlier is worth more than a similar sum received later, because the sum received earlier can be invested to earn interest in the intervening period. For the same reasons, cash paid out later is worth less than a similar sum paid at an earlier date.

title A person's right of *ownership of property. A person in possession of reliable proof of ownership of an asset is said to have **good title**. The documents that prove good title to land, and state the terms on which it is owned, are called **title deeds**.

tiyn A monetary unit of Kazakhstan worth one hundredth of a *tenge.

TLF Abbreviation for *transferable loan facility.

Tobin's Q *See* Q RATIO.

Tobin tax A proposed low-level tax on foreign-exchange dealings. It has been suggested that such a tax could have the effect of restraining destabilizing currency speculation while also raising large sums that could be used to aid developing nations. The tax was proposed by the US economist John Tobin.

toea A monetary unit of Papua New Guinea worth one hundredth of a *kina.

toehold An initial stake in a company obtained as a prelude to an acquisition attempt.

tokkin A special investment fund on the Japanese stock markets owned by companies using their cash surpluses to generate extra income, although their main business is not in the financial markets.

Tokyo Inter Bank Offered Rate (TIBOR) The Japanese equivalent of the *London Inter Bank Offered Rate.

Tokyo round *See* GENERAL AGREEMENT ON TARIFFS AND TRADE.

Tokyo Stock Exchange (TSE) The largest and most important of the eight stock exchanges in Japan, accounting for some 85% of the turnover in Japanese securities. The market is split into three sections. The first section lists some 1200 of the largest issues in the market. Around 70% of first-section companies are also listed in the markets in Osaka and Nagoya. The second section has around 400 stocks, with less stringent listing requirements, similar to the *Alternative Investment Market in the UK. Foreign shares are traded on the third section of the market. The TSE also has an *over-the-counter market in shares registered with the Japanese Securities Dealers Association. A computerized trading system for over-the-counter stocks was established in late 1991. TSE members are either regulars, who deal in securities as principals, or agents (**saitori*), who can only act as intermediaries between regular members. Dealing is now mainly electronic through the Computerized Order Routing and Execution System (**CORES**), although about 150 first-section stocks are still traded by *open outcry on the exchange floor. The main market indicator is the *Nikkei Stock Average of 225 Japanese industrial companies.

tolar (*plural* **tolarji**; SIT) The standard monetary unit of Slovenia, divided into 100 stotin.

tombstone An advertisement in the financial press giving brief deals of the amount and maturity of a recently completed bank facility. The names of the *lead managers are prominently displayed, as well as the co-managers and the managers. It is customary for the borrower to pay although he or she receives little benefit from the advertisement.

too big to fail The idea that some banks will always be supported, because their failure would have an unacceptable effect on the stability of the national or international financial system. If such a bank should get into trouble, it is presumed that the central bank will bail it out. It is further contended that this will make such a bank more willing to take risks. The counterargument is that even if it received aid, there might still be serious consequences for the managers and shareholders of the bank. In any case, the theory only applies to the largest financial institutions. For example, in 1995 the London-based merchant bank Barings plc was allowed to fail after sustaining major losses through irregular trading on the Singapore derivatives market, since the Bank of England could identify no *systemic risk resulting from its failure.

TOPIC Abbreviation for Teletext Output Price Information Computer. This computerized communication system provides brokers and market makers on the *London Stock Exchange with information about share price movements and bargains as they are transacted. Input is from the *Stock Exchange Automated Quotations System (SEAQ). It is now run by a private company independently of the stock exchange.

top slicing A method of assessing the taxable gain on a life-assurance policy. The proceeds of the policy plus all capital withdrawals, less the premiums paid, are divided by the number of years for which the policy has been in force. This amount is added to any other income for the year in which the chargeable event occurred; if this places the taxpayer in a higher tax band, the whole gain is charged at the appropriate marginal rate, i.e. the tax rate in that band less the basic rate of tax. If the sum does not exceed the basic rate tax, no further tax is due.

top up To increase the benefits due under an existing insurance scheme, especially to increase the provision for a pension when a salary increase enables the insured to pay increased premiums.

Toronto Stock Exchange (TSE) The main exchange for Canadian shares; it is larger than either the Montreal or Vancouver markets. The Toronto exchange is computerized and was the first to link with a foreign exchange (the *American Stock Exchange). The main indicators are the Toronto 35 index and the wider TSE 300 Composite index.

total-absorption costing *See* ABSORPTION COSTING.

total income The income of a taxpayer from all sources. This is often referred to as **statutory total income**, which consists of income from sources based on the income of the current year and income from other sources based on income of the preceding year. This artificial concept is used to calculate a person's income tax for a given year.

total profits Profits chargeable to corporation tax (PCTCT), including profits from trading, property, investment income, overseas income, and chargeable gains, less charges.

touch The largest available spread or difference between the bid and offer prices of a security.

touch screen A system of *screen trading in which the operator uses a finger or other pointer to touch the screen in order to activate the system instead of using a keyboard or other system of entry.

town clearing Formerly, a special same-day clearing service for high value cheques drawn on accounts within the City of London and paid into another City account. All other cheques (known as **country cheques**) went into the general clearing system and took two or more days to clear. From 1995 the town clearing service ceased to be available. To guarantee a same-day transfer of funds, bank customers have to use the *telegraphic transfer service.

TPI Abbreviation for *tax and price index.

tracker fund *See* INDEX FUND.

trade **1.** The activity of selling goods or services in order to make a profit. Profits from trade are taxed under *income tax or *corporation tax on income, rather than under *capital gains tax or corporation tax on capital gains. The concept of trade is difficult to define for taxation purposes (*see* BADGES OF TRADE). **2.** To buy or sell in a market.

trade balance *See* BALANCE OF TRADE.

trade barrier Any action by a government that restricts free trading between organizations within that country and the world outside. Tariffs, quotas, embargoes, sanctions, and restrictive regulations all present barriers to free trade.

trade bill A *bill of exchange used to pay for goods. They are usually either held until they mature, as they do not command a favourable discount rate compared to bank bills, or they are discounted by banks.

trade bloc A group of nations united by trade agreements between themselves; for example, the European Union.

trade credit Credit given by one company to another; it usually results when a supplier of goods or services allows the customer a period (e.g. 14 days, 90 days) before expecting an invoice to be settled.

trade creditor One who is owed money by an organization for having provided goods or services to that organization.

trade debt A debt that arises during the normal course of trade.

traded months Those months of the year used in futures and options markets (*see* FUTURES CONTRACT) for stipulating that goods must be delivered or taken up.

traded options Options that can be bought and sold on an exchange, at all times, as opposed to **traditional options**, which, once bought, cannot be resold. *See* EXCHANGE-TRADED OPTION.

trade gap The difference between the value of a nation's imports and the value of its exports. *See also* BALANCE OF PAYMENTS.

trade investment Shares in or loans made to another company with a view to facilitating trade with the other company.

trademark A distinctive symbol that identifies particular products of a trader to the general public. The symbol may consist of a device, words, or a combination of these. A trader may register a trademark at the Register of Trade Marks, which is at the Patent Office (*see* PATENT). This authorizes the trader to enjoy the exclusive right to the trademark for which it was registered. Any manufacturer, dealer, importer, or retailer may register a trademark. Registration is initially for ten years and is then renewable. The right to remain on the register may be lost if the trademark is not used or is misused. The owner of a trademark may assign it or, subject to the Registrar's approval, allow others to use it. If anyone uses a registered trademark without the owner's permission, or uses a mark that is likely to be confused with a registered trademark, the owner can sue for an *injunction and *damages or an *account of profits.

The owner of a trademark that is not registered in the Register of Trade Marks but is identified with particular goods through established use may bring an action for *passing off in the case of infringement.

Tradepoint Investment Exchange A *Recognized Investment Exchange that functions as an *order-driven electronic market for securities in London. Participants are able to trade in the 350 equities comprising FTSE-350 (*see* FINANCIAL TIMES SHARE INDEXES) plus 50 other large company equities. The *London Clearing House acts as the central counterparty (*see* COUNTERPARTY RISK) to all deals carried out through Tradepoint, and the deals are settled through *CREST.

trade reference A reference concerning the creditworthiness of a trader given by another member of the same trade, usually to a supplier. If a firm wishes to purchase goods on credit from a supplier, the supplier will usually ask for a trade reference from another member of the same trade, in addition to a *banker's reference.

trading account The part of a *profit and loss account in which the cost of goods sold is compared with the money raised by their sale in order to arrive at the gross profit.

trading book **1.** The financial obligations held by a dealer or an institution trading on financial markets. *See* BOOK; MAKING A BOOK. **2.** The record of a bank's trading activities and obligations as opposed to its banking obligations. These are those activities of a bank that are seen as financial-market-related and short term. They are required to be marked to market (*see* MARKING TO MARKET) or marked to model (*see* MARKING TO MODEL) and must have adequate capital backing. *Compare* BANKING BOOK.

trading floor An area in a stock exchange, commodity market, financial futures and options market, etc., in which dealers trade by personal contact. In some markets the trading floors have been replaced by *screen trading.

trading halt **1.** The cessation of trading on a financial market when price movements reach the permitted *limit. **2.** The halting of trading in a particular security, usually as a result of a major news development or destabilizing rumour.

trading pit *See* PIT.

trading post The base on the *trading floor from which a *specialist on a US stock exchange operates.

trading profit The profit of an organization before deductions for such items as interest, directors' fees, auditors' remuneration, etc.

traditional options *See* TRADED OPTIONS.

tranche (French: slice) A part or instalment of a large sum of money. In the International Monetary Fund the first 25% of a loan is known as the **reserve** (formerly **gold**) **tranche**. In **tranche funding**, successive sums of money become available on a prearranged basis to a new company, often linked to the progress of the company and its ability to reach the targets set in its *business plan.

tranche CD A *certificate of deposit that has one maturity date but is sold by the issuing bank in portions (*tranches) to other investors.

transaction exposure The risk that the cost of a transaction will change because of exchange-rate movements between the date of the transaction and the date of the settlement.

transfer **1.** The movement of money from one bank account to another. **2.** The movement of funds through the banking system's *clearing house. **3.** A large movement of dollars in the USA through the *fedwire system. **4.** The conveyance of property ownership by the transfer of deeds. **5.** The change of title of ownership of stocks and shares from one owner to a new one by *transfer deed.

transferable Denoting a deed or other document the ownership of which can be transferred freely, e.g. a *negotiable instrument.

transferable loan facility (TLF) A bank loan facility that can be traded between lenders, in order to reduce the credit risk of the bank that provided the loan. It is a form of *securitization but can have an adverse effect on *relationship banking.

Transfer Accounting Lodgement for Investors *See* TALISMAN.

Transfer and Automated Registration of Uncertified Stock *See* TAURUS.

transfer deed A deed that is used to transfer property from one person to another. On the *London Stock Exchange a **stock transfer form** has to be signed by the seller of registered securities to legalize the transaction. This was dealt with by the computerized *TALISMAN system until 1997, when it was taken over by *CREST.

transferee A person to whom an asset is transferred.

transfer form *See* TRANSFER DEED.

transfer of value The reduction in the value of a person's estate by a gratuitous transfer. Such transfers are subject to *inheritance tax in most cases if made in a given period before the date of the donor's death.

transferor A person who transfers an asset to another (the transferee).

transfer payment (transfer income) A payment made or income received in which no goods or services are being paid for. Pensions, unemployment benefits, subsidies to farmers, etc., are transfer payments; they are excluded in calculating *gross national product.

transfer pricing The setting of prices for intra-group or company transfers of goods and services. The pricing may be based on allocating true profits to the individual units, although, in the case of multinational companies, the price may be chosen to avoid paying excessive taxes or duties in one particular country.

transfer risk The risk that goods sold on credit to a foreign buyer may not be paid for in full or on time as a result of a change in exchange-control regulations in the buyer's country.

transfer stamp An impressed stamp on documents relating to the transfer of land, as an acknowledgment that the *stamp duty has been paid.

translation exposure (accounting exposure) A risk that arises from the translation of the assets and liabilities in a *balance sheet into a foreign currency.

transparency 1. An essential condition of a free market in securities, in which transaction prices and volumes of trade are visible for all to see. **2.** The quality of a financial product that makes clear to the purchaser what the front-end and other charges will be.

traveller's cheque A cheque issued by a bank, building society, travel agency, credit-card company, etc., to enable a traveller to obtain cash in a foreign currency when abroad. They may be cashed at banks, exchange bureaus, restaurants, hotels, some shops, etc., abroad on proof of identity. The traveller has to sign the cheque twice, once in the presence of the issuer and again in the presence of the paying bank, agent, etc. Most traveller's cheques are covered against loss.

treasurer 1. A person who is responsible for looking after the money and other assets of an organization. This may include overseeing the provision of the organization's finances as well as some stewardship over the way in which the money is spent. **2.** In more recent times, the manager responsible for an organization's relationship with financial markets.

treasure trove Formerly, gold or silver found on land that had been hidden deliberately and that had no known owner. Treasure trove belonged to the Crown but the finder was recompensed for its value. Under the Treasure Act 1996 treasure was redefined as any item at least 300 years old and containing over 5% precious metal (excluding single coins). All such treasure belongs to the Crown, which will reward the finder.

Treasury 1. The UK government department responsible for the country's financial policies and management of the economy. The First Lord of the Treasury is the Prime Minister, but the Treasury is run by the Chancellor of the Exchequer. **2.** The central finance department of the US government. **3.** The department of a company or financial institution dealing with financial markets.

Treasury bill A *bill of exchange issued by the Bank of England on the authority of the UK government that is repayable in three months. They bear no interest, the yield being the difference between the purchase price and the redemption value. The US Treasury also issues Treasury bills.

Treasury bill rate The rate of interest obtainable by buying a *Treasury bill at a discount and selling it at its redemption value.

Treasury bill tender A weekly sale of Treasury bills to UK *discount houses by the Bank of England. The cost of the bills is set by the **Treasury bill tender rate**.

Treasury bond A bond issued by the US Treasury.

Treasury Investors Growth Receipt *See* TIGR.

Treasury stocks *See* GILT-EDGED SECURITY.

treaty 1. Any formal agreement in writing between nations. A **commercial treaty** relates to trade between the signatories. **2.** A transaction in which a sale is negotiated between the parties involved (**by private treaty**) rather than by auction. **3.** An agreement, usually in reinsurance, in which a reinsurer agrees automatically to accept risks from an insurer, either when a certain sum insured is exceeded or on the basis of a percentage of every risk accepted. With such a treaty an insurer has the confidence and capacity to accept larger risks than would otherwise be possible, as the necessary reinsurance is already arranged.

Treaty of Rome The 1957 treaty that set up the *European Economic Community (EEC), now the *European Union.

Treuhandanstalt The German government agency responsible for privatizing the nationalized industries of the former East Germany, when Germany was reunified in 1990.

Treynor index A risk-adjusted measure of a portfolio's performance. It is calculated by deducting the *risk-free rate of return from the portfolio return and dividing the resulting figure by the *beta coefficient of the portfolio. *Compare* SHARPE RATIO.

Treynor's alpha *See* ALPHA COEFFICIENT.

trial balance A listing of the balances on all the *accounts of an organization with debit balances in one column and credit balances in the other. If the processes of double-entry book-keeping have been accurate, the totals of each column should be the same. If they are not the same, checks must be carried out to find the discrepancy. The figures in the trial balance after some adjustments, e.g. for closing stocks, prepayments and accruals, depreciation, etc., are used to prepare the final accounts (profit and loss account and balance sheet).

trigger option *See* BARRIER OPTION.

trinomial tree A mathematical technique used in certain option-pricing models; it is based on the idea that the market for the *underlying could see a price rise, a price fall, or price constancy at each of various points, and that each of the three outcomes has a separate probability at each point. *Compare* BINOMIAL PROCESS.

triple witching hour The third Friday of each March, June, September, and December, when stock-index options, futures, and individual stock options all expire at the same time. This makes for very volatile trading conditions.

true and fair view Auditors of the published accounts of companies are required to form an opinion as to whether the accounts they audit show a 'true and fair view' of the organization's affairs. This is an important concept in the UK and may be used as an override to depart from legal requirements. Despite its importance there is no legal definition of the expression. The concept is also current in the rest of the European Union and in most of the Commonwealth.

trust **1.** An arrangement enabling property to be held by a person or persons (the *trustees) for the benefit of some other person or persons (the beneficiaries). The trustee is the legal owner of the property but the beneficiary has an equitable interest in it. A trust may be intentionally created or it may be imposed by law (e.g. if a trustee gives away trust property, the recipient will hold that property as constructive trustee for the beneficiary). Trusts are commonly used to provide for families and in commercial situations (e.g. pensions trusts). **2.** A monopoly formed in the USA, in which the owners of merging corporations gave their stock to a board of trustees, who were empowered to act on their behalf. Such monopolies were largely outlawed by the antitrust laws.

trust bank A Japanese bank that both lends and accepts savings; it also carries out trust activities, usually involving property or pension funds.

trust corporation **1.** A body allowed by law to act as a trustee for a will. **2. (trust company)** In the USA, a non-banking organization that can engage in banking activities provided it is chartered by the state authorities. US trust companies can be members of the *Federal Reserve System.

trust deed The document creating and setting out the terms of a *trust. It will usually contain the names of the trustees, the identity of the beneficiaries, and the nature of the trust property, as well as the powers and duties of the trustees. Trusts of land must be declared in writing; trusts of other property need not be although there is often a trust deed to avoid uncertainty.

trustee A person who holds the legal title to property but who is not its beneficial owner. Usually there are two or more trustees of a *trust and for some trusts of land this is necessary. The trustee may not profit from the position but must act for the benefit of the beneficiary, who may be regarded as the real owner of the property. Either an individual or a company may act as trustee. It is usual to provide for the remuneration of trustees in the trust deed, otherwise there is no right to payment. Trustees may be personally liable to beneficiaries for loss of trust property.

trustee in bankruptcy A person who administers a bankrupt's estate and realizes it for the benefit of the creditors (*see* BANKRUPTCY).

trustee investments Investments in which trustees are authorized to invest trust property. In the UK the Trustees Investment Act 1961 regulates the investments of trust property that may be made by trustees. The Act applies unless excluded by a trust deed executed after the Act was passed. Half of the trust fund must be invested in **narrow-range securities**, largely specified in fixed-interest investments. The other half may be invested in **wider-range securities**, most importantly ordinary shares in companies quoted on the London Stock Exchange. In some cases, trustees must take advice before investing. The Act considerably enlarged the range of trustee investments.

trust fund A fund consisting of the assets belonging to a *trust, including money and property, that is held by the *trustees for the beneficiaries.

trust letter A document that assigns goods to a bank as security against a loan and enables the borrower to regain title of the goods in order to sell them to pay off the loan.

trust receipt A document given by a bank holding a borrower's goods as security against a loan (*see* TRUST LETTER), when the borrower takes possession of these goods in order to sell them to pay off the loan.

Truth in Lending Act US consumer protection legislation, dating from 1969, that required lenders to state how they calculated interest on loans and other charges and to express them as an *annual percentage rate. The Act also allows the borrower a 'cooling-off' period, authorizing withdrawal from a financial agreement on a mortgage, within three days of signing a consumer credit agreement.

TSA Abbreviation for The *Securities Association Ltd, which was replaced by the *Securities and Futures Authority Ltd (SFA) in 1991.

TSE **1.** Abbreviation for *Tokyo Stock Exchange. **2.** Abbreviation for *Toronto Stock Exchange.

TT Abbreviation for *telegraphic transfer.

tugrik (Tug) The standard monetary unit of Mongolia, divided into 100 möngös.

turn The difference between the price at which a *market maker will buy a security (*see* BID) and the price at which the market maker will sell it (*see* OFFER PRICE), i.e. the market maker's profit.

Turnbull report A report (1999) providing a framework of *risk management for UK companies. It was prepared by a working party of the Institute of Chartered Accountants in England and Wales and endorsed by the London Stock Exchange.

turnkey system **1.** The planning and execution of a major capital project, in which one company has responsibility for its overall management, so that the client only has to 'turn the key' in order to start the operation. **2.** A computer system that is ready to start work as soon as it is installed. All the necessary programs and equipment are supplied with the system.

turnover **1.** The total sales figure of an organization for a stated period. Turnover is defined in the UK Companies Act 1985 as the total revenue of an organization derived from the provision of goods and services, less trade discounts, VAT, and any other taxes based on this revenue. **2.** More generally, the rate at which at some asset is turned over, e.g. stock turnover is obtained by dividing the total sales figure by the value of the particular asset. **3.** The total value of the transactions on a market or stock exchange in a specified period.

turnover ratio An accounting ratio showing the number of times an item of *working capital has been replaced by others of the same class within a financial period.

turnover tax A tax on the sales made by a business, i.e. on its turnover. *See* SALES TAX.

turn-round rate The total cost of a transaction on a commodity market, including the broker's commission and the fee charged by the *clearing house.

twenty-four-hour trading Round-the-clock dealings in securities, bonds, and currency. In practice, it is not normally carried out from any one office of a securities house; instead, the dealers in one time zone pass on their position to associates in another time zone. Thus, a London office may pass its position to its New York office, which is passed, in turn, to Tokyo, and back to London. Twenty-four-hour trading has been encouraged by the rise in cross-border share trading.

two-tier tender offer A tender offer in a takeover in which shareholders are offered a high initial offer for sufficient shares to give the bidder a controlling interest in the company, followed by an offer to acquire the remaining shares at a lower price. Bidders use this technique in order to provide an incentive to shareholders to accept the initial offer quickly. Such offers are usually for a combination of cash and shares in the bidder's own company. They are illegal in some countries, notably the UK.

tyiyn A monetary unit of Kyrgyzstan worth one hundredth of a *som.

uberrima fides (Latin: utmost good faith) The basis of all insurance contracts. *See* UTMOST GOOD FAITH.

UBR Abbreviation for *Uniform Business Rate.

UCITS Abbreviation for *Undertakings for Collective Investment in Transferable Securities.

UK Balance of Payments An annual publication of the *Office for National Statistics. It is often known as the **Pink Book**.

UK National Accounts An annual publication of the *Office for National Statistics. It is often known as the **Blue Book**. It provides figures for the *gross domestic product and separate accounts of production, income, and expenditure.

ULS Abbreviation for *unsecured loan stock.

ultra vires (Latin: beyond the powers) Denoting an act of an official or corporation for which there is no authority. The powers of officials exercising administrative duties and of companies are limited by the instrument from which their powers are derived. If they act outside these powers, their action may be challenged in the courts. A company's powers are limited by the objects clause in its memorandum of association. It it enters into an agreement outside these objects, the agreement may be unenforceable, although a third party may have a remedy under the Companies Act 1985 if it was dealing with the company in good faith (or there may be other equitable remedies).

umbrella fund An *offshore fund consisting of a *fund of funds that invests in other offshore funds.

unamortized cost 1. The historical cost of a fixed asset less the total depreciation shown against that asset up to a specified date. **2.** The value given to a fixed asset in the accounts of an organization after a revaluation less the total depreciation shown against that asset since it was revalued.

unappropriated profit The part of an organization's profit that is neither allocated to a specific purpose nor paid out in *dividends.

unbundling 1. The separation of a business into its constituent parts, generally by selling off certain subsidiaries or business lines. **2.** The selling off of separate parts of a security, for example its *coupon.

uncalled capital *See* RESERVE CAPITAL.

uncertificated units A small number of units purchased for an investor in a *unit trust by reinvestment of dividends. If the number of units is too small to warrant the issue of a certificate they are held on account for the investor and added to the total when the holding is sold.

uncleared effects Financial documents lodged with a bank for collection, still held by the bank pending the completion of the collection.

uncommitted facility An agreement between a bank and a company in which the bank agrees in principle to make funding available to the company but is under no obligation to provide a specified amount of funding; if a loan is made it will be for only a short period. Examples of an uncommitted facility include a *money market line or an *overdraft. *Compare* COMMITTED FACILITY.

unconditional bid *See* TAKEOVER BID.

unconfirmed letter of credit *See* LETTER OF CREDIT.

unconscionable bargain *See* CATCHING BARGAIN.

UNCTAD Abbreviation for *United Nations Conference on Trade and Development.

undated security A *fixed-interest security that has no *redemption date. *See* CONSOLS.

undercapitalization The state of a company that does not have sufficient *capital or *reserves for the size of its operations. For example, this may be due to the company growing too quickly. Although such a company may be making profits it may be unable to convert these profits sufficiently quickly into cash to pay its debts.

underlying The asset, measure, or obligation on which a *derivative, such as an option or futures contract, is based.

undersubscription *See* OVERSUBSCRIPTION.

Undertakings for Collective Investment in Transferable Securities (UCITS) A set of rules introduced by the European Union in 1989 to regulate the sale of *unit trusts and *investment trusts within the Union.

underwater Describing an asset whose current market price is lower than its purchase price.

underwrite 1. To guarantee an issue of *commercial paper, *euronote, etc., especially by a bank. **2.** To carry out a detailed investigation of the risks involved in making a loan to a particular borrower or in offering an insurance contract, especially by a bank. *See also* UNDERWRITER.

underwriter 1. A person who examines a risk, decides whether or not it can be insured, and, if it can, works out the premium to be charged, usually on the basis of the frequency of past claims for similar risks. Underwriters are either employed by insurance companies or are members of *Lloyd's (*see also* SYNDICATE). The name arises from the early days of marine insurance, when a merchant would, as a sideline, *write* his name *under* the amount and details of the risk he had agreed to cover on a slip of paper. **2.** A financial institution, usually an *issuing house or *merchant bank, that guarantees to buy a proportion of any unsold shares when a *new issue is offered to the public. Underwriters usually work for a commission, and a number may combine together to buy all the unsold shares, provided that the minimum subscription stated in the *prospectus has been sold to the public. *See also* UNDERWRITE. **3.** A person who provides a guarantee for a financial transaction.

u

undischarged bankrupt A person whose *bankruptcy has not been discharged. Such persons must not obtain credit (above £250) without first informing their creditors that they are undischarged bankrupts, become directors of companies, or trade under another name. Undischarged bankrupts may not hold office as a JP, MP, mayor, or councillor. A peer who is an undischarged bankrupt may not sit in the House of Lords.

undisclosed factoring A form of *factoring in which the seller of goods does not wish to disclose that a factor is being used. In these circumstances, the factor buys the goods that have been sold (rather than the debt their sale incurred) and, as an *undisclosed principal, appoints the original seller to act as an agent to recover the debt. The factor assumes responsibility in the case of non-payment so that from the point of view of the seller, the factor offers the same service as in normal factoring.

undisclosed principal A person who buys or sells through an agent or broker and remains anonymous. The agent or broker must disclose when dealing on behalf of an undisclosed principal; failure to do so may result in the agent being treated in law as the principal and in some circumstances the contract may be made void.

undistributable reserves *Retained earnings that may not be distributed according to the Companies Act 1985. They include *share capital, *share premium account, *capital redemption reserve, certain *unrealized profits, or any other reserve that the company may not distribute according to some other act or its own articles of association. They are referred to in the USA as **restricted surplus**.

undistributed profit Profit earned by an organization but not distributed to its shareholders by way of dividends. Such sums are available for later distribution but are frequently used by companies to finance their activities.

undiversifiable risk *See* SYSTEMATIC RISK.

undue influence Unfair pressure exerted on a person to sign a contract that is not a true expression of that person's aims or requirements at the time, but is to the advantage of another party (either a party to the contract or a third party). Such a contract may be set aside by a court.

unearned income Income not derived from trades, professions or vocations, or from the emoluments of office. In the UK, until 1984, it was taxed more heavily than earned income. This was achieved by an investment-income surcharge. In the UK both earned and unearned income are now taxed at the same rates.

unfavourable balance A *balance of trade or *balance of payments deficit.

unfranked income Any type of income from investments that is not *franked investment income.

unfunded pension scheme A pension scheme whose assets do not allow it to cover its liabilities, as, for example, most state pension schemes, which provide funds for the payment of pensions through the contributions of those currently in employment.

Uniform Business Rate (UBR) A UK local tax paid by businesses. The tax is based on a local valuation of the premises they occupy; a uniform rate throughout the UK is fixed by central government. UBR is paid to local authorities as the business equivalent of the *council tax.

uniform price auction A securities *auction in which all the successful bidders receive an allocation at the same price, which is set by the lowest successful bid.

unilateral relief Relief against *double taxation given by the UK authorities for tax paid in another country with which the UK has no double-taxation agreement.

unincorporated business A privately owned business, usually owned by one person, that is not legally registered or recognized as a company. The sole owner has unlimited liability for any debts he or she may incur.

uninsurable risk *See* INSURABLE RISK.

unissued share capital The difference between the nominal *share capital of a company and the issued share capital.

unit banking A system of banking in which a bank must be a single enterprise without branches. This was once common practice in the USA, but regulators have turned against this form of bank, following the collapse of the Continental Illinois Bank.

United Nations Common Fund for Commodities (CFC) *See* UNITED NATIONS CONFERENCE ON TRADE AND DEVELOPMENT.

United Nations Conference on Trade and Development (UNCTAD) A permanent organization set up by the UN in 1964 to encourage international trade, particularly to help developing countries to finance their exports. Under its auspices the **UN Common Fund for Commodities** (CFC) was established in 1989 to provide finance for international commodity organizations to enable *buffer stocks to be maintained and to carry out research into the development of *commodity markets.

United Nations Monetary and Financial Conference *See* BRETTON WOODS CONFERENCE.

unit investment trust *See* UNIT TRUST.

unitization The process of changing an *investment trust into a *unit trust.

unit-linked policy A life-assurance policy in which the benefits depend on the performance of a portfolio of shares. Each premium paid by the insured person is split: one part is used to provide life-assurance cover, while the balance (after the deduction of costs, expenses, etc.) is used to buy units in a *unit trust. In this way a small investor can benefit from investment in a *managed fund without making a large financial commitment. As they are linked to the value of shares, unit-linked policies can go up or down in value. Policyholders can surrender the policy at any time and the *surrender value is the selling price of the units purchased by the date of cancellation (less expenses).

unit of account **1.** A *function of money enabling its users to calculate the value of their transactions and to keep accounts. **2.** The standard unit of currency of a country. **3.** An artificial currency used only for accounting purposes.

unit trust **1.** An investment *trust formed to manage a portfolio, in which small investors can buy units. This gives the small investor access to a diversified portfolio of securities, chosen and managed by professional *fund managers, who seek either high capital gains or high yields, within the parameters of reasonable security. The trustees, usually a commercial bank, are the legal owners of the securities and responsible for ensuring that the managers keep to the terms laid down in the trust deed. Prices of unit trusts are quoted daily, the difference between the bid and offer prices providing a margin for the management costs and the costs of buying and selling. In the USA unit trusts are called **mutual funds** (*see also* OPEN-END TRUST). Many trusts are now available, specializing in various sectors of the market, both at home and abroad; there is also a wide spectrum of trusts catering for both those seeking growth and those seeking income. *See also* UNIT-LINKED POLICY. **2.** A trust scheme (also called a **unit investment trust**) in the USA in which investors purchase **redeemable trust certificates**. The money so raised is used by the trustees to buy such securities as bonds, which are usually held until they mature. Usually both the number of certificates issued and the investments held remain unchanged during the life of the scheme, but the certificates can be sold back to the trustees at any time.

Unit Trust Association (UTA) An association formed to agree standards of practice for the managers of unit trusts for the protection of unit-trust holders and to act as the representative body of **Managers of Authorized Unit Trusts** in dealings with the government and other authorities. It also coordinates control of commissions and charges and has a register of approved agents for selling unit trusts as intermediaries.

Unit Trusts Ombudsman Scheme *See* FINANCIAL OMBUDSMAN SERVICE.

universal banking Banking that involves not only services related to loans and savings but also those involved in making investments in companies. Universal banking is most common in Germany, Switzerland, and the Netherlands. The *Glass–Steagal Act 1933 prohibited universal banking in the USA, but the restrictions placed on it have now been removed. In the UK, it has been largely avoided.

unlimited company A *company whose *shareholders do not benefit from limited liability (*compare* LIMITED COMPANY). Such companies are exempt from filing accounts with the *Registrar of Companies.

unlimited liability A liability to pay all the debts incurred by a business. For a sole proprietor or *partnership, the liability of the owners is not limited to the amount the owner has agreed to invest. All debts of the business must not only be paid out of the *assets of the business but also, if necessary, out of personal assets.

unliquidated damages *See* DAMAGES.

unlisted company *See* UNQUOTED COMPANY.

unlisted securities Securities (usually *equities) in companies that are not on an official stock-exchange list. *See also* ALTERNATIVE INVESTMENT MARKET.

Unlisted Securities Market (USM) A former market established by the *London Stock Exchange in 1980 to trade in shares of small companies, not suitable for the *main market. The USM, which had less stringent listing requirements than the main market, merged with the *third market in 1990 and was replaced by the *Alternative Investment Market in 1995.

unpaid cheque A cheque that has been sent to the payee's bank and then through the clearing process only to be returned to the payee because value cannot be transferred. If the reason is lack of funds the bank will mark the cheque 'refer to drawer'.

unquoted company A company whose securities (*see* UNQUOTED SECURITIES) are not normally available to the public on a stock exchange.

unquoted securities Securities that are not dealt in on any stock exchange. On the London Stock Exchange there are rules for occasional unofficial trading in unquoted securities of small companies or new ventures. Unquoted securities are usually shown in balance sheets valued at cost or market value (if this can be ascertained).

unrealized profit/loss A profit or loss that results from holding *assets rather than using them; it is therefore a profit or loss that has not been realized in cash. *See* REALIZED PROFIT/LOSS.

unsecured creditor A person who is owed money by an organization but who has not arranged that in the event of non-payment specific assets would be available as a fund out of which that person could be paid in priority to other creditors.

unsecured debenture *See* UNSECURED LOAN STOCK.

unsecured debt A debt that is not covered by any kind of collateral.

unsecured loan stock (ULS; **unsecured debenture**) A loan stock or *debenture in which no specific assets have been set aside as a fund out of which the holders could be paid in priority to other creditors in the event of non-payment.

unvalued policy An insurance policy for property that has a sum insured shown for each item although the insurers do not acknowledge that this figure is its actual value. As a result, if a claim is made the insured must provide proof of the value of the item lost, damaged, or stolen before a payment will be made. The policy may have a maximum specified payment. *Compare* VALUED POLICY.

unweighted average *See* WEIGHTED AVERAGE.

unwinding The closing out of a financial position by selling or making an *offsetting transaction.

up and in (or **up and out**) **option** *See* BARRIER OPTION.

upside An upward price movement or gain. *Compare* DOWNSIDE.

upstream Denoting a loan from a subsidiary company to its parent, for example a loan from a subsidiary of a bank to its holding company to enable the holding company to pay its dividends.

uptrend A rising value for a variable.

usance **1.** The time allowed for the payment of short-term foreign *bills of exchange. It varies from country to country but is often 60 days. **2.** Formerly, the rate of interest on a loan.

use of funds A financial statement, used in company accounts, showing how money was spent by a business during the course of a financial year. In some countries it has to be provided according to accounting legislation. *See also* SOURCE AND APPLICATION (DISPOSITION) OF FUNDS.

USM Abbreviation for *Unlisted Securities Market.

US stock exchanges The nine stock exchanges in the USA: the *New York Stock Exchange, *American Stock Exchange, *National Association of Securities Dealers Automated Quotation System, *Pacific Stock Exchange, National Stock Exchange (a small New York exchange dealing in smaller companies not listed elsewhere), Philadelphia Stock Exchange (the oldest exchange in the USA, founded 1790), Boston Stock Exchange, Midwest Stock Exchange, and the Cincinnati Stock Exchange.

usury An excessively high rate of interest. In Christian countries the term was formerly used to condemn all forms of lending on interest, a prohibition that has been maintained by Islam. *See* ISLAMIC FINANCE.

UTA Abbreviation for *Unit Trust Association.

utility theory An analysis and ordering of preferences that is used to explain individual decision-making. The main application in finance is in relation to

u

investment choices. Different structures of utility and *risk preference are considered in *portfolio theory. *See also* PROSPECT THEORY.

utmost good faith (*uberrima fides*) The fundamental principle of insurance practice, requiring that a person wishing to take out an insurance cover must provide all the information the insurer needs to calculate the correct premium for the risk involved. Nothing must be withheld from the insurers, even if they do not actually ask for the information on an application form. The principle is essential because an insurer usually has no knowledge of the facts involved in the risk they are being asked to cover; the only source of information is the person requiring the insurance. If an insured person is found to have withheld information or given false information, the insurer can treat the policy as void and the courts will support a refusal to pay claims.

valium holiday (valium picnic) A colloquial name for a non-trading day on a stock exchange or other commercial market; i.e. a market holiday.

valorization The raising or stabilization of the value of a commodity or currency by artificial means, usually by a government. For example, if a government wishes to increase the price of a commodity that it exports it may attempt to decrease the supply of that commodity by encouraging producers to produce less, by stockpiling the commodity itself, or, in extreme cases, by destroying part of the production.

valuation risk The *risk that arises from problems of valuation. For example, it can be difficult to value a business during the acquisition process or to put an accurate value on an option on the *over-the-counter market.

value added The value added to goods or services by a step in the chain of original purchase, manufacture or other enhancement, and retail. For example, if a manufacturer acquires a partly made component, the value added will be the combination of labour and profit that increase the value of the part before it is sold. *See* VALUE ADDED TAX.

value-added statement (added-value statement) A *financial statement showing how much wealth (value added) has been created by the collective effort of capital, employees, and others and how it has been allocated for a financial period. Value added is normally calculated by deducting materials and bought-in services from *turnover. The value added is then allocated to employees in the form of wages, to shareholders and lenders in the form of dividends and interest, and to the government in the form of taxes, with a proportion being retained in the company for reinvestment.

value added tax (VAT) A charge on taxable supplies of goods and services made by a *taxable person in the course or furtherance of a business. In the UK, each trader (where appropriate) adds VAT to sales and must account to the *Board of Customs and Excise for the *output tax. The *input tax paid on purchases can be deducted from the output tax due. VAT, *indirect taxation that falls on the final customer, was introduced in 1973 when the UK joined the European Economic Community. Unless they are *zero-rated goods and services, *exempt supplies, or taxed at a special rate, all goods and services in the UK now bear VAT at a rate of 17.5%.

value additivity In finance, the rule that the value of the whole must equal the value of the parts.

value-at-risk (VAR) A measure of risk developed at the former US Bank J. P. Morgan Chase in the 1990s, now most frequently applied to measuring *market risk and *credit risk. It is the level of losses over a particular period that will only be exceeded in a certain percentage of cases. A cut-off value for portfolio gains and losses is established that excludes a certain proportion of worst-case results (e.g. the bottom 1% of outcomes); the value-at-risk is then measured relative to that cut-off value. VAR was initially designed to measure the overnight risk in certain market portfolios. It has since developed into a finance industry standard and has been incorporated into the regulatory requirements applying to financial institutions (notably the *Basle Market Risk Amendment issued by the *Bank for International Settlements in 1996). The data used for the value at-risk calculation can be derived from the *variance–covariance matrix of the portfolio, the historical performance of the financial obligations in the portfolio, or by *Monte Carlo simulation. *See also* EXPECTED TAIL LOSSES: RELATIVE VALUE-AT-RISK.

value chain The chain of activities by which a good or service is produced, distributed, and marketed. Each step of the chain (which may consist of the activities of one company or of several) creates different amounts of value for the consumer. The principle underlying the value-chain concept is that a company should examine its costs and performance at each stage and decide, among other things, whether it is best to carry out a particular stage in house or externally. The value chain can provide the basis for a strategic analysis in terms of the search for competitive advantage.

value date **1.** The date on which specified funds become available for use. **2.** The date on which a transaction actually takes place. **3.** The date on which foreign exchange is due to be delivered.

valued policy An insurance policy in which the value of the subject matter is agreed when the cover starts. As a result, the amount to be paid in the event of a total-loss claim is already decided and does not need to be negotiated. *Compare* UNVALUED POLICY.

value for money audit An audit of a government department, charity, or other non-profitmaking organization to assess whether or not it is functioning efficiently and giving value for the money it spends.

value received Words that appear on a *bill of exchange to indicate that the bill is a means of paying for goods or services to the value of the bill. However, these words need not appear on a UK bill as everyone who has signed a UK bill is deemed to have been a party to it for value.

value to the business The value of an *asset taken as the lower of the *replacement cost and the *recoverable amount. The latter is the greater of the *net realizable value and *net present value. It is claimed that generally an asset should never be worth more to a business than its replacement cost, because if the business were deprived of the asset it would replace it. If an asset is not worth replacing it would be sold (net realizable value), unless the net present value were higher. The concept is also known as the **deprival value** and was a feature of *current cost accounting as required by *Statement of Standard Accounting Practice 16.

value transferred The amount by which a donor's estate is diminished by making a *transfer of value. The term is used in the computation of *inheritance tax.

VAR Abbreviation for *value-at-risk.

variable life assurance A *unit-linked policy in which the policyholder can vary the amount of life assurance cover provided.

variable-rate mortgage A *mortgage in which the rate of interest is varied from time to time by the mortgagee (lender) according to market conditions.

variable-rate note (VRN) A *bond, usually with a fixed maturity, in which the interest coupon is adjusted at regular intervals to reflect the prevailing market rate (usually a margin over the *London Inter Bank Offered Rate). A VRN differs from a *floating-rate note in that the margin is not fixed and will be adjusted to take into account market conditions at each coupon setting date.

variable-rate security A security in which the interest rate varies with market rates. *Floating-rate notes, eurobonds, and 90-day *certificates of deposit are examples of variable-rate securities.

variance In statistics, a measure of the dispersion of a distribution of outcomes. It is the square of the *standard deviation. *See* MOMENTS. *See also* SEMI-VARIANCE.

variance analysis An analysis of the difference between a budgeted cost, income, or profit and the actual amounts. This forms the basis of **variance accounting**.

variance–covariance matrix A matrix having as elements the *variances and *covariances of the returns on assets, the variances comprising the main diagonal running from top left to bottom right of the matrix. It is used in the calculation of portfolio variances in *portfolio theory. *See also* VALUE-AT-RISK.

variation margins The gains or losses on open contracts in futures markets, calculated on the basis of the closing price at the end of each day. They are credited by the *clearing house to its members' accounts and by its members to their customers' accounts.

VAT Abbreviation for *value added tax.

vatu (VT) The standard monetary unit of Vanuatu.

vault money *See* TILL MONEY.

VCT Abbreviation for *venture capital trust.

vega A measure of the relation between the value of an *option and the *variance of the price of the *underlying. *See* GREEKS.

velocity of circulation The average number of times that a unit of money is used in a specified period, approximately equal to the total amount of money spent in that period divided by the total amount of money in circulation. The **income velocity of circulation** is the number of times that a particular unit of currency forms part of a person's income in a specified period. It is given by the ratio of the *gross national product to the amount of money in circulation. The **transactions velocity of circulation** is the number of times that a particular unit of currency is spent in a money transaction in a specified period, i.e. the ratio of the total amount of money spent in sales of goods or services to the amount of money in circulation.

vendor placing A type of *placing used as a means of acquiring another company or business. For example, if company X wishes to buy a business from company Y, it issues company X shares to company Y as payment with the prearranged agreement that these shares are then placed with investors in exchange for cash. Vendor placings have been popular with some companies as a cheaper alternative to a *rights issue. *See also* BOUGHT DEAL.

venture capital *See* RISK CAPITAL.

venture capital trust (VCT) An *investment trust that provides venture capital for businesses. The trust managers accept sums of money from investors, who wish to share in the profits (or losses) of the trust. This form of investment has certain tax advantages in the UK, in that any profits are free of capital gains tax and income is untaxed. They have the additional advantages that up to £100,000 can be invested in any year; 20% of any investment in a VCT can be claimed back from previously paid tax, provided the VCT is held for three years. By investing a taxable gain in a VCT that is held for three years, the payment of the capital gains tax is deferred until the VCT investment is sold (and the annual exemptions from capital gains tax can be carried forward).

vertical disintegration The disintegration of a vertically integrated (*see* INTEGRATION) manufacturing and distribution chain as a result of the withdrawal of one stage by a company. For example, a firm may decide that it will be more profitable to close its own distribution network and hand over the responsibility of distribution to another firm.

vertical integration *See* INTEGRATION.

vertical spread A strategy used with *options, consisting of buying a long call option and a short call option with the same exercise date.

vested benefit A benefit owing to a member of a pension scheme, whether or not the member is employed by the organizers of the scheme.

vested interest 1. In law, an interest in property that is certain to come about rather than one dependent upon some event that may not happen. For example, a gift to "A for life and then to B" means that A's interest is **vested in possession**, because A has the property now. B's gift is also vested (but not in possession) because A will certainly die sometime and then B (or B's estate if B is dead) will inherit the property. A gift to C "if C reaches the age of 30" is not vested, because C may die before reaching that age. An interest that is not vested is known as a **contingent interest**. **2.** An involvement in the outcome of some business, scheme, transaction, etc., usually in anticipation of a personal gain.

viatical settlement The purchase by a company set up as a charity of the life assurance policy owned by someone with only a short time to live, to enable that person to make use of the proceeds of the policy during his or her lifetime. The price paid is between the surrender value of the policy and the sum assured, on average about 70% of the sum assured. *Term assurance policies are not eligible for this form of settlement.

visibles Earnings from exports and payments for imports of goods, as opposed to services (such as banking and insurance). The *balance of trade is made up of visibles and is sometimes called the **visible balance.**

volatile Denoting a market, commodity, share, bond, etc., that may be expected to fluctuate greatly and frequently in value.

volatility smile The pattern typically created on a graph when the implied volatility of the *underlying of an option (as derived from an option-pricing model) is plotted against the term of the option. The implied volatility is customarily lowest for options either close to or furthest away from expiry.

volume 1. The space occupied by something. **2.** A measure of the amount of trade that has taken place, usually in a specified period. On the *London Stock Exchange, for example, the number of shares traded in a day is called the volume and the value of these shares is called the *turnover. In commodity markets, the daily volume is usually the number of lots traded in a day.

voluntary arrangement A procedure provided for by the Insolvency Act 1986, in which a company may come to an arrangement with its creditors to pay off its debts and to manage its affairs so that it resolves its financial difficulties. This arrangement may be proposed by the directors, an administrator acting under an *administration order, or a *liquidator. A qualified insolvency practitioner must be appointed to supervise the arrangement. This practitioner may be the administrator or liquidator, in which case a meeting of the company and its creditors must be called to consider the arrangement. The proposals may be modified or approved at this meeting but, once approved, they bind all those who had notice of the meeting. The court may make the necessary orders to bring the arrangement into effect. The arrangement may be challenged in court in the case of any irregularity. The aim of this legislation is to assist the company to solve its financial problems without the need for a winding-up (*see* LIQUIDATION).

voluntary liquidation (**voluntary winding-up**) *See* CREDITORS' VOLUNTARY LIQUIDATION; MEMBERS' VOLUNTARY LIQUIDATION.

vostro account A bank account held by a foreign bank with a UK bank, usually in sterling. *Compare* NOSTRO ACCOUNT.

voting shares Shares in a company that entitle their owner to vote at the annual general meeting and any extraordinary meetings of the company. Shares that carry **voting rights** are usually *ordinary shares, rather than *A shares or *debentures. The company's articles of association will state which shares carry voting rights.

VRN Abbreviation for *variable-rate note.

wafer seal A modern form of seal used on such documents as deeds. It is usually a small red disc stuck onto the document to represent the seal. Almost any form of seal agreeable to all the parties concerned is now acceptable in place of sealing wax.

wagering contract *See* GAMING CONTRACT.

waiter An attendant at the *London Stock Exchange, before screen trading was introduced, and at *Lloyd's, who carries messages and papers, etc. The name goes back to the 17th-century London coffee houses from which these institutions grew, in which the waiters also performed these functions.

waiver The setting aside or non-enforcement of a right. This may be done deliberately or it may happen by the operation of law. For example, if a tenant is in breach of a covenant in a lease and the landlord demands rent in spite of knowing of the breach, the landlord may be held to have waived the right to terminate the lease.

Wall Street 1. The street in New York in which the *New York Stock Exchange is situated. **2.** The New York Stock Exchange itself. **3.** The financial institutions, collectively, of New York, including the stock exchange, banks, money markets, commodity markets, etc.

warehousing 1. The storage of goods in a warehouse. **2.** Building up a holding of shares in a company prior to making a *takeover bid, by buying small lots of the shares and 'warehousing' them in the name of nominees. The purpose is for the bidder to remain anonymous and to avoid having to make the statutory declaration of interest. This practice is contrary to the *City Code on Takeovers and Mergers.

war loan A government stock issued during wartime; it has no redemption date, pays only 3½% interest, and stands at less than half its face value.

warrant 1. A security that offers the owner the right to subscribe for the *ordinary shares of a company at a fixed date, usually at a fixed price. Warrants are themselves bought and sold on *stock exchanges and are equivalent to stock options. Subscription prices usually exceed the market price, as the purchase of a warrant is a gamble that a company will prosper. They have proved increasingly popular in recent years as a company can issue them without including them in the balance sheet. **2.** A document that serves as proof that goods have been deposited in a public warehouse. The document identifies specific goods and can be transferred by endorsement. Warrants are frequently used as security against a bank loan. Warehouse warrants for warehouses attached to a wharf are known as **dock warrants** or **wharfinger's warrants**.

warranty 1. A statement made clearly in a contract (**express warranty**) or, if not stated clearly, understood between the parties to the contract (**implied warranty**). An unfulfilled warranty does not invalidate the contract (as it would in the case of an unfulfilled condition) but could lead to the payment of damages. *See also* FLOATING WARRANTY. **2.** A condition in an insurance policy that confirms that something will or will not be done or that a certain situation exists or does not exist. If a warranty is breached, the insurer is entitled to refuse to pay claims, even if they are unconnected with the breach. For example, if a policy insuring the contents of a house has a warranty that certain locks are to be used on the doors and windows and these are found not to have been used, the insurers could decline to settle a claim for a burst pipe. In practice, however, this does not happen as insurers have agreed that they will only refuse to pay claims if the breach of warranty has affected the circumstances of the claim. **3.** A manufacturer's written promise to repair or replace a faulty product, usually free of charge, during a specified period subsequent to the date of purchase. This is often called a **guarantee**.

wash sale A US name for the sale and purchase by a single investor, or a group in collusion, of a block of securities either simultaneously or in a short space of time to establish a loss or a gain; it may also be used to create the impression that the security in question is trading actively. It is similar to the practice known in the UK as *bed and breakfast. See also* CROSSING.

wasting asset An asset that has a finite life; for example, a lease may lose value throughout its life and become valueless when it terminates. It is also applied to such assets as plant and machinery, which wear out during their life and therefore lose value.

watered stock *See* STOCK WATERING.

WDA Abbreviation for *writing-down allowance.

WDV Abbreviation for *written-down value.

weak-form market efficiency One of three forms of market efficiency defined by Eugene Fama. In a weak-form efficient market it is impossible to achieve *abnormal returns by exploiting publicly available historical information, because this information is already incorporated into market prices. *See* EFFICIENT MARKETS HYPOTHESIS. *Compare* SEMI-STRONG-FORM MARKET EFFICIENCY; STRONG-FORM MARKET EFFICIENCY.

wealth The value of the net assets owned by an individual or group of individuals. It is the value of assets minus the value of liabilities. Economics began as the study of wealth (e.g. Adam Smith's *The Wealth of Nations*) and how it changes during a given period. Keynesian theory tended to place a greater emphasis on *income as the object of study in macroeconomics but it has since been accepted that income only tends to affect the behaviour of individuals as it affects their wealth.

wealth tax A tax used in some European countries, not including the UK, consisting of an annual levy on assets. In practice, the implementation of a wealth tax requires a clear identification of the assets to be charged and an unassailable valuation of these assets.

wedge In *chartist analysis, the pattern produced on a chart when the volatility of a market series declines during a particular time period. A line connecting the market peaks converges on one connecting the troughs.

W

weighted average (**weighted mean**) An arithmetic average that takes into account the importance of the items making up the average. For example, if a person buys a commodity on three occasions, 100 tonnes at £70 per tonne, 300 tonnes at £80 per tonne, and 50 tonnes at £95 per tonne, the purchases total 450 tonnes; the simple average price would be $(70 + 80 + 95)/3 = £81.7$. The weighted average, taking into account the amount purchased on each occasion, would be $[(100 \times 70) + (300 \times 80) + (50 \times 95)]/450 = £79.4$ per tonne.

In calculating the value of a *share index, the share prices are weighted to reflect the volume of shares traded at a particular price. An **unweighted average** is an average calculated on the basis of price only, irrespective of quantity.

weighted average cost of capital The average cost of long-term funding, including both the cost of debt and the post-tax cost of equity.

weighted ballot A *ballot held if a new issue of shares has been oversubscribed, in which the allocation of shares is based on the number of shares applied for and biased towards either the smaller investor or the larger investor.

weightless 1. Denoting a business that has very few tangible assets, especially one involved in Internet trading. **2.** Denoting that part of the economy that is based on ideas and information rather than trade in physical goods.

WGC Abbreviation for *World Gold Council.

white knight A person or firm that makes a welcome *takeover bid for a company on improved terms to replace an unacceptable and unwelcome bid from a *black knight. If a company is the target for a takeover bid from a source of which it does not approve or on terms that it does not find attractive, it will often seek a white knight as a more suitable owner for the company, in the hope that a more attractive bid will be made. *Compare* GREY KNIGHT.

whole (of) life policy A life-assurance policy that pays a specified amount on the death of the life assured. Benefits are not made for any other reason and the cover continues until the death of the life assured, provided the premiums continue to be paid, either for life or until a specified date. They may be *with-profits or *unit-linked policies.

wholesale banking Interbank lending as well as lending to or by other large financial institutions, pension funds, and government agencies. In the USA, wholesale banking also refers to the provision of banking services to the large corporate businesses at special rates.

wholesale deposit A large deposit obtained by a bank, financial institution, or large corporate business.

wholesale market The *money market between banks; the interbank market for short-term loans.

wholly owned subsidiary A *subsidiary undertaking that is owned 100% by a holding company (i.e. there is no *minority interest).

wider-range securities *See* TRUSTEE INVESTMENTS.

will A document giving directions as to the disposal of a person's property after death. It has no effect until death and may be altered as many times as the person (the *testator) wishes. To be binding, it must be executed in accordance with statutory formalities. It must be in writing, signed by the testator or at the testator's direction and in the testator's presence. It must appear that the signature was intended to give effect to the will (usually it is signed close to the last words dealing with the property). The will must be witnessed by two persons, who must also sign the will. The witnesses must not be beneficiaries.

windbill *See* ACCOMMODATION BILL.

winding-up *See* LIQUIDATION.

winding-up order An order given by a British court, under the Insolvency Act 1986, compelling a company to be wound up.

windmill *See* ACCOMMODATION BILL.

window 1. An opportunity to borrow or invest that may be only temporary and should therefore be taken while it is available. **2.** A period during the day during which interbank transfers and clearance may be enacted.

window dressing Any practice that attempts to make a situation look better than it really is. It has been used by accountants to improve the look of balance sheets, although the practice is now deprecated. For example, banks used to call in their short-term loans and delay making payments at the end of their financial years, in order to show spuriously high cash balances.

WIP Abbreviation for *work in progress.

withholding tax Tax deducted at source from *dividends or other income paid to non-residents of a country. If there is a *double-taxation agreement between the country in which the income is paid and the country in which the recipient is resident, the tax can be reclaimed.

without prejudice Words used as a heading to a document or letter to indicate that what follows cannot be used in any way to harm an existing right or claim, cannot be taken as the signatory's last word, cannot bind the signatory in any way, and cannot be used as evidence in a court of law. For example, a solicitor may use these words when making an offer in a letter to settle a claim, implying that the client may decide to withdraw the offer. It may also be used to indicate that, although agreement may be reached on the terms set out in the document, the signatory is not bound to settle similar disputes on the same terms.

without-profits policy A life-assurance or pension policy that does not share in the profits of the office that issued it. *Compare* WITH-PROFITS POLICY.

without recourse (sans recours) Words that appear on a *bill of exchange to indicate that the holder has no recourse to the person from whom it was bought, if it is not paid. It may be written on the face of the bill or as an endorsement. If these words do not appear, the holder does have recourse to the drawer or endorser if the bill is dishonoured. *See also* WITH RECOURSE.

with-profits bond An investment bond that has a cash-in value to some extent protected by the payment and accrual of bonuses.

with-profits policy A life-assurance or pension policy that has additional amounts added to the sum assured, as a result of a profit made on the investment of the fund or funds of the life-assurance office in which the policyholder is entitled to share. *Compare* UNIT-LINKED POLICY; WITHOUT-PROFITS POLICY.

with recourse A *bill of exchange that does not have a *without recourse endorsement or that specifically states that it is "with recourse". Such a bill gives the bank a right to claim the full value of the bill if the customer who has asked the bank to *discount it fails to pay the bill when it matures.

won (W) The standard monetary unit of North Korea and South Korea, divided into 100 chon.

working assets *See* WORKING CAPITAL.

working capital (circulating capital) The part of the capital of a company that is employed in its trading operations. It consists of *current assets (mainly trading stock, debtors, and cash) less *current liabilities. In the normal trade cycle – the supply of goods by suppliers, the sale of stock to debtors, payments of debts in cash, and the use of cash to pay suppliers – the working capital is the aggregate of the net assets involved, sometimes called the **working assets**.

work in progress (WIP) Partly manufactured goods or partly completed contracts. For accounting purposes, work in progress is normally valued at its cost by keeping records of the cost of the materials and labour put into it, together with some estimate of allocated overheads. In the case of long-term contracts, the figure might also include an element of profit. In the USA the usual term is **work in process**.

World Bank The name by which the *International Bank for Reconstruction and Development combined with its affiliates, the *International Development Association and the *International Finance Corporation, is known.

World Gold Council (WGC) An organization set up in 1987 by the major gold producers to stimulate trade in gold. The Council also inaugurated the **Central Bank Advisory Board** in 1992 to develop the involvement of *central banks in the world's gold markets. In the late 1950s world gold production (excluding China and the former USSR) was some 755 tonnes p.a.; in the late 1990s it had increased to 1840 tonnes p.a.

World Trade Organization (WTO) The world trading system founded at the Uruguay round of the *General Agreement on Tariffs and Trade (GATT) in 1994, and superseding GATT in the following year. WTO's aims are to continue the work of GATT in agreeing international trading rules and furthering the liberalization of international trade. WTO has wider and more permanent powers than GATT and extends its jurisdiction into such aspects of trading as *intellectual property rights. The highest authority of WTO is the Ministerial Conference, held at least every two years. As at October 2004 there were 148 members of WTO. Recent meetings of WTO have been met with violent anticapitalist demonstrations in several countries.

writ An order issued by a court. A **writ of summons** is an order by which an action in the High Court is started. It commands the defendant to appear before the court to answer the claim made in the writ by the plaintiff. It is used in actions in tort, claims alleging *fraud, and claims for *damages in respect of personal injuries, death, or infringement of *patent. A **writ of execution** is used to enforce a judgment; it is addressed to a court officer instructing that officer to carry out an act, such as collecting money or seizing property. A **writ of delivery** is a writ of execution directing a sheriff to seize goods and deliver them to the plaintiff or to obtain their value in money, according to an agreed assessment. If the defendant has no option to pay the assessed value, the writ is a **writ of specific delivery**.

write **1.** To cover an insurance risk, accepting liability, under an insurance contract as an *underwriter. **2.** To sell a traded option.

write off **1.** To reduce the value of an asset to zero in a balance sheet. An expired lease, obsolete machinery, or an unfortunate investment would be written off. **2.** To reduce to zero a debt that cannot be collected (*see* BAD DEBT). Such a loss will be shown in the *profit and loss account of an organization.

writer The seller of a traded option. *Compare* TAKER.

writing-down allowance (WDA) A *capital allowance available to a UK trader; from 1 November 1993 it became the only allowance generally available for plant and machinery used in trade, although *first-year allowances have occasionally been introduced for specific types of equipment or business. Any additions to plant and machinery are added to the *written-down value of assets acquired in previous years and the writing-down allowance is calculated as 25% of the total. For cars the allowance is restricted to £3000, for vehicles whose initial cost is in excess of £12,000. For industrial buildings the allowance is calculated at 4% of the initial cost, on the straight-line method of *depreciation. For certain long-life assets it is calculated at 6% in the same way.

written-down value (WDV) The value of an asset for accounting purposes after deducting amounts for depreciation or, in the case of tax computations, for capital allowances.

wrongful trading Trading during a period in which a company had no reasonable prospect of avoiding insolvent *liquidation. The liquidator of a company may petition the court for an order instructing a director of a company that has gone into insolvent liquidation to make a contribution to the company's assets. The court may order any contribution to be made that it thinks proper if the director knew, or ought to have known, of the company's situation. A director would be judged liable if a reasonably diligent person carrying out the same function in the company would have realized the situation: no intention to defraud need be shown. *See* FRAUDULENT TRADING.

WTO Abbreviation for *World Trade Organization.

W

xd Abbreviation for ex dividend (*see* EX-).

xu A monetary unit of Vietnam worth one hundredth of a *dông.

Yankee bond A *bond issued in the USA by a foreign borrower.

yard 1. An informal word for one billion. **2.** An informal name for 100 dollars.

yearling bond A UK local-authority bond that is redeemable one year after issue.

year of assessment *See* FISCAL YEAR.

Yellow Book The colloquial name for *Admission of Securities to Listing*, a book issued by the Council of the *London Stock Exchange that sets out the regulations for admission to the *Official List and the obligations of companies with *listed securities.

yellow sheets A US daily bulletin giving updated prices and other information on bonds. *Compare* PINK SHEETS.

yen (¥) The standard monetary unit of Japan, formerly divided into 100 *sen.

yield 1. The income from an investment expressed in various ways. The **nominal yield** of a fixed-interest security is the interest it pays, expressed as a percentage of its *par value. For example, a £100 stock quoted as paying 8% interest will yield £8 per annum for every £100 of stock held. However, the **current yield** (also called **running yield**, **earnings yield**, or **flat yield**) will depend on the market price of the stock. If the 8% £100 stock mentioned above was standing at a market price of £90, the current yield would be $100/90 \times 8 = 8.9\%$. As interest rates rise, so the market value of fixed-interest stocks (not close to redemption) fall in order that they should give a competitive current yield. The capital gain (or loss) on redemption of a stock, which is normally redeemable at £100, can also be taken into account. This is called the **yield to redemption** (or the **redemption yield**). The redemption yield consists approximately of the current yield plus the capital gain (or loss) divided by the number of years to redemption. Thus, if the above stock had 9 years to run to redemption, its redemption yield would be about $8.9 + 10/9 = 10\%$. The yields of the various stocks on offer are usually listed in commercial papers as both current yields and redemption yields, based on the current market price. However, for an investor who actually owns stock, the yield will be calculated not on the market price but the price the investor paid for it. The annual yield on a fixed-interest stock can be stated exactly once it has been purchased. This is not the case with *equities, however, where neither the dividend yield (*see* DIVIDEND) nor the capital gain (or loss) can be forecast, reflecting the greater degree of risk attaching to investments in equities. Yields on fixed-interest securities and equities are normally quoted gross, i.e. before deduction of tax. **2.** The income obtained from a tax.

yield curve A curve on a graph in which the *yield of fixed-interest securities is plotted against the length of time they have to run to maturity. The yield curve usually slopes upwards, indicating that investors expect to receive a premium for holding securities that have a long time to run. However, when there are expectations of changes in interest rate, the slope of the yield curve may change (*see* TERM STRUCTURE OF INTEREST RATES).

yield gap The difference between the average annual dividend yield on *equities and the average annual yield on long-dated *gilt-edged securities. Before the 1960s yields obtained from UK equities usually exceeded the yields provided by long-dated UK gilts, reflecting the greater degree of risk involved in an investment in equities. In the 1960s, however, rising equity prices led to falling dividend yields causing a *reverse yield gap. This was widely regarded as acceptable, as equities were seen to provide a better hedge against *inflation than fixed-interest securities; thus their greater risk element is compensated by the possibility of higher capital gains.

yield to maturity *See* GROSS REDEMPTION YIELD.

yield to redemption *See* YIELD.

yuan (Y) The standard monetary unit of China, divided into 10 jiao or 100 fen.

zaibatsu A Japanese conglomerate. It differs from a *keiretsu* in having a bank as its dominant member.

Zebra A discounted *zero-coupon bond, in which the accrued income is taxed annually rather than on redemption.

zero-coupon bond A type of *bond or preference share (**zero dividend preference share**) that offers no interest payments but which is sold at a discount to its redemption value. Thus, in effect, the interest is paid at maturity in the redemption value of the bond. Investors sometimes prefer zero-coupon bonds as they may confer more favourable tax treatment. *See also* DEEP-DISCOUNT; TIGR; ZEBRA.

zero dividend preference share *See* ZERO-COUPON BOND.

zero-rated goods and services Goods and services that are taxable for *value added tax purposes but are currently subject to a tax rate of zero. These include:
• certain food items,
• sewerage and water services for non-industrial users,
• periodicals and books,
• charities for certain supplies, such as 'talking books',
• new domestic buildings,
• transport fares for vehicles designed to carry more than 12 passengers,
• banknotes,
• drugs and medicines,
• clothing and footwear for children.

zloty (Zl) The standard monetary unit of Poland, divided into 100 groszy.

Z score A score that strongly indicates whether or not a company will get into financial difficulties. It is based on a regression model (*see* REGRESSION ANALYSIS) using accounting data.

Oxford Companions

'Opening such books is like sitting down with a knowledgeable friend.
Not a bore or a know-all, but a genuinely well-informed chum ... So far
so splendid.'

Sunday Times [of *The Oxford Companion to Shakespeare*]

For well over 60 years Oxford University Press has been publishing
Companions that are of lasting value and interest, each one not only a
comprehensive source of reference, but also a stimulating guide,
mentor, and friend. There are between 40 and 60 Oxford Companions
available at any one time, ranging from music, art, and literature to
history, warfare, religion, and wine.

Titles include:

The Oxford Companion to English Literature
Edited by Margaret Drabble
'No guide could come more classic.'

Malcolm Bradbury, *The Times*

The Oxford Companion to Music
Edited by Alison Latham
'probably the best one-volume music reference book going'

Times Educational Supplement

The Oxford Companion to Western Art
Edited by Hugh Brigstocke
'more than meets the high standard set by the growing number of
Oxford Companions'

Contemporary Review

The Oxford Companion to Food
Alan Davidson
'the best food reference work ever to appear in the English language'

New Statesman

The Oxford Companion to Wine
Edited by Jancis Robinson
'the greatest wine book ever published'

Washington Post

OXFORD

Oxford Paperback Reference

A Dictionary of Psychology
Andrew M. Colman

Over 10,500 authoritative entries make up the most wide-ranging dictionary of psychology available.

'impressive ... certainly to be recommended'
Times Higher Educational Supplement

'Comprehensive, sound, readable, and up-to-date, this is probably the best single-volume dictionary of its kind.'
Library Journal

A Dictionary of Economics
John Black

Fully up-to-date and jargon-free coverage of economics. Over 2,500 terms on all aspects of economic theory and practice.

A Dictionary of Law

An ideal source of legal terminology for systems based on English law. Over 4,000 clear and concise entries.

'The entries are clearly drafted and succinctly written ... Precision for the professional is combined with a layman's enlightenment.'
Times Literary Supplement

OXFORD